ALPHA-KETO ACID DEHYDROGENASE COMPLEXES
ORGANIZATION, REGULATION, AND BIOMEDICAL RAMIFICATIONS

A TRIBUTE TO LESTER J. REED

ANNALS OF THE NEW YORK ACADEMY OF SCIENCES
Volume 573

ALPHA-KETO ACID DEHYDROGENASE COMPLEXES
ORGANIZATION, REGULATION, AND BIOMEDICAL RAMIFICATIONS

A TRIBUTE TO LESTER J. REED

Edited by Thomas E. Roche and Mulchand S. Patel

The New York Academy of Sciences
New York, New York
1989

Library of Congress Cataloging-in-Publication Data

Alpha-keto acid dehydrogenase complexes: organization, regulation, and biomedical ramifications: a tribute to Lester J. Reed / edited by Thomas E. Roche and Mulchand S. Patel.
    p. cm.—(Annals of the New York Academy of Sciences, ISSN 0077-8923; v. 573)
    Includes bibliographical references.
    ISBN 0-89766-539-2 (alk. paper).—ISBN 0-89766-540-6 (pbk.: alk. paper)
    1. Alpha-keto acid dehydrogenase complexes—Congresses. 2. Reed, Lester J.—Congresses. I. Reed, Lester J. II. Roche, Thomas E. III. Patel, Mulchand S. IV. Series.
Q11.N5 Vol. 573
[QP603.A37]
500 s—dc20
[574.19'258]
                                      89-13595
                                       CIP

SP
Printed in the United States of America
ISBN 0-89766-539-2 (cloth)
ISBN 0-89766-540-6 (paper)
ISSN 0077-8923

ANNALS OF THE NEW YORK ACADEMY OF SCIENCES

Volume 573
December 29, 1989

ALPHA-KETO ACID DEHYDROGENASE COMPLEXES: ORGANIZATION, REGULATION, AND BIOMEDICAL RAMIFICATIONS[a]

A TRIBUTE TO LESTER J. REED

Editors and Conference Organizers
THOMAS E. ROCHE and MULCHAND S. PATEL

CONTENTS

Part I. Assembly, Structure, and Catalytic Mechanisms

[a]This volume contains papers from a conference entitled α-Keto Acid Dehydrogenase
Complexes: Organization, Regulation, and Biomedical Aspects—A Conference Honoring Lester
J. Reed, Ph.D.—which was held on November 16–18, 1988, in Austin, Texas, and was
cosponsored by the New York Academy of Sciences and the Clayton Foundation for Research.

Part II. Molecular Cloning of Components

Part III. Regulation of Purified Complexes

Part IV. Cellular Regulation

Part V. Nutritional and Hormonal Control

Part VI. Inborn Errors

Poster Papers

Major financial assistance was received from:

- THE CLAYTON FOUNDATION FOR RESEARCH

Additional financial assistance was received from:

- NATIONAL SCIENCE FOUNDATION

Preface

The conference "α-Keto Acid Dehydrogenase Complexes: Organization, Regulation, and Biomedical Aspects," which was held in Austin, Texas, on November 16–18, 1988, brought together leading investigators—biochemists, molecular biologists, and clinicians—with diversified interests in this field. The conference and this volume are dedicated to Dr. Lester J. Reed, who spawned this field more than three decades ago and still remains at the forefront of research in the area.

The mitochondrial α-keto acid dehydrogenase multienzyme systems are among the most complex enzymes known. They play central roles in cellular metabolism and are major sites of regulation; they are also clinically important. Major new insights into the organization, active-site coupling between components, and intricate metabolite regulation have resulted from recent studies. Inborn errors associated with specific defects in several of the components have been documented, and altered function occurs in association with certain disease states. The complexes have been extensively investigated at levels ranging from the molecular to the whole animal. Several genes encoding components of these complexes, from bacterial and human sources, have been cloned and sequenced, and protein engineering on them has begun. At the other end of the spectrum, the mechanisms by which various hormones regulate the different mitochondrial complexes are just beginning to be elucidated. Many important questions, some of which will undoubtedly require interdisciplinary research efforts, remain to be answered.

Despite the fact that investigations on the α-keto acid dehydrogenase complexes constitute a very active, multifaceted field generating nearly 100 publications per year, prior to this conference there had never been a meeting devoted exclusively to these enzyme systems. Furthermore, enzymologists investigating the bacterial complex had not formally met with investigators studying the enzymes from animal and plant sources. Because of the importance of comparative knowledge at the enzyme and gene levels, such a meeting was critically important. Beyond that, investigators in the area of metabolic regulation (those working with mitochondria, cells, perfused organs, etc.) and clinical investigators had never attended a joint meeting with enzymologists. For these reasons, we felt that it was timely to bring together investigators with different expertise but with a common interest of presenting and discussing recent advances in the structure, function, regulation, and clinical ramifications of these complexes. This highly successful conference was attended by over 100 investigators from all over the world. For them, we believe the conference enhanced the exchange of ideas along with communicating the latest developments; we hope it also stimulated new interactions among participants. The resulting scientific papers, compiled in this volume, demonstrate the dramatic progress that has occurred in recent years and should serve as a unique source for investigators at all levels who want specific information or an overview of current knowledge concerning these enzymes.

We would like to thank the participants for presenting stimulating talks, for fruitful discussions, and for prompt submission of manuscripts. We thank Dr. Lester J. Reed for his invaluable suggestions during the early stages of development of this conference. We are grateful to the New York Academy of Sciences and the Clayton Foundation for Research, Houston, for cosponsoring this conference and to the Clayton Foundation for Research and the National Science Foundation for providing the financial support. We would also like to thank at the Academy Ellen Marks and Carla Manzi for conference management; Bill Boland and Sheila Kane for their help in the production of this volume and Dr. Janet Tannenbaum for editing it; Dr. Daniel Ziegler, Dr. Marvin Hackert, Raquelle Keegan, and Denise Rozwarski of the University of Texas at Austin for the local arrangements for the meeting; and our departmental colleagues at Case Western Reserve University School of Medicine and Kansas State University for thoughtful consultation.

MULCHAND S. PATEL
THOMAS E. ROCHE

Opening Remarks

D. M. ZIEGLER

Clayton Foundation Biochemical Institute
The University of Texas at Austin
Austin, Texas 78712

On behalf of the Clayton Foundation Biochemical Institute, it was a real pleasure to welcome to Austin the participants in this symposium, which brought together biochemists, molecular biologists, and clinicians with a common interest in α-keto acid dehydrogenase complexes. It is only fitting that the first international conference devoted exclusively to this topic was held in Austin where, under the skilled direction of Professor Lester Reed at the University of Texas, most of the fundamental work on the composition, organization, and regulation of these multienzyme complexes was conducted. As any student in biochemistry knows, the α-keto acid dehydrogenase complexes catalyze reactions central to metabolism, and any dysfunction in these complexes, whether acquired or inherited, can lead to serious disease.

This symposium not only paid tribute to Professor Reed for his many accomplishments, but also highlighted the fundamental role of his basic research for recent advances in the diagnosis and treatment of pathological states that are due to impaired functions of one or more of these multienzyme complexes. This conference, like many others sponsored by the New York Academy of Sciences, again illustrates the vital role of basic research for continued advances in our understanding of the molecular events responsible for various pathological states. Although it is often difficult to predict its ultimate applications, it is certain that without basic research by dedicated investigators like Professor Reed, significant advances in clinical practice will not occur.

LESTER J. REED, PH.D.

A Tribute to Lester J. Reed

This conference and volume are a tribute to Dr. Lester J. Reed for his many outstanding contributions to the field of α-keto acid dehydrogenase complexes. Lester gouged out of the forest of biochemical distractions a highway that runs from lipoic acid chemistry to exquisite information on the structure, function, and regulation of α-keto acid dehydrogenase complexes. We wish to pay tribute to Lester for his dedication in this brilliant effort and for his integrity and quiet leadership, which have made lasting impressions on those who have had the privilege to be associated with him.

A Brief Biography

Lester J. Reed was born on January 3, 1925, in New Orleans, Louisiana. He received his B.S. degree at Tulane University in 1943 and completed his Ph.D. under Reynold C. Fuson at the University of Illinois in 1946. Having achieved the latter degree at the ripe old age of 21, he took a position as a postdoctoral research associate with Vincent duVigneaud at Cornell University Medical College from 1946 to 1948.

In 1948, he joined the University of Texas at Austin, where he has been a professor since 1958, director of the Clayton Foundation Biochemical Institute since 1963, and Ashbel Smith Professor since 1984.

Affiliations and Honors

Professor Reed is a member of several professional societies, has served on many advisory councils and editorial boards, and has been the recipient of several honors.

Memberships. Phi Beta Kappa, Sigma Xi, American Chemical Society, American Society for Biochemistry and Molecular Biology, the Protein Society, American Association for the Advancement of Science (Fellow), National Academy of Sciences, American Academy of Arts and Sciences.

Advisory Councils and Editorial Boards. Biochemistry Study Section of the National Institutes of Health; Editorial Board, *Archives of Biochemistry and Biophysics;* Nominating Committee and Executive Committee, Division of Biological Chemistry, American Chemical Society; Membership Committee and Nominating Committee, American Society of Biological Chemists; Editorial Board, *Journal of Biological Chemistry;* Editorial Board, *Biofactors;* U.S. National Committee for the International Union of Biochemistry.

Honors. Eli Lilly and Co. Award in Biological Chemistry (American Chemical Society), 1958; election to the National Academy of Sciences, U.S.A., 1973; Honorary Doctor of Science Degree, Tulane University, 1977; election to the American Academy of Arts and Sciences, 1981; Ashbel Smith Professor, University of Texas, 1984.

Major Contributions to Research on the Structure, Function, and Regulation of
α-Keto Acid Dehydrogenase Complexes

Lester joined the University of Texas at Austin, following his productive studies in synthetic organic chemistry with Fuson and in intermediary metabolism with duVigneaud. In 1949, the pioneering studies of Roger Williams in characterizing B vitamins were being extended in Williams's laboratory to characterizing "acetate-replacing factor." The latter studies were initiated by Esmond Snell at the University of Wisconsin and continued in Texas after Snell moved to Austin. Dr. Williams invited Lester to undertake the characterization of this factor.

The following is a selected list of landmark contributions of Lester Reed to the field of α-keto acid dehydrogenase complexes:

Isolation and characterization of lipoic acid
Identification of the functional form of lipoic acid
Resolution of *Escherichia coli* pyruvate and α-ketoglutarate dehydrogenase complexes and characterization of the components
Utilization of electron microscopy to analyze the structural organization of the bacterial and mammalian complexes
Regulation of the mammalian pyruvate dehydrogenase complex by phosphorylation-dephosphorylation
Isolation and characterization of the pyruvate dehydrogenase kinase and pyruvate dehydrogenase phosphatase
Identification of inner and outer domain structure of the transacylase components
Isolation and characterization of the branched-chain α-keto acid dehydrogenase phosphatase and its inhibitor protein

While establishing the fundamental organization of these quintessential multienzyme complexes, Lester also had a seminal role in formulating concepts concerning the unique properties attendant to the organization of enzymes in a clustered state. The following listing of selected major contributions (arbitrarily divided as convenient) gives a rough time frame for the construction of the Lester J. Reed "highway," as well as a road map for traveling the route. To be honest, my intention was to make a shorter list, but I could not delete from, but only expand on, these significant discoveries. Here, then, is a selected list of Lester's major contributions.

1949–1954

Isolation, characterization, and synthesis of α-lipoic acid: structural and physical characterization, broad distribution and enrichment in mitochondria, high-yield synthesis, ^{35}S-labeled cofactor, analogs.

1954–1958

Functional form of lipoic acid: attachment to ε-amino group of lysine, ATP-requiring (lipoyl-adenylate intermediate) reaction of lipoic acid–activating enzyme, lipoyl-X hydrolase reaction.

1957–1963

Purification of *E. coli* pyruvate and α-ketoglutarate dehydrogenase complexes, flavoprotein nature of the dihydrolipoyl dehydrogenase component, resolution and reconstitution of the *E. coli* pyruvate dehydrogenase complex, characterization of component enzymes, sequence around the ϵ-amino lipoyllysine group, purification of lipoamidase, model reactions, formation of 2-acetyl-thiamin pyrophosphate (PP), other aspects of reaction mechanism of components.

1964–1968

Electron microscopic characterization of complexes, lipoyllysine swinging arm active-site coupling mechanism, transacylase cores composed of 24 E2 subunits arranged with 432 symmetry in cube-like particle, location of the E1 component on the edges and E3 component on the faces of the cubic core, resolution and reconstitution of the *E. coli* α-ketoglutarate dehydrogenase complex, presence of the same E3 component in the pyruvate and the α-ketoglutarate dehydrogenase complexes, purification and molecular organization of the pyruvate and α-ketoglutarate dehydrogenase complexes from bovine kidney, development of concepts concerning unique properties of enzymes that are organized into complexes.

1968–1970

Regulation of the *E. coli* pyruvate dehydrogenase complex by phosphoenolpyruvate, acetyl-CoA, and guanine nucleotides; regulation of bovine kidney and heart and porcine liver pyruvate dehydrogenase complex by phosphorylation and dephosphorylation, ATP-Mg^{2+}–dependent PDH kinase tightly associated with the complex and inhibited by ADP and pyruvate, Mg^{2+}-dependent PDH phosphatase weakly associated with the complex.

1971–1974

X-ray crystallography of inner core of *E. coli* dihydrolipoyl transsuccinylase establishing octahedral (432) symmetry; preparation of the component enzymes of the pyruvate dehydrogenase complexes from bovine kidney and heart, and characterization of their physical and chemical properties; stoichiometry of subunits in the mammalian complexes; subunit ratios based on sedimentation equilibrium molecular weights of purified components of *E. coli* pyruvate and α-ketoglutarate dehydrogenase complexes; multiple phosphorylation sites in mammalian pyruvate dehydrogenase (PDH) and sequence around phosphorylation sites; characterization of PDH kinase: separation of the kinase from the transacetylase, direct pyruvate inhibition, thiamin PP inhibition, transacetylase effect on V_{max} and K_m for PDH_a, and monovalent cation effects on ADP inhibition; role of Ca^{2+} in activating PDH phosphatase by increasing its association with the transacetylase and lowering its K_m for PDH_b; first studies on modulation of steady-state phosphorylation and dephosphorylation; kinetic data supporting multisite ping-pong mechanism of kidney pyruvate dehydrogenase complex.

1975–1979

Kinetic mechanism of bovine kidney transacetylase, data supporting acetyl and electron-pair relay system between lipoyl moieties, purification and properties of bovine kidney branched-chain α-keto acid dehydrogenase complex, acetyl-CoA/CoA and $NADH/NAD^+$ effects on PDH kinase and PDH phosphatase activities, kinetic properties determined with peptide substrates of PDH kinase and PDH phosphatase, details on the sequence around phosphorylation sites, relationship between phosphorylation of specific sites and inactivation of the pyruvate dehydrogenase complex.

1979–1981

Two-domain structure of the transacetylase from *E. coli* and mammalian sources, transacetylation and E2-subunit binding role of inner domain; extended lipoyl-bearing outer domain, capacity of transacetylase domains to bind other components, contribution of structure in the lipoyl domain to the reductive acetylation reaction catalyzed by the E1 component; X-ray crystallography of the inner domain of the *E. coli* transacetylase, establishing 432 symmetry; regulatory properties of the kinase and the phosphatase, utilizing peptide substrates.

1982–1987

Purification and properties of: the pyruvate dehydrogenase phosphatase (FAD-containing 90-kDa regulatory subunit, stimulation by polyamines); the pyruvate dehydrogenase kinase; the branched-chain α-keto acid dehydrogenase phosphatase and a potent protein inhibitor of this phosphatase; and a distinct cation-independent, spermine-stimulated mitochondrial phosphatase. Computer model analysis supporting a multiple random coupling mechanism for active-site coupling through the lipoyl domains of the *E. coli* pyruvate and α-ketoglutarate dehydrogenase complexes.

1986–1988

Purification of bakers' yeast pyruvate dehydrogenase complex and phosphorylation-dephosphorylation by mammalian kinase and phosphatase; cloning of genes of components of the yeast pyruvate dehydrogenase complex.

It should be readily apparent from these latest contributions that Lester is still building the highway and opening new frontiers for further research. During preparations for this conference, Lester gave me a list of 60 students and collaborators who have contributed to the above work. For readers wanting more details about any of this work, I would note that, in addition to his numerous research papers, Lester has written 38 review articles which describe with great clarity the above work and related studies by other researchers.

October 1988

THOMAS E. ROCHE
Kansas State University
Manhattan, Kansas

2-Oxo Acid Dehydrogenase Multienzyme Complexes: Domains, Dynamics, and Design[a]

RICHARD N. PERHAM AND LEONARD C. PACKMAN

Department of Biochemistry
University of Cambridge
Tennis Court Road
Cambridge CB2 1QW, England

INTRODUCTION

The 2-oxo acid dehydrogenase multienzyme complexes catalyze the oxidative decarboxylation of 2-oxo acids, releasing CO_2 and generating the relevant acylCoA. Three principal systems are known; these have as their respective substrates pyruvate, 2-oxoglutarate, and the branched-chain 2-oxo acids related by transamination to valine, leucine, and isoleucine, respectively (for recent reviews of their structure, mechanism and genetics, see Refs. 1 and 2). The reaction catalyzed[3] is shown in schematic form in FIGURE 1. The constituent enzymes of the pyruvate dehydrogenase (PDH) complex are pyruvate decarboxylase (pyruvate dehydrogenase [lipoamide], E1p: EC 1.2.4.1), dihydrolipoamide acetyltransferase (E2p: EC 2.3.1.12), and dihydrolipoamide dehydrogenase (E3: EC 1.8.1.4). The corresponding enzymes of the 2-oxoglutarate dehydrogenase (2OGDH) complex are 2-oxoglutarate decarboxylase (E1o: EC 1.2.4.2), dihydrolipoamide succinyltransferase (E2o: EC 2.3.1.61), and dihydrolipoamide dehydrogenase (E3: EC 1.8.1.4). Similar enzymes constitute the branched-chain 2-oxo acid dehydrogenase complex.[4]

During catalysis, the substrate is attached in thioester linkage to lipoyl-lysine residues (FIG. 1), which form essentially freely rotating swinging arms. The lipoyl-lysine residues are themselves housed in small lipoyl domains which are located in the amino-terminal portions of the E2 polypeptide chains. The carboxyl-terminal portions of the E2 chains comprise larger folded domains that serve at least two known functions: they embody the acyltransferase activity that catalyzes the transfer of the acyl group from the lipoyl-lysine residue to coenzyme A and they aggregate with octahedral (24-mer) or icosahedral (60-mer) symmetry to provide the inner structural core around which the E1 and E3 subunits are assembled. As reviewed elsewhere,[1] the lipoyl domains can move with respect to the bulk of a 2-oxo acid dehydrogenase complex by virtue of the conformational flexibility found in the interdomain segments of the E2 chains, and this movement is an important contributor to the catalytic properties.

Thus, the E2 chains are of particular interest in that they provide the central structural and mechanistic cores of the enzyme complexes. In this article, we review further recent advances in our understanding of the domain structure of the E2 chains, the dynamics of the interdomain segments of polypeptide chain, and the way these

[a]This work was supported by the Science and Engineering Research Council and the Wellcome Trust.

1

might have been utilized in the evolutionary design of the 2-oxo acid dehydrogenase complexes.

DOMAINS AND LINKERS IN THE E2 CHAINS

Knowledge about the domain structures of the E2 chains of 2-oxo acid dehydrogenase complexes has largely been derived from detailed study of the E2p and E2o chains of the PDH and 2OGDH complexes of *Escherichia coli*. The amino acid sequence of the *E. coli* E2p chain (66 kDa) has been deduced from the nucleotide sequence of the

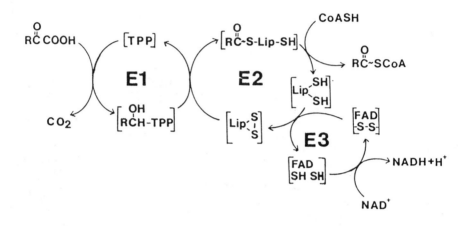

Net Reaction

$$\underset{\substack{|| \\ O}}{RCCOOH} + NAD^+ + CoASH \longrightarrow \underset{\substack{|| \\ O}}{RC} \sim SCoA + NADH + H^+ + CO_2$$

FIGURE 1. The reaction mechanism of oxidative decarboxylation by 2-oxo acid dehydrogenase complexes. $R = CH_3$ for the pyruvate dehydrogenase (PDH) complex; $R = CH_2CH_2COOH$ for the 2-oxoglutarate dehydrogenase (2OGDH) complex; $R = (CH_3)_2CH$, $(CH_3)_2CHCH_2$, or $(CH_3)(C_2H_5)CH$ for the branched-chain 2-oxo acid dehydrogenase complex. TPP, thiamin pyrophosphate; Lip, lipoic acid. (Adapted from Reed.[3])

gene, *ace*F, that encodes it.[5] The amino-terminal half of the chain consists of three highly homologous lipoyl domains, each of about 80 amino acid residues, which can be released from the complex by mild treatment with trypsin or *Staphylococcus aureus* V8 proteinase and which, in this free form, retain their ability to act as substrates for E1p.[6] The residual E2p chain (36 kDa) remains assembled as an octahedral core, still capable of binding E1p and E3 subunits. The cleavage sites for the two proteinases lie in the interdomain segments, which are long (20–30 amino acid residues) and rich in alanine, proline, and charged amino acids (FIG. 2).

The amino acid sequence of the *E. coli* E2o chain has similarly been deduced from the nucleotide sequence of its encoding gene, *suc*B.[7] This differs from E2p in having

Lipoyl domains

```
          1                   20                    40                         60                               80                          100
E2pL1   AIEIKVPDIGADEVE--ITEILVKVGDKVEAEQSLITVEGDKASMEVPSPQAGIVKEIKVSVSGDKTQTGALIMIFDSADGAADAAPAQAEEKKEAAPAAAPAAAA
                                                                                                                 TTV
                                                                                                                ↓↓↓
          101                 120                   140                         160                   180                      200
E2pL2   -KDVNVPDIGSDEVE--VTEILVKVGDKVEAEQSLITVEGDKASMEVPAPFAGTVKEIKVNVGDKVSTGSLIMFEVAGRAGAAAPAA---KQEAAPAAAPAPAAG
                                                                                                    T  V       T
                                                                                                    ↓  ↓       ↓
          201                 220                   240                         260                   280                      300
E2pL3   VKEVNVPDIGGDEVE--VTEVMKVGDKVAAEQSLITVEGDKASMEVPAPFAGVVKELKVNVGDKVKTGSLIMIFEVEGAAPAAAPA---KQEAAPAAKAEAPAAAAPAAAKAEGK
                                                                                                    V               VT  T
                                                                                                    ↓               ↓↓  ↓
          1                   20                    40                         60                               80
E2oL    SSVDILVPDLPESVADATVATWHKKPGDAVVRDEVLVEIETDKVVLEVPASADGILDAVLEDEGTIVTSRQILGRLREGNSAGKETSAKSEEK-ASTPAQRQQAS---------
                                                                                                    V    VT
                                                                                                    ↓    ↓↓
```

E3-binding and inner-core domains

```
          V                   320                   340          360             T V       380                  400                420
E2p     SEFAENDAYVHATPLIRRLAREFGVNLAKVKGTGRKGRILREDVQAVVKEAIKRAEAAPAATGGGIPGMLPWPKVDFSKFGEIEEVELGRIQKISGANLSRNWVMIPHVTHFDKTDIT
                                                                 ↓ ↓
          101                 120                   140          V  160           200
E2o     LEEQNNDAL---SPAIRRLLAEHNLDASAIKGTGVGGRLTREDVEKHLAKAPA---KESAPAAAAPAAQPALAA-------RSEKR-VPMTRLRKRVAERLLEAKNSTAMLTTFNEVNMK

          421                 440                   460             480               500                520                   540
E2p     ELEAFRKQQNEEAAKRKLDVKITPVVFIMKAVAAALEQMPRFNSSLSEDGQRLTLKKYINIGVAVDTPNGLVVPVPFKDVNKKGIIELSREIMTISKKARDGKLTAGEMQGGCFTISSI

          201                 220                   240               260             280                  300                   320
E2o     PIMDLRKQYGEAFEKR-HGIRLGFMSFYVKAVVEALKRYPEVNASI--DGDDVVYHNYFDVSMAVSTPRGLVTPVLRDVDTLGMADIEKKIKELAVKGRDGKLTVEDLTGGNFTITNG

          541                 560                   580               600                620       629
E2p     GGLGTTHFAPIVNAPEVAILGVSKSAMEPVWNGKEFVPRLMLPISLSFDHRVIDGADGARFITIINNTLSDIRRLVM

          321                 340                   360               380              400        404
E2o     GVFGSLMSTPIINPPQSAILGMHAIKDRPMAVNGQVEILPMMYIALSYDHRLIDGRESVGFIVTIKELLEDPTRLLLDV
```

FIGURE 2. Amino acid sequences of the E2p and E2o chains from the PDH and 2OGDH complexes of *E. coli.* Segments of polypeptide chain rich in alanine, proline and charged amino acids, which link folded domains, are *underlined*. Cleavage sites for trypsin (T) and *S. aureus* V8 proteinase (V) are indicated. ●, site of lipoylation of a lysine residue.

only one lipoyl domain, and it has been known for some time that this can be selectively released from the 2OGDH complex by mild treatment with trypsin.[8] It has recently been found that digestion with *S. aureus* V8 proteinase not only releases this lipoyl domain but additionally removes the E3 component.[9] A small folded domain, about 50 residues in length, of E2o could be isolated from the digest, and this domain selectively bound to E3, suggesting that it forms an E3-binding domain in the E2o chain.[9] In the sequence of E2o,[7,10] this E3-binding domain is linked to the lipoyl domain by a region (about 20 residues long) rich in polar and charged amino acids. A region of similar size but rich in alanine and proline residues links the E3-binding domain to the inner core domain (FIG. 2). On the basis of data from more extensive tryptic digestion of the E2p chain of *E. coli*,[9,11] it is thought that a similar E3-binding domain exists in the PDH complex also, but the segment of polypeptide chain linking this domain to the inner core domain is less conspicuously rich in alanine and proline residues (FIG. 2). In both the E2p and E2o chains, the inner core domain, apart from dictating the symmetry of aggregation, and binding the E1p and E1o components, also houses the acyltransferase active site.[9-11] The highly segmented structures of the E2p and E2o chains are represented schematically in FIGURE 3.

Similar results have since been reported for other 2-oxo acid dehydrogenase complexes. The PDH complex of *Bacillus stearothermophilus* differs from the PDH and 2OGDH complexes of *E. coli* in being assembled around an icosahedral E2p core.[12] Treatment of this PDH complex successively with chymotrypsin and trypsin can be used to produce the single lipoyl domain, the E3-binding domain and the residual inner core domain, which show significant homology with their counterparts from the E2p and E2o chains of *E. coli*.[13,14] However, the interdomain segments are somewhat different; the segment (about 37 residues long) linking the lipoyl domain to the E3-binding domain comprises an amino-terminal half dominated by charged and polar residues, similar to the corresponding segment of E2o in *E. coli*, and a carboxyl-terminal half which is rich in alanine and proline residues, characteristic of this region in E2p of *E. coli*. The segment linking the E3-binding domain to the inner core domain is rich in alanine and proline residues, like its *E. coli* counterparts (FIG. 3). An important difference is that the E3-binding domain of the icosahedral PDH complex of *B. stearothermophilus* also appears to be responsible for binding the E1 component, since its loss causes the complex to disassemble to a naked inner core.[15,13]

With the elucidation of the DNA sequences of genes or cDNAs encoding the E2 chains of other 2-oxo acid dehydrogenase complexes, it has become apparent that the structural features of segmented E2 chains are general and widespread. Thus, the E2p chains of the PDH complexes of *Azotobacter vinelandii*,[16] rat liver,[17,18] human placenta,[19,20] and yeast[21,14] and the E2 chains of branched-chain 2-oxo acid dehydrogenase complexes of *Pseudomonas putida*[22] and ox liver[23] can all be divided into one or more amino-terminal lipoyl domains, an E3/E1-binding domain, and an inner-core (transacylase) domain, separated by interdomain segments of unusual amino acid composition (see below). There can be little doubt, therefore, that this is the structural pattern to which all E2 chains conform.

FUNCTIONS OF THE LIPOYL DOMAINS

An obvious question to ask of the PDH complex of *E. coli* is why it has three lipoyl domains in its E2p chain. In an attempt to answer this, the *ace*F gene has been engineered *in vitro* to create E2p chains from which one or two lipoyl domains were deleted. A multienzyme complex was still assembled *in vivo* with these shortened

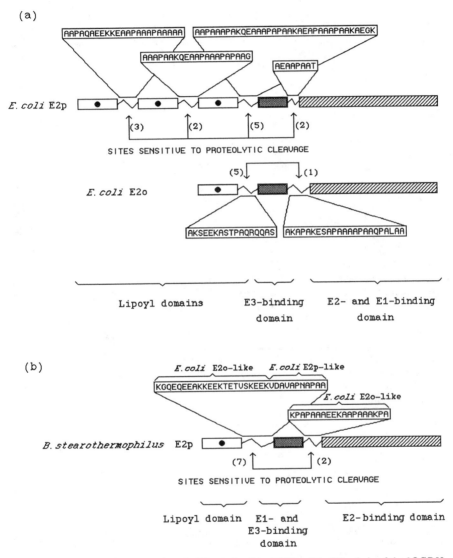

FIGURE 3. Domain structures of (**a**) the E2p chain of the PDH and the E2o chain of the 2OGDH complex from *E. coli* and (**b**) the E2p chain of the PDH complex from *B. stearothermophilus*. The primary structures of the interdomain segments (*jagged lines*) are shown in exploded view. *Numbers in parenthesis* denote the number of identified cleavage sites in limited proteolysis experiments. ●, lipoic acid.

chains, and in each case there was no detectable loss of catalytic activity.[24,25] There is therefore no obvious answer as yet to this question.

On the other hand, lipoyl domains are evidently an important structural feature of all 2-oxo acid dehydrogenase complexes. The reason for this has now been found in an unusual aspect of the first step in the catalytic mechanism, the step catalyzed by E1.[26] Although free lipoic acid and lipoamide can act as substrates in the reactions catalyzed by the E2p and E3 components of the *E. coli* PDH complex,[27] direct reductive acetylation of these compounds by the E1p component does not seem to occur to any appreciable extent.[27,28] However, lipoyl domains excised proteolytically from the complex are reductively acetylated by E1p in the presence of thiamin pyrophosphate (TPP), Mg^{2+}, and pyruvate.[6] Similar results have been obtained with lipoyl domains and E1p components from the ox heart[29] and *B. stearothermophilus*[30] PDH complexes.

A detailed kinetic analysis[26] has revealed that lipoamide is actually a very poor substrate for *E. coli* E1p, with a K_m in excess of 4 mM and a value of k_{cat}/K_m of 1.5 $M^{-1}s^{-1}$. On the other hand, free lipoyl domains from *E. coli* E2p are reductively acetylated much more readily, with a K_m of approx. 26 μM and a value of k_{cat}/K_m of approximately 3.0×10^4 $M^{-1}s^{-1}$, a value some 20,000 times higher than that for lipoamide as substrate. Moreover, it was found that the lipoyl domains from E2p and E2o chains of *E. coli* functioned effectively as substrates only with the E1p and E1o components of their cognate complexes. A lipoylated decapeptide whose amino acid sequence was identical to that surrounding each of the three lipoyl-lysine residues in the *E. coli* E2p chain was ineffective as a substrate for E1p.[26]

The greatly enhanced ability of lipoic acid to act as a substrate that accompanies the attachment of the lipoyl group to a protein domain, and the conferment of specificity by that domain, are not obvious requirements of the chemical mechanism of oxidative decarboxylation (FIG. 1). But, on the assumption that what is true of the *E. coli* PDH and 2OGDH complexes is true of 2-oxo acid dehydrogenase complexes in general, the need for lipoyl domains in the E2 chains is fully apparent. The ineffectiveness of the lipoylated peptide demonstrates that the primary structure around the lipoyl-lysine residue is insufficient to enhance the ability of the dithiolane ring to undergo reductive acylation. It is reasonable to infer that some molecular recognition and interaction between a folded lipoyl domain and its cognate E1 component is an essential part of the E1-catalyzed step in a 2-oxo acid dehydrogenase complex. Understanding the reason for this will clearly repay study.

DYNAMICS OF INTERDOMAIN SEGMENTS IN E2 CHAINS

Based on the sensitivity of the E2 cores to limited proteolysis, and the improved clarity with which an inner core could be seen in the electron microscope after such proteolysis, it was suggested that the lipoylated regions of the E2 chains might protrude outwards between the E1 and E3 subunits in the complexes and might be sufficiently flexible to facilitate movement of the lipoyl-lysine residues between the E1, E2, and E3 active sites.[15,31,32]

The best and most direct evidence for conformational flexibility in the E2 chains has come from ^{1}H-NMR spectroscopy of the 2-oxo acid dehydrogenase complexes (for a review of early work, see Ref. 33). Despite their large sizes (M_r ca. $5-10 \times 10^6$), a wide range of PDH and 2OGDH complexes were found to exhibit a family of sharp resonances (linewidth about 30–50 Hz) in their ^{1}H-NMR spectra, indicative of conformational flexibility that could be localized to the lipoylated regions of their E2 chains.[8,30,34,35] The sharp resonances were dominated by those which, on the basis of their stoichiometry and chemical shifts, could be attributed to substantial numbers of aliphatic side chains, notably those of alanine (or threonine) residues. Moreover, the 500-MHz ^{1}H-NMR spectrum of the lipoyl domain released by chymotryptic digestion of the PDH complex from *B. stearothermophilus* was characteristic of a small folded protein whose tertiary structure was stable even at elevated temperature (45°C).[30] It was tempting, therefore, to suggest that the conformationally mobile segments of the E2 chains must be the long interdomain segments rich in alanine and proline residues.[6,7] Observations based on a combination of NMR spectroscopy and protein engineering of the *E. coli* PDH complex have since amply substantiated that proposal.

As mentioned above, two lipoyl domains can be deleted from the E2p chain of the *E. coli* PDH complex without significant loss of catalytic activity or detectable

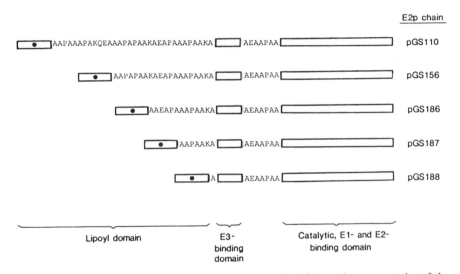

FIGURE 4. Nested deletions in an interdomain linker region. Schematic representation of the domain (*boxes*) and linker structures of E2p chains of *E. coli* with one lipoyl domain and a nested set of deletions in the long sequence rich in alanine and proline joining the lipoyl domain to the E3-binding domain. ●, site of lipoylation of a lysine residue in the lipoyl domain.

impairment of the intramolecular active-site coupling reactions.[24] Similarly, 12 residues can be deleted from the region rich in alanine and proline that links the one remaining lipoyl domain to the E3-binding domain, again without significant effect.[36] These deletions (FIG. 4) were accompanied by corresponding falls in the intensity of the sharp resonances in the 400-MHz ^{1}H-NMR spectrum of the reconstructed (pGS110- and pGS156-encoded) complexes.[11] A more direct, and unequivocal, proof has come from a site-directed mutagenesis experiment. The replacement of Gln-291 (original E2p numbering[5]) with a histidine residue in the region rich in alanine and proline that links the one lipoyl domain to the E3-binding domain in the pGS110-encoded complex (FIG. 5) can be also achieved without damage to the resultant (pGS178-encoded) complex. Two new sharp signals were observed in the aromatic region of the 400-MHz ^{1}H-NMR spectrum of this mutated complex (FIG. 5), with

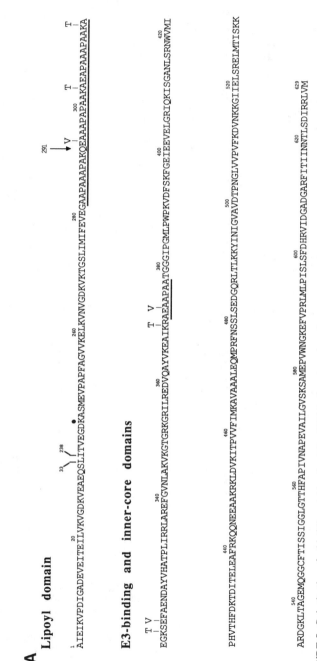

FIGURE 5. Substitution of a histidine residue (position 291) into an interdomain segment. Amino acid sequence (A) of the pGS110-encoded E2p chain of the *E. coli* PDH complex, numbered according to the wild-type E2p chain,[5] with an *arrow* marking the site of the Q291H mutation in the pGS178-encoded E2p chain. ●, site of lipoylation of a lysine residue; T, V, sites of limited proteolysis with trypsin and *S. aureus* V8 proteinase, respectively. The regions rich in alanine and proline are *underlined*.

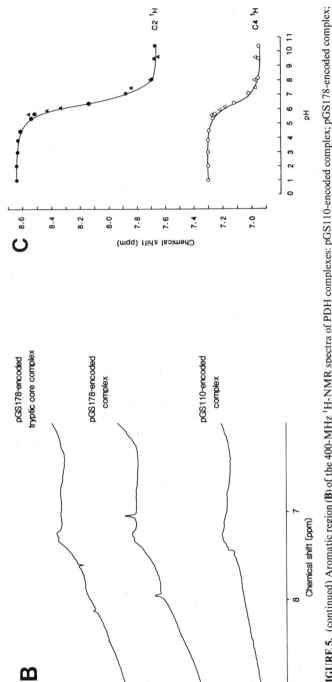

FIGURE 5. (continued) Aromatic region (**B**) of the 400-MHz ^{1}H-NMR spectra of PDH complexes: pGS110-encoded complex; pGS178-encoded complex; tryptic core of the pGS178-encoded complex (36-kDa E2p chain, cleavage at Lys-316; E1p and E3 remain bound). Titration curves (**C**) of a histidine residue at position 291 in the E2p chain of the pGS178-encoded PDH complex and of a histidine residue in a 32-residue synthetic peptide. The amino acid sequence of the peptide was identical to that of the interdomain segment linking the lipoyl domain to the E3-binding domain in the pGS178-encoded E2p chain. The chemical shifts of the C-2 and C-4 protons of the histidine residues in the 400-MHz ^{1}H-NMR spectra were measured relative to internal 3-(trimethylsilyl)-2,2,3,3-tetradeuteropropionic acid (TSP). ● and O, C-2 and C-4 protons, respectively, of the histidine residue in the synthetic peptide; ▲ and △, C-2 and C-4 protons, respectively, of His-291 in the E2p chain of the pGS178-encoded PDH complex.

chemical shifts characteristic of the C-2 and C-4 protons of a histidine residue.[37]Furthermore, the pK_a (6.4) of the new histidine residue in the pGS178-encoded PDH complex[37] was found to be indistinguishable from that of the histidine residue in a 32-residue synthetic peptide whose sequence was identical to that of the interdomain segment,[38] as judged by the pH-dependence of the chemical shifts in the NMR spectra. These are striking results and introduce a novel approach to the study of conformational flexibility in proteins.

Excision of the single lipoyl domain from the E2o chain of the 2OGDH complex of *E. coli* by limited proteolysis with trypsin, now known to be due to cleavage at Arg-100,[10] occurs without any appreciable fall in the sharp resonances attributable to alanine side chains in the ^{1}H-NMR spectrum of the complex.[8] It is likely, therefore, that the source of some of these sharp resonances is the interdomain segment of the E2o chain that links the E3-binding domain to the inner core domain and is conspicuously rich in alanine and proline residues (FIGS. 2 and 3). Similarly, in the 400-MHz ^{1}H-NMR spectra of pGS110- and pGS156-encoded PDH complexes (FIG. 4), another sharp, but small, resonance (at 1.52 ppm) was revealed, which had been masked thitherto by the much larger sharp resonance (at 1.39 ppm) in the spectrum of the wild-type complex with its full complement of three lipoyl domains and interdomain segments.[11] It is conceivable, but not yet proved, that this sharp resonance may derive from the smaller segment rich in alanine and proline that separates the E3-binding domain from the inner core domain in the E2p chain (FIGS. 2 and 3). If, as seems likely, these interdomain segments of the E2p and E2o chains are also conformationally flexible and in turn confer mobility upon the E3-binding domain, it would offer an explanation of earlier fluorescence data which suggest that E3 bound to the *E. coli* PDH complex possesses unexpectedly high mobility.[39]

ROLE OF INTERDOMAIN SEGMENTS IN E2 CHAINS

In the *E. coli* PDH and 2OGDH complexes, the lipoyl-lysine residues can interact with each other by means of an extensive network of intramolecular coupling reactions that permit the transfer of acyl groups between different E2p or E2o subunits in the enzyme core.[40,41] For the PDH complex, it has also been shown that any given E1p subunit can be visited by more than one lipoyl group.[42-44] The superfluity of lipoyl groups, at least in the *E. coli* PDH complex, is emphasized by the demonstration, as noted above, that two of the three lipoyl domains per E2p chain can be deleted by genetic manipulation *in vitro* without apparent effect on the catalytic properties of the complex.[24] The advantages these unusual properties confer on the 2-oxo acid dehydrogenase complexes in terms of catalyzing a multistep reaction and of relieving them of the necessity to adhere to a strict stoichiometry and geometry of assembly have been reviewed elsewhere.[1]

Direct proof that at least one of the interdomain segments of the E2p chain acts to facilitate the system of active-site coupling in the *E. coli* PDH complex has now come from protein engineering experiments.[36,45] A nested set of deletions was created in the long sequence rich in alanine and proline that links the one remaining lipoyl domain to the E3-binding domain in the E2p chain of the pGS110-encoded complex (FIG. 4). In all cases, active PDH complexes were still assembled *in vivo*, despite the deletions in the E2p chains. Shortening the linker to 20 residues (pGS156-encoded complex) was without apparent effect,[36] but cutting it to 13 residues (pGS186-encoded complex) or less (pGS187- and pGS188-encoded complexes) progressively caused substantial falls in the reductive acetylation of the lipoyl domain and corresponding losses in catalytic activity and active-site coupling.[45] This was reflected in poorer growth rates of the relevant strains of *E. coli* on stringent substrates.

Thus, *in vitro* and *in vivo*, there is good evidence that this particular interdomain segment is not concerned with the folding of the recognized protein domains in the E2p chain, that it is not required for the part-reactions of the complex, but that it serves as a linker region to facilitate the transfer of substrate between the successive active sites. Moreover, it has to be more than 13 amino acid residues in length to be fully effective. By extension, it is reasonable to propose that the other interdomain segments in the E2 chains of 2-oxo acid dehydrogenase complexes serve similar purposes.

THE CONFORMATION IN SOLUTION OF SYNTHETIC PEPTIDES REPRESENTING INTERDOMAIN SEGMENTS OF E2 CHAINS

In view of the high M_r (ca. $5-10 \times 10^6$) of the intact 2-oxo acid dehydrogenase complexes, it is clearly going to be difficult to pursue the study of the interdomain segments by means of ^{1}H-NMR spectroscopy of the complexes themselves. We have therefore turned to a study of synthetic peptides.

A 32-residue peptide was synthesized with an amino acid sequence identical to the long segment rich in alanine and proline that links the E3-binding domain to the inner lipoyl domain of the *E. coli* E2p chain (FIGS. 2 and 3). The 400-MHz ^{1}H-NMR spectra of this peptide and of the intact PDH complex were found to bear a striking resemblance to each other (FIG. 6), despite the huge differences in their M_r (ca. 2800 and 5×10^6, respectively).[38,46] This result strongly supports the identification of the segments rich in alanine and proline of the E2p chain as the source of many of the sharp resonances in the ^{1}H-NMR spectrum of the PDH complex (see above) and the view that they must have substantial conformational freedom with respect to the bulk of the complex.

The frequent occurrence of proline in the inter domain segments of the E2 chains suggests that these sequences are unlikely to form highly ordered structures in solution, despite the propensity of alanine residues to enter into α-helices. A circular dichroism study of the synthetic peptide bore this out; the peptide appeared to exist predominantly in an unfolded state in aqueous solution and was induced to fold only partly in the presence of organic solvents.[38] However, close inspection of the ^{1}H-NMR spectrum revealed that the chemical shifts of the alanine α-CH proton resonances were significantly dispersed, the α-CH protons of alanine residues which immediately precede proline resonating downfield (4.60 ppm) from the same protons of the bulk of the alanine residues (which resonated at 4.29 ppm). Moreover, in natural-abundance ^{13}C-NMR spectra, the α-CH and β-CH$_3$ carbon resonance of the alanine residues each occurred as composite signals at two separate chemical shifts and, for the β-CH$_2$ carbon resonance of proline, the signals derived from the *cis* and *trans* isomers about the Ala-Pro peptide bond were well resolved (FIG. 7). This enabled the *cis:trans* ratio to be determined: the Ala-Pro bonds in the synthetic interdomain peptide were found to exist exclusively (>95%) in the *trans* form, in marked contrast with the model peptides Ala-Pro-Gly and Ala-Ala-Pro-Ala, which were found to exist in only 73% and 87% *trans* form, respectively.[38]

The predominance of the *trans* configuration of the Ala-Pro peptide bonds in the synthetic peptide was confirmed by nuclear Overhäuser enhancement (nOe) measurements, and similar experiments with an intact PDH complex containing E2p chains with a single lipoyl domain indicated that this configuration was conserved in the native enzyme.[38] It appears, therefore, that this interdomain segment adopts a

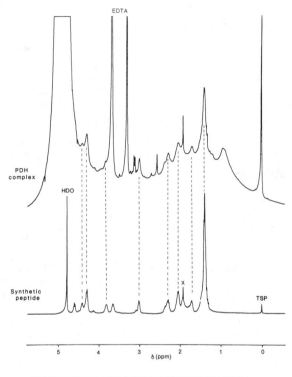

Peptide sequence : AAPAAAPAKQEAAAPAPAAKAEAPAAAPAAKA

FIGURE 6. Comparison of the 400-MHz ¹H-NMR spectra of the wild-type *E. coli* PDH complex and a 32-residue synthetic peptide. The amino acid sequence of the peptide was identical to that of the interdomain segment linking the innermost lipoyl domain to the E3-binding domain in the wild-type E2p chain. The resonances marked × arise from non-protein contaminants.

relatively stiffened conformation in solution, its segmental flexibility restricted around the Ala-Pro peptide bonds, which in turn reduces the number of structures available to it. This could limit the three-dimensional space in which the lipoyl domains are free to move in the complex, a limitation that may have evolved to optimize interaction between the lipoyl domains and the three different active sites in the enzyme complex (see below). Further work is needed on synthetic peptides representing other interdomain segments from the 2-oxo acid dehydrogenase complexes to see how widely these structural findings apply.

DESIGN OF 2-OXO ACID DEHYDROGENASE COMPLEXES

Three features of the structural organization of 2-oxo acid dehydrogenase complexes can now be considered in the light of the recent advances in our knowledge of these unusually complicated enzymes.

First, is there any correlation between the number of lipoyl domains per E2 chain and the symmetry of the E2 core (TABLE 1)? The presence of three lipoyl domains per

E2p chain[5,6] and of only one per E2o chain[7] in the PDH and 2OGDH complexes of *E. coli,* respectively, despite the fact that both are based on E2 cores of octahedral symmetry,[3,47] means that this symmetry is not limited to E2p chains with either just one or three lipoyl domains. This observation is underlined by the ability to create, by *in vitro* genetic manipulation of the *ace*F gene, active *E. coli* PDH complexes with one, two, or three lipoyl domains per E2p chain.[24] Similarly, the PDH complexes of mammalian mitochondria[3] and of the Gram-positive organism *B. stearothermophilus,*[12] are based on E2 cores of icosahedral symmetry. Yet the sequence evidence is now clear that the E2p chain of the *B. stearothermophilus*[13] and yeast,[14,21] enzymes contains one lipoyl domain, whereas that of the human placental enzyme[19,20] and probably also of the rat liver enzyme[17] contains two. However, the E2p chain of

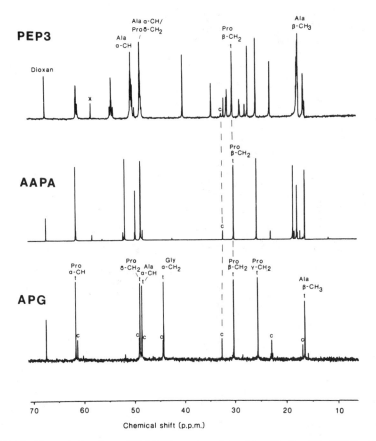

FIGURE 7. Natural-abundance ^{13}C-NMR spectra of peptides Ala-Pro-Gly (**APG**), Ala-Ala-Pro-Ala (**AAPA**), and a 32-residue synthetic peptide (**PEP3**). The amino acid sequence of PEP3 was identical to that of the interdomain segment linking the innermost lipoyl domain to the E3-binding domain in the wild-type E2p chain of *E. coli.* **APG:** 2.5 mg/ml; **AAPA:** 21 mg/ml; and **PEP3:** 30 mg/ml. The resonances arising from the *cis* (**c**) and *trans* (**t**) isomers of several residues are marked. The resonance labeled × in the spectrum for **PEP3** arises from a non-protein contaminant.

TABLE 1. Some Principal Features of the Structure and Assembly of the 2-Oxo Acid Dehydrogenase Complexes

Organism	Gram Stain	Pyruvate Dehydrogenase Complex			2-Oxoglutarate Dehydrogenase Complex			Branched-Chain 2-Oxo Acid Dehydrogenase Complex		
		E2 Core	No. of Lipoyl Domains[a]	E1 Chains	E2 Core	No. of Lipoyl Domains	E1 Chains	E2 core	No. of Lipoyl Domains	E1 Chains
Escherichia coli[3,5-7]	–	Octahedral	3	Single	Octahedral	1	Single			
Salmonella typhimurium[55]	–	Octahedral	(3)	Single	Octahedral[b]	1	Single			
Azotobacter vinelandii[16,56]	–	Octahedral	3	Single	n.k.[c]	n.k.[c]	n.k.[c]			
Pseudomonas spp.[22,57,58]	–	n.k.[c]	n.k.[c]	Single	n.k.[c]	n.k.[c]	n.k.[c]	n.k.[c]	1	Split
Bacillus stearothermophilus[12,50]	+	Icosahedral	1	Split				Icosahedral	1	Split
Bacillus subtilis[50,59]	+	Icosahedral	1	Split	n.k.[c]	n.k.[c]	Single	Icosahedral	1	Split
Neurospora crassa[60,61]		Icosahedral	(1)	Split						
Saccharomyces spp.[21,48,62]		Icosahedral	1	Split	Octahedral[d]	n.k.[c]	n.k.[c]			
Mammals (rat, ox, pig, human)[17,19,20,23,29,63,64]		Icosahedral	2	Split	Octahedral	1	Single	Octahedral	1	Split

[a]Numbers in parentheses denote number of lipoyl domains inferred from the apparent molecular mass of the E2 component on sodium dodecyl sulfate–polyacrylamide gels.

[b]Assumed symmetry based on the similarity of the complex to those of E. coli and pig, whose symmetries are known; see Ref. 56.

[c]n.k., not known.

[d]Tentative assignment; see Ref. 62.

Azotobacter vinelandii, which is Gram-negative, like *E. coli,* also contains three lipoyl domains.[16] As more E2 sequences are determined, it will be interesting to see whether this incipient evidence of correlation is at least sustained for Gram-positive and Gram-negative organisms. What is clear at this stage from the sequence homologies is that the octahedral and icosahedral core-forming E2 chains of prokaryotes and eukaryotes have arisen by divergent evolution from a common ancestor.

Secondly, incipient evidence of another correlation, which has survived thus far, is that the PDH complexes of Gram-positive organisms and eukaryotes are similar in symmetry and subunit structure and distinguished from the PDH complexes of Gram-negative organisms in both regards (TABLE 1).[12] Thus, the former have E2 cores of icosahedral symmetry and E1 components composed of E1α and E1β subunits,[3,12,48] whereas the latter have E2 cores of octahedral symmetry and E1 components composed of unsplit E1 polypeptide chains.[3,47] The PDH complex of *A. vinelandii* (Gram-negative) conforms to this pattern, although it has been suggested that the organization of its E2 core is somewhat different.[49]

The correlation of E1α, E1β chains with an E2 core of icosahedral symmetry for a PDH complex does not extend to the branched-chain 2-oxo acid dehydrogenase complexes. It is satisfied by the branched-chain 2-oxo acid dehydrogenase and pyruvate dehydrogenase complexes of *B. subtilis,* which appear to be one and the same,[50] but it is breached by the branched-chain 2-oxo acid dehydrogenase complexes of mammals. These have split E1α, E1β chains yet are based on E2 cores of octahedral symmetry.[4,51,52] And, although the symmetry of the E2 cores has not been reported, the E1 components of the branched-chain 2-oxo acid dehydrogenase complexes of the Gram-negative organisms *Pseudomonas putida* and *Pseudomonas aeruginosa*[53,54] are also composed of E1α and E1β subunits. So this correlation, too, is poor.

Thirdly, what can we learn about the design of interdomain segments of polypeptide chain from a study of E2 primary structures? The amino acid sequences of the putative interdomain segments drawn from the published primary structures of E2 chains of pyruvate, 2-oxoglutarate and branched-chain 2-oxo acid dehydrogenase complexes from a wide variety of organisms are listed in TABLE 2. Although generally similar, they also differ considerably, ranging from those dominated by alanine and proline residues to some more obviously hydrophilic and charged. Some, indeed, e.g., those of *B. stearothermophilus* E2p, are combinations of these two types,[13] whereas those of the mammalian pyruvate and branched-chain complexes are particularly rich in contiguous proline residues. The interdomain sequences from mammalian E2p chains are almost devoid of charged groups, bearing only an occasional lysine or arginine residue. The hydrophilic nature of the sequences appears to be maintained through an abundance of threonine and serine residues, which is also a feature of one sequence from yeast. Few of the interdomain sequences from prokaryotes or eukaryotes have any aromatic residues, an observation predicted for *E. coli, B. stearothermophilus,* and ox E2p from ^{1}H-NMR experiments.[33] Where such residues do occur, the more hydrophilic tyrosine is chosen; histidine, which has the capacity to become charged, appears to be confined to the carboxyl-terminal ends of the sequences. The sequence linking the inner lipoyl domain to the E3-binding domain in human E2p is so far unique in bearing a cysteine residue. Whether this is involved in a cystine bridge or is reactive to thiol reagents is unknown, but there is potential here to study its interaction with the rest of E2p, E1, and E3.

Thus, it is now quite clear that the interdomain sequences of E2p chains from *E. coli*—the first to be identified—are members of a widely ranging group of structures which differ significantly in absolute sequence yet perform closely related functions. It has already been pointed out[38] that such differences might be the result of careful selection in the course of evolution and could conceivably reflect structural refinement

TABLE 2. Amino Acid Sequences in the Interdomain Segments of the E2 Components of the 2-Oxo Acid Dehydrogenase Complexes from Some Gram-Negative, Gram-Positive, and Eukaryotic Organisms

Organism/Segment[a]	Residues[b]	Sequence
Gram-Negative		
Escherichia coli[5,7]		
E2p L1–L2	82–104	AAPAQAEEKKEAAPAAAPAAAAA
E2p L2–L3	182–204	AGAAAPAAKQEAAPAAAPAPAAG
E2p L3–E3bd	282–316	AAPAAAPAKQEAAAPAPAAKAEAPAAAAPAAKAEGK
E2p E3bd–cat	371–377	AEAAPAA
E2o L–E3bd	82–104	AGKETSAKSEEKASTPAQRQQAS
E2o E3bd–cat	150–172	AKAPAKESAPAAAAPAAQPALAA
Azotobacter vinelandii[16]		
E2p L1–L2	74–115	PAAGAAAAPAEAAAVPAAPTQAVDEAEAPSPGASATPAPAAA
E2p L2–L3	194–219	AQAQPTAPAAAAASPAPAPLAPAAA
E2p L3–E3bd	299–329	AAPSGPRARGSPGQAAAAPGAAPAPAPVGAP
E2p E3bd–cat	381–402	AKEAPAAGAASGAGIPPIPPVD
Pseudomonas putida[22]		
E2b L–E3bd	90–125	AKPAEVPAAPVAAKPEPQKDVKPAAYQASASHEAAP
E2b E3bd–cat	176–197	PQSAAGQTPNGYARRTDSEQVP
Gram-Positive		
Bacillus stearothermophilus[13]		
E2p L–E3bd	86–122	KGQEQEEAKKEEKTETVSKEEKVDAVAPNAPAAEAEA
E2p E3bd–cat	167–189	AGGAKPAPAAAEEKAAPAAAKPA

Eukaryotic

Saccharomyces cerevisiae[21]		
E2p L–E3bd	99–142	SGSDSKTSTKAQPAEPQAEKKQEAPAEETKTSAPEAKKSDVAAP
E2p E3bd–cat	185–222	EKSSKQSSQTSGAAAATPAAATSSTTAGSAPSPSSTAS
Rat[19]		
E2p L1–L2	13–39[c]	ATAATQAAPAPAAAPAAAPAAPSASAP
E2p L2–E3bd	144–175[c]	PQAPPPVPPPVAAVPPIPQPLAPTPSAAPAGP
E2p E3bd–cat	218–240[c]	PTKAAPAAAAAAPPGPRVAPTPA
Human[20]		
E2p L1–L2	97–131	SSAAPTPQAAPAPTPAATASPPTPSAQAPGSSYPP
E2p L2–E3bd	230–265	PQVPPPTPPPVAAVPPTPQPLAPTPSAPCPATPAGP[d]
E2p E3bd–cat	308–330	PSKVAPAPAAVVPPTGPGMAPVP
Human and bovine[23]		
E2b L–E3bd	80–103	EALKDSEEDVVETPAVSHDEHTHQ
E2b E3bd–cat	153–173	GAILPPSPKVEIMPPPPKPKD

[a]Interdomain segments of E2 components of the pyruvate (E2p), 2-oxoglutarate (E2o), and branched-chain 2-oxo acid (E2b) dehydrogenase complexes. The segments linking the lipoyl domains (L1, L2, L3, L) to each other or to the E3-binding domains (E3bd) and segments linking the E3-binding and catalytic domains (cat) are indicated.

[b]The limits of all interdomain segments are uncertain. Evidence that the sequences from *E. coli* and *B. stearothermophilus* link folded structural domains can be found in Refs. 6, 9, 10, 30, 45; the choice of interdomain sequences in other organisms was made by comparison of their E2 sequences with those from *E. coli* and *B. stearothermophilus*.

[c]Sequence inferred from an incomplete cDNA clone; numbering is from the first residue of the deduced sequence, not from the anticipated amino terminus of the mature protein.

[d]*: alanine reported as threonine in Ref. 19.

of these segments to optimize domain movement in catalysis. In all cases, it would appear that the interdomain segments are somewhat extended, as well as conformationally mobile, structures, keeping domains apart in addition to allowing them to move with respect to one another. Further experiments in NMR spectroscopy and protein engineering should throw more light on this fascinating problem, with important lessons to be learned about the folding and conformational flexibility of polypeptide chains in general.

ACKNOWLEDGMENTS

We thank Professor J. R. Guest and Dr. J. S. Miles (University of Sheffield), Dr. E. Appella (National Institutes of Health) and Drs. L. D. Graham, E. D. Laue, S. E. Radford and F. L. Texter (University of Cambridge) for their important collaboration in many of the experiments described here.

REFERENCES

1. PERHAM, R. N., L. C. PACKMAN & S. E. RADFORD. 1987. Biochem. Soc. Symp. **54:** 67–81.
2. MILES, J. S. & J. R. GUEST. 1987. Biochem. Soc. Symp. **54:** 45–65.
3. REED, L. J. 1974. Acc. Chem. Res. **7:** 40–46.
4. YEAMAN, S. J. 1986. Trends Biochem. Sci. **11:** 293–296.
5. STEPHENS, P. E., M. G. DARLISON, H. M. LEWIS & J. R. GUEST. 1983. Eur. J. Biochem. **133:** 481–489.
6. PACKMAN, L. C., G. HALE & R. N. PERHAM. 1984. EMBO J. **3:** 1315–1319.
7. SPENCER, M. E., M. G. DARLISON, P. E. STEPHENS, I. K. DUCKENFIELD & J. R. GUEST. 1984. Eur. J. Biochem. **141:** 361–374.
8. PERHAM, R. N. & G. C. K. ROBERTS. 1981. Biochem. J. **199:** 733–740.
9. PACKMAN, L. C. & R. N. PERHAM. 1986. FEBS Lett. **206:** 193–198.
10. PACKMAN, L. C. & R. N. PERHAM. 1987. Biochem. J. **242:** 531–538.
11. RADFORD, S. E., E. D. LAUE, R. N. PERHAM, J. S. MILES & J. R. GUEST. 1987. Biochem. J. **247:** 641–649.
12. HENDERSON, C. E., R. N. PERHAM & J. T. FINCH. 1979. Cell **17:** 85–93.
13. PACKMAN, L. C., A. BORGES & R. N. PERHAM. 1988. Biochem. J. **252:** 79–86.
14. PACKMAN, L. C. & R. N. PERHAM. 1989. *In* Methods in Protein Sequence Analysis. B. Wittman-Liebold, Ed. Springer Verlag. Berlin. In press.
15. PERHAM, R. N. & A. O. M. WILKIE. 1980. Biochem. Int. **1:** 470–477.
16. HANEMAAIJER, R., A. JANSSEN, A. DE KOK & C. VEEGER. 1988. Eur. J. Biochem. **174:** 593–599.
17. GERSHWIN, M. E., I. R. MACKAY, A. STURGESS & R. L. COPPEL. 1987. J. Immunol. **138:** 3525–3531.
18. YEAMAN, S. J., S. P. M. FUSSEY, D. J. DANNER, O. F. W. JAMES, D. J. MUTIMER & M. F. BASSENDINE. 1988. Lancet **i:** 1067–1070.
19. COPPEL, R. L., L. J. MCNEILAGE, C. D. SURH, J. VAN DE WATER, T. W. SPITHILL, S. WHITTINGHAM & M. E. GERSWIN. 1988. Proc. Natl. Acad. Sci. USA **85:** 7317–7321.
20. THEKKUMKARA, T. J., L. HO, I. D. WEXLER, G. PONS, T.-C. LIU & M. S. PATEL. 1988. FEBS Lett. **240:** 45–48.
21. NIU, X.-D., K. S. BROWNING, R. H. BEHAL & L. J. REED. 1988. Proc. Natl. Acad. Sci. USA **85:** 7546–7550.
22. BURNS, G., T. BROWN, K. HATTER & J. R. SOKATCH. 1988. Eur. J. Biochem. **176:** 165–169.
23. GRIFFIN, T. A., K. S. LAU & D. T. CHUANG. 1988. J. Biol. Chem. **163:** 14008–14014.

24. GUEST, J. R., H. M. LEWIS, L. D. GRAHAM, L. C. PACKMAN & R. N. PERHAM. 1985. J. Mol. Biol. **185:** 743–754.
25. GRAHAM, L. D., J. R. GUEST, H. M. LEWIS, J. S. MILES, L. C. PACKMAN, R. N. PERHAM & S. E. RADFORD. 1986. Philos. Trans. R. Soc. London Ser. A. **317:** 391–404.
26. GRAHAM, L. D., L. C. PACKMAN & R. N. PERHAM. 1989. Biochemistry **28:** 1574–1581.
27. REED, L. J., M. KOIKE, M. E. LEVITCH & F. R. LEACH. 1958. J. Biol. Chem. **232:** 143–158.
28. REED, L. J. 1966. *In* Comprehensive Biochemistry. M. Florkin & E. H. Stotz, Eds. Vol. 14: 99–125. Elsevier. London.
29. BLEILE, D. M., M. L. HACKERT, F. H. PETTIT & L. J. REED. 1981. J. Biol. Chem. **256:** 514–519.
30. PACKMAN, L. C., R. N. PERHAM & G. C. K. ROBERTS. 1984. Biochem. J. **217:** 219–227.
31. BLEILE, D. M., P. MUNK, R. M. OLIVER & L. J. REED. 1979. Proc. Natl. Acad. Sci. USA **76:** 4385–4389.
32. HALE, G. & R. N. PERHAM. 1979. FEBS Lett. **105:** 263–266.
33. ROBERTS, G. C. K., H. W. DUCKWORTH, L. C. PACKMAN & R. N. PERHAM. 1983. Ciba Symp. **93:** 47–62. Pitman Books. London.
34. PERHAM, R. N., H. W. DUCKWORTH & G. C. K. ROBERTS. 1981. Nature **292:** 474–477.
35. DUCKWORTH, H. W., R. JAENICKE, R. N. PERHAM, A. O. M. WILKIE, J. T. FINCH & G. C. K. ROBERTS. 1982. Eur. J. Biochem. **124:** 63–69.
36. MILES, J. S., J. R. GUEST, S. E. RADFORD & R. N. PERHAM. 1987. Biochim. Biophys. Acta **913:** 117–121.
37. TEXTER, F. L., S. E. RADFORD, E. D. LAUE, R. N. PERHAM, J. S. MILES & J. R. GUEST. 1988. Biochemistry **27:** 289–296.
38. RADFORD, S. E., E. D. LAUE, R. N. PERHAM, S. R. MARTIN & E. APPELLA. 1989. J. Biol. Chem. **264:** 767–775.
39. GRANDE, H. J., A. J. W. G. VISSER & C. VEEGER. 1980. Eur. J. Biochem. **106:** 361–369.
40. BATES, D. L., M. J. DANSON, G. HALE, E. A. HOOPER & R. N. PERHAM. 1977. Nature **268:** 313–316.
41. COLLINS, J. F. & L. J. REED. 1977. Proc. Natl. Acad. Sci. USA **74:** 4223–4227.
42. BERMAN, J. N., G.-X. CHEN, G. HALE & R. N. PERHAM. 1981. Biochem. J. **199:** 513–520.
43. STEPP, L. R., D. M. BLEILE, D. K. MCRORIE, F. H. PETTIT & L. J. REED. 1981. Biochemistry **20:** 4555–4560.
44. HACKERT, M. L., R. M. OLIVER & L. J. REED. 1983. Proc. Natl. Acad. Sci. USA **80:** 2907–2911.
45. MILES, J. S., J. R. GUEST, S. E. RADFORD & R. N. PERHAM. 1988. J. Mol. Biol. **202:** 97–106.
46. RADFORD, S. E., E. D. LAUE & R. N. PERHAM. 1986. Biochem. Soc. Trans. **14:** 1231–1232.
47. DANSON, M. J., G. HALE, P. JOHNSON, R. N. PERHAM, J. SMITH & P. SPRAGG. 1979. J. Mol. Biol. **129:** 603–617.
48. KEHA, E. E., H. RONFT & G.-B. KRESZE. 1982. FEBS Lett. **145:** 289–292.
49. HANEMAAIJER, R., A. H. WESTPHAL, T. VAN DER HEIDEN, A. DE KOK & C. VEEGER. 1989. Eur. J. Biochem. **179:** 287–292.
50. LOWE, P. N., J. A. HODGSON & R. N. PERHAM. 1983. Biochem. J. **215:** 133–140.
51. PETTIT, F. H., S. J. YEAMAN & L. J. REED. 1978. Proc. Natl. Acad. Sci. USA **75:** 4881–4885.
52. PAXTON, R. & R. A. HARRIS. 1983. J. Biol. Chem. **257:** 14433–14439.
53. SOKATCH, J. R., V. MCCULLY, J. GEBROSKY & D. J. SOKATCH. 1981. J. Bacteriol. **148:** 639–646.
54. MCCULLY, V., G. BURNS & J. R. SOKATCH. 1986. Biochem. J. **233:** 737–742.
55. SECKLER, R., R. BINDER & H. BISSWANGER. 1982. Biochim. Biophys. Acta **705:** 210–217.
56. BOSMA, H. J. 1984. Ph.D. thesis. Agricultural University, Wageningen. The Netherlands. pp. 27–37.
57. JEYASEELAN, K., J. R. GUEST & J. VISSER. 1980. J. Gen. Microbiol. **120:** 393–402.
58. BURNS, G., T. BROWN, K. HATTER, J. M. IDRISS & J. R. SOKATCH. 1988. Eur. J. Biochem. **176:** 311–317.

59. CARLSSON, P. & L. HEDERSTEDT. 1986. FEMS Microbiol. Lett. **37:** 373–378.
60. MAREK, A. M., H. BESSAM & B. FOUCHER. 1988. Biochem. Biophys. Acta **953:** 289–296.
61. HARDING, R. W., D. F. CAROLINE & R. P. WAGNER. 1970. Arch. Biochem. Biophys. **138:** 653–661.
62. JUNGER, E., H. REINAUER, U. WAIS & J. ULLRICH. 1973. Hoppe-Seyler's Z. Physiol. Chem. **354:** 1655–1658.
63. KOIKE, M. & K. KOIKE. 1976. Adv. Biophys. **9:** 187–227.
64. ZHANG, B., D. W. CRABB & R. A. HARRIS. 1988. Gene **69:** 159–164.

Intermediates in Reductive Transacetylation Catalyzed by Pyruvate Dehydrogenase Complex[a]

PERRY A. FREY, DOUGLAS S. FLOURNOY,
KENNETH GRUYS, AND YUH-SHYONG YANG

Institute for Enzyme Research, Graduate School, and
Department of Biochemistry
College of Agricultural and Life Sciences
University of Wisconsin–Madison
Madison, Wisconsin 53705

The decarboxylation and dehydrogenation of pyruvate is catalyzed by the pyruvate dehydrogenase complex (PDH complex) in a multistep process that involves the sequential and coordinated actions of three enzymes, pyruvate dehydrogenase (E_1), dihydrolipoyl transacetylase (E_2), and dihydrolipoyl dehydrogenase (E_3). These enzymes are the only components of the complex from *Escherichia coli,* which was first isolated and characterized as an intact and fully assembled multienzyme complex by L. J. Reed and his associates.[1] E_1 catalyzes the decarboxylation of pyruvate in a reaction that is thiamin pyrophosphate– (TPP-) dependent. The product of this reaction, 2-(1-hydroxyethylidene)-TPP [$CH_3C(OH)$=TPP], remains tightly bound to E_1. The mechanism of decarboxylation is reasonably well understood, as is the mechanism of acetyl group transfer in reaction **3** and the mechanism of electron transfer from dihydrolipoyl groups on E_2 to NAD^+ in reactions **4** and **5**:

$$CH_3COCO_2^- + E_1TPP + H^+ \rightleftharpoons CO_2 + E_1CH_3C(OH)\text{=}TPP \qquad (1)$$

$$E_1CH_3C(OH)\text{=}TPP + E_2\,\text{—}LipS_2 \rightleftharpoons E_1TPP + E_2\,\text{—}Lip(SH)\text{—}S\text{—}COCH_3 \quad (2)$$

$$E_2\text{—}Lip(SH)\text{—}S\text{—}COCH_3 + CoASH \rightleftharpoons E_2\,\text{—}Lip(SH)_2 + CH_3COSCoA \quad (3)$$

$$E_2\text{—}Lip(SH)_2 + E_3FAD \rightleftharpoons E_2\text{—}LipS_2 + \text{dihydro-}E_3FAD \qquad (4)$$

$$\text{dihydro-}E_3FAD + NAD^+ \rightleftharpoons E_3FAD + NADH + H^+ \qquad (5)$$

Overall Reaction:

$$CH_3COCO_2^- + CoASH + NAD^+ \rightleftharpoons CO_2 + CH_3COSCoA + NADH \quad (6)$$

The least well understood step is reaction **2**, the reductive transacetylation between $E_1CH_3C(OH)$=TPP and a lipoyl (Lip) group on E_2 to give TPP and S-acetyldihydrolipoamide. Several mechanisms can be written for this reaction. The two most commonly proposed are given in FIGURE 1, where they are shown as pathway A and pathway B, both of which involve the tetrahedral addition intermediate between 2-acetylthiamine pyrophosphate (acetyl-TPP) and dihydrolipoamide as a common

[a]Supported by Grant No. DK 28607 from the National Institute of Digestive and Kidney Diseases.

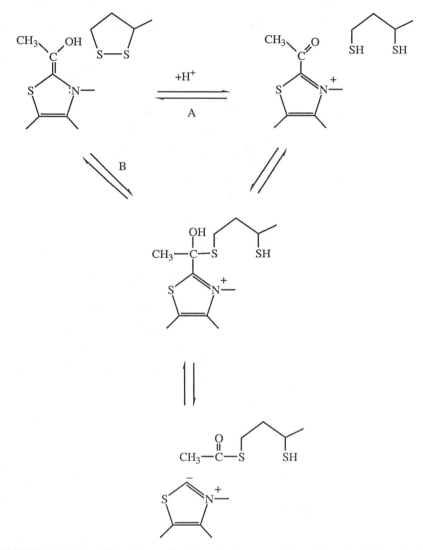

FIGURE 1. Mechanistic pathways for the reductive acetylation of lipoyl cofactors by 2-(1-hydroxyethylidene)-TPP at the active site of pyruvate dehydrogenase (E_1).

intermediate. L. J. Reed first proposed the possibility that acetyl-TPP might be an intermediate in the dehydrogenation of pyruvate. He suggested that $CH_3C(OH){=}TPP$ might reduce lipoamide to form acetyl-TPP and dihydrolipoamide by pathway A in FIGURE 1.[2,3] A sulfhydryl group of dihydrolipoamide would then react as a nucleophile with acetyl-TPP to form S-acetyldihydrolipoamide and regenerate TPP. This is a reasonable mechanism, since $CH_3C(OH){=}TPP$ is an enamine and enamines have reducing properties. And acetyl thiazolium salts can react with mercaptide ions to transfer the acetyl group and form a thioester in nonaqueous solvents, as shown by Reed and his associates.[3]

In pathway B of FIGURE 1, which was proposed by Breslow and by Ingraham,[4,5] the enamine $CH_3C(OH)\!\!=\!\!TPP$ reacts as a carbanion with lipoamide to form the tetrahedral adduct in a single step. This is also a reasonable mechanism, since enamines have carbanionic reactivity. And it is attractive by virtue of the fact that it requires only a single step to reach the tetrahedral adduct from $CH_3C(OH)\!\!=\!\!TPP$ and lipoamide. The electron transfer and group transfer reactions are coupled in this single step. In the former mechanism the electron transfer and group transfer steps are distinct, with electron transfer leading; and the coupling between electron and group transfer processes is kinetic rather than mechanistic.

E_1 and the PDH complex also catalyze reaction **7,** in which ferricyanide is the electron acceptor and water is the acetyl group acceptor:

$$CH_3COCO_2^- + 2\ Fe(CN)_6^{3-} + H_2O \rightarrow CO_2 + 2\ Fe(CN)_6^{4-} + CH_3CO_2^- + 2H^+ \quad (7)$$

This reaction proceeds at the active site of E_1 and presumably does not involve E_2 or E_3 of the PDH complex. Pyruvate is first decarboxylated in reaction **1** in the usual way. The E_1-bound $CH_3C(OH)\!\!=\!\!TPP$ is then oxidized by ferricyanide in reaction **8** to acetyl-TPP, which reacts with water in reaction **9** to form acetate:

$$E_1CH_3C(OH)\!\!=\!\!TPP + 2\ Fe(CN)_6^{3-} \rightarrow E_1CH_3CO\!-\!TPP + 2\ Fe(CN)_6^{4-} + H^+ \quad (8)$$

$$E_1CH_3CO\!-\!TPP + H_2O \rightarrow E_1TPP + CH_3CO_2^- + H^+ \quad (9)$$

It is known from the work of Reed and his associates that phosphate can replace water in reaction **9,** and this leads to the formation of acetyl phosphate according to reaction **10:**

$$\text{Pyruvate} + 2\ Fe(CN)_6^{3-} + P_i \rightarrow CO_2 + 2\ Fe(CN)_6^{4-} + \text{Acetyl-P} \quad (10)$$

It is very likely that acetyl-TPP is an intermediate when ferricyanide is used as the electron acceptor, both in the formation of acetate and in the formation of acetyl phosphate. Reaction **10** suggests that acetyl-TPP at the active site of E_1 can transfer acetyl groups to an acceptor other than water.

The reaction pathways A and B in FIGURE 1 differ most essentially by the involvement of acetyl-TPP and dihydrolipoamide as intermediates in pathway A and not in pathway B. In pathway B, these species could be avoided by the forward decomposition of the tetrahedral adduct to acetyldihydrolipoamide and TPP. The question of whether acetyl-TPP is an intermediate in this reaction is a subject of continuing interest. Recent work described herein suggests that acetyl-TPP and dihydrolipoamide are chemically competent intermediates at the active site of E_1 and that they are actually present in the steady state of the overall reaction of pyruvate, as described in equation **1–6.** The question of regiospecificity in the reaction of lipoate in FIGURE 1, recently reopened by the work of O'Connor et al.,[6] is also resolved in favor of the acetylation of S^8, as shown in FIGURE 1.

REGIOSPECIFICITY IN REDUCTIVE ACETYLATION OF LIPOAMIDE

The question of which sulfur in lipoamide accepts the acetyl group in equation **2** was addressed in 1956 by Gunsalus *et al.,* who showed that S^6-acetyldihydrolipoate

(6-AcDHL) was formed when E_2 catalyzed reaction **11**:[7]

$$\text{dihydrolipoate} + \text{acetyl-CoA} \rightleftharpoons \text{S-acetyldihydrolipoate} + \text{CoA} \qquad (11)$$

The question of regiospecificity was reopened by O'Connor *et al.*, who used [^{13}C]acetyl-CoA and dihyrolipoamide in reaction **11** and observed the formation of both

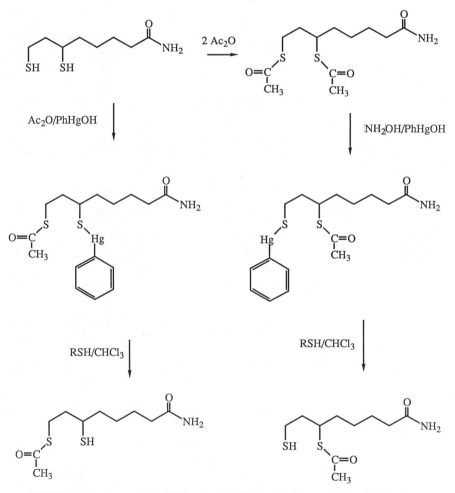

FIGURE 2. Syntheses of 6-AcDHL and 8-AcDHL and their mercuriphenyl derivatives.

6-[^{13}C]AcDHL and 8-[^{13}C]AcDHL by ^{13}C–nuclear magnetic resonance (NMR) spectroscopy.[6] High-resolution NMR was not available at the time of Gunsalus's original work, and the methods that were then available allowed the identification of 6-AcDHL but not of 8-AcDHL, the presence of which would not have been detected. The observations of O'Connor *et al.* indicated that the two isomers are probably rapidly interconverted, so that it would have been difficult to observe which isomer is initially formed.

In a reinvestigation of this question, we have been able to synthesize 8-AcDHL and 6-AcDHL and to measure the rate of their interconversion.[8] The synthetic routes to these compounds, starting with dihydrolipoamide, are outlined in FIGURE 2. Reaction of dihydrolipoamide with one equivalent of acetic anhydride gave preferential acetylation to 8-AcDHL, and the product was quickly trapped by reaction with hydroxymercuribenzene. The major product was S^8-acetyl-S^6-(mecuriphenyl)dihydrolipoamide (8-AcMPDHL). Reaction of dihydrolipoamide with two equivalents of acetic anhydride gave S,S-*bis*-acetyldihydrolipoamide. This compound could be selectively deacetylated by reaction with one equivalent of hydroxylamine to 6-AcDHL, which was quickly trapped by reaction with hydroxymercuribenzene to S^6-acetyl-S^8-(mercuriphenyl)dihydrolipoamide (6-AcMPDHL). The acetyldihydrolipoamides were produced initially in alcoholic solvents and had to be stabilized by reaction with hydroxymercuribenzene because of their tendency to undergo isomerization. Hydroxymercuribenzene was also used later to trap the enzymatic products. The purified mercury derivatives could be distinguished and identified by proton NMR spectroscopy. They were converted to 8-AcDHL and 6-AcDHL by reaction with 3-mercaptopropionic acid in chloroform. They did not undergo isomerization in this solvent.

The interconversion of 8-AcDHL and 6-AcDHL in aqueous solutions is specifically base catalyzed and proceeds to equilibrium with a half-time of 15 seconds at pH 6.5. The equilibrium constant is 3.4 ± 0.14 (SD), favoring 8-AcDHL. This means that in any experiment in which reaction **11** is allowed to proceed for any significant time before isolating the product, both isomers will be isolated. If the products are trapped at various times during the reactions, one might determine which appears first. An effective trapping technique for mercaptans is reaction with a mercurial, since the rate constant[9] for reaction between a sulfhydryl compound and p-(chloromercuri)benzoate is $6 \times 10^6 \ M^{-1}s^{-1}$. In experiments of this type a mixture of 6-AcDHL and 8-AcDHL will always be present at the time of trapping, since isomerization is very fast. Therefore, a mixture of trapped products will be obtained. In the present case, the ratio of 6-AcDHL/8-AcDHL can be determined from the proton NMR spectrum of the isolated, trapped product mixture.

Measurements of the product ratio as a function of the time elapsed prior to trapping show that the initial transacetylation product is 8-AcDHL. The ratio of products (6-AcDHL/8-AcDHL) approaches zero at zero time. And this ratio approaches the equilibrium value with a first-order rate constant that is the same as the rate constant for the conversion of either 8-AcDHL or 6-AcDHL to the equilibrium mixture. Therefore, the enzyme does not catalyze the isomerization reaction, and 8-AcDHL is the only product of the E_2-catalyzed transacetylation from acetyl-CoA to dihydrolipoamide.

TPP-DEPENDENT HYDROLYSIS OF ACETYL-CoA AND SUCCINYL-CoA

The PDH complex and the 2-ketoglutarate dehydrogenase complex from *E. coli* catalyze the hydrolyses of acetyl-CoA and succinyl-CoA, respectively:

$$RCOSCoA + H_2O \xrightarrow{\text{MgTPP/NADH}} RCO_2^- + CoASH + H^+ \qquad (12)$$

$$R = CH3, \ ^-O_2CCH_2CH_2$$

The substrate and cofactor requirements for these reactions indirectly implicate acetyl-TPP and succinyl-TPP as intermediates.[10,11] In each case, the hydrolysis is catalyzed only in the presence of NADH and MgTPP, and hydrolysis requires the presence of all three enzymic components of the complexes. When any of the required cofactors or enzyme components is absent, no hydrolysis can be observed. The values of K_m for acetyl-CoA and succinyl-CoA are comparable to the values for CoA as a substrate in the decarboxylation and dehydrogenation of the 2-ketoacids. The values of k_{cat} are about 0.5% of those for the reactions of the 2-ketoacids.

The cofactor and enzymic requirements for these reactions suggest that the hydrolysis of acetyl-CoA proceeds by the partial reversal of reactions **5, 4, 3,** and **2** in the overall reaction of pyruvate. The most probable reaction sequence is given in FIGURE 3. E_3 catalyzes the reduction by NADH of the lipoyl moieties bonded to E_2. The resulting dihydrolipoyl cofactors are acetylated by acetyl-CoA to S-acetyldihydrolipoyl moieties, which evidently can acetylate TPP at the active site of E_1. The acetyl-TPP so formed can react in reverse with the dihydrolipoyl cofactors or, possibly, undergo hydrolysis to acetate. Alternatively, the reaction might proceed by a pathway that the experimental design was intended to exploit. That is, the dihydrolipoyl cofactor produced by the acetylation of TPP might undergo a second acetylation by acetyl-CoA. This would leave the acetyl-TPP with no opportunity to transfer an acetyl group to a dihydrolipoyl cofactor, and no recourse but to undergo hydrolysis to acetate.

The latter mechanism is favored by the fact that the k_{cat} for hydrolysis is about 0.5% that for the forward reaction, which suggests that a small amount of hydrolysis should be detected during the forward reaction if acetyl-TPP is formed. No such hydrolysis is observed. This means that either acetyl-TPP is not formed in the forward reaction or the hydrolysis of acetyl-CoA in the reverse reaction involves the overacetylation of dihydrolipoyl cofactors. It is known from work described later in this paper that acetyl-TPP is formed in the forward reaction in amounts comparable to those generated in the TPP-dependent hydrolysis of acetyl-CoA. Therefore, it is very likely that the TPP-dependent hydrolysis of acetyl-CoA involves the formation of acetyl-TPP and the overacetylation of dihydrolipoyl groups.

CAPTURE OF ACETYL-TPP BY DIHYDROLIPOAMIDE IN THE E_1 ACTIVE SITE

From reactions **9** and **12,** it is clear that acetyl-TPP is hydrolyzed by water in the active site of E_1. If it is an intermediate in the dehydrogenation of $CH_3C(OH){=}TPP$ by pathway A of FIGURE 1, it must react with the dihydrolipoyl cofactor much faster than it undergoes hydrolysis. Otherwise, acetate would be produced from pyruvate in place of acetyl-CoA. A test of this proposition is to generate acetyl-TPP within the active site of E_1 under conditions in which there is no electron transfer to lipoyl cofactors on E_2 ($E_2{-}LipS_2$). The reactivity of acetyl-TPP toward dihydrolipoamide and water from the solution can then be evaluated. The partitioning of acetyl groups between water and dihydrolipoamide should indicate whether acetyl-TPP is chemically competent to acetylate dihydrolipoamide in aqueous solution.

The test described above is made possible by the reaction according to equation **13** of fluoropyruvate as an alternate substrate for E_1:[12]

$$FCH_2COCO_2^- + H_2O \rightarrow CO_2 + F^- + CH_3CO_2^- + H^+ \tag{13}$$

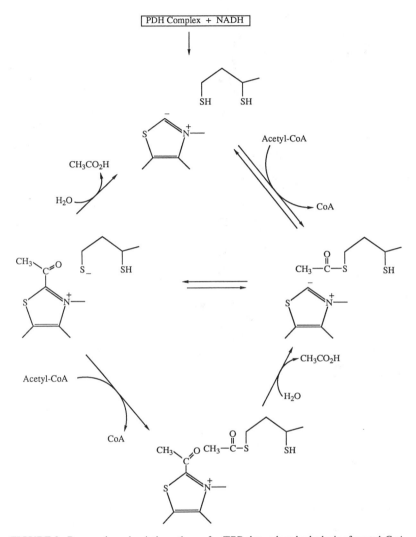

FIGURE 3. Proposed mechanistic pathway for TPP-dependent hydrolysis of acetyl-CoA.

Fluoropyruvate reacts, as illustrated in FIGURE 4, essentially as pyruvate through the decarboxylation step. However, the decarboxylation intermediate is 2-(1-hydroxy-2-fluoroethylidene)-TPP, which spontaneously eliminates fluoride and leads directly to the formation of enolacetyl-TPP. Enolacetyl-TPP undergoes hydrolysis to acetate, presumably after tautomerization to acetyl-TPP.

When the reaction of fluoropyruvate is carried out in the presence of dihydrolipoamide, acetyl-TPP can react with dihydrolipoamide to produce 8-AcDHL or with water to produce acetate. Since dihydrolipoamide is not covalently bonded to E_2, as are the dihydrolipoyl cofactors, it has less assured access to the active site of E_1. Nevertheless, even at modest concentrations of dihydrolipoamide, most of the acetyl-

Fluoropyruvate + pyruvate dehydrogenase (E_1)

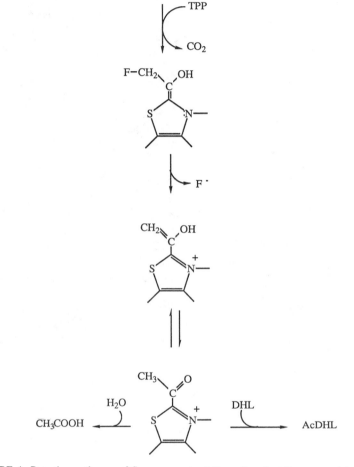

FIGURE 4. Reaction pathways of fluoropyruvate at the active site of pyruvate dehydrogenase (E_1). AcDHL, acetyldihydrolipoate.

TPP is partitioned to dihydrolipoamide; and at saturating concentrations of dihydrolipoamide, over 96% of the acetyl-TPP reacts to form acetyldihydrolipoamide.[13] Very little acetate is formed. Therefore, the acetyl transfer from acetyl-TPP to dihydrolipoamide is chemically competent at the active site of E_1. We shall see that synthetic acetyl-TPP does not react with dihydrolipoamide in aqueous solutions.

SUICIDE INACTIVATION BY FLUOROPYRUVATE

In addition to being an alternate substrate, fluoropyruvate is also a suicide inactivator of pyruvate dehydrogenase (E_1). It inactivates E_1 with time dependence and with TPP-dependence while catalyzing reaction **13,** so that the enzyme gradually loses activity. The inactivation mechanism might proceed by the reaction of a nucleophilic group in the active site of E_1 with either enolacetyl-TPP or acetyl-TPP, as illustrated in FIGURE 5. Reaction of an enzymic nucleophile with enolacetyl-TPP might be an alkylation by a Michael addition reaction. This would generate a covalent linkage between TPP and the enzyme. Alternatively, acetyl-TPP might acetylate an enzymic nucleophile. Recent experiments show clearly that suicide inactivation results from the acetylation of a sulfhydryl group in the active site of E_1. Therefore, the inactivating species may be acetyl-TPP, although the possibility that enolacetyl-TPP might also react to acetylate rather than to alkylate a sulfhydryl group cannot be ruled out.

Suicide inactivation by acetyl-TPP raises doubts about the possibility that acetyl-TPP might be an intermediate in the reaction of pyruvate, since pyruvate is not a suicide substrate. However, fluoropyruvate does not inactivate E_1 in the presence of dihydrolipoamide. Evidently, dihydrolipoamide deacetylates acetyl-TPP at the active site of E_1 much faster than a sulfhydryl group at the active site can react with acetyl-TPP. This prevents inactivation. Should acetyl-TPP arise by pathway A in FIGURE 1, the dihydrolipoyl cofactor would without doubt also deacetylate it much faster than the reaction with the active site–sulfhydryl group could occur.

SYNTHESIS AND PROPERTIES OF ACETYL-TPP

In order to evaluate acetyl-TPP as a possible enzymatic intermediate, we undertook to synthesize this molecule. The synthesis proved to be a straightforward, one-step

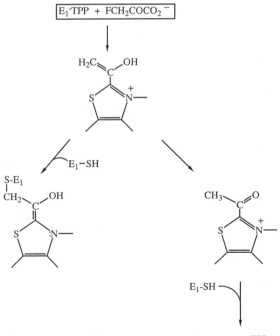

FIGURE 5. Suicide inactivation of pyruvate dehydrogenase (E_1) by fluoropyruvate.

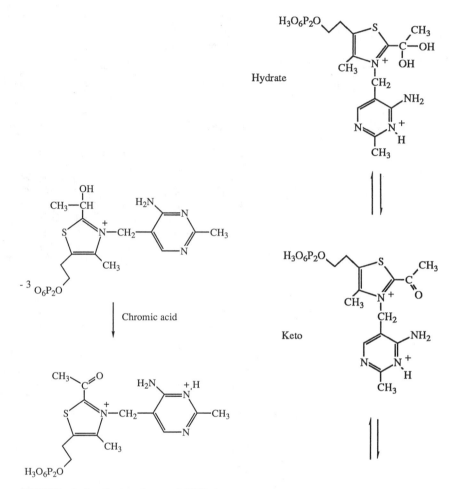

Hydrate

Keto

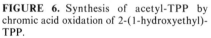

Chromic acid

FIGURE 6. Synthesis of acetyl-TPP by chromic acid oxidation of 2-(1-hydroxyethyl)-TPP.

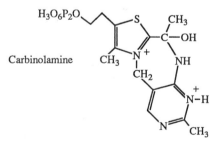

Carbinolamine

FIGURE 7. The three molecular forms of acetyl-TPP. These three forms are in equilibrium in acidic aqueous solutions.

reaction, as illustrated in FIGURE 6.[14] Starting with 2-(1-hydroxyethyl)-TPP, we oxidized it with dilute chromic acid in the presence of a large excess of pyrophosphoric acid to form a complex with the Cr(III) generated by the oxidation. Acetyl-TPP was purified by ion-exchange chromatography in acidic conditions.

Acetyl-TPP is a stable compound in aqueous solutions at pH 2; however, it undergoes hydrolysis to acetate and TPP at higher pH values. The proton NMR spectrum of acetyl-TPP at pH 2 is extremely complex, with more than twice as many signals as expected for a mixture of the keto form and the hydrate. Information from detailed analysis by ^{1}H-, ^{31}P-, and ^{13}C-NMR of acetyl-TPP, [2-[2]H$_3$]acetyl-TPP, and [1-^{13}C]acetyl-TPP is consistent only with the conclusion that the compound exists as an equilibrium mixture of the hydrate, the keto form, and a third form that must be a cyclic structure and is almost certainly the internal carbinolamine adduct shown in FIGURE 7. This is an unexpected adduct, a strained structure with a seven-membered ring. Nevertheless, all of the spectroscopic information suggests this structure and is inconsistent with any other structure. For example, the methylene bridging the thiazolium and pyridinium rings exhibits two proton signals coupled to each other with a coupling constant of about 16 Hz. This is consistent only with a rigid structure, as in the tricyclic structure of the internal carbinolamine in FIGURE 7. Furthermore, the ^{13}C signal for the carbinolamine carbon is broadened by the pyrimidinium nitrogen to which it is bonded, as expected for the carbinolamine. No other structure is consistent with these facts. The ultraviolet spectrum also indicates the presence of three forms of acetyl-TPP, as does the ^{31}P-NMR spectrum. The effects of temperature on the equilibrium mixture are also compatible with the structures assigned in FIGURE 7.

The pH-rate profile for hydrolysis of acetyl-TPP is shown in FIGURE 8. The profile

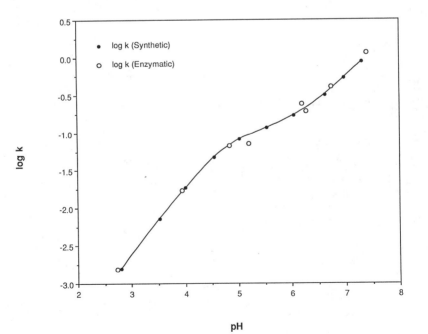

FIGURE 8. The pH-rate profile for the hydrolysis of acetyl-TPP. The filled circles refer to synthetic acetyl-TPP and the open circles to [^{14}C]acetyl-TPP isolated from enzymatic reactions.

is one that is unique in form and characteristic of this compound. At low pH values the slope of the log k_{obs} versus pH profile is $+1$, corresponding to specific base-catalyzed hydrolysis, as reported by Lienhard for a model acetyl thiazolium salt.[15] At pH values above 4.5, the slope decreases, evidently due to the deprotonation of the pyrimidinium ring, leading to a form that hydrolyzes without pH dependence. The slope increases again above pH 6 and once again shows a strong dependence on hydroxide concentration. At low pH values, the hydroxide-catalyzed reaction presumably involves the removal of a proton from the hydrate and breakdown of the resulting anionic adduct:

$$
\begin{array}{c}
\mathrm{OH} \\
|\\
\mathrm{CH_3\!-\!C\!-\!OH} \\
|\\
\mathrm{TPP}
\end{array}
+ \mathrm{OH^-} \rightleftharpoons
\begin{array}{c}
\mathrm{O^-} \\
|\\
\mathrm{CH_3\!-\!C\!-\!OH} \\
|\\
\mathrm{TPP}
\end{array}
\rightarrow \mathrm{CH_3\!-\!COOH} + \mathrm{TPP^-} \qquad (14)
$$

At higher pH values, the predominant form of acetyl-TPP, as determined by proton NMR spectroscopy between pH values of 5 and 6, is the carbinolamine, apparently owing to deprotonation of the pyrimidinium ring. This shift in the equilibrium partitioning of acetyl-TPP among its three forms perturbs the pH-rate profile. The unique pH dependence for the hydrolysis of acetyl-TPP is used in the following experiments to characterize the [14C]acetyl-TPP isolated from enzymatic reactions.

Acetyl-TPP reacts with nucleophiles other than water in aqueous solutions. It reacts with hydroxylamine ($\mathrm{NH_2OH}$) very well at pH 5. However, all efforts to detect a reaction between dihydrolipoamide and acetyl-TPP at pH 5 failed. This contrasts with the enzymatic results described above, in which acetyl-TPP was efficiently captured by dihydrolipoamide in the active site of E_1.

TRAPPING [14C]ACETYL-TPP IN ENZYMATIC REACTIONS

Since acetyl-TPP is stable in acidic aqueous solutions, it should be possible to isolate it from enzymatic reaction mixtures that have been quenched by acid denaturation of the protein. If this is done with a 14C-labeled substrate, and acetyl-TPP is present in the steady state, the [14C]acetyl-TPP should be trapped in a stable form in an acid-quenched reaction. The absence of [14C]acetyl-TPP at detectable levels would place limits on estimates of the level of its viability as an intermediate. The availability of large amounts of the PDH complex from *E. coli* should enable one to make a stringent test of the amount of acetyl-TPP that is present in the steady state when 14C-labeled substrates are used at high specific radioactivity.

The general trapping procedure we use is outlined in FIGURE 9. A reaction mixture is prepared with enzyme, TPP, 14C-labeled substrate, and any other cofactors that may be required. The reaction is initiated by the addition of the 14C-labeled substrate and quenched within a few seconds by the addition of trichloroacetic acid. The precipitate is removed by centrifugation and the supernatant fluid is chromatographed under acidic conditions with carrier acetyl-TPP. Fractions containing [14C]acetyl-TPP and [14C]hydroxyethyl-TPP are pooled and counted. The total label counted is the sum of the two. Since acetyl-TPP is labile to hydrolysis in neutral solutions and hydroxyethyl-TPP is not, the amount of the total product that is [14C]acetyl-TPP can be determined by carrying out the hydrolysis of an aliquot and determining the amount of [14C]acetate produced.

Trapping data are presented in TABLE 1 for a series of experiments with both PDH complex and E_1. In general, [14C]acetyl-TPP can be detected under many conditions.

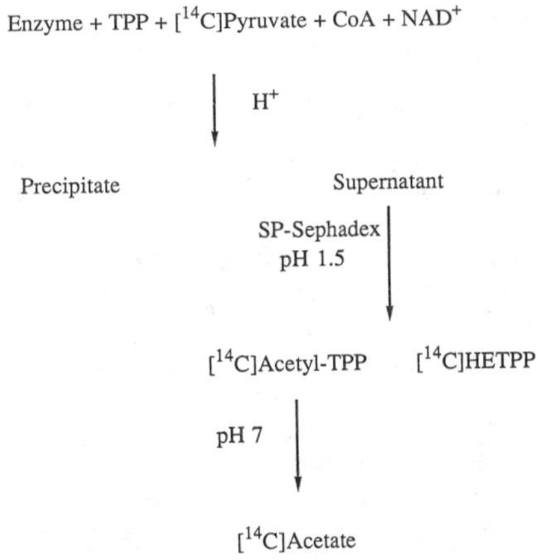

FIGURE 9. Procedure for trapping [^{14}C]ace-
tyl-TPP in enzymatic reactions. HETPP,
hydroxyethyl-TPP.

Enzyme + TPP + [^{14}C]Pyruvate + CoA + NAD$^+$

$\downarrow$ H$^+$

Precipitate   Supernatant

SP-Sephadex
pH 1.5 $\downarrow$

[^{14}C]Acetyl-TPP   [^{14}C]HETPP

pH 7 $\downarrow$

[^{14}C]Acetate

In the complete system, in which [2-^{14}C]pyruvate is being converted to [1-^{14}C]acetyl-
CoA in the presence of the PDH complex of *E. coli*, MgTPP, NAD$^+$ and CoA, the
amount of [^{14}C]acetyl-TPP present in the steady state corresponds to about 0.43% of
the active sites associated with E_1. About 19% of the sites contain
[^{14}C]CH$_3$C(OH)=TPP, as measured by the [^{14}C]hydroxyethyl-TPP isolated in the
acid-quenched reaction. Therefore, about 2% of the total sites occupied by substrate in
the steady state are filled by acetyl-TPP.

Under anaerobic conditions, the amount of [^{14}C]acetyl-TPP is somewhat less
(TABLE 1), but still very easily detected. This experiment is important, because oxygen
can oxidize CH$_3$C(OH)=TPP at the active site and would probably convert it to
acetyl-TPP. Indeed, under pure O$_2$ in the absence of NAD$^+$, the amount of [^{14}C]ace-
tyl-TPP is increased (TABLE 1).

In an experiment not shown in TABLE 1, the enzyme was incubated with
[^{14}C]acetyl-CoA in the presence of NADH and TPP, that is, under conditions in which
the enzyme catalyzes the hydrolysis of acetyl-CoA, and the level of [^{14}C]acetyl-TPP
was measured. It was found to be comparable to that observed in the steady state with
[2-^{14}C]pyruvate. In all experiments in which TPP was omitted, no [^{14}C]acetyl-TPP
could be detected.

Although the levels of [^{14}C]acetyl-TPP in the foregoing experiments were low

TABLE 1. Trapping of Acetyl-TPP

System	^{14}C as % of Active Sites[a]	
	[^{14}C]Acetyl-TPP	[^{14}C]HETPP
PDH complex[b]	0.43	19
Anaerobic	0.17	21
−NAD$^+$ (+O$_2$)	2.4	57
−CoA	0.48	46
−TPP	0.00	0.00
E_1 + ferricyanide	2.8	36

[a]Trapping procedure is outlined in FIGURE 9. HETPP, hydroxyethyl-TPP.
[b]Complete system contains PDH complex of *E. coli*, MgTPP, NAD$^+$, and CoA under aerobic
conditions.

when expressed in terms of the percent of active sites, the amount of material isolated was easily measured. To evaluate the level of labeling, an experiment was carried out in a system that is known to generate acetyl-TPP in the steady state, the oxidative decarboxylation of [2-^{14}C]pyruvate by use of E_1 alone with ferricyanide as the electron acceptor. This reaction follows the course described by reactions **1, 8,** and **9.** In this experiment, the level of [^{14}C]acetyl-TPP was 2.8% of the total sites and 8% of the total sites occupied by the substrate. This result shows that the steady-state level of acetyl-TPP is low owing to its reactivity, even in a system in which it is known to be an intermediate. Since acetyl-TPP at the active site of E_1 is less reactive with water than with dihydrolipoamide (*vide infra*), the lower level of [^{14}C]acetyl-TPP in the complete system with the PDH complex must by expected.

To determine whether the material isolated as [^{14}C]acetyl-TPP actually was this compound and not some other previously unknown substance that releases [^{14}C]acetate in neutral solution, the pH-rate profile for the hydrolysis of [^{14}]acetyl-TPP was determined, using as the substrate the radioactive compound isolated in the above trapping experiments. The pH-rate profile was found to be identical with that of authentic synthetic acetyl-TPP, as shown by the fit of the open symbols (representing the isolated material) to the pH-rate profile of the synthetic acetyl-TPP in FIGURE 8. It is difficult to conceive of another compound exhibiting exactly the same pH-rate profile for hydrolysis as acetyl-TPP. The conclusion that the isolated compound is indeed [^{14}C]acetyl-TPP seems inescapable.

DISCUSSION

There appears to be little doubt that the reaction of lipoyl cofactors in the PDH complex involves S^8 as the site of acetylation, at least by acetyl-CoA. Isomerization is very fast, but it is slower than the turnover rate for this enzyme by a factor of $>10^4$. The determination of the regiospecificity of this reaction in our reinvestigation depended upon the availability of high-field NMR equipment that did not exist at the time this question was first investigated by Gunsalus and co-workers.

The question of the involvement of acetyl-TPP as a compulsory intermediate in the decarboxylation and dehydrogenation of pyruvate remains open. However, the research described here establishes several facts relative to this question. First, the cofactor requirements for the PDH complex–catalyzed hydrolysis of acetyl-CoA suggest that acetyl-TPP is an intermediate in that reaction. And the reaction pathway can be rationalized on the basis that overall reversal of the PDH complex reaction, presumably reversal to acetyl-TPP, is required. Second, acetyl-TPP is chemically competent to transfer an acetyl group to dihydrolipoamide at the active site of E_1. This contrasts with the inability of synthetic acetyl-TPP to acetylate dihydrolipoamide in aqueous solution. Thus, it appears that the microenvironment at the active site facilitates this process. Third, [^{14}C]acetyl-TPP can be isolated from enzymatic reaction mixtures in steady-state turnover with [2-^{14}C]pyruvate as the substrate. [^{14}C]Acetyl-TPP appears during the steady state and disappears upon consumption of the substrate. [^{14}C]Acetyl-TPP is also present during the TPP-dependent hydrolysis of acetyl-CoA catalyzed by the PDH complex.

Acetyl-TPP is present in the steady state of reaction **2,** the reductive acetylation of dihydrolipoyl cofactors by $CH_3C(OH)$=TPP at the active site of E_1. It is not clear, however, that it is a compulsory intermediate. In FIGURE 1, the tetrahedral intermediate is indicated to be connected reversibly with acetyl-TPP and the diydrolipoyl cofactor. Our results show that this connection exists and that it is reversible.

Therefore, acetyl-TPP must be considered as a possible intermediate. To demonstrate that, acetyl-TPP is a compulsory intermediate, its connection with $CH_3C(OH)\!=\!TPP$ by pathway A (FIG. 1) must be proven. Our results do not establish this connection. Neither do our data or any other data establish a connection of $CH_3(OH)\!=\!TPP$ with the tetrahedral adduct via pathway B (FIG. 1). Further experimentation is required to address these questions. However, it is now clear that acetyl-TPP and dihydrolipoyl moieties play a role in reaction **2**.

REFERENCES

1. KOIKE, M., L. J. REED & W. R. CARROLL. 1960. J. Biol. Chem. **235:** 1924–1930
2. DAS, M. L., M. KOIKE & L. J. REED. 1961 Proc Natl. Acad. Sci. USA 47: 753–759.
3. DAIGO, K. & L. J. REED. 1962. J. Am. Chem. Soc. **84:** 659–662.
4. BRESLOW, R. & E. MCNELIS. 1962. J. Am. Chem. Soc. **84:** 2394–2396.
5. WHITE, F. G. & L. L. INGRAHAM. 1962. J. Am. Chem. Soc. **84:** 3109–3111.
6. O'CONNOR, T. P., T. E. ROCHE & J. V. PAUKSTELIS. 1982. J. Biol. Chem. **257:** 3110.
7. GUNSALUS, I. C., L. S. BARTON & W. GRUBER. 1956. J. Am. Chem. Soc. **78:** 1763.
8. YANG, Y.-S. & P. A. FREY. 1986. Biochemistry **25:** 8173–8178.
9. HASINOFF, B. B., N. B. MADSEN & O. AVRAMOVIC-ZIKIC. 1971. Can. J. Biochem. **49:** 742.
10. STEGINSKY, C. A., K. J. GRUYS & P. A. FREY. 1985. J. Biol. Chem. **260:** 13690–13693.
11. CAJACOB, C. A., G. R. GAVINO & P. A. FREY. 1985. J. Biol. Chem. **260:** 14610–14614.
12. LEUNG, L. S. & P. A. FREY. 1978. Biochem. Biophys. Res. Commun. **81:** 274–279.
13. FLOURNOY, D. S. & P. A. FREY. 1986. Biochemistry **25:** 6036–6043.
14. GRUYS, L. J., C. J. HALKIDES & P. A. FREY. 1987. Biochemistry **26:** 7575–7585.
15. LIENHARD, G. E. 1966. J. Am. Chem. Soc. **88:** 5642–5649.

Organization and Functioning of Muscle Pyruvate Dehydrogenase Active Centers

L. S. KHAILOVA, L. G. KOROCHKINA, AND
S. E. SEVERIN

Department of Biochemistry
Moscow State University
Moscow 119899, USSR

The pyruvate dehydrogenase complex (PDC) connects the two major energetic mechanisms—glycolysis and the citric acid cycle. The pyruvate dehydrogenase component (PDH) plays a major role in the functioning and regulation of this multienzyme complex:

1. PDH catalyzes the chemical degradation of pyruvic acid with the formation of carbon dioxide, acetyl residue, and reductive equivalents, which are transferred in the active centers of dihydrolipoate acetyltransferase (E_2) and dihydrolipoate dehydrogenase (E_3) to the terminal acceptors, CoA and NAD.[1,2]
2. PDH carries out the first irreversible and rate-limiting step in the reaction sequence and thus determines the principal kinetic parameters of the enzyme complex.
3. Finally, PDH is the main regulatory center of the multienzyme complex. Activation (dephosphorylation) and inactivation (phosphorylation) of PDC is carried out by the enzymes phosphatase and kinase, which act on the PDH component.[3]

Thus, it was not accidental that Nature has selected the PDH component of the complex to be a major site of genetic damage to the process of pyruvate oxidative decarboxylation.[4] Study of the properties of PDH is therefore a problem of great importance for understanding the mechanism for the functioning and regulation of the PDC. The results of investigations on the active centers of PDH isolated from pigeon breast muscle PDC are discussed in this report. We have used thiamin analogs, modification of the side chains of amino acids at the active site, and spectral transitions to dissect the mechanisms within and interactions between the active centers of the PDH component.

METHODS

The PDC was isolated and purified from pigeon breast muscle by a modified procedure of Jagannatan and Schweet.[5] The PDH was isolated from the highly purified complex by ammonium sulfate fractionation in the presence of 0.5 M KBr.[6] The enzyme was homogeneous, as assessed by sodium dodecyl sulfate polyacrylamide gel electrophoresis.[7] Protein concentration was measured spectrophotometrically. PDH activity was determined by the rate of 2,6-dichlorophenolindophenol (DCPIP) reduction measured spectrophotometrically at 600 nm,[8] using pyruvate or 2-hydroxy-

36

ethyl thiamin pyrophosphate (2-HETPP) as model reaction substrates, or by the rate of the pyruvate:NAD oxidoreductase reaction in the presence of acetyl-CoA.[9] In this case, the multienzyme complex was reconstituted from native or modified PDH and from appropriate amounts of dihydrolipoate acetyltransferase (E_2) and dihydrolipoate dehydrogenase (E_3). The decarboxylase activity of PDH was determined by $^{14}CO_2$ and [2-^{14}C]HETPP production.[10]

Interaction of apo-PDH with thiamin pyrophosphate (TPP) was studied by the circular dichroism (CD) method and spectrophotometrically as described previously.[11] The CD spectra were obtained with a Dichrograph III CNRS-Roussel Jouan in cells of 1-cm path length and at 2×10^{-6} CD density unit sensitivity.

N-Bromosuccinimide was used for modification of tryptophan residues. The number of modified tryptophans was determined from the decrement in protein absorption at 280 nm.[12] Arginine residues were modified by 2,3-butandione, phenylglyoxal, or 4-hydroxy-3-nitrophenylglyoxal[13,14] in 0.05 *M* sodium borate buffer, pH 8.0 and 7.6. Modification and determination of the number of free SH groups were done with *p*-chloromercuribenzoate (pCMB)[15] and 5,5-dithiobis(2-nitrobenzoate) (DTNB).[16] Histidine residues were modified by a freshly prepared solution of diethylpyrocarbonate (DEP) in absolute ethanol. The amount of *N*-carbethoxyhistidine was determined from the increment in protein absorption at 240 nm, taking $E_m = 3200$.[17,18] The kinetics of enzyme inactivation by various modifying agents was followed by the sample withdrawal technique. The kinetic parameters of inactivation were calculated by the method of Ray and Koshland.[19] The absorption spectra and kinetic measurements were performed on Hitachi-124, Hitachi-557, and Cary-219 spectrophotometers. 2-HETPP was synthesized according to Holzer *et al.*[20]

The amount of protein-bound substrate was determined by labeling with [2-^{14}C]pyruvate. The incubation medium contained apo-PDH, TPP, Mg^{2+}, and [2-^{14}C]pyruvate dissolved in 0.01 *M* potassium phosphate buffer, pH 7.0. Aliquots of samples (0.05 ml) were taken at predetermined time intervals and applied to Whatman N3 MM paper filters (2.2 cm). The filters were washed 4 times with cold 10% trichloroacetic acid (TCA), twice with ethanol, and twice with ether. The protein-bound radioactivity count was performed by placing one set of dried filters into a toluene scintillation spectrometer and using an LKB 1210 counter. Simultaneously, a duplicate set of paper filters was placed in a desiccator over performic acid for 18 hr at room temperature as described.[21,22] Then the papers were put into a vacuum dessicator over dry KOH for 12 hr to remove [^{14}C]acetic acid. The difference in the radioactivity of the two sets of papers constituted the amount of the labeled substrate fragment bound to the protein in thioester linkage.[23]

RESULTS AND DISCUSSION

Oligomeric Structure

PDH, isolated from the PDC of pigeon breast muscle, has a molecular weight of about 156,000.[24] In the presence of SDS, the enzyme dissociates into subunits with molecular weights of 41,000 and 37,000, respectively.[7] According to this evidence, the subunit structure of PDH appears to be $(\alpha\beta)_2$. The sedimentation coefficient does not change during the interaction of the apoenzyme with TPP, substrate, or 2-HETPP. These data support the conclusion that the protein tetrameric structure does not change during catalysis.

Structure and Coenzyme Function of TPP in the Active Centers of PDH

To study the nature of the binding and the function of the coenzyme in the active centers of PDH, TPP analogs were used.[a] According to Schellenberger,[25,26] TPP acts by a two-center mechanism in yeast pyruvate decarboxylase. The possibility of a similar mechanism of TPP action for PDH has been studied using 4'-C–substitited analogs of the coenzyme. As can be seen from TABLE 1, all modifications in the amino group as well as the change of this group for an hydroxyl cause a total loss of enzyme activity.

In order to find out what effect the modification of the amino group of the pyrimidine ring might have on the decarboxylase function of the enzyme, experiments were done using pyruvate with the first or second carbon atom labeled. Should decarboxylation occur, one could expect the formation of, respectively, $^{14}CO_2$ or [2-^{14}C]HETPP in the reaction mixture. However, when TPP was replaced by its C-4'–substituted analogs, no products of substrate decarboxylation were detected (see TABLE 1 and FIG. 1). Chromatographic analysis of the reaction products with the use of [2-^{14}C]pyruvate as substrate failed to indicate the formation, in the presence of C-4'–substituted TPP analogs, of any corresponding analogs of "active acetaldehyde" or the "active pyruvate" identified earlier by Holzer[27,28] as an intermediate of the coenzyme-substrate interaction. In contrast, both compounds were seen to form in appreciable amounts in the presence of the natural coenzyme. These experimental data support the conclusion that modification or substitution of the amino group in TPP impairs the mechanism of substrate binding in the active center of holo-PDH. The role of the 4'-NH_2 group is apparently that of providing conditions for the formation of a 2-carbanion, as was suggested earlier,[29,30] or of assisting, together with the pyrimidine ring, in the binding of the substrate to the thiazolium ring.[25]

Participation of the amino group in the two-center catalytic action of TPP is possible when this group is located in close proximity to the second carbon atom of TPP. Such mutual orientation of parts of the TPP molecule has been postulated in the active center of yeast pyruvate decarboxylase.[25,26] A spatial model of TPP that corresponds to its catalytically active conformation in the active center of the yeast enzyme (FIG. 2) suggests that the 4-CH_3 and 6'-CH groups are in direct contact. Any change in the volume of the substituents occupying these positions distorts the situation

TABLE 1. Behavior of TPP Analogs in the PDH Reaction

Substance	V_1 (%)[a]	V_2 (%)[b]	K_m (M)	K_i (M)
TPP (control)	100	100	1×10^{-7}	
4'-N-CH_3-TPP	0	0	1.5×10^{-6}	4.1×10^{-5}
4'-N-$(CH_3)_2$-TPP	0			8.5×10^{-5}
4'-OH-TPP	0	0		2×10^{-8}
6'-CH_3-4-nor-TPP	43		6×10^{-6}	
6'-CH_3-TPP	0		—	—
2-HETPP	90		1×10^{-6}	

[a] V_1, oxidative test with DCPIP.[8]
[b] V_2, production of $^{14}CO_2$.[10]

[a]TPP analogs and pyruvic acid analogs were prepared in the laboratory of A. Schellenberger (Martin Luther University, Halle, GDR).

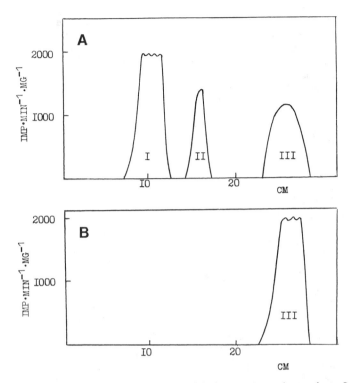

FIGURE 1. Chromatographic analysis of pyruvate dehydrogenase reaction products. Incubation medium contents: [2-^{14}C]pyruvate, 2 mM; TPP, 2.34 mM; MgCl$_2$, 8 mM; PDH, 0.92 mg in 0.8 ml of 0.05 M phosphate buffer, pH 7.0. Incubation time: 3 hr at 25°C. **(A)** in the presence of TPP; **(B)** in the presence of C-4′–substituted analogs of TPP. *Peak I:* [2-^{14}C]HETPP; *Peak II:* [2-^{14}C]carboxyethyl-TPP (?); *Peak III:* [2-^{14}C]pyruvate.

in the region of the active center of TPP, whereas the opposite substitution of proton and methyl should not affect the mutual disposition of the 2-CH and 4′-NH$_2$.

Experiments with the apo-PDH from pigeon breast muscle showed that an additional methyl group in the 6′ position (6′-CH$_3$-TPP) prevents the specific interaction of the analog with apo-PDH (TABLE 1). If this additional group is removed, leaving only one methyl and one proton (in position 4 or 6′), specific binding to the protein is seen to be restored and the analog (6′-CH$_3$-4-nor-TPP) becomes catalytically effective. This result indicates that there is close proximity and intramolecular interaction between the 4′-NH$_2$ and 2-CH groups of the coenzyme in the catalytically active conformation of TPP in the PDH active center—a conformation which appears to be similar to that postulated by Schellenberger[25] for the active center of yeast pyruvate decarboxylase.

The Spectral Characteristics of Holo-PDH

The interaction of apo-PDH with TPP is accompanied by alterations of the CD spectra in the region of optical activity of aromatic amino acids (FIG. 3). A new band appears in the spectral region 320–360 nm, with a diffuse maximum at 330 nm.[11] The appearance of the new band is evidence of the formation of a specific bond in the holoenzyme structure. According to investigations of model systems,[31,32] and also of yeast transketolase,[33,34] this characteristic reflects the formation of the charge transfer complex between the thiazolium ring of TPP (donor of electrons) and the tryptophan indole group (acceptor of electrons).

A linear correlation exists between the changes in the spectral intensity of the charge transfer complex and the rate of the enzymatic reaction during TPP binding. This indicates that the catalytic activity is inherent only in those molecules of the protein-bound coenzyme which are involved in the formation of the charge transfer complex.

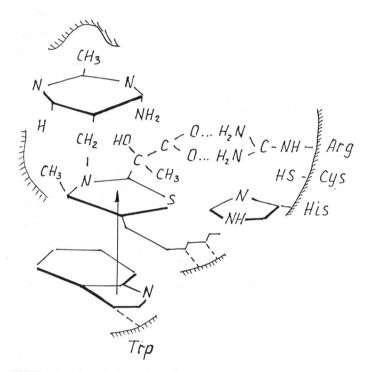

FIGURE 2. A hypothetical scheme for the structure of the PDH active center.

So, the appearance and development of a spectral maximum at 330 nm may serve as an indicator of holo-PDH complex formation. These properties may be used for titration of the coenzyme binding sites and determination of the number of active centers of the enzyme.

Number and Catalytic Efficiency of Active Centers

The data presented in FIGURE 3 suggest the presence of two TPP binding sites in the PDH molecule. Saturation of the first one takes place after addition of one mole of

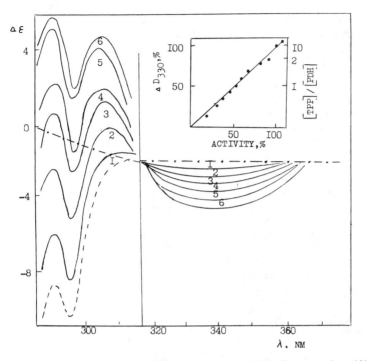

FIGURE 3. Change of CD spectra of apo-PDH with addition of TPP. Concentrations: (*290–315 nm spectra*) apo-PDH, 1.94×10^{-5} *M*; TPP, 0.41×10^{-5} *M* (**I**), 1.22×10^{-5} *M* (**2**), 2.00×10^{-5} *M* (**3**), 2.41×10^{-5} *M* (**4**), 3.51×10^{-5} *M* (**5**), 33.64×10^{-5} *M* (**6**); (*315–370 nm spectra*) apo-PDH, 1.26×10^{-5} *M*; TPP, 0.25×10^{-5} *M* (**I**), 0.50×10^{-5} *M* (**2**), 1.00×10^{-5} *M* (**3**), 1.49×10^{-5} *M* (**4**), 2.45×10^{-5} *M* (**5**), 7.20×10^{-5} *M* (**6**). –·–·–, baseline; – – –, apoenzyme; ——— holoenzyme. *Inset* shows the correlation between PDH activity and the spectral intensity of the charge transfer complex.

TPP. This causes the appearance of half of the maximal value of enzymatic activity. The second site has significantly lower affinity for the coenzyme. After saturation of the second site with TPP, the enzyme acquires maximal catalytic efficiency.

Further evidence for the existence of two active centers in PDH has been obtained using an inactive analog, 4'-OH-TPP,[35] having high affinity for apo-PDH (TABLE 1).

TABLE 2. Interaction of TPP and 2-HETPP with Intact and Modified PDH

	TPP		2-HETPP	
PDH	PDH Activity (%)	$[\theta]_{330}$ (%)	PDH Activity (%)	$[\theta]_{330}$ (%)
Intact enzyme	100	100	44	46
Enzyme modified in one active center by				
4'-OH-TPP	45	42	1	0
DTNB	55	89	—	3
N-Bromosuccinimide	30	50	0	—

Blockade of the first center with this analog results in the formation of a PDH form devoid of CD spectra. The addition to this enzyme form of saturating concentrations of TPP leads to the appearance of only about 50% of the spectral intensity of the charge transfer complex and about half of the maximal value of enzymatic activity (TABLE 2).

It follows from these data that the tetrameric molecule of PDH $(\alpha\beta)_2$ has two active centers, i.e., it is a functional dimer. Each of these centers has identical catalytic efficiency; when catalysis is carried out on only one of the active centers, its activity is equal to half of the maximal value of enzymatic activity.

Identification of Tryptophan Residues in TPP Binding Sites

Modification of the apoenzyme with N-bromosuccinimide results in complete inactivation of PDH and oxidation of two tryptophan residues per mole of the protein.[36] Thus, two tryptophan residues are essential for enzymatic activity (FIG. 4).

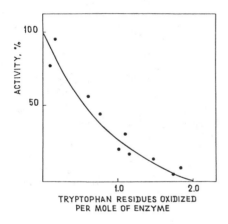

FIGURE 4. Relationship between the residual activity of PDH and the number of modified tryptophan residues (N-bromosuccinimide treatment). PDH concentration, $3 \times 10^{-6}\,M$.

According to observations from investigations on model systems,[31,32] a tryptophan residue can interact with TPP via charge transfer complex formation. In this case, modification of the tryptophan residue should prevent holoenzyme formation. Indeed, oxidation of two tryptophan residues per mole of PDH completely prevents the development of charge transfer complex spectra in the presence of saturating concentrations of TPP (FIG. 5). As can be seen from TABLE 2, the maximal amplitude of the CD spectra for PDH with one oxidized tryptophan residue per mole of the protein was half the value obtained for the saturated holo-PDH, because in this case the holoenzyme is formed by only one active center. These results localize tryptophan residues in TPP binding sites of the PDH active centers as structures essential for the formation of the holoenzyme complex.

Structure of the Substrate Binding Site

The structure of the substrate binding center may be partly characterized by data on substrate specificity.[37] It has been shown that the substrate specificity of the PDC

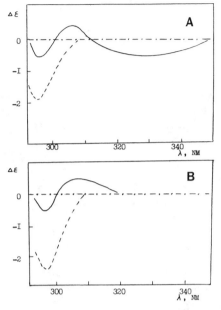

FIGURE 5. Change of CD spectra after addition of TPP to native (**A**) and *N*-bromosuccinimide–modified (**B**) apo-PDH. Concentrations: PDH, 1.26×10^{-5} *M* (**A**), 1.3×10^{-5} *M* (**B**); TPP, 1.97×10^{-5} *M* (**A**), 1.45×10^{-5} *M* (**B**); *N*-bromosuccinimide, 2.52×10^{-5} *M*. —·—·—, baseline, – – –, apoenzyme; ———, holoenzyme.

from pigeon breast muscle is determined by the properties of its PDH component. Similar values for K_m and V_{max} have been obtained only with a limited number of substrates, namely, with pyruvate, α-ketobutyrate, and hydroxypyruvate (TABLE 3). Pyruvate analogs with a branched β substituent or with a substituent longer than the two-carbon fragment show much lower affinity, or no affinity at all, for the holoenzyme. This finding indicates that the active center structure of PDH has steric limitations with respect to the β substituent of pyruvate analogs. Lipophilicity of this group does not appear to be of significance for the binding and catalytic conversion of the substrate.

TABLE 3. Kinetic Behavior of β-Substituted Pyruvate Analogs in PDH Reaction

R—CO—COOH R =	V (%)	K_m (M)
CH₃—	100	6×10^{-6}
C₂H₅—	130	1×10^{-5}
(CH₃)₂CH—	34	4×10^{-3}
(CH₃)(C₂H₅)CH—	0	—
CH₃—CH₂—CH₂—CH₂—	0	—
HO—CH₂—	97	4×10^{-6}
HOOC—CH₂—CH₂—	0	—

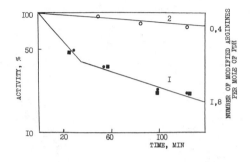

FIGURE 6. Time-course of PDH inactivation by 4-hydroxy-3-nitrophenylglyoxal. (●) apo-PDH, $7.3 \times 10^{-6}\ M$; (■) apo-PDH plus TPP, $2.2 \times 10^{-4}\ M$, and MgCl$_2$, $2.2 \times 10^{-3}\ M$; (○) holoenzyme plus pyruvate, $3.3 \times 10^{-4}\ M$.

The presence of arginine residues in the active centers of PDH was demonstrated by enzyme modification with butandione and with phenylglyoxal and its chromophore analog, 4-hydroxy-3-nitrophenylglyoxal. The kinetics of enzyme inactivation by arginine-specific reagents are biphasic (FIG. 6). Data in TABLE 4 show that the rate constants of inactivation for the fast and the slow phase are essentially different. The reaction is first-order with respect to the concentration of the arginine modifier in both the fast and slow inactivation steps.[13,14,38,39] Therefore, in order to achieve complete inactivation of PDH, it is sufficient to have the binding of only two molecules of the diketone reagent per mole of the protein, modifying the "first," fast-reacting, and the "second," slow-reacting arginine.[40]

Determination of the number of modified arginines by use of 4-hydroxy-3-nitrophenylglyoxal confirmed this stoichoimetry of inactivation, as the complete inactivation of the enzyme coincides with the modification of two arginine residues per mole.[14] The number of modified arginines was decreased when the holoenzyme interacted with the substrate, and under these conditions, the enzyme was protected against inactivation. The effect of complete protection had been observed earlier in the presence of saturating concentrations of pyruvate, hydroxypyruvate or bromopyruvate, but not pyruvamide.[41] These results show that the positively charged arginine residue may be involved in the interaction with the anionic carboxyl of the substrate.

TABLE 4. Kinetics of PDH Inactivation during the Modification of Essential Amino Acid Residues

| Modified Residues | Oxidoreductase Reaction Assayed | Rate Constants ($M^{-1}\ min^{-1}$) | | | |
| | | Inactivation | | Modification | |
		k_{fast}	k_{slow}	k_{fast}	k_{slow}
SH groups	Pyruvate:NAD	1,700	100		
	Pyruvate:DCPIP	1,300	150	4,000	100
	2-HETPP:DCPIP	1,500	110		
Histidine	Pyruvate:NAD	8,000	1,200		
	Pyruvate:DCPIP	9,000	900	10,000	900
	2-HETPP:DCPIP	8,000	800		
Arginine					
2,3-Butandione–modified	Pyruvate:DCPIP	54 ± 17.4	4.4 ± 1.8		
Phenylglyoxal-modified	Pyruvate:DCPIP	66 ± 7.2	4.12 ± 0.68		

It was therefore of interest to examine the effect of modification of arginine residues on the oxidation rate of 2-HETPP used as the substrate of PDH. FIGURE 7 shows that modification of arginine residues completely inactivates PDH in the pyruvate:acceptor oxidoreductase reaction (curve I) but only partly diminishes the velocity of the oxidative conversion of 2-HETPP (curve 2). This observation means that the modified arginine residues are important for the first step of enzyme action, namely, the binding and decarboxylation of pyruvic acid, but are not essential for further oxidative conversion of the intermediate product. The results obtained provide some evidence for the localization of the arginine residues in the substrate binding sites. It is probable that the positively charged guanidinium group of arginine interacts with the departing carboxylic group of pyruvate to form an ionic pair (FIG. 2).

The ability of pyruvate and its analogs to protect the enzyme against inactivation only in the presence of TPP support the conclusion that the formation of the substrate binding site is carried out when formation of holoenzyme complex is completed. On the

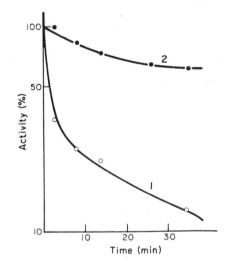

FIGURE 7. Time-course of PDH inactivation in the presence of 2,3-butandione. Residual enzyme activity in the pyruvate:acceptor (**curve 1**) and 2-HETPP:acceptor (**curve 2**) oxidoreductase reactions.

other hand, modification of the essential arginines does not prevent reconstruction of the holoenzyme via charge transfer complex formation (not shown).

Catalytic Mechanism

Model reactions in the presence of artificial electron acceptors are used for studying the PDH enzymatic reaction.[1,8] The formation of 2-HETPP as an intermediate and acetic acid as an end product in these reactions indicates their similarity to the natural catalytic process. 2-HETPP can be also used as a substrate in the PDH reaction.[8] Investigation of this model reaction extends the approaches available for studying the mechanism of PDH action.[39,41]

Kinetic analysis of the 2-HETPP:acceptor oxidoreductase reaction at a constant concentration of one substrate and a varied concentration of the other displayed signs of the "ping-pong" mechanism.[8,41] This observation allows us to suggest that the interaction of PDH with the intermediate α-carbanion of TPP leads to the formation of the substituted form of the enzyme.

Evidence for the formation of the substrate-substituted form of the enzyme during catalysis was obtained in experiments with radioactive pyruvate or TPP. The data in TABLE 5 show that incubation of PDH with [2-^{14}C]pyruvate results in the incorporation of the substrate group into the protein fraction. The label does not attach to the protein if [1-^{14}C]pyruvate is used as the substrate. Simultaneously with enzyme modification by the substrate, enzyme inactivation occurs in a model reaction.[42] The data in TABLE 5 also demonstrate that the formation of substrate-modified PDH is accompanied by TPP fixation in one active center of PDH. As can be seen, the amount of bound substrate and of coenzyme is not equal after gel filtration of the protein. This fact excludes the possibility of substrate group fixation on the protein via the coenzyme molecule, but testifies to their independent binding. The binding of the substrate group is stabilized by trichloroacetic acid, is labile to alkaline treatment and is destroyed by the addition of performic acid,[21] providing evidence for the formation of an acetylthioester bond between the substrate group and the protein moiety.

The appearance of a maximum at 235 nm on the difference absorption spectrum of substrate-substituted PDH[21,41] is consistent with this conclusion concerning the nature of the substrate-enzyme bond. The absorption at 235 nm increases proportionally to protein concentration (FIG. 8). It does not change in the presence of 4 M urea (FIG. 8), but it completely disappears after the addition of hydroxylamine (data not shown). The absorption maximum at 235 nm does not appear when SH groups of the apoenzyme are premodified with pCMB.

The results of inhibitor analysis show that SH groups are essential for the enzymatic activity.[43,45] As implied by the data in TABLE 4, inactivation of PDH in the presence of DTNB is caused by modification of fast- and slow-reacting SH groups. The reaction order for the fast and slow steps of inactivation with respect to inhibitor concentration is equal to unity.[45] Thus only two SH groups per mole are essential for

TABLE 5. Radioactivity in the Protein Fraction after Incubation of PDH in the Presence of [2-^{14}C]TPP or [2-^{14}C]Pyruvate

	[14]C]/PDH (mol/mol)	
Reaction Mixture	Without Performic Acid	Performic Acid Treated
PDH (0.5×10^{-6} M), TPP (5×10^{-5} M), [2-^{14}C]pyruvate (1×10^{-4} M)	1.2[a]	0.12
PDH (0.5×10^{-5} M), TPP (5×10^{-5} M), [2-^{14}C]pyruvate (1×10^{-4} M)	1.5[a]	0.075
PDH (1.5×10^{-5} M), TPP (1.3×10^{-4} M), [2-^{14}C]pyruvate (1.3×10^{-5} M), MgCl$_2$ (1.3×10^{-4} M)	0.35 ± 0.05[b]	—
PDH (1×10^{-5} M), [2-^{14}C]TPP (5×10^{-4} M), pyruvate (5×10^{-5} M)	0.92 ± 0.6[b]	—

[a]The protein was fixed with trichloroacetic acid on paper disks.
[b]The protein was desalted by gel filtration.

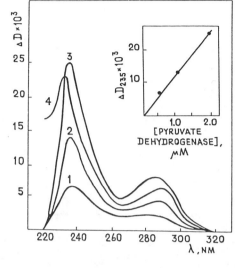

FIGURE 8. Difference absorption spectrum of PDH inactivated by substrate with respect to the absorption spectrum of the holoform. PDH concentrations: 0.5×10^{-6} M **(1)**, 1×10^{-6} M **(2)**, 2×10^{-6} M **(3)**, 2×10^{-6} M plus 4 M urea **(4)**. The concentration ratio for PDH:TPP:MgCl$_2$:pyruvate was 1:5:10:10. *Inset* shows the dependence of absorption at 235 nm on PDH concentration.

PDH activity. Modification of these groups has the same effect on the rate of pyruvate:acceptor and 2-HETPP:acceptor oxidoreductase reactions. Therefore, inactivation of the enzyme by an SH-group modifier is explained by the impairment of one and the same step, common for all the reactions under study. That step is, obviously, the reaction of formation and oxidation of the intermediate α-carbanion in the presence of artificial oxidants or in the PDC containing the native acceptor of acetyl groups and the reductive equivalents—lipoic acid residues.

It may be suggested from the results obtained that the interaction of holo-PDH with pyruvate (or of the apoenzyme with 2-HETPP) in the absence of exogenous oxidants leads to the formation of acetylthioenzyme, which may occur in the enzymatic reaction. This assumption is consistent with the ability of PDH, inactivated in a substrate-dependent manner, to restore its enzymatic activity within the multienzyme complex containing dihydrolipoate acetyltransferase (E_2) and dihydrolipoate dehydrogenase (E_3) in the presence of CoA and NAD.[38] This may occur when acetyl residues and reductive equivalents are transferred by PDH protein groups on the lipoic acid residues bound to E_2.

The formation of acetyl-enzyme during the reaction suggests the existence of an intramolecular mechanism of 2-HETPP oxidation in the active centers of PDH.

Analysis of the rate of substrate-dependent inactivation of PDH at different pH values revealed an essential role of an ionogenic group with pK$_a'$, equal to 6.4.[39] A group with such characteristics may be the histidine imidazole ring. Experiments with photo-oxidation and modification of PDH with diethylpyrocarbonate carried out previously[38,46] likewise established the essential role of histidine residues for enzymatic activity. Modification of these groups similarly affects the rate of pyruvate:NAD, pyruvate:acceptor, and 2-HETPP:acceptor oxidoreductase reactions (TABLE 4).

In the catalytic function of PDH, the 2-HETPP oxidoreductase step depends on the histidine residues to the same extent as does the whole mechanism of action of PDC. Therefore, histidine residues, together with the SH groups of the enzyme, are essential for this step.

Histidine residues apparently do not participate in TPP binding, as the DEP-modified apoenzyme can interact with TPP via charge transfer complex formation,

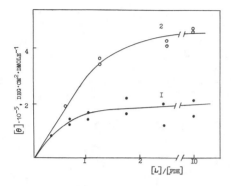

FIGURE 9A. Dependence of PDH molar ellipticity at 330 nm on the amount of added 2-HETPP (**curve I**) or TPP (**curve 2**). PDH concentration: $1.33 \times 10^{-5} M$ (**curve I**), $1.08 \times 10^{-5} M$ (**curve 2**). L, amount of added 2-HETPP (**curve I**) or TPP (**curve 2**).

that is, it can bind the coenzyme. The rate of PDH inactivation by DEP diminishes noticeably only if the holoenzyme interacts with the substrate or with substrate analogs, but, in all cases, the protective effect is not complete (not shown). These results exclude the possibility that histidine residues are involved in substrate binding. It seems more likely that the histidine residues are essential for the catalytic action of the enzyme.

Cooperative Interaction of Active Centers

The biphasic time-course of enzyme inactivation during the modification of essential amino acid residues (TABLE 4) may reflect cooperative interactions of the enzyme active centers. The stoichiometry of the acetylation of PDH upon substrate-dependent modification (TABLE 5) and also the cooperative kinetics of PDH interaction with the substrate and coenzyme[9,47] support this suggestion.

The interaction of apo-PDH with 2-HETPP is more illuminating of the cooperative behavior of the enzyme.[48] FIGURE 9A shows that the addition of 2-HETPP to apo-PDH results in the appearance of a negative Cotton effect at 330 nm (analogous to the interaction of apo-PDH with TPP). However, the maximal spectral change at 330 nm which is induced by apoenzyme interaction with the intermediate product is half of that for the holoenzyme. This may be explained as follows: (1) the structure of the charge transfer complex appears in both active centers of PDH, but its spectral intensity is lower when the apoenzyme interacts with 2-HETPP; or (2) the charge transfer complex is formed only in one of the two centers.

To choose between the above two options, the following experiments were done. One equivalent of TPP was added to apo-PDH to saturate the first center, and the appearance of half of the maximal value for the charge transfer complex spectra was registered (FIG. 9B). After that, an excess of 2-HETPP was added, resulting in a spectral amplitude increase to 100%, that is, a two-fold increase. In the next experiment, the ligand addition order was changed: first the apoenzyme was saturated with 2-HETPP to the maximal development of the charge transfer complex band. The amplitude obtained was 50%—a value indicative of the saturation of one center. After that, an excess of TPP was added. The coenzyme evidently occupied the next active center, as the charge transfer complex intensity doubled.

The results of these simple experiments show that TPP and 2-HETPP added to the apoenzyme in any sequence can interact with the neighboring active centers, leading to the formation of a charge transfer complex of equal spectral intensity regardless of the order of addition. The results reveal that both TPP and 2-HETPP, interacting with a distinct active center of PDH, have a charge transfer complex spectrum with the same characteristics. This means that the half-maximal value of the charge transfer complex spectra observed during 2-HETPP interaction with the apoenzyme must belong to a single center. In other words, PDH exhibits half-of-site reactivity towards 2-HETPP. However, simultaneous interaction of the coenzyme and the intermediate product with neighboring active centers is possible.

The data obtained may be explained in terms of the proposed mechanism of PDH action (FIG. 10). According to this mechanism, the interaction of apo-PDH with 2-HETPP (or of holo-PDH with pyruvate) leads to intramolecular oxidative transfer of the substrate residue on the protein moiety with the formation of the acetylthioenzyme. As a result, in this site TPP becomes free and this transfer is accompanied by the appearance of a charge transfer complex band of 50% intensity. Thus, the half-maximal charge transfer complex spectra, observed during the apo-PDH–2-HETPP interaction, reflects the formation of a free form of holoenzyme, which regenerates as a result of the intramolecular oxidative conversion of the substrate residue.

The half-of-site behavior of PDH in the 2-HETPP conversion catalysis suggests that the acetylation of SH groups in the first active center limits the catalysis of the same reaction in the next active center. Thus, TPP cannot be released from the substrate residue and the holoform in this center does not regenerate (its charge transfer complex value is zero). This is the reason for only a 50% amplitude spectra for the apo-PDH–2-HETPP reaction condition (TABLE 2).

One can check the correctness of the suggested mechanism by blockade of the oxidative transfer of the substrate group to the protein. It may be done, for example, by modification of the SH groups which are postulated to be the acceptor of the acetyl residue. If the SH group is essential for acetylthioenzyme formation, then such modification may prevent development of the charge transfer complex during the interaction of apo-PDH with 2-HETPP.

SH groups were modified by DTNB for enzyme inactivation by half the maximal value, assuming that the SH group of only one active site of the enzyme was affected in this case. Data in TABLE 2 show that the charge transfer complex spectra were not observed during interaction of the modified enzyme with 2-HETPP, while the form of the enzyme supplemented by TPP shows an increase in molar ellipticity at 330 nm to the maximal value.

In another experiment, modification of histidine residues was performed to a residual enzyme activity of 5%. As in the previous case, the modified enzyme could bind TPP (as assessed by charge transfer complex formation) but completely lost the capacity to interact with 2-HETPP (the charge transfer complex was not observed in this case).

FIGURE 9B. Development of the charge transfer complex spectra during sequential interaction of apo-PDH with TPP and 2-HETPP. In the first experiment, TPP (O) was added first, followed by 2-HETPP (■); in the second, the order of addition was changed to 2-HETPP (□) followed by TPP (●). L, amount of added TPP (O, ●) or 2-HETPP (□, ■). PDH concentration: 3.21×10^{-6} M.

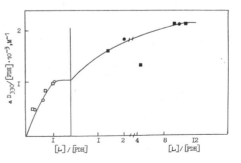

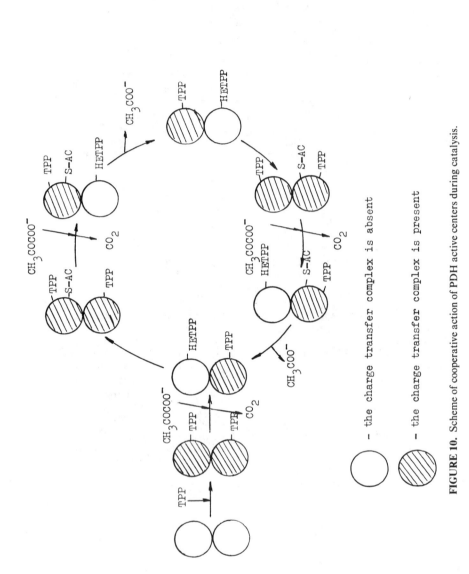

FIGURE 10. Scheme of cooperative action of PDH active centers during catalysis.

As we have shown above, the charge transfer complex band appears as a result of TPP binding in PDH active centers. Data in FIGURE 11 show that holo-PDH interaction with pyruvate results in the disappearance of the charge transfer complex spectrum. The same effect was observed after pyruvate addition to the reaction mixture containing apo-PDH and 2-HETPP (not shown).

Assuming that the deacetylation reaction of the protein is the step limiting the transition of the catalytic mechanism to the next active center, we should be able to observe reaction catalysis in both active centers if conditions for deacetylation of PDH SH groups are maintained. This may occur, for example, in the presence of dithiothreitol (DTT).

The experiment to test this proposal was performed in two ways. The first way was to saturate apo-PDH with 2-HETPP (FIG. 12A). After molar ellipticity reached the limiting value characteristic of coenzyme saturation of one center, DTT was added, leading to a twofold increase in the charge transfer complex band. Its maximal value in

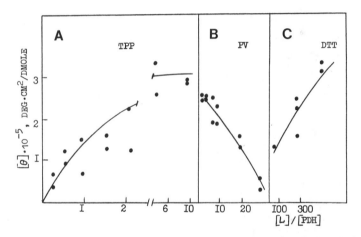

FIGURE 11. Change of the intensity of the CD spectra at 330 nm after the interaction of (**A**) holo-PDH with (**B**) pyruvate (PV) and reversal of the effect (**C**) by DTT. PDH concentration: 1.44×10^{-5} *M*. L, amount of added (**A**) TPP, (**B**) PV, (**C**) DTT.

the presence of DTT was characteristic of the formation of two coenzyme-binding centers.

The other way of performing this experiment was to add 2-HETPP to the apo-PDH solution containing DTT; subsequent development of the charge transfer complex band was observed (FIG. 12B). The maximal value of molar ellipticity was obtained, characteristic of the holoform containing TPP in two active centers, that is, twice as much as during PDH interaction with the intermediate in the absence of DTT.

It is clearly seen in both cases that, in the presence of DTT, the interaction of 2-HETPP with PDH becomes analogous to binding of TPP with two active centers. That is, the substrate-dependent acetylation of the first active center prevents catalysis of the same reaction in the second center until the deacetylation reaction occurs in the first center. The same effect was observed after addition of DTT to the holoenzyme interacting with the substrate (FIG. 11).

Only the bound coenzyme remains after deacetylation of SH groups in the first center. The presence of the coenzyme, as we can see (FIG. 10), does not prevent the conversion of the intermediate in the second center. Thus, 2-HETPP can convert in the second active center only after catalytic cycle termination in the first center.

The experimental data thus demonstrate that the two PDH active centers work in

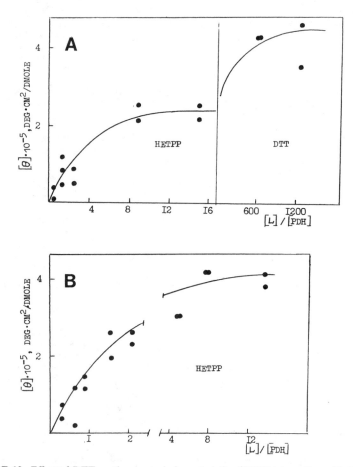

FIGURE 12. Effect of DTT on the spectral characteristic of PDH interacting with 2-HETPP. (**A**) DTT added after 2-HETPP; (**B**) DTT added before 2-HETPP. L, amount of added 2-HETPP (**A**, *left;* **B**) or DTT (**A**, *right*).

turns, affecting each other in such a way that, at each moment of time, different steps of the catalytic mechanism are implemented in each center.[49,50] This means that the intersubunit interaction of PDH may be an essential component of the catalysis and of the regulation of the enzymatic reaction. Such interaction can explain the complete inactivation of PDH upon phosphorylation of only one of the α subunits in the tetrameric molecule[51] and the different rates of acetylation during reduction of lipoic residues and NAD, functioning in the structure of, respectively, the E_2 and E_3 components of the polyenzyme complex.[52,53]

CONCLUSION

Thus, we can conclude that the tetrameric PDH molecule has the structure of the composite dimer, binds two molecules of TPP with different affinity, and has two active centers of equal catalytic efficiency. The tryptophan residue is located in the coenzyme binding site to participate in the formation of the catalytically active TPP conformation. This conformation is characterized by the close proximity of two functionally important groups—the 2-C atom of the thiazolium ring (the center of substrate binding) and the 4'-NH_2 group, essential for substrate binding. The substrate binding site is formed in the structure of holo-PDH; it has limited space in the region of the β group of the substrate and includes an arginine residue interacting with the carboxylic group of pyruvate.

The mechanism of 2-HETPP oxidation in each of the active centers depends on the state of SH groups and the imidazole histidine group. The oxidoreductase PDH activity in the model reaction or in the polyenzyme complex proved to be completely blocked after modification of each of these groups. PDH catalyzes partial conversion of pyruvate with the formation of an intermediate α-carbanion in an incomplete reaction mixture. The α-carbanion is exposed to intramolecular oxidation with the transfer of the acetyl group formed to the protein SH group. The substituted enzyme form has 1–2 acylthioester bonds per mole. The stoichiometry of acetylation, the different reactivity of functional groups, and also the half-of-site interaction of the enzyme with the intermediate reaction product reflect the anticooperative interaction of the active centers, in which at each moment of time different steps of the catalytic mechanism are implemented. The step responsible for the transition of the catalytic mechanism from one active center to the other is a rate-limiting stage of the acetylation-deacetylation of the protein SH group.

REFERENCES

1. SANADY, R. 1963. *In* The Enzymes. P. D. Boyer, Ed. Vol. 7: 307–314. Academic Press. New York-London.
2. REED, L. J. 1974. Acc. Chem. Res. **7:** 40–46.
3. REED, L. J. & D. I. COX. 1966. Annu. Rev. Biochem. **35:** 57–84.
4. KOIKE, K. 1988. *In* Thiamin Pyrophosphate Biochemistry. A. Schellenberger & R. L. Schowen, Eds. Vol. 2: 105–113. CRC Press. Florida.
5. JAGANNATAN, V. & R. S. SCHWEET. 1952. J. Biol. Chem. **196:** 551–562.
6. KHAILOVA, L. S., A. A. GLEMDGA & S. E. SEVERIN. 1970. Biokhimiya (Russ.) **35:** 536–542.
7. KHAILOVA, L. S., M. M. FEIGINA, S. GEORGIU & S. E. SEVERIN. 1970. Biokhimiya (Russ.) **37:** 1312–1314.
8. KHAILOVA, L. S., R. BERNHARDT & G. HUBNER. 1977. Biokhimiya (Russ.) **42:** 113–117.
9. KHAILOVA, L. S., R. BERNHARDT & S. E. SEVERIN. 1976. Biokhimiya (Russ.) **41:** 1391–1396.
10. SEVERIN, S. E., L. S. KHAILOVA & R. BERNHARDT. 1976. Ukr. Biokhim. Zh. **48:** 503–509.
11. KHAILOVA, L. S. & L. G. KOROCHKINA. 1982. Biochem. Int. **5:** 525–532.
12. SPANDE, T. F., N. M. GREEN & B. WITCOP. 1966. Biochemistry **5:** 1926–1933.
13. NEMERYA, N. S., L. S. KHAILOVA & S. E. SEVERIN. 1984. Biochem. Int. **8:** 369–376.
14. KHAILOVA, L. S., N. S. NEMERYA & O. V. LUKIN. 1985. Dokl. Acad. Nauk SSSR (Russ.) **284:** 1495–1498.

15. BOYER, P. D. 1954. J. Am. Chem. Soc. 76: 4331–4337.
16. ELLMAN, G. A. 1959. Arch. Biochem. Biophys. 82: 70–77.
17. KHAILOVA, L. S., B. I. KURGANOV, N. S. NEMERYA & D. R. DAVYDOV. 1987. Molek. Biol. (Mosc.) (Russ.) 21: 758–768.
18. OVADI, J., A. LIBOR & P. ELODI. 1975. Acta Biochim. Biophys. Acad. Sci. Hung. 2: 455–458.
19. RAY, W. J. & D. E. KOSHLAND. 1961. J. Biol. Chem. 236: 1973–1979.
20. HOLZER, H., H. W. GOEDDE & B. ULLRICH. 1961. Biochem. Biophys. Res. Commun. 5: 447–455.
21. KHAILOVA, L. S., O. V. ALEXANDROVITCH & S. E. SEVERIN. 1985. Biochem. Int. 10: 291–300.
22. BARRERA, C. R., G. NAMIHIRA, L. HAMILTON, P. MUNK, M. H. ELEY, T. C. LINN & L. J. REED. 1972. Arch. Biochem. Biophys. 148: 343–358.
23. LYNEN, F. 1967. Biochem. J. 102: 381–400.
24. KHAILOVA, L. S. & E. YU. MOSKALYOVA. 1970. Dokl. Acad. Nauk. SSSR (Russ.) 193: 944–947.
25. SCHELLENBERGER, A. 1982. Ann. N. Y. Acad. Sci. 378: 506–511.
26. SCHELLENBERGER, A. 1967. Angew. Chemie. 79: 1050–1061.
27. HOLZER, H. & E. BEAUCAMP. 1959. Angew. Chem. 71: 776.
28. HOLZER, H. 1961. Angew. Chem. 73: 721–727.
29. BRESLOW, R. 1962. Ann. N. Y. Acad. Sci. 98: 445–452.
30. GALLO, A. A. & H. Z. SABLE. 1974. J. Biol. Chem. 249: 1382–1389.
31. HEINRICH, C. P., D. SCHMIDT & K. NOACK. 1974. Eur. J. Biochem. 41: 555–561.
32. MIEVAL, J. J., J. SUCHY & J. E. BIAGLOW. 1969. J. Biol. Chem. 244: 4063–4071.
33. KOCHETOV, G. A., R. A. USMANOV & V. P. MERZLOV. 1970. FEBS Lett. 9: 265–266.
34. MESHALKINA, L. E. & G. A. KOCHETOV. 1979. Biochim. Biophys. Acta 57: 218–223.
35. KHAILOVA, L. S., L. G. KOROCHKINA & S. E. SEVERIN. 1987. Dokl. Acad. Nauk. SSSR (Russ.) 295: 1020–1023.
36. KOROCHKINA, L. G., L. S. KHAILOVA & S. E. SEVERIN. 1984. Biochem. Int. 9: 491–499.
37. BERNHARDT, R., L. S. KHAILOVA & G. FISHER. 1977. In The Citric Acid Cycle and Mechanism of Its Regulation. p. 85. Moskwa, Nauka (Russ.).
38. KHAILOVA, L. S. & S. E. SEVERIN. 1988. In Thiamin Pyrophosphate Biochemistry. A. Schellenberger & R. L. Schowen, Eds. Vol. 2: 45–60. CRC Press. Florida.
39. KHAILOVA, L. S. & V. S. GOMAZKOVA. 1986. Biokhimiya (Russ.) 51: 2054–2074.
40. LEVY, H. M., P. D. LEBER & E. M. RYAN. 1963. J. Biol. Chem. 238: 3654–3659.
41. SEVERIN, S. E., L. S. KHAILOVA & V. S. GOMAZKOVA. 1986. Adv. Enzyme Regul. 25: 347–375.
42. KHAILOVA, L. S., N. S. NEMERYA & S. E. SEVERIN. 1983. Biochem. Int. 7: 423–432.
43. KHAILOVA, L. S. & O. V. LISOVA. 1981. Dokl. Acad. Nauk. SSSR (Russ.) 259: 505–508.
44. DAS, M. L., M. KOIKE & L. J. REED. 1961. Proc. Natl. Acad. Sci. USA 47: 753–759.
45. KHAILOVA, L. S., O. V. ALEXANDROVITCH & S. E. SEVERIN. 1983. Biochem. Int. 7: 223–233.
46. KHAILOVA, L. S., D. N. KEREEVA & S. E. SEVERIN. 1972. Ukr. Biokhim. Zh. (Russ.) 44: 718–723.
47. KHAILOVA, L. S. & R. BERNHARDT. 1978. FEBS (Fed. Eur. Biochem. Soc.) Proc. Meet. Abstr. 2909. 12th meeting, Dresden.
48. KHAILOVA, L. S. & L. G. KOROCHKINA. 1985. Biochem. Int. 11: 509–516.
49. LAZDUNSKI, M. 1974. Prog. Bioorg. Chem. 3: 81–140.
50. HARADA, K. & R. G. WOLFE. 1968. J. Biol. Chem. 243: 4131–4137.
51. YEAMAN, S. Y., E. T. HUTCHESON, T. E. ROCHE, F. H. PETTIT, J. R. BROWN, L. J. REED, D. C. WATSON & G. H. DIXON. 1978. Biochemistry 17: 2364–2370.
52. AMBROSE-GRIFFIN, M. C., M. J. DANSON, W. G. GRIFFIN, G. HALE & R. N. PERHAM. 1980. Biochem. J. 187: 393–401.
53. FREY, P. A. 1982. Ann. N. Y. Acad. Sci. 378: 250–264.

Properties of Lipoamide Dehydrogenase and Thioredoxin Reductase from *Escherichia coli* Altered by Site-Directed Mutagenesis[a]

CHARLES H. WILLIAMS, JR.,[b,c] NIGEL ALLISON,[d,e]
GEORGE C. RUSSELL,[d] ANDREW J. PRONGAY,[b]
L. DAVID ARSCOTT,[b] SHOMPA DATTA,[b]
LENA SAHLMAN,[b,f] AND JOHN R. GUEST[d]

[b]*Veterans Administration Medical Center and*
Department of Biological Chemistry
University of Michigan
Ann Arbor, Michigan 48105
and
[d]*Department of Microbiology*
Sheffield University
Sheffield S10 2TN
United Kingdom

Lipoamide dehydrogenase and thioredoxin reductase are members of the pyridine nucleotide–disulfide oxidoreductase family of flavoenzymes, which is distinguished by an oxidation-reduction–active disulfide.[1] Other members of the family, glutathione reductase and mercuric reductase, are homologous with lipoamide dehydrogenase in all domains.[2-5] Thioredoxin reductase is homologous with the others only in its two adenosine binding regions; the remainder of the protein, including its active-site disulfide region, appears to have evolved convergently.[6]

Catalysis takes place in two half-reactions, as shown in FIGURE 1 for lipoamide dehydrogenase.[7-9] In the first, dithiol-disulfide interchange effects reduction of the oxidized enzyme (E) to the 2-electron reduced form of the enzyme (EH$_2$); and in the second, the reoxidation of EH$_2$ to E, electrons pass very rapidly via the FAD to NAD$^+$. The distinct roles of the two nascent thiols of EH$_2$ have been demonstrated.[10,11] The thiol nearer the amino terminus reacts almost exclusively with iodoacetamide, and it is this thiol that interchanges with the dithiol substrate; the sulfur nearer the carboxyl terminus interacts with the FAD. Similar results are seen with glutathione reductase[12] and mercuric reductase.[13] The assignment of roles to the two nascent thiols in

[a]This work was supported by the Medical Research Service of the Veterans Administration, by Grant GM21444 from the National Institute of General Medical Sciences (to C. H. W.) and by a Science and Engineering Research Council project grant (to J. R. G.).

[c]Author to whom correspondence should be sent at the V. A. Medical Center (151), 2215 Fuller Road, Ann Arbor, MI 48105.

[e]Current address: Porton Products, Ltd., CAMR, Porton Down, Salisbury SP4 OJG, United Kingdom.

[f]Current address: Department of Biochemistry, University of Umeå, S-90187 Umeå, Sweden.

thioredoxin reductase has been more difficult because both nascent thiols are reactive with all reagents tried.[14] This problem is being solved by site-directed mutagenesis.[15]

In addition to the FAD and the redox-active disulfide, a base is essential for catalysis (FIG. 1). Its function is to deprotonate the dihydrolipoamide for nucleophilic attack on the enzyme disulfide.[16] Glutathione reductase catalysis is in the chemically opposite direction. In this enzyme, the function of the base is to stabilize the nascent interchange thiol as an anion for attack on the glutathione disulfide.[12] The amino acid sequence[17] and X-ray crystallographic structure[18] of human glutathione reductase show that the base is a histidyl residue strongly hydrogen-bonded to a glutamate.[19] The thiol nearer to the amino terminus is positioned for interchange with glutathione, and the other thiol is nearer to the flavin. Thus, the crystal structure and other types of data agree. The structure of *Azotobacter vinelandii* lipoamide dehydrogenase, recently derived, appears to be very similar.[21] It has been suggested that the positive charge of a lysyl residue whose side chain reaches under the flavin ring, from the disulfide compartment to the pyridine nucleotide compartment, modifies the redox potential of the FAD.[20] Three of the mutations described below were used in an attempt to alter slightly the position of this positive charge relative to the flavin ring.

Earlier studies showed that the *Escherichia coli* enzyme is somewhat more complex than the pig heart enzyme (FIG. 2). Whereas in the latter species EH_2 is predominantly the charge transfer complex, in the *E. coli* enzyme at neutral pH, two additional forms are present in significant amounts: in one of these, a proton shift has left the charge transfer thiol protonated and this form is fluorescent; electrons are on the FAD in the other form.[22]

METHODS

Site-directed mutagenesis of *E. coli* lipoamide dehydrogenase[23] and thioredoxin reductase[15,24,25] has been described. The purification and assay of thioredoxin reductase followed established procedures.[15] An *E. coli* strain, JRG1342, having an Lpd⁻ phenotype ($\Delta aroP\text{-}lpd$)[26] and transformed with pJLA504,[27] expressed the wild-type or mutated lipoamide dehydrogenases from λ promoters[23] and was grown in 6 × 1 l of TB broth containing 50 μg/ml ampicillin by shaking in a Lab Line rotary incubator at 30°C. When the A_{600} of the cultures reached 0.6, the temperature was raised to 42°C and incubation was continued for 16–17 hr. The yield of cells was 5.5, 6.0, 7.0, and 5.0

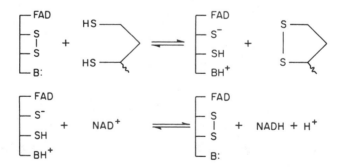

FIGURE 1. Lipoamide dehydrogenase half-reactions: reduction of E to EH_2 by dihydrolipoamide (**upper panel**) and reoxidation of EH_2 to E by NAD⁺ (**lower panel**).

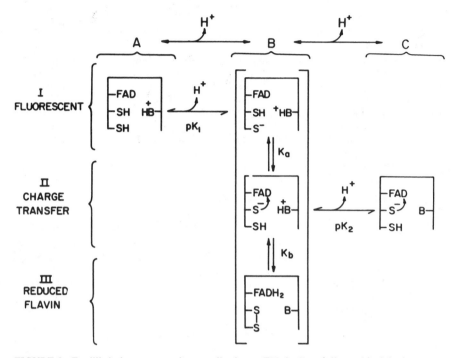

FIGURE 2. Equilibria between species contributing to EH_2 in *E. coli* lipoamide dehydrogenase and the effect of pH. **A**, low pH; **B**, neutral pH; **C**, high pH. (Adapted from Wilkinson & Williams.[22])

g/l for wild type and mutants Glu-188→Asp,[g] His-444→Gln, and Lys-53→Arg/ Glu-188→Asp, respectively. (The numbering for the *E. coli* lipoamide dehydrogenase amino acid sequence is derived from the nucleotide sequence.[28]) Cell were harvested by centrifugation at 6500 rpm for 10 min, homogenized in a minimal volume of 100 m*M* phosphate buffer, 0.3 m*M* EDTA, pH 7.6, containing 25 μ*M* phenylmethylsulfonyl fluoride, and diluted with the same buffer to give 5 ml of suspension/g wet cell weight. Cells were broken in a Branson D610 sonifier using a rosette cell immersed in an ice-salt mixture for 5 bursts of 3 min each. Streptomycin sulfate was added to give a final concentration of 2%, and the suspension was spun in a Beckman L8-70M ultracentrifuge, using the VTI-50 rotor, initially at 25,000 rpm for 20 min and then at 45,000 rpm for an additional hour. The supernatant was fractionated with ammonium sulfate from 35 to 85% saturation, and the precipitate was dissolved in 100 m*M* phosphate buffer, 0.3 m*M* EDTA, pH 7.6. Following extensive dialysis against 10 m*M* phosphate buffer, 0.3 m*M* EDTA, pH 7.6 (buffer A), the solution was applied to a DEAE-TRISACRYL (Pharmacia LKB Biotechnology) column, 2.5 × 11 cm, equilibrated with buffer A. A fraction of protein was eluted by washing with buffer A; elution was continued with a gradient formed from 250 ml each of buffer A, without and with 1 *M* NaCl. The fraction eluting between 0.16 and 0.2 *M* NaCl contained most of the enzyme. After concentration with ammonium sulfate and dialysis against

[g]Designation of mutants: Glu-188→Asp, mutation of Glu-188 to Asp.

50 mM phosphate buffer, 0.3 mM EDTA, pH 7.6 (buffer B), it was further purified by adsorption chromatography on a 2.5 cm × 27 cm calcium phosphate gel column equilibrated with buffer B. The column was washed successively with buffer B and buffer B containing 0.1 M ammonium sulfate, and the enzyme was eluted with buffer B containing 0.3 M ammonium sulfate. In the case of the wild-type enzyme, the A_{280}/A_{450} ratio was 6.4 and the yield was 85 mg.

Since the Glu-188→Asp enzyme did not bind well to calcium phosphate gel, further purification was attempted, following the DEAE step, by apolar chromatography, first on phenyl-Sepharose and then on a hydrophobic interaction column (TSK phenyl-5PW). The yield was poor and the improvement in purity was marginal in both steps; loss of FAD was evident. The A_{280}/A_{455} ratio of the Glu-188→Asp enzyme used in these studies was 11. The His-444→Gln enzyme was not retained by DEAE. Following chromatography on calcium phosphate gel, it was further purified by apolar chromatography on phenyl-Sepharose. The A_{280}/A_{455} was 7.0 and the yield was 95 mg.

Lipoamide dehydrogenase was assayed by following the reduction of acetylpyridine adenine dinucleotide (APAD$^+$) by dihydrolipoamide, measured by a change in absorbance at 363 nm, at 25°C. The assay volume was 2.5 ml of 60 mM phosphate buffer, pH 7.6, containing 0.8 mg/ml bovine serum albumin, 1.4 mM EDTA, 400 μM APAD$^+$, and 80 μM dihydrolipoamide. The turnover number of the wild type enzyme was approximately 500 mol APAD$^+$ oxidized/mol FAD. The turnover number of the Glu-188→Asp mutated enzyme was 1550 mol APAD$^+$ oxidized/mol FAD, or approximately 3 times that of wild-type enzyme.

RESULTS AND DISCUSSION

The nine mutageneses of *E. coli* lipoamide dehydrogenase effected thus far are described in another paper in this volume.[29] Two of the altered enzymes, the Glu-188→Asp and the His-144→Gln, have been extensively purified. For purified enzyme, it is necessary to use the dihydrolipoamide–acetylpyridine adenine dinucleotide assay. Use of the higher-potential APAD$^+$, rather than of NAD$^+$, overcomes the extreme mixed inhibition of the *E. coli* enzyme by NADH; in addition to product inhibition, NADH reduces the active intermediate EH$_2$ to the inactive EH$_4$, the 4-electron reduced form of the enzyme. In crude extracts, NAD$^+$ can be used as the acceptor, presumably because of a very active NADH oxidase. Recently, we have shown with wild-type enzyme that assays using NAD$^+$ as the acceptor are possible in the rapid reaction spectrophotometer, where rates can be established before there is significant buildup of NADH.[30] Steady-state, stopped-flow traces monitoring NADH production at increasing levels of NAD$^+$ showed a pronounced lag at the lowest NAD$^+$ level, while at the highest level, inhibition was apparent within 1.5 s. However, initial rates estimated from the linear phase conformed approximately to a Michaelis-Menten model and quite well to a cooperative binding model. The apparent V_{max} of 400 s^{-1} was approximately half that observed with the pig heart enzyme, where the NADH inhibition is much less severe. These studies examining the steady-state kinetics of catalysis in the physiological direction of the reaction, together with earlier investigations of the kinetics in the opposite direction,[31] as well as the spectral properties of *E. coli* lipoamide dehydrogenase,[22] will form the basis of our comparisons with the enzyme altered by site-directed mutagenesis.

In three of the mutations, we were seeking to alter the position of the Lys-53 side chain charge relative to the isoalloxazine ring: by shortening the ion-pair side chain, as in the Glu-188→Asp mutation, by dispersing the positive charge, as in the Lys-53→Arg mutation, or by using a double mutation which should maintain the overall length of the ion pair. This strategy was worked out in a conversation between one of us (C. H. W.) and Professor Georg E. Schulz, University of Freiberg. There are at least three ways the protein might adjust to accommodate such changes: the ion pair might be weakened or broken, the polypeptide chain carrying Glu-188 might move, or the polypeptide chain containing the Lys-53 might move.

The Glu-188→Asp enzyme has been extensively purified. FIGURE 3 shows the absorbance spectrum of this altered enzyme compared with that of the wild-type enzyme. Changes to the absorbance in the visible region are minimal, primarily a lessening of the resolution of the shoulder at 480 nm. Purification of the other two altered enzymes in this group, the Lys-53→Arg and the Lys-53→Arg/Glu-188→Asp, is in progress.

Lipoamide dehydrogenase in which the base, His-444, has been changed to Gln has been purified to virtual homogeneity and has very low activity in the APAD$^+$ assay—about 0.3 to 0.4% that of wild type. Given that the pH of the assay is 1.7 units below the first pK_a of dihydrolipoamide,[32] it would be expected that the activity would be diminished by 50 to 100 times, if the only function of the base is to deprotonate the

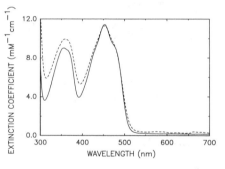

FIGURE 3. Absorbance spectra of wild-type and Glu-188→Asp lipoamide dehydrogenases. The proteins were in 10 mM Na/K phosphate buffer, pH 7.6, 0.3 mM EDTA, at 20°C. *Solid line,* 39.0 μM wild-type enzyme; *dashed line,* 13.6 μM mutated enzyme.

substrate. But, it has been postulated that the base also stabilizes the thiols as thiolates. Absence of this latter function should lead to an additional diminution of activity. Similar levels of activity have been reported for the analogous mutation in glutathione reductase.[33] FIGURE 4a shows spectra resulting from titration of this enzyme by dihydrolipoamide. Even in the early phases of the reduction, no detectable charge transfer is seen. Charge transfer is a direct indication of stabilization of the electron transfer thiol as a thiolate.[34] In a similar equilibrium experiment with the wild-type enzyme (shown in FIGURE 4b),[35] the charge transfer band at 530 nm is obvious; but, as already discussed, in the *E. coli* enzyme, the charge transfer complex is only one of several species present in EH$_2$.[22] When the mutated enzyme is reduced in a stopped flow apparatus, (FIG. 5a) sizable charge transfer builds up over the first 30 s. In a similar experiment with the wild-type enzyme,[1] a high level of charge transfer is almost fully formed in the 3-ms dead time of the rapid-reaction spectrophotometer (FIG. 5b). Thus, in the mutated enzyme, the charge transfer band forms far more slowly and decays more extensively, demonstrating the crucial role of the base in stabilizing the charge transfer complex and, thus, its role in catalysis where the thiolate attacks the FAD.

Conditions for chemical modification of just one of the nascent thiols in *E. coli*

FIGURE 4. Anaerobic titration of lipoamide dehydrogenase with dihydrolipoamide. Spectra were taken at 20°C in conventional spectrophotometers after all changes were complete. **(a)** Spectra of 18.4 μM His-444→Gln enzyme in 0.1 M Na/K phosphate buffer, pH 7.6, 0.3 mM EDTA, titrated with (*top* to *bottom traces*, respectively) 0, 0.21, 0.42, 0.63, 1.05, 1.47, and 9.87 mol dihydrolipoamide per mol enzyme FAD. The spectrum of the oxidized enzyme (*uppermost curve*) overlies that of the enzyme given the first addition of reductant because of incomplete removal of oxygen under these conditions. The small aberration at 550 nm is due to imperfect baseline correction. **(b)** Spectra of 23.5 μM wild-type enzyme in 0.1 M Na/K phosphate buffer, pH 7.6, 1.0 mM EDTA, 30 mM ammonium sulfate, titrated with the indicated amounts (mol) of dihydrolipoamide per mol enzyme FAD or, finally, with dithionite.

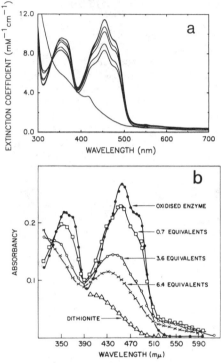

FIGURE 5. Anaerobic reduction of lipoamide dehydrogenase with dihydrolipoamide. **(a)** Spectra of His-444→Gln enzyme were taken, after rapid mixing (ca. 5 ms), using a Tracor Northern diode array spectrometer as the detector. Buildup of charge transfer absorbance (EH$_2$) at 550 nm at (*bottom* to *top traces*, respectively) 0, 3, 6, 9, 12, and 30 s upon reduction with 5.6 mol of dihydrolipoamide per mol enzyme FAD; enzyme was 9.5 μM in 0.12 M Na/K phosphate buffer, pH 7.6, 0.3 mM EDTA, at 20°C after mixing (2-cm light path). **(b)** Spectra of wild-type enzyme: (Δ) oxidized enzyme, (○) EH$_2$, (□) EH$_4$. Spectra of the oxidized and EH$_4$ forms were taken in a conventional spectrophotometer. The composite spectrum of the EH$_2$ form was generated in a series of identical mixings of enzyme with 11 mol dihydrolipoamide per mol enzyme FAD in a rapid reaction spectrophotometer with the detector set at the indicated wavelengths. The enzyme was 18 μM in 0.1 M Na/K phosphate buffer, pH 7.6, 0.3 mM EDTA, at 1°C after mixing (2-cm light path).

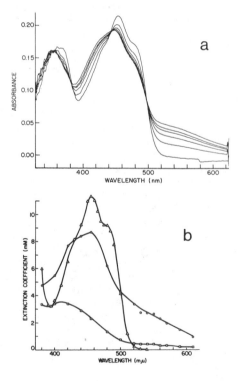

thioredoxin reductase (TRR) were not found,[14] and it was therefore not possible to assign distinct functions to these thiols as had been done with lipoamide dehydrogenase and glutathione reductase.[10,12] Therefore, site-directed mutagenesis has been used to singly modify each thiol to a serine. The properties of the mutated enzymes have allowed us to assign distinct functions to each of the thiols, at least tentatively.[15] FIGURE 6 shows the spectra of the two mutants compared with that of the wild-type enzyme. The differences between the traces may appear unimpressive, but they suggest which cysteine is nearer the FAD. The resolved character of the spectrum of the wild-type enzyme is due to the apolar milieu of the FAD.[36] For the mutated enzyme in which Cys-136 has been changed to serine [TRR(Ser-136,Cys-139)], the spectrum still shows the resolution characteristic of the wild-type enzyme. But in the enzyme

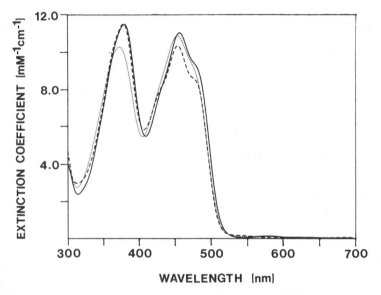

FIGURE 6. Absorbance spectra of wild-type thioredoxin reductase (TRR) and of proteins singly mutated at each thiol group. The proteins were in 0.1 M Na/K phosphate buffer, pH 7.6, 0.3 mM EDTA, at 12°C. *Solid line,* 18.0 μM (wild type) TRR(Cys-136,Cys-139); *dashed line,* 18.8 μM TRR(Ser-136,Cys-139); *dotted line,* 18.5 μM TRR(Cys-136,Ser-139).

which contains Cys-139 substituted with serine [TRR(Cys-136,Ser-139)], the resolved character is lost. This suggests that Cys-139 is closer to the FAD, since the change of this residue to the more polar serine is reflected in an alteration of the flavin spectrum to one characteristic of a more polar milieu.

While purifying the TRR(Ser-136,Cys-139) enzyme, we observed that it turned red upon the addition of ammonium sulfate. This was unexpected, since *E. coli* thioredoxin reductase has not previously been observed to stabilize the charge transfer complex.[37] As shown in FIGURE 7, ammonium ion causes the appearance at long wavelengths of a band very similar in shape to that of the lipoamide dehydrogenase and glutathione reductase charge transfer complexes.[1] An apparent K_d of 54 μM can be calculated after correction for non-specific binding (FIG. 7, inset). Only a limited

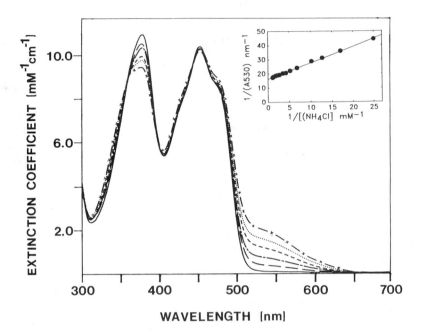

FIGURE 7. Titration of TRR(Ser-136,Cys-139) with 5 M NH$_4$Cl. 42.4 μM TRR(Ser-136,Cys-139) in 0.1 M Na/K phosphate buffer, pH 7.6, 0.3 mM EDTA, was titrated at 12°C with a 5 M NH$_4$Cl solution in 0.1 M Na/K phosphate buffer, 0.3 mM EDTA, pH adjusted to maintain the pH of the enzyme solution at 7.6 throughout the titration. (—) no NH$_4$Cl, (– –) 79 mM NH$_4$Cl, (– – – – –) 98 mM NH$_4$Cl, (- - -) 192 mM NH$_4$Cl; ($\cdots$) 455 mM NH$_4$Cl, and (–x–x–) 833 mM NH$_4$Cl. *Inset:* Benesi-Hildebrand plot of the titration; K_d, 54 μM; E$_{530}$, 1300 M^{-1} cm^{-1}.

number of ions have been tried, but ammonium ion is thus far unique in causing the effect. This result reinforces the suggestion that it is Cys-139 that is interacting with the FAD. If, as with other members of this enzyme family, the two distinct catalytic functions are each carried out by a different nascent thiol, then Cys-136 would perform the initial thiol-disulfide interchange with thioredoxin.

The finding that both thiol-altered enzymes were partially active was totally unexpected.[15] The analogous mutated enzymes in mercuric reductase[38] and lipoamide dehydrogenase[29] were totally without activity in their physiological reactions. The steady-state kinetics of the mutated enzymes have been compared with those of the wild-type enzyme in assays of NADPH-thioredoxin activity linked to 5,5'-dithiobis(2-nitrobenzoic acid) reduction, in which the NADPH concentration was kept constant by glucose-6-phosphate and glucose-6-phosphate dehydrogenase. The K_m values were little changed. The TRR(Ser-136,Cys-139) enzyme had just over 10% activity while the TRR(Cys-136,Ser-139) enzyme appeared to have a V_{max} of about 50% of the wild type. However, with the latter mutant enzyme, the intercept replots of the parallel Lineweaver-Burk plots were not linear, and the V_{max} was extrapolated from the data points for the two highest concentrations. It was therefore an upper limit. It has been suggested, based on the chemical modification studies and from the fact that the substrate for thioredoxin reductase is itself a protein, that the site of thiol-disulfide interchange must be more open in this enzyme than in other members of this enzyme family.[14] It would appear, then, that in this more open active site, the remaining thiol in either mutation of thioredoxin reductase can fairly readily form a mixed disulfide with thioredoxin and that either of these can be reduced by $FADH_2$. This is in contrast to lipoamide dehydrogenase, where only one of the sulfurs can be attacked by the dithiol substrate, or to glutathione reductase, where only one of the nascent thiols can interchange with glutathione. Furthermore, in both these enzymes, interaction with FAD is the unique function of only one of the sulfurs. However, in the mutated thioredoxin reductase enzymes, no new chemistry is required.

FIGURE 8 shows mechanisms for the reoxidation by thioredoxin of each of the two mutated enzymes and indicates the step thought to be partially blocked and thus responsible for their reduced catalytic activities. This picture attempts to suggest that whereas in glutathione reductase the electron transfer thiol and the interchange thiol lie on a line perpendicular to the flavin ring—so that only the electron transfer thiol can interact with the FAD[19]—in thioredoxin reductase the thiols may lie on a less perpendicular line. If the proposal that Cys-139 normally interacts with the FAD is correct, the activity of TRR(Cys-136,Ser-139) (lower line in FIG. 8) would be limited by inefficient electron transfer directly from $FADH_2$ to the mixed disulfide, since this step would have to replace the thiol-disulfide interchange normally initiated by Cys-139. The fact that mutation of Cys-136 to serine results in substantial loss of activity suggests that both thiols have distinct functions, leading to a working hypothesis that Cys-136 is the interchange thiol. Then the activity of TRR(Ser-136,Cys-139) (upper line in FIG. 8) would be limited by inefficient thiol-disulfide interchange with oxidized thioredoxin initiated by Cys-139. The suggested mechanisms for activity in each mutated enzyme re-emphasize the more open active site required by thioredoxin reductase compared to related enzymes in order to accommo-

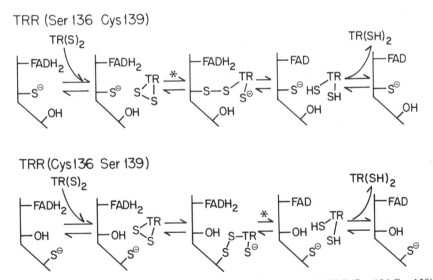

FIGURE 8. Reduction of thioredoxin by reduced forms of (**upper panel**) TRR(Ser-136,Cys-139) and (**lower panel**) TRR(Cys-136,Ser-139). The position of steps possibly responsible for catalytic inefficiencies are indicated by *asterisks*. $TR(S)_2$ and $TR(SH)_2$ are the oxidized and reduced forms of thioredoxin, respectively.

date its protein substrate. However, we are not suggesting that wild-type enzyme is any less specific in dithiol-disulfide interchange than are the other members of this enzyme family.

ACKNOWLEDGMENTS

The authors wish to thank Daniel Domain and David Gamm for help in purifying the enzymes and Eric Baude for assistance in the dihydrolipoamide reductions of the His-444→Gln mutated enzyme.

REFERENCES

1. WILLIAMS, C. H. JR. 1976. Flavin-containing dehydrogenases. *In* The Enzymes, 3rd ed. P. D. Boyer, Ed. Vol. XIII: 89–173. Academic Press. New York.
2. WILLIAMS, C. H. JR., L. D. ARSCOTT & G. E. SCHULZ. 1982. Amino acid sequence homology between pig heart lipoamide dehydrogenase and human erythrocyte gluta-thione reductase. Proc. Natl. Acad. Sci. USA **79:** 2199–2201.
3. RICE, D. W., G. E. SCHULTZ & J. R. GUEST. 1984. Structural relationship between glutathione reductase and lipoamide dehydrogenase. J. Mol. Biol. **174:** 483–496.
4. BROWN, N. L., S. J. FORD, R. D. PRIDMORE & D. C. FRITZINGER. 1983. DNA sequence of a gene from the *Pseudomonas* transposon TN501 encoding mercuric reductase. Biochemis-try **22:** 4089–4095.
5. GREER, S. & R. N. PERHAM. 1986. Glutathione reductase from *Escherichia coli:* Cloning and sequence analysis of the gene and relationship to other flavoprotein disulfide oxidoreductases. Biochemistry **25:** 2736–2742.
6. RUSSEL, M. & P. MODEL. 1988. Sequence of thioredoxin reductase from *Escherichia coli:* Relationship to other flavoprotein disulfide oxidoreductases. J. Biol. Chem. **263:** 9015–9019.
7. MASSEY, V., Q. H. GIBSON & C. VEEGER. 1960. Intermediates in the catalytic action of lipoyl dehydrogenase. Biochem. J. **77:** 341–351.
8. MASSEY, V. & C. VEEGER. 1961. Studies on the reaction mechanism of lipoyl dehydrogen-ase. Biochim. Biophys. Acta **48:** 33–47.
9. SEARLS, R. L., J. M. PETERS & D. R. SANADI. 1961. α-Ketoglutaric dehydrogenase: On the mechanism of dihydrolipoly dehydrogenase reaction. J. Biol. Chem. **236:** 2317–2322.
10. THORPE, C. & C. H. WILLIAMS, JR. 1976. Differential reactivity of the two active site cysteine residues generated on reduction of pig heart lipoamide dehydrogenase. J. Biol. Chem. **251:** 3553–3557.
11. THORPE, C. & C. H. WILLIAMS, JR. 1976. Spectral evidence for a flavin adduct in a monoalkylated derivative of pig heart lipoamide dehydrogenase. J. Biol. Chem. **251:** 7726–7728.
12. ARSCOTT, L. D., C. THORPE & C. H. WILLIAMS, JR. 1981. Glutathione reductase from yeast—Differential reactivity of the nascent thiols in two-electron reduced enzyme and properties of a monoalkylated derivative. Biochemistry **20:** 1513–1520.
13. FOX, B. S. & C. T. WALSH. 1983. Active site peptide of mercuric reductase: Homology to glutathione reductase and lipoamide dehydrogenase. Biochemistry **22:** 4082–4088.
14. O'DONNELL, M. E. & C. H. WILLIAMS, JR. 1985. Reaction of both thiols of reduced thioredoxin reductase with *N*-ethyl maleimide. Biochemistry **24:** 7617–7621.
15. PRONGAY, A. J., D. R. ENGELKE & C. H. WILLIAMS, JR. 1989. Characterization of two active site mutants of thioredoxin reductase from *Escherichia coli.* J. Biol. Chem. **264:** 2656–2664.
16. MATTHEWS, R. G. & C. H. WILLIAMS, JR. 1976. Measurement of the oxidation-reduction potentials for two electron and four electron reduction of lipoamide dehydrogenase from pig heart. J. Biol. Chem. **251:** 3956–3964.
17. UNTUCHT-GRAU, R., G. E. SCHULZ & R. H. SCHIRMER. 1979. The C-terminal fragment of

human glutathione reductase contains the postulated catalytic histidine. FEBS Lett. **105**: 244–248.

18. SCHULZ, G. E., R. H. SCHIRMER, W. SACHSENHEIMER & E. F. PAI. 1978. The structure of the flavoenzyme glutathione reductase. Nature **273**: 120–124.

19. KARPLUS, P. A. & G. E. SCHULZ. 1987. Refined structure of glutathione reductase at 1.54 Å resolution. J. Mol. Biol. **195**: 701–729.

20. PAI, E. F. & G. E. SCHULZ. 1983. The catalytic mechanism of glutathione reductase as derived from X-ray diffraction analyses of reaction intermediates. J. Biol. Chem. **258**: 1752–1757.

21. SCHIERBECK, B. 1988. The three-dimensional structure of lipoamide dehydrogenase from *Azotobacter vinlandii*. Thesis. Groningen University. pp. 74–76.

22. WILKINSON, K. D. & C. H. WILLIAMS, JR. 1979. Evidence for multiple electronic forms of two electron reduced lipoamide dehydrogenase from *Escherichia coli*. J. Biol. Chem. **254**: 852–862.

23. ALLISON, N., C. H. WILLIAMS, JR. & J. R. GUEST. 1988. Overexpression and mutagenesis of the lipoamide dehydrogenase of *Escherichia coli*. Biochem. J. **256**: 741–749.

24. RUSSEL, M. & P. MODEL. 1985. Direct cloning of the *trx*B gene that encodes thioredoxin reductase. J. Bacteriol. **163**: 238–242.

25. RUSSEL, M. & P. MODEL. 1986. The role of thioredoxin in filamentous phage assembly— Construction, isolation and characterization of mutant thioredoxins. J. Biol. Chem. **261**: 14997–15005.

26. GUEST, J. R., H. M. LEWIS, L. D. GRAHAM, L. C. PACKMAN & R. N. PERHAM. 1985. Genetic reconstruction and functional analysis of the repeating lipoyl domains in the pyruvate dehydrogenase multienzyme complex of *Escherichia coli*. J. Mol. Biol. **185**: 743–754.

27. SCHAUDER, B., R. FRANK, H. BLOCKER & J. E. G. McCARTHY. 1987. Inducible expression vectors incorporating the *Escherichia coli atpE* translational initiation region. Gene **52**: 297–283.

28. STEPHENS, P. E., H. M. LEWIS, M. G. DARLISON & J. R. GUEST. 1983. Nucleotide sequence of the lipoamide dehydrogenase gene of *Escherichia coli* K12. Eur. J. Biochem. **135**: 519–527.

29. RUSSELL, G. C., N. J. ALLISON, C. H. WILLIAMS, JR. & J. R. GUEST. 1989. Oligonucleo-tide-directed mutagenesis of the *lpd* gene of *Escherichia coli*. Ann. N. Y. Acad. Sci. This volume.

30. SAHLMAN, L. & C. H. WILLIAMS, JR. 1989. Lipoamide dehydrogenase from *Escherichia coli*—Steady-state kinetics of the physiological reaction. J. Biol. Chem. **264**: 8039–8045.

31. WILKINSON, K. D. & C. H. WILLIAMS, JR. 1981. NADH inhibition and NAD activation of *Escherichia coli* lipoamide dehydrogenase catalyzing the NADH-lipoamide reaction. J. Biol. Chem. **256**: 2307–2314.

32. MATTHEWS, R. G., D. P. BALLOU, C. THORPE & C. H. WILLIAMS, JR. 1977. Ion pair formation in pig heart lipoamide dehydrogenase—Rationalization of pH profiles for reactivity of oxidized enzyme with dihydrolipoamide and 2-electron-reduced enzyme with lipoamide and iodoacteamide. J. Biol. Chem. **252**: 3199–3207.

33. BERRY, A., N. S. SCRUTTON & R. N. PERHAM. 1989. Switching kinetic mechanism and putative proton donor by directed mutagenesis of glutathione reductase. Biochemistry **28**: 1264–1269.

34. MASSEY, V. & S. GHISLA. 1974. Role of charge transfer interactions in flavoprotein catalysis. Ann. N. Y. Acad. Sci. **227**: 446–465.

35. WILLIAMS, C. H., JR. 1965. Studies on lipoyl dehydrogenase from *Escherichia coli*. J. Biol. Chem. **240**: 4793–4800.

36. PALMER, G. & V. MASSEY. 1968. Mechanisms of flavoprotein catalysis. *In* Biological Oxidations. T. P. Singer, Ed.: 263–300. Interscience. New York.

37. O'DONNELL, M. E. & C. H. WILLIAMS, JR. 1983. Proton stoichiometry in the reduction of the FAD and disulfide of *Escherichia coli* thioredoxin reductase—Evidence for a base at the active site. J. Biol. Chem. **258**: 13795–13805.

38. SCHULTZ, P. G., K. G. AU & C. T. WALSH. 1985. Directed mutagenesis of the redox-active disulfide in the flavoenzyme mercuric ion reductase. Biochemistry **24**: 6840–6848.

The Lipoyl-Containing Components of the Mammalian Pyruvate Dehydrogenase Complex: Structural Comparison and Subdomain Roles[a]

THOMAS E. ROCHE, MOHAMMED RAHMATULLAH,
SUSAN L. POWERS-GREENWOOD, GARY A. RADKE,
S. GOPALAKRISHNAN, AND CHRISTINA L. CHANG

Department of Biochemistry
Kansas State University
Manhattan, Kansas 66506

The mammalian pyruvate dehydrogenase complex is presently known to comprise nine distinct subunits. These include the pyruvate dehydrogenase (E1) component (an $\alpha_2\beta_2$ tetramer), the dihydrolipoyl transacetylase (E2) component (postulated to be an α_{60} system organized into a pentagonal dodecahedron), the dihydrolipoyl dehydrogenase (E3) component (an α_2 dimer), the protein X component (oligomeric form not defined), the catalytic (K_c) and the basic subunit (K_b) of the pyruvate dehydrogenase kinase, and the catalytic (P_c) and the FAD-containing subunit (P_f) of the pyruvate dehydrogenase phosphatase. Seven of these subunits bind to the large oligomeric core that is composed of two components—the dihydrolipoyl transacetylase (E2) and the component referred to as protein X (or component X or band 5). A major endeavor in our laboratory during the past few years has been to establish the distinct nature and to sort out the distinct functions of these two lipoyl-bearing components of the mammalian pyruvate dehydrogenase complex. Structural and immunological results indicated that the smaller protein X was distinct from and not derived from transacetylase subunits.[1-7] However, protein X also contains a lipoyl moiety[3-7] that is a substrate[5] for the three reactions—reductive acetylation, transacetylation, and reoxidation—that are catalyzed by the E1, E2, and E3 components, respectively.

Here we will describe sequence evidence[7] that protein X is structurally different from E2 subunits but has a related lipoyl domain. We will present evidence that protein X functions in the binding of the E3 component.[7-9] The domain structure of protein X will also be described,[6] and we will present evidence that the lipoyl domain has a critical role in catalysis in the overall reaction catalyzed by the complex.[7-9]

E2 subunits have been shown to contain two major domains.[10] The inner domain (E2$_I$) associates to form the large oligomeric core and catalyzes the transacetylation reaction.[10] An outer domain fragment encompasses the lipoyl-bearing region (E2$_L$) and is extended and presumably mobile.[10] The E2$_L$ domain, derived from E2 subunits by trypsin treatment, has an anomalously slow mobility in SDS–polyacrylamide gel electrophoresis (SDS–PAGE), giving an apparent M_r of 36,000–38,000, as compared to its behavior during sedimentation equilibrium, which gives a molecular weight of 28,000.[10] Recently we have found that cleavage of E2 subunits by protease arg C

[a] This work was supported by National Institutes of Health Grant DK 18320 and by the Kansas State Agricultural Experiment Station—Contribution No. 89-231-B.

generates a larger outer domain fragment, designated $E2_{LB}$, which, like $E2_L$, separates completely from the $E2_I$ oligomer upon sedimentation of the oligomeric core.[6] Here we will present evidence for the location of the additional structure in $E2_{LB}$ compared to $E2_L$ and demonstrate that this additional structure functions in the binding of the E1 component.[7]

RESULTS AND DISCUSSION

Protease Arg C Treatment

An important tool in our studies has been the use of protease arg C to cleave the $E2\text{-}X\text{-}K_cK_b$ subcomplex. TABLE 1 shows the products obtained by treating the $E2\text{-}X\text{-}K_cK_b$ subcomplex with protease arg C for various periods of time. Fragments were identified on Western blots by their reaction with specific antibodies.[6] Lipoyl domains were identified by their capacity to undergo acetylation and NADH-

TABLE 1. Products Obtained from Treatment of $E2\text{-}X\text{-}K_cK_b$ Subcomplex with Protease Arg C

Products	Duration of Treatment with Protease Arg C[a] (min)		
	10	30–60	240
Associated subunits	$E2\text{-}X_I\text{-}K_cK_b$	$E2\text{-}E2_I\text{-}X_I\text{-}K_c$	$E3_I\text{-}X_I$
Dissociated subunits	X_L	$E2_{LB}$, $E2_L$, X_L	$E2_L$, X_L, K_c
Fragment sizes			27-kDa $E2_{I3}$
	35-kDa X_{I1}	31.5-kDa $E2_{I1}$	28.5-kDa X_{I3}
	ca. 15.5-kDa X_L	27-kDa $E2_{I3}$	
		30.5-kDa X_{I2}	
		28.5-kDa X_{I3}	
		46–49-kDa $E2_{LB}$	
		37–39-kDa $E2_L$	

[a]Treatment at 30°C with arg C protease at a 1:20 ratio to the subcomplex.

dependent alkylation.[6] Initially only the lipoyl domain (X_L) of protein X is removed; then at intermediate times the K_b subunit of the kinase and some of the E2 subunits are cleaved; and at much longer times of treatment all E2 subunits are cleaved.[6] Aprotinin can then be added to inhibit protease arg C. Centrifugation of samples treated for these different times allows isolation of residual subcomplexes (the associated subunits listed in TABLE 1) with compositions $E2\text{-}X_I\text{-}K_cK_b$, $E2\text{-}E2_I\text{-}X_I\text{-}K_c$ (E2:$E2_I$ ratio is about 1:2 when essentially all the K_b is cleaved), and $E2_I\text{-}X_I$. Thus, following the complete removal of the lipoyl domains of the E2 subunits, only the inner domain of protein X remains associated with the oligomeric $E2_I$, and none of the other components binds to the $E2_I\text{-}X_I$ inner core. As indicated in TABLE 1, the X_L, $E2_{LB}$ and $E2_L$ fragments are dissociated and fractionate into the supernatant. (Consideration of kinase subunits will be discussed in another paper[10a] in this volume.

It should also be noted that the X_{I1} fragment is larger than the inner domain fragment and the X_L fragment is much smaller than the outer domain fragment released from E2 subunits.[6] This supports the conclusion that the protein X subunit is distinct from the E2 subunit. The slow cleavage of E2 subunits by protease arg C not only releases the large (46–49 kDa) $E2_{LB}$ fragment but also a 31.5-kDa $E2_{I1}$ fragment[6] that is larger than any inner domain fragments released from the E2 component by trypsin.

Sequence of the Amino Terminus of the Inner and the Outer Domain Fragments of E2 and Protein X Subunits

We have found that the $E2_{LB}$ and $E2_L$ fragments have the same amino-terminal sequence (TABLE 2).[7] Thus, the additional structure in the $E2_{LB}$ fragment is at the carboxyl-terminal end. This sequence of 28 amino acids agrees more closely with the amino acid sequence of the first (26 aligned identities) than with that of the second (18 aligned identities) lipoyl domain of the human E2, as deduced from the cDNA clone for human E2.[11,12] As with intact E2 subunits, the X_L fragment had a blocked amino terminus. Further treatment with trypsin yielded a fragment, designated X_L', that had the amino-terminal sequence shown in TABLE 2.[7] This sequence is different from but clearly related to the amino-terminal sequence of the $E2_L$ fragment.

TABLE 3 shows the amino-terminal sequence of the major 27-kDa $E2_I$ fragment that is generated by protease arg C or trypsin.[7] This sequence aligns with and is closely related to the sequences from the alanine- and proline-rich hinge region of human and rat E2 that is located between the inner (catalytic and E2-subunit binding) domain and a domain related to the E3-binding domain of other transacylase components.[11,12]

TABLE 3 also shows the amino-terminal sequence of a 35-kDa X_I fragment.[7] The sequence is not related to the sequence of the 27-kDa $E2_I$ fragment, nor is it related to any sequence in the human E2. These results are consistent with the results of our previous studies using immunological and structural approaches that suggested that protein X had a lipoyl domain related to the lipoyl domain of the E2 component but that the rest of its structure was not closely related to that of the E2 component.[3]

E1 Binding Region

The E1 component (an $\alpha_2\beta_2$ tetramer), but not the E3 component, reduces the cleavage by trypsin of E2 subunits at 4°C and alters the pattern of cleavage at 22°C. At 22°C, the presence of excess E1 causes the $E2_{LB}$ fragment to be formed.[7] At the same time, the $E1\alpha$ subunit is cleaved, but the $E1\beta$ subunit is resistant to trypsin. In gel filtration studies we have found that the $E2_{LB}$ fragment, but not the $E2_L$ fragment, interacted with the E1 component—specifically with the β subunit(s) of the E1 component (FIG. 1).[7] Thus, the E1 component is bound through an E1 binding domain that is located in E2 subunits between the inner domain and the outer lipoyl-bearing domain.

From analysis of the complete sequence of the human E2 subunit[11,12] and the relative mobilities of the $E2_L$ and $E2_{LB}$ fragments on SDS-PAGE, it seems certain that the additional structure in the 49-kDa $E2_{LB}$ fragment would include and is probably synonymous with the subunit binding domain that has been found in other transacylase subunits.[13-17] In several transacylases, this region has been recognized to participate in binding the E3 component[15,16,18] and in some cases to bind the E1 component.[15,16] We will refer to this region as the $E2_B$ region. TABLE 4 compares the structure of the $E2_B$ region of the human E2 to the corresponding sequences of other transacylase subunits. Interestingly, the $E2_B$ region of the human E2 sequence has the highest number of sequence identities (twenty-five) with the $E2_B$ region of the *Bacillus stearothermophilus* transacetylase. The *B. stearothermophilus* transacetylase subunits share with the mammalian transacetylase subunits the property of being assembled as a 60-subunit

TABLE 2. Amino-Terminal Amino Acid Sequences of $E2_L$, $E2_{LB}$, and X'_L

Fragment Sequenced	Aligned Amino Acid Sequences[a]																													
										10												20								
X'_L			A	G	P	I	K	I	L	M	P	S	L	S	P	T	M	E	E	G	(G/N)	I	V	K	W	L	I	K	E	G
							*				*	*	*	*	*	*	*			*		*			*			*		
$E2_L$ or $E2_{LB}$	S	L	P	P	H	E	K	V	P	L	P	S	L	S	P	T	M	Q	A	G	T	I	A	V	W	E	K	K		
										10										20										

[a]Asterisk (*) designates identical residues aligned. (Table adapted from Rahmatullah *et al.*[7])

TABLE 3. Comparison of the Amino-Terminal Amino Acid Sequences of $E2_I$ and X_I from Bovine Kidney $E2\text{-}X\text{-}K_CK_B$ with Sequences of Human and Rat E2[a]

Source	Amino Acid Sequence																					
Bovine 27-kDa $E2_I$ fragment	A	A	P	T	P	A	A	A	V	P	P	P	S	P	G	V	A	P	V	P	T	G	V
		*	*		*	*	*		*	*	*			*	*		*	*	*	*	*	*	*
Human E2 (residues 311–333)[b]	V	A	P	A	P	A	A	V	V	P	P	T	G	P	G	M	A	P	V	P	T	G	V
	*	*	*			*	*	*		*	*			*		*	*	*		*		*	*
Rat E2[b]	A	A	P	A	A	A	A	A	A	P	P	—[c]	G	P	R	V	A	P	T	P	A	G	V
Bovine 35-kDa X_I fragment	L	S	P	A	A	R	N	I	L	E	K	X[d]	A	L	X[d]	A	N	Q					

[a]Table adapted from Rahmatullah *et al.*[7]
[b]Asterisk (*) indicates that residue is identical to the one in the bovine $E2_I$ fragment.
[c]Gap introduced for alignment.
[d]X, residue could not be determined.

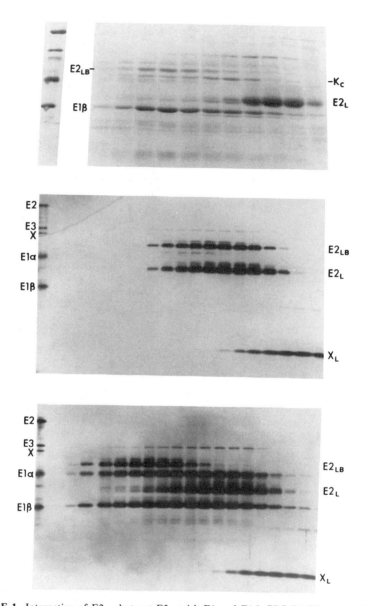

FIGURE 1. Interaction of $E2_{LB}$, but not $E2_L$, with E1 and E1β. SDS-PAGE patterns for gel filtration fractions. Gel filtration was conducted on a Sephacryl S-300 column.[7] (**Middle panel**) profile from the fractionation of the mixture of $E2_{LB}$, $E2_L$, and X_L that was prepared by protease arg C treatment of the $E2$-X-$K_c K_b$ subcomplex followed by pelleting of the oligomeric inner domain.[6] (**Bottom panel**) profile from the fractionation of a 0.4-mg sample of this mixture combined with the E1 tetramer component at a 1:2 ratio. (**Top panel**) profile for an E1β-$E2_{LB}$-$E2_L$ fraction prepared as described in Ref. 7. The SDS-PAGE pattern of the intact complex is shown at the *left* of each panel. Staining in the top panel was with Coomassie blue and in the bottom two panels with a silver stain. ($E2_{LB}$ stains lightly with Coomassie blue.) (From Rahmatullah *et al.*[7] Reprinted from the *Journal of Biological Chemistry* with permission from the American Society of Biochemistry and Molecular Biology.)

TABLE 4. Comparison of the Amino Acid Sequences of the Subunit Binding Domains from Various Transacylases

Transacylase[a]	Sequence[b]
Human[c] E2p[11,12]	GPKGR—VFVSPLAKKLAVEKGIDLTQVKGTGPDGRITKKDIDSFVPSKVAPAP[b] (270 290 310 / 110 130 150)
Escherichia coli E2k[14]	QNNDAL——SPAIRRLLAEHNLDASAIKGTGVGGRLTREDVEKHLAKAPA—KE (330 350 370)
Escherichia coli E2p[13]	AENDAYVHATPLIRRLAREFGVNLAKVKGTGRKGRILREDVQAYVKEAIKRAE (340 360 380)
Azotobacter vinelandii E2p[15]	SRNGAKVHAGPAVRQLAREFGVELAAINSTGPRGRILKEDVQAYVKAMMQKAK (130 150 170)
Bacillus stearothermophilus E2p[16]	GPN—RRVIAMPSVRKYAREKGVDIRLVQGTGKNGRVLKEDIDAFLAGGAKPAP (110 130 150)
Human E2bc[17]	EIKGRKTLATPAVRRLAMENNIKLSEVVGSGKDGRILKEDILNYL—EKQTGAI

[a]E2p, E2k, and E2bc: transacylase components of the pyruvate dehydrogenase, α-ketoglutarate dehydrogenase, and branched-chain α-keto acid dehydrogenase complexes, respectively. Reference numbers are indicated for papers from which sequence data were obtained. (Table adapted from Rahmatullah *et al.*[7])

[b]Sequence of the distinct (i.e., hinged) domain between the lipoyl domain and the inner core domain is shown for the transacylase components of α-keto acid dehydrogenase complexes that have been sequenced. Optimal alignments with the human dihydrolipoly transacetylase (human E2p) sequence[11,12] are presented. For numbering positions of amino acids in the various sequences, each number is centered over the appropriate letter. Asterisk (*) is used to designate a residue identical to the one in the human sequence. The numbering of the sequence for the human E2 is based on assigning as the first residue the serine which is equivalent to the amino-terminal serine of bovine E2L and E2LB (TABLE 2).

[c]At position 272 of human E2p, Patel's laboratory[12] reports a serine and Gershwin's laboratory[11] an aspartic acid residue.

icosahedral core,[19] and the $E2_B$ region of this bacterial transacetylase also binds the E1 component.[16] FIGURE 2 shows a model for the structure of the mammalian transacetylase component and indicates the proposed nature of the $E2_L$, $E2_{LB}$, and $E2_I$ fragments.

Binding of E3 by Protein X

In the remainder of this paper, we will present evidence that protein X has an essential role in the binding of the E3 component in the mammalian pyruvate dehydrogenase complex. The apparent organization of the 60 E2 subunits into a dodecahedron allows for 12 faces as the smallest symmetry unit. This structure is not compatible with the capacity to bind only six E3 dimers. The E3 component must be bound as a dimer (and not as a monomer), since active sites are formed at the interface between subunits. We have found about six protein X molecules per molecule of mammalian pyruvate dehydrogenase complex.[3] Additional insight into the nature of the association of protein X with the E2 component will be given in another paper[10a] in this volume.

We have found that the E3 but not the E1 component selectively protects the protein X component from degradation by trypsin or protease arg C (FIG. 3).[7] Using a protein X–specific antibody (X-IgG) that reacted in ELISA assays with the E2-X subcomplex but not with E2 oligomer prepared free of protein X (cf. below), we found that the X-IgG inhibited reconstitution of the overall reaction of the pyruvate dehydrogenase complex i.e., (E1 and E3 components were added to X-IgG–treated E2-X subcomplex).[7] When the E3 component was added to the E2-X subcomplex prior to addition of X-IgG, it reduced the rate of development of the inhibitory activity of X-IgG on reconstitution. Addition of the E1 component at a level higher than the effective level of E3 gave some reduction in this rate but was less effective than the E3 component. Thus, the E1 component probably interferes with the binding of X-IgG to protein X in a less specific manner than does the E3 component. The above data suggest that the E3 component may bind to the protein X component.

To further investigate this possibility, we prepared the transacetylase in two forms. The first was an oligomeric form of the transacetylase in which protein X and kinase subunits were removed.[8] Resolution of this form involved treatment with 5.5 M urea and 0.4 M NaCl for 90 min at 4°C and separation of the oligomeric E2 on a Sephacryl

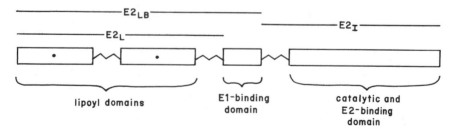

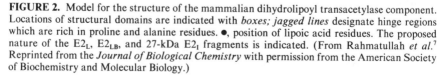

FIGURE 2. Model for the structure of the mammalian dihydrolipoyl transacetylase component. Locations of structural domains are indicated with *boxes; jagged lines* designate hinge regions which are rich in proline and alanine residues. ●, position of lipoic acid residues. The proposed nature of the $E2_L$, $E2_{LB}$, and 27-kDa $E2_I$ fragments is indicated. (From Rahmatullah *et al.*[7] Reprinted from the *Journal of Biological Chemistry* with permission from the American Society of Biochemistry and Molecular Biology.)

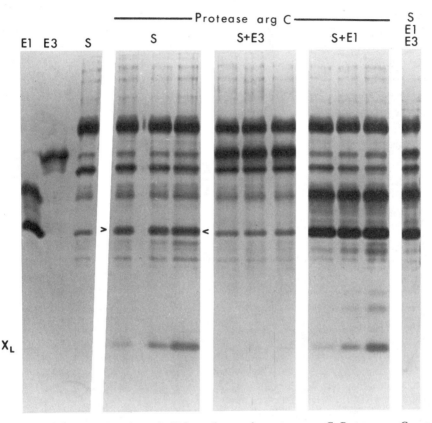

FIGURE 3. E3 protection of protein X from cleavage by protease arg C. Protease arg C was added at 1:40 ratio to total protein, and proteolysis was for 5, 10, or 20 min (**interior panels;** time increases from *left* to *right* in each panel) at 30°C. *Arrows* delineate increase in intensity due to formation of X_I, which comigrates with E1β. S, the E2-X-$K_c K_b$ subcomplex; other symbols are as defined in the text. (From Rahmatullah *et al.*[7] Reprinted from the *Journal of Biological Chemistry* with permission from the American Society of Biochemistry and Molecular Biology.)

S-400 column containing the same chaotropic agents and 0.2 mg/ml Pluronic F-68. The dialyzed product was recovered by pelleting it from 65 min at 180,000 × *g*. The second form was the E1-X_I-$K_c K_b$ subcomplex, which was prepared as described above, by selective removal of the lipoyl domain of protein X by protease arg C and then pelleting of the residual subcomplex.

Both the E2 oligomer and the E2-X_I-$K_c K_b$ subcomplex fully retained transacetylation activity, bound the pyruvate dehydrogenase component, and underwent the reductive acetylation reaction (albeit with a somewhat reduced rate and extent for the reductive acetylation reaction in the case of the E2 oligomer). However, in comparison to the untreated E2-X-$K_c K_b$ subcomplex, the preparations lacking protein X or its lipoyl domain had greatly reduced capacities for binding the E3 component and, in combination with the E1 and E3 components, had greatly reduced activity in the overall reaction catalyzed by the pyruvate dehydrogenase complex.[8] These data

TABLE 5. Properties and Roles of E2 Subunits

Inner domain ($E2_I$) ca. 27 kDa	Forms 60-subunit oligomer Catalyzes transacetylation Retains the inner domain of protein X (X_I)
Lipoyl domain ($E2_L$) ca. 37 kDa (by SDS-PAGE) 28 kDa (by sed. equil.)[a]	Contains two lipoyl domains ($E2_{L1}$ and $E2_{L2}$) Contains structure required for reductive acetylation reaction Participates in transacetylation and electron transfer reactions Is required for regulatory effects on kinase and phosphatase activites
Lipoyl-E1 binding domain ($E2_{LB}$) ca. 47 kDa (by SDS-PAGE)	Contains E1 binding domain ($E2_B$) in addition to lipoyl domains Is required for binding of PDH_a kinase and PDH_b phosphatase[b] May contribute to E3 binding
Hinge regions	Consist of 3 regions: (i) between $E2_{L1}$ and $E2_{L2}$ (ii) between $E2_{L2}$ and $E2_B$ (iii) between $E2_B$ and $E2_I$ Are high in proline and non-polar aliphatic amino acids, particularly alanine

[a]Sed. equil., sedimentation equilibrium.
[b]PDH, pyruvate dehydrogenase.

indicate that protein X, through its X_L domain, enhances the binding of the E3 component and the overall reaction of the complex.

Using this role for protein X as a basis, we have developed an enzyme-linked-assay (ELA) procedure for this component and demonstrated that protein X binds the E3 component in the absence of the E2 component.[9] We have found that the $E2\text{-}X\text{-}K_cK_b$ or the E2-X subcomplex or the $X\text{-}K_cK_b$ fraction (lacking E2 subunits) attached to polystyrene wells binds the E3 component. However, the E2 oligomer or $E2\text{-}X_I\text{-}K_cK_b$ subcomplex was less effective in binding the E3 component, but some binding was observed. The fractions enriched in protein X (but also containing E2 subunits) that eluted after the E2 oligomer from the Sephacryl S-400 column described above had a greater capacity for binding the E3 component than did the native subcomplex or the

TABLE 6. Properties of Protein X

Protein X contains lipoyl group on ca. 15.5-kDa lipoyl domain (X_L).
X_L is different from but related to $E2_{L1}$ and $E2_{L2}$.
Protein X contains 35-kDa inner domain (X_I).
X_I appears not to be a close structural relative of $E2_I$ (on the basis of immunological reactivity, peptide mapping studies, and limited sequence data).
Protein X functions in the binding of the E3 component.
In the absence of the E2 component, the X_L domain is acetylated by pyruvate or acetyl-CoA and is directly reduced by the E3 component.
Additional protein X (functional in the binding of the E3 component) cannot bind to $E2\text{-}X\text{-}K_cK_b$ or $E2\text{-}X_I$ subcomplexes or to the E2 oligomer.

X-K_cK_b fraction lacking E2 subunits. The most likely interpretation of our data is that both protein X and E2 subunits contribute to the binding of E3 subunits.

Further studies are needed to define whether the lipoyl domain of protein X is preferentially used as a substrate by the E3 component. The loss of reconstituted pyruvate dehydrogenase complex activity upon removal of the X_L domain is nearly proportional to the extent of removal of the X_L domain.[9] Furthermore, the protection by the E3 component against removal of the X_L domain leads to maintenance of reconstituted enzyme complex activity.[9] Our results establish an essential role for protein X in the binding of the E3 component and in the overall reaction catalyzed by the mammalian pyruvate dehydrogenase complex.

Properties of the E2 and Protein X Components

TABLES 5 and 6 summarize the properties of the mammalian dihydrolipoyl transacetylase and protein X components based on the above results and the studies of others. Interactions with regulatory enzymes are described in another paper[10a] in this volume.

REFERENCES

1. RAHMATULLAH, M., T. M. JILKA & T. E. ROCHE. 1985. Fed. Proc. **44:** 683.
2. DEMARCUCCI, O. L. & G. LINDSEY. 1985. Eur. J. Biochem. **149:** 641–648.
3. JILKA, J. M., M. RAHMATULLAH, M. KAZEMI & T. E. ROCHE. 1986. J. Biol. Chem. **261:** 1858–1867.
4. DEMARCUCCI, O., J. P. HODGSON & J. G. LINDSAY. 1986. Eur. J. Biochem. **158:** 587–594.
5. RAHMATULLAH, M. & T. E. ROCHE. 1987. J. Biol. Chem. **262:** 10265–10271.
6. RAHMATULLAH, M., S. GOPALAKRISHNAN, G. A. RADKE & T. E. ROCHE. 1989. J. Biol. Chem. **264:** 1245–1251.
7. RAHMATULLAH, M., S. GOPALAKRISHNAN, P. C. ANDREWS, C. L. CHANG, G. A. RADKE & T. E. ROCHE. 1989. J. Biol. Chem. **264:** 2221–2227.
8. GREENWOOD-POWERS, S. L., M. RAHMATULLAH, G. A. RADKE & T. E. ROCHE. 1989. J. Biol. Chem. **264:** 3655–3657.
9. GOPALAKRISHNAN, S., M. RAHMATULLAH, G. A. RADKE & T. E. ROCHE. 1989. Biochem. Biophys. Res. Commun. **160:** 715–721.
10. BLEILE, D. M., M. L. HACKERT, F. H. PETTIT & L. J. REED. 1981. J. Biol. Chem. **256:** 514–519.
10a. ROCHE, T. E., M. RAHMATULLAH, L. LI, G. A. RADKE, C. L. CHANG & S. L. POWERS-GREENWOOD. 1989. This volume.
11. COPPEL, R. L., J. MACNIELAGE, C. SURH, J. VAN DE WATER, T. W. SPITHILL, S. WHITTINGHAM & M. E. GERSHWIN. 1988. Proc. Natl. Acad. Sci. USA **85:** 7317–7321.
12. THELKUMKARA, T. J., H. LAP, I. D. WEXLER, TE-CHANG LIN & M. S. PATEL. 1988. FEBS Lett. **240:** 45–48.
13. STEPHENS, P. E., M. G. DARLISON, H. M. LEWIS & J. R. GUEST. 1983. Eur. J. Biochem. **133:** 481–489.
14. SPENCER, M. E., M. G. DARLISON, P. E. STEPHENS, I. K. DUCKENFIELD & J. R. GUEST. 1984. Eur. J. Biochem. **141:** 361–374.
15. HANEMAAIJER, R., A. JANSSEN, A. DEKOK & C. VEEGER. 1988. Eur. J. Biochem. **174:** 593–599.
16. PACKMAN, L. C., A. BORGES & R. N. PERHAM. 1988. Biochem. J. **252:** 79–86.
17. LAU, K. S., T. A. GRIFFIN, C.-W. C. HU & D. T. CHUANG. 1988. Biochemistry **27:** 1972–1981.
18. PACKMAN, L. C. & R. W. PERHAM. 1986. FEBS Lett. **206:** 193–198.
19. PERHAM, R. N. & A. O. M. WILKIE. 1980. Biochem. Int. **1:** 470–477.

Structure, Expression, and Protein Engineering of the Pyruvate Dehydrogenase Complex of *Escherichia coli*[a]

JOHN R. GUEST,[b] S. JANE ANGIER,
AND GEORGE C. RUSSELL

Department of Microbiology
University of Sheffield
Western Bank
Sheffield S10 2TN
United Kingdom

INTRODUCTION

The advent of molecular genetic techniques for cloning, sequencing and selectively restructuring genes has in recent years led to a rapid acceleration in our ability to probe and understand the structure, function, expression, and assembly of enzymes and multienzyme complexes. This is particularly true in the case of the pyruvate and 2-oxoglutarate dehydrogenase complexes, where their large size and inherent complexity had previously limited progress by the conventional protein chemical approach. Not surprisingly, the well-characterized genes from *Escherichia coli* were the first to be cloned[1,2] and sequenced,[3-7] and the aim of this contribution is to outline what has been learned about the structure, function, and expression of the complexes as a result of sequencing and restructuring these genes.

The pyruvate and 2-oxoglutarate dehydrogenase complexes (PDHC and ODHC, respectively) of *E. coli* contain multiple copies of three enzymatic components, the specific 2-oxo acid dehydrogenase (E1p or E1o) and dihydrolipoamide acyltransferase (E2p or E2o) components and the common dihydrolipoamide dehydrogenase (E3) components. Like other 2-oxo acid dehydrogenase complexes, they catalyze the oxidative decarboxylation of the 2-oxo acid by a series of reactions which generates CO_2 and the correspondong acyl-CoA, as shown in FIGURE 1. The E1 and E3 components are assembled on the edges and faces of the octahedral E2 core components, comprising 24 E2 polypeptide chains; the E1:E2:E3 polypeptide ratios for the complexes are 1.2–1.5:1.0:0.6–0.8 (approximate M_r of complex, 5×10^6) for the PDHC and 0.5:1.0:0.5 (approximate M_r of complex, 3×10^6) for the ODHC.[8,9]

Central to the catalytic mechanism of the complexes are the lipoyl cofactors. These are attached in amide linkage to the N^ϵ-amino groups of specific lysine residues which

[a]This work was supported by the Science and Engineering Research Council.
[b]Author to whom correspondence should be addressed.

are located in specific segments of the E2 chains that protrude from the core.[10,11] This allows the lipoyl-lysine "swinging arms" to interact sequentially with the active sites of the three types of enzymatic component (FIG. 1). There is also evidence for an extensive network of coupling reactions which permits the intramolecular transfer of acyl groups between the lipoyl cofactors of different E2 subunits within the core, such that a single E1 subunit can bring about the reductive acylation of all the lipoyl groups in the E2 core.[12,13] Furthermore, it would appear that each lipoyl cofactor can interact with the active sites of several E1 subunits in the assembled complex, and, conversely, each E1 site can service the lipoyl cofactors of several E2 subunits.[14–16] These forms of active-site coupling would demand a greater degree of mobility within the complexes than that provided by the lipoyl-lysine "swinging arms," and there is indeed direct evidence from ^{1}H-NMR spectroscopy for substantial conformational mobility within the E2 chains.[17] One of the primary aims of our program for genetically restructuring

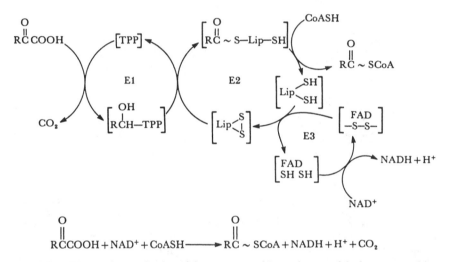

FIGURE 1. The reaction mechanism of the pyruvate and 2-oxoglutarate dehydrogenase multienzyme complexes. **R** = CH_3— for pyruvate, and **R** = $COOHCH_2CH_2$— for 2-oxoglutarate. **TPP**, thiamin pyrophosphate; **Lip**, lipoic acid; **CoA**, coenzyme A.

the complexes has been to identify the source of the conformational mobility and correlate this mobility with active-site coupling and the catalytic function of complexes.

The organization of the genes encoding the PDH and ODH complexes of *E. coli* is illustrated in FIGURE 2. The specific E1 and E2 components are encoded by the *aceEF* and *sucAB* operons in the 3rd and 17th minutes, respectively, of the *E. coli* linkage map, and the common E3 component is encoded by the *lpd* gene, which is adjacent to the *ace* operon.[18] The genes were identified in studies with mutants and the symbols *ace* and *suc* denote the requirement in the respective mutants for supplementary acetate or succinate for aerobic growth in glucose minimal medium. The *lpd* mutants lack the activities of both complexes and therefore require supplementary acetate *and* succinate for best growth under these conditions. The supplements are not required during anaerobic growth on glucose, because other routes are used for acetyl-CoA and succinyl-CoA synthesis, and the PDH and ODH complexes are in fact normally repressed or inhibited during anaerobiosis. The *sucAB* genes form part of a cluster of *E. coli* citric acid cycle genes which includes the citrate synthase gene (*gltA*), four genes encoding the succinate dehydrogenase complex (*sdhCDAB*), and two distal *suc* genes specifying the β and α subunits of succinyl-CoA synthetase (*sucCD*),[19] as shown in FIGURE 2. The significance of this clustering is not known, and the organization of the PDHC and ODHC genes is not universal in bacteria. Thus, the *lpd* gene of *Azotobacter vinelandii* is linked to the succinyltransferase gene,[20] and, in *Pseudomonas putida*, there is an extra *lpd* gene, which is specific for the branched chain 2-oxo acid dehydrogenase complex (BCDHC) and is located at the distal end of the "branched chain" operon.[21]

The *E. coli* genes were originally cloned in phage λ using a strategy which involved a combination of *in vitro* cloning of the adjacent genes (*nadC* and *gltA*) and *in vivo*

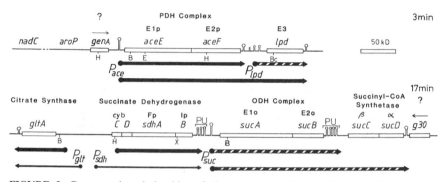

FIGURE 2. Gene-protein relationships of the pyruvate and 2-oxoglutarate dehydrogenase complexes. The structural genes are shown as *open boxes,* drawn to scale; the intergenic regions are not to scale. The mRNA transcripts are indicated by *arrows; arrows with hatching* denote transcripts whose synthesis is particularly coordinated. Regions of potential secondary structure associated with promoters, terminators and palindromic units (**PU**) are denoted by *stem-loops.* Neighboring genes, including those involved in the cloning strategy (***nadC*** and ***gltA***) and the unidentified coding regions (***genA*** and ***g30***) are indicated. The restriction fragments used for promoter cloning are also indicated: ***Pace1***, H–B (711 bp, *Hin*d III–*Bam*H I) in pKO-4; ***Pace2***, H–E (1149 bp, *Hin*d III–*Eco*R I) in pKO-6; ***Plpd***, H–Bc (1662 bp, *Hin*d III–*Bcl* I) in pKO-4; **Pglt** and **Psdh**, B–H (734 bp, *Bam*H I–*Hin*d III), two orientations in pKO-4 and pKO-6, respectively; ***Psuc***, X–B (1379 bp *Xho* I–*Bam*H I) in pKL-300.

extension of the cloned inserts by inducing appropriate λ*nadC* and λ*gltA* lysogens and selecting for λ*nadC-ace-lpd* and λ*gltA-sdh-suc* derivatives.[1,2] The nucleotide sequences of a corresponding 8-kb *aceEF-lpd* segment,[3,5] and a 14-kb *gltA-sdhCDAB-sucABCD* segment[6,7,22,23] were subsequently determined (FIG. 2). The coding regions were identified and translated into primary structures for the E1, E2, and E3 subunits of both complexes, and the mRNA transcripts were mapped in order to identify the promoters and terminators.[24] These analyses provided accurate estimates of the numbers of amino acid residues (a.a.) and molecular weights for each subunit: E1p (885 a.a.; M_r: 99,474), E2p (629 a.a.; M_r: 65,959), E1o (932 a.a.; M_r: 104,805), E2o (404 a.a.; M_r: 43,877), and E3 (473 a.a.; M_r: 50,554). They revealed an unexpected lack of homology between the E1 subunits, but also a remarkable degree of homology between the E2 subunits. They also defined the numbers and relative positions of the lipoyl and catalytic domains and identified the segments rich in alanine plus proline as potential sources both of the characteristic sharp resonances in the ^{1}H-NMR spectra and of the molecular weight anomalies of these subunits. Translating the *lpd* coding region has also confirmed the existence of a high degree of structural homology between lipoamide dehydrogenase (E3) and glutathione reductase, and this homology has proved to be of considerable predictive importance.[25]

TRANSCRIPTIONAL AND REGULATORY ASPECTS

The PDH and ODH complexes play key anabolic and catabolic roles in the metabolism of carbon and nitrogen compounds, so the regulatory mechanisms controlling their expression are likely to be inherently complex. They are induced by their substrates and repressed by glucose and anaerobiosis, and there is some genetic evidence that E1p performs a regulatory role in the expression of the *ace* operon.[18,26] The anaerobic repression has recently been shown to be mediated by the global regulatory system for aerobic respiration, *arcA(dye)*, which represses PDH and ODH synthesis in the absence of oxygen.[27] The basic features of the system for coregulating the expression of the single *lpd* gene with the differentially regulated *ace* and *suc* genes have also emerged as a result of mapping the relevant mRNA transcripts (FIG. 2).[24]

Transcript analysis with S1 nuclease showed that the E1p and E2p subunits are expressed from two types of *ace* transcript, an *aceEF* transcript and a longer *aceEF-lpd* transcript, which extends across the *lpd* gene (FIG. 2). The E1o and E2o subunits are also expressed from two *suc* transcripts (*sucAB* and *sucABCD*), and the E3 subunits can be expressed from an independent *lpd* transcript, as well as from the *aceEF-lpd* transcript. These results confirmed earlier suggestions that the *lpd* gene is a distal gene in the *ace* operon and that it is also capable of independent expression in order to satisfy the E3 requirements of the ODH complex.[26] The transcripts were quantified after growth on different media, and it is clear that the *aceEF-lpd* transcript satisfies the E3 requirements of the PDH complex, whereas independent *lpd* transcription is coregulated with *suc* transcription to meet the needs of the ODH complex. The mechanism of this coregulation is unknown, but it could involve autoregulation of the *lpd* gene by uncomplexed E3 subunits.[18]

The *ace*, *suc* and *lpd* promoter regions are not strikingly similar, nor do they show a particularly strong resemblance to the *E. coli* consensus sequence, suggesting that positive activators may be required for expression.[24] The promoters are situated in regions of hyphenated and unhyphenated dyad symmetry, which could have an important regulatory significance. The *ace*, *suc*, and *lpd* non-coding regions do not appear to share any obvious sequence motifs that could function as binding sites for regulatory proteins such as CRP (the cyclic AMP receptor protein) or ARC (the aerobic respiration control protein[27]), but there is a sequence (AGAACGACCC; boldface denotes conserved nucleobases) near the 5' end of the *lpd* transcript that resembles sequences at comparable positions in the transcripts of some other citric acid cycle genes, *fumA, mdh* and *sdh*.[19] The *lpd* and *suc* promoters have identical −35 regions, which could be important in the coregulation of the *lpd* and *suc* genes. The *suc* and *lpd* promoters would have been expected to contain CRP-binding sites, from the patterns of enzyme and mRNA synthesis (and from the effects of glucose and of Δ*crp* and Δ*cya* mutations on a *suc*-fusion, see below). It is therefore possible that the *suc* genes (and, indirectly, the *lpdgalK* gene) are regulated from the upstream *sdh* promoters (which are associated with CRP sites), even though no *sdh-suc* readthrough transcripts have been detected (FIG. 2). The *ace* promoter differs in being only weakly repressed by glucose.

The activities of the *ace, suc* and *lpd* promoters have been studied by fusion to a promoterless *galK* gene in the pKO and pKL series of plasmid vectors.[29,30] The promoter-containing restriction fragments that were cloned in the *galK* vectors are shown in FIGURE 2, and the resulting specific activities for galactokinase are plotted in FIGURE 3. The most striking result was the very poor activity of the *ace* promoter when present in multiple copies. The activity of P*ace1* was virtually indistinguishable from the vector alone, but P*ace2,* which contains more of the *aceE* structural gene, was sufficiently active to give a Gal+ phenotype in plate tests on EMB-Gal agar. These results contrast with the *lpd* and *suc* promoters, which resembled the *gltA* and *sdh* promoters in having activities comparable to the *gal* promoter (not shown). The weak

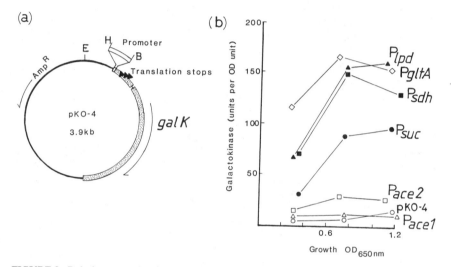

FIGURE 3. Relative strengths of the *ace, suc* and *lpd* promoters estimated by coupling them to a promoterless *galK* gene. (**a**) Cultures of *E. coli* strain N100 (*galK recA13*) were transformed with pKO and pKL derivatives which had the promoter-containing restriction fragments shown in FIGURE 2 cloned upstream of the *gal* region of the vector. (**b**) Samples of toluenized cells were assayed for galactokinase according to McKenney *et al.,*[29] after aerobic growth to different optical densities in L broth. No significant differences in plasmid copy number were detected in parallel β-lactamase assays.

activity of the *ace* promoter was confirmed by constructing a plasmid containing an *aceE-lacZ* translational fusion with the P*ace1* fragment from a different source. In this case, the plasmid conferred a detectable Lac+ phenotype with X-gal, but the β-galactosidase activity of the hybrid protein was less than 0.2% of that obtained with the normal *lac* promoter. Pyruvate, supplied exogenously (25 m*M*) or generated endogenously (in an *aceE* mutant), was a poor inducer of the multicopy *ace* promoter (P*ace2*), but in an *aceE*-deletion strain the promoter activity increased to about 60% of that of the *lpd* and *sdh* promoters. The activity of the *lpd* promoter also increased some 2-fold in a host deleted for the *lpd* gene. These results are indicative of an autogenous regulatory mechanism for the *ace* and *lpd* genes. The *galK* fusions were tested after growth with glucose (1%), and in Δ*crp* Δ*cya* strains, and the results of these tests indicated that P*suc* is subject to catabolite repression but P*lpd* and P*ace2* are not.

Clearly there is still much to be learned about the mechanisms controlling the expression of the *ace, suc,* and *lpd* genes, and, in this respect, the functions of the unidentified genes adjacent to the *ace-lpd* operon (*genA*) and the *suc* operon (*g30*) may be worth investigating (FIG. 2). The nucleotide sequence of *g30* has recently been determined,[68] and its gene product (P30) shares a region of significant sequence homology with the *genA* product (GENA) and with GNTR, a putative regulator of the gluconate operon of *Bacillus subtilis*. It is conceivable that the homologous sequence represents a DNA-binding domain, and, in view of the frequent clustering of functionally related genes in *E. coli*, it is tempting to speculate that *genA* and *g30* could have a hitherto undetected role in the regulation of the adjacent operons.

STRUCTURAL AND FUNCTIONAL IMPLICATIONS OF SEQUENCES HOMOLOGIES

The E1 subunits of the PDH and ODH complexes of *E. coli* exhibit a striking lack of sequence homology.[3,6,31] The lack of homology also extends to the E1α and E1β subunits of the mammalian PDH complexes and the BCDH complexes[32–34] and to several other thiamin pyrophosphate enzymes, such as pyruvate oxidase[35] and pyruvate decarboxylase.[36] It would therefore appear that the E1 subunits of the *E. coli* complexes are not closely related in evolutionary terms, either to each other or to several potentially related enzymes. It will be interesting to see whether this also extends to the single-chain E1o components of the ODH complexes from different sources.

This situation contrasts with the E3 subunit, dihydrolipoamide dehydrogenase (LPDH), which is 40% identical to the human, yeast, and *Azotobacter* enzymes.[37,38,20] There is also a very high degree of sequence homology between LPDH and the related enzymes, glutathione reductase (GR) and mercuric reductase.[5] Indeed, the sequence of *E. coli* LPDH has been fitted to the known three-dimensional structure of human GR. In addition to highlighting the strong conservation of residues in the FAD and NAD(P) binding sites and in the redox centers, this modeling has allowed meaningful predictions to be made concerning the residues that define the cofactor specificity for NAD^+ or $NADP^+$, and the residues that are involved in other specific functions such as the oxygen-sensitivity of LPDH and the preference for passing reducing equivalents from NADPH or to NAD^+ in GR and LPDH, respectively.[25] *In vitro* mutagenesis of the *lpd* gene has confirmed some of these predictions; the results are reported elsewhere in this volume.[39,40]

Homologies between Acyltransferase (E2) Subunits

The sequences of the E2p and E2o of the *E. coli* complexes revealed two highly homologous and highly segmented structures.[4,7,31] As illustrated in FIGURE 4, the amino-terminal half of the E2p chain contains three tandemly repeated and virtually identical lipoyl domains of approximately 80 residues. Each has a potential lipoyl-lysine residue within an identical 18-residue segment. This contrasts with the E2o chain, which contains only one homologous lipoyl domain. In both cases, the lipoyl domains are connected to other highly conserved 50-residue segments, shown to be essential for binding the E3 subunits,[41,42] and therefore designated the E3-binding domains. These are in turn connected to the carboxyl-terminal segments, which constitute two homologous catalytic and inner core–forming domains (230–240 residues; ca. 29 kDa). Here reside the specific acetyltransferase or succinyltransferase activities and the specificities for self assembly (E2-binding) and for binding the corresponding E1 subunits. It would seem reasonable to predict that these binding specificities are defined by the regions of lowest sequence homology, i.e., closest to the amino terminus of the inner core. However, the most striking features in the amino acid sequences are the interdomain linkers (FIG. 4). These are sequences of 20 to 30

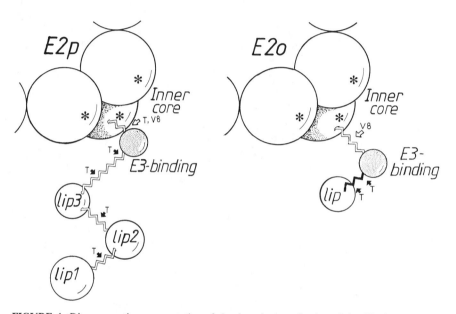

FIGURE 4. Diagrammatic representation of the domain organization of the dihydrolipoamide acyltransferase subunits (**E2p** and **E2o**) of the PDH and ODH complexes. The interdomain linkers (*zig-zags*) are emphasized, those rich in alanine plus proline are denoted by *open zig-zags* and the one which is proline-deficient by the *filled zig-zag*. The major sites of proteolytic cleavage by trypsin (**T**) and *Staphylococcus aureus* V8 protease (**V8**) are indicated by *arrows*; *open arrows* denote sites where cleavage requires prolonged treatment.[41,42] The acyltransferase active sites of the catalytic inner core domains are indicated by *asterisks*.

residues that are either very rich in alanine and proline plus a few charged amino acids (particularly lysine, glutamine, and glutamate) or, in one case, rich in charged residues but proline-deficient. These linker sequences are accessible to proteolytic cleavage by trypsin and *Staphylococcus aureus* V8 protease, and the domain boundaries have, in consequence, been fairly well defined.[9,43] The high alanine content of the linker sequences originally suggested that these linker sequences are the source of the conformational mobility detected by ^{1}H-NMR,[44] because the major resonances had previously been assigned to the β-methyl protons of alanine or threonine.[17] There is also a good correlation between the presence of the alanine-containing linker sequences and the major resonances in that a loss of signal accompanies the proteolytic removal of the lipoyl domains from the E2p subunit, but not from the corresponding E2o subunit, which (unlike the E2p subunit) retains the major alanine-containing linker after trypsin treatment.

The number of known sequences or partial sequences for different E2 subunits is now increasing rapidly and includes the E2p subunits of the PDH complexes from rat and human mitochondria,[45,46,47] *B. stearothermophilus*[48] and *A. vinelandii*,[49] and the branched-chain 2-oxoacyltransferases (E2b) from the mammalian[50,51] and *P. putida*[52] BCDH complexes. They all reveal highly segmented structures with a fundamentally similar organization, despite the differences in subunit content and symmetry of the assembled complexes. Representative sequence alignments are shown in FIGURE 5. Sequence comparisons are interesting with respect to (i) the number of lipoyl domains; (ii) the high degree of sequence conservation in the lipoyl-binding regions of the lipoyl domains, the E3-binding domains, and the distal segments of the catalytic domains; and (iii) the different lengths and compositions of the interdomain linkers.[46] The Gram-negative bacteria have three lipoyl domains per E2p chain, whereas the mammalian E2p chains have two; and the E2p subunits of the Gram-positive bacterium resemble E2o and E2b subunits in having just one lipoyl domain per chain. The reason why some complexes have more than one lipoyl domain is not known. The degree of sequence conservation in the E3-binding domains is consistent with the fact that E3 subunits from one source will often complement the overall enzyme complex activity of E1 and E2 subunits from a heterologous source and can also form hybrid high-molecular-weight complexes. Significantly, the E3-binding domain of the E2b subunit of *P. putida* shares no homology with other E2p or E2o subunits, which probably reflects the unique specificity of the E3 subunit of the bacterial BCDH complex.[52] It is also interesting that the E3-binding domains of the *B. stearothermophilus* and *A. vinelandii* E2p subunits are additionally required for binding the E1p subunits.[48,49]

The Interdomain Linker Sequences

As shown in FIGURE 5, there appear to be three types of polypeptide sequence in the putative interdomain linkers.[46] These are characterized by their different contents of alanine, proline, and charged residues. Thus, there are the linker sequences rich in alanine and proline (AP-rich), which typically have more alanine (or alanine plus valine and glycine) than proline and contain only a small proportion of other (mainly charged) residues (FIG. 5). There are some sequences which are characteristically richer in proline than in alanine, the proline-rich linkers (P-rich), and there are sequences designated proline-deficient (P-deficient), which are deficient in proline but have a high proportion (ca. 50%) of charged residues (FIG. 5). There are no consistent relationships between linker type and position. The highly-conserved segment of the E3-binding domain (boxed in FIG. 5) of the human E2b is flanked by P-deficient and P-rich linkers, whereas these are P-deficient and AP-rich linkers in the *E. coli* E2o chain. The human E2p chain has P-rich and AP-rich linkers in the respective positions, and the linker between the lipoyl domains is AP-rich, but there is an extra segment that fits neither of the three categories and may be part of a larger lipoyl domain. It may also be significant that two of the four AP-rich linkers in the *E. coli* E2p chain are flanked by some high charged P-deficient segments. Unraveling the functional significance of the different types of linker sequence is likely to reveal much about the assembly and mobility of the complexes.

a.

```
E2p.H                                               [MSPHCSTTYLRTLGRTTMFWKTTEGRDGKMAVQEFSEFGLLLQLLGSPGRRYYSLPP]
E2p.E   AIEIKVPDIGADEVE--ITEILVKVGDKVEAEQSLITVEGDKASMEVPSPQAGIVKEIKVSVGDK-TQTGA-LIMIFDSADGAADAPAQQAEEKKEAAPAAAPAAAA
                                                                            *

E2b.H                                               [MLRTWSRNAGKLICVRYFQTCGNVDVLKPNYVCFFGYPSFKYSHPHHFLKTTAALRG]
E2b.H   HQKVPLPSLSPTMQAGTIARWEKKEGDKINEGDLIAEVETDRATVGFESLEECYMAKILVAEGTRDVPIGAIICITVGVGPEDIEAFKNYTLDSSAAPTPQAAPAPTPAATASPPTPSAQAPGSSYPP
        :.* ::.:     ::  .   :: :* ***:: .   *   *  * *:      *
E2p.E   --KDVNVPDIGSDEVE--VTEILVKVGDKVEAEQSLITVEGDKASMEVPAPPAFPAGTVKEIKVNVGDK-VSTGS-LIMVFEVAGEAGAAAPAKQEAAPAAAPAAAG
                                                                            *

E2p.H   QVVQFKLSDIGEGIREVTVKEWVVKEGDTVSQFDSICEVQSDKASVTITSRYDGVIKKLYYNLDDI-AYVGKPL-VDIETEALKDSEEDVVETPAVSHDEHTHQEIKGRKTLA
        : :*  *    .  :  .* .  ** :* : * .* *  *     * *  : .    :  :*: . *
E2p.H   -HMQVVLPALSPTMTGTVQRWEKKVGEKLSEGDLLAEIETDKATIGFEVQEEGYLAKILVPEGTRDVPLGTPLCIIVEKEADISAFADYRPTEVTDLKPQVPPPTPPVAAVPPTPQPLAPTPSTPCPATPAGPKGRVFV
        .   :: :* .*:: .  : .:.  :**:: .  :*  *       *
E2p.E   -VKEVNVPDIGGDEVE--VTEVNVKVGDKVAAEQSLITVEGDKASMEVPAPFAGVVKELKVNVGDK-VKTGS-LIMIFEVEGAAPAAAPAKQEAAAPAPAAKAEAPAAAPAAKAEGKSEFAENDAYVHA
E2o.E   SSVDILVPDLPESVADATVATWHKKPGDAVVRDEVLVEIETDKVVLEVPASADGILDAVLEDEGTT-VTSRQILGRLREGNSACKEISAKSEEKASTPAQRQQASLEEQNNDAL
                                                                            *
```

b.

```
E2b.H   TPAVRRLAMENNIKLSEVVGSGKDGRILKEDILNYIEKQTGAILPPSPKVEIMPPPKPKDMTVPILVSKPPVFTGK
        *   :  :       ::  .  .      . *
E2p.H   DPLAKKLLAAVKGIDLTQVKGTGPDGRITKKDIDSFVPSKVAPAAAVVPPTPGMAPVPTGV
        *    :     :  .:.:* .   ..    : .*
E2p.E   TPLIRRLAREFGVNLAKVKGTGRKGRILEDVQAYVKEAIKRAEAAPAATGGGIPGMLPWRKVDFSK
        *  :: : .   ::  **.:* :.*  ::  :* *
E2o.E   SPAIRRLLAEHNLDASAIKGTGVGGRLTREDVEKHIAKAPAKESAPAAAAPAAQAPALAA
```

c.

```
E2b.H   DKTEPIKGFQKAMVKTMSAALK-----IPHFGYCDEIDLTELVLKREELKPIAFARG--IKLSFMPFFLKYYFSWKS..........
        :  :  *      *   .* .       : ::  *:*     * :  : :*  .  .   :   *  :: :
E2p.H   FTDIPISNIRRVIAQRLM-QSKQ--TIPHYYLLSCKY-GEVLLVRKELNKILEGRG---KISVNDFIIKASALACLKVPEANSS-WMDTV-IRQNHVVDVSVAVSTPAGLITPIVFNAHI
        ::.*  . :* : :::  .       : *   :: .     :   :: :::.       ::. : :**. :  ** ::.   .:  *   ::* * *.**.**.:**::* *::.*
E2p.E   FGEIEEVELGRIQKISGANLSRNWVMIPHVTHFDKTDITELEAFRKQQNEEAAKRKLDVKIPVVFIMKAVAAALEQMPRFNSSLSEDGQRLTLKKYINIGVAVDTPNGLVVPVFKDVNK
        ** :::    :: :..:. :*   :*** .** *.: :***   :  :.: : ::* : :* * :**.*.*** *::* ::: *..: . .: *   :* * *.**.::**:*:.:
E2o.E   RSEKR-VPMTRLRKRVAERLLEAKNSTAMLTTFNEVNMKPIMDLRKQYGEAFEKR-HGIRLGFMSFYVKAVVEALKRYPEVNASI--DGDDVVHNYFDVSMAVSTPRGLVTPVLRDVDT
```

FIGURE 5. Partial amino acid alignments of the dihydrolipoamide acyltransferase subunits of the human and *E. coli* PDH complexes (E2p.H and E2p.E), the human BCDH complex (E2b.H), and the *E. coli* ODH complex (E2o.E).[4,7,47,50,51] The approximate limits of the lipoyl domains (a), the highly conserved segment of the E3-binding domains (b), and the catalytic inner core domains (c) are *boxed*. Identical residues (★) and conservative substitutions (:) are indicated within these segments. The different types of putative interdomain linker sequences[46] are *underlined* as follows: (~~~) rich in alanine + proline, (——) proline-rich, and (....) proline-deficient. The lipoyl lysine residues (K) and the putative active-site histidine residues (H) are marked. The leader sequences of E2p.H and E2b.H are enclosed in *dashed boxes*, though the extent of the former is not known. Fully conserved sites in all catalytic domains (including those known to be in E2p.Rat and E2b of *P. putida*) are indicated by *underlining* of residues within the boxed sequences, and three sites of basic residue conservation are indicated by single dots (•) below residues within the boxed sequences.

The Catalytic Inner Core Domains

The longest and most sustained homologies are in the inner core domains of the PDH and ODH complexes from different sources, particularly in the 180-residue carboxyl-terminal segments (FIG. 5). There are identical residues at 30 sites in the corresponding alignments of all the E2 sequences and partial sequences, including the bacterial E2b sequence[52] and partial sequences of the rat E2p[45,47] (not shown in FIG. 5). There are also a further three sites of basic residue conservation. The conserved residues are primarily glycine (six residues) and proline (five residues), which presumably perform important structural roles, plus some other more specific and functionally significant residues: histidine, serine, threonine, lysine, arginine, and aspartate.

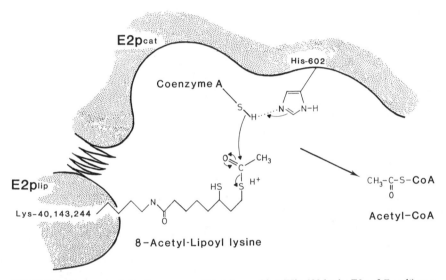

FIGURE 6. Proposed role for the conserved histidine residue (His-602 in the E2p of *E. coli*) as a general base catalyst in the acetyl-transfer reaction. The mechanism derives from that proposed for chloramphenicol acetyltransferase.[54] The corresponding residue involved in succinyl transfer would be His-375 in the E2o subunit of *E. coli*.

Attention has previously been drawn to the most highly conserved region, which contains a consensus sequence (His – – – Asp Gly) that occurs in other enzymes, notably chloramphenicol acetyltransferase (CAT).[53,54] Based on the homology with CAT, it has been suggested that the catalytic mechanism of the dihydrolipoamide acyltransferases resembles that proposed for chloramphenicol acetylation. Thus, the conserved histidine residue (His-602 in E2p.E) is thought to function as a general base for deprotonation of the thiol group of CoA and nucleophilic attack on the carbonyl of the acyl-lipoamide thioester,[19,53] as shown in FIGURE 6.

The CAT monomer is approximately the same size as the putative catalytic inner core domains, and it is conceivable that the proposed catalytic similarity may derive from a more extensive structural homology, based upon a remote ancestral relation-

```
            6     .        20        .        40      .  54
CAT     MNYTKFDVKNWVRREHFEFYRHRLPCGFSLTSKIDITTLKKSLDDSAYK
              ⊢ α₁ ⊣    ⊢--βₐ---⊣   ⊢ α₂ ⊣

          ⊢───── α ─────⊣      ⊢---β----⊣   ⊢── α ──⊣ ⊢── α ──⊣⊢--β--⊣
E2p.E   FGEIEEVELGRIQKISGANLSRNWVMIPHVTHFDKTDITELEAFRKQQNEEAAKRKLDVKITPV
        396 400        .         420      .        440         ,     459


            60          .        80        .        100       .113
CAT     FYPVMIYLIAQAVNQFDELRMAIK-DDELIVWDSVDPQFTVFHQETETFSALSCPYSSD
          ⊢───── α₃ ─────⊣              ⊢--βB---⊣   ⊢-βC-⊣

          ⊢───── α ─────⊣          ⊢----- β ----⊣   ⊢- β --⊣⊢α⊣
E2p.E   VFIMKAVAAALEQMPRFNSSLSEDGQRLTLKKYINIGVAVDTPNGLVVPVFKDVNKKG
        460         .        480        .        500       .    517


            120         .        140       .        160        171
CAT     IDQFMVNYLSVMERYKSDTKLFPQGVTPENHLNISALPWVNFDSFNLNVANFTDYFAP
          ⊢───── α₄ ─────⊣           ⊢--βD--⊣   ⊢- βE-⊣

          ⊢───── α ─────⊣           ⊢--β--⊣   ⊢--β--⊣  ?
E2p.E   IIELSRELMTISKKARDGKLTAGEMQGGCFTISSIGGLGTTHFAPIVNAPEVA
        520         .        540       .        560      570


        172      180                .        200       .        219
CAT     IITMAKYQQEGD-------RLLLPLSVQVHHAVCDGFHVARFINRLQELCNSKLK
          ⊢---βF---⊣       ⊢----βG---⊣    ⊢───── α₅ ─────⊣

          ⊢--β--⊣    ?    ⊢α⊣  ? ⊢        ⊢--β---⊣  ⊢α⊣
E2p.E   ILGVSKSAMEPVWNGKEFVPRLMLPISLSFDHRVIDGADGARFITIINNTLSDIRRLVM
        571      580                .        600       .        620   629
```

(a)

FIGURE 7. Secondary structure prediction for the catalytic inner core of the *E. coli* dihydro-lipoamide acetyltransferase (E2p.E) and comparison with the structure of chloramphenicol acetyltransferase (CAT). (**a**) The sequences of CAT type III and part of E2p.E are approximately aligned with respect to the regions of regular secondary structure that occur in CAT and those that are predicted for E2p.E. α-helices (α) and β-strands (β) are indicated; unmarked segments represent turn or coil, and segments with ambiguous or no predicted structure are indicated by question marks (**?**). (**b**, *facing page*) Diagram of the chain-fold of a CAT monomer viewed down the trimer axis (▲).[54] The active sites are formed at the subunit interfaces in the trimer; the CoA-binding site (**CoA**) and the position of the active-site histidine (*) are indicated. Structural elements for which no counterpart is predicted in E2p are *stippled*.

ship. The fact that the CAT enzyme is trimeric lends further support to this view, because the 24-subunit cores of the *E. coli* complexes are essentially octamers of trimers, and the observed 3-fold rotational symmetry of the complexes could stem therefrom. Weak but potentially significant sequence homologies have been detected,[53] and it is apparent from the three-dimensional structure of CAT that some of these are clustered in the CoA-binding site.[54] This relationship has now been explored by predicting the secondary structures of the catalytic domains of E2p and E2o subunits, using a combination of eight different methods.[56] The results for the E2p subunit are illustrated in FIGURE 7. Although the model is highly speculative, the distribution of predicted α-helices, β-strands and turns or coils in some segments is consistent with the proposed relationship. In particular, the elements making up the Co-A binding site of CAT (α_3 and β_{C-F}) appear to have their counterparts in E2p. A region of coil containing the active-site histidine residue is predicted, but the flanking β-strand (β_G) and α-helix (α_5) are not predicted, even though the corresponding regions show a reasonable degree of sequence homology. There are also discrepancies at the amino-terminal ends which complicate the interpretation, but these could be accommodated if the segment between α_2 and α_3 contains one or two extra elements. So, despite the highly speculative

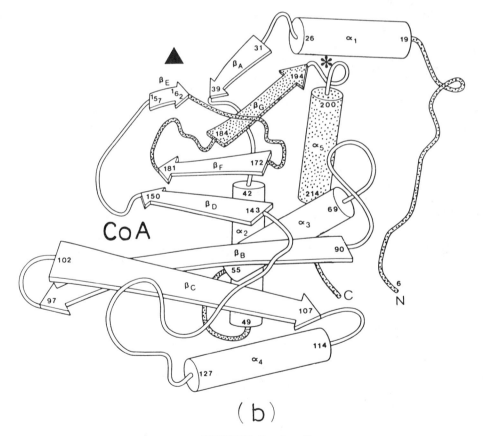

(b)

FIGURE 7. (continued)

nature of these predictions, they do provide a theoretical basis for testing the functions of specific residues.

PROTEIN ENGINEERING OF THE PYRUVATE DEHYDROGENASE COMPLEX

The techniques of restriction enzyme– or oligonucleotide-directed mutagenesis and partial or complete gene synthesis offer unlimited scope for investigating structure-function relationships in enzymes. Thus, it is now possible to restructure a polypeptide chain by the substitution, deletion, or addition of one or more residues or to excise and express individual protein domains by manipulating the corresponding gene.

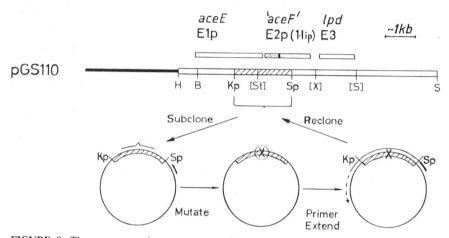

FIGURE 8. The cassette replacement approach to *in vitro* mutagenesis. Plasmid pGS110 contains an *aceEF-lpd* operon encoding an E2p subunit with only one lipoyl domain per chain. The 1.68-kb *Kpn* I– *Sph* I fragment was subcloned in M13mp19 for mutating the lipoyl domain and associated interdomain linker, and the residual 11.5-kb fragment served as the receptor for recloning mutated fragments and expressing the altered complexes from the natural *ace* and *lpd* promoters.[57] Additional restriction sites providing useful cassettes are shown, including artificially engineered sites (in *brackets*): **B**, *Bam*H I; **Kp**, *Kpn* I; **S**, *Sal* I; **Sp**, *Sph* I; **St**, *Sst* I; **X**, *Xho* I.

Cassette Mutagenesis

In the case of the PDH complex, the segment of DNA is too large (ca 7 kb) for facile mutagenesis, so a replaceable cassette approach has been adopted. By this method convenient subsegments of the cloned *aceEF-lpd* operon are transferred to an intermediary plasmid or phage vector for mutation and then returned to the operon for expression.[56,57] This approach is illustrated in FIGURE 8, where a unique *Kpn* I–*Sph* I fragment encoding part of E1p and the lipoyl domain(s) of E2p serves as the cassette, which can be mutated in M13 and religated to a receptor fragment derived from a *aceEF-lpd* plasmid, such as pGS110. The partially deleted operon cloned in pGS110 encodes an E2p subunit having only one lipoyl domain per chain, and this considerably simplifies strategies for mutagenesis of the E2p chain. The versatility of the cassette approach has been increased by using site-directed mutagenesis to create further unique restriction sites at convenient positions for subcloning, without altering the coding properties of the DNA (i.e., by silent mutation). Another important prerequisite of a useful system is that it be able to amplify the expression of the altered protein or enzyme in order to facilitate its purification, and this must be done in a background which is free from contamination with the wild-type product. Both of these requirements have been achieved by coupling relevant *aceEF-lpd* coding regions to the thermoinducible λ promoters in the pJLA series of expression vectors[58] and by using host strains that are deleted for the *ace* or *ace-lpd* genes.[59]

Amplification of the PDH Complex, Subcomplexes, and Individual Domains

A disappointing feature of the PDH complex is the relatively poor amplification obtained by cloning the genes in multicopy plasmids.[59] Because this may be due to stringent control of the *ace* promoter, the *aceEF-lpd* coding region has been cloned immediately downstream of the λ $P_R P_L$ promoters and the efficient *atpE* translational initiator region in the expression plasmid pGS269 (FIG. 9). This involved several steps. Initially, a synthetic double-stranded oligonucleotide linker encoding ten amino-terminal residues of E1p was cloned into the *Nco* I and *Bam*H I sites of the expression vector. An 8.9-kb *Bam*H I–*Sal* I fragment containing the remainder of the operon encoding the PDH complex with only one lipoyl domain per E2p chain was then inserted from pGS110,[56] and the *aceEF-lpd* insert was finally reduced to ca. 6.3 kb by replacing the original *Sph* I–*Sal* I fragment with a shorter fragment containing a *Sal* I site that was created just distal to the *lpd* gene. Thermoinduction of an *aceEF*-deletion strain transformed with pGS269 produced a 20-fold amplification of the PDHC proteins, which increased to 25% of the total soluble protein (FIG. 9). All three subunits were amplified, and a sedimentable complex was formed; but the PDHC activity was only increased 5-fold, and the reason for this discrepancy is as yet unknown. If this problem can be overcome, pGS269 should prove extremely useful for cassette replacement and overexpression of a variety of different PDH complexes, such as those with three, two or no lipoyl domains per E2p chain, which have so far only been expressed from derivatives of pBR322. Similar approaches have already been used to obtain substantial thermoinductions of wild-type and mutant lipoyl domains (pGS203 and pGS204);[60] mutant E2p-E3 subcomplexes that have no lipoyl domains (pGS200); and catalytic inner cores containing E2p chains with neither lipoyl nor E3-binding domains (29-kDa polypeptide) that are expressed with or without uncomplexed E3 subunits (pGS239[61] or pGS223, respectively) (FIG. 10). A similar approach involving cassette replacement and overexpression has been used for studying lipoamide dehydrogenase (E3 subunit); the results are discussed elsewhere.[39,61]

Structure-Function Relationships of Dihydrolipoamide Acetyltransferase (E2p)

As soon as the remarkable segmented structures of the E2 subunits became evident from the nucleotide sequences, they raised obvious questions concerning the functions of individual domains, linker, sequences, and specific residues. Most of these questions could be addressed using an *in vitro* mutagenic approach, and the relevant construc-

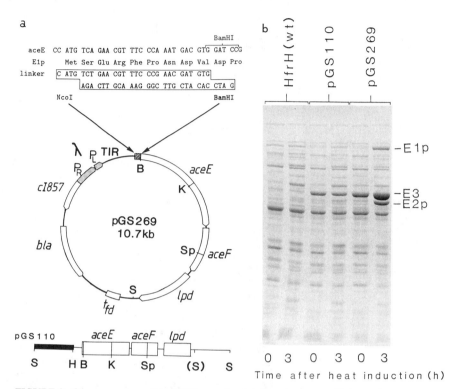

FIGURE 9. Overexpression of the PDH complex. (a) Complementary 28-base oligonucleotides were used to construct an *Nco* I–*Bam*H I linker encoding the amino-terminal segment of E1p to allow precise cloning of the *aceEF-lpd* coding regions downstream of the thermoregulated λ promoters (λP_R and λP_L) and the efficient *atpE* translational initiation region (**TIR**) of the expression vector (pJLA502).[58] The bacterial insert was subsequently shortened by replacing the original *Sph* I–*Sal* I segment with one containing an engineered *Sal* I site just downstream of the *lpd* coding region. Relevant restriction sites are abbreviated as in FIGURE 8. (b) The E1p, E2p, and E3 subunits of a PDH complex with one lipoyl domain per E2 chain were analyzed by denaturing gel electrophoresis and Coomassie blue staining at different times after thermoinduction of an *aceEF*-deletion strain transformed with pGS110 or pGS269; HfrH, wild-type control.

tions were designed, engineered and expressed in our laboratory in Sheffield. In many cases we are indebted to Dr. R. N. Perham and his colleagues in Cambridge for the detailed enzymological characterization and ¹H-NMR spectroscopic analysis of the corresponding complexes. The specific points that have been investigated so far are briefly described in the following paragraphs.

Tandemly Repeated Lipoyl Domains

It is not clear why the E2p subunit of the *E. coli* PDH complex has three homologous lipoyl domains compared with two for the mammalian complex and only one for the E2o subunit of the ODH complex. Indeed, restriction enzyme–mediated deletion of one or two lipoyl domains from the E2p subunit (FIG. 10) had no adverse effects on the assembly or catalytic and active-site coupling activities of the corresponding PDH complexes.[56] In fact, the PDH complex that contains just one hybrid lipoyl domain per E2p chain, expressed by pGS110, has proved to be a very useful starting point for subsequent mutageneses. The deletion of all three lipoyl domains in the pGS179-encoded complex (FIG. 10) had no apparent effect on the assembly of the complex, nor on its ability to transfer acetyl groups between acetyl-CoA and exogenous dihydrolipoamide, but the resulting complex was predictably inactive.[62] Clearly, one lipoyl domain is sufficient, and the reason for the tandem duplication remains obscure. The sequential increases in the length of the deletions in E2p were accompanied by sequential reductions in the discrepancy between the M_r value derived from electrophoretic mobility in denaturing gels and the value calculated from amino acid sequence: for E2p with three lipoyl domains (3-lip), the M_r by electrophoretic mobility was 3-lip, 83,000 versus 66,000 by sequencing; for 2-lip, 69,000 versus 56,000; for 1-lip, 52,000 versus 46,000; and for 0-lip, 37,500 versus 34,500. Thus, a lipoyl domain plus the associated AP-rich linker contributes about 3000–6000 to the discrepancy in M_r values. The interdomain linkers appear to be primarily responsible for the M_r discrepancies, because there is a small residual discrepancy and a correspondingly small AP-rich linker remaining when all three lipoyl domains have been deleted. It has also been observed that deleting residues from an AP-rich linker effects a direct reduction of the M_r discrepancy.[63,64]

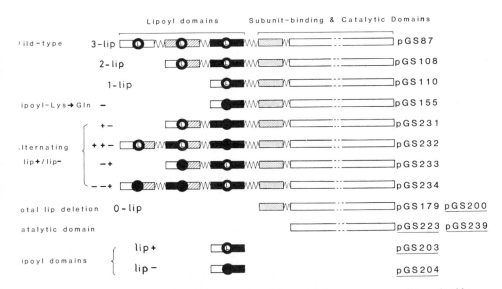

FIGURE 10. Novel E2p polypeptides constructed by restriction enzyme– or oligonucleotide-directed mutagenesis. The plasmid designations refer to plasmids that encode the corresponding PDH complexes, except for those plasmids (*underlined*) which express only the indicated individual domains. lip (**L**), lipoyl domain. *Black, white,* and *hatched* lipoyl domains denote origin of the polypeptide relative to the original 3-lip (**top line**) version.

The Lipoyl-Binding Site and Sequential Acetylation of Lipoyl Domains

An oligonucleotide-directed Lys→Gln substitution confirmed the identity of the lipoyl-binding site in the single hybrid lipoyl domains of the pGS110-encoded PDHC (FIG. 10). Then, to investigate whether sequential transfer of acetyl groups from outer to inner or inner to outer lipoyl domains is an obligatory feature of normal acetyl transfer, genes encoding different combinations of wild-type (lipoylated) and mutant (unlipoylated) lipoyl domains were constructed (FIG. 10; N. J. Allison, J. S. Miles, and J. R. Guest, unpublished observations). The corresponding complexes all retained activity, and only the pGS234-encoded complex, having two mutant lipoyl domains outside a wild-type domain, showed any significant impairment of specific activity and active-site coupling ability (A. Allen and R. N. Perham, personal communication). It would therefore appear that acetyl-transfer between outer and inner lipoyl domains is not essential for activity and that each lipoyl cofactor may be capable of making contact with each type of active site in the assembled complex.

Complementation between Lipoyl and Catalytic Domains

The possibility that complementation may occur between inactive complexes containing catalytic cores with no lipoyl domains, and exogenous lipoyl domains, was

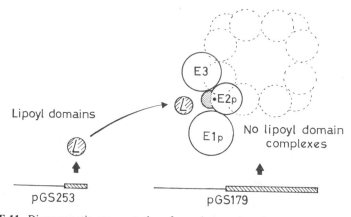

FIGURE 11. Diagrammatic representation of complementation of a mutant PDH complex by exogenous lipoyl domains. Compatible plasmids encoding, respectively, lipoyl domains (pGS253) and a complex lacking lipoyl domains (pGS179) were co-expressed in an *aceEF*-deletion strain to test for nutritional and enzymatic complementation.

investigated by transforming an *aceEF*-deletion strain with two independently select-able and mutually compatible plasmids encoding, respectively, lipoyl-domainless complexes and discrete lipoyl domains (pGS179 and pGS253, respectively; FIG. 11). The transformants expressed an Ace[+] phenotype, as judged by their ability to grow on unsupplemented succinate minimal medium, but no significant PDH complex activity was detected in cell-free extracts. The complementation therefore appears to be very weak, possibly because untethered lipoyl domains cannot successfully invade assem-bled complexes, or because the affinity of the lipoyl domains for the domain-free complex is too low for activity to be retained upon dilution in the cell-free extract. The fact that some complementation occurs can be taken as evidence for at least partial lipoylation of the independent lipoyl domains. Experiments with mixtures of the pGS179-encoded complex and extracts enriched for lipoyl domains (encoded by pGS203) likewise failed to show any significant *in vitro* complementation of enzyme activity.

aceF Subgenes

In vitro mutagenesis of the *aceF* gene has been used to create subgenes that express specific domains. For example, the insertion of stop codons in the interdomain linker region has been used to create subgenes that express the hybrid 9-kDa lipoyl domain of the pGS110 complex (pGS203) and a derivative in the Lys→Gln mutation of pGS155 (pGS204); see FIGURE 10. Subgenes expressing catalytic domains that lack lipoyl domains (35-kDa polypeptide; pGS179 and pGS200) and those that also lack the E3-binding segment (29-kDa polypeptide; pGS223 and pGS239) but retain acetyltransferase activity and aggregate to form subcomplexes with E1p have likewise been created for structural and mechanistic studies (FIG. 10).

Conformational Mobility of the Interdomain Linker Sequences

Protein engineering has been used to confirm that the AP-rich interdomain linkers are the major source of the conformational mobility detected by high-resolution ^{1}H-NMR spectroscopy of the complexes. Deletion of two or of all three lipoyl domains and their associated interdomain linkers produced parallel reductions in the sharp resonances attributed to the β-methyl protons of alanine residues (FIG. 12a)[65] It was also reasoned that if the interdomain linker is conformationally mobile, the introduction of a unique histidine residue in place of Gln-291 in the linker might give rise to diagnostic resonances in the aromatic region of the spectrum of the corresponding (pGS178) complex. The amino acid substitution had no apparent effect on the catalytic activity of the complex, but, as shown in FIGURE 12b, two small signals corresponding to the C-2 and C-4 protons of a mobile histidine residue were detected.[57] This result not only confirms the conformational flexibility of the linker sequence but also demonstrates that the technique is sufficiently powerful to detect a single mobile residue in a large complex having a protomeric molecular weight of ca. 250 kDa. Deletion of 12 residues from the AP-rich linker led to changes in the ^{1}H-NMR spectrum of the corresponding complex (pGS156) which are consistent with the linkers being the source of the sharp resonances,[65] although there were other changes in the pGS156 and pGS178 spectra that have not yet been fully interpreted. Formal proof of these conclusions has come from studies with a synthetic 32-residue polypeptide having the sequence that links the innermost lipoyl domain to the E3-binding domain in the wild-type complex and in the pGS110-encoded complex shown in FIGURE 12b. This polypeptide was found to have a ^{1}H-NMR spectrum that is essentially similar to that of the intact complex.[66]

Active-Site Coupling

The presence of an extensive network of coupling reactions permitting the intramolecular transfer of acyl groups between the lipoyl cofactors of different E2 subunits in the core is a feature of the 2-oxo acid dehydrogenase multienzyme

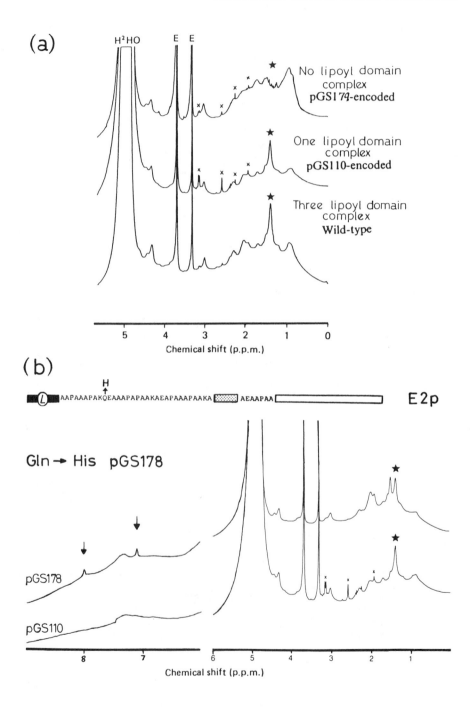

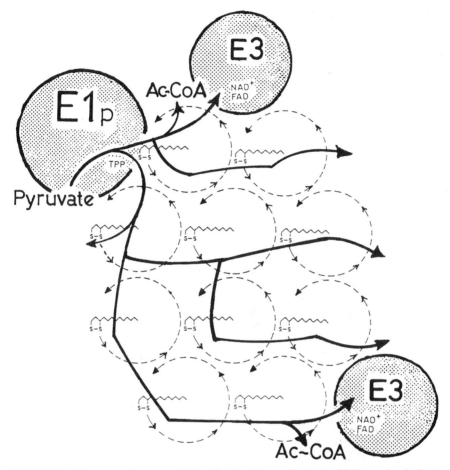

FIGURE 13. Diagrammatic representation of active-site coupling in the PDH complex, indicating the variety of routes that a newly generated acetyl group can take before being transferred to CoA. Representative E1p and E3 components are included, and the interacting lipoyl cofactors denote the network of E2p active sites.

FIGURE 12. ^{1}H-NMR spectra of genetically engineered PDH complexes. (a) Spectra of PDH complexes containing E2p subunits with three (wild-type), one, or no lipoyl domains.[65] Star (★) indicates position of the major sharp resonance other than those due to EDTA (**E, x**). (b) The site of the Glu → His mutation in the interdomain linker of the one–lipoyl-domain E2p component of the pGS178-encoded complex is shown; the lipoyl, E3-binding, and catalytic domains are represented by *filled*, *stippled*, and *open bars*, respectively. The resonances corresponding to a mobile histidine residue in the spectrum of this complex are marked by *arrows;*[57] other symbols are as described in panel (a).

complexes.[12–16, 43] It requires that the lipoyl cofactors attached to different E2 subunits be able to interact with each other, presumably at the acyltransferase active sites; this would seem to be quite feasible if the active sites are formed at the subunit interfaces, as they are in CAT. It also requires that each E1 subunit interacts with more than one E2 subunit, and *vice versa.* Thus, by a series of reductive acylation and transacylation reactions, an acyl lipoamide is generated; the acyl group can then take a variety of

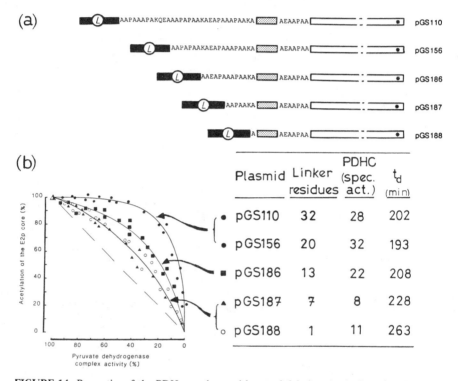

FIGURE 14. Properties of the PDH complexes with nested deletions in the interdomain linker associated with a single lipoyl domain.[63,64] (a) The amino acid sequences of the linker regions are indicated for the E2p components of complexes expressed by specific plasmids, and individual domains are denoted as follows: lipoyl (*dark bars*), E3-binding (*stippled bars*), and catalytic inner core (*open bars*). (b) Acetylation curves (*left*) indicating the degree of active-site coupling (extent of deviation from linearity) and the properties of the altered complexes (*right*) are shown. The number of residues in the linker sequences is indicated, as are the specific activities (spec. act.) of the isolated complexes (μmol substrate transformed/min/mg protein) and the doubling times (t_d) of plasmid-transformants of a mutant lacking the PDH complex for growth with pyruvate.

routes through the E2 core before being discharged, as shown schematically in FIGURE 13. Active-site coupling in the PDH complex is studied using isotopically labeled pyruvate in the absence of CoA and NAD^+ to estimate the degree of acetylation of the E2p core whilst progressively inhibiting the E1p subunit.[67] When plotted against the overall activity of the PDH complex measured in a parallel reaction, the acetylation or servicing curve normally shows that the degree of acetylation is not significantly affected until 70% or more of the complex activity is inhibited (FIG. 14b). This process is thought to be facilitated by flexibility in the E2p subunit. It is not dependent upon the presence of multiple lipoyl domains, because their number can be reduced from three to one without apparent loss of catalytic activity or active-site coupling. Moreover, the ODH complex, which is based on an E2o subunit having only one lipoyl domain, also exhibits active-site coupling. Protein engineering was therefore used to investigate the functional significance of the conformationally mobile interdomain linkers for the active-site coupling ability and the overall catalytic activity of the PDH complex.[63,64]

Starting with the pGS110-encoded complex containing one lipoyl domain, a nested set of deletions was engineered in the 32-residue interdomain linker (FIG. 14). The smallest deletion of 12 residues (pGS156) had no deleterious effects, but longer deletions of 25 and 31 residues (pGS187 and pGS188) produced significant reductions in both PDHC activity and the degree of active-site coupling (FIG. 14). The affected complexes were also impaired in their ability to complement the nutritional lesion of a mutant lacking the PDH complex (FIG. 14), but their E1p, E2p (acetyltransferase) and E3 activities were unimpaired. It is therefore abundantly clear that a direct relationship exists between the length of the AP-rich interdomain linker, the degree of active-site coupling, and the overall specific activity of the complex. The conformationally mobile linker sequences undoubtedly make an important contribution to the efficient processing of the substrate by the complexes. However, the linkers are evidently longer than necessary, because there is no significant impairment until 19 or more residues have been deleted (pGS186; Fig. 14). It should also be noted that active-site coupling and catalytic activity are not entirely abolished by the largest deletion. This could mean that shortening the linker prevents transacetylation between individual E2p subunits but leaves a residual coupling activity that may be indicative of the degree of interaction between the E1p and E2p subunits. Nevertheless, the linker imparts a flexibility which is essential for full active-site coupling and maximum activity of the complex.

CONCLUSION

The molecular genetic approach has been responsible for an acceleration in our understanding of the primary structures of the 2-oxo acid dehydrogenase multienzyme complexes from diverse sources. Comparisons of the sequences are informative, but more important are the opportunities this approach offers for constructing novel complexes with precisely defined structural alterations and for expressing specific domains in order to explore the many problems that still remain concerning the structures of the complexes, the interactions between their subunits, the assembly and dynamics of the complexes, and the detailed molecular basis of their catalytic action.

ACKNOWLEDGMENTS

We are grateful to numerous colleagues, particularly Drs. N. Allison, J. S. Miles, and M. E. Spencer, for permission to review their published and unpublished work, and Drs. P. C. Engel and R. N. Perham (and colleagues) for fruitful collaboration in studies with the genetically engineered complexes.

REFERENCES

1. GUEST, J. R. & P. E. STEPHENS. 1980. J. Gen. Microbiol. **121:** 277–292.
2. SPENCER, M. E. & J. R. GUEST. 1982. J. Bacteriol. **151:** 542–552.
3. STEPHENS, P. E., M. G. DARLISON, H. M. LEWIS & J. R. GUEST. 1983. Eur. J. Biochem. **133:** 155–162.
4. STEPHENS, P. E., M. G. DARLISON, H. M. LEWIS & J. R. GUEST. 1983. Eur. J. Biochem. **133:** 481–489.
5. STEPHENS, P. E., H. M. LEWIS, M. G. DARLISON & J. R. GUEST. 1983. Eur. J. Biochem. **135:** 519–527.
6. DARLISON, M. G., M. E. SPENCER & J. R. GUEST. 1984. Eur. J. Biochem. **141:** 351–359.
7. SPENCER, M. E., M. G. DARLISON, P. E. STEPHENS, I. K. DUCKENFIELD & J. R. GUEST. 1984. Eur. J. Biochem. **141:** 361–374.
8. REED, L. J. 1974. Acct. Chem. Res. **7:** 40–46.
9. PACKMAN, L. C., G. HALE & R. N. PERHAM. 1984. EMBO J. **3:** 1315–1319.
10. BLEILE, D. M., P. MUNK, R. M. OLIVER & L. J. REED. 1979. Proc. Natl. Acad. Sci. USA **76:** 4385–4389.
11. HALE, G. & R. N. PERHAM. 1979. FEBS Lett. **105:** 263–266.
12. BATES, D. L., M. J. DANSON, G. HALE, E. A. HOOPER & R. N. PERHAM. 1977. Nature **268:** 313–316.
13. COLLINS, J. H. & L. J. REED. 1977. Proc. Natl. Acad. Sci. USA **74:** 4223–4227.
14. STEPP, L. R., BLEILE, D. K. MCRORIE, F. H. PETTIT & L. J. REED. 1981. Biochemistry **20:** 4555–4560.
15. BERMAN, J. N. G.-X. CHEN, G. HALE & R. N. PERHAM, R. N. 1981. Biochem. J. **199:** 513–520.
16. HACKERT, M. L., R. M. OLIVER & L. J. REED. 1983. Proc. Natl. Acad. Sci. USA **80:** 2907–2911.
17. ROBERTS, G. C. K., H. W. DUCKWORTH, L. C. PACKMAN & R. N. PERHAM. 1983. Ciba Symp. **93:** 47–62.
18. GUEST, J. R. 1978. Adv. Neurol. **21:** 219–244.
19. MILES, J. S. & J. R. GUEST. 1987. Biochem. Soc. Symp. **54:** 45–65.
20. WESTPHAL, A. H. & A. DEKOK. 1988. Eur. J. Biochem. **172:** 299–305.
21. SYKES, P. J., G. BURNS, J. MENARD, K. HATTER & J. R. SOKATCH. 1987. J. Bacteriol. **169:** 1619–1625.
22. NER, S. S., V. BHAYANA, A. W. BELL, I. G. GILES, H. W. DUCKWORTH & D. P. BLOXHAM. 1983. Biochemistry **22:** 5243–5249.
23. BUCK, D., M. E. SPENCER & J. R. GUEST. 1985. Biochemistry **24:** 6245–6252.
24. SPENCER, M. E. & J. R. GUEST. 1985. Mol. Gen. Genet. **200:** 145–154.
25. RICE, D. W., G. E. SCHULZ & J. R. GUEST. 1984. J. Mol. Biol. **174:** 483–496.
26. LANGLEY, D. & J. R. GUEST. 1979. FEMS Microbiol. Lett. **5:** 5–8.
27. IUCHI, S. & E. C. C. LIN. 1988. Proc. Natl. Acad. Sci. USA **85:** 1888–1892.
28. GUEST, J. R. & I. T. CREAGHAN. 1974. J. Gen. Microbiol. **81:** 237–245.
29. MCKENNEY, K., H. SHIMATAKE, D. COURT, U. SCHMEISNER & M. ROSENBERG. 1981. *In* Gene Amplification and Analysis. J. Chirikjian & T. Papas, Eds. Vol 2: 383. Elsevier North-Holland. New York.
30. SPENCER, M. E., R. J. WILDE & J. R. GUEST. 1986. Soc. Gen. Microbiol. Quart. **13:** M9.
31. SPENCER, M. E., H. M. LEWIS & J. R. GUEST. 1988. *In* Thiamin Pyrophosphate Biochemistry. A. Schellenberger & R. L. Schowen, Eds. Vol 2: 3–11. CRC Press. Boca Raton, Florida.
32. KOIKE, K., S. OHTA, Y. URATA, Y. KAGAWA & M. KOIKE. 1988. Proc. Natl. Acad. Sci. &USA **85:** 41–45.
33. ZHANG, B., M. J. KUNTZ, G. W. GOODWIN, R. A. HARRIS & D. W. CRABB. 1988. J. Biol. Chem. **262:** 15220–15224.
34. BURNS, G., T. BROWN, K. HATTER, J. M. IDRISS & J. R. SOKATCH. 1988. Eur. J. Biochem. **176:** 311–317.
35. GRABAU, C. & J. E. CRONAN. 1986. Nucleic. Acids Res. **14:** 5449–5460.
36. CONWAY, T., Y. OSMAN, J. KONNAN, E. HOFFMANN & L. O. INGRAM. 1987. J. Bacteriol. **169:** 949–954.

37. OTULAKOWSKI, G. & B. H. ROBINSON. 1987. J. Biol. Chem. **262:** 17313–17318.
38. ROSS, J., G. A. REID & I. W. DAWES. 1988. J. Gen. Microbiol. **134:** 1131–1139.
39. RUSSELL, G. C., N. ALLISON, C. H. WILLIAMS, JR. & J. R. GUEST. 1989. Ann. N.Y. Acad. Sci. This volume.
40. WILLIAMS, C. H., JR., N. ALLISON, G. C. RUSSELL, A. J. PRONGAY, L. D. ARSCOTT, S. DATTA, L. SAHLMAN & J. R. GUEST. 1989. Ann. N.Y. Acad. Sci. This volume.
41. PACKMAN, L. C. & R. N. PERHAM. 1986. FEBS Lett. **306:** 193–198.
42. PACKMAN, L. C. & R. N. PERHAM. 1987. Biochem. J. **242:** 531–538.
43. PERHAM, R. N., L. C. PACKMAN & S. E. RADFORD. 1987. Biochem. Soc. Symp. **54:** 67–81.
44. GUEST, J. R., M. G. DARLISON, M. E. SPENCER & P. E. STEPHENS. 1984. Biochem. Soc. Trans. **12:** 220–223.
45. GERSHWIN, M. E., I. A. MACKAY, A. STURGESS & R. L. COPPEL. 1987. J. Immunol. **138:** 3525–3531.
46. FUSSEY, S. P. M., J. R. GUEST, O. F. W. JAMES, M. F. BASSENDINE & S. J. YEAMAN. 1988. Proc. Natl. Acad. Sci. USA **85:** 8654–8658.
47. COPPEL, R. L., L. J. MCNEILAGE, C. D. SURH, J. VAN DER WATER, T. W. SPITHILL, S. WITTINGHAM & M. E. GERSHWIN. 1988. Proc. Natl. Acad. Sci. USA **85:** 7317–7321.
48. PACKMAN, L. C., A. BORGES & R. N. PERHAM. 1988. Biochem. J. **252:** 79–86.
49. HANEMAAIJER, R., A. JANSSEN, A. DEKOK & C. VEEGER. 1988. Eur. J. Biochem. **174:** 593–599.
50. HUMMEL, K. B., S. LITWER, A. P. BRADFORD, A. AITKEN, D. J. DANNER & S. J. YEAMAN. 1988. J. Biol. Chem. **263:** 6165–6168.
51. LAU, K. S., T. A. GRIFFIN, C. C-N. HU & D. T. CHUANG. 1988. Biochemistry **27:** 1972–1981.
52. BURNS, G., T. BROWN, K. HATTER & J. R. SOKATCH. 1988. Eur. J. Biochem. **176:** 165–169.
53. GUEST, J. R. 1987. FEMS Microbiol. Lett. **44:** 417–422.
54. LESLIE, A. G. W., P. C. E. MOODY & W. V. SHAW. 1988. Proc. Natl. Acad. Sci. USA **85:** 4133–4137.
55. ELIOPOULOS, E. E., A. J. GEDDES, M. BRETᵣ, D. J. C. PAPPIN & J. B. C. FINDLAY. 1982. Int. J. Biol. Macromol. **4:** 263–268.
56. GUEST, J. R., H. M. LEWIS, L. D. GRAHAM, L. C. PACKMAN & R. N. PERHAM. 1985. J. Mol. Biol. **185:** 743–754.
57. TEXTER, F. L., S. E. RADFORD, E. D. LAUE, R. N. PERHAM, J. S. MILES & J. R. GUEST. 1988. Biochemistry **27:** 289–296.
58. SCHAUDER, B., R. FRANK, H. BLÖCKER & J. E. G. MCCARTHY. 1987. Gene **52:** 279–283.
59. GUEST, J. R., R. E. ROBERTS & P. E. STEPHENS. 1983. J. Gen. Microbiol. **129:** 671–680.
60. MILES, J. S. & J. R. GUEST. 1987. Biochem. J. **245:** 869–874.
61. ALLISON, N., C. H. WILLIAMS & J. R. GUEST. 1988. Biochem. J. **256:** 741–749.
62. ANGIER, S. J., J. S. MILES, P. A. SRERE, P. C. ENGEL & J. R. GUEST. 1987. Biochem. Soc. Trans. **15:** 832–833.
63. MILES, J. S., J. R. GUEST, S. E. RADFORD & R. N. PERHAM. 1987. Biochim. Biophys. Acta **913:** 117–121.
64. MILES, J. S., J. R. GUEST, S. E. RADFORD & R. N. PERHAM. 1988. J. Mol. Biol. **202:** 97–106.
65. RADFORD, S. E., E. D. LAUE, R. N. PERHAM, J. S. MILES & J. R. GUEST. 1987. Biochem. J. **247:** 641–649.
66. RADFORD, S. E., E. D. LAUE & R. N. PERHAM. 1986. Biochem. Soc. Trans. **14:** 1231–1232.
67. PACKMAN, L. C., STANLEY, C. J. & R. N. PERHAM. 1983. Biochem. J. **213:** 331–338.
68. BUCK, D. & J. R. GUEST. 1989. Biochem. J. **260:** 737–747.

Molecular Cloning of cDNAs for α and β Subunits of Human Pyruvate Dehydrogenase[a]

KICHIKO KOIKE, YOSHISHIGE URATA,
AND MASAHIKO KOIKE

Department of Pathological Biochemistry
Atomic Disease Institute
Nagasaki University School of Medicine
Nagasaki, 852, Japan

INTRODUCTION

Pyruvate dehydrogenase (PDH, EC 1.2.4.1) is found in mitochondria of all mammalian tissues as one of the component enzymes of the PDH multienzyme complex. It catalyzes the first reaction of the coordinated sequence of a CoA- and NAD^+-linked and lipoic acid–mediated oxidative decarboxylation converting pyruvate to acetyl-CoA and CO_2 (reaction 1).[1,2]

$$CH_3COCOOH + CoA—SH + NAD^+ \rightarrow$$

$$CH_3CO—S—CoA + CO_2\uparrow + NADH + H^+ \quad (1)$$

Mammalian PDH has been purified from the complexes isolated from porcine heart,[3–6] bovine kidney and heart,[7,8] and rat heart.[9] These PDHs have been shown to possess similar enzymatic and chemical properties. Porcine PDH is composed of two M_r 41,000 subunits (PDHα) and two M_r 36,000 subunits (PDHβ) in an $\alpha_2\beta_2$ form with a total M_r of 153,000 (determined by sedimentation equilibrium).

The activity of the PDH complex is regulated by two mechanisms, product inhibition by acetyl-CoA and NADH[10,11] and covalent modulation by way of a phosphorylation-dephosphorylation cycle.[12,13] Phosphorylation occurs on three serine residues in the PDHα of bovine kidney and heart[14] and of porcine heart.[15] The amino acid sequences around the phosphorylation sites of PDH from these two species showed high homology.

It has been reported that a genetic PDH deficiency in infants results in progressive neurological disease with persistent lactic and pyruvic acidemia and growth retardation.[16,17] Surprisingly, little is known about the structure and function of human PDH. Molecular cloning and nucleotide sequencing of cDNAs for the two subunits of human PDH should facilitate studies on the protein and gene structures of these two subunits and on their expression. It may also provide information concerning the nature of genetic mutants leading to molecular diseases and aid in carrier detection, prenatal diagnosis, and treatment. Here we report the cloning, complete nucleotide sequences, and deduced amino acid sequences of human PDHα and PDHβ. The amino acid

[a]This work was supported in part by a Grant-in-Aid for Scientific Research on Priority Areas of "Bioenergetics," by a Grant-in-Aid for Scientific Research from the Ministry of Education, Science and Culture, and by grants from the Vitamin B Research Committee.

100

sequences around the amino- and carboxyl-terminal regions and the phosphorylation sites in PDH are also compared with the partial sequences of porcine and bovine enzymes. Some of this work has previously been reported briefly.[18]

EXPERIMENTAL PROCEDURES

Materials

HeLa cells were grown in Eagle's minimal essential medium No. 1 (Nissui, Tokyo) supplemented with 10% calf serum (Gibco Oriental) until they reached a density of 10^7 cells/ml. The HeLa cell cDNA library in the λgt11 expression vector was a generous gift from P. J. Nielsen (Biocenter, University of Basel, Basel).[19] The human foreskin fibroblast cDNA library in plasmid vector pcD was generously provided by H. Okayama (National Institute of Health, Bethesda, MD).

Enzyme Purification, Peptide Sequencing, and Polyclonal Antisera

Porcine heart PDH complex was isolated by a modification of the procedure of Hayakawa *et al.*[3] The complex was separated into its three component enzymes—dihydrolipoamide acetyltransferase (LAT), PDH, and lipoamide dehydrogenase (Fp)—by high-performance gel-permeation chromatography, and PDH was separated into its two different subunits (PDHα and PDHβ).[6] The subunits were reduced and then performic acid–oxidized, or S-carboxymethylated, or S-pyridylethylated. The modified subunits were digested with proteases, and the peptides were fractionated by reverse phase high-performance liquid chromatography. Sequence analysis was performed on a JEOL sequence analyzer (model JAS-570K), an Applied Biosystems gas-phase sequencer (model 477A) coupled to a PTH analyzer (model 120A), and a Beckman sequencer (model 890C). The carboxyl-terminal amino acid sequence was determined by enzymatic hydrolysis with carboxypeptidase Y.[20] The antisera against porcine PDHα and PDHβ were raised in rabbits and were passed through an Affi-Gel 10 and 15 mixed bed (1:1, vol/vol) column to which had been conjugated sonic extracts of *Escherichia coli* strain Y1090.

Antibody Screening of a λgt11 Library

About 5×10^5 plaque-forming units (pfu) of recombinant phage from a HeLa cell cDNA library were screened with anti-PDHα or anti-PDHβ antiserum, respectively, diluted 1:1500 in Tris-buffered saline (TBS) containing 0.5% non-fat dry milk.[19,21] Typically, 3×10^4 pfu were screened per 143 × 103 mm plate by using *E. coli* strain Y1090. Positive plaques were further purified by two cycles of screening at low plaque density with antisera. The positive phage clones (λHPDA, λHPDB) were amplified, digested with *Eco*R I, sized, and purified. The isolated 1.3-kilobase (kb) fragment of λHPDA and 0.4-kb fragment of λHPDB were nick-translated[22] as probes for probe screening.

cDNA Probe Screening of a Plasmid Library

The human foreskin fibroblast cDNA library in the plasmid vector pcD was screened with ^{32}P-labeled nick-translated phage cDNAs for PDHα and PDHβ, respectively. Approximately 3×10^5 individual colonies were screened by colony hybridization.[22,23] Positive clones were purified by two cycles of rescreening at low colony density. Cloned cDNA inserts were isolated by *Bam*H I digestion followed by preparative electrophoresis in agarose gels. The purified inserts were subcloned into plasmid vector pUC19 or expression vector pTZ18R and characterized by restriction endonuclease mapping and *in vitro* transcription and translation.

Sequencing of cDNA

The two entire cDNA inserts were circularized with T4 DNA ligase, sonicated, end-repaired by using nuclease P1 and T4 DNA polymerase, and fractionated into two size ranges (300–500 and 500–800 base pairs) in agarose gels.[24] These two size-class fractions were subcloned into M13mp18 or M13mp19[25] and sequenced by the dideoxynucleotide chain-termination method using universal primer.[26] The inserts subcloned into pUC19 were sequenced by the enzymatic primer-extension method employing synthetic oligodeoxynucleotide primers complementary to selected regions of previously determined sequence.[27]

Fusion Protein Analysis

E. coli Y1090 cells were lysogenized with either λHPDA or λHPDB and induced to promote fusion protein synthesis with isopropyl β-D-thiogalactopyranoside. The fusion proteins were precipitated, dissolved in a SDS–sample buffer, separated in 10% polyacrylamide gels,[28] and electroblotted onto nitrocellulose. The blots were blocked in TBS containing 0.5% non-fat dry milk and incubated for 1 hr in antisera diluted 1:1500 with TBS. Bound antibodies were detected with ^{125}I-labeled protein A and analyzed by fluorography at $-80°C$.

RNA Blot Analysis

Total RNA from HeLa cells was isolated by the guanidine thiocyanate–CsCl method;[29] poly(A)$^+$ RNA was enriched by oligo(dT)-cellulose chromatography.[30] RNA was electrophoresed in 1% agarose gels in the presence of 2.2 M formaldehyde, transferred to nitrocellulose, and hybridized with ^{32}P-labeled probes prepared by nick-translation of pHPDA or pHPDB. Poly(A)$^+$ RNA was translated in a reticulocyte lysate system supplemented with [35S]methionine. Translation products were immunoprecipitated with anti-PDHα or anti-PDHβ antiserum and *Staphylococcus aureus* Cowan I cells as described by Ono *et al.*[31] The precipitates were analyzed by SDS–polyacrylamide gel electrophoresis and fluorography.[31]

RESULTS AND DISCUSSION

Isolation of Human PDHα and PDHβ cDNA Clones in a HeLa Cell Library in λgt11

We had observed that rabbit antisera against porcine heart PDHα and PDHβ cross-reacted highly with human PDHα and PDHβ,[32] respectively. We prepared monospecific rabbit antisera against each of the purified porcine heart subunits, which detected less than 10 ng of these proteins on an electrophoretic immunoblot.

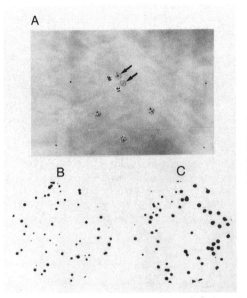

FIGURE 1. Immunological screening of HeLa cell cDNA library in λgt11. (A) Immunopositive clones (*arrows*) for PDH at the first screening. Positive clones (B) for PDHα and (C) for PDHβ at second screening.

The HeLa cell cDNA library in λgt11 was screened by using an antibody procedure described by Nielsen *et al.*[19] A total of 17 positive plaques for PDHα and 11 for PDHβ were detected out of 5×10^5 plaques. The positive plaques were replated and rescreened in two cycles at low density to obtain pure clones, as shown in FIGURES 1A, B, and C. A total of 6 plaques for PDHα and 3 for PDHβ remained positive upon rescreening. The size of inserts of PDHα clone varied from 0.4 to 1.3 kb, and those of PDHβ clone were all 0.4 kb. Clones of 1.3 kb for PDHα and 0.4 kb for PDHβ were selected for further studies and designated as λHPDA and λHPDB, respectively.

The expression vector λgt11 permits insertion of foreign DNA into the structural gene of β-galactosidase and promotes synthesis of fusion proteins. The β-galactosidase fusion proteins of λHPDA and λHPDB, induced by isopropyl β-D-thiogalactopyranoside, were analyzed by immunoblotting. As shown in FIGURE 2, λHPDA and λHPDB

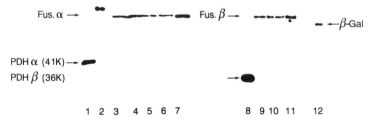

Fus. α →   Fus. β →   − ←β-Gal

PDH α (41K) →
PDH β (36K)   →

1 2 3   4 5 6 7   8 9 10 11   12

FIGURE 2. Immunoblot analysis of λHPDA and λHPDB fusion proteins. Mature PDHα (**lane 1**) and PDHβ (**lane 8**) and cell extracts from isopropyl β-D-thiogalactopyranoside–induced *E. coli* Y1090 cells lysogenized with λHPDA (**lanes 2–7**) and λHPDB (**lanes 9–11**), respectively, were separated by SDS-polyacrylamide gel electrophoresis and electroblotted onto nitrocellulose. **Lanes 1–7** were treated with anti-PDHα antiserum and **lanes 8–11** were treated with anti-PDHβ antiserum. **Lane 12**, β-galactosidase. Bound antibody was detected with ^{125}I-labeled protein A and analyzed by fluorography. Fus. α, β-galactosidase–PDHα fusion protein; Fus. β, β-galactosidase–PDHβ fusion protein; β-Gal, β-galactosidase.

were each expressed as a large fusion protein of M_r 150,000–170,000 (lanes 2–7) or M_r 140,000 (lanes 9–11), respectively, in contrast to β-galactosidase, with M_r 130,000 (lane 12). These results indicated the presence, in λHPDA and λHPDB, of nucleotide sequences encoding partial amino acid sequences of PDHα and PDHβ, respectively.

Isolation of Full-Length Human PDHα and PDHβ cDNA Clones in Plasmids

Nick-translated cDNA fragments derived from λgt11 clones were used to screen a second human foreskin fibroblast cDNA library in plasmids. A total of five positive colonies for PDHα and two for PDHβ were observed upon high-density screening of 3×10^5 colonies. A total of four colonies for PDHα and one for PDHβ remained positive after two cycles of regrowing and rescreening at low density, as shown in FIGURE 3. The size of inserts of PDHα clone varied from 1.0 to 1.8 kb and that of PDHβ was 1.9 kb. A PDHα clone of 1.8 kb and a PDHβ clone of 1.9 kb were designated as pHPDA and pHPDB, respectively, and selected for further studies.

Sequences of pHPDA and pHPDB

Partial restriction maps and sequencing strategies for pHPDA and pHPDB are shown in FIGURE 4. The entire nucleotide sequences of two inserts were determined by the dideoxynucleotide chain-termination procedure using universal and specific primers. The complete nucleotide sequences of pHPDA and pHPDB and the deduced amino acid sequences are shown in FIGURES 5A and 5B, respectively. PDHα cDNA contains 1363 nucleotides, including a poly(A) tail of 30 nucleotides and an open reading frame that begins at position 1 and extends through position 1176. PDHβ cDNA contains 1557 nucleotides, including a poly(A) tail of 41 nucleotides and an

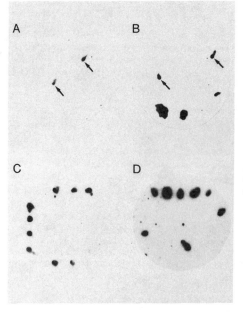

FIGURE 3. Probe screening of a human foreskin fibroblast cDNA library in plasmids by colony hybridization. Positive clones *(arrows)* (**A**) at the first screening for PDHα and (**B**) for PDHβ. Positive clones (**C**) at the third screening for PDHα and (**D**) for PDHβ.

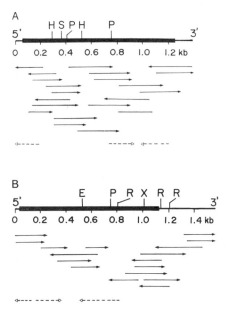

FIGURE 4. Restriction maps and sequencing strategies for (A) PDHα and (B) PDHβ cDNAs. Endonuclease restriciton sites on PDHα and PDHβ cDNA inserts are shown above the lines. **Letters** show the relevant cleavage sites of enzymes: **E**, *Eco*R I; **H**, *Hind* III; **P**, *Pst* I; **R**, *Rsa* I; **S**, *Sma* I; **X**, *Xba* I. **Arrows** show the direction and extent of the nucleotide sequencing by the dideoxynucleotide chain-termination method. **Solid arrows** indicate the fragments obtained by sonication. **Broken arrows** indicate the sequences obtained by the primer-extension method using synthetic oligonucleotide primers.

open reading frame that begins at position 1 and extends through position 1077. A putative leader sequence of PDHα consisting of 29 amino acid residues was identified, yielding a predicted precursor protein of 392 amino acid residues and M_r 43,414 and a mature protein of 363 residues and M_r 40,334. A similar leader sequence of 30 amino acid residues for PDHβ was also identified, yielding a predicted precursor protein of 359 amino acid residues and M_r 39,046 and a mature protein of 329 residues and M_r 35,911. The underlined amino acid sequences (FIG. 5) of the amino-terminal regions of the two subunits are identical with those of the mature porcine PDH. The underlined carboxyl-terminal region (FIG. 5) of the human PDHβ was very similar to that of porcine PDHβ, which was Lys-Phe-Leu-Asn-Ile. However, the carboxyl-terminal residues of human and porcine PDHα were different. The porcine sequence is (Val, Ala)-Leu-Ser-Ile. The amino acid sequences around the three putative phosphorylation sites of human PDHα (amino acid residues 166–174 and 229–242) were identical with the sequences for the phosphorylation sites in bovine and porcine PDHα. Knowledge of the amino acid sequences near the amino and carboxyl termini of the two porcine subunit proteins allowed us to identify the correct reading frame for the DNA sequence. The results showed that there were highly conserved segments of the amino acid sequences among human and porcine PDHs. The homologies of the predicted sequences around the amino termini of the PDHα and PDHβ subunits of the two enzymes are 76% for 66 residues and 79% for 61 residues, respectively, and that of the carboxyl termini of the two PDHβ subunits is 80% for 5 residues. The sequences around the three phosphorylation sites among the three species of PDHα are, as already mentioned, identical.

The nucleotide sequences of human PDHα cDNA reported by Dahl *et al.*[33] and by De Meireleir *et al.*[34] have been carefully examined and compared with our data. We have found several differences. (i) Their entire cDNA inserts possess one *Pst* I

A

```
                                                                    (G)n  TCCTGGGTTGTGAGGAGTCGCCCGTGCCCCCACTGCCTGCTTC          -1
                                                                                                            -   +
Met Arg Lys Met Leu Ala Ala Val Ser Arg  Val Leu Ser Gly Ala Ser Gln Lys Pro Ala  Ser Arg Leu Val Ala Ser Arg Asn Phe
ATG AGG AAG ATG CTC GCC GCC GTC TCC CGC  GTG CTG TCT GGC GCT TCT CAG AAG CCG GCA  AGC AGA CTG GTA GCA TCC CGT AAT TTT        90

Ala Asn Asp Ala Thr Phe Glu Ile Lys Lys  Cys Asp Leu His Arg Leu Glu Gln Gly Pro  Pro Val Thr Leu Thr Arg Glu Glu Asp
GCA AAT GAT GCT ACA TTT GAA ATT AAG AAG  TGT GAC CTT CAC CGG CTC GAA CAG GGC CCT  CCA GTG CTC ACC AGG GAG GAA GAT        180

Gly Leu Lys Tyr Tyr Arg Met Met Arg Val  Leu Ala Met Glu Ala Ala Ser Thr Pro Gln  Leu Tyr Lys Ile Ile Arg Gly Gly Phe
GGG CTC AAA TAC TAC CGA ATG ATG CGC GTA  CTG GCG ATG GAG GCA GCA TCA TCA CAG CAG  CTG TAT AAA ATT ATT CGT GGG GGT TTC       270

Cys His Leu Cys Asp Cys Cys Val Cys Gly  Ala Phe Pro Ser Glu Pro Ser Gln Thr Ile  Ser Gln Ala Lys Gly Lys Gly
TGT CAC TTG TGT GAT TGC TGC GTT TGT GGC  GCT TTT CCG TCC GAG CCA TCA CAG ACC ATC  TCA CAG GCT AAA GGG AAA GGA           360

Thr Ala Leu Ser Pro Gly Ala Phe Ser Glu  Ala Glu Leu Thr Gly Lys Gly Cys Ala Lys  Gly Lys Gly
ACG GCT TTA CTT TCA CCC GGG GCC TTT TCT  GCA GAG CTT ACA GGT GGT TGT GCT AAA GGA           450

Gly Ser Met His Met Tyr Ala Lys Asn Phe  Tyr Gly Asn Gly Val Ile Gly Gln Ile Gln  Gly Ala Phe Glu Ala Tyr Asn Met Ala
GGA TCG CAC ATG TAT GCC AAG AAC TTC TAC  TAT GGC AAT GGC GTG ATC GGT CAG ATA TTC  GAA TTC GAA GCT TAC AAC ATG GCA       540

Ala Leu Trp Lys Leu Pro Cys Ile Ile Pro  Phe Ile Pro Gly Ile Leu Arg Ser Val Glu  Ala Ala Arg Ser Thr Asp
GCT TTG TGG AAA TTA CCT TGT ATC TTC ATT  TTC ATT CCT GGG ATC CTG AGA TCT GTT GAG  GCA GCG CGC AGC ACT GAT        630

Tyr Tyr Lys Arg Asp Gly Arg Val Val Gly  Gln Leu Leu Met Asp Ile Tyr Arg Glu Glu  Ala Thr Phe Ala Ala Ala
TAC TAC AAG AGA GAT GGC AGA GTG GTG GAT  CTG CTG ATG ATC TAT CGT GTT GAG GCA GCA  ACA AGG TTT GCT GCC GCC       720

Tyr Cys Arg Ser Lys Pro Ile Leu Met Gly  Thr Gln Tyr His Gly Ser Met Asp Pro Gly  Val Gly Val Ser Tyr
TAT TGT AGA TCT AAG CCC ATC CTC ATG GGG  ACT CAG TAC TAC CAC GGA TCT ATG GAC GAC  GTC GGA GTC AGT TAC           810

Arg Thr Glu Glu Ala Thr Pro Ile Glu Glu  Ile Glu Asp Ala Gln Phe Ala Thr Ala Asn  Ser Leu Ala Ser Ser
CGT ACA CGA GAA GCA ACG CCT ATT ATT GAG  GAG ATT GAG GAC GAT TTT GCC ACG GCC CCG  CCT GAG AAT GCC AGT        900

Val Glu Lys Leu Gln Ile Glu Lys Val Arg  Glu Lys Ile Glu Asp Ile Phe Ala Asp Pro  Glu Pro Thr Phe
GTG GAA CTA AAG CAG ATT GAA GAG GTG GTG  GAA AAG AGG ATT GAG GCT GCC GAT CCT GAG  GAG CCG ACC TTT           990

Gly Arg Ala Gly His Leu Thr Ala Ala Arg  Ser Phe Val Pro Ile Leu Ser Gly Ser Ser  Leu Ser Gln Ser Val
GGA AGA GCT CTC CAT CTC ACA GCG GCA AGG  AGT GTT GTG CCA ATC CTC AAC GGA TCA AGT  TTA AGT CAG TCA GTT      1080

Lys Gly Arg Arg Thr Phe Thr Gly Leu Pro  Asp Ser Val Leu Lys Val Leu Glu Glu Glu  Asn Pro Val Asn Glu
AAG GGG AGA AGA ACC TTC ACC AGG AGG GGG  GAC AGC GTT CTC AAC TTG GTT GAA GAA GAA  CCA GTC AAT GAA      1170

Ile Gln  *
ATT CAA TGA  AATTCTTGAAACTTCCATTAAGTGTGTAGATTGAGCAGGTAGTAATGCATTAGTGCATTAATTGTACATTATTATTA(A)30   1299
```

B

(The figure shows the nucleotide and deduced amino acid sequence of human PDHβ cDNA, presented in rotated orientation, with codons and corresponding amino acids and nucleotide position numbers 90, 180, 270, 360, 450, 540, 630, 720, 810, 900, 990, 1080, and the 3' untranslated region ending at 1524.)

FIGURE 5. Nucleotide and deduced amino acid sequences of human PDHα and PDHβ cDNAs. PDHα (**A**) and PDHβ (**B**) cDNA sequences were obtained according to the sequencing strategies shown in FIGURE 4. Nucleotides are numbered on the *right*. Amino acid residues identical with those of porcine heart PDHα and PDHβ are *underlined with solid lines*. The sequences around the phosphorylation sites of PDHα (**A**) are *underlined with dashed lines*. The signals for polyadenylation (ATTAAA or AATAAA) are *underlined*: (**A**) nucleotides 1251–1256; (**B**) nucleotides 1461–1466. *, stop codons.

restriction site in contrast to two sites in our insert. (ii) Their sequences possess a 93–base-pair insert (31 amino acid residues) between bases 510 and 511 in our sequence, as shown in FIGURE 6. Consequently, our open reading frame extends about 97 base-pairs downstream beyond their stop codon at position 1282. We could not detect any overlapping sequence with this extra insert in our PDHα cDNA. (iii) We also noticed several base differences among the three cDNAs.

The cloning and sequencing of the PDHα gene have been performed to confirm the involvement of the 93–base-pair insert in the PDHα cDNA. A 15-kb genomic clone for PDHα was isolated and subjected to sequence analysis (manuscript in preparation). Preliminary data indicated that (i) base 510 in our open reading frame is the last base at the 3′ end of one of the exons, (ii) base 511 is the first base at the 5′ end of the next exon, and (iii) the sequence between bases 916 and 1176 is identical with the last exon. Whether the 93–base-pair insert missing in our foreskin fibroblast cDNA sequence is deleted by abnormal splicing or whether those found in the fetal and hepatoma cDNAs are residual introns, still need to be determined by primary structural analysis of these three PDHα cDNAs.

RNA Analysis by Blot Hybridization with pHPDA and pHPDB and by Translation

Blot hybridization analysis (FIG. 7A) of HeLa cell poly(A)$^+$ RNA reveals single hybridization bands for PDHα and PDHβ at about 1.8 kb (lane 2) and 1.7 kb (lane 3), respectively. The clones for PDHα and PDHβ reported here are 1363 and 1557 nucleotides, respectively, representing the PDHα and PDHβ coding and untranslated regions. To confirm the presence of mRNAs specific for PDHα and PDHβ in the HeLa cell poly(A)$^+$ RNA fraction, we carried out *in vitro* translation analysis. The [^{35}S]methionine-labeled translational products were immunoprecipitated and analyzed by SDS-polyacrylamide gel electrophoresis (FIG. 7B). The polypeptides synthesized with the mRNAs were similar in size to the precursor proteins of PDHα with M$_r$

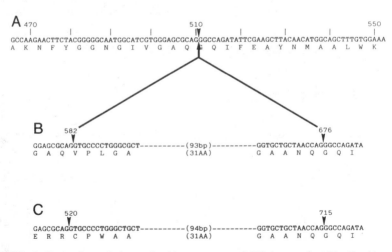

FIGURE 6. Comparison of the nucleotide sequences of (A) human foreskin fibroblast, (B) hepatoma, and (C) fetal liver PDHα cDNAs. The hepatoma and fetal liver PDHα cDNAs have 93–base-pair inserts between bases 510 and 511 in the open reading frame of the human sequence.

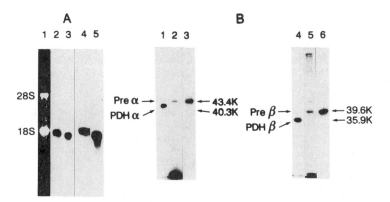

FIGURE 7. Blot hybridization analysis and *in vitro* translation of HeLa cell mRNA. (A) Samples of 5 μg of calf liver rRNA (*lane 1*), 20 μg of poly(A)⁺ RNA from HeLa cells (*lanes 2 and 3*), transcribed PDHα mRNA (*lane 4*) and PDHβ mRNA (*lane 5*) were separated by electrophoresis in a formaldehyde/agarose gel. *Lane 1* was cut and immediately stained with ethidium bromide. *Lanes 2–5* were transferred to nitrocellulose and hybridized to the nick-translated PDHα (*lanes 2 and 4*) or PDHβ (*lanes 3 and 5*) cDNA probes. The film for the radioautogram was exposed at −80°C for 3 hr. (B) Poly(A)⁺ RNA from HeLa cells and the PDHα and PDHβ mRNAs synthesized by *in vitro* transcription were translated by the reticulocyte lysate system. The ³⁵S-labeled cell-free translation products were immunoprecipitated with anti-PDHα and anti-PDHβ antisera and electrophoresed. The radiolabeled polypeptides were detected by fluorography. (*Lane 1*) mature PDHα, (*lane 2*) product (Pre α) translated from poly(A)⁺ RNA, (*lane 3*) Pre α obtained by translation of *in vitro* transcribed PDHα mRNA, (*lane 4*) mature PDHβ, (*lane 5*) product (Pre β) translated from poly(A)⁺ RNA, (*lane 6*) Pre β obtained by translation of *in vitro* transcribed PDHβ mRNA. The samples of mature PDHα and PDHβ were obtained by resolution of the porcine heart PDH complex.

43,000 (lane 2) and PDHβ with M_r 39,000 (lane 5), respectively. The PDHα and PDHβ inserts subcloned into expression vector pTZ18R synthesized mRNAs identical with the PDHα and PDHβ mRNAs obtained by *in vitro* transcription, as shown in FIGURE 7A, lanes 4 and 5; and these mRNAs also synthesized PDHα and PDHβ precursor proteins by in vitro translation, as shown in FIGURE 7B, lanes 3 and 6. These results show that pHPDA and pHPDB contain sequences that are compatible with human PDHα and PDHβ mRNAs.

To understand the pathogenesis of a congenital metabolic disorder involving a PDH defect, it is essential to isolate the genomic DNAs for PDHα and PDHβ and to determine their structure and the mechanism of their expression. Resolution of these questions awaits further study.

SUMMARY

The cDNAs encoding human PDHα and PDHβ were isolated from a HeLa cell cDNA library in the λgt11 expression vector by immunoscreening, followed by colony hybridization from a human foreskin fibroblast cDNA library. Nucleotide sequence analyses of the positive plasmid clones (pHPDA and pHPDB) revealed an insert of 1.36 kilobases (kb) for PDHα and one of 1.69 kb for PDHβ, respectively, allowing us to predict the complete amino acid sequences of the precursor and mature proteins of these two subunits. The amino acid sequences of the amino-terminal regions of the two subunits of human PDH were highly homologous with those of mature porcine PDH. The amino acid sequences of phosphorylation sites determined in PDHα of the bovine and porcine enzymes were also conserved in the human PDHα. Blot analysis of HeLa cell poly(A)$^+$ RNA and the transcriptional product of the two cDNAs showed a single mRNA of 1.8 kb for PDHα and one of 1.7 kb for PDHβ. The precursor proteins of PDHα and PDHβ were detected by immunoprecipitation from an ^{35}S-labeled, cell-free translation system. Our sequence of PDHα cDNA was compared with those of two other origins. The differences among these three PDHα cDNAs have been discussed.

ACKNOWLEDGMENTS

We thank Drs. P. J. Nielsen and H. Okayama for supplying human cDNA libraries.

REFERENCES

1. REED, L. J. 1974. Multienzyme complexes. Acc. Chem. Res. **7:** 40–46.
2. KOIKE, M. & K. KOIKE. 1976. Structure, assembly and function of mammalian α-keto acid dehydrogenase complexes. *In* Advances in Biophysics. M. Kotani, Ed. Vol. 9: 187–227. University of Tokyo Press. Tokyo.
3. HAYAKAWA, T., M. HIRASHIMA, S. IDE, M. HAMADA, K. OKABE, & M. KOIKE. 1966. Mammalian α-keto acid dehydrogenase complexes. I. Isolation, purificaiton, and properties of pyruvate dehydrogenase complex of pig heart muscle. J. Biol. Chem. **241:** 4694–4699.
4. HAYAKAWA, T., T. KANZAKI, T. KITAMURA, Y. FUKUYOSHI, Y. SAKURAI, K. KOIKE, T. SUEMATSU & M. KOIKE. 1969. Mammalian α-keto acid dehydrogenase complex. V. Resolution and reconstitution studies of the pig heart pyruvate dehydrogenase complex. J. Biol. Chem. **244:** 3660–3670.
5. HAMADA, M., T. HIRAOKA, K. KOIKE, K. OGASAHARA, T. KANZAKE & M. KOIKE. 1976. Properties and subunit structure of pig heart pyruvate dehydrogenase. J. Biochem. **79:** 1273–1285.
6. KOIKE, M., Y. URATA, K. KOIKE, A. TSUJI & M. MORIYASU. 1988. Novel separation of the component enzymes of pig heart pyruvate dehydrogenase complex by high-performance liquid chromatography. *In* Thiamin Pyrophosphate Biochemistry. A. Schellenberger & R. L. Schowen, Eds. Vol. 2: 37–43. CRC Press. Boca Raton, Fla.
7. LINN, T. C., J. W. PELLEY, F. H. PETTIT, F. HUCHO, D. D. RANDALL & L. J. REED. 1972. α-Keto acid dehydrogenase complexes. XV. Purification and properties of the component enzymes of the pyruvate dehydrogenase complexes from bovine kidney and heart. Arch. Biochem. Biophys. **148:** 327–342.
8. BARRERA, C. R., G. NAMIHIRA, L. HAMILTON, P. MUNK, M. H. ELEY, T. C. LINN & L. J. REED. 1972. α-Keto acid dehydrogenase complexes. XVI. Studies on the subunit structure of the pyruvate dehydrogenase complexes from bovine kidney and heart. Arch. Biochem. Biophys. **148:** 343–358.
9. MATUDA, S., T. SHIRAHAMA, T. SAHEKI, S. MIURA & M. MORI. 1983. Purification and immunochemical studies of pyruvate dehydrogenase complex from rat heart, and cell-free synthesis of lipoamide dehydrogenase, a component of the complex. Biochim. Biophys. Acta **741:** 86–93.
10. TSAI, C. S., M. W. BURGETT & L. J. REED. 1973. α-Keto acid dehydrogenase complexes. XX. A kinetic study of the pyruvate dehydrogenase complex from bovine kidney. J. Biol. Chem. **248:** 8348–8352.
11. HAMADA, M., K. KOIKE, Y. NAKAULA, T. HIRAOKA, M. KOIKE & T. HASHIMOTO. 1975. A kinetic study of the α-keto acid dehydrogenase complexes from pig heart mitochondria. J. Biochem. **77:** 1047–1056.

12. LINN, T. C., F. H. PETTIT, F. HUCHO & L. J. REED. 1969. α-Keto acid dehydrogenase complexes. X. Regulation of the activity of the pyruvate dehydrogenase complex from beef kidney mitochondria by phosphorylation and dephosphorylation. Proc. Natl. Acad. Sci. USA **62**: 234–241.

13. LINN, T. C., F. H. PETTIT, F. HUCHO & L. J. REED. 1969. α-Keto acid dehydrogenase complexes. XI. Comparative studies of regulatory properties of the pyruvate dehydrogenase complexes from kidney, heart, and liver mitochondria. Proc. Natl. Acad. Sci. USA **64**: 227–234.

14. YEAMAN, S. J., E. T. HUTCHESON, T. E. ROCHE, F. H. PETTIT, J. R. BROWN, L. J. REED, D. C. WATSON & G. H. DIXON. 1978. Sites of phosphorylation on pyruvate dehydrogenase from bovine kidney and heart. Biochemistry **17**: 2364–2370.

15. SUGDEN, P. H., A. L. KERBEY, P. J. RANDLE, C. A. WALTER & K. B. M. REID. 1979. Amino acid sequences around the sites of phosphorylation in the pig heart pyruvate dehydrogenase complex. Biochem. J. **181**: 419–426.

16. KOIKE, M. & K. KOIKE. 1982. Biochemical properties of mammalian 2-oxo acid dehydrogenase multienzyme complexes and clinical relevancy with chronic lactic acidosis. Ann. N.Y. Acad. Sci. **378**: 225–235.

17. KOIKE, K. 1988. Enzymatic studies of the genetic defect of pyruvate dehydrogenase in chronic pyruvic and lactic acidemia. *In* Thiamin Pyrophosphate Biochemistry. A. Schellenberger & R. L. Schowen, Eds. Vol. 2: 105–113. CRC Press. Boca Raton, Fla.

18. KOIKE, K., S. OHTA, Y. URATA, Y. KAGAWA & M. KOIKE. 1988. Cloning and sequencing of cDNAs encoding α and β subunits of human pyruvate dehydrogenase. Proc. Natl. Acad. Sci. USA **85**: 41–45.

19. NIELSEN, P. J., G. K. MCMASTER & H. TRACHSEL. 1985. Cloning of eukaryotic protein synthesis initiation factor genes: Isolation and characterization of cDNA clones encoding factor eIF-4A. Nucleic Acids Res. **13**: 6867–6880.

20. HERMODSON, M. A., R. W. KUHN, K. A. WALSH, H. NEURATH, N. ERIKSEN & E. P. BENDIT. 1972. Amino acid sequence of monkey amyloid protein A. Biochemistry **11**: 2934–2938.

21. YOUNG, R. A. & R. W. DAVIS. 1983. Efficient isolation of genes by using antibody probes. Proc. Natl. Acad. Sci. USA **80**: 1194–1198.

22. MANIATIS, T., E. F. FRITSCH & J. SAMBROOK. 1982. *In* Molecular Cloning: A Laboratory Manual. Cold Spring Harbor Laboratory. Cold Spring Harbor, NY.

23. GRUNSTEIN, M. & D. S. HOGNESS. 1975. Colony hybridization: A method for the isolation of cloned DNAs that contain a specific gene. Proc. Natl. Acad. Sci. USA **72**: 3961–3965.

24. DEININGER, P. L. 1983. Random subcloning of sonicated DNA: Application to shotgun DNA sequence analysis. Anal. Biochem. **129**: 216–223.

25. MESSING, J. 1983. New M13 vectors for cloning. *In* Methods in Enzymology, Recombinant DNA, Part C. R. Wu, L. Grossman, K. Maldave, Eds. Vol. 101: 20–78.

26. SANGER, F., S. NICKLEN & A. R. COULSON. 1977. DNA sequencing with chain-terminating inhibitors. Proc. Natl. Acad. Sci. USA **74**: 5463–5467.

27. SANCHEZ-PESCADOR, R. & M. S. URDEA. 1984. Laboratory Methods. Use of unpurified synthetic deoxynucleotide primers for rapid dideoxynucleotide chain termination sequencing. DNA **3**: 339–343.

28. LAEMMLI, U. K. 1970. Cleavage of structural proteins during the assembly of the head of bacteriophage T4. Nature **227**: 680–685.

29. CHIRGWIN, J. M., A. E. PRZYBYLA, R. MACDONALD & W. J. RUTTER. 1979. Isolation of biologically active ribonucleic acid from source enriched in ribonuclease. Biochemistry **18**: 5294–5299.

30. AVIV, H. & P. LEDER. 1972. Purification of biologically active globin messenger RNA by chromatography on oligothymidylic acid–cellulose. Proc. Natl. Acad. Sci. USA **69**: 1408–1412.

31. ONO, H., N. YOSHIMURA, N. SATO & S. TUBOI. 1985. Translocation of proteins into rat liver mitochondria, existence of two different precursor polypeptides of liver fumarase and import of the precursor into mitochondria. J. Biol. Chem. **260**: 3402–3407.

32. KOIKE, K. & Y. URATA. 1989. Chronic acidemia due to a pyruvate dehydrogenase deficiency in the pyruvate dehydrogenase complex, with evidence of abnormalities of the α- and β-subunits of the enzyme. Ann. N.Y. Acad. Sci. This volume.
33. DAHL, H-H. M., S. M. HUNT, W. M. HUTCHISON & G. K. BROWN. 1987. The human pyruvate dehydrogenase complex. Isolation of cDNA clones for the E1 subunit, sequence analysis, and characterization of the mRNA. J. Biol. Chem. **262:** 7398–7403.
34. DE MEIRELEIR, L., N. MACKEY, A. M. LAM HON WAH & B. H. ROBINSON. 1988. Isolation of a full-length complementary DNA coding for human $E_{1\alpha}$ subunit of the pyruvate dehydrogenase complex. J. Biol. Chem. **263:** 1991–1995.

Molecular Biology of the Human Pyruvate Dehydrogenase Complex: Structural Aspects of the E_2 and E_3 Components[a]

THOMAS J. THEKKUMKARA, GABRIEL PONS,[b]
SUMAIR MITROO, JOYCE E. JENTOFT,
AND MULCHAND S. PATEL[c]

Department of Biochemistry
Case Western Reserve University School of Medicine
Cleveland, Ohio 44106

INTRODUCTION

The mammalian pyruvate dehydrogenase complex (PDC) catalyzes the oxidative decarboxylation of pyruvate to acetyl-CoA according to the overall reaction:

$$\text{Pyruvate} + \text{CoA} + \text{NAD}^+ \rightarrow \text{Acetyl-CoA} + \text{CO}_2 + \text{NADH} + \text{H}^+$$

Mammalian PDC contains multiple copies of six different components: pyruvate dehydrogenase (E_1), dihydrolipoamide acetyltransferase (E_2), dihydrolipoamide dehydrogenase (E_3), protein X, E_1-specific kinase, and phospho-E_1 phosphatase.[1-4] The first three components (E_1, E_2, and E_3) are the major catalytic components. The E_1 component is a tetramer ($\alpha_2\beta_2$) composed of two non-identical subunits (α: M_r, 41,000 and β: M_r, 36,000). $E_1\alpha$ is subject to covalent modification by phosphorylation (inactivation) by its kinase and dephosphorylation (activation) by its phosphatase. The E_2 monomers (60 identical polypeptide chains; M_r, 52,000) interact noncovalently through a core-forming domain (also referred to as the subunit-interacting or catalytic domain), thus forming the central core of the PDC complex. The other components of the complex are attached to this central core by noncovalent interactions. The E_2 monomer contains at least one molecule of lipoic acid in amide linkage to the ϵ-amino group of a lysyl residue in the lipoyl-bearing domain. This, in turn, is connected to the core-forming domain by a trypsin-sensitive hinge region. Thus, E_2 has both catalytic and structural functions. The E_2 core shows icosahedral (532) symmetry, and its morphological subunits are situated at the vertices of a pentagonal dodecahedron.[2,3] A recently identified protein X component in mammalian PDC also contains a covalently linked lipoyl moiety, and the involvement of this protein in the binding of E_1-kinase to the core of the complex has been suggested.[5] E_3, a homodimer (subunit M_r, 51,000), contains one noncovalently attached molecule of FAD per monomer. It reoxidizes the reduced form of the lipoyl moiety linked to the E_2 polypeptides and transfers the electrons to NAD^+, forming NADH. In addition to its presence in the PDC, the E_3 component is also present in two similar complexes, α-ketoglutarate dehydrogenase

[a]The work performed in this laboratory and reported in this review was supported by U.S. Public Health Service Grant AM 20478.

[b]Supported by a Fulbright-Ministerio de Education y Ciencia grant.

[c]Address correspondence to Dr. M. S. Patel, Department of Biochemistry, Case Western Reserve University School of Medicine, 2119 Abington Road, Cleveland, OH 44106.

complex (α-KGDC) and the branched-chain α-keto acid dehydrogenase complex (BCKADC), as well as in the glycine cleavage system.

We and other investigators have independently isolated and characterized full-length cDNA clones for the E_2[6–9] and E_3[10–13] components of PDC from human and other eukaryotic species and have generated the primary amino acid sequences of these two proteins. In this paper, we will present our own findings and review the available information on the primary amino acid sequences of these proteins from both eukaryotes and prokaryotes. Comparison of structures and functions of these two proteins will also be discussed.

STRUCTURAL ASPECTS OF HUMAN PDC-E$_2$

Isolation of Cloned cDNAs for PDC-E$_2$ mRNA

Using specific polyclonal antibodies raised against bovine kidney PDC-E$_2$ (generously provided by Dr. Lester Reed), several PDC-E$_2$ cDNA clones were isolated from a human liver λgt11 cDNA expression library.[14] The characterization of these cDNA clones has been described previously.[8] The identity of these clones was established by matching the deduced amino acid sequence from the nucleotide sequences of these clones with that of previously published partial amino acid sequence of mammalian PDC-E$_2$. Details of one of our E$_2$ cDNA clones are depicted in FIGURE 1.

PDC-E$_2$ cDNA consists of 2583 base-pairs with an open reading frame of 1848 base-pairs, corresponding to a mature protein of 561 amino acids, with a calculated molecular mass of 59,551 daltons and a partial leader sequence of 54 amino acids.[8] The molecular mass increases to 59,927 daltons when two molecules of lipoic acid are covalently linked to mature PDC-E$_2$. Northern blot analysis of RNA isolated from human heart and rat kidney revealed the presence of three hybridizing species of approximately 2.3, 2.9, and 4.0 kilobases (kb) in size[8] (FIG. 2). Coppel et al.[7] have recently isolated from a human placental cDNA library an E$_2$ cDNA clone (2540 bp) with a deduced amino acid sequence of 614 amino acids. Several amino acid residues (numbers 26, 256, 272, and 363–368) in mature human liver PDC-E$_2$[8] differ from the corresponding amino acids in human placental E$_2$.[7] Furthermore, the first 30 amino acid residues of the leader sequence of human placental PDC-E$_2$[7] do not match with

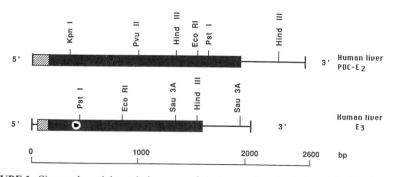

FIGURE 1. Sizes and partial restriction maps of the human liver PDC-E$_2$ and E$_3$ cDNA clones. The *hatched* and *solid boxes* represent coding regions for the leader peptide and mature polypeptide, respectively; *solid lines* represent the noncoding regions of the clone. bp, base-pair.

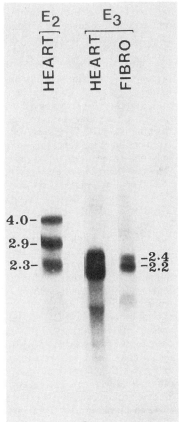

FIGURE 2. Northern blot analysis of RNA from human heart and fibroblasts. The specified amounts of total RNA were fractionated by electrophoresis on a formaldehyde-agarose gel, transferred to a Gene-Screen membrane, and probed.[8,11] E$_2$ **blot:** 25 μg of heart total RNA. E$_3$ **blot:** 20 μg of heart total RNA and 15 μg of poly(A)$^+$ RNA from human skin fibroblasts (FIBRO). The size of the RNA (kb) was determined by comparing its electrophoretic mobility with that of ribosomal RNAs.

the corresponding amino acid sequence in the signal sequence of human liver PDC-E$_2$.[8] Although some of these variations can be ascribed to individual and/or species differences, it is conceivable that the larger differences may be artifactual. Differences are also observed in the numbers and sizes of mRNA species identified from total cellular RNA isolated from human cells by the liver- and placental-specific PDC-E$_2$ cDNAs. In contrast to the detection of three mRNA species (2.3, 2.9 and 4.0 kb in size) by our PDC-E$_2$ cDNA clone,[8] the PDC-E$_2$ cDNA isolated by Coppel *et al.*[7] hybridized with several mRNA species, notably with species of 2.7, 2.9 and 3.2 kb in size. Several different mechanisms (such as the presence of related genes, alternate splicing sites, multiple polyadenylation signals, etc.) could account for these differences. Further analysis is required to clarify these discrepancies.

Primary Structure of Human PDC-E$_2$ and Comparison with E$_2$ from Other α-Keto Acid Dehydrogenase Complexes of Prokaryotic and Eukaryotic Origin

Earlier, Bleile *et al.*[15] showed that limited proteolytic digestion of mammalian PDC-E$_2$ results in the formation of two large fragments, a compact domain (also referred to as the catalytic domain) and a flexible, lipoyl-bearing domain. The deduced amino acid sequence of human PDC-E$_2$ (FIGURE 3) shows the presence of an amino-terminal lipoyl-bearing domain (amino acids 1–254) and the carboxyl-terminal catalytic domain (amino acids 331–561) linked by the E$_3$-binding region (amino acids 254–330). Examination of the lipoyl-bearing domain of human PDC-E$_2$ reveals the presence of two similar, but not identical (55% homology), repeating units of 127 amino acids (FIG. 3). Each repeating unit contains a highly conserved region of 38 amino acids (71% homology, FIG. 4) encompassing the lipoyl-binding lysyl residue and including a carboxyl-terminal region rich in alanine and proline residues. In contrast to mammalian PDC-E$_2$, *Escherichia coli* PDC-E$_2$[16,17] and *Azotobacter vinelandii* PDC-E$_2$[18] contain three repeating units of approximately 100–110 amino acids. However, only one (repeating) unit is present in the lipoyl-bearing domain of PDC-E$_2$ from *Bacillus stearothermophilus*[19] and *Saccharomyces cerevisiae*[9,13] (FIGS. 3 and 5). It should be noted that, in contrast to the presence of two or more lipoyl-binding sites in PDC-E$_2$ from *E. coli, A. vinelandii* and humans, the E$_2$ polypeptides of *E. coli* α-KGDC[17] and BCKADC from *Pseudomonas putida*,[20] bovines[21] and humans[21,22] contain only one lipoyl-binding lysyl residue in a unit composed of about 110 amino acids (FIG. 5). Each repeating unit in these PDC-E$_2$ components shows considerable conservation of amino acid residues in the 38-residue sequence encompassing the lipoyl-binding lysyl residue (FIG. 4). Another difference between *E. coli* PDC-E$_2$ and human PDC-E$_2$ is that the former, but not the latter, contains short internal repeating sequences within each of the three 100-residue repeating units (e.g., internal repeats from amino acids 16 to 34 and 53 to 70 in the first repeating unit).[17] Genetic manipulation of the PDC-E$_2$ gene (*aceF*) in *E. coli* elegantly demonstrated that the overall catalytic activity of PDC and active site coupling are not altered by the removal of up to two of the three lipoyl-bearing repeats in the E$_2$ polypeptide.[23]

Although the carboxyl-terminal region of each repeating unit in PDC-E$_2$ is extremely rich in alanine and proline residues, their relative distribution is quite different between the two repeating units in both the human and the rat PDC-E$_2$. The alanine:proline ratio is >1 (10:9 in human and 16:6 in rat) in repeating unit I and <1 (3:13 in human and 4:13 in rat) in repeating unit II (FIG. 3). This is in contrast to PDC-E$_2$ in *E. coli* and *A. vinelandii*, in which the molar ratio of alanine:proline is relatively constant (>1) among the three repeating units[17,18] (FIG. 3). The significance of these differences is unclear at the present time.

On the basis of sequence homology among the E$_2$ components of the three α-keto acid dehydrogenase complexes, a stretch of 32 amino acids has been identified as an E$_3$-binding site.[22,24] This sequence is also present in human PDC-E$_2$ (amino acids 272–303). In this region, sequence homology as compared to human PDC-E$_2$ is very high for rat PDC-E$_2$ (91%) and *E. coli* PDC-E$_2$ (50%), and also for the E$_2$ components from α-KGDC and BCKADC (40–50%) (FIG. 6). In addition, several amino acid residues within this region are strictly conserved in all the E$_2$ sequences that were compared (FIGS. 4 and 6; see also Ref. 22), suggesting that these amino acids are critical to the recognition of E$_3$.

The catalytic domain (or subunit-binding domain) at the carboxyl-terminal region of PDC-E$_2$ confers specificity for both subunit and substrate interactions. Comparison of the primary amino acid sequences of the catalytic domains of PDC-E$_2$ from four different species revealed that approximately 24% of the amino acids are conserved in these polypeptides (FIG. 3). Although the conserved amino acid residues are distributed throughout the domain, we have identified three separate areas with considerable homologies in this domain (amino acid numbers belong to human PDC-E$_2$: area I, 13 amino acids from 428 to 440 with 62% homology; area II, 22 amino acids from 462 to 483 with 41% homology; and area III, 14 amino acids from 530 to 543 with 36%

```
                    <---------------------------------Lipoyl-bearing domain--------------------------->
H-E2-I    -SLPPH-QKVPLPSLSPTM-QAGTIARWKKKEGDKINEGDLIAEVEDKATVGFESLEECYMAKILVAEGTRDVPIGAIICITVGKPEDIEAFKNYTLDSSAAPTPQAAPAPTPAATASPPTS-AQAPGS        127
H-E2-II   -SYPPHMQ-VLLPALSPTMI-MGTVQRWEKKVGEKLSEGDLLAEIETDKATIGFEVQEEGYLAKILVPEGTRDVPLGTPLCIIVEKEADISAFADYRPTEVTDLKPQVPPTPPVAAVPPTPQ-PLAPTP      254

R-E2-I    ----------------------------------------------------------------------------------------GPEAFKNYTLDSATAAT---QAAPA-PAAAPAAAPAAPSASAPGS  41
R-E2-II   -SYPVHMQIV-LPALSPTMI-MGTVQRWEKKVGEKLSEGDLLAEIETDKATIGFEVQEEGYLAKILVPEGTRDVPLGTPLCIIVEKQEDIAAFADYRPTEVTSLKPQAPPVPPPVAAVPPIPQ-PLAPTP      168

Y-E2      ASYPEHTII-GMPALSPTMTQGNLAA-WTKKEGDLSPGEVIAEIETDKAQMDFEFQEDGYLAKILVPEGTKDIPVNKPIAVYVEDKADVPA-FKDFKLEDSGSDSKTTSKAQPAEPQAEKKQEAPAET-      127

S-E2      A--FEFK-----LPDIGEGI-HEGEIVKWFVKPGDEVNEDDVLCEVQNDKAVVEIPSPVKGKVLEIIVPEGTVATVGQT-L-ITLDAPGYENMTFKGQEQEAK-KEEKTETVSKEEKVDAVA-PNAPAA--    118

E-E2-I    A--IEIK--V--PDIGADF-EVEITEII---VKVGDKVEAEQSLITVEGDKASMEVPSPQAGIVKEIKVSVGDK-TQTGA-L-IMIFDSADGAADAA------PA---QAEEKK--EAA---PAAAPAAAA-   104
E-E2-II   ---KDVN--V--PDIGSD-EVEITEIL---VKVGDKVEAEQSLITVEGDKASMEVPAPFAGTVKEIKVNVGDK-VSTGS-L-IMVFEVA-GEAGAAA-P----AAK-Q-E-----AA--PAAAPAPAA-G    204
E-E2-III  --VKEVN--V--PDIGD-EVEVTEVM---VKVGDKVAAEQSLITVEGDKASMEVPAPFAGVVKELKVNVGDK-VKTGS-L-IMIFEVE-G-AAPAAAP------AK-QEAAAPAPAAKAEAPAA--APAA--    311

A-E2-I    -SEII-R--V--PDIGGDG--EVIELL--VKTGDLIEVEQGLVVLESAKASMEVPSPKAGVVKSVSVKLGDK-LKEGDA--IIELEPAAGAAAAPAEAAAVPAAPTQAVDEARAPSPGASAT-PAPAAA-    116
A-E2-II   -SQ-EVR--V--PDIGSAGKARVIEVL--VKAGDQVOAEQSLIIVLESDKASMEIPSPASGVVESVAIQLNAE-VGTGD-L-ILTLRTT-G-AQA-------QPTAPAAAAASPAPL-APAAAG         221
A-E2-III  P-Q-EVK--V--PDIGSAGKARVIEVL--VKAGDQVOAEQSLIVLESDKASMEIPSPAAGVVESVAVQLNAE-VGTGD--ILTLRVA-GAAPSGPR--A-RGSPGQ----AAAA-PGAAPAP-APVGA--    325


                   <-------------Dihydrolipoamide dehydrogenase binding site------------->
H-E2      SAPCPATP------AGPKGRVFVSPLAKKLAVEKGIDLTQVKGTGPDGRITKKDIDSFVPS----KVAP-A-PAAVPP------>                                               321
R-E2      SA-APAGPK-------GRVFVSPLAKKLAAEKGIDLTQVKGTGPEGRIIKKDIDSFVPT----KAAPAA--AAAAPP------                                                 231
Y-E2      KTSAPEAKKSDVAAPQGRIFASPLAKTIALEKGISLKDVHGTGPRGRITKADIESYLEKSS-KQSSQTSGAAAATPAAAT                                                    206
S-E2      EAEAGPNRR--VIA----MPSVRKYAREKGVDIRLVGGTGKNGRVLKEDIDAFLAGGA-KPAPAAAEKAA-PAAAKPA                                                      189
E-E2      KAE-GKSEFAEND----AYVHATPLIRRLAREFGVNLAKVKGTGRKGRILREDVQAYVKEAI-KRAEAA--------PAAT---                                                378
A-E2      PS----RNG-------AKVHAGPAVRQLAREFGVELAAINSTGPRGRILKEDVQAYVKAMMQKAKEA--------PAA-GAA                                                   390


                   <---------------------------------Catalytic domain--------------------------->
H-E2      TGPGMAPVPTGVFTDIP-ISNIR--RV--IAQR-LMQSKQTIPHYYLSIDVNMGEVLLVRKELNKILEGRS----KISVNDFIIKASALACLKVPEANSSWMDTVIRQNHVVDS--VAVSTPAGLIT     437
R-E2      ---GPRVAPTPAGVFIDIP-ISNIR--RV--IAQR-LMQSKQTIPHYLSVDVNMGEVLVRKELNKMLEGKG---KISVNDFIIKASALACLKVPEANSSWMDTVIRQNHVVDS--VAVSTPAGLIT      346
Y-E2      SSTTAGSAPSPSTASYEDVPISTMRSIIGE---RLL-QSTOGIPSYIVSSKISISK-LLKLRQSLNATANDKYKLSINDLLVKAITVAAKRVPDANAYWLPNENVIRKFKNVDVS--VAVATPTGLLT    328
S-E2      ---TTEGEFPET--RE-KM---SGIR--RA--IAK---                                                                                             211
E-E2      GGGIPGMLPWPKVDFSKFGEIEVELGRIQKISGANLSRNWVMIPHVTHFDKTDITELEAFRKQQNEEAAKRLDVKITPVVFIMKAVAAALEQMPRFNSSLSEDGQRILTKKYINIGVAVDTPNGLVV    507
A-E2      SGAGIPPIP-PVDFAKYGEIEEVPMTRLMQ-IGATNLHRSWLNVPHVTQFESADITELEAFRVAQ-K-AVAEKAGVKLTVLPLLLKACAYLLKELPDFNSSLAFSGQALIRKKVHIGFAVDTPDGLIV    515


                   <---------------------------------Catalytic domain--------------------------->
H-E2      PIVFNAHI-KGVETIANDVVSLATKAREGKLQPHEFQGGTFTISNLGMFGIKNFSAIINPP-QACILAI-GASEDKLVPADNEKGFDVASMMSVTLSCDHRVVDGAVGAQWLAEFRKYLEKPITMLL     561
R-E2      PIVFNAHI-KGLETIASDVVSLASKAREGKLQPHEFQGGTTTISNLGMFGIKNFSAIINPP-QACILAI-GASEDKLVPADNEKGFDVASVMSVTHS----AVIIE-LWMEQ--LE-P-SGLL         457
Y-E2      PIVKNCEA-KGLSQISNEIKELVKRARINKLAPEEFQGGTIC ISNMGMNNAVNMFTSIINPQSTILAIATVERVAVEDAAAENGSFDNQVTITGTFDHRTIDGAKGAEFMKELKTVIENPLEMLL      454
S-E2      ---                                                                                                                              ---
E-E2      P-VFKDVNKKGIIELSRELMTISKKARDGKLTAGEMQGGCFTISSIGGLGTHFAPIVNAPE-VAII----GVSKSAMEPVWNGKEFVPRLMLPISLSFDHRVIDGADGARFITIINNTLSDIRRLVM     629
A-E2      P-VIRNVDQKSLLQLAEAEAELAEKARSKKIGADAMQGACFTISSLGHIGGTAFTPIVNAPE-VAIL----GVSKASMQPVWDGKAFQPRLMLPLSLSYDHRVINGAAAARFTKRLGDLLADIRAILL    637
```

FIGURE 3. Alignment of amino acid sequences of six different PDC-E₂ polypeptides from human (**H**) liver,[8] rat (**R**) liver,[9] *S. cerevisiae* (**Y**),[6] *B. stearothermophilus* (**S**),[19] *E. coli* (**E**),[16] and *A. vinelandii* (**A**).[18] *Hyphens* represent spacing to align the sequences and are not included in the numbering of residues. An amino acid residue present in the aligned position of all six proteins is identified by an *asterisk* (★); a residue present in the aligned position of six or more sequences in the lipoyl-bearing repeating units or of three or more of the proteins in the E₃-binding site or in the catalytic domain is indicated by a *plus* (+) *sign at the bottom of the sequence*. The boundaries of the three domains are indicated by *dashed lines at the top of the sequence*.

		*		
H-PE2 (I)	G D K I N E G D L I A E V E T D K A T V G F E S L E E C Y M A K I L V A E G	(100%)
(II)	G E K L S E G D L L A E I E T D K A T I G F E V Q E E G Y L A K I L L V P E G	(71%)
R-PE2 (II)	G E K A L S P G E V L A E H E T D K A T A A F E V Q E E D G Y L A K I L V P E G	(71%)
Y-PE2	G D Q L S P G E V L C E V Q N D D K K A S M E V P S P V K G K V L E I K V S V G	(59%)
S-PE2	G D E V N E A E Q S L H I T V E G D K A S M E V P A P F A G V V K E I K V N V G	(45%)
E-PE2 (I)	G D K V E A A E Q S L H T T V E G D K A S M E V P A P F A G V V K E L K V N V G	(29%)
(II)	G D K V E A A E Q S L H T T V L E S D K A S M E V P S P K A G V V K E L K V N V G	(29%)
(III)	G D K V A A E Q S L H V H V L E G D A A S M E I P S P K A G V V E S V K L G	(26%)
A-PE2 (I)	G D L I H E V A E Q S L H V L E V Q D K K A S M E I P S P A A G V V E S V A V Q L N	(24%)
(II)	G D L Q V Q A E Q S L H V L E V Q D K K A S M E I P S P A A G V V E S V H I K K L N	(18%)
(III)	G D Q V V S Q F D S H I H H V T S R Y D G S R Y D K L Y Y N L D	(21%)
H-BE2	G D T V S Q F D S H I C E V Q S S D K A S V T H I T S R Y D G V H K K L Y Y N L D	(32%)
C-BE2	G D I H A C D Q V V A D V M T D K A T V E I P S P V S G K V L A L G G Q P G	(32%)
P-BE2	G D A V V R D E V L V E I E T D K V V L E V P A S A D G I L D A V L E D E G	(32%)
E-KE2	G D A V V R D E V L V E I E T D K V V L E V P A S A D G I L D A V L E D E G	(29%)

FIGURE 4. Lipoyl-binding region. Comparison of the amino acid sequences of the 38-residual region surrounding the lipoyl-binding lysyl residue (★) in the repeating units of the lipoyl-bearing domains of the E₂ components of PDC (**P**), BCKADC (**B**) and α-KGDC (**K**) from both prokaryotes and eukaryotes. (**H**) human, (**R**) rat, (**Y**) *S. cerevisiae*, (**S**) *B. stearothermophilus*, (**E**) *E. coli*, (**A**) *A. vinelandii*, (**C**) bovine, and (**P**) *P. putida*. Roman numerals (**I–III**) indicate the repeating unit in this domain. Percent homology with the H-PE₂(I) sequence is shown at *right*. Any amino acid residue present in the aligned position of six or more of the fifteen sequences is enclosed in a *box*.

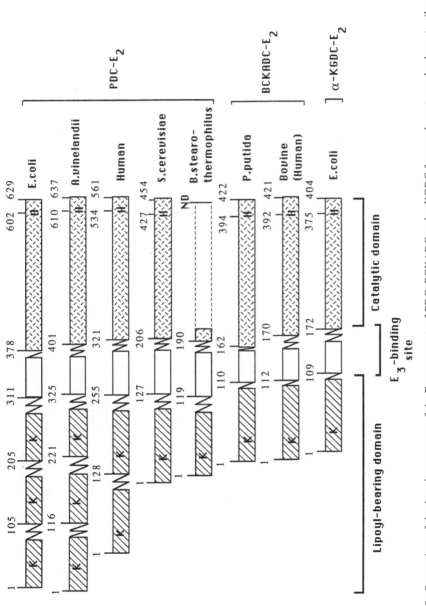

FIGURE 5. Comparison of the domain structures of the E₂ components of PDC, BCKADC and α-KGDC from prokaryotes and eukaryotes (based on a previously described model[23]). The amino acid residues indicating the limits of these domains are approximate. (**K**) lipoyl-binding lysine, (**H**) histidine residue, (▧) lipoyl-bearing repeating units, (☐) E₃-binding site, (▦) catalytic domain, and (Ⱳ) region rich in alanine and proline.

E_3-BINDING SITE

```
H-PE2: 272-303  S P L A K K L A V E K G I D L T Q V K G T G P D G R I T K K D I  (100%)
R-PE2: 182-213  S P L A K K L A A E K G I D L T Q V K G T G P E G R I I K K D I  ( 91%)
Y-PE2: 149-181  S P L A K T I A L E K G I S L K D V H G T G P R G R I T K A D I  ( 69%)
S-PE2: 131-162  M P S V R K Y A R E K G V D I R L V Q G T G K N G R V L K E D I  ( 50%)
E-PE2: 329-360  T P L I R R L A R E F G V N L A K V K G T G R K G R I L R E D V  ( 50%)
A-PE2: 336-367  G P A V R Q L A R E F G V E L A A I N S T G P R G R I L K E D V  ( 41%)
E-KE2: 114-145  S P A I R R L L A E H N L D A S A I K G T G V G G R L T R E D V  ( 41%)
P-BE2: 138-169  S P A V R K R A L D A G I E L R Y V H G S G P A G R I L H E D L  ( 47%)
H-BE2: 113-144  T P A V R R L A M E N N I K L S E V V G S G K D G R I L K E D I  ( 50%)
C-BE2: 113-144  T P A V R R L A M E N N I K L S E V I G S G K D G R I L K E D I  ( 50%)
```

CoA-INTERACTING SITE

```
H-PE2: 530-543  L S C D H R V V D G A V G A  (100%)
R-PE2: 439-444  H S - - - - - - - - - A V I I  ( -- )
Y-PE2: 423-436  G T F D H R T I D G A K G A  ( 57%)
E-PE2: 598-608  L S F D H R V I D G A D G A  ( 79%)
A-PE2: 606-619  L S Y D H R V I N G A A A A  ( 64%)
E-KE2: 371-384  L S Y D H R L I D G R E S V  ( 50%)
P-BE2: 390-403  S S F D H R V V D G M D A A  ( 57%)
C-BE2: 387-400  W S A D H R I I D G A T V S  ( 50%)
```

FIGURE 6. Comparison of the amino acid sequences of the 32-residue region (E_3-binding site) and the 14-residue region (CoA-interacting site) located near the carboxyl terminus of the E_2 components from PDC (**P**), α-KGDC (**K**), and BCKADC (**B**) from human (**H**), rat (**R**), *B. stearothermophilus* (**S**), *S. cerevisiae* (**Y**), *E. coli* (**E**), *A. vinelandii* (**A**), *P. putida*, (**P**), and bovine (**C**) enzymes. Any amino acid residue present in the aligned position for at least five of the ten sequences for the E_3-binding site or at least four of the eight sequences for the CoA-interacting site is enclosed in a *box*. Percent homology with the H-PE_2 sequence is shown at *right*.

homology). The amino acid sequence in area III (specifically the histidyl residue) of PDC-E_2 is most likely to be involved in interacting with CoA.[25] Approximately 50% homology is observed in this CoA-interacting region in the catalytic domain from the E_2 components of BCKADC[20,26] and α-KGDC[17] as compared to the corresponding region in human PDC-E_2 (FIG. 6). We speculate that areas I and II are potential sites for homo- and hetero-subunit interactions in this domain.

STRUCTURAL ASPECTS OF HUMAN E_3

Isolation of Cloned cDNAs from E_3 mRNA

Several prokaryotic and eukaryotic E_3 components have recently been cloned,[10-13,27,28] and their primary amino acid sequences have been deduced and compared with each other and with human glutathione reductase (GR; for review see Ref. 29). Using monospecific polyclonal antibodies raised against pig heart E_3, we isolated two E_3 cDNA clones from a human liver λgt11 cDNA expression library.[11] Their identity as E_3 cDNA was established by matching the deduced amino acid sequence with the known partial amino acid sequence of pig heart E_3. The details of one of these two cDNA clones are presented in FIGURE 1. The nucleotide sequence of the E_3 cDNA clone consists of 2082 base-pairs and contains an open reading frame of 1527 base-pairs encoding the precursor E_3 polypeptide of 509 amino acids. The first 35 amino acids of this precursor protein represent a typical mitochondrial import leader sequence. The mature E_3 of 474 amino acids has a calculated molecular mass of 50,216 daltons, which increases to 50,919 daltons when the molecular mass of 703 daltons for an FAD molecule is added. Our findings on the primary amino acid sequence of human mature E_3[11] are identical (except for differences in two amino acids, Lys-69 versus Thr-69 and Arg-119 versus Gly-119) with those reported independently by Otula-kowski and Robinson.[10] The observation of two hybridizable E_3 mRNA species (2.2 and 2.4 kb) in human tissues[11] is consistent with the presence of two polyadenylation signals located approximately 0.2 kb apart in a human liver E_3 cDNA clone.[10,11]

Comparison of the Primary Amino Acid Sequences of E_3 Components and Structural Similarities of Homologous Flavoproteins

Although the complete amino acid sequence of *E. coli* E_3 was first reported by Stephens *et al.*[27] in 1983, it was only in 1987–1988 that the primary amino acid sequences of E_3 from four additional sources have been presented and compared with the *E. coli* E_3 and glutathione reductase[10-13,28] (for review see Ref. 29). A comparison of the primary amino acid sequence (FIG. 7) of mature E_3 from human liver and from pig heart shows 96% homology. However, the degree of homology decreases as one decends on the evolutionary tree, such that porcine E_3 and *E. coli* E_3 show 96% and 44% homology, respectively, with human E_3.[10,11] Comparison of the primary amino acid sequences of E_3 from human, pig, yeast, *A. vinelandii*, and *E. coli* is shown in FIGURE 7. From crystallographic studies performed at 1.4-Å resolution, the tertiary structure of human erythrocyte GR, a dimeric flavoprotein, has been deduced, and the role of several specific amino acid residues in catalysis has been elucidated.[30-33] The four structural domains in human GR, namely the FAD (residues 1–157), the NADPH (residues 158–293), the central (residues 294–364), and the interface (residues 365–478) domains, have been identified.[30-31] By comparing the primary amino acid sequences of several E_3 components with that of human GR, the four domains can be

```
-----------------------------------------FAD DOMAIN------------------------------------------
       +       ++  ++*    *++*+++++*+++*++++*+++*++++++     +  ++++ +*+  +++  +
E-E3 ---------STEIKTQVVLGAGPAGYSAAFRCADLGLETVIVERYN-------TLGGVCLNVGCIPSKALLHVAKVIEEA--KALAEHGIVFG-EPKTD    81
A-E3 ---------SQKFDVIVIGAGPGGYVAAIKSAQLGLKTALIEKYKGKEGKTALGTCLNVGCIPSKALLDSSYKFHEAH-ESFKLHGISTG-EVAID    86
Y-E3 --------TINKSHDVVIIGGGPAGYVAAIKAAQLGFNTACVEKRG-----KLGGTCLNVGCIPSKALLNNSHLFHQMHTEAQK-RGIDVNGDIKIN    83
P-E3 --------ADQPIDADVTVIGSGPGGYVAAIKAAQLGFKTVCIEKNE------TLGGTCLNVGCIPSKALLNNSHYHMAHGKDFASRGIEMS-EVRLN  84
H-E3 --------ADQPIDADVTVIGSGPGGYVAAIKAAQLGFKTVCIEKNE------TLGGTCLNVGCIPSKALLNNSHYHMAHGKDFASRGIEMS-EVRLN  84
H-GR ACRQEPQPQGPPAAGAVASYDYLVIGGGSGLASARRAAELGARAAVVESH-----KLGGTCVNVGCVPKKVMWNTAVHSEFMH--DHADYGFPSC-EGKFN  95
        <--->  <-------------->  <-------------->             <-------------------->
           βF-3        αI            βF-2                           αII

-----------FAD DOMAIN------------------              >--------><----------NAD (NADPH) DOMAIN----------------
    ++  + +++  *+++  +  +*+ +++++ +++++ +++             ++++++++++*+++++ +++++  ++++++    +++++++++++++++++
E-E3 IDKIRTWKEKVINQLTGGLAG-MAKGRKVKVVNGLGKFTGANTLEVEGEN---------GKTVINFDNAIIAAGSRP-IQLPF-IP-HEDPRIWDSTDALELKEVPE  175
A-E3 VPTMIARKDQIVRNLTGGVAS-LIKANGVTLFEGHGKLLAGKKVEVTAAD--------GSSQVLDTENVILASGSKP-VEIPP-APVDQD-VIVDSTGALDFQNVPG  181
Y-E3 VANFQKAKDDAVKQLTGGIEL-LFKKNKVTYKGNGSFEDETKIRVTPVDGLEGTVKEDHILDVKNIIVATGSEV-TPFPG-IEIDEE-IVSSTGALSLKEIPK    184
P-E3 LEKMMEQKSNAVKALTGGIAH-LFKQNKVVRVNGYGKITGKNQVTATKADG------STEVINTKNILIATGSEV-TPFPG-ITIDED-TVVSSTGALSLKKVPE  179
H-E3 LDKMMEQKSTAVKALTGGIAH-LFKQNKVVHVNGYGKITGKNQVTATKADG------GTQVIDTKNILIATGSEV-TPFPG-ITIDED-TIVSSTGALSLKKVPE  179
H-GR WRVIKEKRDAYVSRLNAIYQNNLTKSHIEIIR-GHAAFTSDPKPTIEVS-G------KKYTAP--HILIATGGMPSTPHESQIPGASL-GITS-DGFQLEELPG  188
   <-------------------->      <--->  <--->  <--->               <-->   <--->   <--->
          αIII              βF-1 βM-3 βM-2   βM-1       βF-4      βN-1      αIV

---------------------NAD (NADPH) DOMAIN------------------------------------------------------------------
  ++++++++*+*+++++++++ +*** +++++         +                    *  +++++++++*+* +++++++ ++ +  ++++ ++ + +++  +    +++++++++**
E-E3 RLLVMGGGIIGLEMGTVYHALGSQIDVVEMFDQVIPAA-DKDIVKVFTKRISKK-FNLMLETKVTAVEAK-EDGIYVTMEGKKAP-AEPQRY-----DAVLVAIGR  272
A-E3 KLGVIGAGVIGELGSVWARLGAEVTVLEAMDKFLPAV-DEQVAKEAQKILTKQGLKILLGARVTGTEVKNKQ---VTVKFVDAEGEKSQAF----DKLIVAVGR  278
Y-E3 RLTIGGGIIGLEMGSVVSRLGSKVTVVEFQPIGASM-DGEVAKATQKFLKKQGLDFKLSTKVISAKRNDDK-NVEIVVEDTKTNKQENLEA--EVLLVAVGR  285
P-E3 KMVVIGAGVIGVELGSVWQRLGADVTAVELLGHVGGIGIDMEVSKNFQRILQKQGFKFKLNTKVIGATKKSDGNIDVSIEAASGGKAEVITC----DVLLVCIGR  280
H-E3 KMVVIGAGVIGVELGSVWQRLGADVTAVELGHVGGVGIDMEISKNFQRIIQKQGFKFKLNTKVTGATKKSDGKIDVSIEAASGGKAEVITC----DVLLVCIGR  280
H-GR RSVIVGAGYIAVEMAGILSALGSKTSLMIRHDKVLRSF-DSMISTNCTEELENAGVEVLKLSG-LEVSMTAVPGRLPVMTMIPDVDCLLWAIGR             291
   <-----------------><---->  <----->         <------->   <-----> <----><--------->< ---->    <----->
       αV      βN-4           αVI         βN-5     βMN-1      βMN-2  βMN-3        βN-2
   βN-3
```

><————————————————CENTRAL DOMAIN——><————————————————INTERFACE DOMAIN————————————

```
        +* +++++++++++++* +*++  +  ++++++++++  +++++++++  *+  ++++  +  ++++  +    +++ ++++++++++++++*+++++   +++++++++++++
E-E3    VPNGKNLDAGKAGVEDDRGFIRVDKDQLRTNV-PHIFAIGDIVGQPMLAHKGVHEGHVAAEVIAGKKHYF--DPKVIPSIAYTEPEVAWVGLTE-KEAKEKGISY   373
A-E3    RPVTTDLLAADSGVTLDERGFIYVDDYCATSV-PGVYAIGDVVRGAMLAHKASEEGVVVAERIAGHKAQM--NYDLIPAVIYTHPEIAGVGKTE-QALKAEGVAI   379
Y-E3    RPYIAGLGAEKIGLEVDKRGRLVIDDQFNSKF-PHIKVVGDVTFGPMLAHKAEEEGIAAVEMLKTGHGHV--NYNNIPSVMYSHPEVAWVGKTE-EQLKEAGIDY   386
P-E3    RPFTQNLGLEELGIELDPRGRIPVNTRFQTKI-PNIYAIGDVVAGPMLAHKAEDEGIICVEGMAGGAVHI--DYNCVPSVIYTHPEVAWVGKSE-EQLKEEGIEY   381
H-E3    RPFTKNLGLEELGIELDPRGRIPVNTRFQTKI-PNIYAIGDVVAGPMLAHKAEDEGIICVEGMAGGAVHI--DYNCVPSVIYTHPEVAWVGKSE-EQLKEEGIEY   381
H-GR    VPNTKDLSLNKLGIQTDDKGHIIVDE-FQNTNVKGIYAVGDVCGKALLTPVAIAAGRKLAHRLFEYKEDSKLDYNNIPTVVFSHPIGTVGLTEDEAIHKYGIEN   395
                                                                                                              ∨
          <->   <->  <---> <--->    <---------->         <---------->         <-->      <->   <-->    αVIII
        β MF-4  βF-8 βF-7  βF-6 βF-5            αVII                    βI-1   βI-2
        <——————————————————————————————————————INTERFACE DOMAIN——————————————————————————————————————>
```

><————————————————————————————INTERFACE DOMAIN——

```
        +++++++++++++++  +++++++++*+++  +++++++++*+++++++++++++++++**+++++++  +++ ++  +  +
E-E3    -ETATFPWAASGRAIASDCADGMTKLIFDKESHRVIGGAIVGTNGGELLGEIGLAIEMCDAEDIALTIHAHPTLHESVGLA--AEVFEGSITDLPNPKAKKK   473
A-E3    -NVGVPFFAASGRAMAANDTAGFVKVIADAKTDRVLGVHVIGPSAAELVQQGAIAMEFGTSAEDLGMMVFAHPALSEALHEA--ALAVSGHAIHVANRKK---   477
Y-E3    -KIGKFPFAANSRAKTNQDTEGFVKILIDSKTERILGAHIIGPNAGEMIAEAGLALEYGASAEDVARVCHAHPTLSEAFKEANMAAYD-KAIHC--------   478
P-E3    -KVGKFPFAANSRAKTNADTDGMVKILGQKSTDRVLGAHIIGPGAGEMINEAALALEYGASCEDIARVCHAHPTLSEAFREANLAASFGKAINF--------   474
H-E3    -KVGKFPFAANSRAKTNADTDGMVKILGQKSTDRVLGAHILGPGAGEMVNEAALALEYGASCEDIARVCHAHPTLSEAFREANLAASFGKSINF--------   474
H-GR    VKTYSTSFTPMYHAVTKRKTKCVMKMVCANKEEKVVGIHMQGLGCDEMLQGFAVAVRMGATKADFDNTVAIHPTSSEELVTLR-------------------   478
        <---------->   <---><---->  <---------->     <--------->  <-------->
        βI-5           βI-4 βI-3          αIX            αX          αXI
        <-->
        βI-5
        <————————————————————————————————————————————————————————————————————————————————————————>
```

FIGURE 7. Alignment of amino acid sequences of E₃ from five different sources: *E. coli* E₃ (E-E₃),[27] *A. vinelandii* E₃ (A-E₃),[28] *S. cerevisiae* E₃ (Y-E₃),[12] porcine heart E₃ (P-E₃),[10] and human liver E₃ (H-E₃).[11] Human erythrocyte glutathione reductase (H-GR)[30] is also shown. These sequences were first aligned by a computer program ("Micro Genie," Beckman) and then readjusted to coincide with the secondary structure of H-GR. *Hyphens* represent spacing to align the sequences and are not included in the numbering. An amino acid residue present in the aligned position of all the six proteins is identified by an *asterisk* (*) at the top, whereas an amino acid residue aligned in three to five proteins is identified by a *plus* (+) *sign*. The boundaries of the four domains are identified by *dashed lines at the top* of the sequence. The structural beta-sheets (β), beta-meander (β M), and alpha-helix (α) are identified by the length of the *dashed line below* the sequences. (F) FAD domain, (N) NAD (NADPH) domain, and (I) interface domain.

identified in the E_3 structures (FIG. 7; also see Ref. 29). Since there is considerable homology at the primary amino acid sequence (33% homology between human GR and human E_3, for instance), GR has been used as a model to predict the secondary structure of E_3[34,35] and to identify likely active-site residues. A detailed structural comparison between human GR and *E. coli* E_3 performed by Rice *et al.*[34] revealed a striking degree of similarity in their structures and strong conservation of amino acid residues at the disulfide active site and in the FAD- and NAD(P)-binding sites. However, in the same study, a significant number of amino acid substitutions were observed in the substrate binding site of these two proteins, indicating their differing substrate specificity.[34] In a separate study of the molecular structure of yeast E_3, elucidated at 4.5-Å resolution by a molecular replacement method using the known structure of human GR, Takenaka *et al.*[35] showed a remarkable identity between these two proteins, except at the amino and carboxyl termini. In both of these studies, the presence of 18 additional residues at the carboxyl terminus of the E_3 has been implicated in substrate recognition. Takenaka *et al.*[35] proposed that the extension of the carboxyl terminus in E_3 forms a narrow entrance for the long chain of the dihydrolipoyl moiety of E_2 to a deep cleft at the interface between the two subunits.

We have compared the secondary structures of human GR and E_3. After the sequences of GR and E_3 were aligned, the sequences associated with each secondary structural element of GR and the corresponding region of E_3 were compared with regard to sequence identity and the nature of sequence substitution, conservation of internal nonpolar and external polar residues in beta-sheets, and conservation of polar and nonpolar faces along the axis of each alpha-helix. The general result of this comparison is shown in TABLE 1 and diagrammed in FIGURE 8.

The most important secondary structural elements conserved in the structural framework of GR are the beta-sheets, because they form the internal cores of the

TABLE 1. Comparison of Human E_3 with GR

	Conservation		
	Sequence		
Secondary Structure	Nonpolar	Polar	Polarity
FAD domain			
Beta-sheet	Conserved	Conserved	Conserved
Beta-meander	Conserved	Variable	Conserved
Helix I	Conserved	Variable	Conserved (rotated)
Helix II	Conserved (half)	Conserved (half)	Conserved (rotated)
Helix III	Variable	Variable	Conserved (rotated)
NAD domain			
Parallel beta-sheet	Conserved	Variable	Conserved
Beta-meander	Variable	Variable	Conserved
Helix IV	Conserved	Conserved	Conserved
Helix V	Conserved	Conserved	Conserved
Helix VI	Variable	Variable	Conserved
Central domain			
Helix VII	Variable	Variable	Conserved
Interface domain			
Flat beta-sheet	Conserved	Conserved	Conserved
Helix VIII	Variable	Variable	Conserved
Helix IX	Conserved	Conserved	Conserved
Helix X	Variable	Variable	Conserved (rotated)
Helix XI	Variable	Conserved (partial)	Reversed

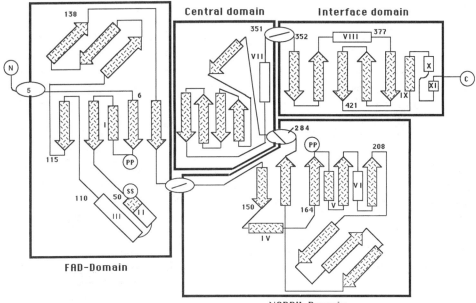

FIGURE 8. Comparison of the chain fold of human GR and human E$_3$ (based on a previous model[31]). Strands of beta-sheets are shown as *arrows* and alpha-helices as *rectangles*. The *open rectangles* indicate helices with little sequence conservation between E$_3$ and GR. The four domains are separately identified by enclosure in *boxes*. *Arabic numbers* indicate amino acid residues of human E$_3$ and *roman numerals* identify alpha-helices. The residues in *ovals* denote domain boundaries. **PP**, pyrophosphate moieties of FAD and NAD; **SS**, the redox-active dithiol (Cys-Cys of E$_3$); **N** and **C**, amino and carboxyl terminus, respectively.

domains (FIG. 8). Every beta-sheet of GR shows a very high degree of sequence identity with the corresponding regions in E$_3$. When substitutions occur in the inner hydrophobic cores of the beta-sheets, the changes are invariably conservative. These findings show that the core structures of E$_3$ and GR are similar.

Alpha-helices, on the other hand, generally pack against internal structural elements in GR and have one face exposed to solvent. The structure of the protein does not depend greatly on the residues in the solvent-exposed face, and, thus, polar residues in these elements need not be conserved for structural reasons. When the alpha-helices of GR and E$_3$ are compared, more differences in sequence and less conservative substitutions are noted, although most of the putative helices in E$_3$ contain a nonpolar face with similar or highly conserved residues relative to the corresponding helix in GR. However, several of the helices, namely, helices II and III in the FAD-binding domain, helix VI in the NAD-binding domain, helix VII in the central domain, and helices VIII, X and XI in the interface domain, show little sequence conservation. Putative E$_3$ helices I, II, III, X and XI may be rotated around their axis relative to the corresponding helices in GR. In E$_3$, the sequence of the putative helix VI is very polar, lacks a distinctive nonpolar face, and is very different from that of helix VI in GR. It is therefore difficult to argue that this sequence should form a helix in E$_3$, except on the basis of packing considerations. Interestingly, helix VI in GR is highly solvent-exposed and does not contribute in any direct way to NADPH binding. The putative alpha-helices in E$_3$ show more variability relative to the corresponding regions in GR,

```
                                FAD-BINDING REGION                                        DISULFIDE ACTIVE SITE REGION

E-E3   7-53   Q V V V L G A G P A G Y S A A F R C A D L G L E T V I V E R Y N - - - - - - T L G G V C L N V G C I P S K   ( 62%)
A-E3   5-57   D V I V I G A G P G G Y V A A I K S A Q L G L K T A L I E K Y K G K E G K T A L G G T C L N V G C I P S K   ( 81%)
Y-E3   7-53   D V V I I G G G P A G Y V A A I K A A Q L G F N T A C V E K R G - - - - - - K L G G T C L N V G C I P S K   ( 85%)
P-E3   8-54   D V T V I G S G P G G Y V A A I K A A Q L G F K T V C I E K N E - - - - - - T L G G T C L N V G C I P S K   (100%)
H-E3   8-54   D V T V I G S G P G G Y V A A I K A A Q L G F K T V C I E K N E - - - - - - T L G G T C L N V G C I P S K   (100%)
H-GR  22-67   D Y L V I G G G S G G L A S A R R A A E L G A R A A V V E S H - - - - - - - K L G G T C V N V G C V P K K   ( 51%)

                      NAD(NADPH)-BINDING REGION

E-E3  176-206  R L L V M G G G I I G L E M G T V Y H A L G S Q I D V V E M F   ( 39%)
A-E3  182-212  K L G V I G A G V I G L E L G S V W A R L G A E V T V L E A M   ( 65%)
Y-E3  185-215  R L T I I G G G I I G L E M G S V Y S R L G S K V T V V E F Q   ( 52%)
P-E3  180-210  K M V V I G A G V I G V E L G S V W Q R L G A D V T A V E L L   (100%)
H-E3  180-210  K M V V I G A G V I G V E L G S V W Q R L G A D V T A V E F L   (100%)
H-GR  189-219  R S V I V G A G Y I A V E M A G I L S A L G S K T S L M I R H   ( 29%)

                       INTERFACE REGION

E-E3  430-462  M G C D A E D I A L T I H A H P T L H E S V G L A - - A E V F E G S I   ( 49%)
A-E3  436-468  F G T S A E D L G M M V F A H P A L S E A L H E A - - A L A V S G H A   ( 40%)
Y-E3  443-476  Y G A S A E D V A R V C H A H P T L S E A F K E A N M A A Y D - K A I   ( 74%)
P-E3  438-471  Y G A S C E D I A R V C H A H P T L S E A F R E A N L A A S F G K A I   ( 97%)
H-E3  438-471  Y G A S C E D I A R V C H A H P T L S E A F R E A N L A A S F G K S I   (100%)
H-GR  453-478  M G A T K A D F D N T V A I H P T S S E E L V T L R                     ( 23%)
```

FIGURE 9. Alignment of amino acid sequences of the specific regions of the FAD (*upper panel*), NAD (NADPH) (*middle panel*), and interface (*lower panel*) domains of E_3 from five different sources: *E. coli* (**E**),[27] *A. vinelandii*, (**A**)[28] *S. cerevisiae*, (**Y**)[12] porcine (**P**),[10] and human (**H**)[11] in comparison to the corresponding sequences of human glutathione reductase (**GR**).[30] An amino acid residue present in the aligned position for at least three of the six sequences is identified by enclosure in a *box*. Percent homology with the H-E_3 sequence is shown at *right*.

consistent with the greater solvent exposure of the alpha-helices in GR. In general, the nonpolar faces of the putative helices in E_3 are conserved, providing further support for the hypothesis of an identical core structure for E_3 and GR.

A second criterion for the structural similarity of the two enzymes is the conservation of relative positions of residues in the active sites, particularly when the substrates or coenzymes are identical or closely related structurally. The FAD is completely buried between the FAD domain and the central domain in GR, and contacts with FAD are made with main-chain atoms and both polar and nonpolar side chains. These contacts for GR can be summarized as follows: (i) the adenosine moiety of FAD binds in a groove between the pleated sheet of the Rossmann fold and the antiparallel beta-meander, (ii) the pyrophosphoryl group of FAD is localized between helix I and helix II (FIG. 8), and (iii) the isoalloxazine moiety of FAD interacts with Cys-63.[32] In E_3, the corresponding residues are highly conserved, (FIG. 9) and most of those that are different represent conservative substitutions. Likewise, the residues that contact NADP in GR are highly conserved in the NAD domain of E_3, except for E_3 residues corresponding to those (Arg-218, His-219, and Arg-224) interacting with the ribose phosphate in GR. The conservation of the residues contacting FAD and NAD^+ is a remarkable observation and nearly convincing evidence by itself that the GR and E_3 proteins fold into almost the same structure, since it is difficult to imagine any other explanation for the high degree of conservation of the residues in E_3 that correspond to residues contacting FAD and NADPH in GR. The interface domain of human GR is involved in the binding of its substrate glutathione, whereas this domain in E_3 recognizes the dihydrolipoyl moiety linked to the E_3 components.

A third criterion for similarity between GR and E_3 is that the subunit-subunit contacts within the dimeric molecule be conserved. In general, sequences in the subunit contact region of GR are conserved or conservatively substituted. When striking changes are observed in the E_3 sequence in this region, an apparent corresponding change can generally be found in a neighboring amino acid in the contact region, leading us to suggest that the intersubunit contact surface is largely the same for GR and E_3.

In summary, we have tested the aligned sequences of GR and E_3 for structural similarity on the basis of three criteria: (i) similarity of secondary structural elements, (ii) conservation of residues in the FAD- and NAD(P)-binding sites, and (iii) conservation of residues in the intersubunit contact region of the dimeric molecules. The correspondence of sequences was convincing by each criterion; taken together, these analyses indicate that the core structure and most of the secondary structural elements of E_3 are the same as those in GR, that the same binding site is formed for FAD in E_3 and GR, that the NAD^+-binding portion of the binding sites is very similar, and that the interface surfaces between subunits of the dimer overlap.

SUMMARY

The availability of the primary amino acid sequences of the E_2 of PDC, α-KGDC and BCKADC from several prokaryotic and eukaryotic species has allowed us to compare the structural aspects of human PDC-E_2 with those of the E_2 components from the other complexes. The PDC-E_2 components from all the species examined so far contain three structurally identifiable regions: the lipoyl-bearing domain, the E_3-binding site, and the catalytic domain. The primary structure of the lipoyl-bearing domain shows considerable variation in its size, ranging from one to three repeating units of approximately 110 amino acids, but essentially preserving its function in the E_2

components. In contrast, the sizes of the E_3-binding site and the catalytic domain of PDC-E_2 from several species are essentially similar and show considerable conservation of specific amino acid residues. Obviously, additional studies are warranted to better understand the structure-function relationships of these domains and the evolutionary conservation of PDC-E_2 in different species.

Similarly, the availability of the primary amino acid sequences of E_3 from several prokaryotes and eukaryotes has also permitted comparison of the structural domains of these proteins with that of the known structure of human GR, a flavoprotein member of the pyridine nucleotide-disulfide oxidoreductase family. Four structural domains (FAD, NAD$^+$, central, and interface domains) have been identified in the E_3 components. On the basis of the comparison of the secondary structural elements of GR and E_3, the core structure of these two proteins are shown to be similar. It is hoped that further analysis of E_3 using site-directed mutagenesis and determination of its crystal structure will provide better insight into its structure-function relationships.

REFERENCES

1. REED, L. J. 1974. Acc. Chem. Res. **7:** 40–46.
2. OLIVER, R. M. & L. J. REED. 1982. Multienzyme complexes. *In* Electron Microscopy of Proteins. J. R. Harris, Ed. Vol. **2:** 1–48. Academic Press. New York.
3. KOIKE, M. & K. KOIKE. 1982. Ann. N.Y. Acad. Sci. **378:** 225–235.
4. WIELAND, O. H. 1983. Rev. Physiol. Biochem. Pharmacol. **96:** 123–170.
5. JILKA, J. M., M. RAHMATULLAH, M. KAZEMI & T. E. ROCHE. 1986. J. Biol. Chem. **281:** 1858–1867.
6. GERSHWIN, M. E., I. R. MACKAY, A. STURGESS & R. L. COPPEL. 1987. J. Immunol. **183:** 3525–3531.
7. COPPEL, R. L., J. MCNEILACE, C. D. SURH, J. V. DE WALTER, T. W. SPITHILL, S. WHITTINGHAM, & M. E. GERSHWIN. 1988. Proc. Natl. Acad. Sci. USA **85:** 7317–7321.
8. THEKKUMKARA, T. J., L. HO., I. D. WEXLER, G. PONS, T-C. LIU & M. S. PATEL. 1988. FEBS Lett. **240:** 45–48.
9. NIU, X-D., K. S. BROWNING, R. H. BEHAL & L. J. REED. 1988. Proc. Natl. Acad. Sci. USA **85:** 7546–7550.
10. OTULAKOWSKI, G. & B. H. ROBINSON. 1987. J. Biol. Chem. **262:** 17313–17318.
11. PONS, G., C. RAEFSKY-ESTRIN, D. J. CAROTHERS, R. A. PEPIN, A. A. JAVED, B. W. JESSE, M. K. GANAPATHI, D. SAMOLS & M. S. PATEL. 1988. Proc. Natl. Acad. Sci. USA **85:** 1422–1426.
12. BROWNING, K. S., D. J. UHLINGER & L. J. REED. 1988. Proc. Natl. Acad. Sci. USA **85:** 1831–1834.
13. ROSS, J., G. A. REID & I. W. DAWES. 1988. J. Gen. Microbiol. **134:** 1131–1139.
14. THEKKUMKARA, T. J., B. W. JESSE, L. HO, C. RAEFSKY, R. A. PEPIN, A. A. JAVED, G. PONS & M. S. PATEL. 1987. Biochem. Biophys. Res. Commun. **145:** 903–907.
15. BLEILE, D. M., M. L. HACKERT, F. H. PETTIT & L. J. REED. 1981. J. Biol. Chem. **256:** 514–519.
16. STEPHENS, P. E., M. G. DARLISON, H. M. LEWIS & J. R. GUEST. 1983. Eur. J. Biochem. **133:** 481–489.
17. SPENCER, M. E., M. G. DARLISON, P. E. STEPHENS, I. K. DUCKENFIELD & J. R. GUEST. 1984. Eur. J. Biochem. **141:** 361–374.
18. HANEMAAIJER, R., A. JANSSEN, A. DE KOK & C. VEEGER. 1988. Eur. J. Biochem. **174:** 593–599.
19. PACKMAN, L. C., A. BORGES & R. N. PERHAM. 1988. Biochem. J. **252:** 79–86.
20. BURNS, G., T. BROWN, K. HATTER & J. R. SOKATCH. 1988. Eur. J. Biochem. **176:** 165–169.
21. LAU, K. S., T. A. GRIFFIN, C-W. C. HU & D. T. CHUANG. 1988. Biochemistry **27:** 1972–1981.

22. HUMMEL, K. B., S. LITWER, A. P. BRADFORD, A. AITKEN, D. J. DANNER & S. J. YEAMAN. 1988. J. Biol. Chem. **263:** 6165–6168.
23. GUEST, J. R., H. M. LEWIS, L. D. GRAHAM, L. C. PACKMAN & R. N. PERHAM. 1985. J. Mol. Biol. **185:** 743–754.
24. PACKMAN, L. C. & R. N. PERHAM. 1986. FEBS Lett. **206:** 193–198.
25. LESLIE, A. G. W., P. C. E. MOODY & W. V. SHAW. 1988. Proc. Natl. Acad. Sci. USA **85:** 4133–4137.
26. GRIFFIN, T. A., K. S. LAU & D. T. CHUANG. 1988. J. Biol. Chem. **268:** 14008–14014.
27. STEPHENS, P. E., H. M. LEWIS, M. G. DARLISON & J. R. GUEST. 1983. Eur. J. Biochem. **135:** 519–527.
28. DE KOK, A. & A. H. WESTPHAL. 1987. Cloning, organization and nucleotide sequence of the *Azotobacter vinelandii* gene for lipoamide dehydrogenase. *In* Flavins and Flavorproteins. D. E. Edmondson & D. B. McCormick, Eds.: 99–102. Walter de Gruyter. Berlin.
29. CAROTHERS, D. J., G. PONS & M. S. PATEL. 1989. Arch. Biochem. Biophys. **268:** 409–425.
30. THIEME, R., E. F. PAI, R. H. SCHIRMER & G. E. SCHULZ. 1981. J. Mol. Biol. **152:** 763–782.
31. KRAUTH-SIEGEL, R. L., R. BLATTERSPIEL, M. SALEH, E. SCHILTZ, R. H. SCHIRMER & R. UNTUCHT-GRAU. 1982. Eur. J. Biochem. **121:** 259–267.
32. UNTUCHT-GRAU, R., R. H. SCHIRMER, I. SCHIRMER & R. L. KRAUTH-SIEGEL. 1981. Eur. J. Biochem. **120:** 407–419.
33. PAI, E. F. & G. E. SCHULZ. 1983. J. Biol. Chem. **258:** 1751–1757.
34. RICE, D. W., G. E. SCHULZ & J. R. GUEST. 1984. J. Mol. Biol. **174:** 483–496.
35. TAKENAKA, A., K. KIZAWA, T. HATA, S. SATO, E-I. MISAKA, C. TAMURA & Y. SASADA. 1988. J. Biochem. **103:** 463–469.

cDNA Cloning of the E1α Subunit of the Branched-Chain α-Keto Acid Dehydrogenase and Elucidation of a Molecular Basis for Maple Syrup Urine Disease[a]

BEI ZHANG, MARTHA J. KUNTZ, GARY W. GOODWIN,
HOWARD J. EDENBERG, DAVID W. CRABB, AND
ROBERT A. HARRIS[b]

Departments of Biochemistry, Medicine, and Medical Genetics
Indiana University School of Medicine
Indianapolis, Indiana 46223

INTRODUCTION

The branched-chain α-keto acid dehydrogenase (BCKDH) complex, a multisubunit mitochondrial enzyme complex, catalyzes the rate-limiting step in the catabolism of leucine, isoleucine, and valine.[1,2] The E1 component [2-oxoisovalerate dehydrogenase (lipoamide); EC 1.2.4.4], composed of E1α and E1β subunits, catalyzes the oxidative decarboxylation of the α-keto acids derived from the branched-chain amino acids. The enzyme is subject to covalent modification; phosphorylation inactivates and dephosphorylation activates the complex.[3–5] E1α is probably the catalytic subunit, and it contains two serine residues which can be phosphorylated by a BCKDH-specific kinase.[6] Furthermore, BCKDH shares significant similarity with pyruvate dehydrogenase (PDH) in subunit structure and regulatory mechanism.[6]

Maple syrup urine disease (MSUD), a genetic disorder inherited in an autosomal recessive fashion, is caused by a deficiency of BCKDH.[7] The disease, which is characterized by ketoacidosis and mental retardation, has been categorized into four clinically different forms: classic, thiamin-responsive, intermediate, and intermittent.[7,8] Biochemical studies indicate that the defects occur most often[9] but not exclusively[10,11] in the E1 component of the BCKDH complex.

In order to gain insight into the structure and regulation of the BCKDH complex and to study the defects of MSUD at the DNA and RNA levels, we cloned the cDNAs encoding the E1α subunits of both rat and human liver BCKDH. We have also studied the molecular basis of MSUD in a family with the classic form of the disease, and the results provide evidence for both a structural and a regulatory mutation in the family.

[a]This work was supported in part by grants from the Riley Memorial Association and the Showalter Foundation, by Public Health Service Grants DK19259, AA06460, AA06434, AA00081, and by a predoctoral fellowship (B. Z.) from the March of Dimes Birth Defects Foundation.

[b]Address correspondence to Robert A. Harris, Ph.D., Department of Biochemistry, Indiana University School of Medicine, Medical Science Building 447, Indiana University Medical Center, 635 Barnhill Drive, Indianapolis, Indiana 46223.

EXPERIMENTAL METHODS

Antibody Screening of Rat Liver cDNA Library

Polyclonal antibodies that specifically react with the E1 component of BCKDH were raised in rabbits as described.[12] The antibodies were used to screen a λgt11 cDNA library constructed from mRNA from adult Sprague-Dawley rat liver (purchased from Clontech Laboratories, Inc.).[13] Briefly, 400,000 individual plaque-forming units were plated on *Escherichia coli* strain Y1090 and grown at 42°C for 4 hr. The plates were then overlaid with nitrocellulose filters saturated with isopropyl-D-thiogalactopyranoside. Following overnight incubation at 37°C, the filters were removed from the plates, washed, and subjected to incubation with the primary antibody. The putative positive plaques were identified by incubation of the filters with goat anti-rabbit IgG-peroxidase, followed by color development. After successive rounds of screening, the clone containing the cDNA insert encoding the E1α subunit was selected with synthetic oligonucleotide probes designed from the known peptide sequence of the E1α phosphorylation sites. The cDNA from the positive clone was then subjected to subcloning and DNA sequencing.

Cloning of Human Liver BCKDH E1α cDNA

A human liver λgt11 cDNA library (kindly provided by Dr. Savio Woo, Houston, Texas) was screened using the cDNA for rat liver BCKDH E1α subunit as the probe.[14] The conditions for plaque lifting, hybridization, and washing were essentially according to Maniatis *et al.*[15] Two positive clones were identified among 500,000 plaque-forming units. The cDNA sequence was determined as described.[14]

Cell Strains and Culture

The normal human fibroblast cell line was obtained from the American Type Culture Collection. Fibroblasts derived from a patient with classic MSUD (GM649) and his father (GM650) and mother (GM651) were purchased from the National Institute of General Medical Sciences Human Genetic Mutant Cell Repository. The cells were cultured and harvested under the conditions described.[16]

Southern and Northern Blot Analysis

Genomic DNA from normal and MSUD fibroblasts was isolated using the method described in Maniatis *et al.*[15] The DNA was digested with different restriction endonucleases, fractionated by electrophoresis, and transferred to nylon membranes. Total RNA was isolated from tissues and fibroblasts by the guanidinium isothiocyanate method[17] and analyzed by electrophoresis and Northern blotting.[18] The blots were probed with cloned cDNAs under the appropriate conditions as described.[12,14,16]

Enzyme Activity Assay and Western Blot Analysis

Cultured fibroblasts were collected by trypsinization and treated with α-chloroisocaproate to activate the BCKDH complex. The total activity of BCKDH was determined radiochemically using [1-^{14}C]ketoisovaleric acid as substrate.[19] Crude mitochondrial extracts from the fibroblasts were prepared[20] and electrophoresed by SDS–polyacrylamide gel electrophoresis (SDS-PAGE).[21] The protein was electroblotted to membranes and analyzed immunochemically using antibodies against the E1 and E2 components of BCKDH.

Analysis of E1α cDNA from MSUD Patient by Polymerase Chain Reaction (PCR) and Allele-Specific Oligonucleotide Hybridization

First-strand cDNA was generated from total RNA by reverse transcription and then subjected to 30–40 cycles of enzymatic amplification using thermal-stable Taq DNA polymerase.[22] Five sets of sense/antisense oligonucleotides used in the amplification were designed on the basis of the normal human and rat cDNA sequences. The amplified cDNAs were subcloned into M13, and four independent clones of each amplified cDNA segment were sequenced. A segment of genomic DNA surrounding codon 394 was also amplified by PCR. In order to study the single base mutation defined in the above study, amplified cDNAs and genomic DNAs were blotted to nylon membranes and subjected to allele-specific oligonucleotide hybridization.[23] The sequences of the probes were GAGCACTACCCACTG (normal) and GAGCACAACCCACTG (mutant).

RESULTS

Isolation of Rat Liver BCKDH E1α cDNA Clone

We have isolated a 1.7-kb cDNA encoding the BCKDH E1α subunit. Translation of the 1323-bp open reading frame of the clone predicts the 24 residues of the previously reported phosphorylation sites 1 and 2 for the bovine kidney and rabbit heart enzymes. In order to locate the amino terminus of the mature E1α peptide within the cDNA, rat liver E1α was purified by reverse phase HPLC, and the sequence of the amino-terminal 15 amino acids was obtained. This sequence was found 40 residues from the beginning of the clone. The deduced amino acid sequence predicts that the mature E1α contains 401 residues and has a calculated M_r of 45,709, which agrees with previous estimates of the M_r (46,000–46,800) by SDS-PAGE.[2] The 40 residues which are upstream from the amino terminus of the mature protein presumably serve as a leader peptide. Northern blots of RNA prepared from rat liver and muscle and probed with the E1α cDNA insert show a single band of mRNA of 1.8 kb in each tissue. This RNA species is more abundant in liver than in muscle, correlating with the higher BCKDH activity in liver.

Cloning and Characterization of Human Liver BCKDH E1α cDNA

A 1552-bp E1α cDNA was isolated from a human liver cDNA library. The cDNA contained a 1134-bp open reading frame encoding a protein of 378 amino acids, followed by 418-bp of untranslated sequence. The clone lacked the amino-terminal 24 codons and the sequence encoding the leader peptide, as compared to the cDNA for the rat enzyme. This sequence was later obtained by amplification of human liver mRNA, using a sense primer based on the corresponding sequence in the rat cDNA.

Comparison of the human BCKDH E1α cDNA with the rat cDNA reveals that the sequences are highly conserved between the two species at both nucleotide and amino acid levels. Within the coding regions, there is 89% sequence identity at the nucleotide level and 96% sequence identity at the amino acid level. The 117 amino acid residues surrounding the phosphorylation sites are completely conserved between human and rat, indicating the importance of this region in the function of the subunit.

BCKDH Activity and Levels of the Protein and Its mRNA in Cultured Fibroblasts from a Normal Human and an MSUD Family

By using radiochemical assay of cell extracts containing completely activated BCKDH, we determined that the total enzyme activities in fibroblasts were 0.202 ± 0.046 nmol substrate/min/mg protein (normal cells), 0.015 ± 0.015 (patient, GM649 cells), 0.114 ± 0.044 (father, GM650 cells), and 0.096 ± 0.010 (mother, GM651 cells). The activity in the fibroblasts derived from the patient with the classic MSUD is less than 10% of normal, whereas the father and mother each have about half of the normal activity. Western blot analysis was performed to determine the protein level of BCKDH complex in cells from the members of this family. Quantification of the blots by densitometry demonstrated that the patient, mother, and father had 12%, 55%, and 59%, respectively, of the normal amount of the immunoreactive E1α, while all the samples contained nearly identical amounts of E2. In addition, the reduction in the amount of E1α was closely paralleled by a reduction in E1β in each family member compared to the normal control. The mRNA level was measured by Northern blot analysis using radioactively labeled human cDNA as the probe. A single mRNA band of 1.8 kb was observed; quantitation of the radioactivity of the band indicated a ratio of 2.1:1.1:2.2:1.0 for normal:patient:father:mother. This result was confirmed by reprobing the filters for β-actin mRNA to normalize the amount of total RNA electrophoresed.

Identification of Tyr→Asn Mutation and Allele-Specific Oligonucleotide Hybridization

To define the mutations at the DNA and RNA level, we cloned and sequenced the cDNA from the patient by reverse transcription of RNA followed by PCR to amplify specifically BCKDH E1α cDNA. The complete coding for the mature E1α protein was amplified in five overlapping segments and sequenced. Only one single base substitution was found: TAC encoding tyrosine at residue 394 was changed to AAC encoding asparagine.

To confirm the presence of the point mutation, sequences flanking codon 394 were amplified from both RNA and genomic DNA of the patient and his parents. Two allele-specific oligonucleotides centered at codon 394 (with one base mismatch) were synthesized and used to probe the slot-blots of the amplified RNA and genomic DNA. The father's RNA and DNA hybridized to both probes, indicating that he was heterozygous for this mutation. The mother's RNA and DNA, on the other hand, hybridized only to the normal probe, demonstrating that she was homozygous for the normal allele with regard to the mutation at codon 394. The patient's DNA hybridized to both probes. In contrast, his RNA hybridized only to the mutant probe, suggesting that, although he was heterozygous at the gene level for the mutation, only the abnormal allele was expressed as RNA.

DISCUSSION

The importance of BCKDH in the catabolism of branched-chain amino acids has been well documented. Molecular cloning of the cDNAs encoding the human and rat liver BCKDH E1α provides the first deduced amino acid sequence for the subunit and allows us to speculate about the structure of the protein. Furthermore, in comparisons of the sequences of human BCKDH and PDH E1α subunits[24-26] considerable amino acid sequence similarity (38%) between the two proteins has been found. The similarity is even more significant in the carboxyl-terminal region, where 49% similarity is found between residues 252–327 (allowing for conservative substitutions). The conservation observed in this region of the two proteins suggests that this region may be involved in enzyme catalysis or coenzyme binding, as well as in phosphorylation of the enzyme.

The availability of the BCKDH E1α cDNA also provides a powerful tool to study the molecular basis of MSUD. With regard to the MSUD family described in this study, the data indicate that the affected child was a compound heterozygote. On the basis of observations that the father is heterozygous for the Tyr→Asn substitution at codon 394 and has the normal level of E1α mRNA but only 59% of the normal level of E1α protein, we propose that the point mutation affects either the translational efficiency of the mRNA or, more likely, the stability of the resulting protein. Although the mother is homozygous for a normal codon 394, she expresses only 50% of the normal E1α mRNA, suggesting that she carries a regulatory mutation which abolishes the expression of mRNA from one of the alleles. MSUD in the patient is thus due to two different mutant alleles: one (inherited from the mother) containing *cis*-acting mutation which essentially eliminates expression of this allele and the other (inherited from the father) containing a point mutation which results in a decreased level of E1α protein. This explains how the patient was genetically heterozygous for the Tyr→Asn substitution, yet expressed only the allele which contains the point mutation.

In conclusion, the results reveal for the first time the defects of MSUD in a family with the classic form of the disease at the DNA and RNA level. The methods established should be applicable for studies of other MSUD families, and we anticipate that many different types of mutations will be found for this clinically heterogeneous disease.

SUMMARY

We have cloned cDNAs encoding human and rat liver BCKDH E1α subunits and deduced the primary structure of the mature protein. The sequences of the cDNA and protein are highly conserved between the two species. Significant sequence similarity has also been found between human BCKDH and PDH E1α subunits. We have studied the molecular basis of MSUD by determining the enzyme activity and levels of BCKDH protein and mRNA, and by enzymatic amplification and sequencing of BCKDH E1α-specific mRNA, from an MSUD patient and his parents. Different mutant alleles were identified in the two parents. The patient was a compound heterozygote, inheriting an allele encoding an abnormal E1α from the father and an allele containing a defect in regulation from the mother. Our results demonstrate that a case of MSUD was caused by structural and regulatory mutations involving the E1α subunit.

REFERENCES

1. PETTIT, F. H., S. J. YEAMAN & L. J. REED. 1978. Purification and characterization of branched chain α-ketoacid dehydrogenase complex of bovine kidney. Proc. Natl. Acad. Sci. USA **75:** 4881–4885.
2. PAXTON, R. & R. A. HARRIS. 1982. Isolation of rabbit liver branched chain α-ketoacid dehydrogenase and regulation by phosphorylation. J. Biol. Chem. **257:** 14433–14439.
3. DAMUNI, Z., M. L. MERRYFIELD, J. S. HUMPHREYS & L. J. REED. 1984. Purification and properties of branched chain α-ketoacid dehydrogenase phosphatase from bovine kidney. Proc. Natl. Acad. Sci. USA **81:** 4335–4338.
4. FATANIA, H. R., K. S. LAU & P. J. RANDLE. 1981. Inactivation of purified ox kidney branched chain 2-oxoacid dehydrogenase complex by phosphorylation. FEBS Lett. **132:** 285–288.
5. PAXTON, R., M. J. KUNTZ & R. A. HARRIS. 1986. Phosphorylation sites and inactivation of branched chain α-ketoacid dehydrogenase isolated from rat heart, bovine kidney, and rabbit liver, kidney, heart, brain and skeletal muscle. Arch. Biochem. Biophys. **244:** 187–201.
6. YEAMAN, S. J. 1986. The mammalian 2-oxoacid dehydrogenases: A complex family. Trends Biochem. Sci. **11:** 293–296.
7. TANAKA, K. & L. E. ROSENBERG. 1983. Disorders of branched chain amino acid and organic acid metabolism. *In* The Metabolic Basis of Inherited Disease. J. B. Stanbury, J. B. Wyngaarden, D. S. Fredrickson, J. L. Goldstein & M. S. Brown, Eds.: 440–473. McGraw-Hill. New York.
8. DANCIS, J., M. LEVITZ & R. G. WESTALL. 1960. Maple sugar urine disease: Branched-chain keto-aciduria. Pediatrics **25:** 72–79.
9. CHUANG, D. T., L. S. KU, D. S. KERR & R. P. COX. 1982. Detection of heterozygotes in maple-syrup-urine disease: Measurements of branched-chain α-ketoacid dehydrogenase and its components in cell cultures. Am J. Hum. Genet. **34:** 416–424.
10. DANNER, D. J., N. ARMSTRONG, S. C. HEFFELFINGER, E. T. SEWELL, J. H. PRIEST & L. J. ELSAS. 1985. Absence of branched-chain α-ketoacid acyltransferase as a cause of maple syrup urine disease. J. Clin. Invest. **75:** 858–860.
11. INDO, Y., A. KITANO, F. ENDO, I. AKABOSHI & I. MATSUDA. 1987. Altered kinetic properties of the branched-chain α-ketoacid dehydrogenase complex due to mutation of the β-subunit of the branched chain α-ketoacid decarboxylase (E1) component in lymphoblastoid cells derived from patients with maple syrup urine disease. J. Clin. Invest. **80:** 63–70.
12. ZHANG, B., M. J. KUNTZ, G. W. GOODWIN, R. A. HARRIS & D. W. CRABB. 1987. Molecular cloning of a cDNA for the E1α subunit of rat liver branched chain α-ketoacid dehydrogenase. J. Biol. Chem. **262:** 15220–15224.
13. YOUNG, R. A. & R. W. DAVIS. 1983. Yeast RNA polymerase II genes: Isolation with antibody probes. Science **222:** 778–782.
14. ZHANG, B., D. W. CRABB & R. A. HARRIS. 1988. Nucleotide and deduced amino acid sequence of the E1α subunit of human liver branched-chain α-ketoacid dehydrogenase. Gene **69:** 159–164.
15. MANIATIS, T., E. F. FRITSCH, & J. SAMBROOK. 1982. Molecular Cloning: A Laboratory Manual. Cold Spring Harbor Press. Cold Spring Harbor, NY.
16. ZHANG, B., H. J. EDENBERG, D. W. CRABB & R. A. HARRIS. 1989. Evidence for both a regulatory mutation and a structural mutation in a family with maple syrup urine disease. J. Clin. Invest. **83:** 1425–1429.
17. CHIRGWIN, J. M., A. E. PRAYBYLA, R. J. MACDONALD & W. J. RUTTER. 1979. Isolation of biologically active ribonucleic acid from sources enriched in ribonuclease. Biochemistry **18:** 5294–5299.
18. THOMAS, P. S. 1980. Hybridization of denatured RNA and small DNA fragments transferred to nitrocellulose. Proc. Natl. Acad. Sci. USA **77:** 5201–5205.
19. CHUANG, D. T. & R. P. COX. 1988. Enzyme assays with mutant cell lines of maple syrup urine disease. Methods Enzymol. **166:** 135–145.

20. MACKALL, J., M. MEREDITH & M. D. LANE. 1979. A mild procedure for the rapid release of cytoplasmic enzymes from cultured animal cells. Anal. Biochem. **95:** 270–274.
21. LAEMMLI, U. K. 1970. Cleavage of structural proteins during the assembly of the head of bacteriophage T4. Nature **227:** 680–685.
22. SAIKI, R. K., D. H. GELFAND, S. STOFEEL, S. J. SCHARF, R. HIGHCHI, G. T. HORN, K. B. MULLIS & H. A. ERLICH. 1988. Primer-directed enzymatic amplification of DNA with a thermostable DNA polymerase. Science **239:** 487–491.
23. FARR, C. J., R. K. SAIKI, H. A. ERLICH, F. McCORMICK & C. J. MARSHALL. 1988. Analysis of RAS gene mutations in acute myeloid leukemia by polymerase chain reaction and oligonucleotide probes. Proc. Natl. Acad. Sci. USA **85:** 1629–1633.
24. DAHL, H-H. M., S. M. HUNT, W. M. HUTCHISON & G. K. BROWN. 1987. The human pyruvate dehydrogenase complex. Isolation of cDNA clones for the E1α subunit, sequence analysis, and characterization of the mRNA. J. Biol. Chem. **262:** 7398–7403.
25. DE MEIRLEIR, L., N. MACKAY, A. M. L. H. WAH & B. H. ROBINSON. 1988. Isolation of a full-length complementary DNA coding for human E1α subunit of the pyruvate dehydrogenase complex. J. Biol. Chem. **263:** 1191–1195.
26. KOIKE, K., S. OHTA, Y. URATA & M. KOIKE. 1988. Cloning and sequencing of cDNAs encoding α and β subunits of human pyruvate dehydrogenase. Proc. Natl. Acad. Sci. USA **85:** 41–45.

Molecular Studies of Mammalian Branched-Chain α-Keto Acid Dehydrogenase Complexes: Domain Structures, Expression, and Inborn Errors[a]

DAVID T. CHUANG

Department of Biochemistry
The University of Texas Southwestern Medical Center
Dallas, Texas 75235

Mammalian mitochondrial branched-chain α-keto acid dehydrogenase complexes (branched-chain complexes) catalyze the oxidative decarboxylation of α-keto acids derived from branched-chain amino acids—leucine, isoleucine and valine—to give rise to the corresponding branched-chain acyl CoAs.[1] In patients with maple syrup urine disease (MSUD), the activity of the branched-chain complex is deficient.[2] The metabolic block at this step results in the accumulation of branched-chain α-keto and amino acids. The clinical consequences are severe, including keto acidosis, mental retardation, brain dysfunctions, and the possibility of death. The prevalence of MSUD is about 1 in 175,000 worldwide. The mammalian branched-chain complex is a multienzyme complex consisting of three catalytic components: a decarboxylase or dehydrogenase (E1b), a transacylase (E2b), and a dehydrogenase (E3) and of two regulatory enzymes: a specific kinase and a specific phosphatase (TABLE 1). The decarboxylase (E1b) consists of α and β subunits. The M_r of the bovine E1b-α subunit is 45,385, as deduced from cloned cDNA.[3] The size of the E1b-β subunit is 37,000, as determined by SDS-polyacrylamide gel electrophoresis. The E1b component has an $\alpha_2\beta_2$ structure with a size of 170,000 daltons, as determined by Sephacryl S-300 column chromatography.[4] The E1α subunit binds thiamin pyrophosphate (TPP), which mediates the decarboxylation of α-keto acids.[5] The transacylase (E2b) component comprises a single species of lipoate-bearing polypeptide. The M_r of the bovine E2b subunit is 46,518, as deduced from cloned cDNA.[6] The M_r of native E2b is 1.1 million, as recently determined by sedimentation equilibrium in my laboratory.[6] The results established a 24-mer structure for the bovine E2b. The subunit compositions of the kinase and the phosphatase are unknown at present. Reed and colleagues have shown that the branched-chain phosphatase exists in two active species, of M_r 460,000 and 33,000.[7] The organization of the branched-chain complex is such that the E2b subunits form a core structure to which E1b, E3, the kinase, and, presumably, the phosphatase are attached through ionic interactions. With this background information, I report here our molecular studies of the mammalian branched-chain complex in the following three areas: (1) the conservation of domain structures in the E2b core, (2) the expression of bovine E2b in *Escherichia coli,* and (3) inborn errors of the branched-chain complex in MSUD.

[a]This work was supported by Grant DK37373 from the National Institutes of Health, Grant 1-1149 from the March of Dimes Birth Defects Foundation, and an institutional grant (RR07175) from the University of Texas Southwestern Medical Center.

TABLE 1. Component Enzymes and Subunits of the Mammalian Branched-Chain Complex

Component	M_r	Prosthetic Group (P) and Cofactor (C)
Branched-chain decarboxylase (E1b)	170,000 $(\alpha_2\beta_2)^a$	TPP^b (C)
α Subunit	45,385^c	Mg^{2+} (C)
β Subunit	37,000	
Dihydrolipoyl transacylase (E2b)	1.1 × 10^6 (α_{24})	Lipoic acid (P)
Subunit	46,518^c	
Dihydrolipoyl dehydrogenase (E3)	110,000 (α_2)	FAD (P)
Subunit	55,000	
Branched-chain kinase	?	Mg^{2+} (C) (?)
Subunit	?	
Branched-chain phosphatase	460,000	None
Subunit	33,000	

^{a}Determined by gel filtration on Sephacryl S-300 column.[4]
^{b}TPP, thiamin pyrophosphate.
^{c}Calculated from amino acid compositions deduced from cDNAs.[3,6]

CONSERVATION OF DOMAIN STRUCTURES

To investigate the highly assembled structure of the E2b core, our approach was to digest the isolated E2b with trypsin. The trypsinized E2b was then examined under the electron microscope, along with undigested E2b. As shown in FIGURE 1, there is virtually no difference between native and trypsinized E2b. These results indicating that trypsinization has no effect on the highly assembled inner core structure are similar to those for other α-keto acid dehydrogenase complexes. The appearance of the assembled inner core is that of a cube. The hypothesized design for the structure is based on the octahedral (432) point-group symmetry proposed for the E2p component of the E. coli pyruvate dehydrogenase complex.[8] According to this model, the compact inner core domain is linked to the outer, extended lipoyl-bearing domain through an exposed trypsin-sensitive hinge region. Every three inner cores form a trimer, with each trimer occupying one of the eight corners of a truncated cube. Mathematically, the architecture will require a 24-mer structure. Tryptic cleavage at the exposed hinges trims away the extended outer domains, leaving the inner core domains intact. The prevalent tetrameric appearance represents a 4-fold symmetry with one face of the cube sitting squarely on the carbon grid.

To determine the composition of tryptic fragments in the inner core domain, we purified the trypsinized E2b by gel filtration with a Sepharose 4B column (data not shown). SDS-polyacrylamide gel electrophoresis revealed that the inner E2b core consists of fragments A ($M_r = 26,000$) and B ($M_r = 22,000$), which are identical to those obtained when the purified E1b-E2b subcomplex is subjected to digestion with increasing concentrations of trypsin (FIGURE 2).[9] As shown in FIGURE 2, the E2b subunit is readily digested to give rise to fragments A and B. Fragment A is converted to B as the trypsin concentration is increased. At a trypsin:complex ratio of 2:1, fragment B is resistant to further digestion. Moreover, the conversion of fragment A to B is accompanied by loss of the transacylase activity. That is, fragment A, not B, is the active species.

To map the lipoyl-bearing domain, we labeled the lipoate residue by reductive acylation with [U-^{14}C]α-ketoisovalerate as substrate. The E1b-E2b subcomplex with a ^{14}C-label at the lipoate residue was then subjected to digestion with increasing concentrations of trypsin, and the digest was resolved by SDS-polyacrylamide gel electrophoresis. As shown in the autoradiogram of the SDS-gel (FIG. 3), the ^{14}C-labeled E2b subunit is readily digested to produce a series of smaller lipoyl-containing radioactive fragments (L_1 to L_5). The digestion pattern with increasing trypsin concentration is a sequential one. That is, E2b is initially digested to produce lipoyl-containing fragment L_1. Fragment L_1 is unstable and quickly converted to fragments L_2 and L_3 as we increase the trypsin concentration. Fragment L_2 is converted to L_3 and then to L_4. Fragment L_4 is also unstable and is readily converted to L_5. Fragment L_5 appears to be a limit peptide which is resistant to further tryptic digestion, even at a trypsin:complex ratio of 2:1.

On the basis of these results from limited proteolysis assays, we have proposed a linear model for the domain structure of bovine E2b.[6] As shown in FIGURE 4, the mammalian E2b subunit contains three folded domains: the lipoyl-bearing, E3-binding, and inner core domains; these are linked in series by two hinge regions. The

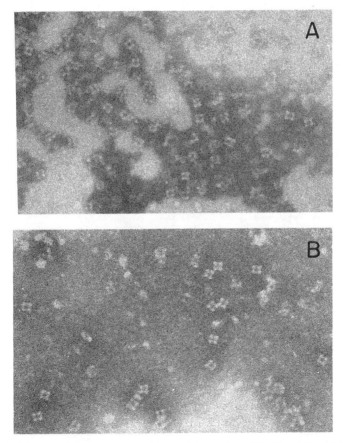

FIGURE 1. Electron micrographs of negatively stained native E2b (**Panel A**) and trypsinized E2b (**Panel B**) of the branched-chain complex from bovine liver. Magnification: 180,000×. (From Chuang *et al.*[9] Reprinted from the *Journal of Biological Chemistry* with permission from the American Society for Biochemistry and Molecular Biology.)

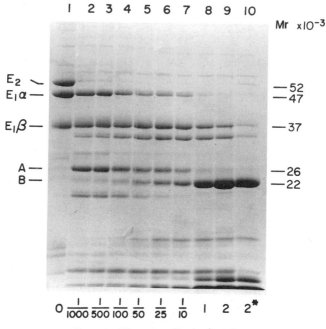

FIGURE 2. Tryptic fragments of the branched-chain complex from bovine liver. The complex was digested with increasing concentrations of trypsin as indicated by the trypsin/complex ratio. Incubations were for 1 hr at 0°C, except for lane 10 (2*), where the digestion was carried out at 25°C for 1 hr. Digestion was terminated by addition of TLCK ($N\alpha$-p-tosyl-L-lysine chloromethyl ketone) and the digest was subjected to SDS-polyacrylamide gel electrophoresis; the gel was stained with Coomassie blue. (From Chuang et al.[9] Reprinted from the *Journal of Biological Chemistry* with permission from the American Society for Biochemistry and Molecular Biology.)

model for the E3-binding domain is based on homologies with the corresponding domain on the E2k subunit of the *E. coli* α-ketoglutarate dehydrogenase complex recently identified by Packman and Perham.[11] The inner core domain contains two trypsin-sensitive sites, i.e., A and B. An initial cleavage at site A produces fragments A and L_1. Fragment A is converted to B upon a further cleavage at site B by a higher concentration of trypsin. Both fragments A and B confer the highly assembled 24-mer structure. Since the conversion of fragment A to B results in a loss of the transacylase activity, a critical portion of the active site is likely to lie between sites A and B on the E2b chain. Assuming sites A and L_1 are identical, we can conclude that the extended region contains five trypsin-sensitive sites, L_1–L_5. A sequential cleavage from sites L_1 to L_5 will generate five lipoyl-containing fragments, L_1–L_5. Fragments L_1 and L_4 are unstable because each contains a hinge region, which is readily removed to produce the next smaller fragment. The hinge region between the lipoyl-bearing and E3-binding domains is less exposed than the one between the E3-binding and inner core domains, since the former requires a higher trypsin concentration for its cleavage to produce fragment L_5. To map epitopic regions on the E2b chain, we have prepared antisera in rabbits, using either native E2b or SDS-denatured E2b as an antigen. The antigenic region recognized by anti-native E2b as determined by Western blot analysis lies between L_1 and L_4 (FIG. 4). The anti–SDS-E2b reacts with a wider spectrum of antigenic determinants on the E2b chain located between site L_4 and the carboxyl end, including the entire inner E2b core.

To substantiate this model for the domain structure, we undertook to clone the E2b subunits of mammalian branched-chain complexes. We initially isolated an incomplete cDNA (1557 bp) encoding human E2b, which did not contain a substantial portion of the inner core sequence.[12] This human E2b cDNA was subsequently used as a probe to isolate two overlapping cDNAs (bE2-5 and bE2-8) of 0.7 and 2.4 Kb in size, respectively, from a λZAP library. The two cDNAs were ligated at the unique *Xba* I site to produce a new construct, bE2-11. Nucleotide sequencing showed that bE2-11 (2701 bp) cDNA encoded the entire precursor of bovine E2b, with 61 amino acid residues in the leader and 421 residues in the mature peptide.[6] The amino-terminal half of the deduced bovine E2b sequence was compared with the corresponding sequences from human E2b,[12] *E. coli* E2p,[13] and *E. coli* E2k[14] (FIG. 5). As expected, there is a high degree of homology between human and bovine E2b in the leader (residues −56

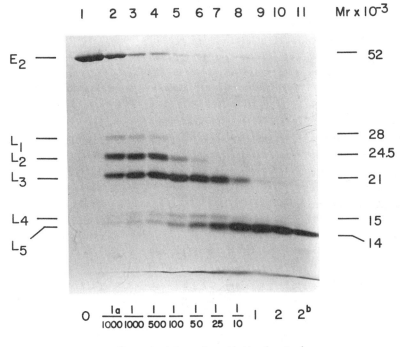

FIGURE 3. Autoradiogram showing lipoyl-containing tryptic fragments separated by SDS-polyacrylamide gel electrophoresis. The lipoyl residue on E2b was radiolabeled by reductive acylation with [U-^{14}C]α-ketoisovalerate as substrate. The complex was then digested with increasing concentrations of trypsin as indicated by the trypsin/complex ratio. Incubations were carried out at 0°C, except for lane 11 (2^b), where the digestion was at 25°C. (From Hu *et al.*[10] Reprinted from the *Journal of Biological Chemistry* with permission from the American Society for Biochemistry and Molecular Biology.)

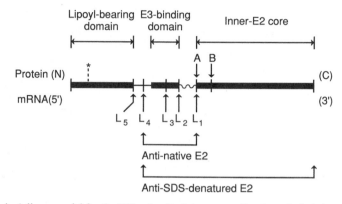

FIGURE 4. A linear model for the E2b subunit of the mammalian branched-chain complex. A, B, L_1, L_2, L_3, L_4, and L_5: trypsin-sensitive sites of native E2b. The A and L_1 sites are identical. *Asterisk:* the position of the lipoyl lysine residue. *Thin solid and wavy lines* between domains: hinge regions. *Brackets:* regions reacting with antibodies to native and denatured E2b, respectively. (From Lau *et al.*[12] Reprinted with permission from *Biochemistry,* copyright 1988, American Chemical Society.)

to -1 in human E2b) and mature peptide regions. The homologies extend to *E. coli* E2p and E2k in the lipoyl-bearing (residues 1–54, human hE2-1) and E3-binding (residues 109–150, human hE2-1) domains. The conservation of primary structures in these two domains is essential for the attachment of lipoic acid by the holoenzyme synthetase, and the binding of E3 component to the E2b chain. There are two putative hinge regions in human E2b. A proline-rich hinge region is located between residues 157 and 171 of human E2b, which aligns well with the hinge region rich in proline and alanine (residues 150–172) of *E. coli* E2k (FIG. 5). A second hinge region rich in charged glutamic acid residues is located between residues 84 and 106 of human E2b. This region lines up with the long hinge region rich in proline and alanine (residues 282–313), which connects the lip3 and E3-binding domains of the *E. coli* E2p chain (FIG. 5). Despite the above alignments, the amino acid sequences in the two hinge regions in mammalian E2b's are significantly different from those in *E. coli* E2p and E2k, notably by the absence of alanine residues. This suggests that the conservation in amino acid residues in the hinge regions is not important, as long as the sequence provides the flexible structure needed for conformational mobility.

Comparison of the inner core domains of rat liver E2p,[15] *E. coli* E2p, and *E. coli* E2k (FIG. 6) indicates that a high degree of conservation also exists in this region. The putative CoA-binding motif Asp-His-Arg-X-X-Asp-Gly[16] is located near the carboxyl terminus of the bovine E2b chain (residues 390–396), which is completely conserved among the four lipoyl-containing proteins. The trypsin-sensitive sites A (residue 175) and B (residue 205) were located by the amino-terminal sequencing of fragments A and B, which are indicated in FIGURE 6. The region between sites A and B on the bovine E2b chain shows little homology to the corresponding segments of other E2 proteins, suggesting that this region is specific for the E2b of the mammalian branched-chain complex. The conservation in the inner core domain can be better illustrated by the diagram shown in FIGURE 7, which indicates the number of residue identities among the inner-core domains of bovine E2b (residues 175–421), *E. coli* E2p (residues 390–629), and *E. coli* E2k (residues 175–404). The 40 residues in the center of the diagram are conserved among all three domains. The results of this comparison are surprising in that the two *E. coli* inner core domains are as related to each other as they are to the bovine E2b inner core domain. This symmetrical relationship suggests that these three domains were derived from a common ancestor and diverged early during evolution.

EXPRESSION OF THE BOVINE TRANSACYLASE IN *E. coli*

To define the structure and function of the E2b component at the molecular level, we have expressed this component of the bovine branched-chain complex in *E. coli*. A *Pst* I site cDNA located at the beginning of the coding region of the constructed bE2-11 cDNA for the bovine E2b precursor allowed us to conveniently subclone the bE2-11 insert into a prokaryotic vector, pKK233-2 (Pharmacia), without introducing foreign amino acid residues (FIG. 8). Recombinant pre-E2b was then expressed in *E.*

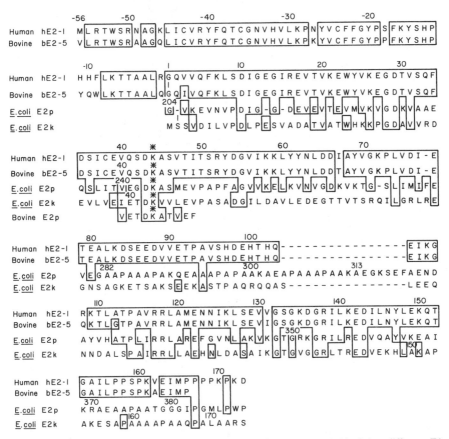

FIGURE 5. Comparison of the sequences for the amino-terminal half of five different E2 proteins. The *E. coli* E2p sequence shown is the lip3 domain. *Open boxes* highlight residues identical to those of human E2b. *Asterisk:* lipoyl lysine (K) residue. (From Lau *et al.*[12] Reprinted with permission from *Biochemistry,* copyright 1988, American Chemical Society.)

```
              A                                          B
              ◆                                          ◆
Bovine E2b   T I P I P I S K P P V F I G K D R T E P V K G F H K A M V K T M S A A L
Rat E2p      F I D I P I S - - - - - - - - - - - - - - N I R R V I A Q R L M Q S K Q
E. coli E2p  K V D F S K F G E I E E V E L G R I Q K I S G A N L S R N W V M I P H -
E. coli E2k  E K R V P M T - - - - - - - - - R L R K R V A E R L L E A K N S T A M -


Bovine E2b   K I P H F G Y C D E V D L T E L V K L R E E L K P I A F A R G I K L S F
Rat E2p      T I P H Y Y L S V D V N M G E V L L V R K E L N K M L E - G K G K I S V
E. coli E2p  - V T H F D K T D I T E L E A F R K Q Q N E E A A K R K - L D V K I T P
E. coli E2k  - L T T F N E V N M K P I M D L R K Q Y G E A F E K R - - H G I R L G F


Bovine E2b   M P F F L K A A S L G L L Q F P I L N A S V D E N C Q N I T Y K A S H N
Rat E2p      N D F I I K A S A L A C L K V P E A N S S W M - D - T V I R Q N H V V D
E. coli E2p  V V F I M K A V A A A L E Q M P R F N S S L S E D G Q R L T L K K Y I N
E. coli E2k  M S F Y V K A V V E A L K R Y P E V N A S I D - - G D D V V Y H N Y F D


Bovine E2b   I G I A M D T E Q G L I V P N V K N V Q I R S I F E I A T E L N R L Q K
Rat E2p      V S V A V S T P A G L I T P I V F N A H I K G L E T I A S D V V S L A S
E. coli E2p  I G V A V D T P N G L V V P V F K D V N K K G I I E L S R E L M T I S K
E. coli E2k  V S M A V S T P R G L V T P V L R D V D T L G M A D I E K K I K E L A V


Bovine E2b   L G S A G Q L S T N D L I G G T F T L S N I G S I G G T Y A K P V I L P
Rat E2p      K A R E G K L Q P H E F Q G G T F T I S N L G M F G I K N F S A I I N P
E. coli E2p  K A R D G K L T A G E M Q G G C F T I S S I G G L G T T H F A P I V N A
E. coli E2k  K G R D G K L T V E D L T G G N F T I T N G G V F G S L M S T P I I N P


Bovine E2b   P E - - - V A I G A L G T I K A L P - R F N E K G E V C K A Q I M N V S
Rat E2p      P Q A C I L A I G A - S E D K L I P - A D N E K G F D V A S - V M S V T
E. coli E2p  P E - - - V A I L G V S K S A M E P - V W N G K E F V P R L - M L P I S
E. coli E2k  P Q - - - S A I L G M H A I K D R P M A V N G Q V E I L P - - M M Y L A


Bovine E2b   W S A D H R I I D G A T V S R F S N L W K S Y L E N P A F M L L D L K ·
Rat E2p      L S C D H R V V D G A V G A Q W L A ...
E. coli E2p  L S F D H R V I D G A D G A R F I T I I N N T L S D I R R L V M ·
E. coli E2k  L S Y D H R L I D G R E S V G F L V T I K E L L E D P T R L L L D V ·
```

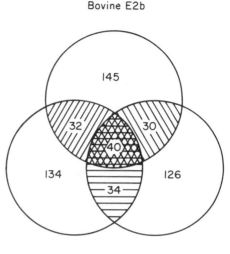

Bovine E2b

E.coli E2p   E.coli E2k

FIGURE 7. Residue identities among the inner core domains of bovine E2b, *E. coli* E2p, and *E. coli* E2k. The values in the *shaded intersecting areas* are the number of residue identities between any two proteins. The 40 residues in the *center* are conserved among all three domains. The values in *unshaded areas* are the number of residues unique to one of the three domains. (From Griffin *et al.*[6] Reprinted from the *Journal of Biological Chemistry* with permission from the American Society for Biochemistry and Molecular Biology.)

coli JM105 cells transformed with pKKbE2-11. The expression was driven by the *trc* promoter in the presence of the inducer isopropylthiogalactoside (IPTG). The recombinant pre-E2b has a molecular weight of 50,000, as determined by SDS-polyacrylamide gel electrophoresis, which is less than that of natural mature E2b $M_r = 52,000$). This difference could be explained by a possible amino-terminal processing of the pre-E2b or by the absence of attached lipoic acid on the recombinant molecule. Lack of lipoic acid attachment was demonstrated by the lack of incorporation of ^{3}H-label into the recombinant pre-E2b when the cells were grown in the presence of ^{3}H-labeled lipoic acid (data not shown).

The recombinant pre-E2b catalyzes the transacylation reaction between [1-^{14}C]isobutyryl-CoA and exogenous dihydrolipoamide,[17] indicating that the inner core domain which contains the active site is folded correctly. To study the assembly of pre-E2b, the lysate of transformed *E. coli* was subjected to gel filtration on a Sepharose 4B column along with natural E2b, and the column fractions were assayed for transacylase activity. The elution profiles indicate that pre-E2b and natural E2b migrate closely with each other (FIG. 9), suggesting that the recombinant pre-E2b is assembled into a 24-subunit quaternary structure as is the natural E2b. Work is in progress to establish the presence of octahedral (432) point-group symmetry in pre-E2b by electron microscopy.

We have recently deleted the pKKbE2-11 vector between various *Pst* I sites to produce three deletion mutants. Linear models of the three deleted polypeptides are shown in FIGURE 10. The recombinant proteins were expressed in *E. coli* and assayed for transacylase activity and antibody reactivities. As described above, the enzyme

◄ FIGURE 6. Comparison of the amino acid sequences of the inner core domains of four E2 proteins. A and B (*diamonds*): locations of trypsin-sensitive site (residues 175 and 205, respectively) as determined by the amino-terminal sequencing of fragments A and B. *Boxed residues* are those identical between any two of the proteins. (From Griffin *et al.*[6] Reprinted from the *Journal of Biological Chemistry* with permission from the American Society for Biochemistry and Molecular Biology.)

assay is based on the transacylation reaction between [1-¹⁴C]isobutyryl-CoA and exogenous dihydrolipoamide. Therefore, a covalently linked lipoyl moiety is not required for activity. The truncation of the region between the E3-binding domain and site B of the inner core domain results in the loss of both enzymatic activity and reactivity with antisera against native E2b (clone Δ115–207) (FIG. 10). Addition of this segment to the inner core domain in the absence of the remainder of the E2b sequence restores both properties (clone Δ−59–114). The truncated inner core domain

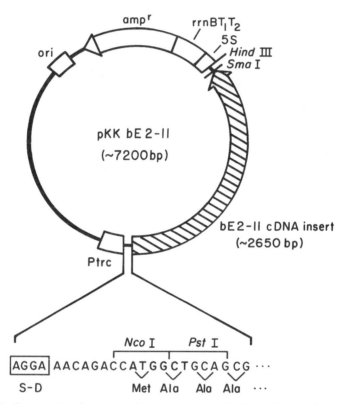

FIGURE 8. Construction of a prokaryotic expression vector for the production of the bovine E2b precursor in *E. coli*. The cDNA (bE2-11) encoding the entire bovine E2b precursor was subcloned into pKK233-2 (Pharmacia). The construction utilized a convenient *Pst* I site to produce an open reading frame in the expression vector which did not alter the region coding for the amino terminus of bovine pre-E2b.

spanning from site B to the carboxyl terminus is neither enzymatically active nor immunochemically reactive with the anti-native E2b (clone Δ−59–207). Antisera to SDS-denatured E2b, on the other hand, react with all three of the truncated E2b proteins, since the antisera contain immunological activity for the inner core domain. The above results, taken together, support the conclusion derived from earlier limited proteolysis studies, that the region between sites A and B of the inner core domain is essential for transacylase activity. Moreover, the antigenicity in native E2b appears to be associated with the proline-rich mobile region between residues 115 and 207.

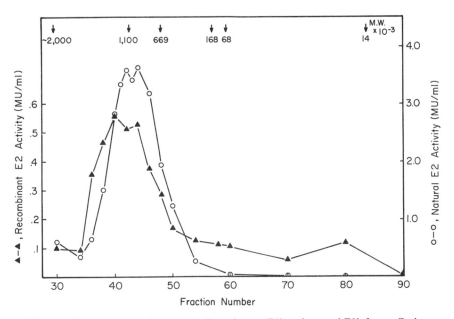

FIGURE 9. Elution profiles of enzymatically active pre-E2b and natural E2b from a Sepharose 4B column. Column fractions were assayed for transacylase activity using [1-^{14}C]isobutyryl-CoA and exogenous dihydrolipoamide as substrates. Different scales are used to express recombinant (*left*) and natural (*right*) E2b activities. ▲, recombinant pre-E2b; ○, natural E2b.

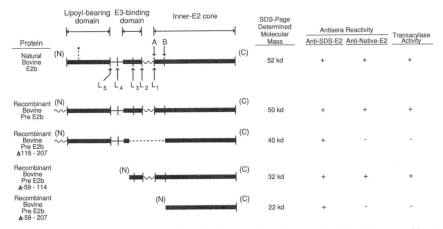

FIGURE 10. Enzymatic activity and antibody reactivity of natural bovine E2b, recombinant bovine pre-E2b, and three deleted (△) recombinant bovine pre-E2b polypeptides. The diagram presents linear models of the domain structure of natural E2b and the four recombinant molecules. The three deleted recombinant pre-E2b polypeptides were expressed using pKKbE2-11 vectors which had deletions between various *Pst* I sites. The molecular mass determined by SDS-PAGE, the antibody reactivity, and the presence of transacylase activity are indicated for each polypeptide.

INBORN ERRORS IN MAPLE SYRUP URINE DISEASE

We are interested in MSUD because the disease provides an excellent model to study how a single mutation would affect the assembly and function of the branched-chain complex. The information derived from these investigations may thus further our understanding of the structure and function of mitochondrial multienzyme systems. MSUD as we know it today has five distinct clinical phenotypes: classical, intermediate, intermittent, thiamin-responsive, and E3-deficient. Our approach is to use cells from various types of MSUD patients as a model to characterize the enzyme deficiency at the protein, mRNA, and DNA levels. To carry out these molecular studies, we isolated cDNAs for the E1b-α and E1b-β subunits of the mammalian branched-chain complex, in addition to the E2b cDNAs that we previously isolated. The full-length bovine E1b-α cDNA is 1,821 bp in length, encoding a leader peptide of 55 amino acids and a mature E1b-α subunit of 400 residues.[3] Subsequently, we isolated a human E1b-α cDNA using a combination of anti-bovine E1b antisera and bovine E1b-α cDNA as probes.[18] The human E1b-α cDNA (1,783 bp) encodes a partial leader peptide of 43 residues and a complete, mature E1b-α subunit of 400 residues. There is 96% amino acid identity between mature bovine and human E1b-α subunits. cDNAs for bovine and human E1b-β subunits have also recently been isolated in this laboratory. The bovine E1b-β cDNA (1,393 bp) specifies a partial presequence of 28 residues and an entire mature polypeptide of 342 residues.[19]

Once the cDNAs for the various subunits of the mammalian branched-chain complex were available, it was possible to perform Northern blotting with poly(A)$^+$ RNA fractions prepared from cultured fibroblasts from normal controls and MSUD

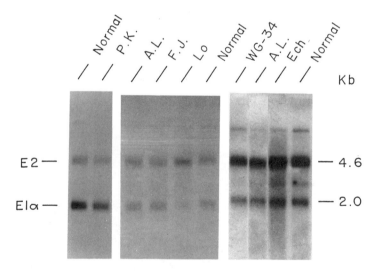

FIGURE 11. Northern blot analysis with poly(A)$^+$ RNA isolated from normal and MSUD fibroblasts. Poly(A)$^+$ RNA (5 μg/lane) was resolved on an 0.8% agarose gel and subjected to Northern blot analysis. A mixed probe consisting of nick-translated human E2b (1.6 kb) and human E1b-α (0.9 kb) cDNAs was used. P.K. (Mennonite), A.L., F.J., and Ech are classical MSUD patients. Lo is an intermediate MSUD patient. WG-34 is a thiamin-responsive patient. (From Fisher et al.[18] Reprinted from the *Journal of Biological Chemistry* with permission from the American Society for Biochemistry and Molecular Biology.)

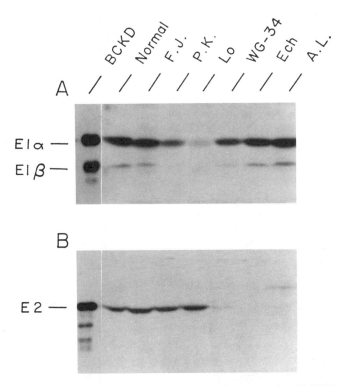

FIGURE 12. Western blot analysis with cellular extracts from normal and MSUD fibroblasts. Cellular extracts (300 μg/lane) from cultured fibroblasts were subjected to Western blot analysis with either a combination of affinity-purified anti–E1b-α and anti–E1b-β (**Panel A**) or anti-E2b (**Panel B**) antibodies as a probe. The clinical phenotypes of the MSUD patients are described in the legend to FIGURE 11. BCKD, branched-chain α-keto dehydrogenase complex. (From Fisher *et al.*[18] Reprinted from the *Journal of Biological Chemistry* with permission from the American Society for Biochemistry and Molecular Biology.)

patients. A mixture of nicked-translated human E1b-α (hE1α-1) and human E2b cDNAs were used as probes. FIGURE 11 shows that E2b (4.6 kb) and E1b-α (2.0 kb) mRNAs are present in normal size and abundance in fibroblasts from classical MSUD patients (P.K., A.L., F.J., and Ech), as well as from a thiamin-responsive patient (WG-34). The level of E1b-α mRNA is significantly reduced in fibroblasts from a patient with intermittent MSUD (Lo), whereas the content of E2b mRNA is normal in cells from this patient. The minor bands present in addition to E2b and E1b-α mRNAs appeared to be non-specific, as their intensities varied depending on the washing conditions. E1b-β mRNA was not measured in this study.

The levels of specific protein subunits (E1b-α, E1b-β, and E2b) of the branched-chain complex in cultured fibroblasts were measured by Western blot analysis. After electrotransfer, resolved proteins from normal and MSUD fibroblasts were blotted with either a mixture of affinity-purified anti–E1b-α and anti–E1b-β antibodies or with anti-E2b antibodies alone. FIGURE 12 (Panel A) shows that E1b-α and E1b-β subunits are present in normal size and abundance in fibroblasts from classical patients F.J., A.L., and Ech and are slightly reduced in cells from thiamin-responsive patient

WG-34. Both E1b-α and E1b-β subunits are nearly absent in cells from intermittent MSUD patient Lo, whereas the levels of both subunits are reduced in cells from the Mennonite patient (P.K.). The E2b subunit exists in normal size and quantity in fibroblasts from patients F.J., P.K. and Lo (FIG. 12, Panel B). By contrast, the E2b subunit is completely absent in cells from patient Ech and markedly reduced in cells from thiamin-responsive patient WG-34 and classical patient A.L.

The E2b subunit of the branched-chain complex was reported also to be absent in lymphoblastoid cell line GM-1366.[20] To elucidate the mechanism for this deficiency, we measured the levels of mRNA and subunits of the branched-chain complex in normal and GM-1366 lymphoblasts. The content of E2b mRNA is markedly lower in GM-1366 lymphoblasts than in normal cells (FIG. 13, upper panel), whereas the level

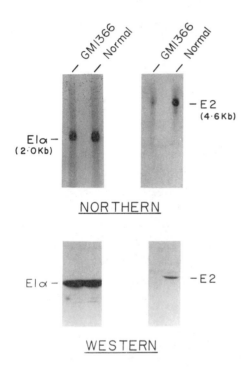

FIGURE 13. The content of mRNA and protein subunits of the branched-chain α-keto acid dehydrogenase complex in E2b-deficient MSUD lymphoblasts (GM-1366). Northern blot analysis (**upper panels**) was carried out with either human E1b-α or human E2b cDNA as a probe. For Western blotting (**lower panels**), affinity-purified anti–E1b-α or combined rabbit antisera to native and SDS-denatured E2b (bovine) were used as a probe. (From Fisher et al.[18] Reprinted from the *Journal of Biological Chemistry* with permission from the American Society for Biochemistry and Molecular Biology.)

of E1b-α mRNA appears to be normal in GM-1366 cells. The reduced E2b mRNA level is consistent with the absence of the E2b subunit in GM-1366 lymphoblasts (FIG. 13, lower panel). The E1b-α mRNA and subunit are present in normal abundance in GM-1366 lymphoblasts.

TABLE 2 shows the activity levels of the branched-chain complex and E1b and E3 components in cultured fibroblasts from classical patients P.K. and F.J., intermittent MSUD patient Lo, and thiamin-responsive patient WG-34. The results indicate that the overall complex and E1b activities are absent in P.K., F.J., and Lo cells and markedly reduced in WG-34 cells (20–40% residual activity). As a control, E3 activity was assayed and shown to be normal in cells from these patients.

The above results obtained with MSUD cells are summarized in TABLE 3. On the basis of the pattern of the contents of mRNA and protein subunits of the branched-

TABLE 2. Enzyme Activities of Branched-Chain Complex and of E1 and E3
Components in Cultured Fibroblasts from Normal Controls and MSUD Patients[a]

Cell Line	Enzyme Activity (nmol product/min/mg protein)[b]		
	Overall Complex	E1 ($\times 10^3$)	E3
Normal	0.09–0.15	7.7–9.5	37.3–51.3
P.K.	0	0.1	57.1
F.J.	0	0	69.6
WG-34	0.02	3.9	52.6
Lo	0	0.06	50.4

[a]Adapted from Fisher et al. [18]

[b]Harvested fibroblasts were treated with 1 mM α-chloroisocaproate at 37°C for 15 min. The treated cells were centrifuged, resuspended in Krebs buffer, and freeze-thaw disrupted for assays of total E1 and complex, and E3 activities.

chain complex, we have tentatively classified these MSUD patients under five distinct molecular phenotypes. These consist of Type I, where the levels of E1b-α mRNA and E1b-α and E1b-β subunits are normal but E1b activity is deficient, as observed with F.J. cells; Type II, where E1b-α mRNA is present in normal quantity, whereas the levels of E1b-α and E1b-β subunits are reduced (P.K.); Type III, where the level of E1b-α mRNA is markedly reduced with a concomitant loss of E1b-α and E1b-β subunits (Lo); Type IV, where the levels of both E2b mRNA and E2b subunit are markedly reduced (GM-1366), and Type V, where E2b mRNA is normally expressed but the E2b subunit is absent or markedly reduced in cells (Ech, A.L., and thiamin-responsive WG-34). These five molecular phenotypes are derived from results of Northern and Western blotting with cells from only 7 MSUD patients. We anticipate that new molecular phenotypes will be identified as more MSUD cell lines are studied. There appears to be no correlation between clinical and molecular phenotypes, since multiple molecular phenotypes are observed within classical MSUD.

The existence of different molecular phenotypes supports the proposal of genetic heterogeneity in MSUD demonstrated previously by complementation studies. The multiple molecular phenotypes probably reflect the large number of genes encoding

TABLE 3. Molecular Phenotypes in Cultured Cells from MSUD Patients[a]

Cell Line	MSUD Phenotype	Molecular Phenotype	E1α		E1β	E2	
			mRNA[b]	Subunit[b]	Subunit[b]	mRNA[b]	Subunit[b]
Normal	None	None	+	+	+	+	+
F.J.	Classical	I	+	+	+	+	+
P.K.	Clasical	II	+	−	−	+	+
Lo	Intermediate	III	−	−	−	+	+
GM-1366	Classical	IV	+	+	N.D.	−	−
Ech	Classical	V	+	+	+	+	−
A.L.	Classical	V	+	+	+	+	−
WG-34[c]	Thiamin-responsive	V	+	+	+	+	−

[a]Adapted from Fisher et al.[18]

[b]+, present in normal size and abundance; −, absent or much reduced in abundance; N.D., not determined.

[c]Thiamin-responsive MSUD patient described by C. Scriver.[21]

the branched-chain complex. The results have thus identified the genetic loci affected in different MSUD patients. Although the specific mutations leading to these phenotypes remain to be elucidated, the following mechanisms can be speculated. In Type I MSUD (F.J.) (TABLE 3), a structural mutation in the E1b-α or E1b-β subunit is likely. The presence of a mutant E1b protein is consistent with a reduced affinity of the branched-chain complex for α-ketoisovalerate in fibroblasts from F.J. On the other hand, a defect in the expression of E1b-α and E2b genes or the synthesis of unstable mRNAs from them is the probable cause for Type III (Lo) and Type IV (GM-1366) MSUD, respectively. The levels of mRNA and subunit are concomitantly reduced or absent in these cells. The absence of both E1b-α and E1b-β subunits in Lo (Type III) is of interest if one assumes the mutation involves only the expression of the E1b-α gene. It is speculated that the E1b-β subunit is expressed at normal levels in these cells but is rapidly degraded because of its failure to assemble into a stable $\alpha_2\beta_2$ structure with E1b-α.

The mechanisms for Type II and Type V are presently uncertain. The results obtained with P.K. cells (Type II; TABLE 3) are consistent with a structural mutation in either the E1b-α or the E1b-β subunit. Alternatively, expression of the E1b-β gene may be deficient in Type II, resulting in a reduced level of the E1b-β subunit. In either case, both E1b-α and E1b-β chains may become unstable as a result of improper folding and assembly, similar to the situation proposed for Type III. P.K. is a member of the Mennonite kindred, where the prevalence of MSUD is 1 in 175 as a result of consanguinity. It is conceivable that a single mutation is transmitted within all the Mennonite families. As for Type V, the lack of detectable E2b subunit in cells expressing normal levels of E2b mRNA, as observed in Ech (FIG. 12), is of interest. This pattern may result from a frame-shift or nonsense mutation or because of the synthesis of an unstable protein. Sequence determination of the Type V transcripts by the polymerase chain reaction, which is in progress, will provide the data to choose among these possibilities.

The classification of the thiamin-responsive (WG-34) patient under type V requires specific comment. The patient was originally described by Scriver et al.[21] to have responded favorably to oral thiamin treatment at a dosage of 10 mg/day. On this regimen, her branched-chain amino acid levels in plasma returned to normal without restriction of dietary proteins. Intact fibroblasts from WG-34 exhibited 40% of the normal decarboxylation rate when incubated with $[1\text{-}^{14}C]\alpha$-ketoisovalerate. Since the level of E2b mRNA is normal while its protein content is low, a point mutation or small deletion is the likely cause for the synthesis of an unstable E2b. We have shown previously that the K_m value of the branched-chain complex for TPP is elevated in WG-34 cells compared to normal cells.[22] Thus, the apparent deficiency in E2b is unexpected, since the E1b-α subunit contains the binding site for TPP.[5] One possible explanation is that the presence of a normal E2b is essential for the efficient binding of TPP to E1b. It has been shown with the chicken glycine-cleavage system that the addition of the lipoate-bearing H-protein causes a conformational change on the pyridoxal phosphate–containing P-protein and significantly increases the affinity of the latter enzyme component for substrate glycine.[23] Whether a similar mechanism exists in the branched-chain complex will have to be studied. Alternatively, Heffelfinger et al.[24] have shown that the E1b-α subunit is protected against chymotryptic digestion by added TPP and α-ketoisocaproate; they have suggested that these reagents stabilize the residual branched-chain complex in thiamin-responsive MSUD in vivo.

In conclusion, the above studies have demonstrated the diversity and complexity of MSUD at the mRNA and protein levels. The molecular phenotype associated with each patient will help develop rational approaches to the management of this metabolic disorder. The isolation of complete cDNAs for subunits of the human branched-chain complex will permit further investigation of different mutations in MSUD at the molecular level. Cloning of the human E1b-α and E2b genes is in progress.

SUMMARY

We have cloned cDNAs encoding the E1b-α, E1b-β, and E2b subunits of the bovine and human branched-chain α-keto acid complexes. The deduced primary structures indicate that the mammalian E2b contains a lipoyl-bearing, an E3-binding, and an inner core domain that are linked in series by two flexible hinge regions. The observed conservation among E2 proteins in each of the three folded domains strongly suggests that the structural cores of α-keto acid dehydrogenase complexes are evolutionarily related. We have expressed bovine pre-E2b in E. coli. The lipoate-free precursor protein is enzymatically active and appears to assemble into a 24-mer structure. Studies with deletion mutants support the proposal that the antigenicity in pre-E2b is associated with the flexible proline-rich hinge region. We have observed five distinct molecular phenotypes in maple syrup urine disease (MSUD) cells, according to the pattern of the branched-chain complex protein subunits and mRNAs present. The results have demonstrated a high degree of genetic heterogeneity in MSUD and have identified the affected genes which must be characterized.

ACKNOWLEDGMENT

The excellent typing assistance of Susan Alexander is appreciated.

REFERENCES

1. REED, L. J., F. M. PETTIT, S. J. YEAMAN, W. M. TEAGUE & D. M. BLEILE. 1980. FEBS Proc. Meet. **60:** 47–56.
2. DANCIS, J., J. HUTZLER & M. LEVITZ. 1963. Biochim. Biophys. Acta **77:** 523–524.
3. HU, C.-W. C., K. S. LAU, T. A. GRIFFIN, J. L. CHUANG, C. W. FISHER, R. P. COX & D. T. CHUANG. 1988. J. Biol. Chem. **263:** 9007–9014.
4. HU, C.-W. C. & D. T. CHUANG. Unpublished observations.
5. STEPP, L. R. & L. J. REED. 1985. Biochemistry **24:** 7187–7191.
6. GRIFFIN, T. A., K. S. LAU & D. T. CHUANG. 1988. J. Biol. Chem. **263:** 14008–14014.
7. DAMUNI, Z., M. L. MERRYFIELD, J. S. HUMPHREYS & L. J. REED. 1984. Proc. Natl. Acad. Sci. USA **81:** 4335–4338.
8. BLEILE, D. M., P. MUNK, R. M. OLIVER & L. J. REED. 1979. Proc. Natl. Acad. Sci. USA **76:** 4385–4389.
9. CHUANG, D. T., C.-W. C. HU, L. S. KU, P. J. MARKOVITZ & R. P. COX. 1985. J. Biol. Chem. **260:** 13779–13786.
10. HU, C.-W. C., T. A. GRIFFIN, K. S. LAU, R. P. COX & D. T. CHUANG. 1986. J. Biol. Chem. **261:** 343–349.
11. PACKMAN, L. C. & R. N. PERHAM. 1986. FEBS Lett. **206:** 193–198.
12. LAU, K. S., T. A. GRIFFIN, C.-W. C. HU & D. T. CHUANG. 1988. Biochemistry **27:** 1972–1981.
13. STEPHENS, P. E., M. G. DARLISON, H. M. LEWIS & J. R. GUEST. 1983. Eur. J. Biochem. **133:** 481–489.
14. SPENCER, M. E., M. G. DARLISON, P. E. STEPHENS, I. K. DUCKENFIELD & J. R. GUEST. 1984. Eur. J. Biochem. **141:** 361–374.

15. GERSHWIN, M. E., I. R. MACKAY, A. STURGESS & R. L. COPPEL. 1987. J. Immunol. **138:** 3525–3531.
16. LESLIE, A. G. W., P. C. E. MOODY & W. V. SHAW. 1988. Proc. Natl. Acad. Sci. USA **85:** 4133–4137.
17. CHUANG, D. T., C.-W. C. HU, L. S. KU, W.-L. NIU, D. E. MYERS & R. P. COX. 1984. J. Biol. Chem. **259:** 9277–9284.
18. FISHER, C. W., J. L. CHUANG, T. A. GRIFFIN, K. S. LAU, R. P. COX & D. T. CHUANG. 1989. J. Biol. Chem. **264:** 3448–3453.
19. CHUANG, J. L., R. P. COX & D. T. CHUANG. Manuscript in preparation.
20. INDO, Y., A. KITANO, F. ENDO, I. AKABOSHI & I. MATSUDA. 1987. J. Clin. Invest. **80:** 63–70.
21. SCRIVER, C. R., C. L. CLOW, S. MACKENZIE & E. DELVIN. 1971. Lancet **1:** 310–312.
22. CHUANG, D. T., L. S. KU & R. P. COX. 1982. Proc. Natl. Acad. Sci. USA **79:** 3300–3304.
23. HIRAGA, K. & G. KIKUCHI. 1980. J. Biol. Chem. **255:** 11671–11676.
24. HEFFELFINGER, S. C., E. T. SEWELL, L. J. ELSAS & D. J. DANNER. 1984. Am. J. Hum. Genet. **36:** 802–807.

DISCUSSION OF THE PAPER

R. N. PERHAM (*University of Cambridge, Cambridge, England*): I am very interested in your expression of the bovine E2b precursor. I thought precursor proteins were not folded.

D. T. CHUANG (*The University of Texas Southwestern Medical Center, Dallas, TX*): The expression of bovine pre-E2b in *E. coli* is an unusual situation. As you know, *E. coli* does not have mitochondria, so the pre-E2b synthesized is not imported into mitochondria and processed. One of our theories is that when you express so much pre-E2b in the cell (the yield is approximately 10% of the total protein in the *E. coli* lysate), these recombinant molecules simply find each other and assemble into a functional enzyme. It is also possible that bacteria do not have cytosolic protein factors to keep the precursor protein from folding. Although the inner core domain is obviously folded and is highly assembled, we still do not know whether the lipoyl-bearing domain is folded. The failure of ^{3}H-labeled lipoic acid to be incorporated into the pre-E2b is consistent with an unfolded structure in the lipoyl-bearing domain. Alternatively, the lipoyl-bearing domain may be folded, but the presence of the presequence may alter the conformation around the lipoyl-attachment site such that the holoenzyme synthetase can no longer recognize the substrate site.

PERHAM: So you are going to do electron microscopy with the pre-E2b protein?

CHUANG: Yes, as I mentioned earlier, we would like to establish the presence of octahedral symmetry in the pre-E2b by electron microscopy.

R. A. HARRIS (*Indiana University School of Medicine, Indianapolis, IN*): I just want to comment on your findings with thiamin-responsive WG-34 cells. We have sequenced the region around the TPP-binding site on the E1b-α of WG-34 cells. It appears to be normal.

Biochemical and Molecular Genetic Aspects of Pyruvate Dehydrogenase Complex from *Saccharomyces cerevisiae*[a]

LESTER J. REED, KAREN S. BROWNING, XIAO-DA NIU,
ROBERT H. BEHAL, AND DAVID J. UHLINGER[b]

*Clayton Foundation Biochemical Institute
and
Department of Chemistry
The University of Texas at Austin
Austin, Texas 78712*

Pyruvate dehydrogenase (PDH) complexes from prokaryotic and eukaryotic sources are composed of multiple copies of three enzymes: pyruvate dehydrogenase (E_1), dihydrolipoamide acetyltransferase (E_2), and dihydrolipoamide dehydrogenase (E_3). These three enzymes, acting in sequence, catalyze the reactions shown in FIGURE 1.[1] E_1 catalyzes both the decarboxylation of pyruvate (reaction 1) and the subsequent reductive acetylation of the lipoyl moiety (reaction 2), which is covalently bound to E_2. E_2 catalyzes the acetyl transfer step (reaction 3), and E_3 catalyzes the reoxidation of the dihydrolipoyl moiety, with NAD^+ as the ultimate electron acceptor (reactions 4 and 5). The eukaryotic PDH complexes contain a minor component of unknown function, designated protein X.[2,3] The eukaryotic PDH complexes, with the possible exception of the yeast PDH complex, also contain small amounts of two specific regulatory enzymes, PDH kinase and PDH phosphatase, which modulate the activity of E_1 by phosphorylation and dephosphorylation.[4-6]

SUBUNIT COMPOSITION AND STRUCTURE OF YEAST PDH COMPLEX

The prokaryotic and eukaryotic PDH complexes are organized about a core consisting of the oligomeric E_2, around which are arranged multiple copies of E_1 and E_3, bound by noncovalent bonds. Two polyhedral forms of E_2 have been observed in the electron microscope, the cube and the dodecahedron (FIG. 2).[7] The former design is exhibited by the E_2 components of the PDH and α-ketoglutarate dehydrogenase (KGDH) complexes of *Escherichia coli* and the mammalian KGDH and branched-chain α-keto acid dehydrogenase complexes. These E_2 components consist of 24 apparently identical subunits arranged with octahedral (432) symmetry. On the other hand, the E_2 components of the PDH complexes from mammalian and avian tissues, fungi, *Bacillus stearothermophilus,* and *Streptococcus faecalis* have the appearance

[a]This work was supported in part by Grant GM06590 from the National Institutes of Health, U.S. Public Health Service.
[b]Present address: Department of Biochemistry, Emory University School of Medicine, Atlanta, Georgia 30322.

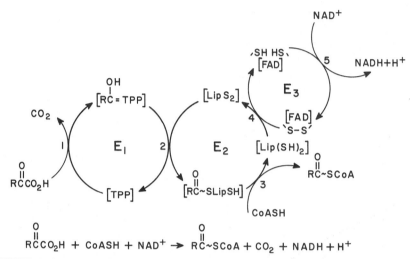

FIGURE 1. Reaction sequence in pyruvate oxidation ($R = CH_3$). **TPP**, thiamin diphosphate; **LipS₂** and **Lip(SH)₂**, lipoyl moiety and its reduced form; **CoASH**, coenzyme A; **FAD**, flavin adenine dinucleotide; **NAD⁺** and **NADH**, nicotinamide adenine dinucleotide and its reduced form; **E₁**, pyruvate dehydrogenase; **E₂**, dihydrolipoamide acetyltransferase; **E₃**, dihydrolipoamide dehydrogenase.

of a pentagonal dodecahedron in the electron microscope and apparently consist of 60 subunits arranged with icosahedral (532) symmetry.

The apparent molecular weights of the subunits of the *Saccharomyces cerevisiae* PDH complex, estimated by sodium dodecyl sulfate-polyacrylamide gel electrophoresis (SDS-PAGE) are $E_1\alpha$, 45,000; $E_1\beta$, 35,000; E_2, 58,000; E_3, 56,000.[8] The molecular weights of E_2 and E_3 calculated from the deduced amino acid sequences are 48,546 and 51,558, respectively.[9,10] Although the subunit stoichiometry of the PDH complex from

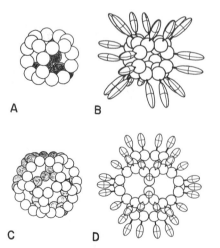

A   B

C   D

FIGURE 2. Interpretive models of the quaternary structure of dihydrolipoamide acyltransferases. (**A**) Model of those acyltransferases consisting of 24 subunits arranged in groups of 3 about the 8 vertices of a cube. (**B**) Model of the 24-subunit acyltransferases illustrating the proposed domain structure. Each of the 24 acyltransferase subunits is represented by one sphere and its attached ellipsoid. The spheres represent the assemblage of compact, inner core domains, and the ellipsoids represent the extended lipoyl domains. (**C**) Model of those acyltransferases consisting of 60 subunits arranged in groups of 3 about the 20 vertices of a pentagonal dodecahedron. (**D**) Model of the 60-subunit acyltransferases illustrating the proposed domain structure. The figure is viewed down a 2-fold axis of symmetry.

S. cerevisiae has not been determined, this complex is similar in size ($s_{20,w} = 77S$), subunit composition, and appearance in the electron microscope to the bovine heart PDH complex, which has a M_r of about 8,500,000 and contains about 30 E_1 tetramers ($\alpha_2\beta_2$) and six E_3 dimers arranged, respectively, on the 30 edges and in the 12 faces of the 60-subunit E_2 core.[11]

A unique architectural feature of dihydrolipoamide acyltransferases, revealed initially by limited proteolysis of the *E. coli* acetyltransferase with trypsin and by electron microscopy, is that the E_2 subunits contain two major domains—an extended, flexible, outer, lipoyl-bearing domain and a compact, inner, catalytic and subunit-binding domain.[12] The assemblage of compact, catalytic and subunit-binding domains constitutes the inner core of E_2, conferring the cubelike or pentagonal dodecahedron-like appearance in the electron microscope (FIG. 2). These findings have been confirmed and extended by studies using molecular genetics[13,14] and ^{1}H-NMR spectroscopy.[15–17] The amino-terminal segment of the E_2 polypeptide chains contains one to three lipoyl domains, followed by a domain that is involved in binding E_3 or E_1 and E_3, and then the catalytic inner core domain (FIG. 3). The domains are linked to each other by protease-sensitive segments that are rich in the conservatively substituted residues alanine, proline, serine, and threonine and in charged amino acid residues. These interdomain linker segments (hinge regions) are thought to provide

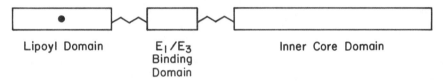

Lipoyl Domain E_1/E_3 Inner Core Domain
                       Binding
                       Domain

FIGURE 3. Diagrammatic representation of the structural domains of dihydrolipoamide acyltransferase (E_2) subunits. The acyltransferases contain one, two, or three lipoyl domains. The domains are connected by hinge regions ($\sim$). The lipoyllysine residue in the lipoyl domain is indicated ($\bullet$).

flexibility to the lipoyl domains, facilitating active-site coupling within these multienzyme complexes. The *E. coli*[13] and *Azotobacter vinelandii*[18] dihydrolipoamide acyltransferases contain three lipoyl domains, the human[19] and rat liver[20,21] acetyltransferases contain two, and the *S. cerevisiae*[9] and *B. stearothermophilus*[22] acetyltransferases contain only one lipoyl domain. The lipoyl moiety is bound in amide linkage to the ϵ-amino group of a lysine residue. There does not appear to be a correlation between the number of lipoyl domains and the structure of the E_2 core, i.e., whether octahedral or icosahedral design.

PHOSPHORYLATION AND DEPHOSPHORYLATION OF YEAST PDH COMPLEX

In eukaryotic cells, the α-keto acid dehydrogenase complexes are located in mitochondria, within the inner membrane–matrix compartment. The activity of PDH complexes from eukaryotic sources, including mammalian, avian, and plant tissues and *Neurospora crassa,* is regulated by a phosphorylation-dephosphorylation cycle.[1,5,23] Phosphorylation by PDH kinase inactivates the complex, and dephosphorylation by PDH phosphatase reactivates the complex. The phosphorylation sites in the mammalian PDH complex are located on three serine residues in the $E_1\alpha$ subunit.[24,25] Attempts thus far to demonstrate PDH kinase activity in *S. cerevisiae* have been unsuccessful.[26,27] However, the purified PDH complex from *S. cerevisiae* is phosphorylated on its $E_1\alpha$ subunits and inactivated in the presence of MgATP and bovine PDH kinase, and the phosphorylated, inactive complex is dephosphorylated and reactivated in the presence of Mg^{2+} and bovine PDH phosphatase[27] (FIG. 4). Tryptic digestion of the ^{32}P-labeled PDH complex yielded a single phosphopeptide, which was purified to homogeneity. The sequence around the phosphorylation site in the yeast $E_1\alpha$ subunit is very similar to the sequence around the major regulatory phosphorylation site in $E_1\alpha$ from bovine kidney and bovine and porcine heart (FIG. 5). These data demonstrate that the *S. cerevisiae* PDH complex possesses the capacity to be regulated by phosphorylation-dephosphorylation, even though PDH kinase activity has not been detected in cell-free extracts of *S. cerevisiae* or in purified preparations of the yeast PDH complex. Whether the kinase is present in low concentration or in an inactive form, or whether biosynthesis of the kinase is suppressed, remains to be determined.

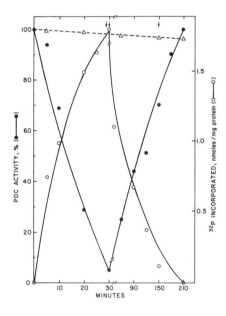

FIGURE 4. Phosphorylation/inactivation of yeast PDH complex by bovine PDH kinase and dephosphorylation/reactivation by bovine PDH phosphatase. The reaction mixture contained 706 μg of highly purified yeast PDH complex, 5 μg of highly purified PDH kinase from bovine kidney, 1 m*M* $MgCl_2$, and 0.1 m*M* [γ-^{32}P]ATP (230,000 cpm/nmole) in 1 ml of 20 m*M* 3-(*N*-morpholino)propanesulfonate buffer (pH 7.2) at 30°C. Aliquots were removed at the indicated times and assayed for PDH complex (PDC) activity (●) and for protein-bound radioactivity (O). At 30 min (*vertical arrows*), unreacted ATP was scavenged by addition of 1 μg of hexokinase and 1 μmole of glucose. At 33 min, 5 μg of highly purified PDH phosphatase from bovine heart and 10 m*M* $MgCl_2$ (final concentration) were added. Five micrograms of bovine heart phosphatase was added subsequently at 150 min. (From Uhlinger *et al.*[27] Reprinted with permission from *Biochemistry*, copyright 1986, American Chemical Society.)

CLONING AND NUCLEOTIDE SEQUENCE OF A cDNA FOR E_3

To gain further understanding of the structure, function, and regulation of eukaryotic PDH complexes, we have undertaken isolation and expression of the genes encoding E_1, E_2, E_3, and protein X from *S. cerevisiae*. We have cloned and sequenced a cDNA encoding E_3,[10] the gene encoding E_2,[9] and a cDNA encoding all but an amino-terminal segment of $E_1\alpha$.

Plaques produced from a yeast cDNA λgt11 library (provided by Hans Trachsel and Michael Altman, Universität Bern, Bern, Switzerland) were screened with rabbit antiserum to the E_3 component of the PDH complex from bakers' yeast. Three positive clones were obtained. One of these clones (pE3-3) also hybridized to a 17-base mixed

Bovine
Porcine
Tyr-His-Gly-His-Ser(P)-Met-Ser-Asp-Pro-Gly-Val-Ser-Tyr-Arg

Yeast   Tyr-Gly-Gly-His-Ser(P)-Met-Ser-Asp-Pro-Gly-Thr-Thr-Tyr-Arg

FIGURE 5. Comparison of amino acid sequences around phosphorylation sites in pyruvate dehydrogenases from bovine kidney and heart,[24] pig heart,[25] and yeast.[27]

oligonucleotide probe corresponding to the amino terminus of E_3. This clone contained an insert of about 2.1 kilobases (kb) (FIG. 6), which was subcloned into the plasmid vector Bluescript (Stratagene) for DNA sequencing. The nucleotide sequence of clone pE3-3 and the deduced amino acid sequence of the protein are shown in FIGURE 7. The precursor of E_3 contains a putative 21-residue presequence that is rich in basic and hydroxylated amino acid residues and is devoid of acidic amino acids. This feature is characteristic of presequences of mitochondrial matrix–inner membrane proteins.[28] The presumed mature protein consists of 478 amino acids and has a calculated M_r of 51,558 (52,344 including a molecule of flavin adenine dinucleotide). Its predicted amino-terminal sequence is virtually identical with the 25-residue amino terminal sequence of the purified protein (underlined in FIG. 7). It is noteworthy that the amino acid sequence surrounding the putative active site cystine (asterisks in FIG. 7) is identical with the sequence reported for the purified protein from pig heart.[29] The complete nucleotide sequence of the E_3 gene from *S. cerevisiae* has also been established.[30] The cDNA and genomic DNA sequences are in agreement within the coding region, except for a one-base mismatch at position $+281$, which does not alter the primary sequence. RNA blot analysis of yeast poly(A)$^+$ RNA shows that the size of the mRNA for E_3 is ca. 1.6 kb. The discrepancy between the size of the mRNA and the size of the cDNA (2.1 kb) indicates that another cDNA was ligated to the E_3 cDNA during the cloning procedures. The flanking region 5′ to the coding region for E_3 shows very strong homology to a portion of the gene encoding enolase in yeast (J. Ross, personal communication). The gene encoding E_3 has been cloned and sequenced from *E. coli*,[31] *A. vinelandii*,[32] and yeast,[30] and the cDNA for E_3 has been cloned and sequenced from yeast,[10] pig adrenal medulla,[33] human liver,[34] and human small cell carcinoma.[33] These E_3 proteins exhibit extensive sequence similarity.

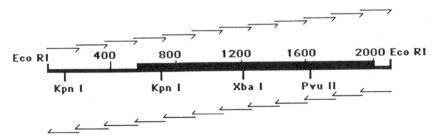

FIGURE 6. Restriction endonuclease map and sequencing strategy for yeast dihydrolipoamide dehydrogenase (E_3) cDNA. *Thick bar* represents the coding region for the enzyme. *Arrows* show the direction and extent of the nucleotide sequencing. (From Browning *et al.*[10] Reprinted with permission from the *Proceedings of the National Academy of Sciences of the United States of America.*)

```
GGGAATTCGCTGGTATCCAAATTGTTGCTGATGACGGTCACCAACCCAGCTAGAA
TTGCTACCGCCATCGAAGAGAAGGCTGCTGAACGTTTGTTGTGAAGGTAACCAAATCG
GTACCTTGTCTGCAATCCATCAAGGCTGTCAAGACTTTCTTTGCTGAAGGGTTGTGGTT
TGGTTTCCCACAGATCTCGGTGAAACTGAAGACACTTTCATTGCTGACTTGGTTGTCGGTT
TAGAACTGGTCAAATCAAGACTGGTCTGCTCAGCTAGATCCGAAAGATTGGCTAAGTTGA
ACCAATTGGTCGAGAATCGAGAAGAATTGGGTGACAAGAACGTGTCTGAAAACT
TCCACCAGGTGACAAGTTGTAAAGTGCTTTAACTAAGAATTATTAGTCTTTCTGCT
ATTTTTCATCATAGTTTAGAACACTTTATATTAACGAATAGTTTATGAATCTATTTAGG
TTTAAAAATTGATACAGTTTTATAAAAAAAAAAAAAAAATTCCACAATGTTAAGA
                                                     M L R
                                                      -21

ATCAGATCACTCCTAAATAATAAGCGTGCTTTTCGTCCACAGTCAGGACATTGACCATT
I  R  S  L  L  N  N  K  R  A  F  S  S  T  V  R  T  L  T  I
                                                        1

AACAAGTCACGTGATGTAGTCATCATCGGTGGTGCTTGTGGTTAGGTGGCTGCTATC
N  K  S  H  D  V  V  I  I  G  G  G  P  A  G  Y  V  A  A  I
        20

AAAGCTGCTCAATTGGGATTTAACACTGCCATGTGTAGAAAAAGAGGCAAATTAGGCCGGT
K  A  A  Q  L  G  F  N  T  A  C  V  E  K  R  G  K  L  G  G
                                                         * *

ACCTGTCTTAACGTTGGTGGATGTATCCCCTCCAAAGCACTTCTAAATAATTCTCATTTATTC
T  C  L  N  V  G  C  I  P  S  K  A  L  L  N  N  S  H  L  F
   * * * * * * *                  * * * * * *

CACCAAATGCATACGGAAGCGCAAAAGAGGAGAATTGACGTCAACGGTGATATCAAAATT
H  Q  M  H  T  E  A  Q  K  R  G  I  D  V  N  G  D  I  K  I
                                                     80

AACGTAGCAAACTTCCAAAAGCTAAGGATGACGTGTTAAGCAATTAACTGAGGTATT
N  V  A  N  F  Q  K  A  K  D  D  A  V  K  Q  L  T  G  G  I
                                                     100

GAGCTTCTGTTCAAGAAAAAATAAGGTCACCTATTATAAAGGTAATGGTTCATTCGAAGAC
E  L  L  F  K  K  N  K  V  T  Y  Y  K  G  N  G  S  F  E  D
                                                      120

GAAACGAAGATCAGAGATCAACTCCCGTTGATGGGTTGGAAGGCACTGTCAAGGAAGACCAC
E  T  K  I  R  V  T  P  V  D  G  L  E  G  T  V  K  E  D  H
                                                      140

ATACTAGATGTTAAGAACATCATAGTCGCCACGGGCTCTGAAGTTACACCCTTCCCGGT
I  L  D  V  K  N  I  I  V  A  T  G  S  E  V  T  P  F  P  G
                                                     160

ATTGAAATAGATGAGGAAAAAATTGTCTCTTCAACAGGTGCTCTTTCGTTAAGGAAATT
I  E  I  D  E  E  K  I  V  S  S  T  G  A  L  S  L  K  E  I
                                                     180

CCCAAAGATTAACCATACTGGTGGAGGAATCATCGGATTGGAAATGGGTTCAGTTTAC
P  K  R  L  T  I  I  G  G  G  I  I  G  L  E  M  G  S  V  Y
                                                     200

TCTAGATTAGGCTCAAGGTTACTGTAGTAGAATTTCAACCTCAAATTGGTGCATCTATG
S  R  L  G  S  K  V  T  V  V  E  F  Q  P  Q  I  G  A  S  M
                                                     220
```

```
GACGGCGAGGTTGCCAAAGCCACCCAAAAGTTCTTGAAAAAAGCAAGGTTTGGACTTCAAA
D  G  E  V  A  K  A  T  Q  K  F  L  K  K  Q  G  L  D  F  K
                                                      240

TTAAGCACCAAAGTTATTTCTGCAAGAGAAGAAACGACGACAAGAACGTCGTCGAAATTGTT
L  S  T  K  V  I  S  A  K  R  N  D  D  K  N  V  V  E  I  V
                                                      260

GTAGAAGATACTAAAACGAATAAGCAAGAAAATTGGAAGTGAAGTTTGCTGGTTGCT
V  E  D  T  K  T  N  K  Q  E  N  L  E  A  E  V  L  L  V  A
                                                      280

GTTGGTAGAAGACCTTACATTGCTGGCTTAGGGGCTGAAAAGATTGGATTGAAGTAGAC
V  G  R  R  P  Y  I  A  G  L  G  A  E  K  I  G  L  E  V  D
                                                      300

AAAAGGGGACGACGCCTAGTCATTGATGACCAATTTAATTCCAAGTTCCCACACATTAAAGTG
K  R  G  R  L  V  I  D  D  Q  F  N  S  K  F  P  H  I  K  V
                                                      320

GTAGGAGATGTTACATTGTCCAATGCTGGCTCAAAGCCGAAGAGGAAGGTATTGCA
V  G  D  V  T  F  G  P  M  L  A  H  K  A  E  E  E  G  I  A
                                                      340

GCTGTCGAAATGTTGAAAACTGGTCACGGTCATGTCAACTATAACAACTTCCTTCGGTC
A  V  E  M  L  K  T  G  H  G  H  V  N  Y  N  N  I  P  S  V
                                                      360

ATGTATTCTCACCCAGAAGTAGCATGGTTGGTAAACCGAAGACAATTGAAAGAAGCC
M  Y  S  H  P  E  V  A  W  V  G  K  T  E  E  Q  L  K  E  A
                                                      380

GGCATTGACTATAAAATTGGTAAGTTCCCTTTGCGGCCAATTCAAGAGCCAAGACCAAC
G  I  D  Y  K  I  G  K  F  P  F  A  A  N  S  R  A  K  T  N
                                                      400

CAAGACACTGAAGGTTTCGTGAAGATTTTGATCGATTCCAAGACCGAGCGTATTTTGGGG
Q  D  T  E  G  F  V  K  I  L  I  D  S  K  T  E  R  I  L  G
                                                      420

GCTCACATTATCGGTCCAAATGCCGGTGAAATGATTGCTGAAGCTGGCTTAGCCTTAGAA
A  H  I  I  G  P  N  A  G  E  M  I  A  E  A  G  L  A  L  E
                                                      440

TATGGCGCTTCCGAGAAGATGTTGCTAGGGTCTGCCATGCTCATCCTACTTTGTCCGAA
Y  G  A  S  A  E  D  V  A  R  V  C  H  A  H  P  T  L  S  E
                                                      460

GCATTTAAGGAAGCTAACATGGCTGCCTATGATAAAGCTATTCATTGTTGAAAACAGGAA
A  F  K  E  A  N  M  A  A  Y  D  K  A  I  H  C

ATAATAAACAGTATAGTATATATATTTATGAAGAACCGCTTAGTATTGAGTAAAAAAAA
AGGAATTC
```

FIGURE 7. Nucleotide sequence of yeast dihydrolipoamide dehydrogenase (E₃) cDNA and the deduced amino acid sequence (one-letter amino acid symbols). The amino-terminal sequence of the enzyme experimentally determined with the purified protein is *underlined*. *Asterisks* represent the putative sequence around the active center cystine. A putative polyadenylylation signal is *overlined*. (From Browning et al.[10] Reprinted with permission from the Proceedings of the National Academy of Sciences of the United States of America.)

2108

CLONING AND NUCLEOTIDE SEQUENCE OF THE E₂ GENE (*LAT1*)

Two positive clones were initially identified by screening a yeast cDNA λgt11 library with rabbit antiserum to yeast E₂.[9] Both inserts, designated E21-1 and E21-2, were subcloned, and their nucleotide sequences were determined. E21-1 contained an insert of 537 bases and had an open reading frame that contained the experimentally determined amino acid sequences of two internal peptides of E₂. (The two peptides were obtained by resolving the purified PDH complex by SDS-PAGE, excising the E₂ band, and digesting the protein *in situ* with *Staphylococcus aureus* V8 protease in a second polyacrylamide gel.[35] After electrophoresis, the peptides were electroblotted onto a poly(vinylidene difluoride) membrane,[36] visualized by staining with Coomassie blue, and subjected to automated sequence analysis.) Insert E21-1 was used as a probe

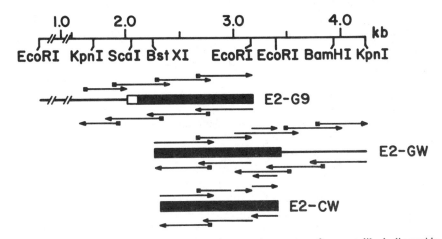

FIGURE 8. Restriction endonuclease map and sequencing strategy for yeast dihydrolipoamide acetyltransferase (E₂) gene (*LAT1*). Two genomic DNA inserts (E2-G9 and E2-GW) and one cDNA insert (E2-CW) was sequenced. *Solid bars* represent the coding regions for the mature enzyme. *Open bar* represents the coding region for the putative presequence. *Arrows* show the direction and extent of the nucleotide sequencing: *arrows beginning with solid boxes* represent sequences determined with synthetic primers based on previously obtained sequences; other *arrows* represent sequences determined with universal or reverse sequencing primers. kb, kilobases. (From Niu *et al.*[9] Reprinted with permission from the *Proceedings of the National Academy of Sciences of the United States of America.*)

to identify two additional clones, E2-GW and E2-CW, containing inserts of 1985 and 1065 bases, respectively. The latter insert was isolated from the cDNA library and the former from a λgt11 yeast genomic DNA library (provided by Richard A. Young and Ronald W. Davis, Stanford University). Sequencing results showed that E2-GW contains the entire nucleotide sequence of E21-1 and brings the open reading frame to a stop codon. To identify the missing portion of the 5′ end of the open reading frame ca. 2×10^6 recombinants from the yeast genomic DNA library were screened with a 915-base DNA fragment from E2-GW. By sizing of the DNA fragments after digestion with *Eco*R I, one of the resulting positive clones was identified as having the 5′ upstream sequence of the open reading frame. This insert, designated E2-G9, was subcloned and sequenced. The restriction map and sequencing strategy for the cDNA and genomic DNA inserts are shown in FIGURE 8. Two genomic DNA inserts, E2-G9

```
AGGAAGAGGCTGAGAACCCTAGATAATTGGTACCGGTGATCACCTCCAGTTTGCACATAC 1740
TATATATCTTCATGTAATACTACATATGTCATAACTTCAATAACTCATACAAGTCATCTG 1800
CTACTATGCTTTGCCGTTTCTACTATCCGTGAAGCGTGACCGGCCCTTCTCACCCCCCGT 1860
GTTACGCAAAGAACAACAAGAGGTCGAGACAACCAACCGGAACGACTAGAAGAGAGGCTG 1920
TTACGTTTCCTGTTTGTTCACGCTCAACATCTTCCATTGCTGTAAACTGCATCCAGTAAA 1980
ATTAATAGTTATTAGCGTACTATGTCTGCCTTTGTCAGGGTGGTTCCAAGAATATCCAGA 2040
               M   S   A   F   V   R   V   V   P   R   I   S   R    -16
             -28
AGTTCAGTACTCACCAGATCATTGAGACTGCAATTGACATGCTACGCATCGTACCCAGAG 2100
 S   S   V   L   T   R   S   L   R   L   Q   L   R   C   Y   A   S   Y   P   E    5
                                                              1
CACACCATTATTGGTATGCCGGCACTGTCTCCTACGATGACGCAAGGTAATCTTGCTGCT 2160
 H   T   I   I   G   M   P   A   L   S   P   T   M   T   Q   G   N   L   A   A    25

TGGACTAAGAAGGAAGGTGACCAATTGTCTCCCGGTGAAGTTATTGCCGAAATAGAAACA 2220
 W   T   K   K   E   G   D   Q   L   S   P   G   E   V   I   A   E   I   E   T    45

GACAAGGCTCAAATGGACTTTGAGTTCCAAGAAGATGGTTACTTAGCCAAGATTCTAGTT 2280
 D   K   A   Q   M   D   F   E   F   Q   E   D   G   Y   L   A   K   I   L   V    65

CCTGAAGGTACAAAGGACATTCCTGTCAACAAGCCTATTGCCGTCTATGTGGAGGACAAA 2340
 P   E   G   T   K   D   I   P   V   N   K   P   I   A   V   Y   V   E   D   K    85

GCTGATGTGCCAGCTTTTAAGGACTTTAAGCTGGAGGATTCAGGTTCTGATTCAAAGACC 2400
 A   D   V   P   A   F   K   D   F   K   L   E   D   S   G   S   D   S   K   T    105

AGTACGAAGGCTCAGCCTGCCGAACCACAGGCAGAAAAGAAACAAGAAGCGCCAGCTGAA 2460
 S   T   K   A   Q   P   A   E   P   Q   A   E   K   K   Q   E   A   P   A   E    125

GAGACCAAGACTTCTGCACCTGAAGCTAAGAAATCTGACGTTGCTGCTCCTCAAGGTAGG 2520
 E   T   K   T   S   A   P   E   A   K   K   S   D   V   A   A   P   Q   G   R    145

ATTTTTGCCTCTCCACTTGCCAAGACTATCGCCTTGGAAAAGGGTATTTCTTTGAAGGAT 2580
 I   F   A   S   P   L   A   K   T   I   A   L   E   K   G   I   S   L   K   D    165

GTTCACGGCACTGGACCCCGCGGTAGAATTACCAAGGCTGACATTGAGTCATATCTAGAA 2640
 V   H   G   T   G   P   R   G   R   I   T   K   A   D   I   E   S   Y   L   E    185

AAGTCGTCTAAGCAGTCTTCTCAAACCAGTGGTGCTGCCGCCGCCACTCCTGCCGCCGCT 2700
 K   S   S   K   Q   S   S   Q   T   S   G   A   A   A   A   T   P   A   A   A    205

ACCTCAAGCACTACTGCTGGCTCTGCTCCATCGCCTTCTTCTACAGCATCATATGAGGAT 2760
 T   S   S   T   T   A   G   S   A   P   S   P   S   S   T   A   S   Y   E   D    225

GTTCCAATTTCAACCATGAGAAGCATCATTGGAGAACGTTTATTGCAATCTACTCAAGGC 2820
 V   P   I   S   T   M   R   S   I   I   G   E   R   L   L   Q   S   T   Q   G    245
```

FIGURE 9. Nucleotide sequence (**above and facing page**) of the yeast *LAT1* gene and the deduced amino acid sequence. The experimentally determined amino acid sequences are *underlined*. A putative polyadenylylation signal is *overlined*. (From Niu et al.[9] Reprinted with permission from the *Proceedings of the National Academy of Sciences of the United States of America*.)

and E2-GW, with a 915-base overlap, contained the nucleotide sequence encoding the precursor of E_2 as well as the 5' and 3' flanking regions. The nucleotide sequence and the deduced amino acid sequence of the protein are shown in FIGURE 9. The genomic DNA sequenced comprised ca. 4.2 kb. However, only the sequence of the E_2 (*LAT1*) gene and its flanking regions are presented in FIGURE 9. The open reading frame of 1446 nucleotides encodes a putative presequence of 28 amino acid residues and a mature protein of 454 amino acid residues, which has a calculated M_r of 48,546 (48,734 including one lipoyl moiety). The deduced amino acid sequence of the mature protein contains the experimentally determined sequences of the amino terminus and two internal peptides of the purified E_2 (underlined in FIG. 9).

RNA blot analysis of yeast poly(A)$^+$ RNA showed that the size of the mRNA is

```
ATTCCATCATACATCGTTTCCTCCAAGATATCCATCTCCAAACTTTTGAAATTGAGACAG 2880
 I  P  S  Y  I  V  S  S  K  I  S  I  S  K  L  L  K  L  R  Q   265

TCCTTGAACGCTACAGCAAACGACAAGTACAAACTGTCCATTAATGACCTATTAGTAAAA 2940
 S  L  N  A  T  A  N  D  K  Y  K  L  S  I  N  D  L  L  V  K   285

GCCATCACTGTTGCGGCTAAGAGGGTGCCAGATGCCAATGCCTACTGGTTACCTAATGAG 3000
 A  I  T  V  A  A  K  R  V  P  D  A  N  A  Y  W  L  P  N  E   305

AACGTTATCCGTAAATTCAAGAATGTCGATGTCTCAGTCGCTGTTGCCACACCAACAGGA 3060
 N  V  I  R  K  F  K  N  V  D  V  S  V  A  V  A  T  P  T  G   325

TTATTGACACCAATTGTCAAGAATTGTGAGGCCAAGGGCTTGTCGCAAATCTCTAACGAA 3120
 L  L  T  P  I  V  K  N  C  E  A  K  G  L  S  Q  I  S  N  E   345

ATCAAGGAACTAGTCAAGCGTGCCAGAATAAACAAATTGGCACCAGAGGAATTCCAAGGT 3180
 I  K  E  L  V  K  R  A  R  I  N  K  L  A  P  E  E  F  Q  G   365

GGGACCATTTGCATATCCAATATGGGCATGAATAATGCTGTTAACATGTTTACTTCGATT 3240
 G  T  I  C  I  S  N  M  G  M  N  N  A  V  N  M  F  T  S  I   385

ATCAACCCACCACAGTCTACAATCTTGGCCATCGCTACTGTTGAAAGGGTCGCTGTGGAA 3300
 I  N  P  P  Q  S  T  I  L  A  I  A  T  V  E  R  V  A  V  E   405

GACGCCGCTGCTGAGAACGGATTCTCCTTTGATAACCAGGTTACCATAACAGGGACCTTT 3360
 D  A  A  A  E  N  G  F  S  F  D  N  Q  V  T  I  T  G  T  F   425

GATCATAGAACCATTGATGGCGCCAAAGGTGCAGAATTCATGAAGGAATTGAAAACTGTT 3420
 D  H  R  T  I  D  G  A  K  G  A  E  F  M  K  E  L  K  T  V   445

ATTGAAAATCCTTTGGAAATGCTATTGTGAGGTTAGAATGAAAATAAAATTCGCCAGTAA 3480
 I  E  N  P  L  E  M  L  L

ATGCGTATCTTGGAGAAAATATCAATTTGTTATTTTGTATATATAAAAAATTAAAAAAAA 3540
AAAAAAAAAAATACTCAAATACTCAAATACGTATACATTATACTGAAATACTTCGCTTGT 3600
GTTCGAATCTAAATCCTCTCTCTCTTCTGTCTCAAATGATATAAATAAATCACGTCAAA 3660
CGGTGCGTCAACATCTTTGTTTTTTCACCTCATGTGGAATTGGTTGAAATTAACAAAGGA 3720
GTGGGATATAGGATATAACGCATAAAGTTTAGCATACTACTTTCGTATATTATTGTTCGG 3780
TGAAAGAAACTAGTTCCCTCTTATCTCTCAATATTTGCCAAAATTAGCTTTTAACAAATA 3840
AACCATGAGTTTCCTACCATCTTTTATCTTAAGCGATGAATCTAAAGAACGTATTTCCAA 3900
AATTTTAACTTTGACTCATAATGTAGCACATTATGGCTGGATCCCATTTGTTTTGTATTT 3960
GGGCTGGGCACACACTTCTAATAGACCAAACTTTTTGAACTTACTGTCTCCGTTACCAAG 4020
TGTTTAAAAACATCAGTTCGATACAACTTGGGTGAGAGAGGGAAGCCCATATTTCCAATTT 4080
TGAATTACTTGACCGTTACTGCAAATAATAAAAATTGACATGTACATAAAGTATATATAT 4140
AATAAAATATAAAATTCATTTTGCATATTGTTATTCTTTCACGCTTTGTTTTGATATGGT 4200
GAAAATTCGAAGTCTCTAGAATGTCCTTTAGGTACC
```

FIGURE 9. (continued)

ca. 1.6 kb. Southern blot analysis of yeast genomic DNA showed that there is a single copy of the *LAT1* gene. Additional analysis indicated that the *LAT1* gene is located on chromosome XIV.

Amino acid sequence comparisons of dihydrolipoamide acetyltransferases from yeast, *E. coli*, and rat liver (FIG. 10) clearly demonstrate that the yeast enzyme has a highly segmented structure similar to that reported for the *E. coli* dihydrolipoamide acetyltransferase and succinyltransferase.[17] The lipoyl domain, comprising the amino-terminal region, is followed by the E_3- (or E_1/E_3-) binding domain, and the catalytic inner core domain (see FIG. 3). These putative domains are connected by interdomain linker segments (hinge regions). The yeast and *E. coli* acetyltransferases exhibit 31% sequence identity for 463 residues, after the introduction of gaps to optimize the alignment. The corresponding value for the yeast and rat liver acetyltransferases is 45% for 440 residues. Conservation of sequence is particularly high around the lipoyllysine residues of the lipoyl domains, in the E_3-binding domains, and in the

Ec   A I E I K V P D   8

```
      I G A D E V E I T E I L V K V G D K V E  28

      A E Q S L I T V E G D •K A S M E V P S P  48

      Q A G I V K E I K V S V G D K T Q T G A  68

      L I M I F D S A D G A A D A A P A Q A E  88

      E K K E A A P A A A P A A A A A K D V N  108

      V P D I G S D E V E V T E I L V K V G D  128

      K V E A E Q S L I T V E G D •K A S M E V  148

Ec    P A P F A G T V K E I K V N V G D K V S  168
Rt                                      G P  2

      T G S L I M V F E V [A] G E [A] G A [A A P A]  188
      E A F K N Y T L D S [A] T A A [A] T Q [A A P A]  22

Ec  - -  [A] K Q E [A A P A A] A P [A] P [A] A [G] - -  204
Yt                                          A [S]  2
Rt  P A  [A] A P A [A A P A A] P S [A] S [A] P [G] S [S]  42

    - - - [V] K E V N V [P D] I G G D E V  E - -  219
  [Y P] E [H] T I [I] G M [P] A L S P T [M] T  Q [G] N  22
  [Y P] V [H] M Q [I] V L [P] A L S P T M T  M [G] T  62

  [V] T E V M V [K V] G D [K] V A A E Q S [L] I T  239
  [L] A A [W] T [K K E] G [D Q] L S P [G] E V [I] A E  42
  [V] Q R [W] E [K K V] G [E K] L S E [G] D L [L] A E  82

  [V E G D K] A S [M] E V P A P F A [G] - V V [K]  258
  [I E T D K A] Q [M] D [F E] F [Q E] D [G] Y L A K  62
  [I E T D K A] T I G [F E] V [Q E] E [G] Y L A K  102

  E [L] K [V] N [V G D K] V K T G S L I M I F E  278
  [I L] - [V] P E G [T] K [D] I [P] V N K [P] I A V Y  81
  [I L] - [V] P E G [T] R [D] V [P] L G T [P] L C I I  121

  [V E G A A] - - [P A A A P] A [K] Q [E] - - - -  292
  [V E D K A D] V [P A F K D] F [K] L [E] D S G [S]  101
  [V E K Q E D] I A [A F A D] Y R P T E V T [S]  141

  - - - - - - A [A A P A] - [P A A] - - [K] A [E]  303
  D S K T S T K [A] Q [P A] E [P Q] A E K [K] Q [E]  121
  L K P Q A P P [P] V [P P] P V [A A] V P [P] I P  161

  [A P A A] A P A A K [A] - [E] - G [K S] E F [A] E  321
  [A P A E] E [T] K T S A [P] E A K [K S] D V [A] A  141
  [Q P L A] P [T] P S A A [P] - - - - - - [A] G  174

  N D A Y [V H A T] P L I R R [L A] R [E F G] V  341
  [P] Q [G R] I [F A S] P L A K T [I A] L [E K G] I  161
  [P] K [G R] V [F V S] P L A K K [L A] A [E K G] I  194

  N [L] A K [V K G T G] R K [G R I] L R E [D] V Q  361
  S [L] K D [V H G T G] P R [G R I] T [K] A [D I] E  181
  D [L L] T Q [V K G T G] P E [G R I] I [K] K [D I] D  214
```

FIGURE 10. *See legend on facing page.*

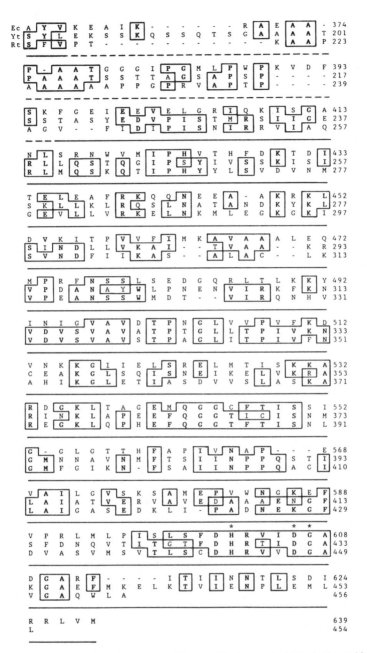

FIGURE 10. Comparison of amino acid sequences (**above and facing page**) of dihydrolipoamide acetyltransferases. The deduced amino acid sequences of the *E. coli* (Ec), yeast (Yt), and rat liver (Rt) enzymes are aligned for maximal homology. The sequence of the rat liver enzyme is incomplete,[20,21] apparently lacking sequences at the amino and carboxyl termini. Lipoyl domains (amino-terminal), E$_3$- or E$_1$/E$_3$-binding domains, and catalytic inner core domains (carboxyl-terminal): *solid lines;* putative interdomain linker segments: *dashed lines.* The lipoyllysine residues in the lipoyl domains are indicated (●), and residues in the putative active site are denoted by *asterisks.* Boxes: regions of sequence identity. (From Niu *et al.*[9] Reprinted with permission from the *Proceedings of the National Academy of Sciences of the United States of America.*)

carboxyl-terminal segment of the catalytic domains. The putative catalytic site is thought to include the highly conserved His-Xaa-Xaa-Xaa-Asp-Gly segment near the carboxyl terminus.[37] In contrast to the *E. coli* acetyltransferase, which contains three lipoyl domains,[13] and the human[19] and rat liver[20,21] acetyltransferases, which contain two lipoyl domains, the yeast acetyltransferase has only one lipoyl domain. In this respect, the yeast dihydrolipoamide acetyltransferase resembles the acetyltransferase from *B. stearothermophilus*.[22] About one-half of the sequence (from the amino terminus) of the latter enzyme has been determined. The two enzymes exhibit 29% sequence identity for 231 residues, after the introduction of gaps to optimize the alignment.

Although the length and composition of the interdomain linker segments vary among the *E. coli*, yeast, and rat liver acetyltransferases, these segments are similar in that they are rich in the conservatively substituted residues alanine, proline, serine, and threonine and in charged amino acid residues. The linker segments of the *E. coli* and rat liver acetyltransferases have a higher content of alanine and proline residues than does the yeast enzyme, whereas the linker segments of the yeast enzyme have a higher content of threonine and serine residues. The interdomain linker segments are thought to be responsible, at least in part, for the relatively slow migration of E_2 in SDS-PAGE, resulting in abnormally high apparent molecular weight values.[38] Thus, the apparent molecular weight of the yeast acetyltransferase estimated by SDS-PAGE is ca. 58,000, whereas the molecular weight calculated from the deduced amino acid sequence is 48,734 (including one lipoyl moiety).

The availability of the structural gene for E_2 should facilitate investigation into mitochondrial import, self-assembly, and structure-function relationships of this oligomeric enzyme. Experiments are in progress to develop yeast and *E. coli* systems for expressing the cloned *LAT1* gene.

REFERENCES

1. REED, L. J. 1974. Acc. Chem. Res. **7:** 40–46.
2. DEMARCUCCI, O. & J. L. LINDSAY. 1985. Eur. J. Biochem. **149:** 641–648.
3. JILKA, J. M., M. RAHMATULLAH, M. KAZEMI & T. E. ROCHE. 1986. J. Biol. Chem. **261:** 1858–1867.
4. LINN, T. C., F. H. PETTIT & L. J. REED. 1969. Proc. Natl. Acad. Sci. USA **62:** 234–241.
5. DENTON, R. M., P. J. RANDLE, B. J. BRIDGES, R. H. COOPER, A. L. KERBEY, H. T. PASK, D. L. SEVERSON, D. STANSBIE & S. WHITEHOUSE. 1975. Mol. Cell. Biochem. **9:** 27–53.
6. REED, L. J. & S. J. YEAMAN. 1987. *In* The Enzymes, 3rd ed. P. D. Boyer & E. G. Krebs, Eds. Vol. **18:** 77–95. Academic Press. Orlando, FL.
7. OLIVER, R. M. & L. J. REED. 1982. *In* Electron Microscopy of Proteins. J. R. Harris, Ed. Vol. **2:** 1–48. Academic Press, London.
8. KRESZE, G.-B. & H. RONFT. 1981. Eur. J. Biochem. **119:** 581–587.
9. NIU, X.-D., K. S. BROWNING, R. H. BEHAL & L. J. REED. 1988. Proc. Natl. Acad. Sci. USA **85:** 7546–7550.
10. BROWNING, K. S., D. J. UHLINGER & L. J. REED. 1988. Proc. Natl. Acad. Sci. USA **85:** 1831–1834.
11. BARRERA, C. R., G. NAMIHIRA, L. HAMILTON, P. MUNK, M. H. ELEY, T. C. LINN & L. J. REED. 1972. Arch. Biochem. Biophys. **148:** 343–358.
12. BLEILE, D. M., P. MUNK, R. M. OLIVER & L. J. REED. 1979. Proc. Natl. Acad. Sci. USA **76:** 4385–4389.
13. STEPHENS, P. E., M. G. DARLISON, H. M. LEWIS & J. R. GUEST. 1983. Eur. J. Biochem. **133:** 481–489.
14. SPENCER, M. E., M. G. DARLISON, P. E. STEPHENS, I. K. DUCKENFIELD & J. R. GUEST. 1984. Eur. J. Biochem. **141:** 361–374.

15. PERHAM, R. N., H. W. DUCKWORTH & G. C. K. ROBERTS. 1981. Nature **292:** 474–477.
16. RADFORD, S. E., E. D. LAUE, R. N. PERHAM, J. S. MILES & J. R. GUEST. 1987. Biochem. J. **247:** 641–649.
17. PERHAM, R. N., L. C. PACKMAN & S. E. RADFORD. 1988. Biochem. Soc. Symp. **54:** 67–81.
18. HANEMAAIJER, R., A. JANSSEN, A. DE KOK & C. VEEGER. 1988. Eur. J. Biochem. **174:** 593–599.
19. COPPEL, R. L., L. J. MCNEILAGE, C. D. SURH, J. VAN DE WATER, T. W. SPITHILL, S. WHITTINGHAM & M. E. GERSHWIN. 1988. Proc. Natl. Acad. Sci. USA **85:** 7317–7321.
20. GERSHWIN, M. E., I. R. MACKAY, A. STURGESS & R. L. COPPEL. 1987. J. Immunol. **138:** 3525–3531.
21. FUSSEY, S. P. M., J. R. GUEST, O. F. W. JAMES, M. F. BASSENDINE & S. J. YEAMAN. 1988. Proc. Natl. Acad. Sci. USA **85:** 8654–8658.
22. PACKMAN, L. C., A. BORGES & R. N. PERHAM. 1988. Biochem. J. **252:** 79–86.
23. WIELAND, O. H. 1983. Rev. Physiol. Biochem. Pharmacol. **96:** 124–170.
24. YEAMAN, S. J., E. T. HUTCHESON, T. E. ROCHE, F. H. PETTIT, J. R. BROWN, L. J. REED, D. C. WATSON & G. H. DIXON. 1978. Biochemistry **17:** 2364–2370.
25. SUGDEN, P. H., A. L. KERBEY, P. J. RANDLE, C. A. WALLER & K. B. M. REID. 1979. Biochem. J. **181:** 419–426.
26. KRESZE, G.-B. & H. RONFT. 1981. Eur. J. Biochem. **119:** 573–579.
27. UHLINGER, D. J., C.-Y. YANG & L. J. REED. 1986. Biochemistry **25:** 5673–5677.
28. VON HEIJNE, G. 1986. EMBO J. **5:** 1335–1342.
29. WILLIAMS, C. H., JR., L. D. ARSCOTT & G. E. SCHULZ. 1982. Proc. Natl. Acad. Sci. USA **79:** 2199–2201.
30. ROSS, J., G. A. REID & I. W. DAWES. 1988. J. Gen. Microbiol. **134:** 1131–1139.
31. STEPHENS, P. E., H. M. LEWIS, M. G. DARLISON & J. R. GUEST. 1983. Eur. J. Biochem. **135:** 519–527.
32. WESTPHAL, A. H. & A. DE KOK. 1988. Eur. J. Biochem. **172:** 299–305.
33. OTULAKOWSKI, G. & B. H. ROBINSON. 1987. J. Biol. Chem. **262:** 17313–17318.
34. PONS, G., C. RAEFSKY-ESTRIN, D. J. CAROTHERS, R. A. PEPIN, A. A. JAVED, B. W. JESSE, M. K. GANAPATHI, D. SAMOLS & M. S. PATEL. 1988. Proc. Natl. Acad. Sci. USA **85:** 1422–1426.
35. CLEVELAND, D. W., S. G. FISCHER, M. W. KIRSCHNER & U. K. LAEMMLI. 1977. J. Biol. Chem. **252:** 1102–1106.
36. MATSUDAIRA, P. 1987. J. Biol. Chem. **262:** 10035–10038.
37. GUEST, J. R. 1987. FEMS Microbiol. Lett. **44:** 417–422.
38. GUEST, J. R., H. M. LEWIS, L. D. GRAHAM, L. C. PACKMAN & R. N. PERHAM. 1985. J. Mol. Biol. **185:** 743–754.

Lipoyl-Containing Components of the Pyruvate Dehydrogenase Complex: Roles in Modulating and Anchoring the PDH Kinase and the PDH Phosphatase[a]

THOMAS E. ROCHE, MOHAMMED RAHMATULLAH,
LIN LI, GARY A. RADKE, CHRISTINA L. CHANG, AND
SUSAN L. POWERS-GREENWOOD

Department of Biochemistry
Kansas State University
Manhattan, KS 66506

The activity of the pyruvate dehydrogenase$_a$ (PDH$_a$) kinase lowers the fraction of the pyruvate dehydrogenase complex that is present in the active form through phosphorylating and concomitantly inactivating the pyruvate dehydrogenase component (PDH, or E1). The pyruvate dehydrogenase$_b$ (PDH$_b$) phosphatase dephosphorylates the α subunit of the E1 component and thereby activates the pyruvate dehydrogenase complex. In this paper, we will describe the role of the lipoyl-containing components— the dihydrolipoyl transacetylase and protein X—in the binding and in the regulation of the kinase and the phosphatase purified from bovine kidney or heart.

PDH$_a$ KINASE

Under conditions that remove the E1 and dihydrolipoyl dehydrogenase (E3) components from the dihydrolipoyl transacetylase (E2) oligomer,[1] the kinase activity and the protein X subunits are retained with the E2 oligomer. Further resolution[2] demonstrated that the kinase comprises a catalytic subunit (designated K$_c$; M_r ca. 46,000) and another subunit (M_r ca. 43,000), which we have shown to have a high isoelectric point,[3] referred to as the basic subunit (designated K$_b$). The latter resolution process also releases a portion of the protein X,[3] a distinct lipoyl-bearing component of the complex (cf. Ref. 3a).

A large number of metabolites, including the various substrates, products, and even a cofactor, thiamin pyrophosphate (TPP), for the overall reaction catalyzed by the complex, are known to affect kinase activity (FIG. 1). The presence of several catalytic and regulatory subunits opens up interesting possibilities for mechanisms of attenuation of kinase activity. Some regulatory effects have been shown to involve allosteric effects. TPP inhibits kinase activity by binding to the E1 component,[4] and this inhibition persists when TPP is converted to the active aldehyde intermediate.[5] Pyruvate and ADP directly inhibit the kinase,[6,7] and the combination synergistically inhibits kinase activity.[7] Our laboratory has presented evidence that stimulations of kinase activity by NADH, acetyl-CoA,[8] or low pyruvate concentrations[9] involve the

[a]This work was supported by National Institutes of Health Grant DK 18320 and by the Kansas State Agricultural Experiment Station—Contribution No. 89-230-B.

168

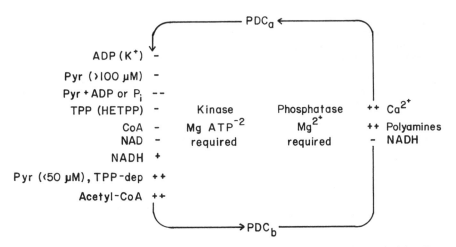

FIGURE 1. Regulatory effects on the PDH_a kinase and the PDH_b phosphatase activity. Pyr, pyruvate; TPP, thiamin pyrophosphate; HETPP, hydroxyethyl thiamin pyrophosphate; TPP-dep, TPP-dependent. $+$, $++$: stimulation; $-$, $--$: inhibition.

introduction of covalent changes. TABLE 1 summarizes the evidence that these stimulatory effects are mediated by the reduction and acetylation of lipoyl moieties within the complex.[10-16] Of particular importance are the data showing that when essentially all the added pyruvate or acetyl-CoA is consumed by acetylation of sites in the complex, there is an associated enhancement of kinase activity for up to 20 acetyl groups incorporated per molecule of complex.[12,13] Inhibitory effects of CoA and NAD^+ appear to involve both reversal of the covalent modifications (e.g., by deacetylation and reoxidation of lipoyl moieties) and direct allosteric inhibition of kinase activity.[15,17]

Because the kinase subunits associate with the E2-X subcomplex and because both the E2 and protein X subunits were potential candidates for the role of facilitating lipoyl-mediated regulation of kinase activity, we conducted studies to determine whether the kinase binds to the E2 or protein X subunit, whether binding is to the inner

TABLE 1. Evidence That Stimulation of Kinase Activity by NADH, Acetyl-CoA, or Pyruvate Is Lipoyl Mediated

Dihydrolipoamide is equivalent to NADH in its capacity (i) to stimulate the kinase and (ii) to enhance acetyl-CoA stimulation.

Arsenite blocks the stimulation by acetyl-CoA but not that by pyruvate.

Pyruvate stimulation requires TPP.

Thiamin thiazalone-PP blocks pyruvate stimulation but not acetyl-CoA stimulation.

The extent of stimulation increases with the extent of acetylation for acetylation of up to 20 sites (i) when pyruvate or acetyl-CoA is the acetylating agent or (ii) when acetyl-CoA is completely consumed in acetylating lipoyl groups (acetylation reaction pulled by CoA removal).

No activation is observed (i) with the kinase associated with purified E1 (restored by addition of E2-X subcomplex but not of $E2_IX_I$ subcomplex) or (ii) when lipoyl groups are alkylated.

Activation can occur (i) with free (e.g., proteolytically released) lipoyl domains or (ii), to low level, with the $X-K_cK_b$ fraction, when the lipoyl group of protein X is reduced and acetylated.

or outer domain of one of these subunits, and whether lipoyl-mediated regulatory effects are facilitated uniquely or more efficiently by the E2 or protein X subunit. We also investigated whether the K_b subunit of the kinase is required for the binding of the kinase or for any regulatory effects on kinase activity.

We have found that the kinase binds to the E2 oligomer in the absence of protein X.[18] Binding does not require the K_b subunit.[16,18] Complete removal of the lipoyl domains (i.e., the $E2_{LB}$ fragment; cf. Ref. 3a) leads to release of the K_c subunit.[16] However, when only ca. 10% of the E2 subunits (i.e., ca. 6 out of 60 subunits) are intact, nearly half of the kinase activity remains associated with the residual subcomplex (FIG. 2.)[16] Thus, intact E2 subunits have a higher affinity for the kinase

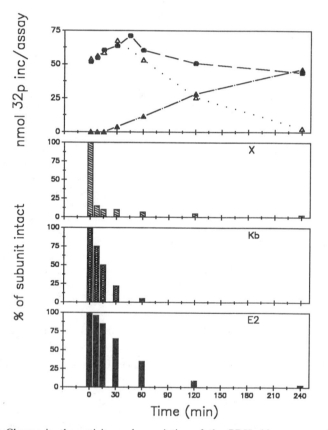

FIGURE 2. Change in the activity and association of the PDH_a kinase upon cleavage of components of the $E2$-X-$K_c$$K_b$ subcomplex by protease arg C. Bottom three panels show the time-dependent decrease in intact protein X, K_b, and E2 subunits. At the indicated times, aprotinin was added and the temperature lowered from 30° to 4°C to terminate the digestion by protease arg C. A portion of each sample was pelleted by centrifugation through a 3-step sucrose gradient. Protein X and E2 subunits were converted by the protease arg C treatment to inner and outer domains that fractionated into the pellet and supernatant fractions, respectively (cf. Ref. 3a). The kinase activity (**top panel:** nmol ^{32}P incorporated/assay) of each sample (●) and of its pellet (△) and supernatant (▲) fractions was measured in the presence of additional E2-X subcomplex, included to allow maximal expression of kinase activity. (Data from tables 2 and 3 of Rahmatullah et al.[16])

than do free lipoyl domains. In the study depicted in FIGURE 2, the K_b subunit was cleaved by protease arg C at a rate that was intermediate between that of the E2 and that of the protein X subunit. Cleavage by protease arg C caused an increase in PDH kinase activity.[16] This increase correlates best with the cleavage of the K_b subunit (FIG. 2).

Although in the absence of E2 subunits (i.e., in an $X-K_cK_b$ fraction) some activation of the kinase occurs in association with the reduction (by NADH) and the acetylation (by pyruvate or acetyl-CoA) of protein X,[15] much greater effects are observed with the intact $E2-X-K_cK_b$ subcomplex. Proteolytic removal of the lipoyl domains of both E2 and protein X lowers kinase activity, but the presence of free lipoyl domains still allows activation of kinase activity through reduction and acetylation of the free lipoyl domains.[15] Other regulatory effects also persist after the release of the lipoyl domains and the cleavages of the K_b subunit.[15] Selective removal of the lipoyl domain of protein X with protease arg C followed by separation of the residual $E2-X_1-K_cK_b$ subcomplex does not decrease activation by NADH, acetyl-CoA, or low concentrations of pyruvate.[16] Furthermore, when most of the lipoyl domains of E2 subunits were released and the residual subcomplexes separated from the freed domains, significant activation of the residual kinase activity was maintained. However, complete removal of lipoyl domains yields an inner domain subcomplex ($E2_1X_1$) that neither binds nor activates the kinase. Thus, it would appear that, in the $E2-X-K_cK_b$ subcomplex, the outer domains of the transacetylase function in the binding of the kinase and facilitate some of the regulatory effects on kinase activity.[16]

We further investigated the capacity of the $E2-X-K_cK_b$ subcomplex, the $E2-X_1-K_cK_b$ subcomplex, and the E2 oligomer (from which most of the protein X was removed) to bind protein X and the kinase subunits of the $X-K_cK_b$ fraction.[18] We initially found both could bind. However, further studies were conducted with an $X-K_cK_b$ fraction carefully treated to completely remove the mercurial agent used in its preparation.[2] Using such an $X-K_cK_b$ fraction in which K_c levels were greater than those of K_b, we found that greater than 14 molecules of kinase could bind to the $E2-X-K_cK_b$ subcomplex or to the $E2-X_1-K_cK_b$ subcomplex.[18] This determination was made after pelleting the residual subcomplexes by centrifugation through a 3-step sucrose gradient. Then, for both the supernatant and pellet fractions, measurements were made of the kinase activity, ATP binding capacity, and the level of subunits, as determined by separation by SDS-PAGE.

In marked contrast to the K_c subunit, after complete removal of the mercurial agent, additional protein X subunits failed to bind to the various subcomplexes.[18] There was no exchange of free protein X with the bound inner domain of protein X when the $E2-X_1-K_cK_b$ subcomplex was used. Even when the E2 oligomer containing a low level of protein X was employed, it also failed to bind free protein X.[18] The protein X in the $X-K_cK_b$ fraction was functional in the binding the E3 component (cf. Ref. 3a) and served as a substrate for the reduction and acetylation of its lipoyl group. We suggest that the binding of protein X may occur during the assembly of the core. Thus, the binding of about 6 subunits of protein X may be controlled by protein synthesis or other mechanisms yet to be elucidated.

TABLE 2 summarizes this new information concerning the function and regulation of the PDH_a kinase.

PDH_b PHOSPHATASE

The pyruvate dehydrogenase phosphatase is a heterodimer composed of a 50-kDa catalytic subunit (P_c) and a 90-kDa subunit (P_f) with a tightly bound FAD.[19,20] The activity of the phosphatase requires millimolar Mg^{2+}. The activity of the phosphatase

TABLE 2. Subunit Roles in the Function and Regulation of the PDH_a Kinase

The K_c subunit of the kinase binds to E2 subunits.

Binding of the K_c subunit requires the outer domain of E2 subunits but does not require the K_b subunit of the kinase.

Lipoyl-mediated effector stimulation of kinase activity is effectively achieved by the lipoyl domain of E2 subunits in the absence of the lipoyl domain of protein X.

Protein X, by itself, can facilitate low levels of stimulation of kinase activity in association with reduction and acetylation of its lipoyl group.

Proteolytic cleavage of the K_b subunit does not cause loss of any known regulatory effects on kinase activity.

Cleavage of the K_b subunit by protease arg C is correlated with an associated increase in kinase activity.

is increased more than 4-fold by the E2-X subcomplex. This activation of the subcomplex[21] requires micromolar Ca^{2+}. The role of Ca^{2+} in activating the phosphatase involves an increased association of the phosphatase with the E2-X subcomplex and a lowering of its K_m for the phosphorylated (inactive) pyruvate dehydrogenase component $(E1_b)$.[21]

Other effectors of phosphatase activity are NADH and polyamines. NADH inhibits the phosphatase activity;[8] thus, NADH exhibits a reciprocal effect on kinase and phosphatase activity that would serve to reduce the activity of the pyruvate dehydrogenase complex. Polyamines increase the activity of the phosphatase, primarily by lowering the K_m for Mg^{2+}, but also by increasing the V_m.[22] Spermine is the most effective polyamine.

As part of the characterization of the mechanism whereby Ca^{2+}, NADH, and spermine modulate phosphatase activity, we wished to characterize the role of the E2-X subcomplex and to further define the roles of the E2 and protein X subunits and their subdomains. We found that the E2-X subcomplex is required for the normal manifestation of the effects of these modulators.[23] A previous study had indicated that NADH directly inhibited the PDH_b phosphatase, thus reducing the dephosphorylation of peptide substrates.[17] However, we wanted to determine how NADH inhibition was altered by the E2-X subcomplex, by Ca^{2+}, and by spermine. In addition, we had observed that free dihydrolipoamide also inhibited the phosphatase, suggesting that NADH might inhibit the phosphatase through its use in the reduction of protein-bound lipoyl moieties. Our studies on the kinase had indicated that free lipoyl domains could elicit regulatory effects. It seemed possible that free lipoyl domains and the E3 component could be present in the assays, which had detected NADH inhibition of the phosphatase with peptide substrates. The E2-X-K_cK_b was the likely source of kinase for phosphorylating the E1 component prior to its digestion with trypsin. Trypsin treatment would lead to release of lipoyl domains from the subcomplex and also release any trypsin-resistant E3 component which is usually present in the E2-X-K_cK_b subcomplex.

In studies using phosphorylated complex, we found that NADH and dihydrolipoamide inhibited PDH_b phosphatase activity to the same extent.[23] The combination gave no further inhibition, consistent with a common mechanism for inhibition. Arsenite alone had no effect on phosphatase activity, but NADH plus arsenite greatly decreased phosphatase activity. That suggested that reduction of lipoyl moieties followed by their reaction with arsenite reduces phosphatase activity. Decreasing the level of Ca^{2+} enhanced NADH inhibition, with the highest fractional inhibition being observed in the absence of Ca^{2+} (albeit this was inhibition of a greatly reduced phosphatase activity). Because Ca^{2+} was thought to be required for the effects of the

E2-X subcomplex on the phosphatase,[21] we investigated this further with resolved components.

Consistent with the requirement for a lipoyl-bearing component, neither NADH nor dihydrolipoamide had any effect on the rate of dephosphorylation of the resolved $E1_b$.[23] The $E2$-X-$K_c K_b$ subcomplex not only greatly enhanced phosphatase activity but also restored inhibition by NADH and dihydrolipoamide. The $E2_I$-X_I subcomplex did not activate the phosphatase beyond the activation achieved with $E1_b$ alone, and it did not allow NADH inhibition. Removal of the lipoyl domain of protein X did not alter NADH inhibition. Further studies showed that the retention of only a small portion of the outer domains of E2 subunits in an $E2_I$-$E2$-X_I subcomplex is sufficient for NADH to inhibit phosphatase activity.

Spermine effects varied from inhibition of the phosphatase, when the $E1_b$ (alone) or $E1_b$ plus the $E2_I$-X_I subcomplex were present, to activation in the presence of the E2-X subcomplex.[23] In the absence of Ca^{2+}, when the E2-X subcomplex alone failed to increase kinase activity, the E2-X subcomplex supported a marked increase in phosphatase activity by spermine (4.8-fold with 1.0 mM spermine and 1.25 mM $MgCl_2$.) With peptide substrates (prepared from ^{32}P-$E1_b$), spermine modestly increased phosphatase activity, and neither Ca^{2+} nor the E2-X subcomplex altered this effect. Thus, spermine binds directly to the phosphatase. From the combination of these results, it would appear that spermine alters the phosphatase so that it preferentially dephosphorylates the peptide substrate or $E1_b$ bound to the E2-X subcomplex but more slowly dephosphorylates free $E1_b$.

Studies using subcomplexes prepared with varying amounts of outer domains removed (by protease arg C treatment and pelleting as in FIG. 2) demonstrated that the lipoyl domains of E2 subunits are critical for efficient function and regulation of the phosphatase. Even when most of the lipoyl domains were removed, the residual $E2_I$-$E2$-X_I subcomplex supported spermine activation of the phosphatase. Since $E1_b$ was present at levels considerably in excess of those of its binding site on the residual subcomplexes and since dephosphorylation of free $E1_b$ by free phosphatase is inhibited by spermine, the observed stimulation would appear to imply that the phosphatase interacts preferentially with the lipoyl domains of the residual intact E2 subunits and/or with a conformationally altered $E1_b$ bound to those intact E2 subunits.

In further studies, the E2 oligomer (prepared free of protein X, cf. Ref. 3a) gave an 8-fold enhancement of phosphatase activity. A 40% greater enhancement was observed

TABLE 3. Properties of the PDH_b Phosphatase

P_c: 50,000-kDa subunit; catalytic.

P_f: 90,000-kDa subunit; contains FAD.

Phosphatase activity requires Mg^{2+}.

The activity is increased >4-fold by the E2-X subcomplex (requires Ca^{2+}).

The role of Ca^{2+} in activating phosphatase involves (i) an increased association of $P_c P_f$ with the E2-X subcomplex ($E2_I X_I$ will not substitute) and (ii) a lowering of its K_m for $E1_b$.

NADH inhibition requires the E2-X subcomplex ($E2_I X_I$ will not substitute).

Dihydrolipoamide gives inhibition equivalent to that obtained with NADH.

Spermine (and other polyamines) activates the phosphatase by greatly lowering its K_m for Mg^{2+} and by increasing its V_m.

Spermine activation (i) changes to inhibition in the absence of the E2-X subcomplex ($E1_b$ as substrate) and (ii) increases dephosphorylation of peptide substrates (this activity is unaffected by the E2-X subcomplex).

Removal of the X_L domain from protein X does not alter any of the above effects.

The $E2_L$ domain contributes to all the effects on phosphatase function and regulation that require the E2-X subcomplex.

---

with the $E2\text{-}X\text{-}K_cK_b$ subcomplex. Possibly, not all the E2 subunits retained a completely native structure following the treatments used to prepare the E2 oligomer. The large enhancement in the absence of protein X suggests that protein X does not have a major role in the functioning of the phosphatase.

TABLE 3 summarizes the basic properties of the PDH_a phosphatase and new information concerning the subunit requirements for the function and regulation of the PDH_b phosphatase.

REFERENCES

1. LINN, T. C., J. W. PELLEY, F. H. PETTIT, F. HUCHO, D. D. RANDALL & L. J. REED. 1972. Arch. Biochem. Biophys. **148:** 327–342.
2. STEPP, L. R., F. H. PETTIT, S. J. YEAMAN & L. J. REED. 1983. J. Biol. Chem. **258:** 9454–9458.
3. RAHMATULLAH, M., J. M. JILKA, G. A. RADKE & T. E. ROCHE. 1986. J. Biol. Chem. **261:** 6515–6523.
3a. ROCHE, T. E., M. RAHMATULLAH, S. L. POWERS-GREENWOOD, G. A. RADKE, S. GOPALAKRISHNAN & C. L. CHANG. 1989. This volume.
4. ROCHE, T. E. & L. J. REED. 1972. Biochem. Biophys. Res. Commun. **48:** 840–846.
5. CAREY, M. 1984. Ph.D. dissertation. Kansas State University. Manhattan, KS.
6. HUCHO, F., D. D. RANDALL, T. E. ROCHE, M. W. BURGETT, J. W. PELLEY & L. J. REED. 1972. Arch. Biochem. Biophys. **151:** 328–340.
7. PRATT, M. L. & T. E. ROCHE. 1979. J. Biol. Chem. **254:** 7191–7196.
8. PETTIT, F. H., J. W. PELLEY & L. J. REED. 1975. Biochem. Biophys. Res. Commun. **65:** 575–582.
9. COOPER, R. H., P. J. RANDLE & R. M. DENTON. 1974. Biochem. J. **143:** 625–641.
10. ROCHE, T. E. & R. L. CATE. 1976. Biochem. Biophys. Res. Commun. **72:** 1375–1383.
11. CATE, R. L. & T. E. ROCHE. 1978. J. Biol. Chem. **253:** 496–503.
12. CATE, R. L. & T. E. ROCHE. 1979. J. Biol. Chem. **254:** 1659–1665.
13. RAHMATULLAH, M. & T. E. ROCHE. 1985. J. Biol. Chem. **260:** 10146–10152.
14. RAHMATULLAH, M., T. E. ROCHE, J. M. JILKA & M. KAZEMI. 1985. Eur. J. Biochem. **150:** 181–187.
15. JILKA, J. M., M. RAHMATULLAH, M. KAZEMI & T. E. ROCHE. 1986. J. Biol. Chem. **261:** 1858–1867.
16. RAHMATULLAH, M., S. GOPALAKRISHNAN, G. A. RADKE & T. E. ROCHE. 1989. J. Biol. Chem. **264:** 1245–1257.
17. REED, L. J., F. H. PETTIT, S. J. YEAMAN, W. M. TEAGUE & D. M. BLEILE. 1980. *In* Enzyme Regulation and Mechanisms of Action. P. Mildner & P. Rico Eds.: 477–486. Pergamon Press. Oxford.
18. LI, L., G. A. RADKE, S. L. POWERS-GREENWOOD, M. RAHMATULLAH, S. GOPALAKRISHNAN & T. E. ROCHE. Manuscript in preparation.
19. TEAGUE, W. M., F. H. PETTIT, T-L. WU, S. R. SILBERMAN & L. J. REED. 1982. Biochemistry **21:** 5585–5592.
20. PRATT, M. L., J. F. MAHER & T. E. ROCHE. 1982. Eur. J. Biochem. **125:** 349–355.
21. DAMUNI, Z., J. S. HUMPHREYS & L. J. REED. 1975. Biochem. Biophys. Res. Commun. **65:** 575–582.
22. PETTIT, F. H., T. E. ROCHE & L. J. REED. 1972. Biochem. Biophys. Res. Commun. **49:** 563–571.
23. RAHMATULLAH, M. & T. E. ROCHE. 1988. J. Biol. Chem. **263:** 8106–8110.

The Pyruvate Dehydrogenase Complex from Anaerobic Mitochondria of the Parasitic Nematode *Ascaris suum:* Stoichiometry of Phosphorylation and Inactivation[a]

RICHARD KOMUNIECKI AND JULIA THISSEN

Department of Biology
University of Toledo
Toledo, Ohio 43606

INTRODUCTION

The pyruvate dehydrogenase complex (PDC) occupies a unique position in the mitochondrial metabolism of the parasitic nematode *Ascaris suum.*[1,2] In early larval stages, the PDC functions like its mammalian counterpart and supplies acetyl-CoA for tricarboxylic acid (TCA) cycle oxidation.[3] In contrast, in the adult where mitochondrial metabolism is largely anaerobic, the PDC uses pyruvate generated intramitochondrially and supplies acetyl-CoA and reducing power needed to drive its unique fermentative metabolism.[4,5] Adult body wall muscle mitochondria lack a functional TCA cycle, and β-oxidation operates in the synthetic direction.[5,6] Instead of oxygen, unsaturated organic acids are used as terminal electron-acceptors, and the NADH-dependent reductions of fumarate and 2-methyl branched-chain enoyl CoA's are coupled to site I, electron-transport associated energy generation.[7,8] Acetate, propionate, succinate, 2-methylbutyrate, and 2-methylvalerate accumulate as end products of malate-dependent mitochondrial metabolism.[1,2] Intramitochondrial NADH/NAD and acyl CoA/CoA ratios are dramatically elevated in these anaerobic organelles. It was therefore initially surprising to find that they contained substantial PDC activity, since elevation of these ratios potently inhibits the activity of the mammalian PDCs.[9-11] This inhibition results from both end-product inhibition and the stimulation of PDH_a kinase, which catalyzes the phosphorylation and inactivation of the α subunit of pyruvate dehydrogenase (E1α). Indeed, in other anaerobic eukaryotes, the PDC is either absent or not regulated by covalent modification, as in *Saccharomyces cerevisiae.*[12]

CHARACTERIZATION OF PDC ACTIVITY IN *A. suum* BODY WALL MUSCLE

The ascarid PDC appears to be structurally similar to its mammalian counterpart, although the mobilities of its subunits during SDS–polyacrylamide gel electrophoresis (SDS-PAGE) differ from those of the corresponding mammalian subunits (FIG. 1).

[a]Much of this work was supported by NIH Grant AI 18427 to R. K.

175

When the ascarid PDC is purified from body wall muscle without prior activation, it yields six major bands during SDS-PAGE.[13,14] While not readily dissociated using techniques described for the mammalian complex, dihydrolipoyl transacetylase (E2), dihydrolipoyl dehydrogenase (E3), E1α, and E1β have been definitively identified.[13,14,17] Since phosphorylation of E1α decreases its mobility during SDS-PAGE, the

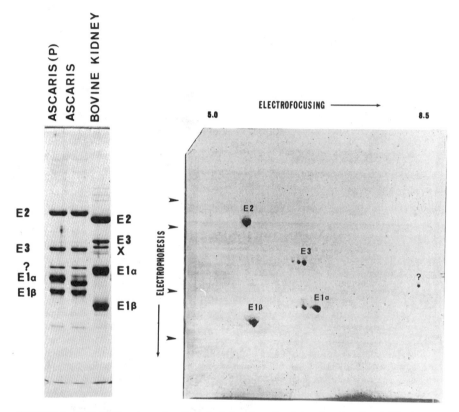

FIGURE 1. (*left*) SDS–polyacrylamide gel electrophoresis of the phosphorylated (P) *A. suum* PDC, dephosphorylated *A. suum* PDC, and dephosphorylated bovine kidney PDC. Samples (15 µg protein) were loaded onto 10% SDS–polyacrylamide slab gels, electrophoresed according to Laemmli,[26] and stained with 0.5% Coomassie brilliant blue. ?, 45-kDa subunit.

FIGURE 2. (*right*) Two-dimensional gel electrophoresis of the purified *A. suum* PDC. Dephosphorylated *A. suum* PDC (20 µg protein) was electrophoresed according to O'Farrell,[27] as modified by Henslee and Srere.[28] Molecular weight standards (*arrowheads*): phosphorylase (92,000), bovine serum albumin (67,000), ovalbumin (45,000), and carbonic anhydrase (31,000).

complex can be seen to contain a mixture of phosphorylated and dephosphorylated E1α when purified without activation or when immunoprecipitated directly from muscle homogenates.[13,28] Matuda *et al.*[19] have recently suggested that the altered mobility of the ascarid E1α could be the result of the activity of a Mg^{2+}-dependent protease, largely on the basis of their inability to demonstrate significant PDH_a kinase or PDH_b

phosphatase activity in their preparations of ascarid PDC. The present study conclusively demonstrates that this is not the case and provides data on the reversible phosphorylation-dephosphorylation of the ascarid complex. The inability of previous workers to demonstrate this reversible phosphorylation-dephosphorylation may have resulted from their use of hydroxyapatite chromatography to purify the complex, which inactivates the PDH_a kinase, and from the presence of Mg^{2+} concentrations (1 mM) which are too low to fully activate PDH_b phosphatase.[11,14,19] The sixth major subunit of ascarid PDC, with an apparent M_r of 45,000, does not appear to correspond to the protein X recently identified in mammalian PDCs.[20,31] Its pI ($>$ pH 8) is much more basic than that the of mammalian X (FIG. 2) and, more importantly, its predicted acetylation with [2-^{14}C]pyruvate could not be demonstrated.[19,20] Judging from the patterns on immunoblots of larval homogenates probed with antisera prepared against the adult ascarid PDC, it appears that this novel component is less abundant in the PDC of aerobic second-stage larvae than in the adult (Komuniecki, unpublished observations). This observation suggests that it may play a regulatory role in these anaerobic ascarid mitochondria, perhaps by inhibiting PDH_a kinase activity.

In isolated *A. suum* mitochondria, the PDC is phosphorylated and only 20% active, but substantial activity is still present, even under physiological conditions favoring inactivation.[14] To maintain PDC activity under these unfavorable conditions, total PDC content in adult ascarid body wall muscle is greater than the values reported from any other source, in spite of the fact that the final specific activity of the purified *A. suum* PDC ($<$ 5 μmol NADH formed/min/mg protein) is lower than the values reported for yeast or mammals (10–20 μmol NADH formed/min/mg protein).[11,13] The reason for this lower specific activity is not clear. The ascarid complex is recovered in high yield and appears to be fully dephosphorylated during purification.[18] Many of the kinetic parameters of the adult ascarid PDC also have been subtly modified to maintain activity under the reducing conditions present in these unique organelles.[14,15] For example, both overall PDC activity and the stimulation of PDH_a kinase are less sensitive to elevated NADH/NAD ratios than they are in PDC from other sources.[14,15] In addition, pyruvate and propionate, inhibitors of the mammalian PDH_a kinase, are of physiological importance in *A. suum*, since their concentrations are elevated during ascarid mitochondrial metabolism.[9,16] In fact, the apparent K_m for pyruvate of the ascarid PDC is much higher than the K_m values reported for the mammalian complexes, which may permit pyruvate to accumulate to inhibitory levels in *A. suum*.[15]

REGULATION BY PHOSPHORYLATION-DEPHOSPHORYLATION

In mammalian pyruvate dehydrogenase complexes, three distinct phosphorylation sites have been identified.[21-23] Inactivation is largely associated with the phosphorylation of site 1, and it appears that both the PDH_a kinase and PDH_b phosphatase exhibit distinct preferences for individual phosphorylation sites.[21-23] PDH_a kinase appears to phosphorylate site 1 before sites 2 and 3, and PDH_b phosphatase appears to dephosphorylate site 2 before site 1. It has been argued that the major role of phosphorylation at sites 2 and 3 is to inhibit the reactivation of the complex by preventing dephosphorylation of site 1 by PDH_b phosphatase.[23,24] In contrast to results reported for mammalian PDCs, phosphorylation of the ascarid complex parallels inactivation, and no additional phosphorylation is observed after inactivation is complete[14,18] (FIG. 3). Conversely, when the phosphorylated complex is reactivated with partially purified *A. suum* PDH_b phosphatase, a similar linear relationship

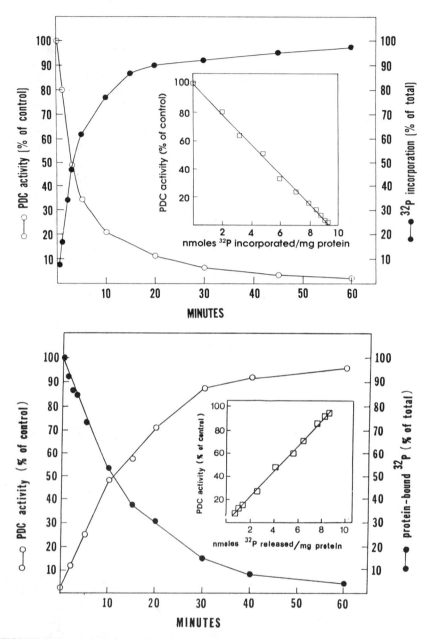

FIGURE 3. Regulation of ascarid PDC activity by phosphorylation-dephosphorylation. To assay PDH$_a$ kinase activity (**upper panel**), purified PDC was incubated as described previously and assayed either spectrophotometrically for PDC activity or by scintillation counting for protein-bound ^{32}P.[14,18] PDH$_b$ phosphatase was purified from isolated *A. suum* mitochondria through the DEAE-sepharose chromatography step previously described for the purification of the bovine kidney PDH$_b$ phosphatase.[28] These preparations could be concentrated by ultrafiltration (Micro-centricon, Amicon) and stored at $-70°$C in 40 mM MOPS buffer (pH 7.3), 300 mM KCl, 20% (w/v) glycerol, 0.1 mM EGTA, 0.5 mM dithiothreitol for 1 month with little loss of activity. PDH$_b$ phosphatase activity (**lower panel**) was assayed according to Pratt *et al.*,[29] except that Ca^{2+}, which inhibited the *A. suum* PDH$_b$ phosphatase, was omitted from the assay mixture.

TABLE 1. Comparison of Amino Acid Sequence Data for *A. suum,* Mammalian, and Yeast Phosphopeptides from PDC

A. suum
Tyr-Ser-Gly-His-Ser(P)-Met-Ser-Asp-Pro-Gly-Thr-Ser(P)-Tyr-Arg
Mammalian[a]
Tyr-His-Gly-His-Ser(P)-Met-Ser-Asp-Pro-Gly-Val-Ser(P)-Tyr-Arg
Saccharomyces cerevisiae[b]
Tyr-Gly-Gly-His-Ser(P)-Met-Ser-Asp-Pro-Gly-Thr-Thr-Tyr-Arg

[a]Described in Ref. 22.
[b]Described in Ref. 25.

between dephosphorylation and reactivation is observed, and no dephosphorylation occurs without reactivation (FIG. 3).

Tryptic digestion of the fully phosphorylated *A. suum* PDC yields a single tetradecapeptide containing two phosphorylated serine residues.[18] Its amino acid sequence is very similar to that of the tryptic phosphopeptide containing phosphorylation sites 1 and 2 isolated from mammalian PDC or that of a phosphopeptide isolated from a yeast PDC phosphorylated with the mammalian PDH$_a$ kinase (TABLE 1). At partial phosphorylation, three phosphopeptides can be isolated by anion-exchange HPLC, which correspond to the two monophosphorylated (TA1 and TA2) and the diphosphorylated (TA12) tetradecapeptide, based on amino acid analysis of cyanogen bromide–cleavage peptides.[18] Using this technique to identify site-specific phosphorylation, we have demonstrated that the strict preference of the PDH$_a$ kinase for site 1, as observed in mammalian complexes, apparently is not operative in *A. suum* (TABLE 2). Site 1 of the ascarid E1α initially is phosphorylated more rapidly than is site 2, but at 50% inactivation, 41% of the incorporated phosphoryl groups are incorporated into site 2. In addition, substantial amounts of peptide monophosphorylated at site 2 also accumulate, suggesting that prior phosphorylation at site 1 is not necessary for

TABLE 2. Distribution of ^{32}P in Tryptic Phosphopeptides from *A. suum* PDC

Time[a] (min)	PDC activity (% inactivation)	Total ^{32}P (nmoles/mg protein)	Radioactivity in Peptides (%)			% Maximum Radioactivity	
			TA1	TA2	TA12	Site 1	Site 2
0.5	16	1.63	61	24	15	24.9	11.5
1	31	3.00	49	20	31	43.2	23.8
2	54	5.01	30	12	58	66.0	45.8
3	74	6.55	25	11	64	83.3	62.9
5	87	7.64	12	8	80	88.7	81.9
30	98	8.92	1	3	96	96.0	98.0
60	99	8.96	1	2	97	97.0	99.0

[a]*A. suum* PDC was phosphorylated with PDH$_a$ kinase and [γ-^{32}P]ATP. At the indicated times, aliquots were removed and assayed for PDC activity, total protein-bound phosphoryl groups, and the distribution of radioactivity in the three tryptic phosphopeptides derived from E1α. (Adapted from Thissen and Komuniecki.[18])

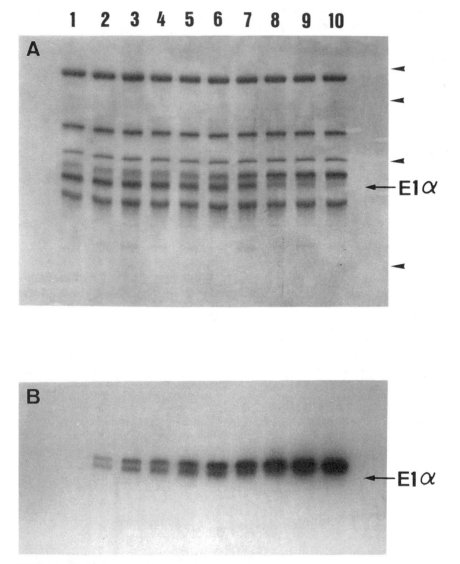

FIGURE 4. SDS-polyacrylamide gel electrophoresis (**A**) and autoradiography (**B**) of the *A. suum* pyruvate dehydrogenase complex phosphorylated with $[\gamma\text{-}^{32}P]ATP$ and PDH$_a$ kinase from 0 to 100%. The PDC was phosphorylated and then electrophoresed as described in FIGURE 1. *Lane 1,* dephosphorylated pyruvate dehydrogenase complex; *lanes 2–10,* aliquots removed from the incubation mixture at 0.33, 0.67, 1, 2, 3, 5, 10, 15, and 30 min., respectively. E1α, dephosphorylated α subunit of pyruvate dehydrogenase. (From Thissen and Komuniecki.[18] Reprinted from the *Journal of Biological Chemistry* with permission from the American Society for Biochemistry and Molecular Biology.)

phosphorylation at site 2, in contrast to the pattern observed previously for the mammalian PDH_a kinase.[20,21] As mentioned above, phosphorylation also causes a marked decrease in mobility of the E1α subunit on SDS–polyacrylamide gels. In fact, when the PDC is phosphorylated with [γ-^{32}P]ATP, separated by SDS-PAGE, and autoradiographed, two radiolabeled bands are present during the initial stages of phosphorylation (FIG. 4). One band corresponds to the lower mobility form of phosphorylated E1α observed on Coomassie blue–stained gels, and the other is intermediate in apparent M_r between the dephosphorylated and fully phosphorylated forms of E1α. At full phosphorylation, only the band corresponding to the lower mobility form of phosphorylated E1α is present. From a comparison of these results with those for the incorporation of ^{32}P into TA1, TA2, and TA12, it appears that these two radiolabeled bands correspond to the mono- and diphosphorylated forms of E1α and that both E1α subunits of the $\alpha_2\beta_2$ tetramer are fully phosphorylated at complete inactivation.[18]

In summary, the results of these studies demonstrate that, while the ascarid PDC is in some ways similar to its mammalian counterpart, its regulation is modified to permit its functioning in the unique reducing environment found in mitochondria of adult *A. suum* body wall muscle.

ACKNOWLEDGMENT

We would like to thank Rebecca Castle for the preparation of two-dimensional gels.

REFERENCES

1. SAZ, H. J. 1981. Annu. Rev. Physiol. **43:** 323–341.
2. KOHLER, P. 1985. Mol. Biochem. Parasitol. **17:** 1–18.
3. BARRETT, J. 1976. *In* Biochemistry of Parasites and Host-Parasite Relationships. H. Vanden Bossche, Ed.: 117–123. Elsevier, Amsterdam.
4. RIOUX, A. & R. KOMUNIECKI. 1984. J. Comp. Physiol. **154:** 349–354.
5. WARD, C. & D. FAIRBAIRN. 1970. J. Parasitol. **56:** 1009–1012.
6. KOMUNIECKI, R., P. R. KOMUNIECKI & H. J. SAZ. 1981. J. Parasitol. **67:** 841–846.
7. SAZ, H. J. 1971. Comp. Biochem. Physiol. **39B:** 627–637.
8. KOMUNIECKI, R., S. FEKETE & J. THISSEN-PARRA. 1985. J. Biol. Chem. **260:** 4770–4777.
9. BARRETT, J. & I. BEIS. 1973. Comp. Biochem. Physiol. **44A:** 331–340.
10. KOMUNIECKI, R., T. CAMPBELL & N. RUBIN. 1987. Mol. Biochem. Parasitol. **24:** 147–154.
11. KOMUNIECKI, R., P. R. KOMUNIECKI & H. J. SAZ. 1979. Biochem. Biophys. Acta **571:** 1–11.
12. KRESZE, G. B. & H. RONFT. 1981. Eur. J. Biochem. **119:** 581–587.
13. MATUDA, S., K. NAKANO & T. SAHEKI. 1986. Biochem. Int. **13:** 599–608.
14. THISSEN, J., S. DESAI, P. MCCARTNEY & R. KOMUNIECKI. 1986. Mol. Biochem. Parasitol. **21:** 129–138.
15. KOMUNIECKI, R., M. WACK & M. COULSON. 1983. Mol. Biochem. Parasitol. **8:** 165–176.
16. KOMUNIECKI, R., P. R. KOMUNIECKI & H. J. SAZ. 1981. J. Parasitol. **67:** 601–608.
17. KOMUNIECKI, R. & H. J. SAZ. 1979. Arch. Biochem. Biophys. **196:** 239–247.
18. THISSEN, J. & R. KOMUNIECKI. 1988. J. Biol. Chem. **263:** 19092–19097.
19. MATUDA, S., K. NAKANO, Y. URAGUCHI, S. MATUO & T. SAHEKI. 1987. Biochim. Biophys. Acta **926:** 54–60.
20. JILKA, J. M., M. RAHMATULLAH, M. KAZEMI & T. E. ROCHE. 1986. J. Biol. Chem. **261:** 1858–1867.

21. SUGDEN, P. H., A. L. KERBEY, P. J. RANDLE, C. A. WALLER & K. REID. 1979. Biochem. J.
    181: 419–426.
22. YEAMAN, S. J., E. T. HUTCHESON, T. E. ROCHE, F. PETTIT, J. R. BROWN, L. J. REED, D. C.
    WATSON & G. H. DIXON. 1978. Biochemistry **17:** 2364–2370.
23. SALE, G. J. & P. J. RANDLE. 1982. Biochem. J. **203:** 99–108.
24. SALE, G. J. & P. J. RANDLE. 1982. Biochem. J. **206:** 221–229.
25. UHLINGER, D. J., C. YUANG & L. J. REED. 1986. Biochemistry **25:** 5673–5677.
26. LAEMMLI, U. K. 1970. Nature **227:** 680–685.
27. O'FARRELL, P. H. 1975. J. Biol. Chem. **250:** 4007–4021.
28. HENSLEE, J. G. & P. A. SRERE. 1979. J. Biol. Chem. **254:** 5488–5497.
29. PRATT, M. L., J. R. MAHER & T. E. ROCHE. 1982. Eur. J. Biochem. **125:** 349–355.
30. DESAI, S., J. THISSEN, B. A. DODD, E. F. DUBRUL & R. KOMUNIECKI. 1987. Mol. Biochem.
    Parasitol. **23:** 203–209.
31. DEMARCUCCI, D. L. & J. G. LINDSAY. 1985. Eur. J. Biochem. **149:** 641–648.

Regulation of the α-Keto Acid Dehydrogenase Complexes and Their Involvement in Primary Biliary Cirrhosis

S. J. YEAMAN,[a,b] M. F. BASSENDINE,[c,d] D. FITTES,[a]
D. R. HODGSON,[a,e] L. HESELTINE,[a] H. J. BROWN,[a,f]
D. J. MUTIMER,[c] O. F. W. JAMES,[c]
AND S. P. M. FUSSEY[a,g]

[a]Department of Biochemistry and Genetics and
[c]Department of Medicine
University of Newcastle upon Tyne
NE2 4HH
United Kingdom

REGULATION OF α-KETO ACID DEHYDROGENASE COMPLEXES

The activity of each mammalian α-keto acid dehydrogenase complex is under acute control.[1] In the cases of the pyruvate dehydrogenase complex (PDC) and the branched-chain α-keto acid dehydrogenase complex (BCKADC), this control, by hormones and dietary factors, is exerted primarily via reversible phosphorylation of the α subunit of the α-keto acid dehydrogenase (E1) component.[1,2] The activity of the α-ketoglutarate dehydrogenase complex (KGDC) is apparently not controlled by phosphorylation, but is sensitive to changes in the intramitochondrial concentrations of various allosteric effectors. In particular, the presence of free Ca^{2+} ions decreases the affinity of the complex for α-ketoglutarate and mediates the increase in activity observed in response to Ca^{2+}-mobilizing hormones such as adrenaline in the heart and vasopressin and the α-adrenergic effects in the liver.[3]

Multisite Phosphorylation of PDC and BCKADC

Both PDC and BCKADC are subject to multisite phosphorylation on the α subunit of the E1 component.[2,4] In the case of PDC, there are three phosphorylation sites, two of which (sites 1 and 2) are in close proximity in the primary structure[5,6] and are located in the carboxyl-terminal third of the polypeptide,[7-9] site 3[5] is located some 60 residues to the amino-terminal side of sites 1 and 2. Work in this laboratory in recent years has concentrated on regulation of BCKADC by reversible phosphorylation. This complex has two phosphorylation sites.[10-12] The sequence around site 1 is homologous to that of site 1 in PDC[11,13] (TABLE

[b]Lister Institute Research Fellow.
[d]Supported by the Sir James Knott Trust.
[e]Held a Vacation Scholarship from the Wellcome Trust.
[f]Held a Schoolteacher Fellowship from the Biochemical Society.
[g]Holder of a Research Studentship from the Science and Engineering Research Council, U.K.

1). Interestingly, however, the phosphorylatable serine residue at site 2 in PDC is absent in BCKADC, being replaced by an alanine residue. The protein sequence predicted from a cDNA clone of the α subunit indicates that phosphorylation site 1 is located in a highly conserved region corresponding in position in the polypeptide to the position of site 1 in the α subunit of PDC,[14,15] i.e., in the carboxyl-terminal third of the polypeptide. Site 2 in BCKADC is ten residues to the carboxyl side of site 1, in a region showing little homology with the α subunit of PDC. Evidence obtained using purified complexes and components indicates that phosphorylation of the respective site 1 in each complex is responsible primarily for inactivation of that complex, via a dramatic reduction in V_{max}.[5,10,12,13]

Despite the similarities between the primary structures around the principal phosphorylation site on each E1, the kinase responsible for inactivation of each complex is apparently specific for that complex. Free PDC kinase will act on homogeneous preparations of free E1[5] and also on a synthetic peptide corresponding to the sequence around phosphorylation site 1.[16] Interestingly, although the serine residues of sites 1 and 2 were present on the synthetic peptide, only site 1 was subject to phosphorylation by the kinase.[16] Similarly, when free E1 is phosphorylated by kinase, the kinase shows a marked preference for site 1 over sites 2 and 3.[5] No such information is available as yet for BCKADC kinase, and, indeed, this kinase has not yet been successfully resolved from the dihydrolipoyl transacylase (E2) component of the complex.

TABLE 1. Primary Structure at Major Phosphorylation Sites on BCKADC and PDC

	SITE 1		SITE 2
	↓		↓
BCKADC	Ile-Gly-His-His-Ser(P)	-Thr-Ser-Asp-Asp-Ser-Ser- Ala -	Tyr-Arg- Ser(P)-
	SITE 1	SITE 2	
	↓	↓	
PDC	Tyr-His-Gly-His- Ser(P) -Met-Ser-Asp-Pro-Gly-Val-Ser(P)-	Tyr-Arg-Thr-	

PDC and BCKADC Kinases

PDC kinase has been purified to homogeneity[17] and is relatively well characterized.[4,17] It consists of a catalytic α subunit of M_r 48,000 and a β subunit of M_r 45,000, which has been postulated to serve a regulatory function.

In contrast, the polypeptide(s) comprising BCKADC kinase have not been identified and nothing is known of the structure of this enzyme. Clearly, it will be of interest to learn, probably from cloning studies, of the possible structural relationship of the two kinases and also of any possible relationship with well-characterized cytoplasmic protein kinases.

Physiological Regulation of BCKADC

The liver is the major site of branched-chain amino and keto acid catabolism. In rats fed a high protein diet, BCKADC is essentially fully dephosphorylated and active.[18–20] Feeding a diet restricted in protein causes a dramatic decrease in BCKADC activity,[19–21] this decrease occurring within 1–2 days, with the final value relating to the protein content of the diet.[19] Several mechanisms may contribute to the decreased activity of the complex under conditions of low protein intake. It is known that BCKADC has a relatively broad specificity, oxidizing five substrates with comparable kinetic parameters.[22,23] All five substrates are potent inhibitors of BCKADC kinase,[22] and high circulating levels of these keto acids in animals fed the high-protein diet are likely to inhibit the kinase and to maintain the complex in its dephosphorylated form. Low protein intake decreases the activity state of the complex, partly due to decreased inhibition of the kinase but also due to an observed stable increase in kinase activity.[24] Furthermore, the total amount of BCKADC may decrease in response to a low protein diet, but the question of whether this effect occurs remains controversial.[19–21, 25]

Starvation of rats previously fed a high-protein diet has little effect on the total activity or the activity state of hepatic BCKADC. However, starvation of rats previously maintained on a low-protein diet causes a dramatic increase in the activity state of the complex,[19,20] consistent with the utilization of keto acid under conditions of restricted calorie intake.

PRIMARY BILIARY CIRRHOSIS

Primary biliary cirrhosis (PBC) is a chronic cholestatic liver disease in which the epithelial cells of the small bile ducts are the principal target of end-organ damage.[26,27] PBC was initially considered a rare disease which was diagnosed almost only at a late stage and following operation for "surgical obstruction" to the biliary tree, but, recently, recognition of cases earlier in the evolution of this disease has enabled a more accurate estimate of the incidence of PBC to be made. In Northern Britain and Scandinavia, PBC has a prevalence of between 90 and 150 cases per 1,000,000,[28] and in Europe it is now the commonest indication for liver transplantation.[29]

Primary Biliary Cirrhosis as an Autoimmune Disease

PBC is a multisystem autoimmune disease, characterized by the presence of circulating autoantibodies targeted against mitochondrial antigens. Berg and co-workers showed that PBC sera react with trypsin-sensitive antigens localized on the inner mitochondrial membrane.[30] These anti-mitochondrial antibodies (AMA) can be detected by indirect immunofluorescence in greater than 99% of patients with PBC.[31] Furthermore, the finding of a significant AMA titer ($\geq 1:40$) has been shown to be strongly suggestive of PBC, even in the absence of symptoms and in the presence of normal blood test results for liver function, including that for serum alkaline phosphatase.[32]

The M2 Autoantigens

Demonstration of AMA by indirect immunofluorescence lacks complete diagnostic specificity for PBC, however, as AMA may also be found in other disorders (e.g., myocarditis, syphilis) using this technique. A PBC-specific mitochondrial autoantigen, termed M2, has been characterized and is defined by two serological criteria: first, by a positive reaction in immunoassays with the ATPase fraction released by chloroform extraction of beef heart submitochondrial particles[33] and, second, by the demonstration of two to five antigenic determinants in a Western immunoblot of this ATPase fraction or total mitochondrial extracts.[34–38] These polypeptide constituents of the M2 autoantigen have reported molecular masses of around 80–68 kDa (M2a), 64–60 kDa (M2b), 56–50 kDa (M2c), 48–43 kDa (M2d), and 36 kDa (M2e).[39] The discrepancies reported in the number and the molecular masses of the M2 antigens are likely to be mainly methodological, reflecting different antigen preparations and AMA detection techniques, as well as differences in the buffer systems employed in the SDS–polyacrylamide gel electrophoresis (SDS-PAGE) procedures. Serum autoantibodies to the 70-kDa (M2a) polypeptide have been found in 85–95% of patients with PBC.[40] The cDNA encoding part of this 70-kDa antigen has been cloned and sequenced from a rat liver cDNA library,[41] and, subsequently, a full-length human cDNA has been cloned and sequenced.[42] The predicted protein sequence derived from the the rat liver cDNA did not lead to identification of the protein antigen. In retrospect, this is surprising, as the antigen shows a high degree of homology at the protein level to its bacterial counterpart, which had been cloned and sequenced several years previously.[43]

Identification of the M2 Autoantigens

Detailed inspection of the predicted protein sequence of this 70-kDa M2a antigen strongly suggested its identity to be the E2 component of the mammalian PDC.[44] In particular, it contains a 10-residue section identical in sequence to that surrounding the lipoic acid attachment site on bovine PDC E2.[45] The identity of the 70-kDa antigen as PDC E2 was confirmed by immunoblotting of PBC patients' sera with purified PDC E2 protein. In our initial study,[44] sera from 38/40 (95%) patients with PBC reacted positively with PDC E2, whilst no sera from 39 controls gave a positive response. Furthermore, all PBC patients' sera that recognized E2 also cross-reacted with protein X,[44] an additional lipoate-containing component of PDC.[46,47] Both the E2 and X components of PDC have characteristics that have previously been reported for the M2 autoantigen.[44] It has been shown independently by another laboratory that the autoantibodies in PBC sera cross-react with PDC E2 and that they inhibit the overall catalytic activity of PDC.[48]

Following the identification of the E2 of PDC as the 70-kDa antigen in PBC, the high degree of structural homology between the E2 components of all three α-keto acid dehydrogenase complexes prompted us to investigate whether the E2 components of mammalian KGDC and BCKADC were also autoantigens in PBC. We have been able to confirm this is the case by immunoblotting the PBC patients' sera with purified E2 protein from KGDC and BCKADC.[49] An immunoblot of a PBC serum recognizing all three E2 components is shown in FIGURE 1.

Specificity and Class of Autoantibodies

When preparations of the E1-E2 subcomplex of bovine KGDC (2 μg, containing approximately equal amounts of E1 and E2) were immunoblotted with PBC patients' sera at a dilution of 1:100 or greater, it was found that 87 of 129 (67%) of the sera contained IgG antibodies that strongly reacted with KGDC E2. None of the sera from 77 control subjects (49 subjects with non-PBC chronic liver disease, 12 healthy normal women, 16 subjects with primary Sjogrens syndrome) reacted with KGDC E2. Similarly, when preparations of BCKADC E2 (1 μg protein) were immunoblotted with the same sera (dilution of 1:100 or greater), IgG autoantibodies were found in 70 of 129 (54%) of PBC patients. 125 of the 129 PBC patients' sera (97%) contained IgG autoantibodies to at least one E2 component.

We have also found by immunoblotting that IgM antibodies to purified E2 components of the α-keto acid dehydrogenase complexes are found in a large percentage of PBC patients' sera. Of the same 129 PBC patients, 123 possessed IgM autoantibodies to PDC E2 (and protein X), 61 had IgM against E2 of BCKADC, and 110 had IgM directed against E2 of KGDC. Two of the four PBC patients whose sera contained no IgG antibodies to any E2 component possessed IgM antibodies to both PDC E2 (and X) and KGDC E2. The two PBC patients who possessed no detectable IgG or IgM antibodies to any of the four identified M2 antigens (under the immunoblot conditions outlined above) had early histological Stage I disease. Only 2/77 controls showed any reactivity against the purified antigens—these patients had "mixed" autoimmune liver disease and were positive for AMA, as detected by indirect immunofluorescence.

The presence of a particular subclass of antibodies to the E2 polypeptides may be of

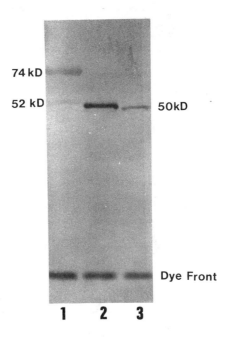

FIGURE 1. Purified antigens (containing 1 μg of E2) were subjected to SDS-PAGE, transferred to nitrocellulose, and incubated with a PBC serum at a dilution of 1:1000. Detection of human IgG antibodies was by use of secondary goat anti-human IgG (γ-chain–specific), peroxidase-conjugated antibodies, with 4-chloro-1-naphthol as substrate. **Lane 1,** E2 and X components of PDC; **lane 2,** E2 of BCKADC; **lane 3,** E1-E2 subcomplex of KGDC.

relevance in the pathogenesis of PBC, in view of the different biological properties of the various immunoglobulin isotypes. For instance, IgG3 has a greater capacity to fix complement (via the classical pathway) than do other IgG subclasses. IgM is also a potent activator of the complement pathway. PBC patients classically have raised serum levels of IgM. A 4–5-fold increase in serum levels of IgG3 has been demonstrated in all histological stages of PBC,[50] lymphocytes from patients with PBC spontaneously secrete high levels of IgG3 in culture,[51] and AMA in PBC is predominantly of the IgG3 subclass (as assessed by indirect immunofluorescence).[52] A predominance of IgG3- and IgM-isotype AMA against the recombinant fused 70-kDa mitochondrial polypeptide[53] (now identified as PDC E2) has also been demonstrated.

Bacterial and Yeast Antigens

Anti-mitochondrial antibodies in PBC have been shown to cross-react with bacterial[40] and yeast[54] proteins. The high degree of structural homology between mammalian and bacterial α-keto acid dehydrogenase complexes also raised the question of whether PBC patients' sera recognized purified bacterial and yeast E2 polypeptides. We have been able to demonstrate that they do by immunoblotting of PBC patients' sera with purified *Escherichia coli* PDC E2 (gift of Professor J. R. Guest, University of Sheffield, U.K.) and with yeast (*Saccharomyces cerevisiae*) PDC E2 (gift of Dr. J. G. Lindsay, University of Glasgow, U.K.). Serial dilution of PBC patients' sera to 1:80,000 showed no obvious difference in their reactivity against the yeast E2 compared to the bovine E2 and X components of PDC. It remains to be determined whether "anti-mitochondrial" antibodies arise initially in response to exposure to bacterial or yeast E2 polypeptides, thus making the basis of this "autoimmune" reactivity the resemblence between a specific foreign molecule and a molecule of self.

Although antibodies to the E2 components of PDC, KGDC and BCKADC (plus protein X of PDC) appear to be uniquely found in PBC, their role in the pathogenesis is uncertain. More detailed molecular dissection of both B and T cell reactivity to these purified proteins should help to clarify the mechanism of autoreactivity and should lead both to an understanding of the etiology of PBC and to the development of immunotherapeutic strategies.

Possible Role of Lipoic Acid in the Immune Response

As all four identified M2 autoantigens have lipoyl domains, the question is raised of whether this domain contains the main immunogenic region (MIR) of the polypeptides. We have been able to confirm that it does in the case of PDC E2 by immunoblotting of PBC patients' sera against partial proteolytic digests of the purified protein. The lipoate residue(s) of PDC E2 was acetylated using [2-^{14}C]pyruvate and subjected to limited proteolysis by trypsin, cleaving E2 into two major domains, the inner catalytic domain and the lipoate-containing domain.[55] Western blotting of the digested E2 showed that only the radioactive lipoate domain was recognized by the autoantibodies.

In addition to its presence in the α-keto acid dehydrogenase complexes, lipoic acid has been found in only one other protein, namely, the H-protein of the glycine cleavage system (molecular mass 13.9 kDa), which possesses a single lipoic acid moeity linked to a lysine residue.[56] This raised the question of whether this protein was also an M2 autoantigen. However, immunoblotting against purified chicken liver H-protein (gift of Professor Y. Motokawa, Takushima, Japan) has shown that PBC patients' sera do not recognize this lipoate-containing protein (unpublished observations). Furthermore, addition of excess lipoic acid (1 mM) or lipoamide (1 mM) in the immunoblotting procedure did not absorb out the reactivity of PBC patients' sera against purified E2 components of the α-keto acid dehydrogenases. However, lipoic acid has been shown to be a mitogen,[57] and it is effective in restoring the antibody responses of immunosuppressed mice,[58] so it is possible that lipoic acid plays a role in development of antibodies to the E2 polypeptides.

The MIR has also been studied by use of the recombinant protein derived from the partial rat liver cDNA clone.[59] It was demonstrated that one recombinant fusion protein (nucleotides 76–679, encompassing the lipoyl domain) contains the MIR recognized by sera from PBC patients. Furthermore, a 20 amino acid synthetic peptide (residues 81–100, including the lysine residue to which the lipoic acid moeity would be attached in the native protein) was able to absorb out reactivity of PBC sera to the original recombinant rat PDC E2, but only for sera at a dilution of 1:80,000.

Clearly, the exact role of the lipoic acid cofactor in the immunoreactivity of the E2 components has yet to be established. As the amino acid sequences flanking the lipoyl-lysine residues of lipoate-containing proteins (including chicken liver H-protein) are highly conserved,[60] and since PBC sera recognize two, three, or four lipoate-containing proteins, but not chicken liver H-protein, it is clear that the MIR recognized by PBC antisera is complex. Features of secondary and tertiary structure unique to each lipoyl domain must be important with respect to their antigenicity.

CONCLUSIONS

The E2 components of the α-keto acid dehydrogenase complexes are the major M2 autoantigens in PBC, with the lipoic acid residues playing a major role in antibody recognition. The E2 polypeptides may be used diagnostically in a serological test, as autoantibodies to at least one of the E2 polypeptides are found in over 98% of PBC patients' sera and not in sera from patients with other liver diseases. However, the initial event in production of autoantibodies is not clear. Do the B cells respond to antigens present during bacterial or yeast infections, producing antibodies that then cross-react with human proteins, or *vice versa?* Could some of the E2 polypeptides be mistargeted to the cell surface during synthesis, leading to recognition by the circulating B-cells?

Furthermore, the role of the antibodies in the pathogenesis of the disease is unclear, as there is strong evidence to suggest that the primary mechanism of bile duct injury in PBC is T cell–mediated cytotoxicity.[61] Do the T cell epitopes lie on the E2 components of the complex, or perhaps on one of the other components, such as E3, which is common to all three α-keto acid dehydrogenase complexes? In this regard, it should be noted that, for hepatitis B virus, priming of the immune system with an internal core antigen, recognized by T cells, can result in the primed T cells' helping B cells to react with a second protein on the viral surface.[62]

REFERENCES

1. YEAMAN, S. J. 1986. Trends Biochem. Sci. **11:** 293–296.
2. YEAMAN, S. J. 1989. Biochem. J. **257:** 625–632.
3. DENTON, R. M. & J. G. MCCORMACK. 1985. Am. J. Physiol. **249:** E543–E554.
4. REED, L. J. & S. J. YEAMAN. 1987. *In* The Enzymes. P. D. Boyer & E. G. Krebs, Eds. Vol. XVIII: 77–95. Academic Press Inc. Orlando, FL.
5. YEAMAN, S. J., E. T. HUTCHESON, T. E. ROCHE, F. H. PETTIT, J. R. BROWN, L. J. REED, D. C. WATSON & G. H. DIXON. 1978. Biochemistry **17:** 2364–2370.
6. SUGDEN, P. H., A. L. KERBEY, P. J. RANDLE, C. A. WALLER & K. B. M. REID. 1979. Biochem. J. **181:** 419–426.
7. DAHL, H.-H. M., S. M. HUNT, W. M. HUTCHISON & G. K. BROWN. 1987. J. Biol. Chem. **262:** 7398–7403.
8. KOIKE, K., S. OHTA, Y. URATA, Y. KAGAWA & M. KOIKE. 1988. Proc. Natl. Acad. Sci. USA **85:** 41–45.
9. DE MEIRLEIR, L., N. MACKAY, A. M. L. H. WAH & B. H. ROBINSON. 1988. J. Biol. Chem. **263:** 1991–1995.
10. COOK, K. G., R. LAWSON & S. J. YEAMAN. 1983. FEBS Lett. **157:** 59–62.
11. COOK, K. G., R. LAWSON, S. J. YEAMAN & A. AITKEN. 1983. FEBS Lett. **164:** 47–50.

12. COOK, K. G., A. P. BRADFORD, S. J. YEAMAN, A. AITKEN, I. M. FEARNLEY & J. E. WALKER. 1984. Eur. J. Biochem. **145:** 587–591.
13. PAXTON, R., M. KUNTZ & R. A. HARRIS. 1986. Arch. Biochem. Biophys. **244:** 187–201.
14. ZHANG, B., M. J. KUNTZ, G. W. GOODWIN, R. A. HARRIS & D. W. CRABB. 1987. J. Biol. Chem. **262:** 15220–15224.
15. HU, C.-W. C., K. S. LAU, T. A. GRIFFIN, J. L. CHUANG, C. W. FISHER, R. P. COX & D. T. CHUANG. 1988. J. Biol. Chem. **263:** 9007–9014.
16. MULLINAX, T. R., L. R. STEPP, J. R. BROWN & L. J. REED. 1985. Arch. Biochem. Biophys. **243:** 655–659.
17. STEPP, L. R., F. H. PETTIT, S. J. YEAMAN & L. J. REED. 1983. J. Biol. Chem. **258:** 9454–9458.
18. WAGENMAKERS, A. J. M., J. T. G. SCHEPENS, J. A. M. VELDHUIZEN & J. H. VEERKAMP. 1984. Biochem. J. **220:** 273–281.
19. HARRIS, R. A., S. M. POWELL, R. PAXTON, S. E. GILLIM & H. NAGAE. 1985. Arch. Biochem. Biophys. **243:** 542–555.
20. SOLOMON, M., K. G. COOK & S. J. YEAMAN. 1987. Biochim. Biophys. Acta **931:** 335–338.
21. MILLER, R. H., R. S. EISENSTEIN & A. E. HARPER. 1988. J. Biol. Chem. **263:** 3454–3461.
22. JONES, S. M. A. & S. J. YEAMAN. 1986. Biochem. J. **237:** 621–623.
23. PAXTON, R., P. W. D. SCISLOWSKI, E. J. DAVIS & R. A. HARRIS. 1986. Biochem. J. **234:** 295–303.
24. ESPINAL, J., M. BEGGS, H. PATEL & P. J. RANDLE. 1986. Biochem. J. **237:** 285–288.
25. PATSTON, P. A., J. ESPINAL, J. M. SHAW & P. J. RANDLE. 1986. Biochem. J. **235:** 429–434.
26. KAPLAN, M. M. 1987. New Engl. J. Med. **316:** 521–528.
27. JAMES, S. P., J. H. HOOFNAGLE, W. STROBER & E. A. JONES. 1983. Ann. Intern. Med. **99:** 500–512.
28. MYSZOR, M. F. & O. F. W. JAMES. 1989. *In* Progress in Liver Diseases. H. Popper & F. Schaffner, Eds. Vol. IX. Grune & Stratton. New York. In press.
29. BISMUTH, H., D. CASTAING, B. G. ERICZON, J. B. OTTE, K. ROLLES, B. RINGE & M. SLOOF. 1987. Lancet **ii:** 674–676.
30. BERG, P. A., D. DONIACH & I. M. ROITT. 1967. J. Exp. Med. **126:** 277–290.
31. MUNOZ, L. E., H. C. THOMAS, P. J. SCHEUER, D. DONIACH & S. SHERLOCK. 1981. Gut **22:** 136–140.
32. MITCHISON, H. C., M. F. BASSENDINE, A. HENDRICK, M. K. BENNETT, G. BIRD, A. J. WATSON & O. F. W. JAMES. 1986. Hepatology **6:** 1279–1284.
33. BERG, P. A., R. KLEIN, J. LINDENBORN-FOTINOS & W. KLOPPEL. 1982. Lancet **ii:** 1423–1426.
34. LINDENBORN-FOTINOS, J., H. BAUM & P. A. BERG. 1985. Hepatology **5:** 763–769.
35. FRAZER, I. H., I. R. MACKAY, T. W. JORDAN, S. WHITTINGHAM & S. MARZUKI. 1985. J. Immunol. **135:** 1739–1745.
36. MENDEL-HARTVIG, I., B. D. NELSON, L. LOOF & T. H. TOTTERMAN. 1985. Clin. Exp. Immunol. **62:** 371–379.
37. MAEDA, T., Y. YAMAMOTO & S. ONISHI. 1986. Acta Hepatol. Jpn. **27:** 753–761.
38. ISHII, H., S. SAIFUKU & T. NAMIHISA. 1986. Hepatology **7:** 134–136.
39. BERG, P. A. & R. KLEIN. 1988. Hepatology **8:** 200–201.
40. BAUM, H. & C. PALMER. 1985. Mol. Aspects Med. **8:** 201–234.
41. GERSHWIN, M. E., I. R. MACKAY, A. STURGESS & R. L. COPPEL. 1987. J. Immunol. **138:** 3525–3531.
42. COPPEL, R. L., L. J. MCNEILAGE, C. D. SURH, J. VAN DE WATER, T. W. SPITHILL, S. WHITTINGHAM & M. E. GERSHWIN. 1988. Proc. Natl. Acad. Sci. USA **85:** 7317–7321.
43. STEPHENS, P. W., H. M. LEWIS, M. G. DARLISON & J. R. GUEST. 1983. Eur. J. Biochem. **133:** 481–498.
44. YEAMAN, S. J., S. P. M. FUSSEY, D. J. DANNER, O. F. W. JAMES, D. J. MUTIMER & M. F. BASSENDINE. 1988. Lancet **i:** 1067–1070.
45. BRADFORD, A. P., S. HOWELL, A. AITKEN, L. A. JAMES & S. J. YEAMAN. 1987. Biochem. J. **245:** 919–922.
46. DE MARCUCCI, O. & J. G. LINDSAY. 1985. Eur. J. Biochem. **149:** 641–648.

47. JILKA, J. M., M. RAHMATULLAH, M. KAZEMA & T. E. ROCHE. 1986. J. Biol. Chem. **261:** 1858–1867.
48. VAN DE WATER, J., D. FREGEAU, P. DAVIS, A. ANSARI, D. DANNER, P. LEUNG, R. COPPEL & M. E. GERSHWIN. 1988. J. Immunol. **141:** 2321–2324.
49. FUSSEY, S. P. M., J. R. GUEST, O. F. W. JAMES, M. F. BASSENDINE & S. J. YEAMAN. 1988. Proc. Natl. Acad. Sci. USA **85:** 8654–8658.
50. FLOREANI, A. P., P. BIRD, H. MITCHISON, O. F. W. JAMES & M. F. BASSENDINE. 1987. Italian J. Gastroenterol. **19:** 325–328.
51. BIRD P., J. E. CALVERT, H. MITCHISON, N. R. LING, M. BASSENDINE & O. F. W. JAMES. 1988. Clin. Exp. Immunol. **71:** 475–480.
52. RIGGIONE, O., R. P. STOKES & R. A. THOMPSON. 1983. Br. Med. J. **286:** 1015–1016.
53. SURH, C. D., A. E. COOPER, R. L. COPPEL, P. LEUNG, A. AHMED, R. DICKSON & M. E. GERSHWIN. 1988. Hepatology **8:** 290–295.
54. GHADIMINEJAD, I., D. WILKIE & H. BAUM. 1988. J. Bioenerg. Biomembr. **20:** 243–259.
55. BLEILE, D. M., M. L. HACKERT, F. H. PETTIT & L. J. REED. 1981. J. Biol. Chem. **256:** 514–519.
56. FUJIWARA, K., K. OKAMURA-IKEDA & Y. MOTOKAWA. 1986. J. Biol. Chem. **261:** 8836–8841.
57. OHMORI, H., T. YAMAUCHI & I. YAMAMOTO. 1986. Jpn. J. Pharmacol. **42:** 135–140.
58. OHMORI, H., T. YAMAUCHI & I. YAMAMOTO. 1986. Jpn. J. Pharmacol. **42:** 275–280.
59. VAN DE WATER, J., M. E. GERSHWIN, P. LEUNG, A. ANSARI & R. L. COPPEL. 1988. J. Exp. Med. **167:** 1791–1799.
60. BRADFORD, A. P., A. AITKEN, F. BEG, K. G. COOK & S. J. YEAMAN. 1987. FEBS Lett. **222:** 211–214.
61. YAMADA, G., I. HYODO, K. TOBE, M. MUZINO, T. NISHIHARA, T. KOBOYASHI & M. NAGASHIMA. 1986. Hepatology **6:** 385–391.
62. MILICH, D. R., A. MCLACHLAN, G. B. THORNTON & J. L. HUGHES. 1987. Nature **329:** 547–549.

Regulation of the Pyruvate Dehydrogenase Complexes in Plants[a]

DOUGLAS D. RANDALL,[b] JAN A. MIERNYK,
TUNG K. FANG, RAYMOND J. A. BUDDE,
AND KATHRYN A. SCHULLER

Biochemistry Department
University of Missouri-Columbia
Columbia, Missouri 65211

INTRODUCTION

Plants and animals have many metabolic processes in common. Convergent evolution has resulted in striking similarities in metabolic regulation. Superimposed upon the similarities, however, are differences arising from characteristic organismal requirements. The pyruvate dehydrogenase complex (PDC) in plant cells is illustrative of both the similarities in metabolic processes and the differences dictated by the need to respond to diverse external stimuli. Plants are unique in containing two distinct, spatially separated types of PDCs, one within the mitochondrial matrix and the other in the plastid stroma. Each type of PDC has characteristic structural, catalytic, and regulatory properties.[1] The mitochondrial location is typical for the PDC in eucaryotic organisms, where it serves as a primary entry point for carbon into the citric acid cycle. The plastid PDC provides both acetyl-CoA and NADH for fatty acid and isoprenoid biosynthesis. Thus, the first mechanism, and one of the most important, for regulation of plant PDCs is by compartmentation.

In contrast to mammalian cells and microbes, all *de novo* fatty acid biosynthesis by plant cells occurs within the plastids.[2] This is true for the chloroplasts in light-grown leaves, the chromoplasts in fruits and floral tissues, and the leucoplasts and amyloplasts in seeds and other non-green tissues. Plant cells also contain two glycolytic pathways, the classical cytoplasmic pathway and a second metabolic sequence within the plastids.[3] It was a search for the connecting link between the pyruvate produced by plastid glycolysis and the acetyl-CoA necessary for fatty acid synthesis which led Dennis and his associates to discovery of the PDC within the leucoplasts of developing castor oil seeds.[4,5] Observations concerning the occurrence of plastid PDC were subsequently extended to green tissues.[6,7] The chloroplast PDC not only produces acetyl-CoA for fatty acid biosynthesis, but also is the only known source to date for NADH in the chloroplast.[8]

[a]Research from the authors' laboratory was supported by the National Science Foundation (DMB-8506473) and the Missouri Agricultural Experiment Station. This is journal report number 10695 from the Missouri Agricultural Experiment Station.
[b]Address correspondence to Douglas D. Randall, 117 Schweitzer Hall, University of Missouri, Columbia, MO 65211.

Another feature unique to green plant cells is the existence of two separate systems for electron transport–coupled synthesis of ATP: oxidative phosphorylation in mitochondria and photophosphorylation in chloroplasts. In the dark, only oxidative phosphorylation is operative. In the light, photophosphorylation is operative, but it is controversial as to whether oxidative phosphorylation is additionally operative.[9] If oxidative phosphorylation is operative in illuminated plant cells, it is not clear if it is supported by the citric acid cycle or by an alternative substrate such as glycine from photorespiration. The mitochondrial PDC occupies an ideal position for regulation of carbon flow into the citric acid cycle during photosynthesis.

This paper will describe what is known about regulation of plant PDCs. The informed reader will note that progress in understanding plant systems has lagged behind that made with mammals and microbes. While there are manifold reasons for this lag, a major contributing factor is the low abundance of mitochondria per unit fresh weight of plant material. The mitochondrial PDC has been purified only a single time from a plant source, *Brassica oleracea* florets.[10] A truly herculean effort resulted in the reduction of approximately 500 kg of broccoli to 1 mg of pure mitochondrial PDC!

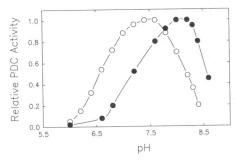

FIGURE 1. In vitro activity of the plant mitochondrial (O) and plastid (●) pyruvate dehydrogenase complexes as a function of assay pH.

GENERAL PROPERTIES OF PLANT MITOCHONDRIAL PYRUVATE DEHYDROGENASE COMPLEXES

Mammalian mitochondrial PDC has an $s_{20,w}$ of 70–90S,[11] corresponding to a native M_r of $7–8 \times 10^6$. The broccoli mitochondrial PDC is somewhat smaller at 59.3S.[10] Analysis of pea mitochondrial PDC by SDS–polyacrylamide gel electrophoresis (SDS-PAGE) plus Western blotting has shown subunits of M_r 97,700, 67,400, 58,100, 43,300, and 37,000.[8] The M_r 58,100 subunit is lipoyl dehydrogenase, while the 43,000 and 37,000 polypeptides are most probably the α and β subunits, respectively, of pyruvate dehydrogenase (PDH).

The substrate and cofactor requirements of plant mitochondrial PDCs are typical of the complex from non-plant sources. Catalytic rates with 2-oxybutyrate, the only substrate other than pyruvate utilized by plant PDCs, are only 10% of the rates with pyruvate.[10] Like mammalian complexes, plant PDCs have a multisite ping-pong kinetic mechanism.[12] Typical Michaelis constants are 125 μM, 94 μM, 5 μM, 80 nM, and 0.4 mM for pyruvate, NAD, CoA-SH, Mg-TPP and Mg^{2+}, respectively. *In vitro* activity of plant mitochondrial PDCs is maximal around pH 7.5, with half-maximal rates at pH 6.8 and 8.5 (FIG. 1).

IN VITRO REGULATION OF THE PLANT MITOCHONDRIAL PYRUVATE DEHYDROGENASE COMPLEX

Product Inhibition

All plant mitochondrial PDCs examined to date are inhibited by the products of the overall reaction, NADH and acetyl-CoA. Inhibition is linearly competitive with CoA and NAD.[12-14] Generally, the K_i values for acetyl-CoA are greater than the K_m values for CoA-SH, and increasing the acetyl-CoA/CoA-SH ratio results in a linear increase in inhibition. In contrast, K_i values for NADH are 5-to 10-fold lower than the K_m values, and increasing the NADH/NAD ratio around the complex results in a logarithmic increase in inhibition. These patterns suggest that PDC is most sensitive to product inhibition by NADH.

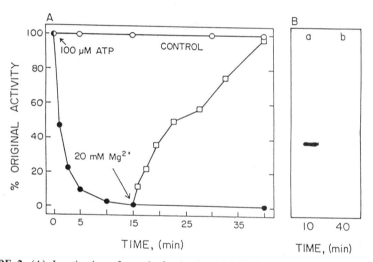

FIGURE 2. (A) Inactivation of pea leaf mitochondrial PDC by phosphorylation (●) and reactivation by dephosphorylation (□). **(B)** Analysis by immunoprecipitation, SDS-PAGE, and autoradiography of samples taken 10 and 40 min after addition of $[\gamma\text{-}^{32}P]$ATP (From Miernyk and Randall.[25] Reprinted with permission from *Plant Physiology.*)

Reversible Phosphorylation of Pyruvate Dehydrogenase

The demonstration that plant mitochondrial PDCs could be inactivated in an ATP-dependent manner, and subsequently reactivated through a Mg^{2+}-stimulated process, indicated that plant mitochondrial PDCs were most likely regulated by covalent modification in the same manner as the mammalian PDCs[15-18] (FIG. 2). Phosphorylation was verified by assay of ^{32}P incorporation from $[\gamma\text{-}^{32}P]$ATP with lysed mitochondria, followed by purification of the complex[16] and by crossed-rocket immunoelectrophoresis.[18] Dephosphorylation was shown by loss of ^{32}P from the complex, as demonstrated by autoradiography of agarose electrophoresis gel patterns of the PDC.[18] These studies were the first to demonstrate regulation of the activity of a plant enzyme by a phosphorylation-dephosphorylation mechanism. We have subsequently shown that mitochondrial PDCs from all plant tissues examined, i.e., green leaves, etiolated tissues, roots, developing and germinating seeds, etc., across a broad phylogenetic spectrum, are all inactivated-reactivated by phosphorylation-dephosphorylation of a single subunit of M_r 43,300.[1] This subunit corresponds to the M_r 41,000 subunits of the mammalian PDCs, or the E1α subunit of the pyruvate dehydrogenase component of the complex. As with the mammalian complex, it is a serine residue that is phosphorylated during inactivation; we also have evidence for additional serine phosphorylations on the 43,300 subunit that are not related to the activation state, as is found with the mammalian complexes.[19] Antibodies to a synthetic peptide corresponding to the 14 amino acid tryptic fragment containing phosphorylation sites one and two of bovine PDH yielded positive signals on Western blots for bovine, porcine or yeast PDCs but not for plant mitochondrial or plastid PDCs.[20] The synthetic peptide also does not serve as a substrate for the plant phosphorylation system but is a substrate for the mammalian PDH kinase. This suggests that the phosphorylation site of the plant mitochondrial PDC may be significantly different.

Metabolite Regulation

A number of mitochondrial matrix metabolites were examined as potential modulators of PDC activity. None of the metabolites tested stimulated PDC activity *in vitro,* and only the adenylates had a significant inhibitory effect.[12,13,21] Inhibition by ADP was linearly competitive with respect to CoA-SH, with a K_i of 0.6 mM, which is similar to the concentration reported for the plant mitochondrial matrix. AMP was slightly inhibitory, but only at values far in excess of reported *in vivo* concentrations.[21] Glyoxylate, a photorespiratory metabolite in leaf tissue, inhibited competitively against pyruvate (K_i, 51 μM); however, there is no evidence that glyoxylate enters plant mitochondria.[21]

Plant Mitochondrial Pyruvate Dehydrogenase Kinase

The PDH kinase has been studied with the mitochondrial PDC from pea seedlings and from the endosperm of *Ricinus communis* seeds. The kinase is lost from the complex or inactivated during purification; thus, all studies to date with the plant enzyme have used either partially purified PDC that retains kinase activity or mitochondrial extracts. Activity of plant PDH kinases is optimal at pH 7.5, with Mg-ATP as the preferred phosphoryl donor but with quite a broad nucleotide specificity. The K_m for Mg-ATP is 2.5 μM, certainly supporting the conclusion that if the PDH kinase is not regulated, the PDC must always be inactive (phosphorylated). Preliminary data indicated that the eight amino acid peptide corresponding to phosphorylation site one of the bovine complex is not a substrate for the plant PDH kinase, but substitution of a threonine for serine in the peptide resulted in an effective phosphoryl acceptor. This is obviously in conflict with data indicating that serine is the phosphorylated amino acid in plant PDCs. Further study will resolve this problem.

Since the low abundance of the plant PDH kinase has precluded its isolation and purification, we have attempted to estimate its M_r by incubation with 8-azido-[α-^{32}P]-ATP, followed by photolysis, immunoprecipitation, SDS-PAGE, and autoradiography. This strategy indicated that the M_r is about 53,000, which is considerably larger than the 48,000 catalytic subunit of the mammalian PDH kinase.

In vitro effectors of the plant PDH kinase activity include ADP, pyruvate, acetyl-CoA, NADH, citrate, 2-oxoglutarate, and monovalent cations.[22,23] Inhibition by

ADP is competitive with ATP, as it is for the mammalian PDH kinase. In contrast to their stimulatory effect on the mammalian kinase, acetyl-CoA and NADH inhibit the plant enzyme. Inhibition by acetyl-CoA is competitive with Mg-ATP, and NADH is non-competitive with respect to Mg-ATP. We have not established as yet the basis for this difference. Citrate inhibition of PDC inactivation also does not fit the expected pattern, since one would think that an increasing citrate concentration would indicate decreased citric acid cycle activity and demand for acetyl-CoA in the mitochondria. However, this pattern of regulation may indicate that there are alternate uses for citrate and/or acetyl-CoA outside the mitochondria that depend upon carbon flow through PDC and subsequent export of the citrate.

As with the mammalian PDH kinase, pyruvate inhibition of the plant enzyme is competitive with respect to ATP, with a K_i of about 60 μM in the presence of saturating TPP concentrations. In the absence of TPP, the pyruvate inhibition *in vitro* is reduced about 6-fold.[24] The pyruvate analog dichloroacetate also inhibits phosphorylation, and this inhibition is very much enhanced by TPP. With intact mitochondria TPP does not appear to inhibit the kinase in the presence of K^+ or NH_4^+, but it is a very effective inhibitor (10–100 μM TPP) of the kinase when K^+ or NH_4^+ is removed from disrupted mitochondria by dialysis.[23] Most likely, the TPP inhibition of kinase activity is overridden by the stimulation of the kinase by K^+ and/or NH_4^+ in undialyzed mitochondria. Na^+ (100 μM) enhances the TPP inhibition of kinase activity in intact mitochondria.

Pea leaf PDH kinase is inhibited by Na^+ and simulated by millimolar K^+ and micromolar NH_4^+.[23] The stimulation by NH_4^+ could be very significant in light of potential photorespiratory control of the citric acid cycle during photosynthesis (see *in situ* studies, below). K^+ does not affect the ADP inhibition of the plant kinase activity as it does with the mammalian kinase.[21] The details of concentration requirements and the mechanisms of action of these effector metabolites remain to be established, but the data so far obtained point to a number of differences as well as similarities between the plant and the mammalian PDCs and between their modes of regulation.

Plant Mitochondrial Phospho–Pyruvate Dehydrogenase Phosphatase

The plant phospho-PDH (P-PDH) phosphatase requires a divalent cation for activity, with activation by $Mg^{2+} > Mn^{2+} > Co^{2+}$ and K_m values of 3.8, 1.7, and 1.4 mM, respectively.[25] Ca^{2+}, monovalent cations, and polyamines do not activate the plant phosphatase. Micromolar Ca^{2+} antagonizes Mg^{2+}-dependent dephosphorylation of the plant PDC (FIG. 3), in contrast to the stimulation of the mammalian P-PDH

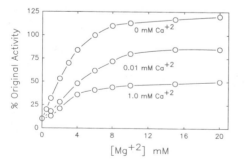

FIGURE 3. Calcium inhibition of the magnesium-dependent reaction of the phosphorylated pea mitochondrial pyruvate dehydrogenase complex.

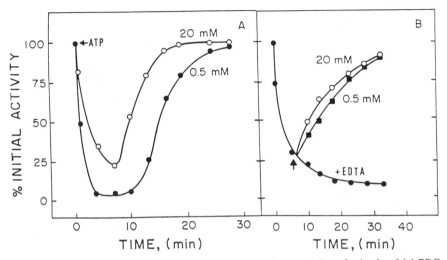

FIGURE 4. Effect of magnesium on the inactivation and reactivation of mitochondrial PDC activity. Mitochondria permeablized with 0.01% Triton X-100 were incubated (pH 7.6, 20°C) with 0.5 mM or 20 mM MgCl$_2$ as indicated, and inactivation was initiated with 200 μM ATP. Aliquots were withdrawn at the times indicated and assayed for PDC activity. **(A)** Different concentrations of magnesium were added initially with the ATP (←) to discern the effect of magnesium on inactivation and reactivation. **(B)** PDC was inactivated in the presence of 0.5 mM MgCl$_2$. At 6 min (↑), the reaction mixture was divided into three parts, and either the concentration of magnesium was changed as indicated or 2 mM EDTA was added. (From Budde & Randall.[26] Reprinted with permission from *Plant Physiology*.)

phosphatase by Ca^{2+}. Calmodulin does not enhance the Ca^{2+} effect, and EGTA only slightly stimulates the plant phosphatase activity.[25] The only metabolite that has any effect on this phosphatase is orthophosphate, which inhibits slightly. Fluoride inhibits the plant phosphatase, but vanadate and molybdate do not. The *in vitro* rates of the P-PDH phosphatase are usually 10–20% of the PDH kinase rates.

Results of *in vitro* studies indicate that the PDC is receptive to regulation by product inhibition and reversible phosphorylation. The activity rates of the regulatory enzymes are such that in the absence of effectors the *in vivo* complex will be inactive at all times, i.e., our data indicate that PDH kinase rates are about 6 times the P-PDH phosphatase rates. Pyruvate appears to be the metabolite with the greatest potential for controlling the PDH kinase activity and thus adjusting the steady-state PDC activity *in vivo*. To determine the physiological significance of the *in vitro* results, we have undertaken *in situ* studies using highly purified, intact and functional mitochondria.

REGULATION OF MITOCHONDRIAL PYRUVATE DEHYDROGENASE COMPLEX ACTIVITY *IN SITU*

Intact mitochondria purified from green pea seedlings were used in experiments under various respiratory states as measured by O$_2$ electrode, with concomitant determination of the steady-state PDC activity. While most *in vitro* results were generally verified in the *in situ* studies, there were differences in the degree of regulation and order of importance of the various effectors.

In contrast to mammalian PDC, changes in the ATP:ADP ratio over a 20-fold range (0.25–5 mM) have little or no effect on the activation state of the plant mitochondrial PDC.[24] The degree of pyruvate inhibition of PDH kinase *in situ* increased about 2-fold, and TPP enhanced the pyruvate inhibition 2- to 3-fold. The PDC in intact mitochondria is inactivated by exogenously added ATP and remains inactivated until the ATP is removed by addition of excess glucose and hexokinase or is hydrolyzed by the F_1-ATPase from the broken mitochondria that contaminate the preparation of intact mitochondria.[26] Once the ATP is removed, the PDC is reactivated (FIG. 4), and this reactivation occurs at 0.5 mM Mg^{2+}, which is 20- to 40-fold less

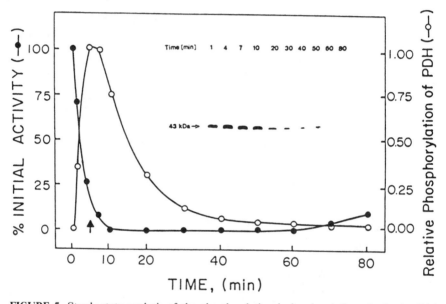

FIGURE 5. Steady-state analysis of the phosphorylation-dephosphorylation of mitochondrial PDH *in situ*. Intact pea leaf mitochondria were incubated (25 mM TES-NaOH, pH 7.5, 20°C) with 0.5 mM MgCl$_2$, and inactivation was initiated with 200 μM [γ-^{32}P]ATP (10^8 dpm/μmole). At the times indicated, aliquots were assayed for PDC activity (●) and aliquots were taken for SDS-PAGE and analyzed by autoradiography. At 7 min (↑) 300 μM of non-labeled ATP, 4 mM phosphocreatine, 6 units of creatine phosphokinase and 5 μg/ml of oligomycin were added to keep PDC phosphorylated and inactive. **Insert:** Autoradiography of the samples assayed for relative phosphorylation (O) of the PDH 43-kDa subunit (From Budde and Randall.[26] Reprinted with permission from *Plant Physiology*.)

magnesium than is needed for *in vitro* reactivation.[26] While the *in situ* concentration of Mg^{2+} may exceed 0.5 mM, permeablizing the mitochondria with 0.01% Triton X-100 results in identical reactivation at 0.5 mM Mg^{2+} or 20 mM Mg^{2+} (FIG. 4B). Incubation of the permeablized mitochondria with 20 mM Mg^{2+} did not stimulate reactivation but, in fact, inhibited the PDH kinase (FIG. 4A). Again, identical results were obtained with non-permeablized mitochondria. This is in direct contrast to the observation that the P-PDH phosphatase activity after partial enrichment of the PDC requires much higher Mg^{2+} concentration.[25] Ca^{2+}, which inhibits PDH kinase activity and stimulates the phosphatase of the mammalian PDCs, is without effect on the *in situ* activity of the plant PDC. EGTA treatment of permeablized mitochondria did not affect the relative rates of either inactivation or reactivation.[26]

The reversible phosphorylation of PDC is a steady-state phenomenon which is easily seen when intact mitochondria are incubated with [^{32}P]ATP to inactivate the complex and then the radioactive label is chased by the addition of excess unlabeled ATP.[26] The label in the 43,300 band (Elα subunit) is maximal with maximal inactivation, but, although this label is chased out, activity is not recovered (FIG. 5). Pulse-labeling with a limited amount of labeled ATP showed that the level of labeling and the activity of PDC changed in a reciprocal fashion. This indicates that the kinase and the phosphatase are both active at the same time and that the kinase activity must be inhibited in order to reach a steady-state level of PDC activity. This is further supported by experiments involving pyruvate oxidation monitored by O_2 electrode, plus sampling to determine the activation state of PDC.[27] FIGURE 6 shows O_2 electrode traces of the oxidation of different substrates and the steady-state level of PDC. The level of PDC activity reflects the amount of pyruvate present by exogenous addition or by generation within the mitochondria by malic enzyme.[27] When mitochondria are oxidizing other substrates, including the photorespiratory metabolite glycine, the PDC is quickly inactivated or inhibited by phosphorylation to a new steady-state level.[27] The inactivation of PDC when the mitochondria are oxidizing glycine (FIG. 6C) reflects ATP generation from oxidative phosphorylation, increases in NADH from rapid glycine oxidation, and NH_4^+ stimulation of the PDH kinase.[23]

We have also observed that some mitochondrial preparations appear to be uncoupled when oxidizing pyruvate but well coupled when oxidizing malate or 2-oxoglutarate. The steady-state level of PDC activity of these apparently uncoupled mitochondria is about 100%. The apparent lack of coupling can be relieved by adding oxaloacetate, malate, or carnitine to serve as acetyl acceptors, allowing regeneration of the CoA-SH.[28] Measurement of the CoA pool verified that the acetyl-CoA:CoA-SH ratio was greater than 2.5 when the mitochondria appeared uncoupled with pyruvate. Thus, *in situ,* acetyl-CoA is a more effective product inhibitor than predicted from the *in vitro* results, which point to the preeminence of the NADH:NAD ratio.[21]

The *in situ* studies are just beginning, but it is obvious that we must determine the levels of the various metabolites in the mitochondria in order to understand how the plant PDC is regulated through either the mode of covalent modification or that of metabolite effectors. Preliminary experiments have indicated that shortly after leaf tissue is illuminated and photosynthesis and photorespiration are underway, the PDC is inactivated to a very low steady-state level (R. J. A. Budde and D. D. Randall, unpublished observations). If the tissue is placed in the dark or photosynthesis is chemically inhibited, the steady-state level of PDC activity increases to almost maximal levels. Prolonged darkness results in a high steady-state level of PDC activity. This certainly supports our original hypothesis that the mitochondrial PDC is the logical site to limit carbon flow into the citric acid cycle during photosynthesis. Alternate carbon sources such as glycine are oxidized to generate the ATP by oxidative phosphorylation.

LONG-TERM DEVELOPMENTAL REGULATION

While most research on the PDC in plant systems has addressed short-term, acute regulation, long-term developmental control of enzyme activity must also be considered. During germination of castor oil seeds there is a characteristic pattern of change

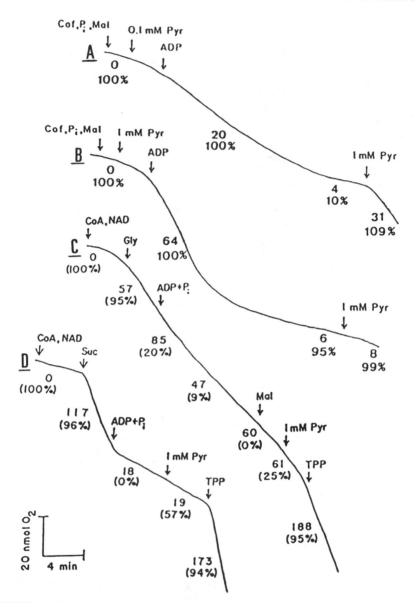

FIGURE 6. Effect of pyruvate, glycine, and succinate on the *in situ* activation level and phosphorylation of PDC. Respiring mitochondria were incubated with the indicated substrate in the presence of cofactors (Cof: NAD, coenzyme A, TPP), orthophosphate (P_i), 0.1 mM sparker malate (Mal), and 0.15 mM ADP. Oxygen uptake was monitored by O_2 electrode. Oxygen uptake rates (nmoles O_2 uptake/min/mg mitochondrial protein) are indicated by *numbers* on the traces. *Percentages* indicate percent of active PDC in aliquots taken from O_2 electrode chamber. (**A**) 0.1 mM pyruvate as substrate; (**B**) 1 mM pyruvate as substrate; (**C**) 1 mM glycine (Gly) as substrate; (**D**) 1 mM succinate (Suc) as substrate. The addition of 1 mM pyruvate, following the initial substrate, resulted in activation of PDC, as seen in (**A**), (**C**), and (**D**). The addition of thiamine pyrophosphate (TPP) enhanced the pyruvate activation by enhancing the pyruvate inhibition of PDH kinase.[26]

in the activity of the mitochondrial PDC.[29] There is no activity in mitochondrial preparations from imbibition through day three of germination, followed by a rapid increase in activity to a peak at day five, then a sharp decrease as tissue senescence begins. A qualitatively similar pattern of change was observed for cytoplasmic, glyoxysomal, and other mitochondrial enzyme activities, making it unlikely that the changes in PDC activity are entirely due to differences in phosphorylation state. The developmental regulation of PDC activity must include control of both the rate of synthesis of the complex and the rate of its degradation. There is as yet no information on the synthesis and turnover of the component proteins of the PDC in plant cells, but the germinating castor oil seed promises to be an effective system in which to study these processes.

GENERAL PROPERTIES OF THE PLASTID PYRUVATE DEHYDROGENASE COMPLEX

While the plastid PDC catalyzes the same overall reaction[8,30,31] and has the same kinetic mechanism[32] as the mitochondrial PDC, it is structurally distinct. A marked instability has hampered estimation of the native M_r of the pea and maize mesophyll chloroplast PDCs by rate-zonal sedimentation.[8,30] It was possible, however, to demonstrate that the chloroplast PDC is intermediate in size between the *Escherichia coli* (M_r 4.3×10^6) and bovine mitochondrial (M_r 6–8×10^6) PDCs.[8] It has been suggested by Treede and Heise[30] that the instability or lack of tight association of the component enzymes of plastid PDCs may permit individual subcomplexes to function in support of other reactions, for example, synthesis of acetolactate for branched-chain amino acids. Subunit analyses of plastid and mitochondrial PDCs by SDS-PAGE plus Western blotting showed significant differences.[8,14] At this time, the only subunit of the plastid PDCs which has been unequivocally identified is that of lipoyl dehydrogenase, with an M_r of 58,000.

The *in vitro* catalytic characteristics of plastid PDCs are generally similar to those of mitochondrial PDCs. A possible exception is the Michaelis constant for NAD, which is approximately half of the value for the mitochondrial complex (49 μM [4 species] versus 94 μM [6 species]).

IN VITRO REGULATORY PROPERTIES OF PLASTID PYRUVATE DEHYDROGENASE COMPLEXES

Product Inhibition

As is the case with bacterial and mitochondrial PDCs, the plastid complex is sensitive to product inhibition by NADH and acetyl-CoA. Inhibition by NADH is competitive with respect to NAD, and K_i values are around 20 μM.[32–34] The inhibition by acetyl-CoA is competitive with respect to CoA-SH, and K_i values are also around 20 μM. The pea chloroplast PDC was assayed at ratios of NADH to NAD and of acetyl-CoA to CoA-SH from 0 to 4.4, at fixed total pyridine nucleotide and coenzyme A concentrations of 100 μM and 20 μM, respectively.[32] The plastid complex, like the mitochondrial complex, was much more sensitive *in vitro* to the ratio of NADH to NAD, with a ratio of 0.2 giving 50% inhibition, than to that of acetyl-CoA to CoA, which required a ratio of 2.2 for 50% inhibition.

Reversible Phosphorylation

Plastid PDCs resemble the bacterial complexes rather than the mitochondrial PDCs in that they are not regulated by reversible phosphorylation[1] (FIG. 7). In green plant tissues, fatty acid biosynthesis is light-driven.[35] Thus, the demand for acetyl-CoA and NADH in the plastid stroma is greatest at the same time that the ATP concentration, produced by photophosphorylation, is the highest. Under these circumstances, regulation of the plastid PDC by phosphorylation would be counterproductive. It is possible to phorphorylate the plastid complex *in vitro* using heterologous protein kinases, but there is no change in activity associated with this phosphorylation.[1]

Metabolite Regulation

The *in vitro* activity of pea chloroplast PDC is insensitive to physiological concentration of intermediates of glycolysis, the reductive pentose-phosphate pathway, or amino acid metabolism.[32] Inorganic phosphate inhibited activity by 24% at 10 mM. Common terpenoids, acetyl-CoA–derived products of plastid metabolism, were without effect on the *in vitro* activity of plastid PDC. There was, however, a significant (57%) inhibition by 50 μM oleic acid and a 36% stimulation by palmitic acid. Other fatty acids, acyl-CoA's, and acyl-ACPs were without effect, suggesting that the oleate and palmitate effects are specific.[32] The fatty acid effects could be an additional component of the fine regulation of plastid PDC activity.

Light Regulation

The pH optima of the plastid PDCs are more alkaline than that of the mitochondrial complex[6,8,30] (FIG. 1). The K_m of the pea chloroplast PDC for pyruvate is lowest at the pH optimum for the complex, 8.0, and increases sharply at pH values more acidic or alkaline than 8.0. The values for V_{max} are largely unaffected by changes in pH

$M_r \times 10^3$

205 –

116 –
97.4 –

67 –

45 – ▬   ▬

29 –

A   B   C   D

FIGURE 7. Autoradiograph of phosphorylation of pea seedling and castor oil seed endosperm PDCs *in vitro*. Samples are pea leaf mitochondria (**A**), pea leaf chloroplasts (**B**), *Ricinus* endosperm leucoplasts (**C**), and *Ricinus* endosperm mitochondria (**D**). In each case, the organelles in 1 ml of 100 mM TES-KOH, pH 7.5, containing 2 mM dithiothreitol, 20 mM NaF, and 10 μM leupeptin were disrupted by use of a Polytron. After removal of membranous material by centrifugation, the supernatant was incubated for 20 min at room temperature with [γ-^{32}P]ATP at a final concentration of 200 μM. Phosphorylation was terminated by the addition of 0.1 ml of rabbit anti-broccoli mitochondrial PDC antibodies, and the samples were incubated at 4°C for 12 hr. The immunoprecipitates were washed, dissociated, and analyzed by SDS-PAGE and autoradiography.

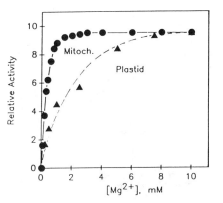

FIGURE 8. PDC activity as a function of Mg^{2+} concentration. The mitochondrial PDC (●) was partially purified from pea leaves and dialyzed. The chloroplast PDC (▲) was partially purified and desalted on G-25 Sephadex.

between 7.0 and 9.0.[1] Plastid PDCs require greater concentrations of divalent cations for maximum *in vitro* activity than do mitochondrial PDCs[8,30] (FIG. 8). When illuminated, the plastid stroma becomes more alkaline, and there is an increase in concentration of free Mg^{2+} and Ca^{2+}. Both of these changes would activate the PDC. It has further been noted that the plastid PDC is unstable in an oxidizing environment[8] and that reducing equivalents produced during photosynthesis are transferred to the plastid stroma via the ferredoxin-thioredoxin system,[36] which may protect the chloroplast PDC *in vivo*. Finally, plastid PDCs are relatively insensitive to inhibition by ATP and NADPH,[5,32] metabolites which would increase in concentration in illuminated chloroplasts. Overall, then, there is substantial evidence supporting the proposal that chloroplast PDC activity is regulated by the changes in physical environment which accompany the dark-light transition. This type of regulatory mechanism has not been reported for mitochondrial or microbial PDCs.

CONCLUSION

Plants are unique in having two distinct types of PDCs localized within different subcellular compartments. Most of the kinetic and regulatory properties of plant

TABLE 1. Regulation of Pyruvate Dehydrogenase Complexes

Regulatory Mechanism	Procaryotic		Eucaryotic			
	E. coli	*B. subtilis*	*N. crassa* Mitochondria	Mammalian Mitochondria	Plant Mitochondria	Plant Plastid
Product inhibition	+++	+++	+++	+++	+++	+++
Metabolite regulation	+++	+++	?	+	+	+
Protein turnover	+	+	?	?	+	?
Covalent modification	−	−	+++	+++	+++	−
Regulatory proteins	?	?	?	+	?	?
Light/dark transition	−	−	−	−	−	+++

mitochondrial PDCs are similar to those of the mammalian complexes. The PDCs within plastids of plant cells are in many ways more similar to the bacterial complexes than to mitochondrial PDCs. Both types of plant PDCs have evolved unique regulatory features in response to particular metabolic requirements and environmental factors (TABLE 1).

We have recently developed a method for assaying mitochondrial PDC activity *in situ*. While in many cases the results of *in situ* measurements have confirmed and extended results obtained *in vitro* with the partially purified complex, there have also been several instances where the results of experiments with isolated intact mitochondria have clarified interpretations based solely upon *in vitro* results. Examples include observations on the divalent cation concentrations required for activation of P-PDH phosphatase, and the regulatory importance of acetyl-CoA/CoA-SH. Future use of a combination of both methods will result in a more thorough understanding of this important regulatory system.

REFERENCES

1. MIERNYK, J. A., P. J. CAMP & D. D. RANDALL. 1985. Regulation of plant pyruvate dehydrogenase complexes. Curr. Top. Plant Biochem. Physiol. **4:** 175–190.
2. OHLROGGE, J. B., D. N. KUHN & P. K. STUMPF. 1979. Subcellular localization of acyl carrier protein in leaf protoplasts of *Spinacia oleracia*. Proc Natl. Acad. Sci. USA **76:** 1194–1198.
3. DENNIS, D. T. & J. A. MIERNYK. 1982. Compartmentation of non-photosynthetic carbohydrate metabolism. Annu. Rev. Plant Physiol. **33:** 27–50.
4. REID, E. E., C. R. LYTTLE, D. T. CANVIN & D. T. DENNIS. 1975. Pyruvate dehydrogenase complex activity in proplastids and mitochondria of developing castor bean endosperm. Biochem. Biophys. Res. Commun. **62:** 42–47.
5. REID, E. E., P. THOMPSON, C. R. LYTTLE & D. T. DENNIS. 1977. Pyruvate dehydrogenase complex from higher plant mitochondria and proplastids. Plant Physiol. **59:** 842–848.
6. WILLIAMS, M. & D. D. RANDALL. 1979. Pyruvate dehydrogenase complex from chloroplasts of *Pisum sativum*. Plant Physiol. **64:** 1099–1103.
7. ELIAS, B. A. & C. V. GIVAN. 1979. Localization of pyruvate dehydrogenase complex in *Pisum sativum* chloroplasts. Plant Sci. Lett. **17:** 115–122.
8. CAMP, P. J. & D. D. RANDALL. 1985. Purification and characterization of the pea chloroplast pyruvate dehydrogenase complex. A source of acetyl-CoA and NADH for fatty acid biosynthesis. Plant Physiol. **77:** 571–577.
9. GRAHAM, D. 1980. Effects of light on "dark" respiration. *In* The Biochemistry of Plants. D. D. Davis, Ed. Vol. 2: 526–580. Academic Press. New York.
10. RUBIN, P. M. & D. D. RANDALL. 1977. Purification and characterization of pyruvate dehydrogenase complex. Arch. Biochem. Biophys. **178:** 342–349.
11. LINN, T. C., J. W. PELLEG, F. H. PETTIT, F. HUCHO, D. D. RANDALL & L. J. REED. 1972. α-Keto acid dehydrogenase complexes. XV. Purification and properties of the component enzymes of the pyruvate dehydrogenase complexes from bovine kidney and heart. Arch. Biochem. Biophys. **148:** 327–342.
12. RUBIN, P. M., W. L. ZAHLER & D. D. RANDALL. 1978. Plant pyruvate dehydrogenase complex: Analysis of the kinetic properties and metabolite regulation. Arch. Biochem. Biophys. **188:** 70–77.
13. RANDALL, D. D., P. M. RUBIN & M. FENKO. 1977. Plant pyruvate dehydrogenase complex purification, characterization and regulation by metabolites and phosphorylation. Biochim. Biophys. Acta **485:** 336–349.
14. RAPP, B. J., J. A. MIERNYK & D. D. RANDALL. 1987. Pyruvate dehydrogenase complexes from *Ricinus communis* endosperm. J. Plant Physiol. **127:** 293–306.
15. RANDALL, D. D. & P. M. RUBIN. 1977. Plant pyruvate dehydrogenase complex. II. ATP-dependent inactivation and phosphorylation. Plant Physiol. **59:** 1–4.

16. RUBIN, P. M. & D. D. RANDALL. 1977. Regulation of plant pyruvate dehydrogenase complex by phosphorylation. Plant Physiol. **60:** 34–39.

17. RAO, K. P. & D. D. RANDALL. 1980. Plant pyruvate dehydrogenase complex: Inactivation and reactivation by phosphorylation-dephosphorylation. Arch. Biochem. Biophys. **200:** 461–466.

18. RANDALL, D. D., M. WILLIAMS & B. J. RAPP. 1981. Phosphorylation-dephosphorylation of pyruvate dehydrogenase complex from pea leaf mitochondria. Arch. Biochem. Biophys. **207:** 437–444.

19. YEAMAN, S. J., E. T. HUTCHESON, T. E. ROCHE, F. H. PETTIT, J. R. BROWN, L. J. REED, D. C. WATSON & G. H. DIXON. 1978. Sites of phosphorylation on pyruvate dehydrogenase from bovine kidney and heart. Biochemistry **17:** 2364–2370.

20. MIERNYK, J. A. & D. D. RANDALL. 1989. A synthetic peptide–directed antibody as a probe of the phosphorylation site of pyruvate dehydrogenase. J. Biol Chem. **264:** 9141–9144.

21. MIERNYK, J. A. & D. D. RANDALL. 1987. Some kinetic and regulatory properties of the pea mitochondrial pyruvate dehydrogenase complex. Plant Physiol. **83:** 306–310.

22. MIERNYK, J. A. & D. D. RANDALL. 1987. Some properties of plant mitochondrial pyruvate dehydrogenase kinase. *In* Plant Mitochondria. A. L. Moore & R. B. BEACHEY, Eds.: 223–226. Plenum Publishing Corp. New York.

23. SCHULLER, K. A. & D. D. RANDALL. 1989. Regulation of pea mitochondrial pyruvate dehydrogenase complex: Does photorespiratory ammonium influence mitochondrial carbon metabolism? Plant Physiol. **89:** 1207–1212.

24. BUDDE, R. J. A. & D. D. RANDALL. 1988. Regulation of pea mitochondrial pyruvate dehydrogenase complex activity: Inhibition of ATP-dependent inactivation. Arch. Biochem. Biophys. **258:** 600–606.

25. MIERNYK, J. A. & D. D. RANDALL. 1987. Some properties of pea mitochondrial phospho-pyruvate dehydrogenase phosphatase. Plant Physiol. **83:** 311–315.

26. BUDDE, R. J. A. & D. D. RANDALL. 1988. Regulation of steady state pyruvate dehydrogenase complex activity in plant mitochondria: Reactivation constraints. Plant Physiol. **88:** 1026–1030.

27. BUDDE, R. J. A., T. K. FANG & D. D. RANDALL. 1988. Regulation of the phosphorylation of mitochondrial pyruvate dehydrogenase complex *in situ:* Effects of respiratory substrates and calcium. Plant Physiol. **88:** 1031–1036.

28. FANG, T. K., R. J. A. BUDDE, D. D. RANDALL & J. A. MIERNYK. 1989. *In situ* regulation of the plant mitochondrial pyruvate dehydrogenase complex by product inhibition. Manuscript submitted.

29. RAPP, B. J. & D. D. RANDALL. 1980. Pyruvate dehydrogenase complex from germinating castor bean endosperm. Plant Physiol. **65:** 314–318.

30. TREEDE, H.-J. & K.-P. HEISE. 1986. Purification of the chloroplast pyruvate dehydrogenase from spinach and maize mesophyll. Z. Naturforsch. **41c:** 149–155.

31. LIEDVOGEL, B. 1985. Acetate concentration and chloroplast dehydrogenase complex in *Spinacia oleracia* leaf cells. Z. Naturforsch. **40c:** 182–188.

32. CAMP, P. J., J. A. MIERNYK & D. D. RANDALL. 1988. Some kinetic and regulatory properties of the pea chloroplast pyruvate dehydrogenase complex. Biochim. Biophys. Acta **933:** 269–275.

33. THOMPSON, P., E. E. REID, C. R. LITTLE & D. T. DENNIS. 1977. Pyruvate dehydrogenase complex from higher plant mitochondria and proplastids: Kinetics. Plant Physiol. **59:** 849–853.

34. THOMPSON, P., E. E. REID, C. R. LITTLE & D. T. DENNIS. 1977. Pyruvate dehydrogenase complex from higher plant mitochondria and proplastids: Regulation. Plant Physiol. **59:** 854–858.

35. ROUGHAN, P. G., T. KAGAWA & H. BEEVERS. 1980. On the light dependency of fatty acid synthesis by isolated spinach chloroplasts. Plant Sci. Lett. **18:** 221–228.

36. BUCHANAN, B. B. 1980. Role of light in regulation of chloroplast enzymes. Annu. Rev. Plant Physiol. **31:** 341–374.

The Role of Ca²⁺ in the Hormonal Regulation of the Activities of Pyruvate Dehydrogenase and Oxoglutarate Dehydrogenase Complexes[a]

GUY A. RUTTER,[b,c] JAMES G. McCORMACK,[d]
PETER J. W. MIDGLEY,[b] AND RICHARD M. DENTON[b]

[b]Department of Biochemistry
School of Medical Sciences
University of Bristol
Bristol, BS8 1TD
United Kingdom
and
[d]Department of Biochemistry
University of Leeds
Leeds, LS2 9JT
United Kingdom

INTRODUCTION

The oxo-acid dehydrogenase complexes play a central role in determining the supply of NADH for the respiratory chain. For example, regulatory properties of the mammalian complexes allow tissues to oxidize appropriate fuels depending on availability.[1] An important example of this fuel selection is the near complete inhibition of the pyruvate dehydrogenase complex (PDC) and hence carbohydrate oxidation in certain tissues during fasting.[1] However, the regulatory properties of the complexes must also be such as to allow the overall rate of NADH production within mitochondria to match the needs of the cell. In the case of both PDC and the oxoglutarate dehydrogenase complex (OGDC), an important means of achieving this appears to be through activation of the two complexes by Ca²⁺.[2,3]

Many hormones and other external stimuli cause an increase in the cytoplasmic concentration of Ca²⁺ in mammalian cells. Such increases initiate many different responses, such as the stimulation of muscle contraction, secretion, and certain anabolic pathways, depending on the target tissue. These stimulated functions utilize ATP; thus, it is necessary for the rate of ATP supply from mitochondrial metabolism to be increased to meet increased requirements under these circumstances (FIG. 1). Until recently, it had been widely assumed that such increases in mitochondrial ATP synthesis were initiated by increases in ADP/ATP ratios—yet such increases are not generally observed.[4]

[a]This work was supported by grants from the Medical Research Council, British Diabetic Association, British Heart Foundation, Percival Waite Salmond Bequest, and Lister Institute.
[c]Address all correspondence to Professor R. M. Denton, Department of Biochemistry, School of Medical Sciences, University of Bristol, Bristol, BS8 1TD, United Kingdom.

This main goal of this short paper will be to review the effects of Ca^{2+} on the activities of pyruvate dehydrogenase and oxoglutarate dehydrogenase complexes as observed in studies on the separated complexes and also on complexes located within intact or permeabilized mitochondria. We will then summarize some of the approaches that can be used to explore the importance of changes in the intramitochondrial concentration of Ca^{2+} on the effects of hormones and other extrinsic factors. The focus will be mainly on the rat heart and its response to adrenaline or increased work load, as this has been the system studied the most intensively. Aspects of this topic have also been reviewed recently by Hansford[5] and by Crompton.[6]

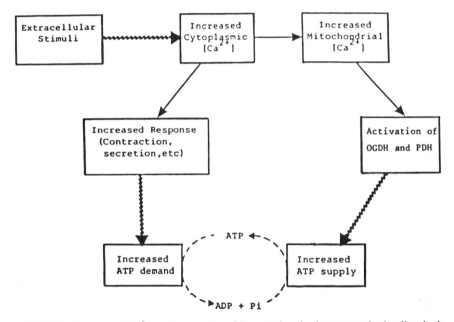

FIGURE 1. The role of Ca^{2+} in the coupling of hormonal and other external stimuli to both energy-requiring intracellular responses and the enhanced formation of ATP by mitochondria through the activation of pyruvate dehydrogenase complex (**PDH**) and oxoglutarate dehydrogenase complex (**OGDH**).

EFFECTS OF Ca^{2+} ON THE ACTIVITIES OF THE OXO-ACID DEHYDROGENASE COMPLEXES

Studies on Isolated Enzymes

The first Ca^{2+}-sensitive mitochondrial dehydrogenase to be recognized was the pyruvate dehydrogenase complex. The Mg^{2+}-requiring pyruvate dehydrogenase–phosphate–phosphatase was found to be activated about five- to tenfold by Ca^{2+} at all Mg^{2+} concentrations, with a $K_{0.5}$ value of about 1 μM.[7] With isolated preparations of phosphatase, the action of Ca^{2+} seems to be to decrease the apparent K_m for phosphorylated pyruvate dehydrogenase component at saturating Mg^{2+} concentrations,[8] but, in addition, Ca^{2+} also decreases the K_m for Mg^{2+}.[7] Studies on pyruvate dehydrogenase kinase from pig heart have also revealed a small inhibitory effect of submicromolar concentrations of Ca^{2+} on this enzyme, which potentially could act to reinforce the stimulatory effects of Ca^{2+} on the phosphatase in bringing about an increase in PDC activity.[9]

Subsequently, it was found that OGDC could also be activated by Ca^{2+}.[10] However, this complex is not regulated by reversible phosphorylation. The effect of Ca^{2+} is directly on the activity of the dehydrogenase, possibly through binding to the E1 (oxoglutarate dehydrogenase) component.[11] The principal effect of Ca^{2+} is to greatly diminish the K_m value for oxoglutarate[10] (TABLE 1). In the absence of other additions, the $K_{0.5}$ for Ca^{2+} is in the range 0.5 to 1 μM, close to the sensitivity of the pyruvate dehydrogenase system. The K_m of the complex for oxoglutarate can also be modified by changes in the ATP/ADP ratio and pH so that, overall, a truly remarkable range of K_m values can be observed (TABLE 1).

The enzyme preceding OGDC in the citrate cycle is NAD^+-isocitrate dehydrogenase, and this enzyme is also activated by Ca^{2+}.[12] As with OGDC, Ca^{2+} acts directly on this enzyme to lower its K_m value for substrate. However, although the response of NAD^+-isocitrate dehydrogenase to changes in Ca^{2+} is comparable to that of the two oxo-acid dehydrogenase complexes, its sensitivity to Ca^{2+} is rather less.

FIGURE 2 and TABLE 2 illustrate the differences in the Ca^{2+} sensitivity of preparations of pyruvate dehydrogenase phosphatase, OGDC, and NAD^+-isocitrate dehydrogenase, all derived from rat heart and assayed under similar conditions. The sensitivity to Ca^{2+} of OGDC—and, to a more marked extent, that of NAD^+-isocitrate dehydrogenase—is influenced by the ATP/ADP ratio,[13] so that at high values of this ratio the enzyme tends to become less sensitive to Ca^{2+} (TABLE 2). This phenomenon appears not to be exhibited by the pyruvate dehydrogenase system (see also below).

Neither the branched-chain oxo-acid dehydrogenase complex nor its associated kinase and phosphatase appear to be sensitive to micromolar concentrations of Ca^{2+}.[15]

Studies on Mitochondria

Extensive studies have been carried out to explore the calcium sensitivities of PDC and OGDC within intact coupled mitochondria from rat heart and many other tissues.[2-6] In all cases, increases in the extramitochondrial concentration of Ca^{2+} were found to cause broadly parallel activations of both dehydrogenases.

TABLE 3 summarizes some of our observations with mitochondria from rat heart and liver. In uncoupled mitochondria, where there is little or no gradient of Ca^{2+} across the inner mitochondrial membrane, half-maximal effects are evident at about 1 μM

TABLE 1. Effects of Ca^{2+} and Other Regulators on the K_m for Oxoglutarate of Pig Heart 2-Oxoglutarate Dehydrogenase

Adenine Nucleotide	pH	K_m for Oxoglutarate (mM)[a]	
		≤ 1 nM Ca^{2+}	ca. 20 μM Ca^{2+}
1.5 mM ATP	7.2	24.5	0.79
None	7.2	8.6	0.34
1.5 mM ADP	7.2	0.84	0.075
1.5 mM ADP	7.0	0.40	0.049

[a]Data are taken from McCormack & Denton[10] or are unpublished observations of J. G. McCormack. Under all conditions, half-maximal effects of Ca^{2+} are achieved in the range 0.1–1 μM.

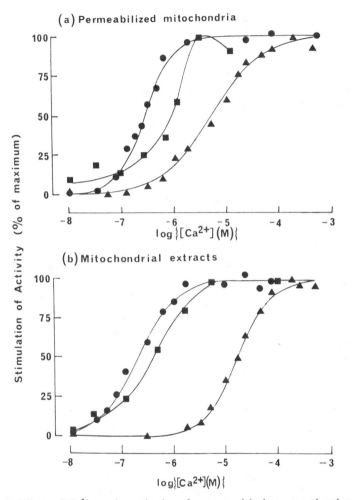

FIGURE 2. Effects of Ca^{2+} on the activation of pyruvate dehydrogenase phosphatase (■), OGDC (●), and NAD^+-isocitrate dehydrogenase (▲) in (a) toluene-permeabilized rat heart mitochondria or (b) extracts of rat heart mitochondria. Results are taken from Rutter & Denton[13] (oxoglutarate dehydrogenase and NAD^+-isocitrate dehydrogenase), Rutter[25] (pyruvate dehydrogenase phosphatase assayed within permeabilized mitochondria), and Pask[14] (pyruvate dehydrogenase phosphatase in mitochondrial extracts). Enzyme activities were assayed in the presence of ADP, with the exception of the assays for pyruvate dehydrogenase phosphatase in mitochondrial extracts. Calculated $K_{0.5}$ values are given in TABLE 2.

Ca^{2+}. In coupled mitochondria incubated in media containing 10 m*M* NaCl and 1 m*M* $MgCl_2$, half-maximal effects are apparent at about 0.4 μM. These are conditions which correspond to those occurring *in vivo;* thus, these observations allow the important conclusion that within cells, increases in the cytoplasmic concentration of Ca^{2+} within the physiological range of 0.05–3 μM may result in increases in the activities of the two dehydrogenases.[16,17]

TABLE 2. $K_{0.5}$ Values for Ca^{2+} of Rat Heart Pyruvate Dehydrogenase-Phosphate (PDHP) Phosphatase, 2-Oxoglutarate Dehydrogenase Complex, and NAD^+-Isocitrate Dehydrogenase

Enzyme	Additions	$K_{0.5}$ Value (μM) for Ca^{2+}	
		Permeabilized Mitochondria[a]	Mitochondrial Extracts[a]
PDHP phosphatase	None	—	0.43
	0.2 mM ADP	0.77	—
	0.2 mM ATP	0.74	—
OGDC	1.5 mM ADP	0.28	0.21
	1.5 mM ATP	0.81	2.12
NAD^+-isocitrate dehydrogenase	1.5 mM ADP	5.4	15
	1.5 mM ATP	41.0	43

[a]Data taken from Rutter & Denton,[13] from Rutter[25] (PDHP phosphatase in permeabilized mitochondria), or from Pask[14] (PDHP phosphatase in extracts). *Dash,* not done.

The gradient of Ca^{2+} ions across the mitochondrial inner membrane is determined by the relative activities of the systems which transfer Ca^{2+} into and out of mitochondria.[3,5,6,18] Uptake of Ca^{2+} occurs by a uniporter which is driven by the larger electrical gradient across the inner membrane. This uniporter is inhibited by ruthenium red and also by Mg^{2+} ions. Transfer of Ca^{2+} out of mitochondria occurs mainly by an electroneutral exchange of Ca^{2+} for 2 Na^+. In the absence of both Na^+ and Mg^{2+} ions, a much greater gradient of Ca^{2+} ions across the inner membrane would be expected. This is borne out by the parallel activation of both PDC and OGDC at a much lower range of extramitochondrial Ca^{2+} concentrations (TABLE 4).

The above results suggest strongly that the sensitivity of pyruvate dehydrogenase and OGDC to activation by Ca^{2+} for the enzymes located within intact mitochondria is very similar to that observed for the enzymes isolated from mitochondria. Direct evidence confirming this has been obtained recently from studies in which the Ca^{2+}

TABLE 3. Effect of Treatment with Hormones and Other Agents on the PDC Activity and on the Total Calcium Associated with Rapidly Prepared Mitochondrial Fractions in the Perfused Rat Heart and Liver

Preparation	Treatment	PDC Activity[a] (% total)	Estimated Total Mitochondrial Calcium[a] (nmol/mg protein)
Rat heart	Control	10	1.8
	Adrenaline	41	4.2
	High calcium	42	—
	Ruthenium red	11	—
	Adrenaline + ruthenium red	13	—
	High calcium + ruthenium red	13	—
Rat liver	Control	5	1.2
	Vasopressin	27	2.1
	Vasopressin + glucagon	45	4.9

[a]Data taken from McCormack & England[32] and Crompton *et al.*[34] (rat heart), and Assimacopoulos-Jeannet *et al*[39] (rat liver). Total PDC activity was determined for complex fully dephosphorylated by incubation with PDH-phosphate–phosphatase.

concentration within rat heart mitochondria has been measured using quin-2 and fura-2.[19-21] FIGURE 3 shows the sensitivity of the two dehydrogenases within coupled rat heart mitochondria to increases in the intramitochondrial concentration of Ca^{2+}, as determined by parallel measurements of the fluorescence of intramitochondrial fura-2. The calculated $K_{0.5}$ values for activation by intramitochondrial Ca^{2+} were 535 nM for PDC and 376 nM for OGDC.

There are some serious limitations to using isolated enzymes or intact mitochondria for the study of the effects of Ca^{2+} on the activity of the two dehydrogenase complexes. Although the properties of the isolated complexes are relatively easily studied, they may not be a faithful reflection of the properties of the complexes when they are located within mitochondria. On the other hand, studies on the kinetic properties within conventional preparations of mitochondri lack precision. This is because the concentrations of substrates, products, and effectors are not always known accurately

TABLE 4. Persistence of Activation of PDC and OGDC in Mitochondria Prepared from Intact Tissue Preparations Previously Exposed to Hormones Which Increase Activity of PDC[a]

	PDC Activity (% total) in Incubated Mitochondria[b]			OGDC Activity (% V_{max}) in Incubated Mitochondria[c]		
Source of Mitochondria	No Additions	NaCl	Ca^{2+}	No Additions	NaCl	Ca^{2+}
Rat heart perfused with medium containing						
No hormone	8	8	45	23	25	65
Adrenaline	20	7	47	35	24	—
Liver from rats injected with						
No hormone	12	13	49	8	8	33
Adrenaline	20	14	51	13	8	35

[a]Data taken from McCormack & Denton[37] (rat heart) and McCormack[38] (rat liver), from which full details can be obtained. In brief, after exposure to appropriate concentrations of hormone, tissue was rapidly homogenized and mitochondria prepared at 0°C in Na-free media containing EGTA. Mitochondria were then incubated at 30°C for 5 min in KCl-based medium containing respiratory substrates, EGTA, and, where indicated, additions of NaCl (10 mM) or sufficient Ca^{2+} to maximally activate either PDC or OGDC. *Dash*, not done.
[b]Total PDC activity is for fully dephosphorylated complex.
[c]V_{max} is activity at saturating concentration of 2-oxoglutarate.

and often cannot be varied independently; moreover, the activities of the dehydrogenases have to be measured somewhat indirectly. Recently we have employed a different approach which circumvents these problems. This is to study the kinetic properties of the two dehydrogenase complexes within mitochondria made permeable to all small molecules (less than about 2000 Da) by controlled treatment with toluene, as first described by Matlib *et al.*[22]

In the case of PDC, the use of toluene-permeabilized mitochondria has the added advantage of allowing for the first time the activity of PDC to be followed continuously while changes in phosphorylation are occurring.[23-25] This approach was first applied to mitochondria from rat epididymal adipose tissue[23,24] and subsequently to mitochondria from rat heart (FIG. 4). When the reactivation of fully phosphorylated PDC within permeabilized adipose tissue mitochondria was followed on initiating phosphatase

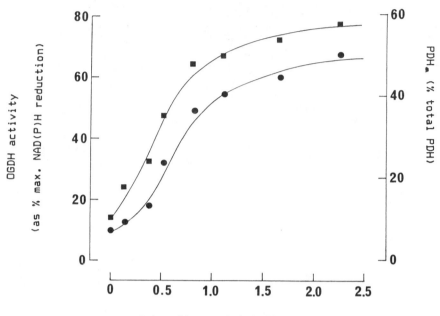

FIGURE 3. Sensitivity to intramitochondrial Ca^{2+} concentration ($[Ca^{2+}]$) of the steady-state levels of pyruvate dehydrogenase complex activity (PDH_a, ●) and oxoglutarate dehydrogenase complex activity (OGDH, ■) within intact fura-2–loaded rat heart mitochondria incubated in KCl-based medium in the absence of added Na^+ and Mg^{2+}. Data are from McCormack et al.[21]

activity by addition of Mg^{2+} with or without Ca^{2+}, a number of interesting observations were made. In the absence of Ca^{2+}, and at a low concentration of Mg^{2+}, there was a clear lag period before the maximum rate of reactivation was achieved. In the presence of Ca^{2+}, all evidence of the lag period was lost and a faster rate of reactivation was evident. The lag phase was also lost if reactivation was initiated by a high concentration of Mg^{2+}.[24] A likely explanation of the lag period at low concentrations of Mg^{2+} is that the dephosphorylation of phosphorylation site 1 on the pyruvate dehydrogenase component (which mainly determines the activity of pyruvate dehydrogenase complex) is inhibited until the dephosphorylation of sites 2 and 3 has occurred. The effect of Ca^{2+} or high concentrations of Mg^{2+} may be to overcome the inhibitory effects of sites 2 and 3.[24]

With permeabilized rat heart mitochondria, similar effects of Ca^{2+} were found,[4,25] but the lag phase in the absence of Ca^{2+} was less evident (FIG. 4). In part this may be related to the rapidity of the reactivation process in these mitochondria. In the presence of Mg^{2+} and Ca^{2+}, the $t_{1/2}$ for the reactivation process was less than 15 s in the permeabilized rat heart mitochondria. This is much more rapid than the process observed in permeabilized rat adipose tissue mitochondria, where the comparable value for the $t_{1/2}$ is 200–300 s. More detailed studies of the effects of Mg^{2+} and Ca^{2+} in both types of permeabilized mitochondria have shown that the effect of Ca^{2+} on the phosphatase when it is located within mitochondria is to decrease the K_m for Mg^{2+}: there is little or no effect of Ca^{2+} at saturating concentrations of Mg^{2+}. Studies with rat adipose tissue mitochondria made permeable to divalent metal ions by the ionophore A23187 gave similar results.[26] These findings are in marked contrast to those with isolated preparations of the phosphatase where, as mentioned above, a large activation by Ca^{2+} is evident at all Mg^{2+} concentrations. However, the concentration of Mg^{2+} giving half-maximal effects in the permeabilized mitochondria was about 0.5 μM[24,25]—similar to that found with the isolated enzyme at a saturating concentration of Mg^{2+} (FIG. 2, TABLE 2).

Damuni and Reed[27] have purified and characterized a divalent cation–independent protein phosphatase from bovine kidney mitochondria which is active towards phosphorylated pyruvate dehydrogenase complex. This phosphatase appears to be very

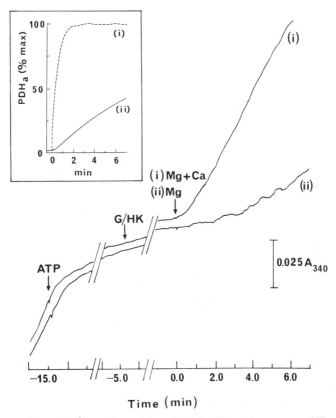

FIGURE 4. Effect of Ca^{2+} on the activity of PDC within toleune-permeabilized rat heart mitochondria. Permeabilized mitochondria (ca. 25 μg protein/ml) were incubated in KCl-poly(ethyleneglycol)–based medium, and PDC activity was measured by following the production of NADH at A_{340}. At the times indicated, 0.2 mM ATP was added to cause phosphorylation and inactivation of the complex, followed by 1 U/ml hexokinase plus 10 mM glucose (G/HK) to convert the ATP to ADP. Reactivation of the complex by endogenous phosphatase was then initiated by adding either (i) 30 μM Mg^{2+} plus 25 μM Ca^{2+} or (ii) 30 μM Mg^{2+} alone (the concentrations given are for the free, unbound ions). Increases in the level of active pyruvate dehydrogenase complex (PDH_a) following the addition of metal ions (**inset**) were obtained by fitting the data to an integrated first-order rate equation. Data are taken from Rutter.[25]

inactive in the mitochondria of rat heart or adipose tissue, as there is little or no reactivation of pyruvate dehydrogenase in the absence of divalent metal ions.[24,25]

We have also carried out extensive studies into the kinetic properties of oxoglutarate dehydrogenase in toluene-permeabilized rat heart mitochondria and compared its properties to those of NAD^+-isocitrate dehydrogenase measured under the same conditions. Some results are summarized in FIGURE 2 and TABLE 2. These studies confirm that the sensitivity of OGDC to Ca^{2+} tends to be somewhat greater than that of pyruvate dehydrogenase phosphatase, especially in the presence of high ADP/ATP ratios, but the differences between the sensitivities to Ca^{2+} of the two dehydrogenase complexes are small. In contrast, the $K_{0.5}$ for Ca^{2+} of NAD^+-isocitrate dehydrogenase is at least an order of magnitude greater, especially at low ADP/ATP ratios (TABLE 2).

THE ROLE OF CHANGES IN INTRAMITOCHONDRIAL Ca^{2+} IN THE HORMONAL REGULATION OF OXIDATIVE METABOLISM

Studies on Rat Heart

In the rat heart perfused with medium containing glucose, β-adrenergic agonists, increased work load, and other positive inotropic agents increase the force of contraction in the heart by elevating peak concentration of Ca^{2+} in the sarcoplasm. At the same time, there are increases of up to twofold in O_2 uptake and hence flux through the citrate cycle and of up to fourfold (TABLE 3) in the proportion of PDC in its active form. These increases occur with little or no change in the calculated ADP concentration.[28–31]

Evidence that changes in the level of intramitochondrial Ca^{2+} are important in bringing about changes in intramitochondrial oxidative metabolism has come mainly from three different approaches. The first approach has been the use of ruthenium red, which inhibits the uptake of Ca^{2+} into mitochondria.[32] Addition of ruthenium red to the perfusing medium essentially blocks the effects of inotropic agents on PDC activity (TABLE 3), while having little or no effect on contraction or phosphorylase a content.[32] Similarly, Hansford[33] has shown that ruthenium red does not prevent increases in the level of cytoplasmic Ca^{2+} in quin-2–loaded myocytes subjected to various treatments designed to elicit such a response but does block accompanying increases in PDC activity.

Secondly, measurements have been made of the total amount of mitochondrial Ca^{2+}, using both rapid subcellular fractionation[34] (TABLE 3) and X-ray probe analysis.[35] Positive inotropic agents were found to increase the amount of total calcium, and, moreover, the range of values found (1–5 nmol/mg) protein) was roughly within the range shown to be associated with changes in the activity of the dehydrogenase in studies on isolated mitochondria.[5,19,20,36]

The most convincing and direct evidence that positive inotropic agents do act on intramitochondrial oxidative metabolism via changes in the intramitochondrial concentration of Ca^{2+} has come from the third approach as, illustrated in TABLE 4. This approach depends on the rapid preparation of mitochondria at 0°C in media containing EGTA but no Na^+, conditions under which there is little transfer to Ca^{2+} into or out of the organelles. Activations of PDC initiated by prior hormone treatment of the tissues are then found to persist not only during the preparation of the mitochondria but also during their subsequent incubation at 30°C in sodium-free medium containing respiratory substrates and EGTA (TABLE 4).[37] Increases in the activity of OGDC (at subsaturating concentrations of oxoglutarate) are also apparent in these mitochondira. (TABLE 4). However, these increases are lost if Na^+ is added to the mitochondrial incubation medium. Since these effects of Na^+ are blocked by diltiazem, which inhibits the sodium-dependent pathway for Ca^{2+} efflux, it can be concluded that the increases in the activities of both pyruvate dehydrogenase and oxoglutarate dehydrogenase are the result of increases in the Ca^{2+} concentration in the mitochondria from the stimulated hearts.[37] This conclusion is reinforced by the finding that incubation of the mitochondria with sufficient Ca^{2+} to elicit maximal stimulation also results in the disappearance of the differences between the activities of the two dehydrogenases in mitochondria from control hearts and the activities in those from stimulated hearts (TABLE 4).

Studies on Rat Liver

Exposure of liver cells to α_1-adrenergic agonists, vasopressin, angiotensin, and, to a lesser extent, glucagon, results in increases in cytoplasmic Ca^{2+}. Again, as seen in the heart, these are increases in O_2 uptake, citrate cycle flux, and PDC activity (TABLE 3) with no increase in the apparent concentration of ADP. As with the rat heart, these changes in mitochondrial oxidative metabolism appear to be brought about by increases in the intramitochondrial concentration of Ca^{2+}.[38,39] Thus, the total calcium associated with mitochondria is increased within the appropriate range (TABLE 3). Moreover, increases in the activities of both PDC and OGDC are evident in mitochondria prepared from livers exposed to adrenaline (TABLE 4). These increases are lost on incubation of the mitochondria with Na^+ (to deplete them of Ca^{2+}), and addition of Ca^{2+} sufficient to maximally activate the dehydrogenases elevates their activities to the same level in preparations from adrenaline-treated or control livers (TABLE 4). Unfortunately, the addition of extracellular ruthenium red to liver cells does not appear to result in appreciable inhibition of Ca^{2+} uptake into mitochondria, either because the dye enters the cells very slowly or because it is metabolized or sequestered within the cells.

GENERAL COMMENTS

Altogether, there is now substantial evidence from studies in rat heart and liver that the activities of both PDC and OGDC may be regulated by changes in the intramitochondrial concentration of Ca^{2+}. Moreover, this mechanism would appear to play an important role in bringing about the increases in oxidative metabolism and ATP formation which are observed when the tissues are exposed to hormones or other extrinsic agents which increase the cytoplasmic concentration of Ca^{2+}. It seems reasonable to expect that this mechanism will prove to be of rather general importance in many tissues of higher animals. However, the two dehydrogenases from non-vertebrate sources do not exhibit Ca^{2+} regulation,[40] and, thus, this type of regulation should probably be considered as a later evolutionary refinement. Its advantage to general metabolic homeostasis is that the Ca^{2+} activation of the dehydrogenases may allow increased formation of NADH for the respiratory chain and hence increased ATP synthesis without diminishing the important $NADH/NAD^+$ and ATP/ADP ratios.[2,3]

Many aspects of the role of Ca^{2+} within mitochondria are unresolved. For example, what might be the importance of the apparent lower sensitivity of NAD^+-isocitrate dehydrogenase to Ca^{2+} compared to that of the two oxo-acid dehydrogenase complexes? Is this a device for increasing the range of intramitochondrial calcium ion concentrations which can influence the rate of the citrate cycle?

Very little is known about the Ca^{2+} binding sites of the dehydrogenases. Our efforts to identify a separate calcium-binding component associated with any of the enzymes have been unsuccessful; it seems more likely that Ca^{2+} binds to integrated domains within components of the dehydrogenase systems. The relationships between such domains will be of considerable interest and may give clues to the evolution of the Ca^{2+} sensitivity of the dehydrogenase in higher animals.

We view the main role of the calcium transport system in mitochondria as a means whereby the intramitochondrial concentration of Ca^{2+} may be regulated.[2,3] This proposal is in direct contrast to earlier suggestions that its major role is to allow mitochondria to buffer or regulate the cytoplasmic concentration of Ca^{2+}.[41] It has been calculated that, in the heart, the beat-to-beat changes in the cytoplasmic concentration of Ca^{2+} probably greatly exceed the kinetic capacity of the mitochondrial Ca^{2+} transport system.[6] As a result, it was concluded that oscillations in the intramitochondrial concentration Ca^{2+} will be quite small and that the level of Ca^{2+} within mitochondria will essentially only reflect "time-average" changes in cytoplasmic concentrations. However, it has recently been reported that appreciable changes in PDC activity may occur within each heart beat,[42] suggesting that it may be necessary to reassess this conclusion.

REFERENCES

1. RANDLE, P. J. 1986. Biochem. Soc. Trans. **14:** 799–806.
2. DENTON, R. M. & J. G. MCCORMACK. 1980. FEBS Lett. **119:** 1–7.
3. DENTON, R. M. & J. G. MCCORMACK. 1985. Am. J. Physiol. **249:** E543–E554.
4. DENTON, R. M., J. G. MCCORMACK, P. J. W. MIDGLEY & G. A. RUTTER. 1987. Biochem. Soc. Symp. **54:** 127–143.
5. HANSFORD, R. G. 1985. Rev. Physiol. Biochem. Pharmacol. **102:** 1–72.
6. CROMPTON, M. 1985. Curr. Top. Membr. Transp. **25:** 231–276.
7. DENTON, R. M., P. J. RANDLE & B. R. MARTIN. 1972. Biochem. J. **128:** 161–163.
8. PETTIT, F. H., T. E. ROCHE & L. E. REED. 1972. Biochem. Biophys. Res. Commun. **49:** 563–571.
9. COOPER, R. H., P. J. RANDLE & R. M. DENTON. 1974. Biochem. J. **143:** 625–641.
10. MCCORMACK, J. G. & R. M. DENTON. 1979. Biochem. J. **180:** 533–544.
11. LAWLIS, V. B. & T. E. ROCHE. 1981. Biochemistry. **20:** 2519–2524.
12. DENTON, R. M., D. A. RICHARDS & J. G. CHIN. 1978. Biochem. J. **176:** 899–906.
13. RUTTER, G. A. & R. M. DENTON. 1988. Biochem. J. **252:** 181–189.
14. PASK, H. 1976. Ph.D. Thesis. University of Bristol. Bristol, U.K.
15. RANDLE, P. J., P. A. PATSTON & J. ESPINAL. 1987. *In* The Enzymes. P. D. Boyer & E. G. Krebs, Eds. Vol. 18: 97–121. Academic Press. Orlando, FL.
16. DENTON, R. M., J. G. MCCORMACK & N. J. EDGELL. 1980. Biochem. J. **190:** 107–117.
17. MCCORMACK, J. G. 1985. Biochem. J. **231:** 581–585.
18. AKERMAN, K. E. O. & D. G. NICHOLLS. 1983. Rev. Physiol. Biochem. Pharmacol. **95:** 149–201.
19. LUKAS, G. L., A. KAPUS & A. FONYO. 1988. FEBS Lett. **229:** 219–223.
20. DAVIS, M. H., R. A. ALTSHULD, D. W. JUNG & G. P. BRIERLEY. 1987. Biochem. Biophys. Res. Commun. **149:** 40–45.
21. MCCORMACK, J. G., H. M. BROWNE & N. J. DAWES. 1988. Biochim. Biophys. Acta **973:** 420–427.
22. MATLIB, M. A., W. A. SHANNON & P. A. SRERE. 1977. Arch. Biochem. Biophys. **179:** 396–407.
23. THOMAS, A. P. & R. M. DENTON. 1988. Biochem. J. **238:** 93–101.

24. MIDGLEY, P. J. W., G. A. RUTTER, A. P. THOMAS & R. M. DENTON. 1987. Biochem. J. **241:** 373–377.
25. RUTTER, G. A. 1988. Ph.D. Thesis. University of Bristol. Bristol, U.K.
26. THOMAS, A. P., T. A. DIGGLE & R. M. DENTON. 1986. Biochem. J. **238:** 83–91.
27. DAMUNI, Z. & L. J. REED. 1987. J. Biol. Chem. **262:** 5133–5138.
28. NEELY, J. R., R. M. DENTON, P. J. ENGLAND & P. J. RANDLE. 1972. Biochem. J. **128:** 147–159.
29. KATZ, L. A., A. P. KORETSKY & R. S. BALABAN. 1988. Am. J. Physiol. **255:** H185–H188.
30. SOBOLL, S. & R. BUNGER. 1981. Hoppe-Seyler's Z. Physiol. Chem. **362:** 125–132.
31. FROM, A. H. L., S. P. MICHURSKI, S. D. ZIMMER & K. UGURBIL. 1986. FEBS Lett. **206:** 257–261.
32. MCCORMACK, J. G. & P. J. ENGLAND. 1983. Biochem. J. **214:** 581–585.
33. HANDSFORD, R. G. 1987. Biochem. J. **241:** 145–151.
34. CROMPTON, M., P. KESSAR & I. AL-NASSER. 1983. Biochem. J. **216:** 333–342.
35. WENDT-GALLITELLI, M. F. 1986. Basic Res. Cardiol. **81:** 25–32.
36. LUKAS, G. L. & A. KAPUS. 1987. Biochem. J. **248:** 609–613.
37. MCCORMACK, J. G. & R. M. DENTON. 1984. Biochem. J. **218:** 235–247.
38. MCCORMACK, J. G. 1985. Biochem. J. **231:** 581–595.
39. ASSIMACOPOULOS-JEANNET, F., J. G. MCCORMACK & B. JEANRENAUD. 1986. J. Biol. Chem. **261:** 8799–8804.
40. MCCORMACK, J. G. & R. M. DENTON. 1981. Biochem. J. **196:** 619–624.
41. AKERMAN, K. E. O. & D. G. NICHOLLS. 1983. Rev. Physiol. Biochem. Pharmacol. **95:** 149–201.
42. KRAUSE, E.-G. & I. BEYERDOERFER. 1988. J. Mol. Cell. Cardiol. In press.

Regulation of the Mitochondrial Multienzyme Complexes in Complex Metabolic Systems[a]

MERLE S. OLSON

Department of Biochemistry
The University of Texas Health Science Center
7703 Floyd Curl Drive
San Antonio, Texas 78284-7760

INTRODUCTION

For the past two decades my laboratory has actively been involved in the delineation of mechanisms which regulate the various α-keto acid dehydrogenase multienzyme complexes. Until very recently our perspective in this area of research has been to design experiments which demonstrate the regulatory characteristics of these important multienzyme complexes in intact metabolic systems, e.g., intact mitochondria, isolated cells, and, especially, isolated perfused organs. We have attempted to benefit from the insight that the enzymologists among us have provided as to the regulatory properties of the purified enzyme complexes to discern the regulatory characteristics of these multienzyme complexes as they participate in the physiological responses of intact cells or tissues. In the interest of brevity and to avoid unnecessary redundancy in this volume, it is not my purpose in this paper to provide an extensive review of the relevant literature in this area of research. I will iterate only the experimental approach of my laboratory and the perspectives developed therefrom as to the regulatory responses of the pyruvate and the branched-chain α-keto acid dehydrogenase complexes and of glycine synthase (i.e., the glycine cleavage enzyme), a much less well investigated multienzyme system quite analogous to the α-keto acid dehydrogenase complexes, which are the focal point of this volume.

FIGURE 1 illustrates the general location in the crucial energy-generating or catabolic pathways of most aerobic cells of the various multienzyme complexes under examination in my laboratory. Because of the strategic metabolic location of these enzyme complexes in important catabolic pathways and because of the unique regulatory properties of these systems, it seems essential for us to understand the impact of metabolic or physiological state transitions on the stimulation or inhibition of these complexes in intact tissues under as close to *in situ* conditions as possible.

PYRUVATE DEHYDROGENASE COMPLEX

In keeping with the geographical location and certainly the unofficial spirit of the conference on which this volume is based, the enzymatic mechanism of the pyruvate dehydrogenase multienzyme complex has been reformulated and is depicted in FIGURE

[a]Supported by grants from the NIH (HL-24654 and DK-19473) and the Robert A. Welch Foundation (AQ-728).

2. The three catalytic components of this enzyme complex, i.e., the pyruvate dehydrogenase (E_1), the dihydrolipolyl transacetylase (E_2), and the dihydrolipolyl dehydrogenase (E_3), effect the oxidative decarboxylation of pyruvate, generating the three products of the reaction, CO_2, acetyl-CoA, and NADH plus H^+. Implied but not stated explicitly in the pictorial analogy shown in FIGURE 2 (see star) is the fact that a primary site of regulation of this enzyme complex occurs on the pyruvate dehydrogenase component of the complex (i.e., here in Austin[b]).

The regulation of the pyruvate dehydrogenase complex (PDC), summarized in FIGURE 3, occurs by two quite different mechanisms. The first involves covalent modification by a cyclic AMP–independent protein kinase, which phosphorylates and inactivates the pyruvate dehydrogenase (E_1) component of the complex, and dephosphorylation of the complex by a specific phosphoprotein phosphatase. The second is a direct inhibitory effect of two of the products of the PDC reaction, acetyl-CoA and

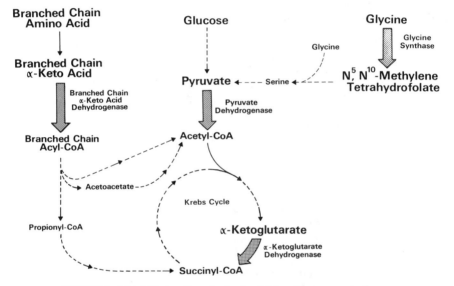

FIGURE 1. Metabolic location of mitochondrial multienzyme complexes.

NADH. Also of some importance is the sensitivity of the covalent modification regulatory system to the divalent metal cations magnesium and calcium.

Our contributions to this area of regulation of PDC have concerned the regulatory characteristics of this system in isolated heart and liver mitochondria and in isolated perfused heart and liver preparations. In the early 1970s we demonstrated that the intramitochondrial ATP concentration was not the sole determinant of the activity of PDC,[1] but that divalent metal cations were crucial components in this regulatory system.[2,3] We were among the first laboratories to recognize that changing (increasing) the intramitochondrial $NADH/NAD^+$ and acetyl-CoA/CoASH ratios leads to an inactivation of PDC[4] under conditions where the ATP/ADP ratio of the mitochondrial

[b]EDITOR'S NOTE: Dr. Lester J. Reed, to whom the conference and this volume are a tribute, has been affiliated with the University of Texas at Austin since 1948.

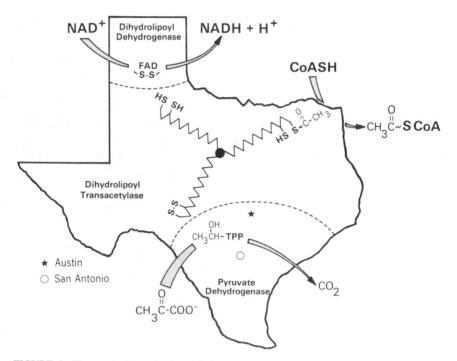

FIGURE 2. The catalytic mechanism of the pyruvate dehydrogenase multienzyme complex: Texas style.

suspension is held constant. Also, at this time we were able to demonstrate the phosphorylation/inactivation of PDC in an intact beef heart mitochondrial system.[5]

Our investigation of the regulation of PDC in the isolated perfused heart and liver demonstrated several important characteristics of this regulatory system. In the perfused heart we demonstrated that minute-by-minute metabolic flux through the PDC reaction could be monitored by infusing [1-¹⁴C]pyruvate and measuring ¹⁴CO₂ in the effluent perfusate. Flux measurements combined with the ability to measure the activation state of this enzyme complex in extracts of freeze-clamped hearts allowed us to determine the proportion of the changes in flux through the PDC reaction which was due to inactivation/activation by the kinase/phosphatase system.[6] Also, we demonstrated the importance of the concentration of the substrate, pyruvate, in the regulation of the heart complex.[7]

In the course of these studies of the regulatory properties of the heart pyruvate dehydrogenase complex, we demonstrated that short chain-length fatty acids, especially odd chain-lengths, more especially propionate, caused an interesting perturbation in the regulation of PDC. Infusion of propionate into a perfused rat heart oxidizing [1-¹⁴C]pyruvate caused an immediate and precipitous decrease in the metabolic flux through PDC without affecting the activation state of the complex. Upon further perfusion with propionate, the flux recovered as the activation state of the complex increased from ca. 30–40% active to nearly 100% active in the presence of propionate. This apparent inactivation of the kinase reaction was attributed to an effect of an increase in the mitochondrial propionyl-CoA and a decrease in the acetyl-CoA level caused by the introduction of propionate into the system.

In a collaborative study with Dr. Roland Scholz (University of Munich), we investigated the regulatory characteristics of PDC in the isolated perfused rat liver. We were most interested in the effect of fatty acids (i.e., ketogenic conditions) on the regulation of the PDC reaction. We observed that the infusion of fatty acids into livers in the presence of a low, physiological concentration (0.05 mM) of pyruvate actually stimulated the decarboxylation of [1-^{14}C]pyruvate. However, at higher concentrations of pyruvate, the often observed inhibition of PDC was seen.[8–11] On the basis of our experimental results in this series of studies, we proposed that the mechanism by which fatty acids or any other precursors of acetoacetate (i.e., α-ketoisocaproate, acetate, or β-hydroxybutyrate) cause the stimulation of PDC in the liver was by an exchange transport mechanism via the monocarboxylate translocator. This suggestion is illustrated schematically in FIGURE 4, which indicates that when ketogenesis (intramitochondrial acetoacetate synthesis) is stimulated at low cytosolic pyruvate levels, pyruvate-acetoacetate exchange on the translocator is stimulated. One consequence of the increase in mitochondrial pyruvate is to cause an inhibition of the pyruvate dehydrogenase kinase, leading to an activation of the pyruvate dehydrogenase complex.[12] As shown in FIGURE 5, an increase in the mitochondrial pyruvate level increases both pyruvate carboxylation (i.e., gluconeogenesis) and pyruvate decarboxylation (i.e., PDC activity). The activation of glucose production (i.e., pyruvate

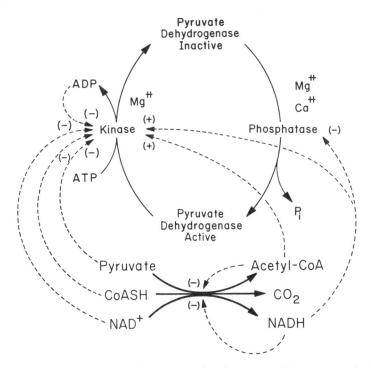

FIGURE 3. The regulation of the pyruvate dehydrogenase multienzyme complex.

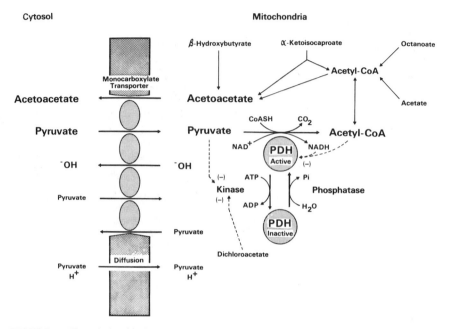

FIGURE 4. The relationship between exchange transport of pyruvate and acetoacetate on the mitochondrial monocarboxylate translocator and the regulation of the pyruvate dehydrogenase complex. PDH, pyruvate dehydrogenase complex.

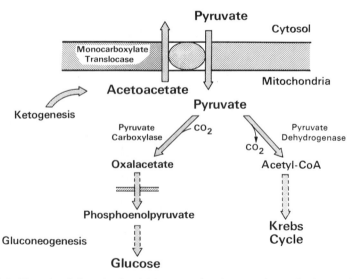

FIGURE 5. The role of the mitochondrial monocarboxylate translocase in the regulation of pyruvate carboxylation and decarboxylation.

carboxylation) was shown not to be due to changes in the mitochondrial acetyl-CoA level, which would itself activate pyruvate carboxylase.[12]

More recently we have developed an interest in the effect of the monovalent metal cation potassium on the activity of the pyruvate dehydrogenase kinase. We have demonstrated that potassium is required for the catalytic activity of the kinase.[13–15] Moreover, in the beef-heart enzyme complex, potassium is required to observe the inhibition of the kinase by thiamin pyrophosphatase and 5,5′-dithio-bis-(2-nitrobenzoic acid) (DTNB).[15]

Several studies were conducted to characterize the sensitivity of the PDC regulatory mechanisms to α- and β-adrenergic agonists in the liver and heart, respectively. We demonstrated that PDC was activated in the heart by β-adrenergic agonists. While this effect was a pure β response in the heart, the actual regulatory effect exerted on PDC occurred via a calcium-mediated stimulation of the dephosphorylation of the pyruvate dehydrogenase component by its phosphatase.[16] On the other hand, we concluded that α-adrenergic agonists have no effect on the activation state of PDC in the perfused rat liver, even though α agonists perturb the intracellular calcium levels of the hepatocytes. We concluded that in the intact liver either hepatic mitochondrial calcium levels do not change upon α-agonist stimulation or that any change may be superfluous if the basal intramitochondrial calcium level is already high enough to saturate the pyruvate dehydrogenase phosphatase.[17] In another study, we attempted to employ the activity state of the pyruvate dehydrogenase complex in perfused cardiac tissue as a monitor or probe of intramitochondrial calcium levels during the onset of global myocardial ischemia.[18] We were able to demonstrate that, at low perfusate pyruvate concentrations, the induction of low-flow ischemia lead to a very pronounced inactivation of the complex, while at high perfusate pyruvate concentrations (e.g., 5 mM), PDC was actually activated by the ischemic challenge. In the end, caution is advised in interpreting changes in the activation state of this enzyme complex during physiological state transitions because the interactions of the substrates and various other regulatory species are complex.

At present our work has turned toward the problem of multienzyme complex assembly. We have developed a 2-dimensional agarose gel electrophoresis system for separating large multimeric complexes and have demonstrated the utility of this electrophoresis system in separating complexes and subcomplexes of the α-keto acid dehydrogenase systems.[19] With this separation system and a library of monoclonal antibodies to the subunits of the respective enzyme complexes, we hope to be able to characterize intermediates in the assembly pathway for the pyruvate and branched-chain dehydrogenase multienzyme complexes.

BRANCHED-CHAIN α-KETO ACID DEHYDROGENASE COMPLEX

The branched-chain α-keto acid dehydrogenase complex (BCKDC) reaction is acknowledged to be the rate-determining step in the metabolism of the three branched-chain amino acids, leucine, isoleucine, and valine (FIG. 6). Because of the many similarities in the catalytic and regulatory properties of PDC and BCKDC from mammalian tissues, we performed experiments designed to characterize the regulatory properties of the branched-chain enzyme complex in mitochondrial and perfused organ (i.e., heart and liver) systems.[20–30] The major foci of these experiments were (a) to demonstrate that branched-chain α-keto acids are translocated across the mitochondrial membrane via an α-cyanocinnamate–sensitive monocarboxylate translocator;[21] (b) to develop evidence that metabolic flux rates through the BCKDC reaction could be monitored in perfused organ systems by infusing the 1-^{14}C–labeled branched-chain α-keto or amino acids;[20] (c) to demonstrate the activation/inactivation of the branched-chain multienzyme complex by a phosphorylation/dephosphorylation system in mitochondrial and perfused organ systems (see FIG. 7);[23–27] and (d) to show that the regulation of the branched-chain α-keto acid dehydrogenase by covalent modification was sensitive to various hormonal manipulations, e.g., treatment with α-adrenergic agonists in the liver[26] and both α- and β-adrenergic agonists in the heart.[27,29,30] Of particular interest in these studies was the apparent reciprocal

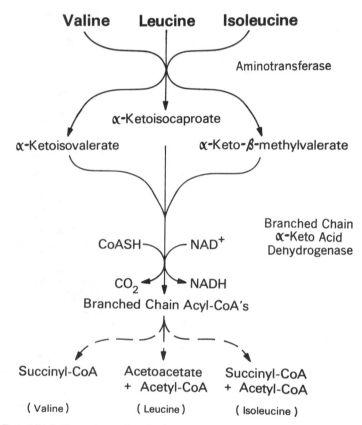

FIGURE 6. Metabolic pathway for the branched-chain amino acids, valine, leucine, and isoleucine.

regulation that the substrates for the pyruvate and the branched-chain α-keto acid dehydrogenase components have on their respective enzyme complexes (see FIG. 8). We were able to demonstrate in cardiac-derived preparations that, while pyruvate activates PDC by inhibiting its kinase, the branched-chain α-keto acid α-ketoisocaproate inhibits the pyruvate dehydrogenase by activating the pyruvate dehydrogenase kinase. On the other hand, pyruvate inactivates BCKDC by stimulating the branched-chain dehydrogenase kinase, while the homologous substrate, α-ketoisoca-

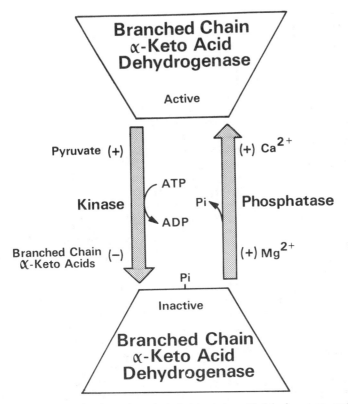

FIGURE 7. The regulation of the branched-chain α-keto acid dehydrogenase multienzyme complex by covalent modification.

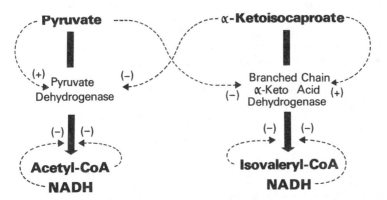

FIGURE 8. The reciprocal regulation of the pyruvate and branched-chain α-keto acid dehydrogenase complexes by pyruvate and by branched-chain α-keto acids.

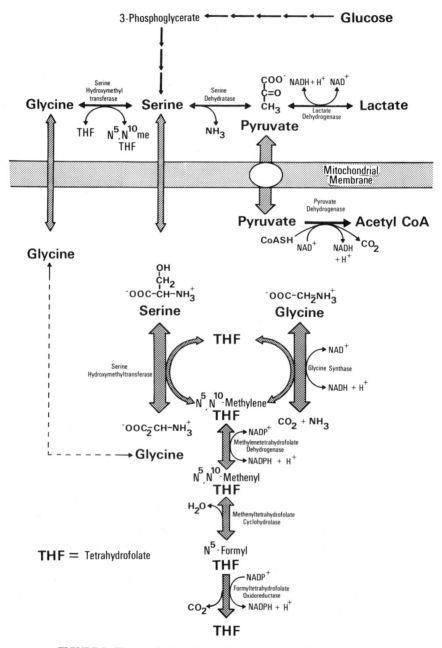

FIGURE 9. The metabolic pathways for glycine catabolism in the liver.

proate, stimulates BCKDC by inhibiting the kinase. Both α-keto acid dehydrogenase complexes are inhibited by NADH and the homologous acyl-CoA products of the respective reactions. These various interactions are probably important in the metabolic control scenarios operating during transitions from a well-fed (high carbohydrate) to a prolonged fasting (protein catabolic) situation, where the relative exposure of the mitochondrial enzyme complexes to various α-keto acid substrates changes substantially.

GLYCINE SYNTHASE

Glycine is catabolized in mammals, primarily in the liver, by two separate but related mechanisms (FIG. 9). Glycine can be converted either to serine via the serine

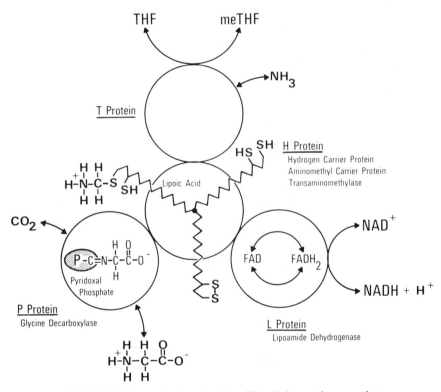

FIGURE 10. The catalytic mechanism of the glycine synthase reaction.

hydroxymethyltransferase or to CO_2, NH_3, N^5,N^{10}-methylene tetrahydrofolate, and NADH via the glycine cleavage system (i.e., glycine synthase). We became interested in the glycine cleavage system shown in FIGURE 10 because of its mechanistic similarities to the α-keto acid dehydrogenase complexes. Again, as in our studies of the α-keto acid dehydrogenase complexes, our primary interest in the glycine cleavage system concerned its regulation in intact metabolic preparations. We were able to demonstrate that the activity of the glycine cleavage system could be monitored in liver mitochondria and in perfused liver by measuring the production of $^{14}CO_2$ from infused [1-^{14}C]glycine and that, during the time-course of our experiments, nearly all of the $^{14}CO_2$ found in the reaction mixture or in the effluent perfusate was due to the glycine cleavage reaction. The activity of the glycine cleavage system was very sensitive to the metabolic state of the preparation being examined.[31,32] Maximal rates of glycine decarboxylation were observed in uncoupled mitochondria, where the oxidation-reduction states of the NAD(H) and NADP(H) redox couples were highly oxidized. In fact, the glycine cleavage enzyme was particularly sensitive to the NADPH level of liver mitochondria. Short chain-length fatty acids (e.g., propionate) were effective in activating the glycine cleavage system due to their effects (oxidation) on the mitochondrial NADPH content.[33] In ther perfused liver, it was demonstrated that any metabolic perturbation which lead to an oxidation of the NAD(H) or NADP(H) redox couples activated glycine cleavage.[32,34] This finding was particularly striking under conditions of enhanced ureogenesis, in which the NADP(H) redox system is highly oxidized.[34] These data obtained from this experimental treatment of the glycine cleavage system are of interest in explaining some of the pronounced hyperglycinemias observed in a variety of clinical disorders, which result either as a consequence of genetic lesions in the glycine cleavage system itself (non-ketonic hyperglycinemias) or of perturbations in other metabolic pathways (ketonic hyperglycinemias), such as in branched-chain α-keto acid dehydrogenase deficiency or in organic acidemias of various etiologies.

SUMMARY

During the past two decades, I and the members of my laboratory have enjoyed very much contributing to the body of knowledge concerning the α-keto acid dehydrogenase complexes. We would hope that some of our work has allowed those interested in this area a perception as to how these interesting enzyme complexes are regulated in intact metabolic systems. And last, but certainly not least, I have treasured both my professional relationship and my personal friendship with Lester Reed. His work and his presence in this field of inquiry serve as a gold standard for all of us.

REFERENCES

1. SCHUSTER, S. M. & M. S. OLSON. 1972. J. Biol. Chem. **247:** 5088–5094.
2. SCHUSTER, S. M. & M. S. OLSON. 1972. Biochemistry **11:** 4166–4172.
3. SCHUSTER, S. M. & M. S. OLSON. 1974. J. Biol. Chem. **249:** 7159–7165.
4. BATENBURG, J. J. & M. S. OLSON. 1976. J. Biol. Chem. **241:** 1364–1370.
5. SCHUSTER, S. M., M. S. OLSON & C. A. ROUTH. 1975. Arch. Biochem. Biophys. **171:** 745–752.
6. OLSON, M. S., S. C. DENNIS, M. S. DeBUYSERE & A. PADMA. 1978. J. Biol. Chem. **253:** 7369–7375.
7. DENNIS, S. C., M. S. DeBUYSERE, A. PADMA & M. S. OLSON. 1979. J. Biol. Chem. **254:** 1252–1258.
8. SCHOLZ, R., M. S. OLSON, A. SCHWAB, U. SCHWABE, C. NOELL & W. BRAUN. 1978. Eur. J. Biochem. **86:** 519–530.
9. DENNIS, S. C., M. DeBUYSERE, R. SCHOLZ & M. S. OLSON. 1978. J. Biol. Chem. **253:** 2229–2237.
10. ZWIEBEL, F. M., U. SCHWABE, R. SCHOLZ & M. S. OLSON. 1982. Biochemistry **21:** 346–353.

11. PATEL, T. B., M. S. DEBUYSERE, R. SCHOLZ & M. S. OLSON. 1982. Arch. Biochem. Biophys. **213:** 573–584.
12. PATEL, T. B., L. L. BARRON & M. S. OLSON. 1984. J. Biol. Chem. **259:** 7525–7531.
13. ROBERTSON, J. G., L. L. BARRON & M. S. OLSON. 1986. J. Biol. Chem. **261:** 76–81.
14. PAWELCZYK, T., R. A. EASOM & M. S. OLSON. 1988. Biochem. J. **253:** 819–825.
15. ROBERTSON, J. G., L. L. BARRON & M. S. OLSON. 1989. J. Biol. Chem. **264:** 11626–11631.
16. HIRAOKA, T., M. S. DEBUYSERE & M. S. OLSON. 1980. J. Biol. Chem. **255:** 7604–7609.
17. FISHER, R. A., S. TANABE, D. B. BUXTON & M. S. OLSON. 1985. J. Biol. Chem. **260:** 9223–9229.
18. PATEL, T. B. & M. S. OLSON. 1984. Am. J. Physiol. **246:** 858–864.
19. EASOM, R. A., M. S. DEBUYSERE, M. S. OLSON & P. SERWER. 1989. Proteins Struct. Funct. Genet. **5:** 224–232.
20. BUFFINGTON, C. K., M. S. DEBUYSERE & M. S. OLSON. 1979. J. Biol. Chem. **254:** 10453–10458.
21. PATEL, T. B., P. P. WAYMACK & M. S. OLSON. 1980. Arch. Biochem. Biophys. **201:** 629–635.
22. WAYMACK, P. P., M. S. DEBUYSERE & M. S. OLSON. 1980. J. Biol. Chem. **255:** 9773–9781.
23. PATEL, T. B., L. L. BARRON & M. S. OLSON. 1981. Arch. Biochem. Biophys. **212:** 452–461.
24. PATEL, T. B., L. L. BARRON & M. S. OLSON. 1981. J. Biol. Chem. **256:** 9009–9115.
25. PATEL, T. B. & M. S. OLSON. 1982. Biochemistry. **21:** 4259–4264.
26. BUXTON, D. B., L. L. BARRON & M. S. OLSON. 1982. J. Biol. Chem. **257:** 14318–14323.
27. BUXTON, D. B. & M. S. OLSON. 1982. J. Biol. Chem. **257:** 15026–15029.
28. BUXTON, D. B., L. L. BARRON, M. K. TAYLOR & M. S. OLSON. 1984. Biochem. J. **221:** 593–599.
29. HILDEBRANDT, E. F. & M. S. OLSON. 1987. Biochem. J. **248:** 423–428.
30. HILDEBRANDT, E. F., D. B. BUXTON & M. S. OLSON. 1988. Biochem. J. **250:** 835–841.
31. HAMPSON, R. K., L. L. BARRON & M. S. OLSON. 1983. J. Biol. Chem. **258:** 2993–2999.
32. HAMPSON, R. K., M. K. TAYLOR & M. S. OLSON. 1984. J. Biol. Chem. **259:** 1180–1185.
33. HAMPSON, R. K., L. L. BARRON & M. S. OLSON. 1984. Biochemistry **23:** 4604–4610.
34. HAMPSON, R. K., S. M. ROBERTSON & M. S. OLSON. 1989. Arch. Biochem. Biophys. In press.

Regulation of Substrate Availability for the Branched-Chain α-Keto Acid Dehydrogenase Enzyme Complex[a]

SUSAN M. HUTSON

Department of Biochemistry
Bowman Gray School of Medicine of
Wake Forest University
Winston-Salem, North Carolina 27103

The branched-chain α-keto acid dehydrogenase enzyme complex (BCKDH) catalyzes the first irreversible step in the catabolism of the three essential branched-chain amino acids, leucine, isoleucine, and valine. The substrates for the BCKDH, the branched-chain α-keto acids (BCKA), α-ketoisovalerate (KIV), α-ketoisocaproate (KIC), and α-keto-β-methylvalerate (KMV), are products of the branched-chain aminotransferase reaction, which is the first step in catabolism of these amino acids. The enzyme which catalyzes this reaction is the branched-chain aminotransferase (BCAT). The BCAT is widely distributed among tissues, with high activity in heart and kidney and very low activity in liver.[1] BCKDH activity is regulated by phosphorylation and dephosphorylation of the E1α subunit; and under normal dietary conditions the complex is almost completely in the active state in liver, while only about 10% is active in skeletal muscle.[2-4] Since branched-chain α-keto acids are released from perfused skeletal muscle, it has been suggested that muscle is a major site of branched-chain amino acid transamination, while liver is thought to be a major site of branched-chain α-keto acid oxidation.[5]

Another level of control is suggested by the intracellular location of BCKDH and BCAT within different organs and tissues. BCKDH is a mitochondrial matrix enzyme, and the tissue content of the enzyme complex will vary directly with the tissue mitochondrial content. The subcellular distribution of BCAT between mitochondria and cytosolic compartments varies among different tissues.[6] A mitochondrial transporter for branched-chain α-keto acids has been characterized.[7] This transport system provides the link between the mitochondrial and cytosolic compartments for branched-chain α-keto acid substrates. In the present study, the role of the intracellular compartmentation of the BCAT as well as the function of branched-chain α-keto acid transport in influencing BCKDH flux in different tissues will be discussed.

EXPERIMENTAL PROCEDURES

Preparation of Mitochondria and Transport Procedures

Heart mitochondria were prepared from male Sprague-Dawley rats using the protease Nagase as described by LaNoue *et al.*[8] Skeletal muscle, liver, and kidney mitochondria were prepared by the methods described in Ref. 6. α-Keto acid uptake by

[a]This work was supported by NIH Grant No. DK-34738.

230

isolated mitochondria was measured using the standard conditions at 8°C described in Ref. 9.

Measurement of Branched-Chain α-Keto Acid and Amino Acid Oxidation in Isolated Mitochondria

The rate of branched-chain α-keto acid or branched-chain amino acid oxidative decarboxylation and transamination were measured using 1-^{14}C–labeled BCKA or BCAA, as described by Hutson et al.[1] The standard incubation medium contained the following components: 125 mM KCl; 2.5 mM potassium phosphate; 2.5 mM MgCl$_2$; 3 mM L-carnitine; 20 mM MOPS, pH 7.0 at 37°C; 1.0 mg/ml mitochondrial protein. Mitochondria were incubated for 5 min before the reaction was started by addition of labeled substrate. When the distribution of branched-chain α-keto acids between intra- and extramitochondrial compartments was measured, mitochondria were separated from the incubation medium by rapid centrifugation, and α-keto acids in the extramitochondrial medium were determined as described.[1]

RESULTS AND DISCUSSION

Characteristics of the Mitochondrial Branched-Chain α-Keto Acid Transport System

With the apparent compartmentation of the first two enzymes in branched-chain amino acid metabolism between the mitochondrial and cytosolic compartments in the cell, the question arose as to which mechanism the branched-chain α-keto acids used to cross the mitochondrial inner membrane. Originally, it was assumed that the branched-chain α-keto acids used the pyruvate or "mono-carboxylate" carrier, but the existence of a transporter for these α-keto acids was proposed by Patel et al.[10] Systematic investigation of branched-chain α-keto acid transport revealed that these α-keto acids cross the mitochondrial inner membrane on a transport system which is distinct from that of pyruvate.[7] The branched-chain α-keto acid transporter operates via proton symport, and a schematic representation of this type of transporter is shown in FIGURE 1. Certain kinetic characteristics of this transport system[9] have important metabolic consequences. First, concentration of branched-chain α-keto acids inside the more alkaline matrix compartment will be favored. Second, net efflux of mitochondrially generated α-keto acids would be expected to be slower than their exchange. The data also indicate that branched-chain α-keto acid transport can be regulated by pH changes within the physiological range. However, the role of transport in branched-chain amino acid metabolism depends, in many respects, on the relative activities of the mitochondrial and cytosolic BCAT in each tissue. Indeed, the subcellular distribution of the aminotransferase actually determines the degree to which catabolism and anabolism are compartmentalized within the cell.

Subcellular Distribution of BCAT in Rat Tissues

Recently, we have shown that BCAT in rat heart is located exclusively in the mitochondria.[1] This study was followed by a systematic examination of the mitochondrial aminotransferase activity and distribution in other tissues thought to be involved

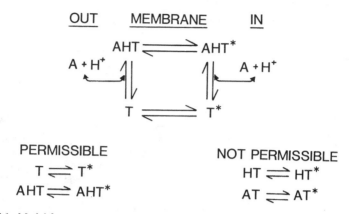

FIGURE 1. Model for cotransport of a proton (H$^+$) with an α-keto acid anion (A). T represents the transporter when it is oriented on the external surface of the inner mitochondrial membrane, and T* represents the inward orientation of the transporter. (From Hutson.[9] Reprinted from the *Journal of Biological Chemistry* with the permission of the American Society for Biochemistry and Molecular Biology, Inc.)

in metabolism of branched-chain amino acids.[6] Results of this examination of BCAT activity in mitochondria isolated from rat tissues are summarized in TABLE 1. BCAT activity was highest in heart and skeletal muscle mitochondria. Considerable activity was found in kidney cortex mitochondria, with the lowest activity found in mitochondria isolated from brain. No detectable activity was found in liver mitochondria. When total tissue activity was calculated using citrate synthase as a mitochondrial marker enzyme, it appeared that in mixed skeletal muscle some of the BCAT activity was extramitochondrial (see TABLE 1). Of the non-muscle tissues tested, activity appeared to be mitochondrial in kidney cortex and predominantly cytosolic in brain. The highest total tissue activity was found in heart muscle. In other tissues, total BCAT activity per g wet-weight of tissue relative to heart was, kidney, 0.80; brain, 0.36; skeletal muscle, 0.25; and liver, 0.01.

Heart is an oxidative working muscle. The skeletal muscle taken from the rat hindquarter consisted of a variety of fiber types with differing mitochondrial content. Thus, the possibility that the distribution might not be uniform among different types of muscle was investigated, and the results are summarized in TABLE 2. In soleus, which is composed of about 89% slow-twitch red fibers and 11% fast-twitch red

TABLE 1. Mitochondrial Branched-Chain Aminotransferase (BCAT) Activity

Mitochondrial Source	BCAT Activity	
	U/mg Protein[a]	% Total Tissue Activity
Heart	71.7 ± 4.2	104
Mixed skeletal muscle	71.9 ± 5.6	63
Kidney cortex	54.8 ± 2.3	97
Brain	15.0 ± 0.5	26
Liver	N.D.[b]	0

[a]A unit (U) of BCAT was defined as 1 nmol valine formed/min at 37°C (pH 7.8) with substrate concentrations of 15 mM isoleucine and 1.0 mM [1-^{14}C]KIV.[6]

[b]N.D., not detectable.

TABLE 2. Distribution of BCAT Activity between the Cytosolic and Mitochondrial Compartments in Different Skeletal Muscles from the Rat Hindquarter

Skeletal Muscle	BCAT Distribution[a] (% mitochondrial)
Mixed	64 ± 1
Soleus	103 ± 1
White gastrocnemius	30 ± 1

[a]BCAT activity was determined at three different KIV and isoleucine concentrations. Total tissue mitochondrial BCAT activity at each KIV and isoleucine concentration was calculated from the mitochondrial activity (units/unit citrate synthase) multiplied by tissue citrate synthase activity (units citrate synthase/g wet tissue).[6]

fibers,[11] all of the activity could be accounted for by the mitochondria. However, in white gastrocnemius, which consists of about 91% fast-twitch white fibers and 9% fast-twitch red fibers,[11] at least 70% appeared to be extramitochondrial. The difference in compartmentation of BCAT in these skeletal muscles suggest that there are functional differences among fiber types in skeletal muscles which catabolize these amino acids.

Branched-Chain Amino Acid Metabolism in Tissues with Mitochondrial BCAT

A scheme for branched-chain amino acid metabolism in muscles where BCAT is mitochondrial is shown in FIGURE 2. In the heart,[1] the diaphragm,[12] skeletal muscles with high red-fiber content,[6] and the kidney cortex, branched-chain α-keto acid formation will depend on the mitochondrial matrix pH, α-ketoglutarate–to–glutamate ratio in the mitochondria, and intramitochondrial branched-chain amino acid concentrations. In these tissues, the BCKA transporter probably operates primarily in the direction of efflux.

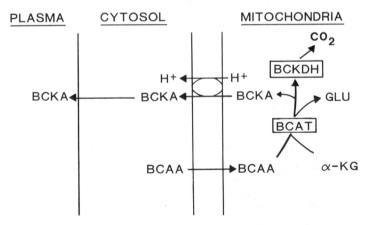

FIGURE 2. A scheme for branched-chain amino acid metabolism in tissues where branched-chain aminotransferase is a mitochondrial enzyme. BCAA, branched-chain amino acid; BCAT, branched-chain aminotransferase; BCKDH, branched-chain α-keto acid dehydrogenase enzyme complex; α-KG, α-ketoglutarate; GLU, glutamate, BCKA, branched-chain α-keto acid.

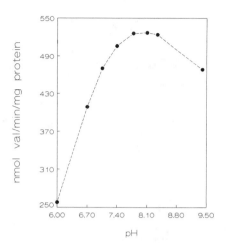

FIGURE 3. Influence of pH on branched-chain aminotransferase (BCAT) activity. A partially purified preparation of BCAT from isolated rat heart mitochondria was used. The assay system was as described.[1]

The pH optimum for the rat heart mitochondrial BCAT was investigated using detergent treated heart mitochondria and a partially purified aminotransferase preparation. The activity profile versus pH was the same for both preparations, and the data for the partially purified preparation are shown in FIGURE 3. Aminotransferase activity exhibited a broad alkaline pH optimum around pH 8.0. Activity fell off sharply below pH 7.0 These data are in the same range as the pH optima (pH 8.0–8.6) that have been reported for BCAT isoenzymes purified from rat and hog tissues (for review see Ref. 13). Thus, the alkaline environment in the mitochondrial matrix will favor transamination. Solely on the basis of pH differences between the cytosolic and mitochondrial compartments, transamination would be favored in the mitochondrial over the cytosolic compartment.

The role of transamination and BCKA transport were investigated in isolated rat heart mitochondria. Transamination of leucine (0.2 mM) versus increasing α-ketoglutarate concentration is shown in FIGURE 4. At physiological concentrations of

FIGURE 4. Effect of varied α-ketoglutarate concentrations ([α-KG]) on leucine transamination in rat heart mitochondria. Initial rates of leucine transamination at 37°C were measured as described.[1] The concentration of [1-^{14}C]leucine was 0.20 mM, and malate was 0.10 mM. Means and standard errors of the means (*vertical bars*) for the data from 3–7 separate experiments are shown.

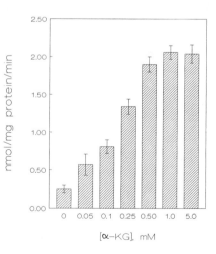

leucine, the rate of leucine transamination increased progressively with increasing concentrations of α-ketoglutarate, and transamination was nearly maximal at 0.5 mM added α-ketoglutarate. Results were similar with valine except that maximal rates of transamination were about half that of leucine, and rates were maximal at 0.5 mM α-ketoglutarate. Hence, branched-chain amino acid transamination was most sensitive to changes in α-ketoglutarate concentration within the physiological range for cytosolic α-ketoglutarate, that is, <0.5 mM α-ketoglutarate. However, the rate of transamination was higher than that of oxidation at all α-ketoglutarate concentrations tested, and α-keto acids accumulated. FIGURE 5 shows extramitochondrial accumulation of KIC from leucine transamination during a 20-min incubation in the absence and presence of rotenone. Rotenone, which inhibits oxidation of mitochondrial NADH via the electron transport chain, was added to partially inhibit oxidative decarboxylation of KIC, produced by transamination of leucine in the mitochondria. Addition of rotenone resulted in a significant increase in mitochondrial release of KIC, with essentially no effect on total transamination (FIG. 5). Thus, the primary effect of the

FIGURE 5. Leucine transamination and release of α-ketoisocaproate (KIC) in isolated rat heart mitochondria in the presence and absence of rotenone. Transamination and KIC formation from [1-^{14}C]leucine, at 37°C, were measured as described.[1] Additions were 0.20 mM [1-^{14}C]leucine, 0.5 mM α-ketoglutarate, 0.1 mM malate, and (as indicated) 0.3 μM rotenone. Transamination (▲) was the same with and without rotenone. KIC release is shown with (●) and without (○) rotenone. Mean values are presented from triplicate determinations which did not differ more than 10%.

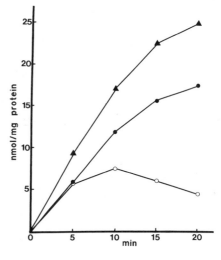

inhibition of leucine oxidation by rotenone addition was increased release of KIC by the mitochondria.

Because the cytosolic pH is around 7.0 and the matrix pH 7.6–7.8, branched-chain α-keto acid concentrations could be 4–6-fold higher in the mitochondria than in the cytosol. Unlike branched-chain α-keto acids, which can concentrate inside the mitochondria, the amino acids are zwitterions at physiological pH and presumably enter the mitochondria via a neutral carrier or by diffusion. We could not measure any accumulation of leucine or valine in rat heart mitochondria. Thus, mitochondrial branched-chain amino acid concentrations probably are equal to or less than cytosolic concentrations. The effect of branched-chain amino acid transport on the rate of transamination remains to be determined.

Using our data[6,14] and that of others,[15–18] we compared estimates of total tissue activity of BCKDH and BCAT in heart and skeletal muscle (TABLE 3). In both tissues, but especially in skeletal muscle, total tissue BCKDH activity was considerably lower than that of BCAT. However, comparison of rates of branched-chain α-keto acid oxidative decarboxylation[1] and branched-chain amino acid transamination[1] (FIG. 4) at physiological concentrations of branched-chain amino and α-keto acids suggests that mitochondrial oxidative capacity was equal to or greater than that of mitochondrial transamination. In heart, the capacity of the mitochondria to transaminate leucine at physiological concentrations (0.20 mM) with α-ketoglutarate (0.25 mM) was about 27% of the rate of oxidation of KIC (10–20 μM). Differences were lower in skeletal muscle. In skeletal muscle the activity state of the complex is $\leq$10% under normal dietary conditions,[3,4] which results in BCKDH activity being rate-controlling for oxidation in skeletal muscle. Maximal activation of about 40% was only observed in the postprandial state in rats fed a 50% protein diet.[3] In perfused skeletal muscle, transamination always exceeded oxidation.[19] Therefore, in tissues with intramitochondrial BCAT—muscles with high red fiber content, heart, and possibly kidney—the activity state of BCKDH will influence significantly the rate of branched-chain α-keto acid release from the tissue.

TABLE 3. Comparison of BCKDH and BCAT Activities in Muscle Tissues

Muscle Type	Tissue Capacity (μmol KIV metabolized/g wet tissue/min)	
	BCKDH[a]	BCAT[b]
Heart	0.5–1.7	4.3
Mixed skeletal muscle	0.11–0.16	1.1
Soleus	0.24	

[a] Oxidation of KIV by BCKDH. Tissue activities at 37°C were estimated from data in Refs. 14–18, adjusted for differences in branched-chain α-keto acid substrate and assay temperature.
[b] Transamination of KIV by BCAT. Data from Ref. 6.

Metabolism in Tissues with Cytosolic and Mitochondrial BCAT

The hypothetical scheme shown in FIGURE 6 is representative of branched-chain amino acid metabolism in tissues where BCAT activity is found predominantly in the cytosol, i.e., brain and muscles with high white fiber content. In muscles where BCAT activity is found in both subcellular compartments, it is not yet known whether the aminotransferase is located solely in the mitochondria in one fiber type and solely in the cytosol in another. At least in brain, BCAT is primarily cytosolic with some mitochondrial activity. The pH gradients across the cell membranes favor the presence of low concentrations of branched-chain α-keto acids in the cytosol. However, since reported values for BCKDH activity in brain are 20–100 times less than values for BCAT activity,[20] BCKDH activity would be expected to limit catabolism in this tissue.

In muscles with a low content of mitochondria and with significant amounts of cytosolic aminotransferase, one can speculate that keto acid release may represent a higher proportion of total transamination than in muscles with higher mitochondria content. The compartmentalization of transamination in both cytosol and mitochondria means that relative rates of transamination will fluctuate with the α-ketoglutarate-to–glutamate ratio in both compartments, and communication between the two branched-chain α-keto acid pools will occur via the transporter. Since exchange catalyzed by the mitochondrial branched-chain α-keto acid transporter is considerably faster than efflux,[7,9] equilibration of the two branched-chain α-keto acid pools should be rapid.

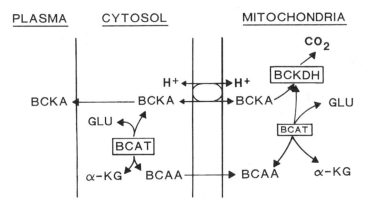

FIGURE 6. A scheme for branched-chain amino acid metabolism in tissues with cytosolic and mitochondrial branched-chain aminotransferase. BCAA, branched-chain amino acid; BCAT, branched-chain aminotransferase; BCKDH, branched-chain α-keto acid dehydrogenase enzyme complex; α-KG, α-ketoglutarate; GLU, glutamate; BCKA, branched-chain α-keto acid.

Liver Branched-Chain Amino Acid Metabolism

FIGURE 7 diagrams branched-chain amino acid metabolism in liver. No BCAT was detectable in liver mitochondria, and tissue activity was a hundredfold lower than in heart muscle. In rats fed a normal diet, the BCKDH complex is nearly 100% active,[2,21] and, as shown in TABLE 4, hepatic BCKDH activity is in 40-fold excess over hepatic branched-chain aminotransferase activity. Therefore, the liver is poised for oxidation of branched-chain α-keto acids. Indeed, in isolated hepatocytes incubated with physiological concentrations of amino acids, glucose, and pyruvate under a variety of hormonal conditions, oxidation of 100 μM KIC was rapid and was essentially complete by 90 min, while metabolism of 200 μM leucine was <1% (Hutson *et al.*, unpublished

LIVER

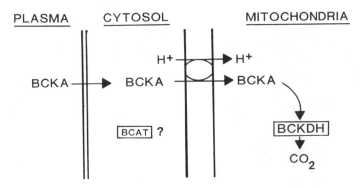

FIGURE 7. A scheme for branched-chain amino acid metabolism in liver. Abbreviations are as in the legend to FIGURE 6.

TABLE 4. Comparison of BCKDH and BCAT Activities in Rat Liver

Tissue BCKDH Activity[a] (units/g liver)[b]	Tissue BCAT Activity (units/g liver)[b]
2200	53

[a] Miller et al.[4]

[b] Unit = 1 nmol product/min/g liver at 37°C.[6] BCKDH and BCAT activities were measured with KIV and KIV plus isoleucine as substrates, respectively.

observations). In liver, mitochondrial branched-chain α-keto acid transport must operate primarily in the direction of uptake followed by oxidative decarboxylation.

Purification of the BCAT from Rat Heart Mitochondria

In order to quantitate the mitochondrial BCAT enzyme and determine whether the cytosolic and mitochondrial enzymes are the same isoenzyme form, work is now in progress to purify the mitochondrial aminotransferase from rat heart. The SDS–polyacrylamide gel electrophoretic pattern obtained for our current preparation resolved under reducing conditions is shown in FIGURE 8. The protein we have purified that has BCAT activity (Lane B) appears on the stained gel to have a molecular mass of 42 kDa; with prestained standards, the value is 45 kDa. Thus, the rat heart mitochondrial enzyme has a molecular mass considerably lower than the 75 kDa that has been reported for the hog heart enzyme, but it is within the range reported for BCAT isoenzymes purified from rat tissues.[13]

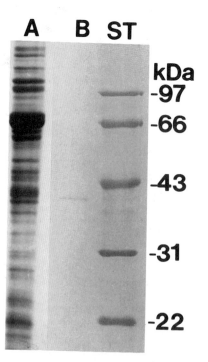

FIGURE 8. SDS–polyacrylamide gel electrophoretic pattern of branched-chain aminotransferase (BCAT) purified from rat heart mitochondria. **Lane ST** has standard proteins. **Lane A** shows the initial mitochondrial matrix extract, obtained as the supernatant after centrifugation of the disrupted mitochondria at 100,000 × g, and **Lane B** shows the protein that has BCAT activity.

SUMMARY

The tissue distribution of BCAT and BCKDH is largely responsible for the unique metabolism of branched-chain amino acids in rat tissues. Because BCKDH is a mitochondrial enzyme, tissue capacity for branched-chain amino acid oxidation will be a function of mitochondrial specific activity and tissue mitochondrial content, as well as the activity state of the BCKDH complex. In muscle tissues, the activity of the BCKDH appears to restrict branched-chain amino acid oxidation. Therefore, in muscle, transamination exceeds oxidation. Depending on muscle fiber type, the branched-chain α-keto acid transporter operates primarily as either an efflux or an exchange pathway and keto acids are released from the tissue. The liver contains very low cytosolic BCAT activity and no mitochondrial BCAT. Since the BCKDH is largely in the active state in hepatic tissue, the liver is a major site of branched-chain amino acid oxidation. Thus, control of the metabolism of these essential amino acids *in vivo* is achieved through distribution and regulation of the activity of the first two enzymes in the catabolic pathway.

REFERENCES

1. HUTSON, S. M., D. FENSTERMACHER & C. MAHAR. 1988. J. Biol. Chem. **263:** 3618–3625.
2. ZHANG, B., R. PAXTON, G. W. GOODWIN, Y. SHIMOMURA & R. A. HARRIS. 1987. Biochem. J. **246:** 625–631.
3. BLOCK, K. P., R. P. AFTRING, W. B. MEHARD & M. G. BUSE. 1987. J. Clin. Invest. **79:** 1349–1358.
4. MILLER, R. H., R. S. EISENSTEIN & A. E. HARPER. 1988. J. Biol. Chem. **263:** 3454–3461.
5. HARPER, A. E., R. H. MILLER & K. P. BLOCK. 1984. Annu. Rev. Nutr. **4:** 409–454.
6. HUTSON, S. M. 1988. J. Nutr. **118:** 1475–1481.
7. HUTSON, S. M. & S. L. RANNELS. 1985. J. Biol. Chem. **260:** 14189–14193.
8. LANOUE, K. F., F. M. H. JEFFRIES & G. K. RADDA. 1986. Biochemistry **25:** 7667–7675.
9. HUTSON, S. M. 1987. J. Biol. Chem. **262:** 9629–9635.
10. PATEL, T. B., P. P. WAYMACK & M. S. OLSON. 1980. Arch. Biochem. Biophys. **201:** 629–635.
11. ARMSTRONG, R. B. & R. O. PHELPS. 1984. Am. J. Anat. **171:** 259–272.
12. SNELL, K. & D. A. DUFF. 1985. Biochem. J. **225:** 737–743.
13. ICHIHARA, A. 1985. *In* Transaminases. P. Christen & D. E. Metzler, Eds. Vol. 2: 430–438. John Wiley & Sons, New York.
14. HUTSON, S. M. 1986. J Biol. Chem. **261:** 4420–4425.
15. GILLIM, S. E., R. PAXTON, G. A. COOK & R. A. HARRIS. 1983. Biochem. Biophys. Res. Commun. **111:** 74–81.
16. WAGENMAKERS, A. J. M., J. T. G. SCHEPENS, J. A. M. VELDHUIZEN & J. H. VEERKAMP. 1984. Biochem. J. **220:** 273–281.
17. AFTRING, R. P., K. P. BLOCK & M. G. BUSE. 1986. Am. J. Physiol. **250:** E599–E604.
18. PATSTON, P. A., J. ESPINAL, J. M. SHAW & P. J. RANDLE. 1986. Biochem. J. **235:** 429–434.
19. ZAPALOWSKI, C., S. M. HUTSON & A. E. HARPER. 1981. *In* Metabolism and Clinical Implications of Branched Chain Amino and Ketoacids. M. Walser & J. R. Williamson, Eds.: 239–244. Elsevier Scientific Publishing Co., Inc. New York.
20. BROSNAN, M. E., A. LOWRY, Y. WASI, M. LOWRY & J. T. BROSNAN. 1985. Can. J. Physiol. Pharmacol. **63:** 1234–1238.
21. BLOCK K. P., B. W. HEYWOOD, M. G. BUSE & A. E. HARPER. 1985. Biochem. J. **232:** 593–597.

Activation of Pyruvate Dehydrogenase Complex by Ca^{2+} in Intact Heart, Cardiac Myocytes, and Cardiac Mitochondria

RICHARD G. HANSFORD, RAFAEL MORENO-SÁNCHEZ,[a]
AND BOHDAN LEWARTOWSKI

Gerontology Research Center
National Institute on Aging
National Institutes of Health
Francis Scott Key Medical Center
Baltimore, Maryland 21224

INTRODUCTION

The discovery that dehydrogenase enzymes may be activated by Ca^{2+} ions in the range of concentrations found within cells[1-5] prompted the suggestion that this activation may provide a mechanism whereby mitochondrial oxidations are enhanced during periods of elevated tissue work load.[6,7] This may allow the closer balance of energy supply and demand, especially in excitable tissues. In this article we describe the results of some recent work in which we have tried to define more closely the conditions under which two α-ketoacid dehydrogenase complexes, *viz.*, the pyruvate dehydrogenase complex (PDC) and the 2-oxoglutarate dehydrogenase complex (OGDC), respond to increased work load in the heart and the role of mitochondrial Ca^{2+} concentrations in this process.

By increasing the amount of catalytically active protein, in the case of PDC,[2,3,8] or by increasing the affinity of the dehydrogenase for its substrate, in the case of OGDC,[5,9] activation by Ca^{2+} ions leads to more active reduction of NAD. It has been suggested that this permits the mitochondria in activated tissues to maintain higher $NADH/NAD^+$ ratios than would otherwise be possible.[10,11] In this paper we also examine the quantitative relationship between mitochondrial $NADH/NAD^+$ ratios and the flux through oxidative phosphorylation, as measured by the O_2 consumption of isolated cardiac mitochondria when the activities of pyruvate and 2-oxoglutarate dehydrogenase complexes are varied by varying either substrate concentration or the availability of Ca^{2+}.

METHODS AND MATERIALS

The preparation of rat heart mitochondria, loading of the mitochondria with the fluorescent Ca^{2+}-chelating agent indo-1,[12] and the measurement of PDC activity were all as described by Moreno-Sánchez and Hansford.[13] The preparation of isolated cardiac myocytes and the measurement of cytosolic free Ca^{2+} concentration was as

---

[a]Present address: Instituto Nacional de Cardiología, Departmento de Bioqúimica, Juan Badiano No. 1, Tlalpan, 14080 México D.F., Mexico.

described by Hansford and Lakatta[14] and Moreno-Sánchez and Hansford.[13] Other experimental details are given in the appropriate figure legends and tables.

RESULTS AND DISCUSSION

Relationship between Content of Active Pyruvate Dehydrogenase Complex and Intramitochondrial Free Ca^{2+} Concentration

Ca^{2+} ions activate pyruvate dehydrogenase phosphatase[2,3,8] and thereby tend to increase the amount of the catalytically active, dephospho-PDC (PDC$_a$). We have recently studied the Ca^{2+}-ion concentration-dependence of this process when PDC is present in its natural locale, within the mitochondrial matrix compartment. In these experiments, suspensions of cardiac mitochondria were loaded with the fluorescent Ca^{2+}-chelating agent indo-1,[12] by exposure to the membrane-permeant acetoxymethylester form. The concentration of free, ionized Ca^{2+} within the mitochondrial matrix ([Ca^{2+}]$_m$) can then be inferred from the fluorescence of the indo-1, after an appropriate calibration procedure.[13] Other, recent work has used the analogous chelating agent fura-2 for the same purpose.[15,16]

FIGURE 1A shows that addition of a Ca^{2+}-EGTA buffer stabilizing the level of free Ca^{2+} at 830 nM to a suspension of mitochondria loaded with indo-1 and oxidizing succinate in the presence of low (ca. 10 nM) extramitochondrial Ca^{2+} results in a large, rapid increase in [Ca^{2+}]$_m$. After a steady-state has been achieved, addition of ruthenium red initiates a progressive decline in [Ca^{2+}]$_m$. This is expected, as ruthenium red blocks the uptake of Ca^{2+} into mitochondria, whereas the egress pathway remains active.[17] Egress occurs by exchange of Ca^{2+} for 2 Na$^+$,[17,18] which is permissible in the medium used ([Na$^+$] = 10 mM). Prior exposure to ruthenium red (FIG. 1B) prevents the Ca^{2+} added to the incubation medium from raising [Ca^{2+}]$_m$—consistent with the above reasoning. When samples of mitochondria withdrawn at the time-points indicated in FIGURE 1A were assayed for PDC$_a$ content, it was found that PDC$_a$ declined progressively with [Ca^{2+}]$_m$ (FIG. 1, *inset*). This experiment shows the practicality of following the kinetics of changes in [Ca^{2+}]$_m$ and PDC$_a$ content; a more precise relation of steady-state values of PDC$_a$ to [Ca^{2+}]$_m$ is given below.

FIGURE 2A presents the results of an analogous experiment in which an addition of ADP subsequent to the Ca^{2+}-EGTA buffer resulted in a further increase in PDC$_a$ content and an apparent further increase in [Ca^{2+}]$_m$, as judged from an increase in the fluorescence of indo-1 at 400 nm. Repetition of the experiment, with fluorescence recorded at 490 nm (FIG. 2B), also revealed an increase in fluorescence in response to the addition of ADP. This response is paradoxical, as the indo-1/Ca^{2+} chelate fluoresces maximally at 400 nm, whereas the unbound indo-1 fluoresces maximally at 490 nm.[12] Thus, an increase in [Ca^{2+}]$_m$ should result in optical records at 400 and 490 nm which are mirror images. An experiment with fluo-3, another Ca^{2+}-chelating agent, which fluoresces maximally at a longer wavelength (530 nm) and has a higher K_d value for Ca^{2+} (approximately 0.4 μM), also gave an increase in fluorescence in response to ADP (FIG. 2C). Evidently, there is some optical artifact involved, possibly due to a conformational change of the mitochondrial membranes caused by ADP. Thus, the increase in PDC$_a$ content with ADP may follow from an increase in [Ca^{2+}]$_m$, or it may be due to a direct inhibitory effect of ADP on pyruvate dehydrogenase kinase, as documented previously.[19] Addition of the uncoupling agent carbonylcyanide *p*-trifluoromethoxyphenylhydrazone (FCCP) in the experiment of FIGURE 2A resulted in a fall in [Ca^{2+}]$_m$, suggestive of an initial gradient of [Ca^{2+}]$_m$/[Ca^{2+}]$_o$ of more than

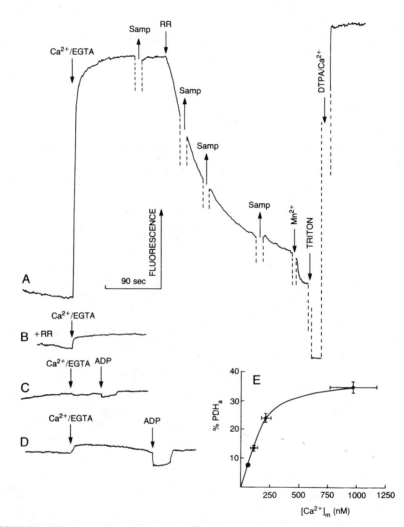

FIGURE 1. Effect of ruthenium red on $[Ca^{2+}]_m$ and PDC_a (% PDH_a) content. The fluorescent chelating agent indo-1 was used to follow changes in $[Ca^{2+}]_m$ of cardiac mitochondria oxidizing succinate, in the presence of rotenone. (**Panel A**) Addition of a Ca^{2+}-EGTA buffer stabilizing the level of free Ca^{2+} at 830 nM to mitochondria respiring in the presence of EGTA results in a large increase in $[Ca^{2+}]_m$; the subsequent addition of ruthenium red (RR) causes a progressive reversal. Addition of Triton X-100 plus $MnCl_2$ allows the determination of minimal fluorescence; subsequent addition of a molar excess of the Ca^{2+} salt of diethylenetriamine–N,N,N',N'',N''-pentaacetic acid (DTPA/Ca^{2+}) allows the determination of maximal fluorescence. Given the K_d of the Ca^{2+}/indo-1 chelate, these values allow computation of the value of $[Ca^{2+}]_m$ corresponding to any point on the fluorescence recording. (**Panel B**) Ruthenium red (RR) was added prior to Ca^{2+}-EGTA. (**Panels C** and **D**) The mitochondria were not loaded with indo-1. **Panel E** presents the content of PDC_a at the points of sampling (Samp) indicated in **panel A:** results from 3 mitochondrial preparations were used to compile these data (mean ± SEM). Full experimental details are given in Moreno-Sánchez & Hansford.[13] (From Moreno-Sánchez & Hansford.[13] Reprinted with permission from the *Biochemical Journal*.)

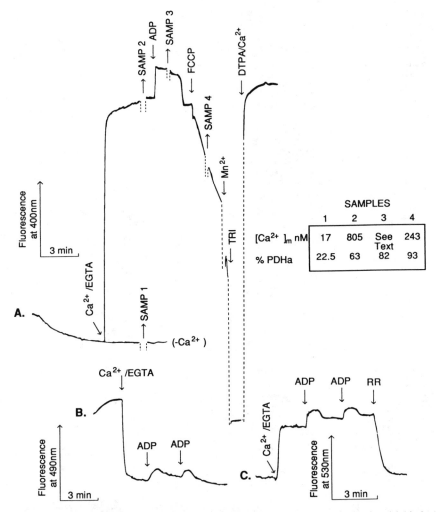

FIGURE 2. Effect of ADP and an uncoupling agent on the fluorescence of mitochondrial indo-1 and on PDC$_a$ content (%PDH$_a$). (**A, B**) Mitochondria were loaded with indo-1 (ca. 2 mg of protein/ml) as described in Moreno-Sánchez and Hansford.[13] (**Panel A**) The respiratory substrate was 5 m*M* glutamate plus 5 m*M* malate; (**panel B**) the substrate was 20 m*M* succinate in the presence of 2.5 µ*M* rotenone. Where indicated, a Ca²⁺-EGTA buffer was added to give 1.2 µ*M* free Ca²⁺. ADP was added to 1.5 m*M* in **A** and 0.15 m*M* in **B**; FCCP was added to 1 µ*M*. Samples of the suspension (50 µl) for the estimation of PDC$_a$ were withdrawn at the points indicated (SAMP). (**Panel C**) Mitochondria (1.6 mg of protein/ml), loaded by exposure to 5 µ*M* fluo-3 AM in the presence of 1 m*M* ADP for 30 min at 26°C, were incubated with 20 m*M* succinate (plus 2.5 µ*M* rotenone) as substrate. Where indicated, Ca²⁺-EGTA was added to give 0.4 µ*M* free Ca²⁺, ADP to give 1 m*M*, and ruthenium red (RR) to give 0.5 µ*M*. Note that in all of these experiments (**A, B, C**), the incubation medium contained 10 m*M* Na⁺ and 5 m*M* P$_i$, but no Mg²⁺.

unity ($[Ca^{2+}]_o$ is the concentration of extramitochondrial free Ca^{2+}). This conclusion is not iron-clad, however, as small values of membrane potential ($\Delta\psi$) and ΔpH, which can remain in the presence of an uncoupling agent,[20] can affect the mitochondrial Ca^{2+} transport cycle. The increase in PDC_a content at this juncture is not unexpected, as FCCP will decrease $NADH/NAD^+$ and ATP/ADP ratios, and this itself will favor an increased PDC_a content, as shown previously (see Hansford[10] for review).

When PDC interconversion was allowed to achieve a steady-state, 9 min after the addition of Ca^{2+}-EGTA buffers, relationships between PDC_a content and $[Ca^{2+}]_m$ of the type shown in FIGURE 3 were obtained. Regardless of the respiratory substrate

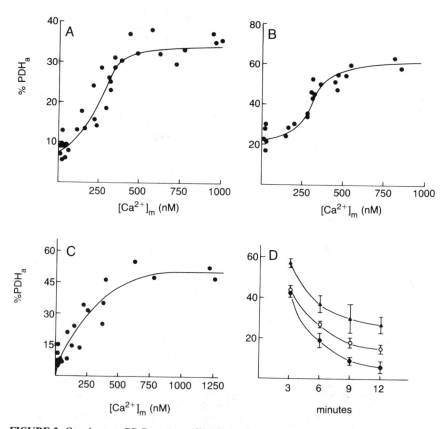

FIGURE 3. Steady-state PDC_a content (%PDH_a) of mitochondria as a function of $[Ca^{2+}]_m$. In **panels A, B,** and **C,** the PDC_a content of mitochondria was sampled 9 min after the imposition of known values of $[Ca^{2+}]_o$, using Ca^{2+}-EGTA buffers. At this time, interconversion of the enzyme is at or near a steady-state (**panel D**). $[Ca^{2+}]_m$ was calculated from the fluorescence of mitochondrial indo-1. (**Panel A**) The oxidizable substrate was 20 mM succinate (plus 2.5 μM rotenone). (**Panel B**) The substrate was 5 mM glutamate plus 5 mM malate. (**Panel C**) The substrate was succinate, but the experiments differed from those in A in that $MgCl_2$ was added to 2 mM prior to the addition of the Ca^{2+}-EGTA buffer. (**Panel D**) Time-course of inactivation of PDC_a in the presence of (▲) glutamate (5 mM) + malate (5 mM) + ATP (1 mM); (O) succinate (20 mM) + rotenone (2.5 μM); or (●) succinate (20 mM) + rotenone (2.5 μM) + ATP (1 mM). Full details are given in Moreno-Sánchez & Hansford.[13] (From Moreno-Sánchez & Hansford.[13] Reprinted with permission from the *Biochemical Journal*.)

TABLE 1. Effect of Depolarization of the Plasma Membrane on the PDC_a Content of Isolated Cardiac Myocytes[a]

Condition[b]	PDC_a[c]	
	% of Total	n
Increasing K⁺		
5 mM KCl	31.7 ± 1.4	32
20 mM KCl	39.5 ± 0.6	4
40 mM KCl	49.5 ± 4.6	6
55 mM KCl	49.3 ± 3.6	8
80 mM KCl	60.6 ± 3.9	11
Increasing K⁺ + ruthenium red (RR)		
5 mM KCl + RR	31.5 ± 2.7	3
40 mM KCl + RR	38.7 ± 2.3	3
55 mM KCl + RR	35.2 ± 3.0[d]	5
80 mM KCl + RR	37.8 ± 3.3[e]	7
Veratridine		
5 μM Veratridine	37.6 ± 4.5	6
25 μM Veratridine	51.0 ± 1.9	10
25 μM Veratridine + 0.2 mM ouabain	57.6 ± 3.9	8
25 μM Veratridine + 0.2 mM ouabain + RR	35.8 ± 2.0[f]	10

[a]Adapted from Hansford.[44]

[b]Suspensions of rat cardiac myocytes were incubated and sampled for PDC_a content as previously described. The basal medium contained 5 mM KCl; higher concentrations of K⁺ were achieved by mixing volumes of an isotonic medium in which K⁺ replaced Na⁺ ions. Sampling was done 10 min after the addition to the suspension of K⁺-containing medium or of veratridine plus ouabain, as appropriate. Where indicated, ruthenium red was added 3 min before the K⁺-containing medium or veratridine, to give a concentration of 12 μM.

[c]Data are presented as means ± SEM; the number of preparations (n) is indicated. Note that values of PDC_a are significantly lower in the presence of ruthenium red than in otherwise identical incubations omitting ruthenium red.

[d]$p < 0.05$.

[e]$p < 0.005$.

[f]$p < 0.001$.

used, and of the presence of free Mg^{2+}, the $S_{0.5}$ value for activation was determined to be approximately 300 nM. This value rests upon a determination of the K_d for the intramitochondrial indo-1/Ca^{2+} chelate of 95 nM.[13] If this value is in fact higher, as it is when determined in simple aqueous solution considered close in ionic strength to the mitochondrial matrix,[12,16] then the calculated $S_{0.5}$ for PDC activation is raised accordingly. Despite these uncertainties about absolute quantitation of $[Ca^{2+}]_m$, it is clear that these fluorescent chelating agents provide a powerful tool for the continuous monitoring of mitochondrial Ca^{2+} and that PDC interconversion when the enzyme is in its intramitochondrial milieu shows a sensitivity to Ca^{2+} which is very similar to that originally shown for the purified pyruvate dehydrogenase phosphatase, assayed under less natural conditions in the spectrophotometer cuvette.[21]

Response of Pyruvate Dehydrogenase Complex to Interventions Which Raise $[Ca^{2+}]_c$ in Isolated Cardiac Myocytes

Although experiments with isolated cardiac mitochondria show that PDC_a content responds to changes in $[Ca^{2+}]_o$ which are similar to these thought to occur in the cytosol of cardiac myocytes[22-24] (see also, FIG. 3), more convincing evidence for the physiological significance of this response requires the study of myocytes or bulk muscle preparations. Isolated cardiac myocytes offer some advantages for such a study in that the concentration of free cytosolic Ca^{2+} ($[Ca^{2+}]_c$) is not only regulated by the same mechanisms as in bulk muscle, but can additionally be measured more easily. We have subjected suspensions of isolated rat cardiac myocytes to procedures which

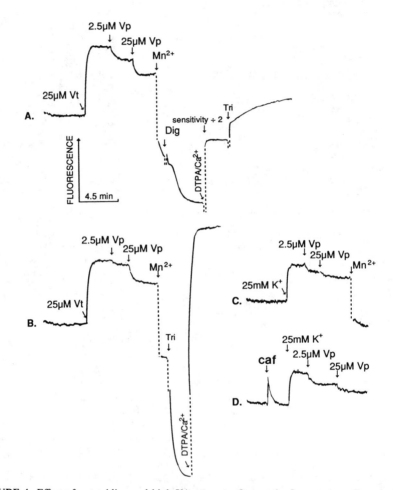

FIGURE 4. Effect of veratridine and high K^+ concentration on the fluorescence of rat cardiac myocytes loaded with indo-1 and quin-2. Cardiac myocytes (2.2 mg of protein/ml) were incubated with 10 μM indo-1/AM (**A**) or 35 μM quin-2/AM (**B–D**) for 30 min at 37°C with orbital shaking (140 rpm) in 2 ml of a medium comprising (in mM) 116 NaCl, 5.4 KCl, 1 NaH_2PO_4, 25 HEPES-Tris, 1 $CaCl_2$, 1 $MgSO_4$, 22 D-glucose, and 0.5% bovine serum albumin; final pH, 7.4. Cells were then washed by centrifugation and resuspended by addition of 2 ml of medium equilibrated with 100% O_2 at 37°C. The external Ca^{2+} concentration was 2 mM for **A, C** and **D**, and 1 mM for **B**. Veratridine (Vt), verapamil (Vp) and KCl (K^+) were added at the indicated concentrations. Other additions, as indicated, were 0.2 mM $MnCl_2$ (Mn^{2+}), 25 μM digitonin (Dig), 5 mM diethylenetriamine pentaacetic acid/10 mM $CaCl_2$ ($DTPA/Ca^{2+}$), 0.1% (v/v) Triton X-100 (Tri), and 10 mM caffeine (caf). The sensitivity of the recorder was diminished in **A** by a factor of 2 after the addition of $DTPA/Ca^{2+}$.

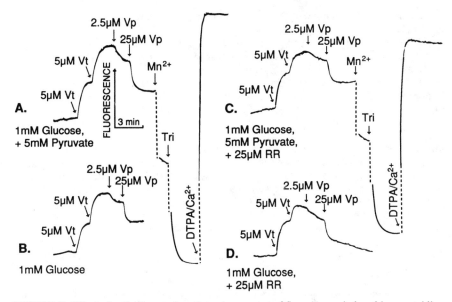

FIGURE 5. Effect of ruthenium red on the enhancement of fluorescence induced by veratridine in quin-2–loaded cardiac myocytes. Cardiac myocytes (3.2 mg of protein/ml) were loaded by exposure to 25 μM quin-2/AM for 15 min, essentially as described for FIGURE 4. In C and D, 25 μM ruthenium red (RR) was added 7 min prior to the addition of quin-2/AM; cells were then collected by centrifugation and resuspended in 2 ml of fresh medium to give the indicated final concentrations of substrates. The Ca^{2+} concentration was 2 mM and the albumin concentration was 0.125 mg/ml; other conditions were as described for FIGURE 4.

depolarize the plasma membrane and thereby raise [Ca^{2+}]$_c$ and have measured the impact of the procedures upon PDC$_a$ content. TABLE 1 shows that depolarization of the plasma membrane with increasing K$^+$ ion concentrations in the suspending medium caused a graded increase in PDC$_a$ content, consistent with a supposed increase in [Ca^{2+}]$_c$ in response to depolarization (see below). Exposure to veratridine, an alkaloid which potentiates the opening of plasma membrane Na$^+$ channels and hence causes depolarization,[25,26] also gives an increase in PDC$_a$ content. Most significantly in the context of this discussion, prior treatment with ruthenium red, which inhibits uptake of Ca^{2+} by mitochondria,[27] greatly blunted the effect of depolarization in increasing PDC$_a$ content.

Repetition of these procedures in suspensions of myocytes containing the fluorescent Ca^{2+}-chelating agents quin-2[28] or indo-1 allowed us to estimate the changes in [Ca^{2+}]$_c$ which accompanied these maneuvers. FIGURE 4 shows that addition of 25 μM veratridine results in a large and rapid increase in [Ca^{2+}]$_c$, which is then partially reversed by plasma membrane Ca^{2+} antagonists. Comparison of the results of the experiments shown in panels B, C, and D of FIGURE 4, all of which employed the same cell preparation and loading with quin-2, shows that addition of 25 mM KCl (to give a final K$^+$ concentration of 30 mM) results in a somewhat smaller increase in [Ca^{2+}]$_c$ than does the addition of 25 μM veratridine; part of the response to addition of KCl reflects the release of Ca^{2+} from the sarcoplasmic reticulum, as judged by a lower rate of rise after the prior depletion of reticular Ca^{2+} stores with caffeine[14] (cf. FIGS. 4C, D). Reference to TABLE 1 shows that 40 mM K$^+$, which is higher than the K$^+$ concentration used in FIGURE 4, is needed to increase PDC$_a$ content to the same degree seen with 25 μM veratridine; thus, effects of these agents on $[Ca^{2+}]_c$ and on PDC_a content are essentially congruent.

When cardiac myocytes are pretreated with a high concentration of ruthenium red and then exposed to veratridine, the response of $[Ca^{2+}]_c$ is not diminished by the ruthenium red (FIG. 5). Indeed, when allowance is made for the optical quenching by ruthenium red, which can be assessed on the basis of the span between maximal fluorescence ($DTPA/Ca^{2+}$) and minimal fluorescence (Mn^{2+} plus Triton X-100), the increase in $[Ca^{2+}]_c$ is found to be slightly larger in cells treated with ruthenium red. Thus, for PDC to be activated in response to the depolarization of the cardiac myocyte, it is necessary for $[Ca^{2+}]_c$ to rise and for some of this Ca^{2+} to be transported into the mitochondria. When the latter process is inhibited with ruthenium red, dehydrogenase activation is greatly attenuated (TABLE 1). This finding reinforces evidence from an earlier study in which ruthenium red was found to largely prevent PDC activation in response to positive inotropic interventions in the intact heart[29]; the present study is stronger in that it shows directly that ruthenium red does not prevent the depolarization-induced increase in $[Ca^{2+}]_c$.

Response of Pyruvate Dehydrogenase Complex to Electrical Stimulation of the Isolated Perfused Heart

As a means of exploring the sensitivity to Ca^{2+} ions of PDC interconversions in a more physiologically intact setting, we determined the PDC_a content of isolated perfused rat hearts as a function of electrical stimulation (TABLE 2). Although several studies have shown increased PDC_a content of perfused hearts as a function of increased work performance, elicited by increased left atrial influx and/or increased systolic pressure,[31–33] or by adrenergic stimulation,[32,34] we are not aware of any study on the effect of electrical stimulation as such. It is seen in TABLE 2 that, when rat hearts are perfused with a medium containing 10 mM glucose and 0.1 mM octanoate, stimulation at 5 Hz raises PDC_a from 7.7% in the resting heart to 41% of maximal activity. This substrate combination was chosen as mimicking the *in vivo* situation, where fatty acids are available for oxidation, influencing the balance of PDC interconversion.[35] Octanoate was chosen instead of the more physiological long-chain fatty acids, as it is actively oxidized by rat heart[35] and avoids solubility and surfactant problems.

At the time of writing this paper, we have information that this electrical-stimulation protocol raises the mitochondrial Ca content of guinea-pig hearts when this is measured by atomic absorption spectrophotometry (B. Lewartowski and R. G. Hansford, unpublished observations) or by ^{45}Ca content at steady-state (A. Proko-pezuk, E. Wasilewska, and B. Lewartowski, unpublished observations), following a rapid isolation of mitochondria using the procedure of McCormack and Denton.[36] Unfortunately, we have not yet acquired results for the rat, to allow comparison with the enzyme data in TABLE 2. We were at some pains in this work to avoid conditions of very high work load, which have been used in much of the previous work and which could conceivably generate some degree of hypoxia in a heart perfused with saline solutions. We also sought to avoid beta-adrenergic stimulation by placing the bipolar electrode at the very tip of the right ventricle and using stimuli of slightly supra-threshold strength; inclusion of 1 μM propranolol in some of the experiments did not diminish the increase in PDC_a content due to stimulation. Although these results are consistent with a role of Ca^{2+} in regulating PDC_a content in response to electrical stimulation, they clearly are not definitive. We plan to buttress these findings by measuring other known effectors of enzyme interconversion. The direct experiment, of trying to prevent mitochondrial gain of Ca^{2+} by use of ruthenium red, did not attenuate in any way the increase in PDC_a due to electrical stimulation—in contrast to the earlier work of McCormack and England[29] and our experiments with isolated myocytes. We presume that access for this highly charged compound is inadequate in the intact heart.

Relation of Dehydrogenase Activation to Oxidative Phosphorylation

The biological advantage of dehydrogenase activation in response to high work loads may be that the redox potential gradient of the respiratory chain is maximized,

TABLE 2. Effect of Electrical Stimulation on the PDC_a Content of Isolated Perfused Rat Hearts

	PDC$_a$	
Condition[a]	% of OGDC[b]	% of Total PDC[c]
Rest	4.2 ± 0.6 ($n = 6$)	7.7
Stimulated (4–5 Hz)	22.5 ± 4.1 ($n = 4$)	41
Working	40.1 ± 5.8 ($n = 5$)	74
Stimulated ($+10$ mM pyruvate)	54.4 ± 5.1 ($n = 5$)	100

[a]The "rested" and "stimulated" rat hearts were perfused at 37°C, using the Langendorf method, with a medium of composition: 137 mM NaCl, 7.4 mM KCl, 11.9 mM NaHCO$_3$, 10 mM Na-HEPES, 0.42 mM NaH$_2$PO$_4$, 1.8 mM CaCl$_2$, 1.05 mM MgSO$_4$, 11.0 mM D-glucose, and 0.1 mM Na-octanoate. The final pH was adjusted to 7.35 with NaOH after equilibration with an atmosphere of 95% O$_2$:5% CO$_2$. To enforce quiescence ("rest"), the A-V bundle was crushed: no contractions were observed for several minutes prior to freezing. To stimulate the heart ("stimulated"), a bipolar electrode was placed on the endocardium of the apex of the right ventricle: the frequency was 4–5 Hz, the duration of the pulses 0.1 msec, and the voltage was slightly suprathreshold. Hearts were stimulated for 5 min prior to freeze clamping. The "working" heart was basically the preparation of Neely,[45] with an aortic hydrostatic pressure of 80 cm of water. The frequency of stimulation was 3 Hz and the cardiac output was in the range of 18–32 ml/min, plus coronary flow of 8–12 ml/min. To achieve complete conversion of PDC to PDC_a, a protocol was adopted involving electrical stimulation (4–5 Hz) of hearts perfused with medium omitting octanoate and containing 10 mM Na-pyruvate.

[b]PDC and OGDC activities were determined in extracts of freeze-clamped heart made using a buffer which minimizes interconversion of pyruvate dehydrogenase. For details, see Hansford.[44]

[c]PDC_a is calculated as a percentage of total PDC activity, making the assumption that complete activation of the enzyme complex occurs in the presence of 10 mM pyruvate and that OGDC activity (as measured under V_{max} conditions) is invariant in these various protocols.

allowing high fluxes through oxidative phosphorylation without the necessity of letting the adenine nucleotide phosphorylation potential fall.[10] The mechanism of this is the maintenance of high $NADH/NAD^+$ ratios. The question arises as to whether we can demonstrate that the activation by Ca^{2+} of pyruvate and 2-oxoglutarate dehydrogenase complexes does result in the generation of high $NADH/NAD^+$ ratios when flux through oxidative phosphorylation is high. We have approached this question with both isolated mitochondria and isolated cardiac myocytes.

In experiments with isolated cardiac mitochondria oxidizing 2-oxoglutarate (FIG. 6) in the presence of ADP, increasing the concentration of 2-oxoglutarate results in increased $NADH/NAD^+$ ratios and, concomitantly, increased rates of respiration. Increasing the value of $[Ca^{2+}]_o$ from 5 nM to 1.2 μM, at a non-saturating concentra-

FIGURE 6. Relation between NAD(P)H content and rate of ADP-stimulated respiration of heart mitochondria oxidizing 2-oxoglutarate. Mitochondria (2.2 mg of protein/ml) were incubated at 25°C in 2 ml of a medium comprising 120 mM KCl, 25 mM K-MOPS, 0.5 mM EGTA, 5 mM potassium phosphate, 10 mM NaCl; final pH, 7.2. The concentration of 2-oxoglutarate (αKG) was varied from 0.24 mM to 10 mM (*filled circles*). After 5 min, 1 mM ADP was added and the rate of O$_2$ uptake and the steady-state level of reduction of nicotinamide nucleotides were measured in parallel experiments with the same mitochondrial preparation. Reduced nicotinamide nucleotide was determined by differential absorbance of the mitochondrial suspension at 340–370 nm.

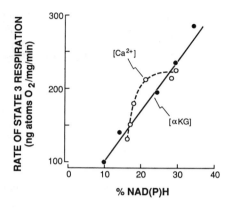

In a separate set of experiments (*empty circles*), mitochondria (1.3 mg of protein/ml) were incubated with 1 mM 2-oxoglutarate for 2 min and the concentration of free Ca^{2+} was then increased by addition of Ca^{2+}-EGTA buffers: the range of free Ca^{2+} concentrations was from 10 nM to 1.2 μM. After 3 min, 1 mM ADP was added and O$_2$ uptake and reduced nicotinamide nucleotides were determined. The percentage of reduction of NAD(P) shown was calculated on the basis of minimal reduction in the absence of added substrate and the presence of 1 mM ADP, and maximal reduction in the presence of 5 mM glutamate, 5 mM malate, and 2.5 μM rotenone. Further experiments in which nicotinamide nucleotides were determined in extracts of mitochondria have confirmed that changes in reduction under the conditions shown above can be attributed essentially completely to changes in NADH content: the contribution from NADPH is almost invariant in coupled mitochondria.

tion of 2-oxoglutarate (1 mM) also gave progressive increases in NADH/NAD$^+$ ratio and in flux. The fact that the two curves do not superimpose in this, representative, experiment suggests that the role of Ca^{2+} is not confined to increasing the affinity of OGDC for its substrate.[5,9] A possible explanation is that Ca^{2+} is also activating the adenine nucleotide translocase or ATP-synthase of the mitochondria,[37,38] thus activating both the generation and consumption of the proton electrochemical gradient which mediates oxidative phosphorylation.[39] Besides these interesting finer points, it is clear that increasing the Ca^{2+} concentration to which mitochondria are exposed can increase both the mitochondrial NADH/NAD$^+$ ratio and the flux through oxidative phosphorylation, as indexed by O$_2$ consumption. This is in keeping with the concepts on the interplay between dehydrogenase activity and oxidative phosphorylation advanced previously.[10] A similar relation between state-3 O$_2$ uptake and the mitochondrial NADH/NAD$^+$ ratio has recently been reported by Koretsky and Balaban[40] in a study which employed different substrates, but not alterations in the Ca^{2+} concentration, to vary dehydrogenase activity. It is noted that a process of energy dissipation due to enhanced Ca^{2+} cycling across the mitochondrial membrane[17,41] would increase O$_2$ uptake, but decrease the NADH/NAD$^+$ ratio. Such a process may obtrude when values of [Ca^{2+}]$_o$ are in excess of 1 μM (in the presence of 1 mM Mg^{2+} and 10 mM Na$^+$), but it is clearly not occurring here (FIG. 6).

At the level of intact cardiac myocytes, the activation of dehydrogenases by Ca^{2+} is also important in maintaining high NADH/NAD$^+$ ratios under conditions of depolarization of the plasma membrane (FIG. 7). In these experiments, 5 μM veratridine was used to partially depolarize the cells, thus increasing [Ca^{2+}]$_c$, and cellular NADH was monitored by fluorescence. Under these conditions, the major contributor to changes in fluorescence is mitochondrial NADH, which clearly relates closely to the parameter of thermodynamic interest, $NADH/NAD^+$. It is seen that under conditions of limited substrate supply to the mitochondria, veratridine elicits a greater oxidation of NADH in cells pretreated with ruthenium red than in cells without this inhibitor; but in the presence of saturating concentrations of pyruvate, the presence of ruthenium red is immaterial (FIG. 7). Although treatment with veratridine, especially at concentrations above 5 μM, causes these myocytes to lose their characteristic morphology in a process which takes several minutes, no such changes in morphology are evident during the response of NADH to veratridine shown in FIGURE 7. Thus, in this case it is clear that pretreatment of the cells with ruthenium red has caused a decrease in total dehydrogenase activity when energy demand is stimulated by depolarization of the plasma membrane. A reasonable inference is that the inhibitor has penetrated the cells during

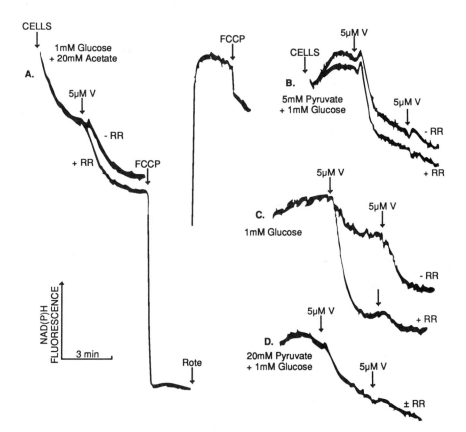

FIGURE 7. Effect on ruthenium red on the response of cardiac myocyte NAD(P)H content to depolarization with veratridine. Myocytes (3.2 mg of protein/ml) were incubated in 2 ml of medium at 37°C in the presence or absence of 25 μM ruthenium red (RR) for 30 min. Cells were then centrifuged and resuspended in 2 ml of fresh medium to give the indicated concentrations of substrates. Additions were as follows: 5 μM veratridine (V), 4 μM FCCP, and 12.5 μM rotenone (Rote). A second addition of FCCP, after rotenone, in A showed the quenching associated with the uncoupling agent itself. Fluorescence of the cell suspension was excited at 333 nm and collected at wavelengths longer than 460 nm; it reflects largely NADH and NADPH.

the preincubation, without the necessity of the plasma membrane permeability properties being compromised in a gross shape change, and prevents the Ca^{2+} signal from reaching the Ca^{2+}-sensitive dehydrogenases within the mitochondrial matrix. There may be a difference in permeability to ruthenium red between isolated myocytes and the intact heart (see above).

Thus, Ca^{2+}-linked activation of the dehydrogenases minimizes the degree to which the $NADH/NAD^+$ ratio falls in this experimental protocol. In the living animal, the action potential of the cardiac myocytes is quite short and $[Ca^{2+}]_c$ is not maintained at an elevated value, as it is in the protocol of FIGURE 7. An increased rate of stimulation or activation is instead signaled to the mitochondria by an increased "time-averaged" $[Ca^{2+}]_c$, resulting from both a more rapid heartbeat and possibly higher systolic transients in $[Ca^{2+}]_c$. The latter may be of particular importance, owing to the profoundly sigmoidal relation between $[Ca^{2+}]_o$ and rates of mitochondrial Ca^{2+} uptake.[17] Evidence is equivocal on whether the $NADH/NAD^+$ ratio, as determined by surface fluorescence of the isolated, intact heart, rises or falls in response to increased stimulation.[11,42] Almost certainly the answer obtained will depend upon the substrate with which the heart is perfused. In this context, recent NMR studies of the *in situ* dog heart revealed no decrease in the ATP/ADP ratio on stimulation with catecholamines.[43] This result, which deserves further experimental scrutiny, suggests that the extra flux through oxidative phosphorylation is being driven by an increased mitochondrial $NADH/NAD^+$ ratio, this being a consequence of the activation by Ca^{2+} of the α-keto acid dehydrogenase complexes.

REFERENCES

1. HANSFORD, R. G. & J. B. CHAPPELL. 1967. Biochem. Biophys. Res. Commun. **27:** 686–692.
2. DENTON, R. M., P. J. RANDLE & B. R. MARTIN. 1972. Biochem. J. **128:** 161–163.
3. PETTIT, F. H., T. E. ROCHE & L. J. REED. 1972. Biochem. Biophys. Res. Commun. **49:** 563–571.
4. DENTON, R. M., D. A. RICHARDS & J. G. CHIN. 1978. Biochem. J. **176:** 899–906.
5. McCORMACK, J. G. & R. M. DENTON. 1979. Biochem. J. **180:** 533–544.
6. HANSFORD, R. G. 1985. Rev. Physiol. Biochem. Pharmacol. **102:** 1–72.
7. DENTON, R. M. & J. G. McCORMACK. 1985. Am. J. Physiol. **249:** E543–E554.
8. RANDLE, P. J., R. M. DENTON, H. T. PASK & D. SEVERSON. 1974. Biochem. Soc. Symp. **39:** 75–87.
9. LAWLIS, V. B. & T. E. ROCHE. 1981. Biochemistry **20:** 2512–2518.
10. HANSFORD, R. G. 1980. Curr. Top. Bioenerg. **10:** 217–278.
11. KATZ, L. A., A. P. KORETSKY & R. S. BALABAN. 1987. FEBS Lett. **221:** 270–276.
12. GRYNKIEWICZ, G., M. POENIE & R. Y. TSIEN. 1985. J. Biol. Chem. **260:** 3440–3450.
13. MORENO-SÁNCHEZ, R. & R. G. HANSFORD. 1988. Biochem. J. **256:** 403–412.
14. HANSFORD, R. G. & E. G. LAKATTA. 1987. J. Physiol. **390:** 453–467.
15. DAVIS, M. H., R. A. ALTSCHULD, D. W. JUNG & G. P. BRIERLEY. 1987. Biochem. Biophys. Res. Commun. **149:** 40–45.
16. GUNTER, T. E., D. RESTREPO & K. K. GUNTER. 1988. Am. J. Physiol. **255:** C304–C310.
17. CROMPTON, M. 1985. Curr. Top. Membr. Transp. **25:** 231–276.
18. CROMPTON, M., M. CAPANO & E. CARAFOLI. 1976. Eur. J. Biochem. **69:** 453–462.
19. HUCHO, F., D. D. RANDALL, T. E. ROCHE, M. W. BURGETT, J. W. PELLEY & L. J. REED. 1972. Arch. Biochem. Biophys. **151:** 328–340.
20. COLL, K. E., S. K. JOSEPH, B. E. CORKEY & J. R. WILLIAMSON. 1982. J. Biol. Chem. **257:** 8696–8704.
21. McCORMACK, J. G. & R. M. DENTON. 1980. Biochem. J. **190:** 95–105.
22. HANSFORD, R. G. & L. COHEN. 1978. Arch. Biochem. Biophys. **191:** 65–81.
23. DENTON, R. M., J. G. McCORMACK & N. J. EDGELL. 1980. Biochem. J. **190:** 107–117.

24. HANSFORD, R. G. 1981. Biochem. J. **194:** 721–732.
25. HONERJÄGER, P. & M. REITER. 1975. Naunyn-Schmiedeberg's Arch. Pharmacol. **289:** 1–28.
26. HORACKOVA, M. & G. VASSORT. 1974. Pfluegers Arch. **352:** 291–302.
27. MOORE, C. L. 1971. Biochem. Biophys. Res. Commun. **42:** 298–305.
28. TSIEN, R. Y., T. POZZAN, & T. J. RINK. 1982. J. Cell Biol. **94:** 325–334.
29. MCCORMACK, J. G. & P. J. ENGLAND. 1983. Biochem. J. **214:** 581–585.
30. ILLINGWORTH, J. A. & R. MULLINGS. 1976. Biochem. Soc. Trans. **4:** 291–292.
31. PEARCE, F. J., E. WALAJTYS-RODE & J. R. WILLIAMSON. 1980. J. Mol. Cell. Cardiol. **12:** 499–510.
32. BÜNGER, R., B. PERMANETTER, O. SOMMER & S. YAFFE. 1982. Am. J. Physiol. **242:** H30–H36.
33. KOBAYASHI, K. & J. R. NEELY. 1983. J. Mol. Cell. Cardiol. **15:** 369–382.
34. MCCORMACK, J. G. & R. M. DENTON. 1981. Biochem. J. **194:** 639–643.
35. LATIPÄÄ, P. M., K. J. PEUHKURINEN, J. K. HILTUNEN & I. E. HASSINEN. 1985. J. Mol. Cell. Cardiol. **17:** 1161–1171.
36. MCCORMACK, J. G. & R. M. DENTON. 1984. Biochem. J. **218:** 235–247.
37. MORENO-SÁNCHEZ, R. 1985. J. Biol. Chem. **260:** 4028–4034.
38. MORENO-SÁNCHEZ, R. 1985. J. Biol. Chem. **260:** 12554–12560.
39. MITCHELL, P. 1979. Eur. J. Biochem. **95:** 1–20.
40. KORETSKY, A. P. & R. S. BALABAN. 1987. Biochim. Biophys. Acta **893:** 398–408.
41. NICHOLLS, D. G. 1978. Biochem. J. **176:** 463–474.
42. ILLINGWORTH, J. A., W. C. L. FORD, K. KOBAYASHI & J. R. WILLIAMSON. 1975. Recent Adv. Stud. Card. Struct. Metab. **8:** 271–290.
43. BALABAN, R. S., H. L. KANTOR, L. A. KATZ & R. W. BRIGGS. 1986. Science **232:** 1121–1123.
44. HANSFORD, R. G. 1987. Biochem. J. **241:** 145–151.
45. NEELY, J. R., H. LIEBERMEISTER, E. J. BATTERSBY & H. E. MORGAN. 1967. Am. J. Physiol. **212:** 804–814.

Targeting of 2-Oxo Acid Dehydrogenase Complexes to the Mitochondrion[a]

J. GORDON LINDSAY

Department of Biochemistry
University of Glasgow
Glasgow G12 8QQ
Scotland, United Kingdom

INTRODUCTION

The complex internal organization of the eukaryotic cell necessitates that nuclear-coded polypeptides, which are synthesized on cytoplasmic ribosomes, must be translocated across one or more internal membranes to their correct intracellular or extracellular destinations.[1,2] In the overall context of intracellular traffic, delivery and import of polypeptides to the mitochondrion is an area of special interest for the following reasons: (*a*) there is a considerable flow of polypeptides to this organelle, which is particularly abundant in tissues such as liver and heart, constituting 10–20% of total cellular protein; (*b*) proteins directed to the surface of the organelle must then be delivered to the proper mitochondrial sublocation, namely, matrix, inner membrane, intermembrane space, or outer membrane, and (*c*) in several cases, assembly of multimeric complexes of the inner membrane, e.g., cytochrome c oxidase, requires the coordinated expression and regulated interplay of the products both of mitochondrial and of nuclear genetic systems.[3]

In the case of the pyruvate dehydrogenase (PDC), 2-oxoglutarate dehydrogenase (OGDC) and branched-chain 2-oxo acid dehydrogenase (BCDC) multienzyme complexes, the individual polypeptides must be nuclear coded, since all the translation products of the mitochondrial genome have been identified as components of the major respiratory chain complexes of the inner membrane involved in oxidative phosphorylation.[4] The high M_r values (2.0–8.5×10^6), organizational complexity, multiple cofactor requirements, and relatively simple polypeptide compositions of these three analogous mitochondrial complexes make them attractive models for studying their biosynthesis, import, processing, and maturation to functional assemblies. PDC, OGDC and BCDC are each composed of multiple copies of three separate enzymes: E1, E2, and E3. A substrate-specific, TPP-requiring dehydrogenase (E1), distinct for each complex, catalyzes the oxidative decarboxylation of the appropriate 2-oxo acid and is responsible for the reductive acylation of covalently bound lipoic acid on lipoamide acyltransferase (E2). These E2 enzymes form the multimeric "core" structures which mediate the eventual transfer of acyl groups to CoASH via a network of interacting lipoyl moieties. Finally, reoxidation of reduced lipoyl groups is promoted by a common, FAD-linked lipoamide dehydrogenase (E3), with the concomitant production of NADH.[5,6]

The transit time for movement of mitochondrial precursor forms into the organelle is short, approximately 5–10 min, leading to difficulties in detection of these precursors. However, translocation is an energy-linked process requiring both ATP[7]

[a]Continued financial support for this work has been provided by SERC, U. K.

254

and an intact electrochemical gradient,[8] $\Delta\mu_{H^+}$, across the inner membrane. Thus, it is possible to promote accumulation of newly synthesized precursors in a reversible manner by incubating mammalian cell cultures in the presence of uncouplers of mitochondrial energy production, e.g., 2,4-dinitrophenol (2,4-DNP) or carbonyl cyanide trifluoromethoxyphenylhydrazone (FCCP).

In this study, an immunological approach is adopted to identify and characterize the initial cytosolic translation products of the constituent enzymes of PDC, OGDC, and BCDC in pig kidney (PK-15), bovine kidney (NBL-1), and Buffalo rat liver (BRL) cells. Some special features of the E2 precursors relating to their variable stabilities, extended presequences, and immunologically distinct conformations are described, as well as differences in the affinity of E3 for the E2 core structure in these cell lines. The possibility that some substages in the formation of these multienzyme complexes occur prior to mitochondrial uptake is also discussed.

MATERIALS AND METHODS

Materials

Pig kidney (PK-15), bovine kidney (NBL-1), and Buffalo rat liver (BRL) cells were all purchased from Flow Laboratories, Irvine, U.K. Routine culturing of cells was performed in Glasgow-modified Eagle's medium supplemented with 10% (v/v) newborn calf serum (BRL cells) or 5% and 10% (v/v) fetal calf serum (PK-15 cells and NBL-1 cells, respectively). Fresh ox hearts and kidneys were generously supplied free of charge by Alan Jess, Boneless Beef Co., Sandyford Abattoir, Paisley, U.K. Pansorbin, a 10% (w/v) suspension of fixed *Staphylococcus aureus* cells, Cowan I strain, standardized for IgG binding capacity in immunoprecipitation studies, was the product of Calbiochem-Behring.

L-[^{35}S]Methionine (1330 Ci/mmol) and Na^{125}I (carrier free) were purchased from Amersham International. N-[2-^{3}H]Ethylmaleimide was the product of New England Nuclear. Methionine-free medium for isotopic incorporation studies was obtained from GIBCO-BRL, Paisley, U.K. X-ray film, either X-Omat S or X-Omat XAR 5, was obtained from Kodak (U.K.).

Lipoamide dehydrogenase (E3) from pig heart was purchased from Calbiochem-Behring. Protein A was obtained from Sigma (G.B.) Ltd., and low-M_r marker proteins from Pharmacia, U.K.

Phenylmethanesulfonyl fluoride, p-aminobenzamidine, 1,10-phenanthroline, leupeptin, and 2,4-dinitrophenol (2,4-DNP) were commercially available from Sigma (G.B.) Ltd. Carbonyl cyanide p-trifluoromethoxyphenylhydrazone (FCCP) came from Aldrich Chemical Company. Iodogen (1,3,4,6-tetrachloro-3α,6α-diphenylglycouril) was bought from Pierce and Warriner (Chester, U.K.)

Preparation of PDC, OGDC, and BCDC and Individual Enzymes or Subunits

PDC and OGDC from bovine heart were purified to near homogeneity ($\geq$95%), essentially as described by Stanley and Perham,[9] with minor modifications.[10] BCDC from bovine kidney was isolated as described by Lawson and co-workers.[11] Enzymic activity for all three multienzyme complexes was assayed by monitoring NADH formation at 340 nm[12] after addition of the appropriate 2-oxoacid substrate. Full details of the methodology for production of antisera to native PDC, OGDC, and the individual gel-purified subunits have been reported previously.[10,13] A similar regime has been employed in the case of BCDC and its constituent polypeptides.

Analysis of Antibody Cross-Reactivity and Specificity by Immunoblotting

Mitochondrial and whole cell extracts and purified multienzyme complexes were resolved on 10% (w/v) SDS-polyacrylamide slab gels, transferred electrophoretically onto nitrocellulose paper, and processed for the detection of immune complexes with ^{125}I-labeled protein A, as reported in earlier publications.[10,13,14]

Metabolic Labeling of Cultured Mammalian Cells, Immunoprecipitation, and Fluorography

Incubation conditions for metabolic incorporation of [35S]methionine into cultured mammalian cells and accumulation of mitochondrial precursor "pools" have been described previously.[14] Immunoprecipitation protocols were adapted from a method originally devised by Mosmann *et al.*[15] SDS-polyacrylamide gel electrophoresis and fluorographic analyses were performed on 10% (w/v) slab gels, basically employing the Laemmli gel system. Fluorographic detection of newly synthesized polypeptides was achieved by the method of Chamberlain.[16] The procedure for preparation of N-[3H]ethylmaleimide–modified PDC and OGDC for use as M_r markers has been reported previously.[10]

RESULTS

For analysis of molecular events in the biosynthesis, targeting, and assembly of PDC, OGDC, and BCDC, a range of antisera was first produced to the native, intact complexes with the purity and polypeptide compositions shown in FIGURE 1. Subunit M_r values for the mature polypeptides in each complex were determined by estimation of their mobilities on SDS-polyacrylamide gels (Laemmli gel system) with reference to a set of calibrated M_r marker proteins. In all cases, comparisons were made on the same gel and M_r estimates represent an average of three values differing by no more than ± 1000. The final list of M_r determinations was (*a*) PDC (FIG. 1, lane 5): E2, 70,000; E3, 55,000; protein X, 51,000; E1α, 42,000; and E1β, 36,000; (*b*) OGDC (lane 3): E1, 96,000; E3, 55,000; and E2, 48,000; (*c*) BCDC (lane 4): E2, 50,000; E1α, 46,000; and E1β, 37,000. These M_r values are similar to those reported previously in the literature, except for the E2 of BCDC, which exhibited a slightly higher mobility than expected, i.e., 50,000 M_r compared to the reported M_r of 52,000.[11] As seen in FIGURE 1, this polypeptide migrates slightly ahead of protein X of PDC, which has been reported previously to have an M_r value of 51,000 $\pm$ 1000.[10] It should be noted that BCDC, prepared according to Lawson *et al.*,[11] contains little or no detectable E3. Thus, E3 has to be added to the assay mixture, otherwise only low levels (5–10% of maximum) of BCDC activity can be measured.

A surprising feature of antibodies raised to intact PDC or OGDC is that the E3 component is found to induce a negligible immune response relative to the other subunits.[10] This phenomenon can be attributed to a high degree of conservation of the common E3 enzyme, a fact confirmed recently from comparative nucleotide sequence analysis of the *Escherichia coli*,[17] *Saccharomyces cerevisiae*,[18] and human[19] E3 genes.

For more detailed study of individual precursors, a comprehensive range of antisera was produced to the constituent enzymes of the complexes or to their gel-purified subunits, e.g., protein X and the E1α and E1β polypeptides of PDC and BCDC. In the case of E3, it was possible to produce a high-titer antibody to the native enzyme by administering a large amount (5–10 mg) of lipoamide dehydrogenase to rabbits in a series of subcutaneous and intramuscular injections.

Examples of the quality of antisera produced by these procedures, as exhibited by their high sensitivity and specificity in immunoblotting, are illustrated in FIGURES 2 and 3, in which mitochondrial and cellular extracts (FIGS. 2B, 2D, and 3A: Coomassie blue–stained profiles) from several permanent cell lines are probed by immune replica analysis with a variety of subunit-specific antisera. In FIGURES 2A and 2C, immune complex formation is shown with anti-E2– (PDC) and anti-E1α– (PDC) specific sera, respectively, while FIGURES 3B and 3C depict similar profiles with anti-E1β (PDC) and anti-E3 sera, respectively. In each case, the respective polyclonal serum cross-reacts exclusively with the parent antigen, even in SDS extracts of whole cells. Differing M_r values for the E2 subunit (FIG. 2A), in particular, are evident, with a lower M_r form of the enzyme observed in BRL cells in comparison with bovine or

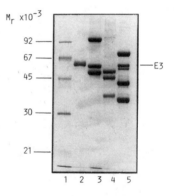

FIGURE 1. Comparison of subunit compositions and estimation of M_r values of the constituent polypeptides of PDC, OGDC and BCDC. Samples of purified pig heart E3, bovine heart PDC and OGDC, and bovine kidney BCDC were subjected to electrophoresis on 10% (w/v) SDS-polyacrylamide slab gels and stained with Coomassie blue. Lane 1, low M_r marker proteins; lane 2, pig heart E3 (4 μg); lane 3, OGDC (10 μg); lane 4, BCDC (10 μg); lane 5, PDC (15 μg).

porcine cell lines. This finding is consistent with the previously reported M_r of 68,000 for E2 in purified rat liver PDC as opposed to 70–74,000 for the ox heart complex.[20] Lack of reactivity of our subunit-specific E2 antiserum with the 51,000 M_r species (protein X) always observed in pure PDC preparations was one of the early indications that protein X was a distinct lipoyl-bearing polypeptide and not a degradation product of E2, as supposed previously.[13,21,22] The precise function of protein X is currently under active investigation.[23]

It is also clear that PDC subunits are expressed at high levels in these three cell lines, confirming their suitability for *in vivo* studies on biosynthesis, targeting, and assembly. Similar immunoblotting analyses were conducted with anti-OGDC and anti-BCDC sera (not shown), again revealing that both multienzyme complexes were readily detectable in these cultured mammalian cells.

Precursor levels of the constituent subunits of PDC, OGDC, and BCDC were enhanced by accumulating cytoplasmic pools of these polypeptides in 2,4-DNP or FCCP-inhibited cell cultures incubated in the presence of [^{35}S]methionine. Specific detection was achieved by fluorographic analysis of the immunoprecipitated product(s) after resolution on SDS-polyacrylamide gels. In FIGURE 4A, the pre-E1 (lanes 1

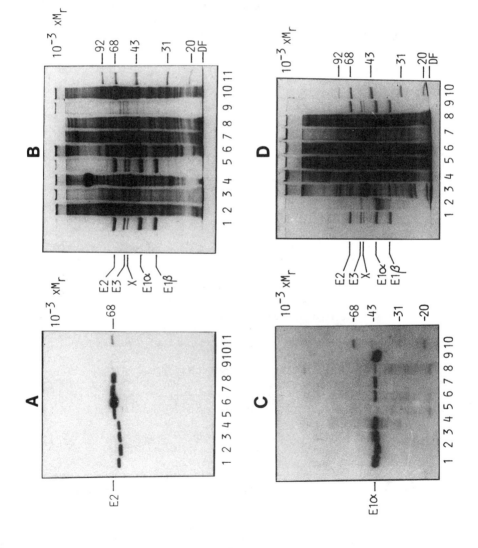

FIGURE 2. Immunoblotting analysis of dihydrolipoyl acetyltransferase (E2) and pyruvate dehydrogenase (E1α subunit) of PDC in mitochondrial and cellular extracts. Purified PDC and various cell extracts were resolved by electrophoresis on 10% (w/v) SDS-polyacrylamide slab gels, which were used for immunoblotting analysis with antiserum raised against the E2 subunit (A), or the E1α subunit (C); parallel gels were stained with Coomassie blue (B and D). **Panels A and B:** (*lanes 1 and 5*) PDC, 0.1 μg (A) or 12 μg (B) protein; (*lane 2*) SDS extract of BRL cells, 80 μg (A) or 60 μg (B); (*lane 3*) BRL mitochondria, 40 μg; (*lane 4*) rat liver mitochondria, 40 μg; (*lane 6*) ox heart mitochondria, 15 μg (A) or 50 μg (B); (*lane 7*) SDS extract of NBL-1 cells, 80 μg (A) or 50 μg (B); (*lane 8*) SDS extract of PK-15 cells, 80 μg (A) or 50 μg (B); (*lane 9*) PK-15 mitochondria, 20 μg; (*lane 10*) PK-15 cytosol, 60 μg; (*lane 11*) ¹²⁵I-labeled M_r markers. **Panels C and D:** (*lanes 1 and 9*) PDC, 1 μg protein (C) or 12 μg (D); (*lane 2*) partially purified subunit E1α, 0.2 μg (C) or 3 μg (D); (*lane 3*) ox heart mitochondria, 40 μg; (*lane 4*) rat liver mitochondria, 80 μg (C) or 50 μg (D); (*lane 5*) SDS extract of NBL-1 cells, 90 μg (C) or 70 μg (D); (*lane 6*) SDS extract of BRL cells, 80 μg; (*lane 7*) BRL mitochondria, 60 μg; (*lane 8*) SDS extract of PK-15 cells, 120 μg (C) or 80 μg (D); (*lane 10*) ¹²⁵I-labeled M_r markers. DF, dye front.

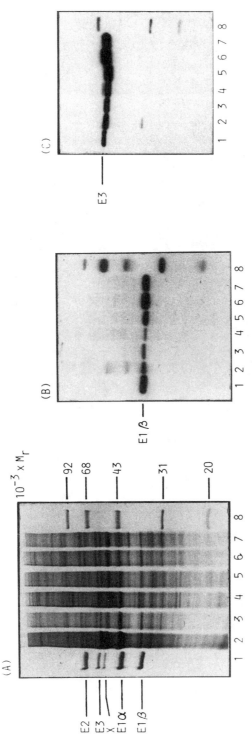

FIGURE 3. Immunological detection of PDC subunit E1β and lipoamide dehydrogenase (E3) in various cell extracts. Samples of purified PDC and cell extracts from cultured cells were subjected to electrophoresis on a 10% (w/v) SDS-polyacrylamide gel. Proteins resolved were transferred onto nitrocellulose paper and employed for immunoblotting analysis with antisera to the E1β subunit (**B**) or to the E3 enzyme (**C**). A similar gel was stained with Coomassie blue (**A**). **Panels A, B, and C:** (*lane 1*) PDC: 12 μg (**A**), 0.25 μg (**B**), and 1 μg protein (**C**); (*lane 2*) SDS extract of NBL-1 cells: 60 μg (**A**), 40 μg (**B**), and 40 μg (**C**); (*lane 3*) NBL-1 mitochondria: 50 μg (**A**), 40 μg (**B**), and 40 μg (**C**); (*lane 4*) SDS extract of BRL cells: 60 μg; (*lane 5*) BRL mitochondria: 50 μg; (*lane 6*) SDS extract of PK-15 cells: 60 μg; (*lane 7*) PK-15 mitochondria: 50 μg; (*lane 8*) ¹²⁵I-labeled M_r standards.

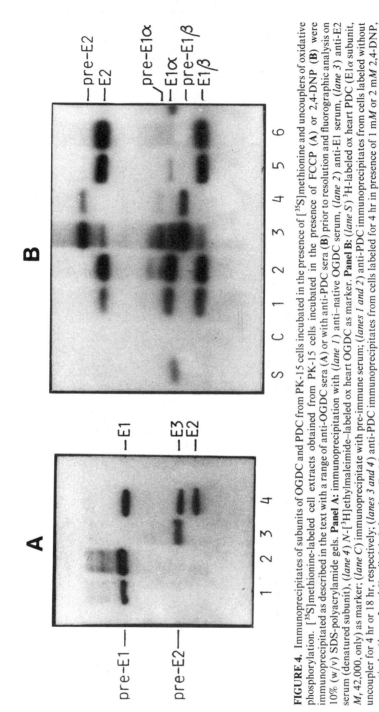

FIGURE 4. Immunoprecipitates of subunits of OGDC and PDC from PK-15 cells incubated in the presence of [^{35}S]methionine and uncouplers of oxidative phosphorylation. [^{35}S]methionine-labeled cell extracts obtained from PK-15 cells incubated in the presence of FCCP (**A**) or 2,4-DNP (**B**) were immunoprecipitated as described in the text with a range of anti-OGDC sera (**A**) or with anti-PDC sera (**B**) prior to resolution and fluorographic analysis on 10% (w/v) SDS-polyacrylamide gels. **Panel A:** immunoprecipitation with (*lane 1*) anti–native OGDC serum, (*lane 2*) anti-E1 serum, (*lane 3*) anti-E2 serum (denatured subunit), (*lane 4*) N-[^{3}H]ethylmaleimide–labeled ox heart OGDC as marker. **Panel B:** (*lane S*) ^{3}H-labeled ox heart PDC (E1α subunit, M_r 42,000, only) as marker; (*lane C*) immunoprecipitate with pre-immune serum; (*lanes 1 and 2*) anti-PDC immunoprecipitates from cells labeled without uncoupler for 4 hr or 18 hr, respectively; (*lanes 3 and 4*) anti-PDC immunoprecipitates from cells labeled for 4 hr in presence of 1 mM or 2 mM 2,4-DNP, respectively; (*lanes 5 and 6*) cells labeled as described for *lanes 3 and 4*, then "chased" for 40 min in fresh, non-radioactive medium without 2,4-DNP.

and 2) and pre-E2 (lane 3) states of OGDC are shown to have M_r values of 98,000 and 56,000 compared to 96,000 and 48,000 for the respective mature species. Immunoprecipitation of the precursor form of the lipoate succinyltransferase (core) enzyme (E2) is possible only with IgG raised to the mature, denatured E2 polypeptide (lane 3), whereas IgG directed against native OGDC, which cross-reacts with both E1 and E2 components on immunoblots,[10] is ineffective (lane 2). Confirmation of the identity of the higher M_r products as the appropriate precursor states of E1 and E2 was gained (a) by monitoring their conversion to the mature polypeptides after removal of uncoupler and (b) by immunocompetition studies in which immune complex formation was induced after addition of competing amounts of purified non-radioactive enzyme.[14]

A similar example is depicted in FIGURE 4B, illustrating the appearance of pre-E2, pre-E1α, and pre-E1β forms of PDC in PK-15 cells incubated for 4 hr in the presence of [^{35}S]methionine and 1 mM or 2 mM 2,4-DNP (lanes 3 and 4). At intermediate levels of uncoupler (1 mM), processing is only partially arrested, as evidenced by the simultaneous appearance of newly synthesized precursor and mature forms of the subunits. Similar results can be achieved employing 5 μM or 10 μM FCCP to dissipate the mitochondrial membrane potential. Rapid processing of cytosolic precursors to mitochondrially located native enzymes occurs within 30 min when cultures are incubated in fresh medium minus 2,4-DNP and in the presence of excess, non-radioactive methionine (lanes 5 and 6). In each case, identification of individual precursor polypeptides was confirmed by immunocompetition analysis and immunoprecipitation with the relevant subunit-specific antiserum. As for OGDC, the pre-E2 of PDC showed a greatly reduced mobility on SDS-polyacrylamide gels, exhibiting an apparent M_r value of 77,000 $\pm$ 1000, compared to 70,000 for mature E2. Independent precursors for both the E1α, M_r 42,000, and E1β, M_r 36,000, subunits of pyruvate dehydrogenase (E1) could be detected, with apparent M_r values of 44,500 and 39,000, respectively.

Successful accumulation of a large number of mitochondrial precursors in the cytoplasmic compartment over a period of 3–4 hr implies that the majority of these initial products of translation are stable, since they are not rapidly degraded when import into mitochondria is prevented by the action of uncouplers. In FIGURE 5A, the appearance of PDC precursors is monitored in rat liver (BRL) cells and their relative stabilities are assessed by further incubation of 2,4-DNP–inhibited cultures for 1–3 hr after replacement of [^{35}S]methionine-containing medium with fresh medium containing excess unlabeled methionine. It is clear that the pre-E2, pre-E1α, and pre-E1β species are retained in the cytoplasm and are only slowly degraded, to approximately equal extents, over a period of several hours. They also remain in a translocation-competent state, since rapid processing to mature polypeptides occurs on removal of 2,4-DNP (not shown). In contrast, the pre-E1α of PDC is much less stable in PK-15 cells, where it is only poorly accumulated and is often aberrantly processed on release of inhibitor.[24] In NBL-1 cells, the pre-E2 of BCDC is so rapidly degraded that no significant accumulation of this species can be achieved; however, it is readily detectable and quite stable in PK-15 cells (G. H. D. Clarkson, unpublished observations).

Immunoprecipitates of intact PDC from BRL cells contain an extra polypeptide, M_r 55,000, which was identified as the lipoamide dehydrogenase (E3) component by immunocompetition studies. Variations in the affinity of E3 for intact PDC have been observed in PK-15 and NBL-1 cells by employing anti-PDC sera which have no detectable titer of antibody to this component.[24] Thus, this enzyme is precipitated in some cases by virtue of its physical association with the E2 core assembly. In FIGURE 5A, however, the anti-PDC serum was from a late bleed after multiple boosts of the rabbit with PDC, which had induced a significant level of antibody to E3, as evidenced

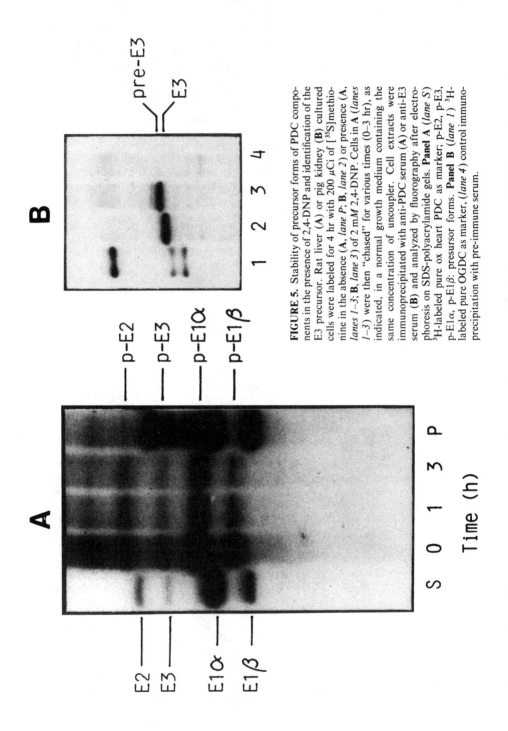

FIGURE 5. Stability of precursor forms of PDC components in the presence of 2,4-DNP and identification of the E3 precursor. Rat liver (**A**) or pig kidney (**B**) cultured cells were labeled for 4 hr with 200 μCi of [³⁵S]methionine in the absence (**A**, *lane P*; **B**, *lane 2*) or presence (**A**, *lanes 1–3*; **B**, *lane 3*) of 2 mM 2,4-DNP. Cells in A (*lanes 1–3*) were then "chased" for various times (0–3 hr), as indicated, in a normal growth medium containing the same concentration of uncoupler. Cell extracts were immunoprecipitated with anti-PDC serum (**A**) or anti-E3 serum (**B**) and analyzed by fluorography after electrophoresis on SDS-polyacrylamide gels. **Panel A** (*lane S*) ³H-labeled pure ox heart PDC as marker; p-E2, p-E3, p-E1α, p-E1β: presursor forms. **Panel B** (*lane 1*) ³H-labeled pure OGDC as marker, (*lane 4*) control immunoprecipitation with pre-immune serum.

by immunoblotting analysis. Specific detection of the precursor of this enzyme (FIGURE 5B) was accomplished by employing subunit-specific IgG raised to purified pig heart E3. Pre-E3 has an apparent M_r value of 57,000, indicating the presence of an amino-terminal presequence of approximately M_r 2000, in close agreement with the size predicted from sequence analysis of the human E3 gene.[19]

TABLE 1 provides a comprehensive survey of the apparent subunit M_r values of the precursor and mature forms of the constituent enzymes of each of these three multienzyme complexes. All of the individual subunits of the distinct substrate-specific dehydrogenases (E1) and the common E3 enzyme examined to date are synthesized initially as higher M_r forms with presequences in the M_r range of 2000–3000, i.e., approximately 15–25 amino acids in length. An interesting feature is that cytoplasmic forms of all three separate lipoate acyltransferase (E2) "core" enzymes have lengthy

TABLE 1. Comparison of the M_r Values of Precursor and Mature Forms of the Constituent Polypeptides of PDC, OGDC and BCDC

	Apparent M_r Value[a]	
Polypeptide	Mature Form	Precursor Form
E1		
PDC: α	42,000	44,500
PDC: β	36,000	39,000
OGDC	96,000	98,000
BCDC: α	46,000	49,000
BCDC: β	37,000	N.D.
E2		
PDC	70,000[b]	77,000[b]
OGDC	48,000	56,000
BCDC	50,000	56,500
E3	55,000	57,000
Protein X: PDC	51,000	N.D.

[a]All values, averaged from 3 separate determinations of samples from bovine or pig kidney cells, differed by ± 1000 or less. M_r values were estimated by SDS-polyacrylamide gel electrophoresis; further details can be found in the MATERIALS AND METHODS section and additional references.[14,24] Data on precursors to BCDC polypeptides were from unpublished observations (G. H.D. Clarkson & J. G. Lindsay). N.D., not detected.

[b]In rat liver cells, these values correspond to 68,000 and 76,000 ± 1000 for the mature and precursor forms, respectively.

presequences in the M_r range of 6000–8000, indicating a specialized function for these signal sequences in addition to that of directing mitochondrial import. No precursor states of the E1β subunit of BCDC and of protein X of PDC could be detected in either PK-15 or NBL-1 cells. In the case of the E1β of BCDC, this result reflected the weak titer of antibody raised to this polypeptide, whereas for protein X, additional factors may include its low abundance relative to its companion PDC subunits and its low methionine content.

DISCUSSION

Biosynthesis and maturation of multimeric complexes such as PDC, OGDC and BCDC is necessarily a multistage process involving an ordered sequence of molecular events, which are only understood in general terms at present. Data included in this paper represent our initial efforts in a more detailed investigation of the underlying mechanisms leading to the formation of intact, functional assemblies in the mitochondrial matrix/inner membrane compartment. Like the majority of mitochondrial precursors, the initial cytosolic translation products of the three multienzyme complexes each contain amino-terminal extensions which are proteolytically cleaved, apparently in a single-step process, during, or shortly after, entry into the organelle.

The most striking feature in examining the nature of these precursors is the presence of extended presequences on each of the distinctive lipoate acyltransferase enzymes, which comprise the 60-meric (PDC) or 24-meric (OGDC, BCDC) multisubunit core structures to which tetrameric or dimeric E1 and dimeric E3 enzymes are attached in the native complexes. This observation has been confirmed directly in the case of BCDC by nucleotide sequence analysis of cDNA clones of the human/bovine E1 genes, isolated by immunological screening of expression libraries,[25] housed in λ phage.

Mitochondrial presequences in general exhibit considerable variability in size, with a range of M_r 1500–10,000. There are several indications that elongated signal sequences contain information additional to that which is present in the short (20–25 amino acid) amino-terminal sequence—normally all that is required for targeting the precursor to the organelle. Since it appears that all mitochondrial precursors are preprogrammed by their amphiphilic amino-terminal sequences to be delivered into the matrix compartment,[26] hydrophobic "location" sequences must also be present at an appropriate region in the presequence, distal to the amino-terminus, to direct polypeptides to the intermembrane space, the outer, or the inner membrane.[27] In one case, subunit 9 of the mitochondrial ATP synthetase complex, the protein is synthesized with a 66 amino acid amino-terminal sequence which is very basic and hydrophilic, apparently maintaining this small (81 amino acid), hydrophobic polypeptide in a soluble state during its passage through the cytoplasm to the mitochondrial surface.[28]

In the case of the three lipoate acyltransferase enzymes, a specific property of this group of polypeptides is that they are required to assemble into complex multimeric "core" structures, presumably after proteolytic removal of the amino-terminal presequence, shortly after uptake into the mitochondrion. Immunological data for the pre-E2 of OGDC have demonstrated that antibody raised to native E2 fails to recognize the precursor form of this enzyme, which is readily immunoprecipitated, however, by antibody raised to the denatured E2 subunit. This finding is consistent with the idea that the pre-E2 of OGDC exists in a dissimilar conformation to the native, aggregated "core" assembly, since antibody to a native enzyme is elicited primarily against noncontiguous, three-dimensional epitopes on the surface of the polypeptide, while antibody raised to the denatured protein is predominantly against linear (5–8 amino acids) sequence elements.[29] Thus, the elongated presequences on E2 precursors may limit the tendency of these polypeptides to form aggregates prior to mitochondrial uptake by promoting formation of a stable conformational state which is distinct to that found in the functional E2 core assembly.

Recent attention has also focused on the necessity for newly synthesized precursors to be maintained in a loosely-folded, translocation-competent state to facilitate their movement across mitochondrial and other internal membranes, e.g., the endoplasmic reticulum.[30] It appears that proteins belonging to a class of well-documented, highly conserved polypeptides known as heat shock proteins, exhibiting ATP-dependent "unfoldase" activity, may be essential for promoting formation of this translocation-competent state.[31,32] It is unclear whether interaction with elongated E2 signal sequences may be important in mediating this process. It will be interesting to determine if any substages in the assembly of E2 core structure, e.g., the interaction of pre-E2 to form trimers, occur in the cytoplasm, since a number of mitochondrial precursors, e.g., the adenine nucleotide translocase,[33] are found in oligomeric states at this stage. In this connection, preliminary evidence from this laboratory indicates that the pre-E1α and pre-E1β forms of PDC and BCDC may associate strongly prior to uptake into the mitochondrion.

Current research is concerned with elucidating at a molecular level the sequence of molecular events involved in the targeting, maturation, and assembly of these three multienzyme complexes. At present, our major objectives are (*a*) to examine whether addition of specific cofactors, e.g., lipoic acid, represents an obligatory step in the processing/assembly pathway, as is the case for heme insertion into cytochromes c and c$_1$,[34,35] and (*b*) to investigate the role of cytosolic and intramitochondrial protein factors in guiding the delivery and ordered assembly of these complicated multimeric aggregates.

ACKNOWLEDGMENTS

J. G. L. gratefully acknowledges the major contributions made to this work by three successive Ph.D. students—one for each complex—Olga G. L. De Marcucci (PDC), Anne Hunter (OGDC), and George H. D. Clarkson (BCDC).

REFERENCES

1. REID, G. A. 1985. Curr. Top. Membr. Transp. **24:** 295–336.
2. PFANNER, N. & W. NEUPERT. 1987. Curr. Top. Bioenerg. **15:** 177–219.
3. HAY, R., P. BOHNI & S. GASSER. 1984. Biochim. Biophys. Acta **779:** 65–87.
4. CHOMYN, A., P. MARIOTTINI, M. W. J. CLEETER, C. J. RAGAN, A. MATSUNO-YAGI, Y. HATEFI, R. F. DOOLITTLE & G. ATTARDI. 1985. Nature **314:** 592–597.
5. REED, L. J. 1984. Acc. Chem. Res. **7:** 40–46.
6. YEAMAN, S. J. 1986. Trends Biochem. Sci. **11:** 293–296.
7. CHEN, W-J. & M. G. DOUGLAS. 1987. Cell **49:** 651–658.
8. GASSER, S. M., G. DAUM & G. SCHATZ. 1982. J. Biol. Chem. **257:** 13034–13041.
9. STANLEY, C. & R. N. PERHAM. 1980. Biochem. J. **191:** 147–154.
10. DE MARCUCCI, O. G. L., A. HUNTER & J. G. LINDSAY. 1985. Biochem. J. **226:** 509–517.
11. LAWSON, R., K. G. COOK & S. J. YEAMAN. 1983. FEBS Lett. **157:** 54–58.
12. BROWN, C. R. & R. N. PERHAM. 1976. Biochem. J. **155:** 419–427.
13. DE MARCUCCI, O. G. L. & J. G. LINDSAY. 1985. Eur. J. Biochem. **149:** 641–648.
14. HUNTER A. & J. G. LINDSAY. 1986. Eur. J. Biochem. **155:** 103–109.
15. MOSMANN, T. R., R. BOWMAL & A. R. WILLIAMSON. 1979. J. Immunol. **9:** 511–516.
16. CHAMBERLAIN, J. 1979. Anal. Biochem. **98:** 132–135.
17. STEPHENS, P. E., H. M. LEWIS, M. G. DARLISON & J. R. GUEST. 1983. Eur. J. Biochem. **135:** 219–297.
18. BROWNING, K. S., O. J. UHLINGER & L. J. REED. 1988. Proc. Natl. Acad. Sci. USA **85:** 1821–1824.
19. PONS, G., C. RAEFSKY-ESTRIN, D. J. CAROTHERS, R. A. PEPIN, A. A. JAVED, B. W. JESSE, M. K. GANAPATHI, D. SAMOLS & M. S. PATEL. 1988. Proc. Natl. Acad. Sci. USA **85:** 1422–1426.
20. MATUDA, S., T. SHIRAMA, T. SAHEKI, S. MIURA & M. MORI. 1983. Biochim. Biophys. Acta **741:** 86–93.
21. DE MARCUCCI, O. G. L., J. A. HODGSON & J. G. LINDSAY. 1986. Eur. J. Biochem. **158:** 587–594.
22. HODGSON, J. A., O. G. L. DE MARCUCCI & J. G. LINDSAY. 1986. Eur. J. Biochem. **158:** 595–600.

23. HODGSON, J. S., O. G. L. DE MARCUCCI & J. G. LINDSAY. 1986. Eur. J. Biochem. **171:** 609–614.
24. DE MARCUCCI, O. G. L., G. M. GIBB, J. DICK & J. G. LINDSAY. 1988. Biochem. J. **251:** 817–823.
25. LAU, K. S., T. A. GRIFFIN, C-W. W. HU & D. T. CHUANG. 1988. Biochemistry **27:** 1972–1981.
26. HASE, T., O. MULLER, H. REIZMAN & G. SCHATZ. 1984. EMBO J. **3:** 3157–3164.
27. HURT, E. C., B. PESOLD-HURT, K. SUDA, W. OPPLINGER & G. SCHATZ. 1985. EMBO J. **4:** 2961–2968.
28. VIEBROCK, A., A. PERZ & W. SEBALD. 1982. EMBO J. **1:** 565–571.
29. WESTHOF, E., D. ALTSCHUCH, D. MORAS, A. C. BLOOMER, A. MONDRAGON, A. KLUG & M. H. V. VAN REGENMORTEL. 1984. Nature **311:** 123–126.
30. EILERS, M. & G. SCHATZ. 1986. Nature **322:** 228–232.
31. DESHAIES, R. J., B. D. KOCH, M. WERNER-WASHBURNE, E. A. CRAIG & R. SCHEKMAN. 1988. Nature **322:** 800–805.
32. CHIRICO, W., G. WATER & G. BLOBEL. 1988. Nature **332:** 805–810.
33. ZIMMERMAN, R. & W. NEUPERT. 1980. Eur. J. Biochem. **109:** 217–229.
34. OHASHI, A., J. GIBSON, I. GREGOR & G. SCHATZ. 1982. J. Biol. Chem. **257:** 13042–13047.
35. HENNIG, B. & W. NEUPERT. 1981. Eur. J. Biochem. **81:** 533–544.

Chairman's Remarks

Thoughts on the Role of Branched-Chain α-Keto Acid Dehydrogenase Complex in Nitrogen Metabolism

ALFRED E. HARPER[a]

Departments of Biochemistry and Nutritional Sciences
College of Agricultural and Life Sciences
University of Wisconsin-Madison
Madison, Wisconsin 53706

The group of papers following these introductory remarks deals with nutritional and hormonal control of α-keto acid dehydrogenase complexes. The activities of these enzyme complexes and the flux of substrate through them are controlled by a variety of regulatory mechanisms, several of which have been described in the preceding papers of this volume. These mechanisms respond to changes in the nutritional and hormonal state of the organism. The basis for some of these responses is described in the papers to follow in this section.

From 50% to 80% of the energy sources in the diets of omnivores must be channeled through the pyruvate dehydrogenase system. For the human adult, this represents 250–400 g of glucose each day; yet, during periods without food and especially during starvation, glucose conservation is essential. The reaction of the pyruvate dehydrogenase complex, which commits pyruvate to oxidation or channeling into lipids or steroids, is essentially irreversible. Continued flux through this pathway during periods of carbohydrate deprivation could lead to depletion of the body pool of glucose. Although glucose can be synthesized from amino acids and intermediates of the glycolytic pathway, reserves of these precursors are limited. Erythrocytes and the renal medulla have an absolute requirement for glucose; nerve cells also have an obligatory requirement for glucose, at least until blood concentrations of ketone bodies rise enough to reduce this need.[1] It is not surprising, therefore, that a highly sensitive system of regulatory mechanisms should have evolved for control of the pyruvate dehydrogenase complex, which is central in the metabolic pathway by which organisms derive energy from carbohydrate.

It should also not be surprising that a shift from the fed-to-starved or starved-to-fed state should initiate regulatory responses of the pyruvate dehydrogenase system, as described by SUGDEN, or that insulin should be involved, as discussed in the papers by WIELAND and by DENTON.

It is much more difficult to understand, in fact it seems almost incongruous, that a similar intricate regulatory system has evolved for control of the catabolism of the branched-chain amino acids. The papers by HARRIS and by HUTSON provide considerable detail about this system. The branched-chain α-keto acid dehydrogenase complex is involved primarily, although its specificity is not absolute,[2] in the oxidation of the carbon skeletons of only the three branched-chain amino acids. These comprise about 20% of most dietary proteins. In usual human diets they provide only about 80 of the

[a]Address correspondence to Dr. A. E. Harper, Department of Biochemistry, University of Wisconsin-Madison, 420 Henry Mall, Madison, WI 53706.

1500–3000 kcal of energy derived daily by human adults from food and not more than 2.5–5.0% of potential dietary energy sources. This raises a question, if one accepts parsimony as a guiding principle in the process of evolution, as to what function is served by having an intricate regulatory system, comparable to that for a key step in the major pathway of energy utilization, for the catabolism of a small group of amino acids.

Pathways for the catabolism of most indispensable amino acids are confined to the liver. With the possible exceptions of the pathways for degradation of phenylalanine and tryptophan—precursors of a variety of aromatic compounds, including neurotransmitters—these catabolic pathways do not have elaborate controls. Flux of amino acids through these pathways depends primarily on substrate concentration and on the concentration of the initial degradative enzyme. The initial reaction in the degradation of most indispensable amino acids is essentially irreversible, and surpluses of them are oxidized rapidly by the liver, even in preference to glucose. The remainder, after passing through the liver, are degraded little, if at all, in peripheral tissues and therefore remain available for synthesis of proteins throughout the body.[3]

Catabolism of the branched-chain amino acids differs in several respects from that of the other indispensable amino acids. The enzymes for degradation of the branched-chain amino acids are distributed ubiquitously in tissues throughout the body rather than being confined primarily to the liver. The initial step in their degradation is a highly reversible transamination. The activity of the branched-chain aminotransferase is low in liver but high in other organs and tissues, so a high proportion of the branched-chain amino acids pass through the liver unaltered, to be degraded in peripheral tissues, especially muscle.[4]

With a highly active branched-chain aminotransferase distributed widely throughout the body, continued flux of substrate through this enzyme, with subsequent oxidation of the α-keto acids formed, would create the potential for depletion of the carbon skeletons of the branched-chain amino acids, which cannot be synthesized by the body. As deficiencies of branched-chain amino acids do not occur, even in animals with a low protein intake, regulation of the branched-chain α-keto acid dehydrogenase complex, the enzyme system catalyzing the second step in branched-chain amino acid catabolism, apparently provides a conservation mechanism which prevents depletion of these essential carbon skeletons, just as regulation of the pyruvate dehydrogenase complex provides a conservation mechanism which prevents depletion of glucose during starvation. In fact, in studies on intact animals using doubly labeled leucine, up to 80% of the branched-chain α-keto acids formed during transamination are found to be reaminated.[5,6]

If the complex regulatory system for control of branched-chain amino acid catabolism had evolved only as a mechanism which prevented depletion of the essential carbon skeletons of the branched-chain amino acids, thereby conserving them as substrates for protein synthesis in peripheral tissues, restriction of the catabolic pathway to the liver, with regulation being accomplished merely through substrate control (K_m control), would have provided a more parsimonious evolutionary solution. That this unique regulatory system did evolve raises a further question as to whether it does not serve some additional function.

I would suggest that catabolism of the branched-chain amino acids, with branched-chain α-keto acid dehydrogenase complex as a key regulatory enzyme, plays a critical, central role in nitrogen metabolism in the body. I shall return to this point, but first I should like to change direction and turn away for a few moments from the major interest of this volume, carbon metabolism, and shift toward the metabolism of nitrogen and some interactions of branched-chain amino acids in the body.

TABLE 1. Arterial Concentrations and Arteriovenous Differences (A-V) in Concentrations of Amino Acids in Blood Across the Forearm of Human Subjects after Ingestion of Meat Providing 50 g of Protein[a]

Amino Acid	Arterial Concentration (mmol/l)		A-V Difference (mmol/l)	
	Basal[b]	60–150 min (Ave)	Basal[b]	60–150 min (Ave)
Leu	119	265	−2	+33
Ile	69	163	−8	+20
Val	204	336	−2	+17
Glu	175	195	+16	+24
Gln	558	633	−39	−42
Ala	244	348	−39	−6
$\sum$ 5 AA[c]	611	739	−26	−4
Lys + Arg	260	476	−7	+20

[a]Based on values from Felig.[8]
[b]Basal: after overnight fast.
[c]$\sum$ 5 AA: sum of values for Gly, Tyr, Phe, His, and Trp.

Most of the branched-chain amino acids absorbed from the intestine pass through the liver, owing to the low activity of the branched-chain aminotransferase there,[7] and are transported to other organs.[8] Blood concentrations of branched-chain amino acids rise more after a meal than do those of most other amino acids (TABLE 1). Muscle, which makes up 40% of body weight, takes up branched-chain amino acids readily. They account for about 50% of the amino acids taken up by muscle.[8–10]

The initial step in the metabolism of the branched-chain amino acids taken up by muscle, transamination, generates branched-chain α-keto acids, the substrates for the reaction of the branched-chain α-keto acid dehydrogenase complex, and glutamate (FIG. 1, upper left). Glutamate can undergo transamination with pyruvate and

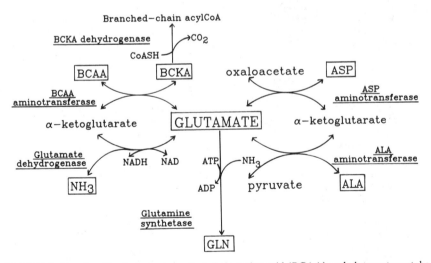

FIGURE 1. Relationships between branched-chain amino acid (BCAA) and glutamate metabolism. BCKA, branched-chain α-keto acids.

oxaloacetate to yield alanine and aspartic acid, respectively, and amidation, which produces glutamine. It can also provide ammonia, through the glutamate dehydrogenase reaction, for glutamine synthesis. Thus, nitrogen from the branched-chain amino acids can be channeled readily into several key intermediates of nitrogen metabolism in the body.

I should now like to extend this excursion in order to examine the roles played by glutamate and glutamine in nitrogen metabolism generally in the body. During absorption from the intestine, glutamate and glutamine undergo catabolism. They serve as major energy sources for this organ.[11] Their nitrogen is released into the portal blood largely in alanine, where it is removed highly efficiently by the liver.[12] As a result, the blood pools of glutamate and aspartate are small, only about 0.2 mmol/l, and arteriovenous difference measurements (TABLE 1) indicate that the amount of glutamate taken up by muscle after a meal represents only about 17% of total amino acid uptake; aspartate uptake is much less.[9] Intracellular pools of glutamate and glutamine in muscle, however, are large; the glutamine pool can be as high as 20 mM and amount totally to as much as 365 mmol.[13] In view of the low glutamate uptake into muscle, the glutamate and glutamine in the intracellular pools must be largely synthesized *in situ*.

Also, alanine and glutamine are released continuously from muscle.[8,9,14] About 60% of the total nitrogen released by muscle is in the form of glutamine and alanine.[8–10] The proportions can differ widely (TABLE 1), because glutamine release tends to remain constant, whereas alanine release declines after a meal.[9] Alanine serves as a highly soluble, nontoxic vehicle for transport of nitrogen to the liver, where it is incorporated into urea. The glutamine released is taken up by the kidney to provide ammonia for maintenance of acid-base balance. Lund & Williamson[14] have estimated that the human kidney takes up 46–68 mmol or 7–10 g of glutamine a day. Also, the amount of glutamine taken up by the human intestine as an energy source is estimated to equal or exceed that removed by the kidney.

Nitrogen for maintenance of muscle pools of glutamate and glutamine, and for synthesis of glutamine released and subsequently taken up by kidney and intestine, must be replenished from nitrogen sources in blood. Glutamate and aspartate, as was mentioned, represent less than 20% of total muscle amino acid uptake; alanine is released rather than being taken up by muscle; most of the other amino acids from blood do not undergo catabolism in muscle. This leaves the branched-chain amino acids, which represent 50% of muscle amino acid uptake, as the main source of nitrogen available for replenishment of the muscle glutamate and glutamine pools.

Muscle contains the complement of enzymes needed to incorporate amino groups from the branched-chain amino acids into either the α-amino or amide groups of glutamine[4] (FIG. 1). Activity of branched-chain aminotransferase is high in muscle; and branched-chain α-keto acid dehydrogenase complex, the catalyst for removal of the keto acid product, is present largely in the inactive phosphorylated form.[4] As a result, a high proportion of the branched-chain α-keto acids formed are reaminated to branched-chain amino acids, which remain available for glutamate synthesis or for recirculation to other organs and tissues.[5,6] A portion of the branched-chain α-keto acids formed is released from muscle.[14,15] Concentrations of branched-chain amino acids rise more in blood and remain elevated longer than those of other amino acids after an animal or human subject has consumed protein.[9,16] This further helps to maintain the supply of branched-chain amino acids for uptake into muscle.

The pathway for incorporation of branched-chain amino nitrogen into glutamine amide nitrogen has not been established with certainty. Glutamate can be deaminated to provide ammonia for glutamine synthesis, but the activity of glutamate dehydrogenase is low in muscle,[4,14] so glutamate degradation by this reaction is probably limited.

Glutamate concentration in muscle is 2.0 mM or higher; and aspartate aminotransferase activity is high, so formation of aspartate from oxaloacetate and glutamate (FIG. 1) should occur readily. Aspartate formation is probably limited by oxaloacetate supply, as the aspartate pool in muscle is small; but in studies with a muscle preparation *in vitro*, aspartate was formed rapidly when branched-chain amino acids were incubated in the presence of a mixture of pyruvate, α-ketoglutarate, and oxaloacetate (enol form).[17] Aspartate is the amino donor for regeneration of adenosine monophosphate (AMP) from inosinic acid in muscle, via the purine nucleotide cycle (FIG. 2). Deamination of the AMP formed in this reaction by AMP deaminase, the activity of which is high in muscle, can serve, for glutamine synthesis, as an alternate pathway to the glutamate dehydrogenase reaction for generation of ammonia[18] from the amino groups of the branched-chain amino acids. Which of these pathways predominates

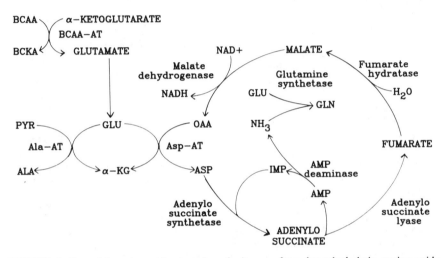

FIGURE 2. Potential pathway for transfer of nitrogen from branched-chain amino acids (BCAA) to the amide group of glutamine (GLN). BCKA, branched-chain α-keto acids; BCAA-AT, branched-chain amino acid aminotransferase; PYR, pyruvate; OAA, oxaloacetate; α-KG, α-ketoglutarate; Ala-AT, alanine-glutamate aminotransferase; Asp-AT, aspartate-glutamate aminotransferase; IMP, inosinic acid; AMP, adenosine monophosphate.

may be in question, but incorporation of ^{15}N from ^{15}N-labeled valine and leucine into the amide nitrogen of glutamine was observed by Golden[19] to occur readily *in vivo*.

Muscle glutamine production rates have been estimated for human subjects to be about 50 mmol/day.[13] Usual protein intakes provide about 153 mmol of branched-chain amino acids daily. The observed level of glutamine production could thus be provided readily by muscle, which is the major site of branched-chain amino acid metabolism.

Great difficulty is encountered in estimating glutamate and glutamine synthesis and turnover rates because of compartmentation of these amino acids in pools that exchange slowly with the plasma pool. From the few estimates that are available, it is clear that production rates are extremely high—on the order of 500 mmoles/day in fasting adult men.[13] One value for fed subjects of 1200 mmol/day approximates total daily nitrogen intake.[20] There must obviously be extensive recycling of glutamate and glutamine nitrogen. Nitrogen from alanine taken up by the liver can be channeled through transamination into glutamate and aspartate and into glutamine. There are no estimates of the amounts of these amino acids that must be synthesized daily from ingested amino acids to maintain the large glutamate and glutamine pools in tissues (in muscle, 84 mmol of glutamate and 365 mmol of glutamine) and to provide for obligatory losses of these two amino acids.[13] It is, thus, not possible to estimate total synthesis nor the relative importance of liver and muscle as sites of glutamine synthesis. Studies of arteriovenous differences in amino acid concentrations across organs and tissues indicate that both muscle and liver release glutamine for export to kidney and intestine, where it is used extensively.[13,14] The continuous production of glutamine by muscle, observed under a variety of conditions, indicates that the contribution by this tissue is substantial,[14,20] and evidence from *in vivo* and *in vitro* studies indicates that branched-chain amino acids serve effectively as sources of nitrogen for this function.[4,14,19]

This brings us back to the reaction of the branched-chain α-keto acid dehydrogenase complex, which commits the branched-chain α-keto acids to oxidation or channeling into other irreversible pathways for which the branched-chain acyl-CoA products are substrates (FIG. 1). Regulation of this system, with the dehydrogenase complex in muscle ordinarily 90% or more in the inactive form, limits the rate of oxidation of the branched-chain α-keto acids and results in a high rate of their reamination to the amino acids.[5,6] Only if branched-chain amino acids accumulate in tissues, as they do when protein or branched-chain amino acid intake is high, as discussed by HARRIS, and both muscle and liver branched-chain α-keto acid dehydrogenase complexes are activated,[21–23] do rates of branched-chain amino acid oxidation increase appreciably, and almost linearly, with increasing intake.[24] Regulatory mechanisms for control of the branched-chain α-keto acid dehydrogenase complex would thus appear to function in peripheral tissues in mammals mainly as a system for diverting the branched-chain α-keto acids away from, rather than into, the irreversible oxidative pathway. This not only conserves three essential amino acids required for protein synthesis, but conserves major donors of nitrogen for the synthesis of several amino acids that play key roles in overall nitrogen metabolism in the body.

Regulation of the branched-chain α-keto acid dehydrogenase complex can thus contribute in a major way to channeling of nitrogen from the branched-chain amino acids into glutamate to maintain intracellular pools of glutamate and aspartate in organs other than liver, and into glutamine, in particular, which is released from muscle to provide ammonia for the kidney and is a major source of energy for the intestine. Viewed in this way, the branched-chain α-keto acid dehydrogenase complex, rather than being merely a system for regulating the oxidative decarboxylation of a small group of branched-chain α-keto acids, assumes central importance in the metabolism of nitrogen, comparable to the role of the pyruvate dehydrogenase complex in the metabolism of energy sources. It then becomes much more understandable that the pathway for catabolism of the branched-chain amino acids should be controlled by an intricate and sensitive series of regulatory mechanisms resembling those for the pyruvate dehydrogenase complex.

REFERENCES

1. NEWSHOLME, E. A. & A. R. LEECH. 1983. Biochemistry for the Medical Sciences. pp. 192–194. John Wiley and Sons. New York.
2. DIXON, J. L. & A. E. HARPER. 1984. J. Nutr. **114:** 1025–1034.
3. HARPER, A. E. 1974. *In* The Control of Metabolism. J. D. Sink, Ed.: 49–74. Pennsylvania State University Press. University Park, PA.

4. HARPER, A. E., R. H. MILLER & K. P. BLOCK. 1984. Annu. Rev. Nutr. **4:** 409–454.
5. NISSEN, S. & M. W. HAYMOND. 1981. Am. J. Physiol. **241:** E72–E75.
6. MATTHEWS, D. E., D. M. BIER, M. J. RENNIE, R. A. EDWARDS, D. HALLIDAY, D. J. MILWARD & G. A. CLUGSTON. 1981. Science **214:** 1129–1131.
7. SHINNICK, F. L. & A. E. HARPER. 1976. Biochim. Biophys. Acta **437:** 477–486.
8. FELIG, P. 1975. Annu. Rev. Biochem. **44:** 933–955.
9. ELIA, M. & G. LIVESEY. 1983. Clin. Sci. **64:** 517–526.
10. ABUMRAD, N. N. & B. MILLER. 1983. J. Parenter. Enteral. Nutr. **7:** 163–170.
11. WINDMUELLER, H. G. & A. E. SPAETH. 1975. Arch. Biochem. Biophys. **17:** 662–672.
12. ISHIKAWA, E. 1976. Adv. Enzyme Regul. **14:** 117–136.
13. DARMAUN, D., D. E. MATTHEWS & D. M. BIER. 1986. Am. J. Physiol. **251:** E117–E126.
14. LUND, P. & D. M. WILLIAMSON. 1985. Br. Med. Bull. **41:** 251–256.
15. HARPER, A. E. & C. ZAPALOWSKI. 1981. *In* Nitrogen Metabolism in Man. J. Waterlow & J. Stephen, Eds.: 97–115. Applied Science Publishers. London.
16. PETERS, J. C. & A. E. HARPER 1985. J. Nutr. **115:** 382–398.
17. CREE, T. C. 1980. Ph.D. Thesis. pp. 51–83. University of Wisconsin. Madison, WI.
18. LOWENSTEIN, J. M. 1972. Physiol. Rev. **52:** 382–414.
19. GOLDEN, M. H. 1981. *In* Nitrogen Metabolism in Man. J. C. Waterlow & J. M. L. Stephen, Eds.: 109–110. Applied Science Publishers. London.
20. GOLDEN, M. H., P. JAHOOR & A. A. JACKSON. 1982. Clin. Sci. **62:** 299–305.
21. BLOCK, K. P., P. AFTRING, W. B. MEHARD & M. G. BUSE. 1987. J. Clin. Invest. **79:** 1349–1353.
22. MILLER, R. H., R. S. EISENSTEIN & A. E. HARPER. 1988. J. Biol. Chem. **263:** 3454–3461.
23. HARRIS, R. A., R. PAXTON, G. W. GOODWIN, M. J. KUNTZ, Y. SHIMONURA & A. HAN. 1986. Biochem. Soc. Trans. **14:** 1005–1008.
24. HARPER, A. E. & E. BENJAMIN. 1984. J. Nutr. **114:** 431–440.

Insulin, Phospholipase, and the Activation of the Pyruvate Dehydrogenase Complex: An Enigma[a]

OTTO H. WIELAND, T. URUMOW, AND P. DREXLER

Institut für Diabetesforschung
Krankenhaus München-Schwabing
München, Federal Republic of Germany

INTRODUCTION

It is now almost 20 years ago that Lester Reed and his colleagues in Austin discovered that the mitochondrial pyruvate dehydrogenase complex (PDC) is an interconvertible enzyme system whose activity is controlled by phosphorylation-dephosphorylation.[1,2] Shortly afterwards it was shown that insulin promoted PDC activation in rat epididymal adipose tissue incubated *in vitro*[3] and that this activation was due to conversion of the inactive phosphorylated form (PDC_b) to the active dephosphorylated form (PDC_a)[4,5] of the enzyme. This insulin effect on PDC received much attention, because it could plausibly explain earlier observations of Winegrad and Renold, who, in 1958, showed that insulin stimulates the conversion of glucose into fat in adipose tissue,[6] a pathway where PDC plays a pivotal rate-controlling role.[7] Ever since, PDC activation by insulin has been studied in many laboratories, including our own in Munich.

In this paper we shall try to give a critical appraisal of the state of knowledge regarding the effect of insulin on PDC. Moreover, we shall point out some special properties of the insulin stimulation of PDC which, on the basis of our own experience and that of others, we found to be responsible for the fact that it turned out to be frustratingly difficult to gain a satisfactory comprehension of the mechanism underlying this well-documented activation of PDC by insulin. In TABLE 1 are listed some of the characteristic properties of the insulin stimulation of PDC in the fat cell system. A few of them shall be discussed here in some more detail.

The question of which of the two regulatory enzymes for PDC, the kinase or the phosphatase, is the target of insulin has been studied in our laboratory using intact fat cells. In these experiments, shown in FIGURE 1, cells were incubated with dichloroacetate (DCA) at concentrations sufficient to maximally inhibit the kinase. Accordingly, the activation of PDC by phosphatase was enhanced. When insulin was then given in addition to DCA, the rate of PDC activation was still further enhanced beyond that obtained with DCA alone. These findings obtained in intact fat cells can best be explained by insulin activation of the phosphatase, as has been also suggested by others.[12]

It has long been known that the activation of PDC requires the presence of glucose or another metabolizable sugar. More recently we have shown that *myo*-inositol can partially replace glucose in the activation of PDC by insulin.[8] These results are

[a]This work was supported by the Deutsche Forschungsgemeinschaft, Bad Godesberg.

TABLE 1. Characteristic Features of the Insulin Activation of PDC in Adipose Tissue

Insulin activates at physiological concentrations (K_a ca. 10 μU/ml).
Activation is rapid (in minutes).
Insulin activates via pyruvate dehydrogenase phosphatase activation.
Activation requires the presence of a metabolizable sugar. (This requirement can partially be replaced by *myo*-inositol.)
Insulin does not change the mitochondrial ATP/ADP ratio.
The activation persists in mitochondria isolated from insulin-treated fat cells.
Cyclic AMP is not responsible for the effect of insulin on PDC.
Insulin activation cannot be demonstrated in isolated fat cell mitochondria.
PDC activation by insulin has been demonstrated in white and brown adipocytes, fibroblasts, BC$_3$H myocytes, and lactating mammary gland but not in liver.

illustrated in FIGURE 2. Further studies using ^{14}C-labeled *myo*-inositol failed to demonstrate any $^{14}CO_2$ formation, thus excluding the possibility that this compound is a metabolizable substrate in fat cells. One might speculate therefore that *myo*-inositol is required for the insulin effect because it serves as substrate for *de novo* biosynthesis of membrane inositol phospholipids in fat cells. However, formation of the relevant inositol phospholipids must be relatively fast. Further studies are needed to resolve this problem.

Since the mitochondrial ATP/ADP ratio is a major determinant of the phosphorylation state of the PDC system, we have measured the concentrations of ATP and ADP in the mitochondrial compartment of isolated fat cells. For that purpose we have adopted the digitonin fractionation procedure[9,10] originally proposed by Tager and his colleagues for studies of the subcellular distribution of metabolites in hepatocytes.[11] This technique requires only a few minutes. It is therefore much more rapid than conventional methods for preparation of mitochondria, thus reducing the hazards of metabolite change during preparation of mitochondria. Such experiments clearly showed that insulin does not cause a change of the mitochondrial ATP/ADP ratio, excluding the possibility that such a change is responsible for the increased formation of PDC$_a$[9,10] (TABLE 2). It should be further noted in TABLE 2 that the changes in PDC activity which one observes in extracts from insulin-treated whole cells are still demonstrable in extracts of the particulate mitochondrial fraction from these cells. Thus, the changes induced by insulin appear to be stable and to persist in mitochondria for some time, a phenomenon which has been studied in more detail by Denton and his group.[12]

FIGURE 1. Insulin activates PDC through activation of pyruvate dehydrogenase phosphatase. Isolated rat fat cells were incubated at 37°C in HEPES buffer, pH 7.4, containing 2.5% bovine serum albumin and 1 mM glucose, as described.[14] Further additions were insulin, 100 μU/ml; or dichloroacetate (DCA), 5 mM; or insulin plus DCA. At the times indicated, samples were rapidly centrifuged through dinonylphthalate, frozen in liquid N$_2$, and then extracted for spectrophotometric determination of PDC (*PDHa*) and total PDC activity as described elsewhere.[14]

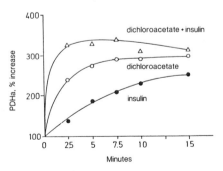

FIGURE 2. PDC activation (*PDHa*) by insulin requires glucose, which can be partially replaced by *myo*-inositol. Isolated rat fat cells were incubated at 37°C in the HEPES buffer described in the legend to FIGURE 1. Where glucose was added, its concentration was 1 mM. The concentration of added *myo*-inositol was 10 mM and of insulin was 100 μU/ml. After 15 min, the samples were frozen in liquid N$_2$ and then further processed for PDC determination as described.[14] Mean values ± SEM from 6 experiments are shown.

PHOSPHOLIPASE C AND INSULIN ACTION

With the recent emphasis on a possible role of inositol glycans as second messengers of insulin action (for review see Ref. 13), interest was renewed in phosphatidylinositol metabolism. Our laboratory was among the first to consider a possible role for the products of phospholipase C action in PDC activation by insulin. We shall recapitulate the experiences of our laboratory which led us to a rather skeptical and critical view of the possible involvement of phospholipase C activation in insulin action. Let us begin by considering the activation of phospholipase C in homogenates of fat cells treated with insulin and with the similarities between the activation of phospholipase C and that of PDC. These studies[14] were motivated by the earlier studies of Blecher,[15] Rodbell,[16] Rosenthal & Fain,[17] and others who showed that exposure of adipose tissue to phospholipase C mimics several insulin effects, including activation of PDC.[18] FIGURE 3 shows an experiment from our own laboratory comparing activation of PDC by phospholipase C and by insulin in rat epididymal fat cells in the presence of glucose. When fat cells were incubated with insulin, the hormonal stimulation of PDC activity was paralleled by an increase of a phosphatidylinositol diesterase (phospholipase C) activity (FIG. 4). The insulin concentrations required for half-maximal activation of this phospholipase were quite similar to those required for PDC activation, i.e., in the 5–10 μU/ml range. Analysis of nearly 40 experiments on activation of both phospholipase and PDC at saturating concentrations of insulin (100 μU/ml) gave on average a 2.2-fold activation of each of these enzymes.

TABLE 2. Effect of Insulin on the Mitochondrial ATP/ADP Ratio and PDC Activation[a]

Source of Extracts	Additions to Whole Cells	PDC$_a$ (% of total)	ATP/ADP
Whole cells	None	29	4.3
	Insulin (1 mU/ml)	51[b]	4.9
Pellet fraction	None	30	2.1
	Insulin (1 mU/ml)	51[b]	2.2

[a]The experiments were carried out according to Ref. 9. Isolated rat fat cells were fractionated with digitonin after incubation with or without insulin as indicated. Mean values from 10 experiments are given.[9]

[b]p vs. controls < 0.01.

FIGURE 3. Activation of PDC (PDH_a) in isolated adipocytes by insulin, 100 μU/ml, (●) or *Clostridium perfringens* phospholipase C, 75 ng/ml, (○) as a function of time. Controls: (□). Mean values ± SEM from at least 7 experiments carried out in the presence of glucose are given. (From Koepfer-Hobelsberger & Wieland.[14] Reprinted with permission from *Molecular and Cellular Endocrinology*.)

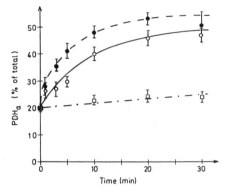

However, caution is warranted. In these experiments, phospholipase activity was determined in the supernatant from frozen and subsequently homogenized cells. The assay was carried out essentially as described by Craven and DeRubertis,[19] with a sample containing 15–40 μg protein and 1.1 mM phosphatidylinositol as substrate in Tris-maleate buffer, pH 7.5, containing 1–2.5 mM Ca^{2+}. Phosphatidylinositol was dispersed in the buffer by sonication. The reaction was stopped after incubation at 37°C for 10 min by addition of perchloric acid, and acid soluble phosphorus was measured with ascorbate and ammonium molybdate for color development. Under the conditions described, the release of acid-soluble phosphorus was nearly linear up to 10 min.[31]

In all our experiments, the release of phosphate from phosphatidylinositol was stimulated by insulin to a greater or lesser extent. However, when instead of unlabeled phosphatidylinositol, tracer amounts of phosphatidyl-[³H]inositol were used as substrate and instead of phosphate, water-soluble ³H radioactivity was measured, the results were erratic. We have not yet been able to resolve this discrepancy.

Based on the assumption that insulin simultaneously activates phospholipase C and PDC in rat adipocytes, it seemed plausible to look for activation of PDC by products of the classical phospholipase C action. And, indeed, inositol trisphosphate (IP₃) markedly stimulated PDC activity in isolated permeabilized rat fat cells.[8] IP₃ caused, in a concentration-dependent manner, a more than 3-fold increase of the active form of PDC (PDC$_a$) without changing total PDC activity (FIG. 5). This effect is comparable

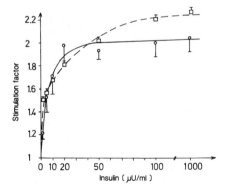

FIGURE 4. Response of phospholipase C (○) and PDC (□) activities to insulin in adipocytes. Fat cells were incubated for 10 min with increasing concentrations of insulin.[14] The stimulation factor is the ratio of the enzyme activity in the presence of insulin to the basal activity in the absence of insulin. Mean values ± SEM of 5 experiments are given. (From Koepfer-Hobelsberger & Wieland.[14] Reprinted with permission from *Molecular and Cellular Endocrinology*.)

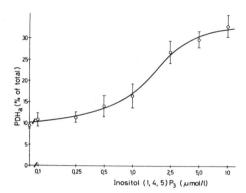

FIGURE 5. Activation of PDC (*PDH$_a$*) by IP$_3$. Permeabilized fat cells were incubated for 10 min at 37°C with increasing concentrations of IP$_3$ and further processed as described.[8] Maximal effect was obtained at 5–10 μM IP$_3$. (From Koepfer-Hobelsberger & Wieland.[8] Reprinted with permission from *FEBS Letters.*)

to the well-documented PDC stimulation by insulin in intact adipocytes. Notably, IP$_3$ had no effect on PDC activity when it was added to isolated fat cell mitochondria (data not shown). However, studies on the specificity of IP$_3$ activation indicated that all sorts of phosphate sugar esters activated PDC in permeabilized rat adipocytes (TABLE 3). It should be noted that these compounds were no longer active after removal of the phosphate group by treatment with alkaline phosphatase. Taking the results as a whole, we can say that we failed to obtain convincing evidence that insulin activation of PDC in adipocytes is mediated by IP$_3$.

POSSIBLE MEDIATORS OF INSULIN ACTIVATION OF PDC

Besides inositol phosphates and other phosphate esters, several other substances have been reported to mimic insulin action on PDC activity in fat cells. Some of these substances are listed in TABLE 4.

TABLE 3. Effects of Phosphate Esters on PDC Activity

	PDC Activity[b]		
		Treated with Alkaline Phosphatase[c]	
Compounds[a] (5 μM)	Untreated	Native	Boiled
Insulin, 100 μU/ml	340	—	—
IP$_3$	270	90	230
Glucose-6-P	218	100	170
Glucose-1-P	160	100	160
Fructose-1,6-P$_2$	215	100	190
Fructose-2,6-P$_2$	150	117	150
GAP	260	130	230
DHAP	180	90	135
ATP	225	—	—

[a] Isolated epididymal rat fat cells were incubated at 37°C for 10 min in HEPES buffer containing 2.5% bovine serum albumin, 1 mM glucose, and 0.001–0.0005% purified digitonin.[32] GAP, glyceraldehyde-3-phosphate; DHAP, dihydroxyacetone phosphate.

[b] Cell extraction and PDC determination were as described,[14] except that total PDC activity was routinely measured in parallel cell incubations with dichloroacetate. The activity of PDC in control cells without additions was taken to be 100%.

[c] To study the influence of the phosphate ester bond, the compounds were treated prior to use with immobilized alkaline phosphatase (Sigma) either in the native form or after boiling.

TABLE 4. Substances Mimicking Insulin Action on PDC

H_2O_2
Calcium ions
G Proteins
Metabolites of the phosphatidylinositol pathway
Second messengers (phosphoinosit glycans)
Glycolytic metabolites

H_2O_2

A second messenger role was ascribed to H_2O_2 because it produces many insulin effects, including reversible activation of PDC in fat cells and fat cell mitochondria.[10,30] In adipocytes, H_2O_2 production can be monitored by the rate of [14C]formate oxidation to $^{14}CO_2$. As shown in FIGURE 6A, insulin leads to an increase of H_2O_2 production paralleled by an increase of PDC activity, confirming previous results.[10,20,21] However, when H_2O_2 production was stimulated by exogenously added glucose oxidase instead of insulin, PDC activity remained unchanged. As shown in FIGURE 6B, aminotriazole,[22] which inactivates the catalase-H_2O_2 complex I, attenuated both the glucose oxidase–dependent and the insulin-dependent stimulation of formate oxidation. However, it did not affect activation of PDC by insulin. These results showing that H_2O_2 production and PDC activation can be changed independently do not support the proposed messenger role for H_2O_2 in PDC activation by insulin.

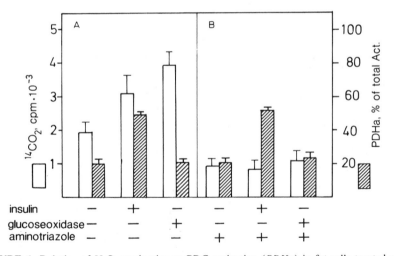

FIGURE 6. Relation of H_2O_2 production to PDC activation (*PDHa*) in fat cells treated with insulin. Isolated fat cells were incubated for 30 min at 37°C in the HEPES medium described in the legend to FIGURE 1. Further additions, as indicated, were insulin, 100 μU/ml; glucose oxidase (Boehringer Mannheim), 100 μg/ml; aminotriazole (Sigma), 50 mM. H_2O_2 production was monitored by the rate of formate oxidation, which was measured by following the formation of $^{14}CO_2$ from [14C]formate.[20] [14C]formate corresponding to about 700,000 cpm was added per assay as tracer; the final concentration of sodium formate was 0.2 mM. For PDC determination, the cells were treated and further processed as described.[14]

Calcium

There is more and more evidence that intracellular calcium is an essential participant in insulin signal transduction,[23] although the specific interactions of Ca^{2+} in the insulin effector systems are not yet understood. Recent studies using the Ca^{2+} chelator fura-2 have established that insulin produces a rise of intracellular $[Ca^{2+}]$ in adipocytes, which was attributed to an increased influx through the plasma membrane rather than to mobilization of Ca^{2+} from intracellular stores.[24] It was also shown that chelation of intracellular Ca^{2+} by quin-2 prevents several insulin effects in adipocytes, such as stimulation of glucose transport, glucose oxidation, and antilipolysis.[25] In our laboratory, we were able to demonstrate that incubation of fat cells with quin-2–acetoxymethylester (quin-2–AM) abolished the insulin-dependent activation of PDC (Fig. 7). The insulin effect was maintained by addition of Ca^{2+} and the calcium ionophore A 23187. These observations support the concept that intracellular Ca^{2+} is an essential component of the insulin effector system and are hard to reconcile with the view that insulin action on PDC in adipocytes is by a calcium-independent mechanism.[26]

G PROTEINS AND PHOSPHATIDYLINOSITOL METABOLISM

Finally, we wish to introduce briefly another aspect of phosphatidylinositol metabolism which deserves attention, namely, the involvement of guanine nucleotide–binding regulatory proteins (G proteins). Several reports have described in cell-free preparations effects of hormones on phospholipase C activity which are dependent on the presence of guanine nucleotides. In addition, nonhydrolyzable GTP analogs have been shown to activate phospholipases. The putative G protein that appears to be involved in phospholipase C activation has not been identified. It is pertussis toxin–sensitive in some cells but not in others (for review see Ref. 27). Among the hormones whose actions are amplified by a G protein is vasopressin, which also activates PDC in fat cells and other cells. A scheme of the reactions of phosphatidylinositol metabolism is shown in Figure 8. We have recently shown that guanosine-5'-O-(3-thiotriphosphate) (GTPγS) not only stimulates phospholipase C activity in membranes from human placenta and from rat liver but also activates phosphatidylinositol 4-phosphate kinase activities in these membranes.[28,29] The latter activation, which is shown in

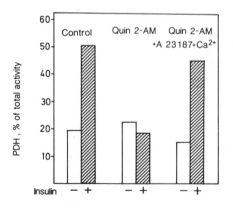

FIGURE 7. Attenuation of insulin activation of PDC (*PDH*) by quin-2 loading of fat cells. Fat cells were incubated in HEPES medium as described in the legend to Figure 1, except that Ca^{2+} was omitted. The cells were first incubated for 15 min at 37°C in the presence of 100 μM quin-2–AM alone or in combination with 0.5 μM A 23187 and $CaCl_2$, 1.2 mM. Insulin, 100 $\mu U/ml$, was then added and incubations were continued for a further 10 min. Controls received dimethyl sulfoxide at the concentrations used as solvent. For further treatment of cells and PDC determination, see Ref. 14. The experiment was repeated three times with similar results. Results of a representative experiment are shown.

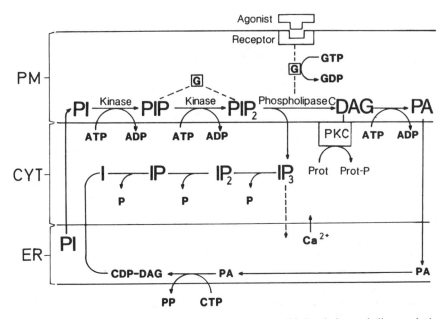

FIGURE 8. Schematic view of the reactions of phosphatidylinositol metabolism and the involvement of regulatory G proteins. PM, plasma membrane; CYT, cytosol; ER, endoplasmic reticulum; PI, phosphatidylinositol; PIP, phosphatidylinositol 4-phosphate; PIP$_2$, phosphatidylinositol 4,5-bisphosphate; DAG, diacylglycerol; PA, phosphatidic acid; PKC, protein kinase C; IP$_3$, inositol 1,4,5-trisphosphate; IP$_2$, inositol 1,4-bisphosphate; IP, inositol monophosphate; I, *myo*-inositol. (Adapted from Exton.[33])

FIGURE 9, appears to be mediated by a different putative G protein than that involved in activation of the phospholipase, since it is elicited by higher GTPγS concentrations than those required for the former effect. Moreover, this latter G protein is cholera toxin sensitive[29] (FIG. 10).

CONCLUSIONS

There are two mainstreams of thought on the mechanism of signal transfer from the insulin receptor in the plasma membrane to the intracellular target. One proposal is for a phosphorylation-dephosphorylation cascade triggered by activation of the receptor tyrosine kinase by the hormone, the other implies formation of second messengers like in the classical case of hormone-stimulated cyclic AMP formation. The two possibilities need not be mutually exclusive. However, a conceptual difficulty arises in the application of either of these regulatory pathways to insulin activation of PDC because of location of PDC in the mitochondrial inner membrane–matrix space, which introduces the problem of accessibility. Moreover, the fact that insulin activation persists upon isolation of mitochondria is not readily reconciled with the involvement of a short-lived messenger and/or a readily reversible phosphorylation-dephosphorylation reaction. Therefore, whatever the mechanisms of signal transduction may be, two additional aspects have to be considered: (1) the means by which the

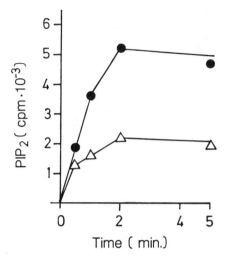

FIGURE 9. Stimulation of PIP$_2$ formation by GTPγS in rat liver membranes. Membranes were incubated with [γ-^{32}P]ATP in the absence (△) or presence (●) of 100 μM GTPγS. At the times indicated, samples were extracted with chloroform-methanol; and phospholipids were separated, spotted by autoradiography, and counted as described.[29]

activated form of PDC persists and (2) the changes in the intramembraneous location of PDC required to make the enzyme accessible to the cellular transduction network which transmits the insulin signal from the plasma membrane receptor to PDC.

Finally, we wish to consider an aspect of insulin action that also has deeply influenced our way of thinking about insulin action on PDC, that is, the idea that the

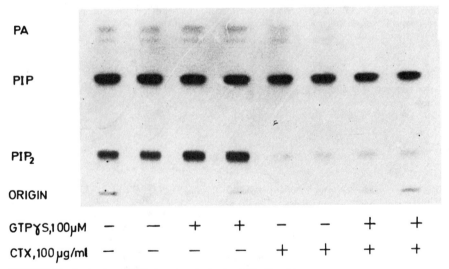

FIGURE 10. Activation of PIP phosphorylation by GTPγS and its attenuation with cholera toxin treatment. Liver membranes were incubated with [γ^{32}P]ATP for 2 min at 25°C with or without GTPγS. The membranes were preincubated, as indicated, with or without cholera toxin (CTX) as described.[29] Phospholipids were extracted and separated on silica-gel plates (a radioautograph is shown), excised, and counted. For quantitative data, see Ref. 29. PA, phosphatidic acid; PIP, phosphatidylinositol 4-phosphate; PIP$_2$, phosphatidylinositol 4,5-bisphosphate; GTPγS, guanosine 5'-O-(3-thiotriphosphate). CTX, cholera toxin. (From Urumow & Wieland.[29] Reprinted with permission from *Biochimica et Biophysica Acta*.)

many pleiotropic actions of insulin can all be reduced to one, single, regulatory process. In our case, it means that, for example, glycogen synthase is activated by insulin in the same manner as is PDC. But, as outlined above, such a view neglects the different location of the two enzymes and other differences in the activation pattern. Thus, even in one particular differentiated cell type insulin might employ different means to affect cellular metabolism. If we accept that multiple mechanisms are involved, clearly we should direct our attention to determining how these different and independent mechanisms of insulin action are interrelated and coordinated. Certainly, there is still a lot to do, and further speculation does not seem profitable before more data become available.

ACKNOWLEDGMENTS

We thank Mr. P. Delly for the artwork and Mrs. D. Lehmeier and Mrs. D. Berberich for typing the manuscript. In particular, we are indebted to Prof. E. J. M. Helmreich, Würzburg, for valuable discussions.

REFERENCES

1. LINN, T. C., F. H. PETTIT & L. J. REED. 1969. Proc. Natl. Acad. Sci. USA **62:** 234–241.
2. WIELAND, O. H. 1983. Rev. Physiol. Biochem. Pharmacol. **96:** 124–170.
3. JUNGAS, R. L. 1970. Endocrinology **86:** 1368–1375.
4. DENTON, R. M., H. G. COORE, B. R. MARTIN & P. J. RANDLE. 1971. Nature **231:** 115–116.
5. WEISS, L., G. LÖFFLER, A. SCHIRMANN & O. H. WIELAND. 1971. FEBS Lett. **15:** 229–231.
6. WINEGRAD, A. I. & A. E. RENOLD. 1958. J. Biol. Chem. **233:** 267–273.
7. WIELAND, O. H., E. A. SIESS, G. LÖFFLER, C. PATZELT, R. PORTENHAUSER, U. HARTMANN & A. SCHIRMANN. 1973. Symp. Soc. Exp. Biol. **27:** 371–400.
8. KOEPFER-HOBELSBERGER, B. & O. H. WIELAND. 1984. FEBS Lett. **176:** 411–413.
9. PAETZKE-BRUNNER, I., H. SCHÖN & O. H. WIELAND. 1978. FEBS Lett. **93:** 307–311.
10. WIELAND, O. H. & I. PAETZKE-BRUNNER. 1981. *In* Metabolic Interconversion of Enzymes. H. Holzer, Ed.: 134–142. Springer. Berlin, Heidelberg, New York.
11. ZUURENDONK, P. F. & J. M. TAGER. 1974. Biochim. Biophys. Acta **333:** 393–399.
12. DENTON, R. M., J. G. McCORMACK, P. J. W. MIDGLEY & G. A. RUTTER. 1987. Biochem. Soc. Symp. **54:** 127–143.
13. SALTIEL, A. R. & P. CUATRECASAS. 1988. Am. J. Physiol. **255**(Cell Physiol. **24**): C1–C11.
14. KOEPFER-HOBELSBERGER, B. & O. H. WIELAND. 1984. Mol. Cell. Endocrinol. **36:** 123–129.
15. BLECHER, M. 1965. Biochem. Biophys. Res. Commun. **21:** 202–209.
16. RODBELL, M. 1966. J. Biol. Chem. **241:** 130–139.
17. ROSENTHAL, J. W. & J. N. FAIN. 1971. J. Biol. Chem. **246:** 5888–5895.
18. HONEYMAN, T. W., W. STROHSNITTER, C. R. SCHEID & J. SCHIMMEL. 1983. Biochem. J. **212:** 489–498.
19. CRAVEN, P. A. & F. R. DeRUBERTIS. 1983. J. Biol. Chem. **258:** 4814–4823.
20. MUCHMORE, D. B., S. A. LITTLE & C. DeHAEN. 1981. J. Biol. Chem. **256:** 365–372.
21. MUKHERJEE, S. P., R. H. LANE & W. S. LYNN. 1978. Biochem. Pharmacol. **27:** 2589–2594.
22. MARGOLIASH, E., A. NOVOGRODSKY & A. SCHEJTER. 1969. Biochem. J. **74:** 339–350.
23. McDONALD, J. M. & H. A. PERSHADSINGH. 1985. *In* Molecular Basis of Insulin Action. M. P. Czech, Ed.: 103–117. Plenum Press. New York.
24. DRAZNIN, B., M. KAO & E. SUSSMAN. 1987. Diabetes **36:** 174–178.
25. PERSHADSINGH, H. A., D. L. SHADE, D. M. DELFERT & J. M. McDONALD. 1987. Proc. Natl. Acad. Sci. USA **84:** 1025–1030.

26. DENTON, R. M., J. G. McCORMACK & A. P. THOMAS. 1986. Ann. N.Y. Acad. Sci. **488:** 370–384.
27. FAIN, J. N., M. A. WALLACE & R. J. H. WOJCIKIWICZ. 1988. FASEB J. **2:** 2569–2574.
28. URUMOW, T. & O. H. WIELAND. 1986. FEBS Lett. **207:** 253–257.
29. URUMOW, T. & O. H. WIELAND. 1988. Biochim. Biophys. Acta. **972:** 232–238.
30. PAETZKE-BRUNNER, I., O. H. WIELAND & G. FEIL. 1980. FEBS Lett. **122:** 29–32.
31. WIELAND, O. H., B. KÖPFER-HOBELSBERGER, T. URUMOW & G. GALLWITZ. 1986. *In* Mechanisms of Insulin Action. B. Belfrage, J. Donner & P. Stralfors, Eds.: 249–261. Elsevier Science Publishers. Amsterdam.
32. CORNELL, N. W. & A. M. JANSKI. 1980. Biochem. Int. **186:** 423–429.
33. EXTON, J. H. 1988. Rev. Physiol. Biochem. Pharmacol. **111:** 117–224.

Studies into the Mechanism Whereby Insulin Activates Pyruvate Dehydrogenase Complex in Adipose Tissue[a]

RICHARD M. DENTON,[b] PETER J. W. MIDGLEY,
GUY A. RUTTER, ANDREW P. THOMAS,[c] AND
JAMES G. McCORMACK[d]

Department of Biochemistry
School of Medical Sciences
University of Bristol
Bristol, BS8 1TD
United Kingdom

INTRODUCTION

Exposure of rat epididymal adipose tissue or isolated fat cells to insulin leads to a two- to threefold increase in the activity of the pyruvate dehydrogenase complex (PDC) within a few minutes.[1-3] The effect is an important component of the means whereby insulin stimulates the conversion of glucose into fatty acids and has been studied extensively in several laboratories. It is now also evident that insulin increases PDC activity in other tissues which are important sites of fatty acid synthesis, namely, liver,[4,5] lactating mammary gland,[6] and brown adipose tissue.[7] However, the effects in liver appear to be rather less than in the other tissues.

From measurements of PDC activity before and after incubation with pyruvate dehydrogenase phosphatase in the presence of added Mg^{2+} and Ca^{2+},[8,9] it was deduced in early studies that insulin increased the proportion of the pyruvate dehydrogenase complex in its active non-phosphorylated form. Subsequently, techniques have been devised which allow the direct demonstration of the extent of dephosphorylation of the α subunits of pyruvate dehydrogenase within fat cells.[10] Much evidence has now accumulated which suggests that the effects of insulin on PDC are not secondary to the well-established effects of insulin on either glucose transport or triacylglycerol metabolism.[9,11,12] Over the years, many hypotheses have been put forward for the mechanism whereby insulin binding to receptors on the outside of the fat cell leads to the activation of PDC within the mitochondria.[9-13] These have included inhibition of the kinase by decreases in intramitochondrial ATP/ADP or acetyl-CoA/CoA ratios,[14,15] as well as activation of the phosphatase by calcium ions[16,17] or by a low-molecular-weight mediator.[18-24]

An important and interesting characteristic of the effect of insulin on PDC activity is its persistence during the isolation of fat cell mitochondria and their subsequent

[a]Supported by grants from the Medical Research Council, British Diabetic Association, and Percival Waite Salmond Bequest.
[b]Address correspondence to Professor R. M. Denton.
[c]Present address: Department of Pathology, Thomas Jefferson University, Philadelphia, PA 19107.
[d]Present address: Department of Biochemistry, University of Leeds, Leeds, LS2 9JT, U.K.

incubation under a wide variety of conditions.[16,25,26] This paper is mainly concerned with the further study of this phenomenon in order to explore the means whereby insulin activates PDC. The concluding section also contains a detailed appraisal of the mitochondrial assay system used in a number of laboratories[18-24] as a means of detecting putative mediators of insulin action on PDC. Finally, a distinction is made between the short- and long-term actions of insulin on the pyruvate dehydrogenase system.

PERSISTENCE OF INSULIN ACTIVATION OF PYRUVATE DEHYDROGENASE COMPLEX

Some examples of the persistence of the insulin activation of PDC during isolation and subsequent purification of mitochondria from both white and brown adipose tissues of the rat are given in TABLE 1. In these studies, mitochondria were prepared in ice-cold sucrose-based medium containing EGTA, reduced glutathione, and albumin and then incubated at 30°C in a KCl-based medium containing EGTA and an

TABLE 1. Persistence of the Insulin Activation of Pyruvate Dehydrogenase Complex during Isolation and Subsequent Incubation of Mitochondria from White and Brown Adipose Tissue

Preparation[a]	Mitochondrial PDC Activity[b] (% total)	
	Control Tissue	Insulin-treated Tissue
Rat epididymal white adipose tissue		
Intact tissue (*in vivo* insulin)	10	35[c]
Intact tissue (*in vitro* insulin)	22	58[c]
Freshly isolated mitochondria	33	60[c]
Incubated mitochondria		
No additions to standard medium	16	35[c]
Plus 0.5 mM ADP	37	80[c]
Plus 1 mM pyruvate	31	50[c]
Plus 10 mM NaCl	15	30[c]
Plus 0.5 μM Ca^{2+} (Ca-EGTA buffer)	40	59[c]
Plus 10 mM NaCl and 0.5 μM Ca^{2+}	40	60[c]
Rat interscapular brown adipose tissue		
Intact tissue (*in vivo* insulin)	13	31[c]
Freshly isolated mitochondria	13	25[c]
Incubated mitochondria		
No additions to standard medium	7	14[c]
Plus 0.5 mM GDP	3	3
Plus 0.5 mM GDP and 5 mM pyruvate	13	20[c]

[a]The exposure of the tissues to insulin *in vivo* was manipulated by injections of either anti-insulin serum (control) or glucose (insulin-treated) and *in vitro* (white adipose tissue only) by incubation of the tissue for 30 min in bicarbonate-buffered medium with (insulin-treated) or without (control) insulin (1 mU/ml). Mitochondria were prepared in sucrose-based medium containing EGTA and albumin and then incubated in 125 mM KCl, 20 mM Tris, 5 mM phosphate, pH 7.3, for 5 min at 30°C. This standard incubation medium also contained for white adipose tissue mitochondria 2 mM EGTA, 5 mM oxoglutarate, and 0.5 mM malate and for brown adipose tissue mitochondria 2 mM EGTA, 10 mM oxoglutarate, 1 mM malate, and defatted albumin (1 mg/ml).
[b]Data taken from Denton *et al.*[26] and Marshall *et al.*[27]
[c]Effect of insulin, $p < 0.01$ versus control value.

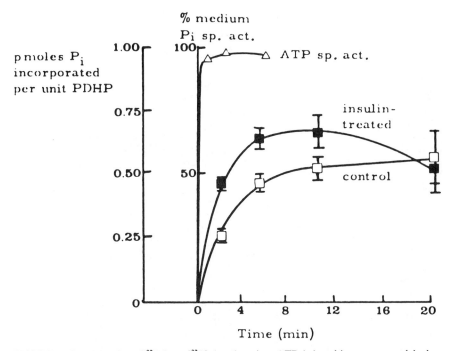

FIGURE 1. Incorporation of ^{32}P from [^{32}P]phosphate into ATP ($\triangle$) and into pyruvate dehydrogenase phosphate (*PDHP*) within mitochondria prepared from control ($\square$) and insulin-treated (■) adipose tissue. Mitochondria were incubated in medium containing phosphate (0.2 mM), 2-oxoglutarate (5 mM), and malate (0.5 mM) for 3 min to achieve steady-state levels of PDC activity (15% and 35% of total activity in, respectively, the mitochondria from control and insulin-treated tissue) before addition of ^{32}P$_i$. Methods as given by Hughes & Denton.[16]

oxidizing substrate, usually oxoglutarate and malate. However, very similar results are obtained with other substrates such as palmitoyl-carnitine and succinate.

Pyruvate dehydrogenase kinase can be regulated by a number of metabolites, including pyruvate and ADP, which inhibit, and NADH and acetyl-CoA, which activate.[9,11] It can be seen from TABLE 1 that addition of either pyruvate or ADP to white adipose tissue mitochondria leads to an increased proportion of PDC in its active form but not to a loss of the effect of insulin. The intramitochondrial concentrations of the potential kinase regulators ATP, ADP, NAD, NADH, acetyl-CoA and, CoA were all measured in white fat mitochondria incubated with oxoglutarate and malate as substrate. Insulin treatment did not produce any changes which could result in inhibition of kinase activity,[26] suggesting that insulin may cause activation of the phosphatase. In fact, further evidence for this view had been obtained in earlier studies in which the rate of the kinase reaction was measured directly from the incorporation of ^{32}P$_i$ into pyruvate dehydrogenase phosphate by rat epididymal adipose tissue mitochondria incubated under steady-state conditions.[16] As shown in FIGURE 1, the specific radioactivity of ATP within the mitochondria approaches that of the medium phosphate within seconds, and, hence, the initial rate of incorporation of P$_i$ into pyruvate dehydrogenase phosphate is a measure of the rate of the kinase reaction. In mitochondria from insulin-treated adipose tissue, the rate is actually increased. The simplest interpretation of this observation is that the major effect of insulin is to cause a stimulation of the dephosphorylation of pyruvate dehydrogenase and that this in turn leads to an increased turnover of the pyruvate dehydrogenase phosphorylation-dephosphorylation cycle under the steady-state conditions studied. If the increase in PDC activity had been due to inhibition of the kinase, a decrease in turnover would have been expected.

Studies on brown adipose tissue mitochondria also indicate that the major acute effect of insulin on PDC activity is exerted through an increase in phosphatase activity.[26,28] As shown in TABLE 1, manipulation of plasma insulin levels by injection of anti-insulin serum or glucose demonstrates that there is a marked insulin-dependent increase of PDC activity. This effect, like that in white adipose tissue mitochondria, persists during the preparation and subsequent incubation of mitochondria. However, with these mitochondria the effects of prior exposure to insulin are no longer evident if the mitochondria are incubated with GDP and albumin. These are conditions in which brown adipose tissue mitochondria become fully coupled, and it appears that the kinase activity is sufficiently great to cause the virtually complete conversion of the complex to its inactive, phosphorylated form in the mitochondria from both control and insulin-treated tissue. However, if kinase activity is somewhat diminished by, for example, the addition of pyruvate, then increases in PDC activity are observed, with the increase being greater in the mitochondria from insulin-treated tissue.[26] More detailed time-course studies show that the rate of dephosphorylation is markedly greater in these mitochondria, again pointing to the activation of the phosphatase as being important in insulin action.[26]

Until recently, the only known regulators of pyruvate dehydrogenase phosphatase were Ca^{2+}, Mg^{2+}, and NADH. Since no changes in either mitochondrial Mg^{2+} or NADH were found,[26] the possibility that insulin might act through changes in mitochondrial Ca^{2+} had to be considered.[27] Studies with rat heart and liver[30] have provided excellent evidence that Ca^{2+} is important in the activation of PDC by hormones which act through increases in cytoplasmic Ca^{2+}. It was realized that if insulin were to increase intramitochondrial Ca^{2+}, such an increase would be unlikely to be secondary to an increase in the cytoplasmic concentration of Ca^{2+}. Insulin treatment does not, in general, result in intracellular effects such as the activation of glycogen breakdown, which would be expected to follow an increase in cytoplasmic levels of Ca^{2+}. Nevertheless, it was found that increases in PDC activity in rat epididymal adipose tissue comparable to those observed with insulin could be observed in tissue incubated in medium with an elevated concentration of calcium.[27]

Approaches that had been successful in establishing a role for Ca^{2+} in the regulation of PDC by hormones which increase cytoplasmic Ca^{2+} in heart and liver were therefore applied to the effects of insulin on PDC in adipose tissue. These clearly showed that insulin did not activate pyruvate dehydrogenase phosphatase through an increase in mitochondrial Ca^{2+}. The main evidence was as follows:

1. Activation of PDC in mitochondria from insulin-treated tissue persists not only when Na^+ is added to the incubation medium but also when mitochondria are incubated with a concentration of Ca^{2+} which gives maximal activation (TABLE 1). Separate studies showed that addition of Na^+ caused essentially the complete loss of intramitochondrial calcium.[27]

2. There was no evidence that activation of the other two Ca^{2+}-sensitive intramitochondrial dehydrogenases (NAD-isocitrate dehydrogenase and oxoglutarate dehydrogenase complex) accompanied the increased activity of PDC in mitochondria from insulin-treated adipose tissue.[27]

3. Addition of ruthenium red did not block the effect of insulin on PDC activity in intact tissue but did block the effects of high calcium concentrations in the medium.[27]

To date, we have been unable to detect any changes in phosphatase activity in extracts of mitochondria from insulin-treated tissue.[27,31] We therefore explored the use of permeabilized mitochondria as a means of investigating in greater detail the basis of the increased activation of PDC in adipose tissue. The mitochondria were either made permeable rather specifically to Mg^{2+} and Ca^{2+} by incubation with A23187 in the presence of an uncoupler[31] or made permeable to all substances up to a molecular weight of about 2000 by treatment with toluene. As explained in another paper[30] in this volume, the latter preparation has the great advantage that the activity of PDC can be followed continuously.

In FIGURE 2, two pairs of traces are shown for assays of PDC activity with toluene-permeabilized mitochondria from control or insulin-treated adipose tissue. At the start of the traces, neither kinase nor phosphatase is active, and the activity of PDH_a is essentially the same as that of the source tissue, with a clearly increased activity in the mitochondria from insulin-treated adipose tissue. Addition of $CaCl_2$ and $MgCl_2$ resulted in activation of the phosphatase and conversion of all the complex into its active, non-phosphorylated form so that the insulin effect was no longer present. Addition of ATP allowed both kinase and phosphatase to act simultaneously, with the result that a new intermediate steady-state activity was achieved. The insulin-induced activation of PDC again became apparent under these conditions. Similar results were obtained when the sequence of additions was reversed, with kinase activation before initiation of the phosphatase reaction. With both of the protocols used in FIGURE 2, the effect of insulin was subsequently lost if either the phosphatase or kinase was again allowed to act alone, resulting in total activation or near-complete inactivation, respectively. This was accomplished by removing ATP to inhibit the kinase or by adding fluoride ions to block the phosphatase. This approach clearly shows that the effect of insulin persists in toluene-permeabilized mitochondria but does not allow clear-cut conclusions as to whether changes in kinase or in phosphatase activity are involved. The protocols employed in FIGURE 3 address this point. The PDC was first inactivated by treatment with ATP, and the excess ATP was then removed by hexokinase in the presence of glucose. The time-course of reactivation on addition of a limiting concentration of Mg^{2+} was then followed. It is evident that under these conditions the phosphatase activity is greater in mitochondria from insulin-treated tissue, as assessed by observing the time-course of either acetyl-CoA formation or NADH formation. The figure also illustrates the use of sodium fluoride to block phosphatase activity after a fixed time as a further means of demonstrating the increased phosphatase activity after exposure of the tissue to insulin.

Using the approaches illustrated in FIGURES 2 and 3, it was found that effects of insulin were evident at all Ca^{2+} concentrations but lost at high Mg^{2+} concentrations. More detailed studies confirmed that insulin acts on the phosphatase by changing its apparent K_m for Mg^{2+}.[31,32] FIGURE 4 shows the effects of varying Mg^{2+} concentrations on the steady-state PDC activity in experiments carried out as in FIGURE 2 (traces a and b) in the absence of Ca^{2+}. The calculated K_a for Mg^{2+} was diminished from 0.36 mM in control permeabilized mitochondria to 0.16 mM in those from insulin-treated tissue.

DISCUSSION AND CONCLUSIONS

Our studies clearly show that the activating effect of insulin on PDC persists during the isolation and subsequent incubation of adipose tissue mitochondria and that the effect even persists, albeit probably somewhat diminished, in toluene-permeabilized mitochondria. Study of these mitochondrial preparations has indicated that the

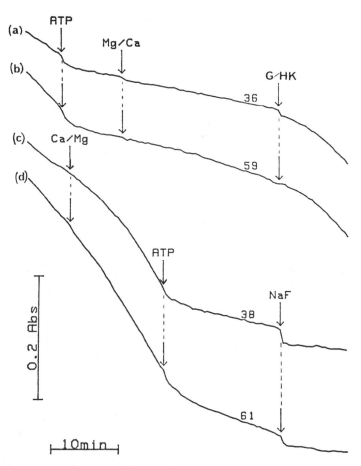

FIGURE 2. Persistent elevation of PDC activity in permeabilized mitochondria prepared from insulin-treated adipose tissue. Adipose tissue mitochondria from control (**a, c**) and insulin-treated (**b, d**) tissues were treated for a brief period with toluene, and PDC activity was followed by measuring acetyl-CoA production as the decrease in absorption at 460 nm, resulting from the acetylation of aminophenylazobenzene sulphate.[32] Additions were made as follows: ATP, 0.2 mM ATP plus 50 μM $MgCl_2$; Mg/Ca, $CaCl_2$ plus $MgCl_2$ to give 0.9 μM Ca^{2+} plus 0.2 mM Mg^{2+}; G/HK, 10 mM glucose plus 1.4 U/ml hexokinase; NaF, 25 mM sodium fluoride. Data replotted from Thomas & Denton.[32] *Numbers* on the traces are the calculated rates of PDC activity in arbitrary units.

activation of PDC may be largely explained by the stimulation of the phosphatase by a calcium-independent mechanism. The stimulation is characterized by a decrease in the apparent K_m of pyruvate dehydrogenase phosphatase for Mg^{2+}. Such a mechanism could only be relevant in the intact cell if the free Mg^{2+} concentration in mitochondria is sufficiently low; certainly it would have to be less than 1 mM. Recent studies[33,34] indicate that this condition is met.

Similar changes in the kinetic properties of the phosphatase can be observed on exposure of purified preparations to the polyamine spermine.[31,35] However, it seems most unlikely that insulin could act simply by increasing the mitochondrial concentration of spermine, since the concentration of spermine throughout cells is high and insulin appears to have little or no short-term effects on its concentration.[36] Moreover, addition of spermine to toluene-permeabilized mitochondria has no discernible effect on phosphatase activity, although it would be expected to enter such mitochondria freely.[32] In any case, if the effect of insulin were due to an increase in the mitochondrial concentration of a small water-soluble molecule such as a polyamine, it would not be expected to persist in toluene-permeabilized mitochondria. Perhaps the simplest explanation of our observations is that insulin may cause a change in the interaction of

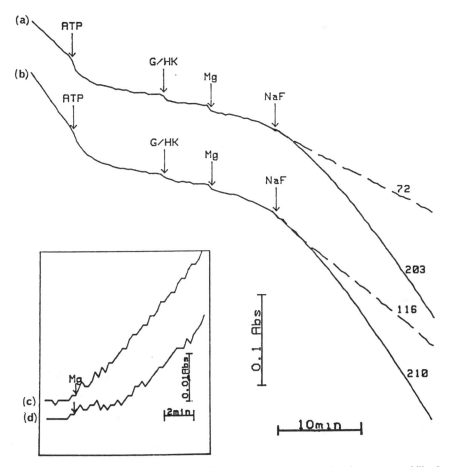

FIGURE 3. Different activities of pyruvate dehydrogenase phosphatase in toluene-permeabilized mitochondria from control (**a, d**) and insulin-treated (**b, c**) adipose tissue. Activity was followed (**a** and **b**) by measuring acetyl-CoA production as in FIGURE 2 and (**c** and **d**) by direct measurement of NADH production as absorbance at 340 nm. Traces after addition of NaF are shown as *broken lines;* continuous lines show the increase in PDC$_a$ in the absence of NaF. Mg, sufficient MgCl$_2$ was added to give 0.3 mM Mg^{2+}; other additions are as given in FIGURE 2. Further experimental details are given in the text and in Thomas & Denton.[32]

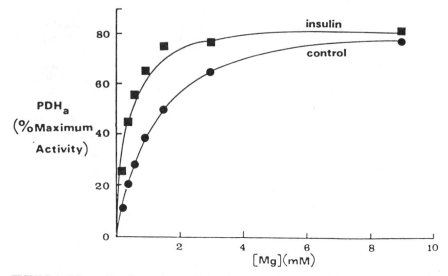

FIGURE 4. Effects of insulin on the sensitivity of pyruvate dehydrogenase phosphatase to Mg^{2+}. Toluene-permeabilized mitochondria from control (●) and insulin-treated (■) tissue were incubated as in FIGURE 3, and steady-state values of pyruvate dehydrogenase complex activity (PDH_a) were obtained in the presence of 0.2 mM ATP, 100 μM Ca^{2+}, and various Mg^{2+} concentrations. Results are replotted from Thomas & Denton.[32]

the pyruvate dehydrogenase system with a large-molecular-weight component within mitochondria and that this interaction is lost on complete lysis of mitochondria, explaining the lack of persistence of the insulin effect in mitochondrial extracts. An attractive possibility is that this large-molecular-weight component may be in the inner-mitochondrial membrane and hence might be directly involved in the transmission of the insulin signal across this membrane.

It is difficult to reconcile our findings with the view that insulin activates pyruvate dehydrogenase phosphatase through the increased formation of small-molecular-weight mediator molecules at the plasma membrane, as initially proposed by Jarett and colleagues.[18,20] Recently, Saltiel[23,27] has suggested that these mediator molecules may be inositol phosphate glycans of molecular weight about 1000, and supporting evidence for this proposal has been obtained by others.[38–40] However, although there is mounting evidence that insulin may activate an appropriate specific phospholipase C to cause the increased formation of inositol phosphate glycans from glycolipid precursors, it seems that their release may be restricted to the outside of the cell.[39] Hence, if such molecules are to be important in the regulation of the pyruvate dehydrogenase system, they would have to be transferred across both the plasma membrane and the mitochondrial inner member, a process which would certainly not be typical for phosphorylated oligosaccharides.

It would seem appropriate at this point to make some comments about the basic PDC assay system which has been widely used to follow the insulin-mimicking activities of putative insulin mediators, including preparations likely to contain inositol phosphate glycans.[18–24] The assay involves following the apparent changes in PDC activity in mitochondria that have previously been frozen and thawed in a 50 mM phosphate–based medium containing 50 μM $CaCl_2$ and 50 μM $MgCl_2$ and then incubated in the same medium in the presence or absence of mediator preparations.

The system has a number of features that suggest it may be far from optimal for studying the stimulation of PDC and may be particularly prone to artifacts. The features in question include the use of changes in the rate of decarboxylation of [1-^{14}C]pyruvate as an indirect means of following pyruvate dehydrogenase dephosphorylation. This assay can be complicated by significant blank rates of $^{14}CO_2$ production and the fact that only the activity of PDC in fully broken mitochondria would be adequately detected. In addition, the free Mg^{2+} concentration in the assay is about 5

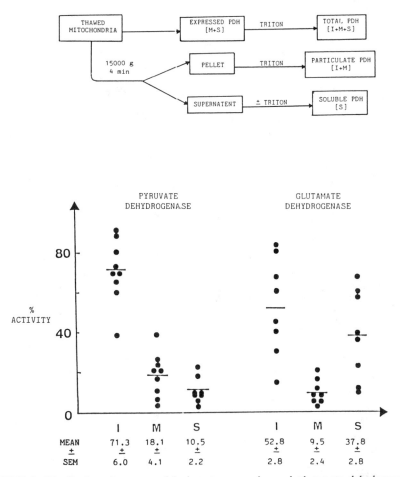

FIGURE 5. Distribution of pyruvate dehydrogenase complex and glutamate dehydrogenase (**lower panel**) in eight separate preparations of rat fat cell mitochondria which had been frozen and thawed once when suspended at about 10 mg/ml in 50 mM potassium phosphate buffer, pH 7.4. Activities of pyruvate dehydrogenase complex (*PDH*) and glutamate dehydrogenase in the frozen and thawed preparations were assayed[46] before and after centrifugation and/or treatment with 0.1% Triton to cause complete disruption of the preparation (see scheme in **upper panel**). From these assays, the proportion (as % total activity) of the dehydrogenases within intact mitochondria (I), associated with mitochondrial membranes (M), or apparently soluble (S) was calculated. Previously unpublished data of Midgley & Denton.

μM, which is far below the K_m of the phosphatase for Mg^{2+} (which is in the range 0.2–1 mM). It follows that contamination of mediator preparations with Mg^{2+} may give rise to increases in phosphatase activity. However, the weakest aspect of the assay is in the use of previously frozen mitochondria. As illustrated in FIGURE 5, this results in the damage of a variable proportion of the mitochondria at the start of the assay. In eight apparently identical preparations, the proportion of total PDC within intact mitochondria (I) varied from under 40% to over 90%, with the remainder either attached to membranes (M) or apparently released into the medium (S). Glutamate dehydrogenase exhibited a similarly variable distribution. It is important to stress that the activities calculated as within mitochondria were latent and only expressed on the addition of Triton. Morever, it was found that during subsequent incubation in the medium containing $CaCl_2$ and $MgCl_2$, there was evidence of an increase in the proportion of latent PDC—apparently due to resealing of membranes originally containing attached PDC. Clearly, it may well be possible for mediator preparations to contain components which influenced this process and hence the proportion of the pyruvate dehydrogenase measured in the assay for enzymic activity.

In our view, the use of intact coupled mitochondria or fully toluene-permeabilized mitochondria is more appropriate for the study of putative mediator molecules on the

TABLE 2. Effects of Insulin on the Activity of Pyruvate Dehydrogenase Complex in Rat Epididymal Adipose Tissue from Control, Starved, and Diabetic Rats

	PDC Activity after Incubation[a] (% total)	
Source of Tissue	No Hormone	Insulin
Normal rat	36	68[b]
Starved rat (48 hr)	18	37[b]
Alloxan-diabetic rat	16	45[b]

[a]Tissue was preincubated for 30 min before being transferred to fresh bicarbonate-buffered medium containing fructose (2 mg/ml); it was then incubated in the presence or absence of insulin (1 mU/ml) for 30 min at 37°C. Data taken from Stansbie et al.[46]

[b]Effect of insulin, $p < 0.01$ versus value for no hormone present during incubation.

pyruvate dehydrogenase system than is use of frozen mitochondrial preparations, in which PDC and its interconverting kinase and phosphatase are present in an ill-defined and changing mixture of environments. To date, we have not ourselves found any convincing effects of a range of different preparations of "mediators" on the activity of PDC within either intact or permeabilized mitochondria.

Finally, it needs to be emphasized that this paper has been concerned with the mechanism whereby insulin activated PDC activities within the span of a few minutes. This effect of insulin appears to be restricted to tissues which carry out fatty acid synthesis and is exerted through a stimulation of the phosphatase. Insulin also has long-term effects on the pyruvate dehydrogenase system, which have been extensively studied by Randle, Kerbey, and colleagues.[41–45] These studies have shown that decreases in PDC activity in heart muscle, liver, and other tissues in long-term insulin-deficient states, such as starvation and alloxan diabetes, are caused by an increase in kinase activity, perhaps via a kinase activator protein. These effects are reversed over 24–28 hr by refeeding or insulin injections. Similar effects of starvation and diabetes can be observed on PDC activity in adipose tissue.[46] However, as shown in TABLE 2, the effects are not reversed on incubation for a short period with a high concentration of insulin in vitro, clearly illustrating the separate mechanisms involved in the short- and long-term actions of insulin. Recently, Marchington et al.[47] have demonstrated the inhibition of kinase activity in hepatocytes cultured in the presence of physiological concentrations of insulin for 4 hr. It will be of interest to see if longer-term incubation of fat cells with insulin will also result in changes in kinase activity, as well as in that of the phosphatase.

REFERENCES

1. JUNGAS, R. L. 1971. Metabolism **20:** 43–53.
2. DENTON, R. M., H. G. COORE, B. R. MARTIN & P. J. RANDLE. 1971. Nature **231:** 113–116.
3. WEISS, L., G. LOFFLER, A. SCHIRMANN & O. H. WIELAND. 1971. FEBS Lett. **15:** 229–231.
4. TOPPING, D. L., A. GOHEER, H. G. COORE & P. A. MAYES. 1977. Biochem. Soc. Trans. **5:** 1000–1001.
5. ASSIMACOPOULOS-JEANNET, F., J. G. McCORMACK, M. PRENTKI, B. JEANRENAUD & R. M. DENTON. 1982. Biochim. Biophys. Acta **717:** 86–90.
6. BAXTER, M. A., M. A. GOHEER & H. G. COORE. 1979. FEBS Lett. **97:** 27–31.
7. McCORMACK, J. G. & R. M. DENTON. 1977. Biochem. J. **166:** 627–630.
8. SEVERSON, D. L., R. M. DENTON, H. T. PASK & P. J. RANDLE. 1974. Biochem. J. **140:** 225–237.
9. DENTON, R. M., P. J. RANDLE, B. J. BRIDGES, R. H. COOPER, A. L. KERBEY, H. T. PASK, D. L. SEVERSON, D. STANSBIE & S. WHITEHOUSE. 1975. Mol. Cell. Biochem. **9:** 27–52.
10. HUGHES, W. A., R. W. BROWNSEY & R. M. DENTON. 1980. Biochem. J. **192:** 469–481.
11. WIELAND, O. H. 1983. Rev. Physiol. Biochem. Pharmacol. **96:** 123–170.
12. EVANS, G. & R. M. DENTON. 1977. Biochem. Soc. Trans. **5:** 1288–1291.
13. DENTON, R. M. & W. A. HUGHES. 1978. Int. J. Biochem. **9:** 545–552.
14. WIELAND, O. H., L. WEISS, G. LOEFFLER, I. BRUNNER & S. BARD. 1974. In Metabolic Interconversion of Enzymes. E. H. Fisher, E. G. Krebs & H. Newell, eds.: 117–129. Springer. Berlin.
15. PAETZKE-BRUNNER, I., H. SCHON & O. H. WIELAND. 1978. FEBS Lett. **93:** 307–311.
16. HUGHES, W. A. & R. M. DENTON. 1976. Nature **264:** 471–473.
17. WIELAND, O. H., B. KOPFER-HOBELSBERGER, T. VRUMOW & B. GALLWITZ. 1986. In Mechanisms of Insulin Action. P. Belfrage, J. Donner, & P. Stralfors, Eds.: 249–261. Elsevier. Amsterdam.
18. SEALS, J. R. & L. JARETT. 1980. Proc. Natl. Acad. Sci. USA **77:** 77–81.
19. SEALS, J. R. & M. P. CZECH. 1980. J. Biol. Chem. **255:** 6529–6531.
20. KIECHLE, F. L., L. JARETT, N. KOTAGEL & D. A. POPP. 1981. J. Biol. Chem. **256:** 2945–2951.
21. SALTIEL, A. R., M. I. SIEGEL, S. JACOBS & P. CUATRECASAS. 1982. Proc. Natl. Acad. Sci. USA **79:** 3513–3517.
22. SUZUKI, S., T. TOYOTA, S. TAMURA, K. KIKUCHI, S. TSUIKI, L. HUANG, C. VILLAR-PALASI, J. LARNER & Y. GOTO. 1987. J. Biol. Chem. **262:** 3199–3204.
23. SALTIEL, A. R. 1987. Endocrinology **120:** 967–972.
24. GOTTSCHALK, W. K. & L. JARETT. 1988. Arch. Biochem. Biophys. **261:** 175–185.
25. SEVERSON, D. L., R. M. DENTON, H. T. PASK & P. J. RANDLE. 1974. Biochem. J. **140:** 225–237.
26. DENTON, R. M., J. G. McCORMACK & S. E. MARSHALL. 1984. Biochem. J. **217:** 441–452.
27. MARSHALL, S. E., J. G. McCORMACK & R. M. DENTON. 1984. Biochem. J. **218:** 249–260.
28. McCORMACK, J. G. 1982. Prog. Lipid. Res. **21:** 195–223.
29. REED, L. J. & S. J. YEAMAN. 1987. In The Enzymes. P. D. Boyer & E. G. Krebs, Eds. Vol. **18:** 77–96.
30. RUTTER, G. A., J. G. McCORMACK, P. J. W. MIDGLEY & R. M. DENTON. 1989. This volume.
31. THOMAS, A. P., T. A. DIGGLE & R. M. DENTON. 1986. Biochem. J. **238:** 83–91.
32. THOMAS, A. P. & R. M. DENTON. 1986. Biochem. J. **238:** 93–101.

33. CORKEY, B. E., J. DUSZYNSKI, T. L. RICH, B. MATSCHINSKY & J. R. WILLIAMSON. 1986. J. Biol. Chem. **261:** 2567–2574.
34. JUNG, D. W. & G. P. BRIERLEY. 1986. J. Biol. Chem. **261:** 6408–6415.
35. DAMUNI, Z., J. S. HUMPHREYS & L. J. REED. 1984. Biochem. Biophys. Res. Commun. **124:** 95–99.
36. DENTON, R. M. 1986. Adv. Cyclic Nucleotide Protein Phosphorylation Res. **20:** 293–341.
37. SALTIEL, A. R., J. A. FOX, P. SHERLINE & P. CUATRECASAS. 1986. Science **233:** 967–972.
38. MATO, J. M., K. L. KELLY, A. ALBER & L. JARETT. 1987. J. Biol. Chem. **263:** 2131–2137.
39. ALVAREZ, J. F., I. VARELA, J. M. RUIZ-ALBUSAC & J. M. MATO. 1988. Biochem. Biophys. Res. Commun. **152:** 1455–1462.
40. LARNER, J., L. C. HUANG, F. W. SCHWARTZ, A. S. OSWALD, T.-Y. SHEN, M. KINTER, G. TANG & K. ZELLER. 1988. Biochem. Biophys. Res. Commun. **151:** 1416–1426.
41. RANDLE, P. J. 1986. Biochem. Soc. Trans. **14:** 799–806.
42. RANDLE, P. J., S. J. FULLER, A. L. KERBEY, G. J. SALE & T. C. VARY. 1984. Horm. Cell. Regul. **9:** 139–150.
43. KERBEY, A. L. & P. J. RANDLE. 1982. Biochem. J. **206:** 103–111.
44. KERBEY, A. L., I. J. RICHARDSON & P. J. RANDLE. 1984. FEBS Lett. **176:** 115–119.
45. DENYER, G. S., A. L. KERBEY & P. J. RANDLE. 1986. Biochem. J. **239:** 347–354.
46. STANSBIE, D., R. M. DENTON, B. J. BRIDGES, H. T. PASK & P. J. RANDLE. 1976. Biochem. J. **154:** 225–236.
47. MARCHINGTON, D. R., A. L. KERBEY, A. E. JONES & P. J. RANDLE. 1987. Biochem. J. **246:** 233–236.

Insulin Mediators and the Control of Pyruvate Dehydrogenase Complex[a]

J. LARNER, L. C. HUANG, S. SUZUKI, G. TANG,
C. ZHANG, C. F. W. SCHWARTZ, G. ROMERO,
L. LUTTRELL, AND A. S. KENNINGTON

Department of Pharmacology
University of Virginia School of Medicine
Charlottesville, Virginia 22908

HISTORICAL

Just a year after insulin was discovered in Toronto by virtue of its hypoglycemic effect, its discoverers found that this hormone increased both glycogen and fat in the organs of animals injected with it.[1] We now know at the molecular level that glycogen synthase and pyruvate dehydrogenase complex (PDC), the first rate-limiting enzymes in the respective metabolic pathways involved in these effects, are each activated by insulin-induced dephosphorylation.[2] The discovery by Linn, Pettit, and Reed[3] that PDC was controlled by covalent phosphorylation in a manner analogous to glycogen synthase had two important effects: (1) it broadened the significance of covalent phosphorylation beyond the boundaries of glycogen metabolism, where it had been contained up to that time, to include lipid metabolism, and (2) it was the second example, following our work on glycogen synthase,[4] of a biosynthetic enzyme activated by dephosphorylation and inactivated by phosphorylation. These early examples, together with the prior examples of the activation of phosphorylase and phosphorylase b kinase by covalent phosphorylation, led to the current generalization that biosynthetic enzymes are activated by dephosphorylation, but degradative enzymes are activated by phosphorylation. This mechanism provides simultaneous fail-safe control of both synthesis and degradation.

INTRODUCTION

Today we recognize two major signaling mechanisms in the action of insulin: (1) altered polypeptide phosphorylation, both increased and decreased, and (2) generation of novel putative mediator molecules which are able to mimic some but not all of insulin's actions either on intact cells or in isolated enzyme systems.[2]

Although we recognize that both the activation by insulin of glycogen synthase and that of PDC are by a similar control mechanism, clear distinguishing features of the two responses have emerged. For example, Kang Cheng in our laboratory has shown that when rat adipocytes are incubated with insulin and then removed from the insulin by changing to a fresh medium, the stimulated state of glycogen synthase reverts to

[a]This work was supported by NIH Grants (AM 14334 and 22125), the University of Virginia Diabetes Center, the Pratt Fund of the University of Virginia, and an American Heart Association Grant (VHA 870027) to G. R.

normal in about 20 min, while the stimulated state of PDC is maintained for the entire 30-min time period studied[5] (FIG. 1). This indicates a distinct difference in the "off" rate of insulin action in these two systems, in keeping with the proposed existence of two separate putative mediators, which we will detail below.

PUTATIVE INSULIN MEDIATORS

On the basis of considerable early work in our laboratory and others demonstrating that insulin inactivated[6] and desensitized the cyclic AMP–dependent protein kinase,[7] maintaining it in its holoenzyme form,[8] we devised the first assay to detect the putative insulin mediator. Detection of such a mediator required demonstration of insulin-selective inhibition of the cyclic AMP–dependent protein kinase by boiled extracts prepared from insulin-treated as compared to control tissue. We originally provided the first evidence for a putative insulin mediator in 1974.[9] Our first full paper[10] demonstrated that such an activity was detected in a specific Sephadex G-25 column fraction, fraction two, corresponding to molecular weight 1000–1500. When Sephadex G-25 column fractions containing this material prepared in our laboratory were assayed in a blind fashion in Jarett's laboratory in St. Louis, fraction two was again identified by its stimulatory activity on the mitochondrial pyruvate dehydrogenase (PDH) phosphatase.[11] Subsequent work in our laboratory[12] demonstrated that the putative mediator of this PDH phosphatase stimulation sized slightly larger than the kinase inhibitor on a Sephadex G-15 column (FIG. 2). Laura Huang in our laboratory has now shown[13] that both putative mediators are readily separated by selective elution with HCl after adsorption on the anion exchanger AG1. The putative mediator for the insulin-induced activation of the PDH phosphatase stimulation is eluted at pH 2, while

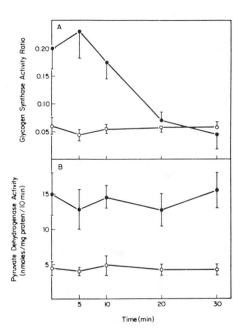

FIGURE 1. Differential effects of insulin on glycogen synthase (**upper panel**) and pyruvate dehydrogenase (**lower panel**) after the termination of insulin action. Adipocytes (20%) were incubated with (●) or without (○) insulin (1 mU/ml) at 37°C for 20 min. After incubation, the cells were washed three times with fresh Krebs-Ringer bicarbonate buffer containing 2 mM glucose and 3% bovine serum albumin, pH 7.4, and resuspended in the same buffer and incubated at 37°C. Aliquots (1 ml) were removed at the indicated times, and the enzyme activities were measured as described.[5] Data represent means ± SE from three experiments performed on different days.

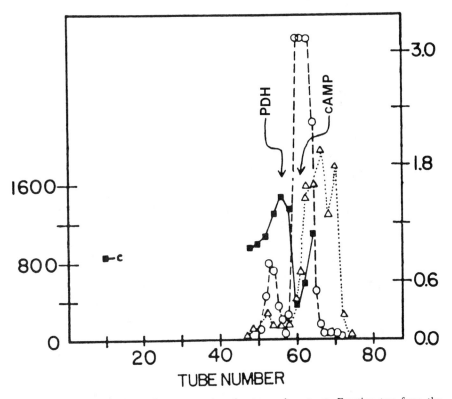

FIGURE 2. Sephadex G-15 chromatography of rat muscle extract. Fraction two from the Sephadex G-25 column was pooled, lyophilized, and applied to a Sephadex G-15 column (2.5 cm × 90 cm) in 50 mM formic acid. Fractions were analyzed for absorbance at 230 nm (O), ninhydrin reactivity (△) and the ability to stimulate phosphoprotein phosphatase 1 (■). *Arrows* indicate the relative elution positions of the PDH phosphatase mediator (PDH: 1,500 daltons) and cyclic AMP–dependent kinase mediator (cAMP: 1,200 daltons). Control phosphatase activity (c) was 900 cpm. **Left axis**, phosphatase activity (cpm); **right axis**, absorbance.

the cyclic AMP–dependent protein kinase inhibitor is eluted at pH 1.3–1.5. The putative insulin mediator that acts to increase the fraction of PDC in the active form will be referred to as the *PDC mediator*. The general chemical characteristics of these putative mediators include heat- and mild acid–stability, lability to alkali, non-adsorption to charcoal, absence of significant UV absorption, acid character, molecular size 1000–1500, and the presence of amino acids and carbohydrates on acid hydrolysis.

Chemical Composition of the Two Putative Mediators

We have now purified the two putative mediators from rat liver to essential homogeneity by following the control-insulin difference through a series of steps. They migrate as single ninhydrin-staining spots on several solvent systems. In the example

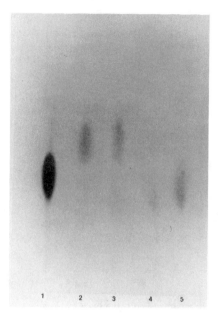

FIGURE 3. Chromatogram of purified mediators. The purified mediators were chromatographed on a thin-layer plate developed in isopropanol:pyridine:acetic acid:H_2O (8:8:1:4). Spots were visualized by ninhydrin spray. (**Lane 1**) galactosamine standard; (**lane 2**) PDH mediator from control rat liver, (**lane 3**) PDH mediator from insulin-treated rat liver; (**lane 4**) cyclase/kinase mediator from control rat liver; (**lane 5**) cyclase/kinase mediator from insulin-treated rat liver.

shown in FIGURE 3, the putative PDH phosphatase mediator has an R_f of 0.52, while the kinase inhibitor—which also inhibits the catalytic subunit of adenylate cyclase— migrates with an R_f of 0.34.

Little progress was made in elucidating the chemical structure of these substances over a number of years until the discovery in 1986 of a class of inositol-containing oligosaccharides that mimicked insulin action on a number of metabolic enzymes.[14] These observations have been independently confirmed by Mato *et al.*[15] and by Larner *et al.*[13]

TABLE 1 demonstrates that the carbohydrate constituents determined by gas chromatograph–mass spectrometry (GC/MS) after acid hydrolysis of the two putative mediators are similar but not identical. As shown, the putative PDH phosphatase mediator contains D–*chiro*-inositol, galactosamine, and mannose, while the cyclic AMP–dependent protein kinase inhibitor contains *myo*-inositol, glucosamine, and galactose. We have strong evidence that both putative mediators also contain

TABLE 1. GC/MS Data of Purified Hydrolyzed Mediators

Compound	Retention Times		Characteristic M/E			
PDH phosphatase mediator						
Mannose	9:25	10:11	191	204	217	435
Galactosamine	9:58	10:32		203	216	304
chiro-Inositol	10:43			305	318	507
Ethanolamine	4:59		174	262		
Kinase mediator						
Ethanolamine	4:59		174	262		
Galactose	9:22	9:53	204	217	435	
Glucosamine	9:27	9:44	203	216	304	
myo-Inositol	10:41		305	318	507	

ethanolamine, organic phosphorous, and, possibly, amino acids as well. There is significant agreement among the various laboratories on the chemical composition of these substances. They contain inositol, phosphate, amino sugar, and an undetermined number of neutral sugars. Their actual role in the mechanism of insulin action is yet to be determined. Nevertheless, because of their insulin-like biochemical effects and the stimulatory action of insulin in generating these compounds, it has been proposed that they constitute putative second messengers in the mechanism of insulin action. Early experiments from Jarett's laboratory indicated that addition of the unresolved putative mediator to adipocytes activated both PDC and glycogen synthase.[16]

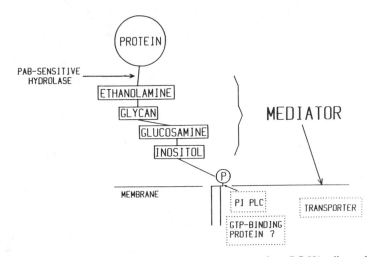

FIGURE 4. Model for the mechanism of PDC mediator release from BC_3H1 cell membranes. It is proposed that the glycophospholipid anchor of a membrane protein is a primary source of insulin mediator. Insulin activates, possibly by a protein phosphorylation process, two hydrolytic enzymes. The first of these is a protease (or possibly a phosphodiesterase) that is inhibited by *p*-aminobenzamidine (PAB) and that hydrolyzes the protein or the anchor in a position distal to inositol. This enzyme releases the protein from its anchor and generates a glycophospholipid similar to those described by Saltiel *et al.*[14] and Mato *et al.*[15] The second hydrolytic enzyme is a phospholipase C (PI PLC), the activity of which is apparently modulated by a GTP-binding protein sensitive to pertussis toxin. This enzyme cleaves the inositolphosphate-glycerol bond, releasing diacylglycerol and the mediator. The mediator is thus released to the extracellular medium and is transported into the cell by yet another component of the system.

Formation of Insulin Mediators

This constellation of components leads to the notion (FIG. 4) that the putative mediator originates from a unique class of proteins, termed *PIG tailed,* (phosphatidyl-inositol-glycan tailed) which are linked to the external surface of cells by a novel phospholipid glycan anchor. Work by Romero in our laboratory has demonstrated that two hydrolytic steps are apparently required to release the putative mediator during insulin action: a presumed proteolytic event specifically inhibited by *p*-aminobenzam-idine and detected by the release of alkaline phosphatase and of the putative PDC mediator into the medium, and a phospholipase C cleavage specifically inhibited by pertussis toxin pretreatment and detected by the release of diacylglycerol and of the putative PDC mediator into the medium.[17] The two mediators therefore presumably arise from similar but non-identical PIG-tailed proteins. As shown in the model proposed, (FIG. 4) a receptor or transporter is required to carry the externally formed putative mediator into the cell of origin (autocrine mechanism) or a neighboring cell (paracrine). Independent evidence from Mato's laboratory[18] supports the proposal of an extracellular site of putative mediator (also termed modulator). These workers recently used chemical labeling procedures to demonstrate that about 85% of the putative modulator precursor glycophospholipids are located on the outer surface of the cell membrane.

Further additional studies have documented an extracellular site of action of insulin. Proteoheparan sulfate[19] and lipoprotein lipase[20] have each been shown to be released by insulin into the extracellular medium, presumably by a phospholipase C cleavage, since the inositol glycan anchor is present on each of the released products. The time-course of this action of insulin is much slower (30–60 min) than the very much more rapid effect of insulin to release mediator reported herein. In addition, an inositol-containing oligosaccharide with modulator-like properties has been shown to

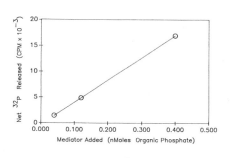

FIGURE 5. Concentration-dependence of the effect of mediator on phosphatase activity. Purified mediator was added to the phosphatase incubation mixture as indicated. The incubation mixture contained 50 mM imidazole, pH 7.4, 1 mM dithiothreitol, 10% glycerol, 0.05 mM CaCl$_2$, 10 mM MgCl$_2$, 0.2% bovine serum albumin, and phosphatase in a final volume of 40 μl. After 2 min of pre-incubation at 30°C, the reaction was initiated by the addition of 10 μl [^{32}P]PDH (190,000 cpm). The mixture was kept at 30°C for 4 min, and 40 μl was then spotted onto a piece of Whatman filter paper (2 cm × 2 cm). The paper was washed in 10% trichloroacetic acid and counted in a scintillation counter.

be released into the cell culture medium constitutively in the absence of added insulin.[21] All these reports provide further strong support to our proposal for a mechanism involving an extracellular site of action of insulin and of an extracellular initial or early location of the mediator.

Action of the Mediator on Pyruvate Dehydrogenase Phosphatase

Purified PDC mediator acts to stimulate soluble homogeneous PDH phosphatase to enhance dephosphorylation of [^{32}P]PDH. Newman *et al.*[22] have previously reported effects of mediator on soluble PDH phosphatase. In collaboration with Dr. Zahi Damuni and with homogeneous phosphatase supplied by Dr. Lester Reed, we have recently been able to demonstrate a linear stimulation of added mediator on the phosphatase reaction (FIG. 5). The stimulation occurs in the low micromolar or high nanomolar range of added mediator (as measured in terms of its content of organic phosphate). Mediator inactivated by nitrous acid deamination (TABLE 2) is inactive in

TABLE 2. Inactivation of the Putative Insulin Mediator by Nitrous Acid

Additions	Mitochondrial PDC Activity ($[^{14}C]CO_2$ released from $[1\text{-}^{14}C]$pyruvate)		Phosphatase Activity (^{32}P released from $[^{32}P]$PDH)	
	Cpm	% Control	Cpm	% Control
None	1,495	100	50,583	100
Mediator	2,730	182	67,212	133
Nitrous acid–treated mediator	1,448[a]	97[a]	53,777[b]	107[b]

[a]Purified mediator was incubated with 0.1 *M* sodium nitrite, pH 4.0, for 2 hr at room temperature.
[b]Purified mediator was incubated with 0.5 *M* sodium nitrite, pH 3.5, for 15 hr at room temperature.

this assay, as well as in the mitochondrial assay. In the presence of 50 μM Ca^{2+} and with increasing Mg^{2+} concentrations, mediator stimulates at both limiting and maximally activating Mg^{2+} concentrations (FIG. 6). This is reminiscent of the stimulations observed with mitochondria isolated from insulin-treated cells[23] and is similar to polyamine effects on the purified PDH phosphatase.[24] These studies open the field to further detailed mechanistic studies of this reaction in the future.

S. Suzuki in our laboratory[25] has shown that ATP-Mn^{2+}, the specific substrate for tyrosine kinase autophosphorylation in the insulin receptor, also markedly stimulates mediator formation. This evidence suggests a link between mediator formation, activation, or entry into the cell and receptor tyrosine phosphorylation via a phosphorylation event.

An alternate mechanism of putative modulator formation has been proposed by the laboratories of Saltiel[14] and Jarett.[15] These laboratories provide evidence that the putative modulator arises from an intracellular glycophospholipid precursor by an insulin-activated phospholipase C cleavage alone. This is in keeping with the absence of ethanolamine or amino acids in their putative modulator preparations. Perhaps two separate mechanisms are activated by insulin inside and outside the cell; or, alternatively, perhaps the effects of insulin observed on the intracellular glycophospholipid precursor simply reflect a "pull" secondary to an initial action of insulin on the external PIG-tailed protein precursor. Further work will be required to clarify the chemistry of the respective mediator and modulator molecules and the mode of their formation. But a distinct new chapter has now been added to the story of the mechanism of action of insulin.

FIGURE 6. Effect of $MgCl_2$ on the stimulatory effect of mediator. The $MgCl_2$ concentration in the phosphatase incubation mixture was varied as indicated. Phosphatase activity was determined as described in FIGURE 5, except that the amount of mediator added was 0.06 nmol organic phosphate.

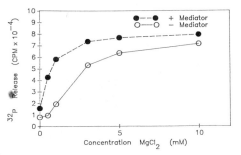

REFERENCES

1. BANTING, F. G., C. H. BEST, J. B. COLLIP, J. J. R. MACLEOD & E. C. NOBLE. 1963. *In* Selected Papers of Charles H. Best. pp. 84–87. Univ. of Toronto Press. Toronto.
2. LARNER, J. 1988. Banting memorial lecture: Insulin signaling mechanisms. Diabetes **37**: 262–275.
3. LINN, T. C., F. H. PETTIT & L. J. REED. 1969. α-Keto acid dehydrogenase complexes X. Regulation of the activity of the pyruvate dehydrogenase complex from beef kidney mitochondria by phosphorylation and dephosphorylation. Proc. Natl. Acad. Sci. USA **62**: 234–241.
4. FRIEDMAN, D. L. & J. LARNER. 1963. Interconversion of two forms of muscle UDPG-glucan transglucosylase by a phosphorylation-dephosphorylation reaction sequence. Biochemistry **2**: 669–675.
5. CHENG, K. & J. LARNER. 1987. "Stable" effects of insulin and isoproterenol on adipocyte pyruvate dehydrogenase. Arch. Biochem. Biophys. **256**: 699–702.
6. SHEN, L. C., C. VILLAR-PALASI & J. LARNER. 1970. Hormonal alteration of protein kinase sensitivity to 3′ 5′-cyclic AMP. Physiol. Chem. Phys. **2**: 536–544.
7. WALKENBACH, R. J., R. HAZEN & J. LARNER. 1978. Reversible inhibition of cyclic AMP dependent protein kinase by insulin. Mol. Cell. Biochem. **19**: 31–41.
8. GUINOVART, J., J. C. LAWRENCE & J. LARNER. 1978. Hormonal effect on fat cell adenosine 3′,5′-monophosphate dependent protein kinase. Biochem. Biophys. Acta **539**: 181–194.
9. LARNER, J., L. C. HUANG, G. BROOKER, F. MURAD & T. B. MILLER. 1974. Inhibitor of protein kinase formed in insulin treated muscle. Fed. Proc. **33**: 261.
10. LARNER, J., G. GALASKO, K. CHENG, A. A. DEPAOLI-ROACH, L. HUANG, P. DAGGY & J. KELLOGG. 1979. Generation by insulin of a chemical mediator that controls protein phosphorylation and dephosphorylation. Science **206**: 1408–1410.
11. JARETT, L. & J. R. SEALS. 1979. Pyruvate dehydrogenase activation in adipocyte mitochondria by an insulin-generated mediator from muscle. Science **206**: 1406–1408.
12. CHENG, K., M. THOMPSON, C. SCHWARTZ, C. MALCHOFF, S. TAMURA, J. CRAIG, E. LOCKER & J. LARNER. 1985. Multiple intracellular peptide mediators of insulin action. *In* Molecular Basis of Insulin Action. M. P. Czech, Ed.: 171–182. Plenum Publ. Co. New York.
13. LARNER, J., L. C. HUANG, C. F. W. SCHWARTZ, A. S. OSWALD, T.-Y. SHEN, M. KINTER, G. TANG & J. LARNER. 1988. Rat liver insulin mediator which stimulates pyruvate dehydrogenase phosphatase contains galactosamine and D-chiroinositol. Biochem. Biophys. Res. Commun. **151**: 1416–1426.
14. SALTIEL, A. R., J. A. FOX, P. SHERLINE & P. CUATRECASAS. 1986. Insulin-stimulated hydrolysis of a novel glycolipid generates modulators of cAMP-phosphodiesterase. Science **233**: 967–972.
15. MATO, J. M., K. L. KELLEY, A. ABLER & L. JARETT. 1987. Identification of a novel insulin sensitive glycophospholipid from H35 hepatoma cells. J. Biol. Chem. **262**: 2131–2137.
16. JARETT, L., E. H. A. WONG, S. L. MACAULAY & J. A. SMITH. 1985. Insulin mediators from rat skeletal muscle have differential effects on insulin-sensitive pathways of intact adipocytes. Science **227**: 533–535.
17. ROMERO, G., L. Luttrell, A. ROGOL, K. ZELLER, E. HEWLETT & J. LARNER. 1988. Phosphatidylinositol-glycan anchors of membrane proteins: Potential precursors of insulin mediators. Science **240**: 509–511.
18. ALVAREZ, J. F., I. VARELA, J. M. RUIZ-ALBUSAC & J. M. MATO. 1988. Localization of the insulin-sensitive phosphatidylinositol glycan at the outer surface of the cell membrane. Biochem. Biophys. Res. Commun. **152**: 1455–1462.
19. ISHIHARA, M., N. S. FEDARKO & H. E. CONRAD. 1987. Involvement of phosphatidylinositol and insulin in the coordinate regulation of proteoheparan sulfate metabolism and hepatocyte growth. J. Biol. Chem. **262**: 4708–4716.
20. CHAN. B. L., M. P. LISANTI, E. RODRIGUEZ-BOULAN & A. R. SALTIEL. 1988. Insulin-stimulated release of lipoprotein lipase by metabolism of its phosphatidylinositol anchor. Science **241**: 1670–1672.
21. WITTERS, L. A., T. D. WATTS, G. W. GOULD, G. E. LIENHARD & E. M. GIBBS. 1988.

Regulation of protein phosphorylation by insulin and an insulinomimetic oligosaccharide in 3T3-L1 adipocytes and Fao hepatoma cells. Biochem. Biophys. Res. Commun. **153:** 992–998.

22. NEWMAN, J. D., J. M. ARMSTRONG & J. BORNSTEIN. 1985. Assay of insulin mediator acitvity with soluble pyruvate dehydrogenase phosphatase. Endocrinology **116:** 1912–1919.

23. THOMAS, A. P., T. A. DIGGLE & R. M. DENTON. 1986. Sensitivity of pyruvate dehydrogenase phosphate phosphatase to magnesium ions. Biochem. J. **238:** 83–91.

24. DAMUNI, Z., J. S. HUMPHREYS & L. J. REED. 1984. Stimulation of pyruvate dehydrogenase phosphatase activity by polyamines. Biochem. Biophys. Res. Commun. **124:** 95–99.

25. SUZUKI, S., T. TOYOTA, S. TAMURA, K. KIKUCHI, S. TSUIKI, L. HUANG, C. VILLAR-PALASI, J. LARNER & Y. GOTO. 1987. ATP-Mn^{2+} stimulates the generation of a putative mediator of insulin action. J. Biol. Chem. **262:** 3199–3204.

Nutritional and Hormonal Regulation of the Activity State of Hepatic Branched-Chain α-Keto Acid Dehydrogenase Complex[a]

ROBERT A. HARRIS, GARY W. GOODWIN,[b]
RALPH PAXTON,[c] PAUL DEXTER, STEVEN M. POWELL,
BEI ZHANG, AMY HAN, YOSHIHARU SHIMOMURA,[d]
AND REID GIBSON

Department of Biochemistry
Indiana University School of Medicine
635 Barnhill Drive
Indianapolis, Indiana 46223

INTRODUCTION

The branched-chain α-keto acid dehydrogenase complex (EC 1.2.4.4 + no EC number for the dihydrolipoamide acyltransferase + EC 1.8.1.4) is the rate-limiting enzyme in the catabolism of the branched-chain amino acids. This complex is an intramitochondrial enzyme subject to regulation by covalent modification.[1-3] Phosphorylation causes inactivation and dephosphorylation causes activation of the complex. The kinase responsible for phosphorylation of the complex is sensitive to inhibition by branched-chain α-keto acids,[3,4] α-chloroisocaproate,[5,6] and dichloroacetate.[7,8] The phosphatase is subject to inhibition by an inhibitory protein and by nucleoside tri- and diphosphates.[9] Control of the activity state of the complex in various tissues of the intact animal has been the subject of numerous investigations from this and other laboratories.[10-15] We report here a summary of our findings concerning the nutritional and hormonal regulation of the activity state of the hepatic enzyme.

EXPERIMENTAL METHODS

Source of Materials

Branched-chain α-keto acid dehydrogenase complex and broad-specificity phosphoprotein phosphatase were isolated from rat or rabbit liver by procedures given

[a]This work was supported in part by grants from the Showalter Foundation, the Public Health Service (DK19259), and the Indiana Heart Association.

[b]Current address: Department of Biochemistry, University of Washington, Howard Hughes Medical Institute, Seattle, WA 98195.

[c]Current address: Department of Biological Sciences, Texas Tech University, Lubbock, TX 79409.

[d]Current address: Institute of Health and Sports Sciences, University of Tsukuba, Tsukuba, Ibaraki 305, Japan.

previously.[1,8,10,11] α-Chloroisocaproate was obtained from Dr. Ronald Simpson of Sandoz, Inc.

Assay of Branched-Chain α-Keto Acid Dehydrogenase Complex, Its Kinase, and Branched-Chain α-Keto Acids

Rats were killed by cervical dislocation. Livers were removed and freeze-clamped with Wollenberger clamps precooled in liquid N_2. The tissue, pulverized to a fine powder in liquid N_2, was extracted as described previously[11,16] using protease inhibitors to prevent inactivation of enzymes by proteolysis, EDTA to inhibit phosphatases, and α-chloroisocaproate to inhibit branched-chain α-keto acid dehydrogenase kinase. The extracts were assayed for enzyme activity as described previously[11,16] before and after activation of the complex by the action of the broad-specificity phosphoprotein phosphatase. Total activities were obtained by incubation with phosphatase. The activity state (percent of total activity) was taken as the activity obtained without phosphatase versus that after incubation with phosphatase. Branched-chain α-keto acid dehydrogenase kinase activity was measured as the first-order rate constant for ATP-mediated inactivation of the dehydrogenase complex.[17] Branched-chain α-keto acids were measured enzymatically as described previously.[18]

Flux Measurements through the Branched-Chain α-Keto Acid Dehydrogenase Complex with Isolated Hepatocytes

Hepatocytes were isolated from male Wistar rats fed low-protein diets.[19] Hepatocytes were incubated at 37°C in Krebs-Henseleit buffer supplemented with 2.5% bovine albumin, under an atmosphere of 95% O_2, 5% CO_2. 1-[14C]-labeled α-ketoisovalerate was added to a final concentration of 0.2 mM, and the incubation was conducted for 15 min. The reaction was terminated with acid, and the CO_2 was collected as described previously.[19]

RESULTS

Effect of Dietary Protein Level and Starvation on the in Vivo Activity State of Hepatic Branched-Chain α-Keto Acid Dehydrogenase Complex

The branched-chain α-keto acid dehydrogenase complex is completely active (i.e., completely dephosphorylated) in the liver of rats maintained on Purina chow diet (minimum 23% protein diet). Feeding rats for several days on protein-restricted diets results in inactivation of the complex (6% active with 0% protein diet; 10% active with 8% protein diet; 58% active with 20% protein diet).[11] In contrast to protein starvation, complete withdrawal of food from the rats (starvation) up to the longest period of time tested (5 days) causes no inactivation of the complex.[17] Starvation of rats previously fed an 8% protein diet results in activation of the complex.[11,15] Protein excess in the diet places the complex in the completely activated state (95% active with 30% protein diet; completely active with 50% protein diet.[11]

Effect of Diabetes on the Activity State of Hepatic Branched-Chain α-Keto Acid Dehydrogenase Complex

Diabetes induced by the injection of streptozotocin has the same effects as starvation, i.e., it causes no change in the activity state with Purina chow–fed rats but results in activation of the complex with low-protein–fed animals.[10,20]

Effect of Dietary Protein Level, Starvation, and Diabetes on Blood Concentrations of the Branched-Chain α-Keto Acids

Feeding rats restricted protein diets results in low blood levels of branched-chain α-keto acids (12 μM with 0% protein diet; 19 μM with 8% protein diet; 28 μM with 20% protein diet).[17] Starvation of rats for 48 hr or streptozotocin-induced diabetes results in elevated levels of the keto acids (20 μM for control animals; 32 μM for starved; 100 μM for diabetic).[17,19]

Effect of Branched-Chain α-Keto Acids on the Activity State of the Dehydrogenase Complex in Isolated Hepatocytes

The branched-chain α-keto acid dehydrogenase complex exists largely in the inactive state in hepatocytes isolated from low-protein–(8% protein diet) fed rats.[19] Activation of and increased flux through the complex result from preincubation of the hepatocytes with the branched α-keto acids.[19] The keto acid obtained by transamination of leucine (α-ketoisocaproate) is the most effective inhibitor of the dehydrogenase kinase.[3,4]

Effect of Cycloheximide on the In Vivo *Activity State of the Dehydrogenase Complex and on Blood Levels of Branched-Chain α-Keto Acids*

Injection of cycloheximide into rats maintained on a low-protein diet (FIG. 1) results in activation of the complex (P. Dexter and R. A. Harris, unpublished observations). A striking increase in blood levels of the branched-chain α-keto acids occurs concurrently with activation of the complex (Fig. 1).

Effect of Dietary Protein Level, Starvation, and Diabetes on the Activity of Branched-Chain α-Keto Acid Dehydrogenase Kinase

Branched-chain α-keto acid dehydrogenase kinase activity varies inversely with the dietary protein content, i.e., the lower the protein content the greater the kinase activity (measured as first-order rate constant: 2.4 min^{-1} for 0% protein diet; 2.3 for 8% protein diet; 1.5 for 20% protein diet; 0.7 for 30% protein diet; 0.5 for 50% protein diet) (Ref. 17; G. W. Goodwin, unpublished observations). Starvation for 48 hr and induction of diabetes with streptozotocin also resulted in diminished kinase activity (results not shown).

DISCUSSION

The liver plays an important role in the disposal of excess dietary branched-chain amino acids. These amino acids are essential for protein synthesis in every cell but, when present in excess, must be oxidized to avoid the toxic effects that occur in maple syrup urine disease. The liver is largely devoid of branched-chain amino acid aminotransferase activity but contains considerable branched-chain α-keto acid dehydrogenase complex activity. The excess branched-chain amino acids are transaminated in the extrahepatic tissues to keto acids which, in turn, are released into the blood,

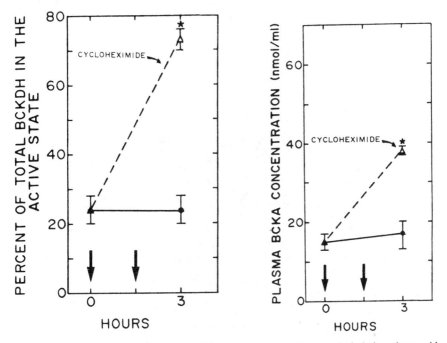

FIGURE 1. Effect of cycloheximide on the activity state of the branched-chain α-keto acid dehydrogenase complex (BCKDH) and plasma branched-chain α-keto acid (BCKA) concentration. Cycloheximide-treated rats (△) received intraperitoneal injection of cycloheximide (0.5 mg/kg) at times indicated by *large arrows*. Control rats (●) were injected with saline.

taken up by the liver, and oxidatively decarboxylated by the branched-chain α-keto acid dehydrogenase complex (see FIG. 2 and reviews in Refs. 21 and 22). Because the branched-chain α-keto acids are potent inhibitors of branched-chain α-keto acid dehydrogenase kinase,[3,4] they have the potential to act as feed-forward activators for their decarboxylation. As described above, the branched-chain α-keto acid concentration of the blood varies directly with the dietary protein level, and branched-chain α-keto acids activate the branched-chain α-keto acid dehydrogenase complex in hepatocytes prepared from low-protein–fed rats. Thus, the activity state of the branched-chain α-keto acid dehydrogenase complex is likely determined in part by the accumulation of branched-chain α-keto acids produced by transamination of the branched-chain amino acids not required for protein synthesis.

Starvation of an animal for all sources of calories does not have the same effect as protein starvation has on the activity state of the hepatic branched-chain α-keto acid dehydrogenase complex. Indeed, starvation of animals previously protein-starved results in activation of the branched-chain α-keto acid dehydrogenase complex. This finding is reasonable because there is a need of substrates for gluconeogenesis to maintain blood glucose in the starved state. Valine and isoleucine are gluconeogenic and must, therefore, be used to meet the body's need for glucose. The concentrations of the branched-chain amino acids and their corresponding keto acids rise in the starved state, presumably because of increased proteolysis of tissue proteins. Inhibition of branched-chain α-keto acid dehydrogenase kinase by the branched-chain α-keto acids probably contributes to maintaining the dehydrogenase complex in the completely

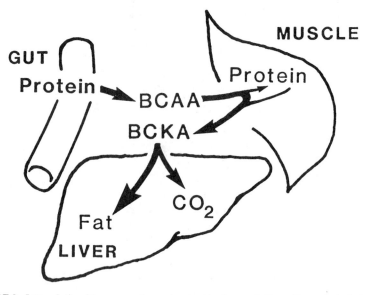

FIGURE 2. Interrelationships among tissues involved in the catabolism of branched-chain amino acids (BCAA). BCKA, branched-chain α-keto acids.

active, dephosphorylated state in this nutritional condition. As expected, induction of diabetes by streptozotocin treatment has the same effects as starvation on the activity state of the dehydrogenase complex. Loss of insulin control of tissue proteolysis undoubtedly contributes to the elevation of the level of branched-chain amino acids and keto acids that occurs in this condition. Indeed, inducing or maintaining the active form of the dehydrogenase complex in the diabetic state must serve to blunt the increase in the blood level of branched-chain amino acids that could otherwise occur.

The cycloheximide experiment was designed to test the hypothesis that regulation of the activity state of the branched-chain α-keto acid dehydrogenase complex is tightly coupled to the requirement for branched-chain amino acids for protein synthesis. The working hypothesis was that inhibition of protein synthesis *in vivo* would result in elevated levels of the branched-chain amino acids and the corresponding keto acids, and that the latter would trigger, via inhibition of branched-chain α-keto acid dehydrogenase kinase, an activation of the hepatic branched-chain α-keto acid dehydrogenase complex. This effect was found in the present study with animals previously maintained on a low-protein diet. Thus, even in a nutritional state in which the animal is starving for protein, inhibition of protein synthesis results in activation of the oxidative pathway for disposal of the branched-chain amino acids. This study provides additional evidence that the activity state of the dehydrogenase complex is subject to short-term regulation by blood levels of the branched-chain α-keto acids. These results were in fact predictable from the previous findings of others. A paradoxical increase in activity of the hepatic complex in response to cycloheximide was reported many years ago in the important paper by Wohlhueter and Harper.[23] That study was carried out prior to our current appreciation of the regulation of the complex by covalent modification. The present work establishes that dephosphorylation of the complex explains the increase in enzyme activity caused by cycloheximide.

Protein malnutrition results in an increase in activity of the kinase responsible for inactivation of the branched-chain α-keto acid dehydrogenase complex. Espinal *et al.*[24] reported previously that complete absence of protein from the diet results in a substantial increase in kinase activity. We have found an inverse correlation between kinase activity and the activity state of the dehydrogenase complex in response to variation in dietary protein intake. Thus, an undefined adaptive mechanism adjusts the activity of the kinase to effect decreased (protein-starved state) or increased (protein-excess state) activity of the dehydrogenase complex. Regulation of kinase activity can be achieved in the short term by rapid changes in branched-chain α-keto acid concentration and in the long term by the more direct means of changing the amount of total kinase activity. The exact mechanism responsible for the adaptive change in kinase activity remains to be established.

SUMMARY

The hepatic branched-chain α-keto acid dehydrogenase complex plays an important role in regulating branched-chain amino acid levels. These compounds are essential for protein synthesis but are toxic if present in excess. When dietary protein is deficient, the hepatic enzyme is present in the inactive, phosphorylated state to allow conservation of branched-chain amino acids for protein synthesis. When dietary protein is excessive, the enzyme is in the active, dephosphorylated state to commit the excess branched-chain amino acids to degradation. Inhibition of protein synthesis by cycloheximide, even when the animal is starving for protein, results in activation of the hepatic branched-chain α-keto acid dehydrogenase complex to prevent accumulation of branched-chain amino acids. Likewise, the increase in branched-chain amino acids caused by body wasting during starvation and uncontrolled diabetes is blunted by activation of the hepatic branched-chain α-keto acid dehydrogenase complex. The activity state of the hepatic branched-chain α-keto acid dehydrogenase complex is regulated in the short term by the concentration of branched-chain α-keto acids (inhibitors of branched-chain α-keto acid dehydrogenase kinase) and in the long term by alteration in the total branched chain α-keto acid dehydrogenase kinase activity.

REFERENCES

1. PAXTON, R. & R. A. HARRIS. 1982. Isolation of rabbit liver branched chain α-ketoacid dehydrogenase and regulation by phosphorylation. J Biol Chem. **257:** 14433–14439.

2. ODESSEY, R. 1982. Purification of rat kidney branched-chain oxoacid dehydrogenase complex with endogenous kinase activity. Biochem. J. **204:** 353–356.
3. LAU, K. D., H. R. FATANIA & P. J. RANDLE. 1982. Regulation of the branched-chain 2-oxoacid dehydrogenase kinase reaction. FEBS Lett. **144:** 57–62.
4. PAXTON, R. & R. A. HARRIS. 1984. Regulation of branched chain α-ketoacid dehydrogenase kinase. Arch. Biochem. Biophys. **231:** 48–57.
5. HARRIS, R. A., R. PAXTON & A. A. DEPAOLI-ROACH. 1982. Inhibition of branched chain α-ketoacid dehydrogenase kinase activity by α-chloroisocaproate. J. Biol. Chem. **257:** 13915–13918.
6. SHIMOMURA, Y., M. J. KUNTZ, M. SUZUKI, T. OZAWA & R. A. HARRIS. 1988. Monovalent cations and inorganic phosphate alter branched chain α-ketoacid dehydrogenase kinase activity and inhibitor sensitivity. Arch. Biochem. Biophys. **266:** 210–218.
7. SANS, R. M., W. W. JOLLY & R. A. HARRIS. 1980. Studies on the regulation of leucine catabolism. Mechanism responsible for oxidizable substrate inhibition and dichloroacetate stimulation of leucine oxidation by the heart. Arch. Biochem. Biophys. **200:** 336–345.
8. PAXTON, R. & R. A. HARRIS. 1984. Clofibric acid, phenylpyruvate, and dichloroacetate inhibition of branched chain α-ketoacid dehydrogenase kinase *in vitro* and in perfused rat heart. Arch. Biochem. Biophys. **231:** 58–66.
9. DAMUNI, Z. & L. J. REED. 1987. Purification and properties of the catalytic subunit of the branched chain α-ketoacid dehydrogenase phosphatase from bovine kidney mitochondria. J. Biol. Chem. **262:** 5129–5132.
10. GILLIM, S. E., R. PAXTON, G. A. COOK & R. A. HARRIS. 1983. Activity state of the branched chain α-ketoacid dehydrogenase complex in the heart, liver, and kidney of model, 48-h fasted, diabetic, low-protein fed, and high-protein fed rats. Biochem. Biophys. Res. Commun. **111:** 74–81.
11. HARRIS, R. A., R. PAXTON, G. W. GOODWIN & S. M. POWELL. 1985. Physiological covalent regulation of rat liver branched chain α-ketoacid dehydrogenase. Arch. Biochem. Biophys. **243:** 542–555.
12. PATSTON, P. A., J. ESPINAL & P. J. RANDLE. 1984. Effects of diet and of alloxan-diabetes on the activity of branched-chain 2-oxo acid dehydrogenase complex and of activator protein in rat tissues. Biochem. J. **222:** 711–719.
13. DIXON, J. L. & A. E. HARPER. 1984. Effects of plasma amino acid concentrations and hepatic branched-chain α-ketoacid dehydrogenase activity of feeding rats diets containing 9 or 50% casein. J. Nutr. **114:** 1025–1034.
14. WAGENMAKERS, A. J. M., J. T. G. SCHEPENS & J. H. VEERKAMP. 1984. Effect of starvation and exercise on actual and total activity of the branched-chain 2-oxo acid dehydrogenase complex in rat tissues. Biochem. J. **223:** 815–821.
15. SOLOMON, M., K. G. COOK & S. J. YEAMAN. 1987. Effect of diet and starvation on the activity state of branched-chain 2-oxoacid dehydrogenase complex in rat liver and heart. Biochim. Biophys. Acta **931:** 335–338.
16. GOODWIN, G. W., B. ZHANG, R. PAXTON & R. A. HARRIS. 1988. Determination of activity and activity state of branched-chain α-ketoacid dehydrogenase in rat tissues. Methods Enzymol. **166:** 189–200.
17. GOODWIN, G. W. 1989. Regulation of valine catabolism. Ph.D. Thesis. Indiana University, Indianapolis, IN.
18. GOODWIN, G. W., M. J. KUNTZ, R. PAXTON & R. A. HARRIS. 1987. Enzymatic determination of branched-chain α-ketoacids. Anal. Biochem. **162:** 526–539.
19. HAN, A. C., G. W. GOODWIN, R. PAXTON & R. A. HARRIS. 1987. Activation of branched-chain α-ketoacid dehydrogenase in isolated hepatocytes by branched chain α-ketoacids. Arch. Biochem. Biophys. **258:** 85–94.
20. GIBSON, R. G., G. W. GOODWIN, S. E. FINEBERG & R. A. HARRIS. 1989. Effects of diabetes and insulin on the total activity and activity state of hepatic branched chain α-ketoacid dehydrogenase complex. J. Cell Biol. **107:** 633a.
21. HARPER, A. E., R. H. MILLER & K. P. BLOCH. 1984. Branched-chain amino acid metabolism. Annu. Rev. Nutr. **4:** 409–454.
22. HARRIS, R. A., R. PAXTON, S. M. POWELL, G. W. GOODWIN, M. J. KUNTZ & A. C. HAN.

1986. Regulation of branched-chain α-ketoacid dehydrogenase complex by covalent modification. Adv. Enzyme Regul. **25:** 219–237.

23. WOHLHUETER, R. M. & A. E. HARPER. 1970. Coinduction of rat liver branched chain α-ketoacid dehydrogenase activities. J. Biol. Chem. **245:** 2391–2401.

24. ESPINAL, J., M. BEGGS, H. PATEL & P. J. RANDLE. 1986. Effects of low-protein diet and starvation on the activity of branched-chain 2-oxo acid dehydrogenase kinase in rat liver and heart. Biochem. J. **237:** 285–288.

The Role of Regulation of Tissue Pyruvate Dehydrogenase Complex Activity during the Starved-to-Fed Transition[a]

M. C. SUGDEN AND M. J. HOLNESS

Department of Biochemistry
London Hospital Medical College
Turner Street
London, E1 2AD
United Kingdom

INTRODUCTION

The oxidative decarboxylation of pyruvate to acetyl-CoA, catalyzed by the mitochondrial pyruvate dehydrogenase complex (PDC), is the first physiologically irreversible reaction in the oxidative pathway of glucose metabolism. There are two alternative metabolic fates for acetyl-CoA generated via the PDC reaction. In most tissues, the metabolic fate of acetyl-CoA is predominantly its complete oxidation to CO_2 via the tricarboxylic acid (TCA) cycle, and in general the oxidation of lipid fuels (fatty acids and/or ketone bodies) can substitute for the oxidation of pyruvate for energy production (the glucose/fatty acid cycle[1]). In lipogenic tissues (e.g., liver, adipose tissue, and lactating mammary gland), acetyl-CoA entering the TCA cycle via PDC can additionally be utilized for fatty acid synthesis via the condensation of acetyl-CoA with oxaloacetate to form citrate, efflux of citrate to the cytoplasm, and cleavage of citrate by ATP-citrate lyase. This sequence regenerates oxaloacetate and acetyl-CoA in the cytoplasm, where acetyl-CoA enters the lipogenic pathway via acetyl-CoA carboxylase. Since the accumulation of citrate can occur only when the supply of acetyl-CoA via flux through PDC exceeds carbon flux through the span of the TCA cycle from citrate to oxaloacetate, the availability of citrate for lipid synthesis can increase only when energy demands are satisfied. In liver, the formation of citrate via such an overflow mechanism in the fed state is closely paralleled by the formation of ketone bodies in the starved state. In this latter instance, however, PDC is relatively inactive, acetyl-CoA is provided predominantly by the β-oxidation of fatty acids, and citrate synthesis is limited by the oxaloacetate supply.[2-4]

The oxidation of pyruvate is not necessarily confined to those tissues in which it is generated. In tissues which have low oxidative capacity and/or exhibit high rates of glycolysis, a proportion of the available pyruvate is converted to lactate, which is released into the circulation. Such tissues may include skeletal muscle, the skin, mature red blood cells, the renal medulla, and nervous tissue. After refeeding, the gut may also be an important site of lactate production, with conversion of dietary carbohydrate to lactate occurring during absorption.[5-7] While heart and kidney and, in some circumstances, skeletal muscle can utilize blood-borne lactate, up to 70% of total lactate removal is hepatic.[8] However, the hepatic fate of lactate, after its reconversion

[a]This work was supported by the U.K. Medical Research Council; The British Heart Foundation; Hoescht U.K. Ltd.; Bucks., U.K.; and KabiVitrum Ltd., Middx., U.K.

314

to pyruvate, is not exclusively restricted to energy production or lipid synthesis. In starvation, where hepatic ATP requirements can be met by the β-oxidation of fatty acids, pyruvate is utilized for glucose synthesis via glucose-6-phosphate formation (gluconeogenesis). Entry of pyruvate into the gluconeogenic pathway also occurs after refeeding carbohydrate to previously starved rats,[9] but, in this case, the glucose-6-phosphate is preferentially used for glycogenesis rather than for glucose production.[10-13]

In this review, we shall attempt to define the extent to which regulation of the activity of PDC during the starved-to-fed transition is important in determining the alternative metabolic fates of pyruvate (gluconeogenesis, glycogenesis, oxidation, lipid synthesis) within the liver. We also discuss the possibility that there may be interorgan cooperation to ensure the disposal of dietary carbohydrate in a way which is of optimal benefit to the organism as a whole.

REGULATION OF PDC ACTIVITY

The mechanisms involved in the regulation of PDC activity are summarized in FIGURE 1. PDC is regulated by reversible phosphorylation,[14,15] a limitation on the rate of pyruvate oxidation being imposed by the percentage of the complex in the active (dephosphorylated) form. This percentage is determined by the relative activities of two specific enzymes, pyruvate dehydrogenase (PDH) kinase (phosphorylating) and PDH phosphatase (dephosphorylating). Starvation is associated with net phosphorylation of the complex.[16,17] In tissues, such as heart and skeletal muscle, where PDC is important solely for ATP production, the increased state of PDC phosphorylation is thought to be secondary to an increase in the activity of PDH kinase, rather than to a decrease in the activity of PDH phosphatase.[18-20] Increases in PDH kinase activity may be achieved as a consequence of increased mitochondrial acetyl-CoA/CoA (and possibly $NADH/NAD^+$) concentration ratios, conditions associated with decreased flux through PDC, secondary to end-product inhibition.[17] Such increases may occur concomitantly with diminished inhibition of PDH kinase activity by pyruvate.[17]

It has been clearly demonstrated that increases in mitochondrial acetyl-CoA/CoA and $NADH/NAD^+$ concentration ratios result from increased oxidation of lipid fuels.[21] The oxidation of lipid fuels may also decrease pyruvate availability via suppression of glycolysis at the level of phosphofructokinase-1[22,23] and glucose phosphorylation/uptake[24] (in liver, this may be coupled with stimulation of gluconeogenesis). Long-term starvation is associated with adaptive increases in PDH kinase activity,[18,19,25] achieved in part by increases in the specific activity of a protein activator of PDH kinase (kinase activator protein, KAP).[26-28] However, in contrast to the relatively rapid effects of increases in fat oxidation on PDH kinase activity, these changes are relatively slow in onset,[29] and, once invoked, may be envisaged to provide a hysteresis mechanism to avoid transient increases in PDC activity under conditions where the restoration of an exogenous carbohydrate supply is not assured.

In lipogenic tissues, some of which (e.g., white adipose tissue) do not efficiently oxidize fatty acids or ketone bodies, an increase in the PDH kinase–to–PDH phosphatase activity ratio may additionally be achieved as a consequence of deactivation of PDH phosphatase as a result of a decrease in the insulin concentration.[30,31] In liver, evidence has been presented suggesting that there is stringent control of the activities of both PDH kinase and PDH phosphatase.[32] Such dual control may be necessary because of the unique role of liver in glycogen storage and in the production of lipid substrates (lipoproteins and ketone bodies) for use by peripheral tissues.

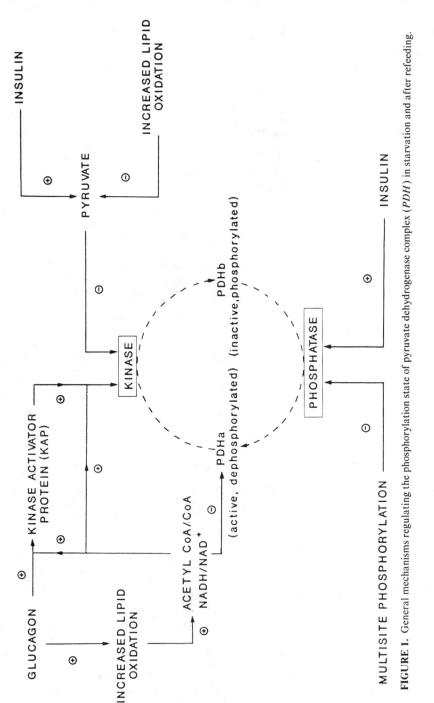

FIGURE 1. General mechanisms regulating the phosphorylation state of pyruvate dehydrogenase complex (*PDH*) in starvation and after refeeding.

THE RESPONSE TO STARVATION

Increases in whole-body glucose turnover occur in response to insulin infusion in post-absorptive rats.[33] However, from a comparison of the individual responses of a range of tissues (including brain, adipose tissue, and skeletal muscle) to prolonged (48 hr) starvation, it appears that the major factor restricting glucose uptake and utilization is not the decline in insulin concentration, but the preferential oxidation of lipid fuels, particularly by working muscles with initially high rates of glucose utilization, including the heart.[24] Hepatic glucose utilization may also be suppressed under conditions where fatty acid oxidation is increased, both at the level of glycolysis (phosphofructokinase-1)[22,23] and at the level of pyruvate oxidation.[21]

The concept that the operation of the glucose/fatty acid cycle is of critical importance for glucose conservation in prolonged starvation is supported by the pattern of changes in circulating substrate concentrations observed over a 48-hr starvation period. (FIG. 2a). Blood glucose concentrations decline by ca. 50%, the decrease in glycemia being closely paralleled by a decrease in blood lactate. The decreased availability of these carbohydrate-derived fuels is accompanied by increased availability of lipid-derived fuels (fatty acids, ketone bodies). However, while the most marked decrease in glycemia occurs between 4 and 24 hr of starvation, glucose concentrations are maintained for the subsequent 24 hr, during which time high blood fatty acid and ketone body concentrations are observed. Over this latter period, glucose concentrations are maintained via gluconeogenesis as hepatic glycogen stores are exhausted (FIG. 2a; TABLE 1). Glycemia decreases and lactate concentrations increase if gluconeogenesis is inhibited, for example, by the administration of 3-mercaptopicolinate (MPA), an inhibitor of PEP-carboxykinase[35-37] (TABLE 1).

Maintenance of glycemia in the absence of exogenous (i.e., dietary) glucose is facilitated by partial or total inactivation of PDC. The inactivation profiles for liver, heart, and kidney, three tissues of high oxidative capacity, are shown in FIGURE 2b. With the possible exception of the brain, such inactivation has been demonstrated to occur in all tissues studied.[16,17] The importance of PDC inactivation for glucose homeostasis once hepatic glycogen is depleted is that the metabolism of glucose is thus restricted to its conversion to lactate (or related C_3 intermediates, such as alanine). Such intermediates can be recycled to glucose via gluconeogenesis[38] (FIG. 3).

Both hypolactatemia and hypoglycemia are observed in 48 hr–starved rats when PDC activity is increased, for example, by pharmacological suppression of PDH kinase activity by dichloroacetate (DCA)[39,40] (TABLE 1). Whereas essentially complete reactivation of PDC is achieved in heart, kidney, and skeletal muscle, reactivation of hepatic PDC is not observed[40] (TABLE 1), although an increase in hepatic PDC activity can be effected in response to DCA in rats starved for less prolonged periods[39] or if glucose is additionally administered[40] (TABLE 2). The finding that the efficacy of PDC reactivation in response to DCA might be critically dependent on the length of the antecedent period of starvation raised the possibility that adaptive changes in the regulation of the complex might modulate the response to refeeding.

REFEEDING AFTER PROLONGED (48 HOUR) STARVATION

PDC Activities and Carbon Recycling after Glucose Refeeding

The response to refeeding carbohydrate or a mixed diet involves repletion of hepatic glycogen[12,13,37,40–43] (TABLE 2; see also TABLE 4, below). Our interest in the regulation of PDC activity during the starved-to-fed transition first arose when it

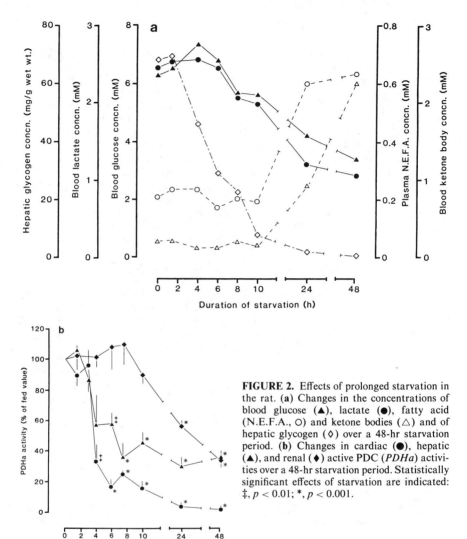

FIGURE 2. Effects of prolonged starvation in the rat. (**a**) Changes in the concentrations of blood glucose (▲), lactate (●), fatty acid (N.E.F.A., ○) and ketone bodies (△) and of hepatic glycogen (◇) over a 48-hr starvation period. (**b**) Changes in cardiac (●), hepatic (▲), and renal (◆) active PDC (*PDHa*) activities over a 48-hr starvation period. Statistically significant effects of starvation are indicated: ‡, $p < 0.01$; *, $p < 0.001$.

became apparent that the hepatic capacity for net glucose phosphorylation is diminished during starvation and that the precursors utilized for hepatic glycogen synthesis include C_3 derivatives of glucose (predominantly lactate) as well as glucose itself.[9,44] Studies in intact animals[10,37,41] and with isolated liver preparations[37,45–47] indicated the involvement of the gluconeogenic pathway in hepatic glycogen synthesis from these C_3 derivatives. Thus, for example, hepatic glycogenesis during the first 2 hr after the administration of glucose is blocked when gluconeogenesis is inhibited with MPA[37,48] (TABLE 2). The existence of the indirect (gluconeogenic) pathway of hepatic glycogenesis necessitates not only that carbon flux from glucose to lactate should continue (or

TABLE 1. Effects of Inhibition of Gluconeogenesis and Reactivation of PDC on Concentrations of Hepatic Glycogen and Blood Metabolites and on Tissue Activities of Activated PDC (PDCa) in 48-hr–Starved Rats

Response	Fed ad libitum	48-hr Starved[a]		
		Control	3-Mercaptopicolinate[b]	Dichloroacetate[b]
Hepatic glycogen[c] (mg/g wet wt.)	68.1 ± 0.3	0.9 ± 0.2	1.4 ± 0.3	1.6 ± 0.4
Blood metabolites[d] (mM)				
Glucose	6.28 ± 0.45	4.47 ± 0.18	1.66 ± 0.16**	3.37 ± 0.26*
Lactate	2.52 ± 0.33	1.23 ± 0.11	2.67 ± 0.17***	0.35 ± 0.02***
PDCa activity[e] (% of fed value)				
Liver	100	21 ± 2	18 ± 3	22 ± 1
Heart	100	14 ± 2	9 ± 2	60 ± 5***
Kidney	100	37 ± 2	33 ± 5	93 ± 7***
Skeletal muscle	100	13 ± 2	13 ± 4	146 ± 12**

[a]Female albino Wistar rats (180–220 g) were administered 3-mercaptopicolinate (20 mg/100 mg body wt.) to inhibit gluconeogenesis or dichloroacetate [0.25 ml of a 5% (w/v) solution] to reactivate PDC by intraperitoneal injection 2 hr before sampling.
[b]Statistically significant effects of 3-mercaptopicolinate or dichloroacetate are indicated: *, $p < 0.05$; **, $p < 0.01$; ***, $p < 0.001$.
[c]Glycogen concentrations were determined in extracts of freeze-clamped liver.
[d]Blood glucose and lactate concentrations were determined in KOH-neutralized $HClO_4$ extracts of arterial blood.[34]
[e]PDCa activities were measured in freeze-clamped tissue extracts.[21]

possibly even increase) after refeeding, but also that the gluconeogenic pathway should continue to compete effectively with PDC for available pyruvate (FIG. 4).

The identity of the site(s) of the initial metabolism of glucose to its C_3 breakdown products during the first 2 hr after refeeding remains controversial.[6,7,40,49,50–56] However, in three of the tissues known to be capable of oxidation of exogenous (i.e., circulating) lactate (liver, heart, skeletal muscle),[8,57] PDC activities remained low for at least 2 hr after the administration of glucose to 48-hr–starved rats (TABLE 2). This delayed reactivation contrasted with more immediate increases in PDC activities in kidney (TABLE 2) and adipose tissue,[32,40,58] but the possibility that it might be of quantitative importance for sparing C_3 precursors for hepatic glycogenesis was indicated by inhibition of hepatic glycogen deposition when glucose was administered in combina-

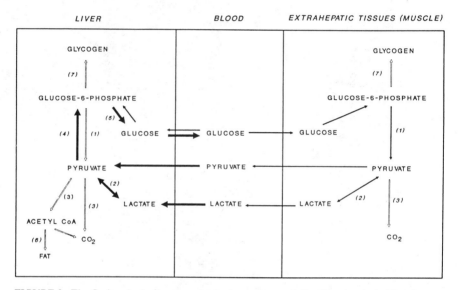

FIGURE 3. The Cori cycle. In the starved rat, glucose is metabolized by glycolysis (1) to lactate (2) in extrahepatic tissues. Pyruvate oxidation (3) is markedly inhibited. Pyruvate and lactate are transferred through the circulation to the liver and resynthesized to glucose (4, 5). In the liver, pyruvate oxidation (3) and utilization of pyruvate for lipid (6) and glycogen (7) synthesis are inhibited (*white arrows*).

tion with DCA[40] (TABLE 2). This inhibition was associated with a decline in blood lactate concentrations, but blood glucose concentrations were unaffected by DCA[40] (TABLE 2).

The Role of PDC in Determining the Fate (Glycogenesis versus Lipogenesis) of Hepatic Pyruvate

Changes in rates of hepatic lipid synthesis observed in fed rats after the administration of glucose (TABLE 3) or after acute exposure to anti-insulin serum[59] are not associated with changes in PDC activity, and it is generally considered that acetyl-CoA carboxylase, rather than PDC, is flux-generating. However, acetyl-CoA carboxylase

TABLE 2. Effects of Inhibition of Gluconeogenesis and Reactivation of PDC on Hepatic Glycogen Repletion, Blood Metabolite Concentrations, and Tissue PDCa Activities in Response to Intragastric Glucose in 48-hr-Starved Rats

Response	Fed ad libitum	48-hr Starved[a]		
		Control	3-Mercaptopicolinate[b]	Dichloroacetate[b]
Hepatic glycogen[c] (mg/g wet wt.)	68.1 ± 0.3	11.4 ± 0.9	1.4 ± 0.5***	2.8 ± 1.3***
Blood metabolites[d] (mM)				
Glucose	6.28 ± 0.45	8.06 ± 0.57	5.95 ± 0.56*	6.80 ± 0.53
Lactate	2.52 ± 0.33	2.46 ± 0.27	2.10 ± 0.16	0.41 ± 0.03***
PDCa activity[e] (% of fed value)				
Liver	100	21 ± 4	13 ± 3	105 ± 2***
Heart	100	21 ± 3	14 ± 4	80 ± 4***
Kidney	100	94 ± 7	85 ± 5	95 ± 6
Skeletal muscle	100	16 ± 3	14 ± 3	98 ± 14***

[a]Female albino Wistar rats (180–220 g) were administered glucose (2 mmol/100 g body wt.) intragastrically at 2 hr before sampling. 3-Mercaptopicolinate (20 mg/100 g body wt.) to inhibit gluconeogenesis or dichloroacetate [0.25 ml of a 5% (w/v) solution] to reactivate PDC was injected intraperitoneally at the time of glucose administration.
[b]Statistically significant effects of 3-mercaptopicolinate or dichloroacetate are indicated: *, $p < 0.05$; ***, $p < 0.001$.
[c]Glycogen concentrations were determined in extracts of freeze-clamped liver.[34]
[d]Blood glucose and lactate concentrations were determined in KOH-neutralized $HClO_4$ extracts of arterial blood.[34]
[e]PDCa activities were measured in freeze-clamped tissue extracts.[21]

cannot be flux-generating unless it is saturated with substrate (cytoplasmic acetyl-CoA). In the fed state, cytoplasmic acetyl-CoA is derived from carbohydrate via PDC, citrate synthase, and ATP-citrate lyase; and, as a consequence, marked inhibition of lipogenesis is observed after the administration of ($-$)-hydroxycitrate, a potent and specific inhibitor of ATP citrate lyase[60] (TABLE 3). As lactate and pyruvate act as precursors for lipid synthesis as well as for glycogen synthesis via the indirect pathway,[47,61,62] it was attractive to speculate[13,40] that the retarded reversal of starvation-induced decreases in hepatic PDC activity on refeeding after prolonged (48 hr) starvation might ensure the preferential use of precursors for glycogen repletion under conditions where glycogen synthesis from glucose itself might be restricted because of diminished glucokinase activity. The administration of glucose to starved rats, where PDC remains low, failed to elicit substantial increases in rates of hepatic lipogene-

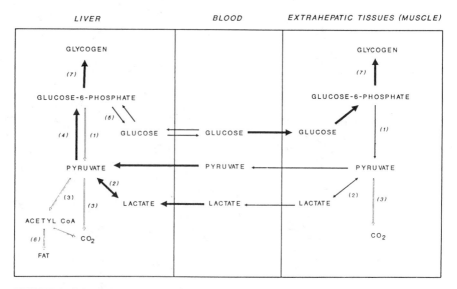

FIGURE 4. Schematic representation of carbohydrate fluxes during the initial (0–2 hr) period of refeeding after 48-hr starvation. Glucose is metabolized by glycolysis (**1**) to lactate (**2**) in extrahepatic tissues. Pyruvate oxidation (**3**) in liver and muscle remains suppressed. In the liver, pyruvate is utilized for glycogen synthesis via gluconeogenesis (**4, 7**), rather than for lipid synthesis (**6**). Glucose is utilized directly for glycogen synthesis (**7**) in muscle.

sis,[40,58,63,64] whereas marked increases in lipogenic rates are observed in the fed state (where hepatic PDC activity is high)[59,64] and in previously starved glycogen-storage-disease (*gsd/gsd*) rats, in which hepatic glycogen concentrations are maintained in starvation due to the absence of phosphorylase *b* kinase[65] (TABLE 3).

Chow versus Glucose Refeeding

The preceding experiments suggested that a continued restriction on pyruvate oxidation during the acute phase of refeeding might facilitate flux from glucose to

TABLE 3. Hepatic PDC Activities and Rates of Lipogenesis after Acute Administration of Glucose or (−)-Hydroxycitrate to Fed or 48-hr-Starved Rats

Rats[a]	PDCa Activity[b,c] (mU/U of citrate synthase)	Lipogenic Rate[c,d] (μg atoms of H/hr per g wet wt.)
Normal		
Fed	25.7 ± 2.6	20.6 ± 1.8
Fed + (−)-hydroxycitrate	—	11.6 ± 2.1***
Fed + glucose	26.9 ± 2.9	40.8 ± 2.3***
48-hr Starved	9.3 ± 0.6	6.6 ± 0.2
48-hr Starved + (−)-hydroxycitrate	—	7.8 ± 0.6
48-hr Starved + glucose	9.4 ± 0.8	8.4 ± 1.2
48-hr Starved + glucose + (−)-hydroxycitrate	—	9.0 ± 0.8
Glycogen-storage-disease		
48-hr Starved	8.7 ± 1.4	5.6 ± 0.7
48-hr Starved + glucose	25.5 ± 4.4*	14.9 ± 2.0***

[a]Female albino Wistar rats or female glycogen-storage-disease rats (a substrain of the NZR/Gd line) were administered glucose (2 mmol/100 g body wt.) intragastrically 1–2 hr before sampling. (−)-Hydroxycitrate (0.085 mmol/100 g body wt.) was given at 1 hr before sampling.

[b]PDCa and citrate synthase activities were measured in freeze-clamped liver extracts.[21]

[c]Statistically significant effects of glucose or (−)-hydroxycitrate are indicated: *, $p < 0.05$; ***, $p < 0.001$.

[d]Rates of lipogenesis were estimated as ^{3}H incorporation from ^{3}H$_2$O into tissue-saponifiable fatty acid.[59]

lactate to glycogen. However, it remained possible that the response to the provision of glucose alone might not be representative of the normal response to refeeding a mixed diet. It is known, for example, that dietary amino acids are required for optimal rates of hepatic glycogenesis[66] and for achieving reversal of starvation-induced increases in skeletal muscle proteolysis after refeeding.[67] Furthermore, the predominant dietary carbohydrate is starch or sucrose rather than glucose: the effects of chow refeeding are blocked by acarbose, a glucosidase inhibitor.[54] Perhaps more importantly, the amount of glucose provided in these acute glucose refeeding experiments was restricted. While the amount provided (360 mg/100 g body wt.) could sustain the rates of glucose oxidation observed in the fed state (19.2 mg of glucose/hr per 100 g body wt.[68]) for ca. 19 hr, ca. 35% of the glucose load is utilized for skeletal muscle glycogen deposition.[69] It was therefore considered important to compare the acute response to the provision of glucose or a complete diet *ad libitum*.

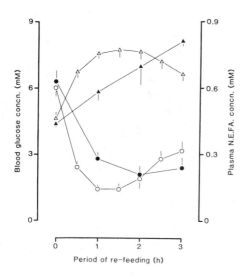

FIGURE 5. A comparison of the effects of glucose or chow refeeding on blood glucose and fatty acid concentrations in 48-hr-starved rats. Glucose (2 mmol/100 g body wt.; △, O) was administered by intragastric tube while rats were under ether anesthesia; standard laboratory chow (52% carbohydrate; 16% protein; 2% lipid; 30% nondigestible residue; ▲, ●) was provided *ad libitum*. Glucose concentrations (△, ▲) were measured in KOH-neutralized $HClO_4$ extracts of whole blood; nonesterified fatty acid (N.E.F.A.) concentrations (O, ●) were measured in plasma. Rats were sampled at 0.5-hr intervals for up to three hours.

Increases in glycemia in response to glucose were less sustained than those observed in response to chow (FIG. 5). Furthermore, while both chow and glucose refeeding decreased the blood fatty acid concentration, the decline in fatty acid levels in response to glucose was partially reversed after 2.5–3.0 hr (FIG. 5). Rates of hepatic glycogenesis after the provision of chow were also considerably higher than those observed when glucose alone was provided (TABLE 4). Nevertheless, neither restoration of hepatic PDC activity nor substantial increases in lipogenesis were observed within 2 hr of chow refeeding (TABLE 4). Furthermore, the response of PDC in extrahepatic tissues to the administration of chow *ad libitum* was essentially similar to that observed in response to the administration of glucose. Thus, renal PDC was reactivated immediately (see below), whereas only limited (26%) reactivation of cardiac PDC was observed.[26] It therefore appeared that delayed reactivation of tissue PDC after refeeding might be of physiological relevance and might be linked to sequestration of available carbohydrate as glycogen, avoiding its irreversible loss as CO_2.

TABLE 4. A Comparison of the Effects of Glucose or Chow Refeeding on Hepatic Glycogenesis and Lipogenesis in 48-hr–Starved Rats

Rats[a]	PDCa Activity[b] (% fed value)	Glycogen[b,c] (mg/g wet wt.)	Glycogen Synthesis Rate[c,d] (µg atoms of H/hr per g wet wt.)	Lipogenic Rate[d] (µg atoms of H/hr per g wet wt.)
48-hr Starved	35.4 ± 8.6	1.5 ± 0.2	9.9 ± 3.2	6.6 ± 0.5
48-hr Starved + glucose	37.4 ± 2.7	11.0 ± 1.1	118.0 ± 7.0	7.9 ± 0.6
48-hr Starved + chow	40.5 ± 7.0	19.1 ± 3.3*	169.8 ± 13.0**	8.5 ± 1.3

[a] Female albino Wistar rats (180–220 g) were sampled 2 hr after the intragastric administration of glucose (2 mmol/100 g body wt.) or the provision of chow *ad libitum*.
[b] PDCa activities and glycogen concentrations were measured in freeze-clamped liver extracts.[21]
[c] Statistically significant differences between glucose-fed and chow-fed rats are indicated: *, $p < 0.05$; **, $p < 0.01$.
[d] Rates of lipogenesis and glycogen synthesis were estimated as ^3H incorporation from ^3H_2O into tissue-saponifiable fatty acid or into glycogen, respectively.[13]

RESTORATION OF OXIDATIVE CAPACITY

Hepatic PDC and Liver Glycogen Repletion

Since hepatic glycogen concentrations achieved only ca. 17% of the fed value within 2 hr of glucose refeeding in the short-term studies described above, the time-course for complete hepatic glycogen repletion was compared with that for restoration of hepatic PDC activity after more prolonged periods of chow refeeding[13] (FIG. 6). Glycogen deposition was initiated between 1 and 2 hr after the administration of chow, and, thereafter, concentrations steadily increased, reaching ca. 54% repletion by 4 hr. Rates of glycogen synthesis increased for the first 2 hr, were maintained for a further hour, and subsequently declined. Reactivation of hepatic PDC occurred concurrently with the diminution in the rate of glycogen synthesis (after 3–4 hr of chow refeeding). Nevertheless, despite the restoration of hepatic PDC activity to approximately the value observed in the fed state, net glycogen deposition continued to occur during the period from 4 to 8 hr after the provision of chow. Therefore, although the maintenance of a low hepatic PDC activity may facilitate glycogen deposition via the indirect pathway during the initial (0–2 hr) refeeding period, there is no evidence that pyruvate oxidation via PDC necessarily precludes net glycogen deposition.

During the initial period after refeeding, there is good evidence for the predominant use of C_3 derivatives of glucose for hepatic glycogenesis.[9,44] The direct contribu-

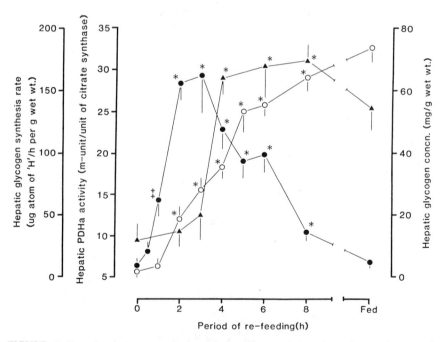

FIGURE 6. Hepatic glycogen synthesis and deposition and hepatic active PDC (*PDHa*) activities after chow refeeding of 48-hr–starved rats. Glycogen synthesis rates (●), glycogen concentrations (○), and PDHa activities (▲) were measured as described in Ref. 13. Points at extreme *right* (Fed) indicate values for fed rats. Statistically significant effects of refeeding are indicated: ‡, $p < 0.01$; *, $p < 0.001$.

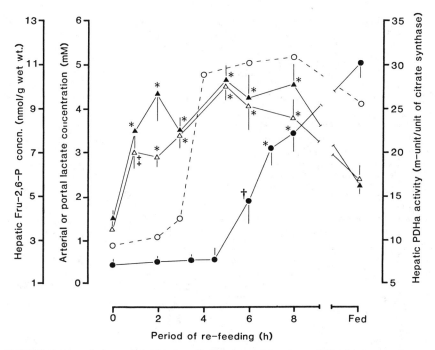

FIGURE 7. Hepatic fructose-2,6-bisphosphate and arterial and portal blood lactate concentrations after chow refeeding of 48-hr–starved rats. Fructose-2,6-bisphosphate (Fru-2,6-P$_2$, ●) and arterial (△) and portal (▲) lactate concentrations were measured as described in Ref. 13. The time-course of hepatic PDC reactivation (*PDHa*) is shown for comparison (○). Points at extreme *right* (Fed) indicate values for fed rats. Statistically significant effects of refeeding are indicated: †, $p < 0.05$; ‡, $p < 0.01$; *, $p < 0.001$.

tion of glucose itself may, however, increase as the refeeding period is extended. Hepatic glucokinase activities are restored about 5 hr after refeeding,[70] and hepatocytes from starved rats cultured with glucose for a comparable period show increases in the relative contribution of direct glucose utilization to total glycogen synthesis.[71] It remains unclear whether the temporal association between PDC reactivation and the diminished rate of glycogen synthesis indicates a regulatory association or is merely coincidental.

The Source of Pyruvate for Oxidation

The restoration of the capacity of the liver for carbohydrate oxidation at ca. 3–4 hr after refeeding does not necessarily indicate a complete reversal of hepatic carbon flux from gluco/glycogenesis towards glycolysis and lipogenesis. In the liver, net glycolytic flux is critically dependent on the concentration of fructose-2,6-bisphosphate, a potent activator of 6-phosphofructo-1-kinase.[72] This decreases by 80% after prolonged starvation (from ca. 10 nmol/g to ca. 2 nmol/g),[13,43,72–74] and increases in response to chow refeeding in an inverse relationship to the rate of glycogenesis.[74] This suggests that a high rate of hexose phosphate utilization (as a result of activation of glycogen synthase) may limit the activity of 6-phosphofructo-2-kinase (the enzyme responsible for the fructose-2,6-bisphosphate synthesis) via a limitation of precursor supply.[74] Significant increases in hepatic fructose-2,6-bisphosphate concentrations do not precede PDC reactivation (FIG. 7), and, on the basis of studies with isolated hepatocytes, where glycolytic flux is negligible at a fructose-2,6-bisphosphate concentration of < 5 nmol/g,[73] it would be anticipated that significant glycolytic flux from glucose would be observed only after ca. 6 hr of refeeding, i.e., subsequent to PDC reactivation.

The potential nevertheless exists for hepatic generation of lactate and pyruvate from substrates entering glycolysis at the level of triose phosphate, from dietary amino acids and possibly from alanine derived from skeletal muscle. However, on the basis of the marked and sustained increases in both portal and arterial lactate concentrations (FIG. 7), it seems more likely that lactate and pyruvate predominantly derived from glycolysis in extrahepatic tissues are used as oxidative substrate by the liver.

The time-courses for the reactivation of renal and cardiac PDC after chow refeeding of 48-hr–starved rats are shown in FIGURE 8. As we have noted previously, renal PDC reactivation is essentially complete within 2 hr of the administration of chow. In contrast, the reactivation of cardiac PDC is even more retarded than that of liver. Limited (26%) reactivation is observed over the first 2 hr, but the activity remains $< 30\%$ of the fed value for at least the first 6 hr after the provision of chow. While skeletal muscle PDC activity was not measured in this study, its regulation does

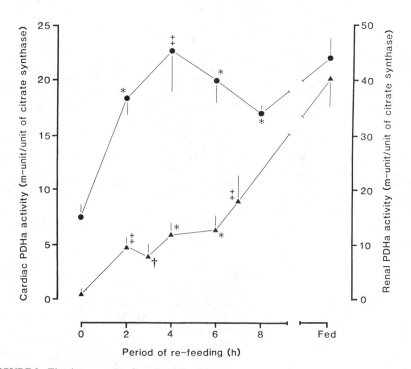

FIGURE 8. The time-courses of cardiac (▲) and renal (●) PDC reactivation (*PDHa*) after chow refeeding of 48-hr–starved rats. Points at extreme *right* (Fed) indicated values for fed rats. Statistically significant effects of refeeding are indicated: †, $p < 0.05$; ‡, $p < 0.01$; *, $p < 0.001$.

LIVER   BLOOD   EXTRAHEPATIC TISSUES (MUSCLE)

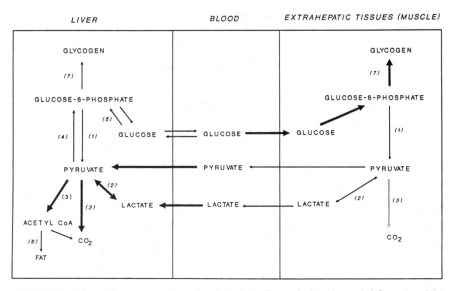

FIGURE 9. Schematic representation of carbohydrate fluxes during the period from 4 to 8 hr after the administration of chow to 48-hr–starved rats. Glucose is metabolized by glycolysis (**1**) to lactate (**2**) in extrahepatic tissues. Pyruvate oxidation (**3**) remains suppressed (*white arrow*) in muscle but not in liver. A proportion of acetyl-CoA derived from carbohydrate is used for hepatic lipid synthesis (**6**). Hepatic glycogen repletion (**7**) nears completion, but muscle glycogen synthesis (**7**) continues.

not differ substantially from that of heart,[20] and, thus, skeletal muscle pyruvate oxidation may also remain suppressed.

The inactivation of tissue PDC which occurs in starvation has been envisaged as a means to recycle carbon towards hepatic glucose synthesis. The delayed reactivation of PDC in certain tissues during the starved-to-fed transition may spare pyruvate for oxidative use by the liver under conditions where hepatic glycolysis from glucose is restricted (FIG. 9).

Although the restoration of the oxidative capacity of the liver may be associated with a redirection of pyruvate metabolism from glucose-6-phosphate formation to acetyl-CoA formation, the potential fate (oxidation or lipid synthesis) of any acetyl-CoA generated remained undefined. The relationship between the restoration of PDC activity and the pattern of changes in rates of hepatic lipogenesis was therefore investigated.

The Role of PDC in Restoration of Rates of Hepatic Lipogenesis

The decrease in the rate of hepatic lipogenesis observed in response to prolonged (24–48 hr) starvation is associated with diminished sensitivity of lipogenesis to acute (2 hr) stimulation by carbohydrate[13,40,58,63,64,74] and acute inhibition by (−)-hydroxycitrate[58,60,75] (TABLE 3). These findings could indicate that carbohydrate, utilized via citrate, ceases to become the predominant lipogenic precursor. Although starvation is associated with phosphorylation and inactivation of acetyl-CoA carboxylase and decreased maximal activities of acetyl-CoA carboxylase and fatty acid synthase, evidence that the major restriction on the rate of lipid synthesis after refeeding was not imposed at the level of acetyl-CoA carboxylase and fatty acid synthase was obtained using MPA.[37,76] When glucose was administered in combination with MPA, conditions permitting the cytoplasmic accumulation of oxaloacetate, rates of lipogenesis comparable to those found in the fed state were observed within 2 hr. While the mechanism(s) by which such increases were achieved were not elucidated, the results clearly indicated that neither the activity state of acetyl-CoA carboxylase nor the maximal capacity of the lipogenic pathway distal to ATP-citrate lyase is rate-limiting for fatty acid synthesis immediately after refeeding. The time-course of changes in rates of lipogenesis occasioned by refeeding was therefore investigated in detail in order to delineate the time at which sensitivity to (−)-hydroxycitrate was restored and to examine whether restoration of (−)-hydroxycitrate sensitivity bore any temporal relationship to the time-course of PDC reactivation and the potential for the provision of acetyl-CoA from carbohydrate for lipogenesis.[13]

The rate of lipogenesis measured in rats treated with (−)-hydroxycitrate showed a modest, steady increase over the refeeding period (FIG. 10a). This rate gives an estimate of the rates of utilization of cytoplasmic acetyl-CoA derived from precursors other than citrate. In contrast, the total rate of lipogenesis [measured in rats not treated with (−)-hydroxycitrate] showed a marked increase during the period from 4 hr to 6 hr after refeeding (FIG. 10a). It may therefore be concluded that the rate of supply of substrate via ATP-citrate lyase assumes quantitative significance for lipogenesis from about 4 hr after the initiation of refeeding. Thus, as shown in FIGURE 10b, a close temporal relationship exists between hepatic PDC reactivation and the use of citrate as a precursor for lipid synthesis. This strongly suggests that the total rate of lipogenesis during the initial (0–3 hr) phase of the starved-to-fed transition is limited

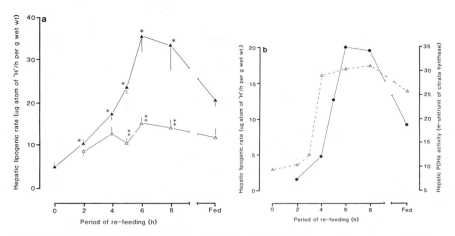

FIGURE 10. (a) Rates of hepatic lipogenesis in 48-hr–starved rats after chow refeeding. Lipogenesis was measured by the incorporation of ^3H from ^3H_2O into lipid (▲). One group of rats was treated with (−)-hydroxycitrate to inhibit the use of citrate as lipogenic precursor (△). Points at extreme *right* (Fed) indicate values for fed rats. Full experimental details are given in Ref. 13. Statistically significant effects of refeeding are indicated: ‡, $p < 0.01$; *, $p < 0.001$. **(b)** The time-course of changes in rates of (−)-hydroxycitrate–sensitive lipogenesis (●). The time-course of hepatic PDC reactivation (*PDHa*) is shown for comparison (△). Points at extreme *right* (Fed) indicate values for fed rats.

TABLE 5. Effects of Insulin Administration on Hepatic PDC Activities in Control, 2-Tetradecylglycidate- or Dichloroacetate-Treated, 48-hr–Starved Rats

Treatment[a]	Hepatic PDC Activity (mU/U of citrate synthase)		
	Control	2-Tetradecylglycidate	Dichloroacetate
NaCl			
2 hr	7.3 ± 0.5	8.0 ± 2.5	5.8 ± 0.7
Insulin			
0.25 hr	5.8 ± 0.9	30.3 ± 0.7***	17.4 ± 8.9
0.5 hr	6.5 ± 1.3	21.2 ± 0.7***	81.6 ± 11.6***
2.0 hr	4.0 ± 2.0	50.4 ± 5.2***	—

[a]Female albino Wistar rats (180–220 g) were administered 2-tetradecylglycidate (2.5 mg/100 g body wt.) or dichloroacetate [0.25 ml of a 5% (w/v) solution] by intraperitoneal injection 2 hr before sampling. Insulin (2 units) or 0.15 M NaCl was administered subcutaneously at the times indicated.

[b]PDCa activities were measured in freeze-clamped liver extracts.[21] Statistically significant effects of insulin are indicated: ***, $p < 0.001$.

by the inability to utilize carbohydrate via PDC and citrate synthase, and increased use of carbohydrate for lipogenesis occurs concomitantly with PDC reactivation.

A Role for Continued Fat Oxidation in Directing Carbon Flux on Refeeding after Prolonged Starvation

Although refeeding is associated with an immediate decrease in the availability of circulating fatty acids,[13,40] (FIG. 5) hepatic long-chain acyl-CoA concentrations remain high for at least 2 hr, the major decline in concentration occurring between 2 hr and 4 hr.[77] This decline bears a striking correlation with hepatic PDC reactivation, reduced use of C_3 derivatives of glucose for hepatic glycogenesis via the indirect (gluconeogenic) pathway, and increased hepatic lipogenesis. It might therefore be tempting to conclude that coordinated changes in the direction of hepatic carbon flux after refeeding are achieved through a reversal of the metabolic effects of lipid oxidation, with decreased β-oxidation permitting PDC reactivation via deactivation of PDC kinase, and diversion of available acetyl-CoA towards citrate synthesis and lipogenesis. However, neither culture of hepatocytes from starved rats in the absence of exogenous fatty acid[78] nor inhibition of mitochondrial fat oxidation by the administration of 2-tetradecylglycidate,[21] an inhibitor of overt carnitine palmitoyl transferase (CPT-1), leads to hepatic PDC reactivation (TABLE 5). Consequently, it appears that changes in rates of mitochondrial fat oxidation have a permissive rather than an active role in hepatic PDC reactivation.

In 48-hr–starved rats pretreated for 2 hr with 2-tetradecylglycidate, increases in hepatic PDC activity are observed within 15–30 min of the administration of insulin (TABLE 5). In view of the ability of insulin to stimulate PDH phosphatase in other lipogenic tissues,[30,31] together with some evidence for a direct effect of insulin on hepatic PDH phosphatase in the fed state,[79,80] it is tempting to invoke a role for an increase in PDH phosphatase activity in achieving rapid increases in hepatic PDC activity. Nevertheless, as insulin administration alone did not lead to reactivation (TABLE 5), it appears that increased activity of PDH phosphatase is insufficient in itself to achieve reactivation.

We propose that an increase in hepatic PDC activity via increased PDH phosphatase can be achieved only under conditions where PDH kinase activity is suppressed. This is the case in the fed state, but not during the initial phase of the starved-to-fed transition. When PDH kinase is inhibited by DCA, insulin elicits rapid hepatic PDC reactivation in previously starved rats[32] (TABLE 5).

REFEEDING AFTER SHORT-TERM STARVATION

Wieland et al.[81] observed rapid reactivation of hepatic PDC in response to refeeding in rats starved for 24 hr, and the response of hepatic PDC to DCA also appeared to be increased if the duration of starvation was decreased from 48 hr to 24 hr (see above).[39] We therefore considered it important to determine whether the immediacy of the response of tissue PDC to refeeding was dependent on the antecedent period of starvation. McGarry et al.[82] demonstrated that starvation for only 6–12 hr induces profound effects on hepatic carbohydrate metabolism, including glycogen depletion (see also FIG. 2a) and activation of gluconeogenesis; and, as shown in FIGURE 2b, whereas PDC activities remain high for 2–3 hr after food removal, both hepatic and cardiac PDC activities are considerably diminished within 6 hr of the onset of starvation. The responses of hepatic PDC to chow refeeding in rats previously starved for either 6, 24 or 48 hr are compared in FIGURE 11a.

The major consequence of a decrease in the period of starvation preceding refeeding on the response of hepatic PDC was a diminution in the duration of the lag phase prior to significant reactivation. Thus, whereas there is a delay of 3–4 hr before hepatic PDC reactivation in 48-hr–starved rats, reactivation was observed within 1 hr of refeeding of 6-hr–starved rats, with an intermediate period of hysteresis in 24-hr–starved rats. The duration of starvation also influenced the reactivation profile of cardiac PDC (FIG. 11b). While limited reactivation of cardiac PDC was observed within 1 hr of refeeding in rats previously starved for 24 hr, no reactivation was observed in rats starved for 48 hr, and the extent of reactivation during this initial period was increased if the antecedent period of starvation was diminished to 6 hr. Thus, reactivation of cardiac PDC to values not significantly different from those observed in the fed state was achieved in 6-hr–starved rats, whereas only 30–35% reactivation was observed in 24-hr–starved rats. Renal PDC activity was unaffected by short-term (6 hr) starvation or refeeding, whilst refeeding of 24-hr– or 48-hr–starved rats led to immediate reactivation (FIG. 11c).

CONCLUDING REMARKS

Mechanisms Leading to Retarded PDC Reactivation after Refeeding

In at least two tissues, starvation has a progressive effect to restrict the extent of PDC reactivation observed immediately after refeeding. There are two mechanisms which may account for this. First, phosphorylation of sites on the PDH component of the complex in addition to that which is required for inactivation inhibits PDC reactivation by PDH phosphatase.[83] Multisite phosphorylation is observed in 48-hr–starved rats but is minimal in fed rats.[84] Secondly, the specific activity of PDH kinase and kinase activator protein increase progressively with the duration of starvation.[26,29]

In both liver (isolated hepatocytes)[78] and heart (intact animals),[26] the reactivation

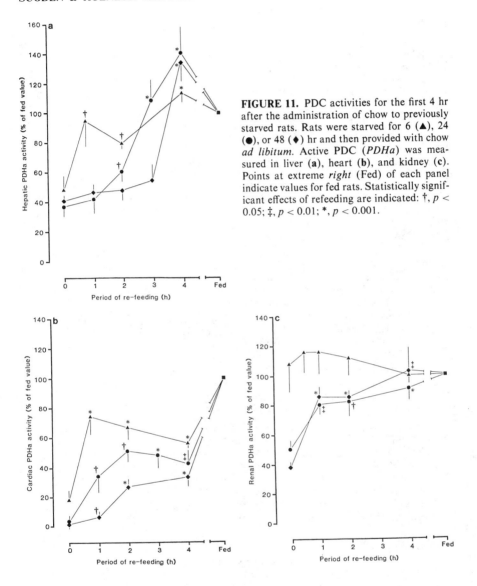

FIGURE 11. PDC activities for the first 4 hr after the administration of chow to previously starved rats. Rats were starved for 6 (▲), 24 (●), or 48 (♦) hr and then provided with chow *ad libitum*. Active PDC (*PDHa*) was measured in liver (**a**), heart (**b**), and kidney (**c**). Points at extreme *right* (Fed) of each panel indicate values for fed rats. Statistically significant effects of refeeding are indicated: †, $p < 0.05$; ‡, $p < 0.01$; *, $p < 0.001$.

of PDC after prolonged starvation has been correlated with a reversal of starvation-induced increases in PDH kinase. The expression of such increases may be permitted by a continued bias towards the mitochondrial oxidation of lipid. Thus, in liver at least, long-term adaptations to starvation include an increase in the maximal activity of CPT-1 and a decline in its sensitivity to inhibition by malonyl-CoA, neither of which changes are immediately reversed on refeeding.[85] On the basis of the refeeding experiments described in this review, it appears that such adaptive changes assume regulatory importance for periods of starvation exceeding 24 hr and may be initiated between 6 and 12 hr after food withdrawal.

Oxidative Substrates during the Starved-to-Fed Transition

In this review, we have suggested that during the initial period of refeeding after prolonged starvation, hepatic energy requirements continue to be met by the oxidation of lipid. However, we have not considered the energy requirements of heart and skeletal muscle, where pyruvate oxidation may be restricted for an even more protracted period. Such requirements may be met by the non-oxidative metabolism of glucose or, as in liver, by the continued use of lipid, which may include endogenous triacylglycerol and exogenous lipoproteins in addition to available fatty acids and ketone bodies.

There are two indications that, in heart at least, lipid-derived fuels continue to be oxidized. First, the concentration of fructose-2,6-bisphosphate (which is dictated by the availability of hexose monophosphate, and may also be inversely related to the rate of fat oxidation[22]) remains low.[86] This may impose a restraint on glycolytic flux. Secondly, in anesthetized, starved rats the intravenous administration of 2-tetradecyl-glycidate leads to immediate PDC reactivation, associated with a decline in the acetyl-CoA/CoA concentration ratio.[21]

The situation in skeletal muscle is less clear-cut, as energy requirements are dictated by contractile activity. However, as in heart and liver, a restriction on glycolytic flux may be imposed by the maintenance of a low concentration of fructose-2,6-bisphosphate.[86] Because in skeletal muscle the response to refeeding includes repletion of any glycogen loss occasioned by starvation,[56] it is attractive to speculate that the continued oxidation of lipid fuels may spare carbohydrate until glycogen stores are replenished. In rats starved for shorter periods, glycogen loss is less extensive, and, consequently, glycogen repletion, glycolysis, and pyruvate oxidation may occur concomitantly after refeeding.

Glucose Recycling during the Fed-to-Starved Transition

Total glucose turnover in rats starved for 3–6 hr is almost twice that found after 24 hr of starvation,[87] even though in at least two tissues (heart, liver) PDC activity is diminished. It therefore remains possible that suppression of pyruvate oxidation may precede suppression of glucose utilization via glycolysis. Under such circumstances, the liver may act as a lactate buffer, with the direction of available carbon towards glucose, glycogen, oxidation, or lipogenesis as dictated by the precise hormonal and nutritional conditions. An accelerated rate of glucose-lactate recycling provides metabolic flexibility while minimizing carbon loss.

ACKNOWLEDGMENTS

The authors would like to thank Elizabeth Cook, David Kelm, Peter MacLennan, Paul Schofield and David Watts for their skilled technical assistance.

REFERENCES

1. RANDLE, P. J., E. A. NEWSHOLME & P. B. GARLAND. 1964. Biochem. J. 93: 652–665.
2. LEHNINGER, A. L. 1946. J. Biol. Chem. 164: 291–306.
3. WIELAND, O., L. WEISSEL & I. EGER-NEUFELDT. 1964. Adv. Enzyme Regul. 2: 85–99.
4. KREBS, H. A. 1966. Adv. Enzyme Regul. 4: 339–353.

5. HOPKIRK, T. J. & D. BLOXHAM. 1977. Biochem. Soc. Trans. **5:** 1294–1297.
6. ABUMRAD, N. N., A. D. CHERRINGTON, P. E. WILLIAMS., W. W. LACY & D. RABIN. 1982. Am. J. Physiol. **242:** E398–E406.
7. BJORKMAN, O., M. CRUMP & R. W. PHILLIPS. 1984. J. Nutr. **114:** 1413–1420.
8. COHEN, R. D. & H. F. WOODS. 1983. Diabetes **32:** 181–191.
9. MCGARRY, J. D., M. KUWAJIMA, C. B. NEWGARD, D. W. FOSTER & J. KATZ. 1987. Annu. Rev. Nutr. **7:** 51–73.
10. SHIKAMA, H. & M. UI. 1978. Am. J. Physiol. **235:** E354–E360.
11. NEWGARD, C. B., D. W. FOSTER & J. D. MCGARRY. 1984. Diabetes **33:** 192–195.
12. HOLNESS, M. J. & M. C. SUGDEN. 1987. Biochem. J. **247:** 627–634.
13. HOLNESS, M. J., P. A. MACLENNAN, T. N. PALMER & M. C. SUGDEN. 1988. Biochem. J. **252:** 325–330.
14. LINN, T. C., F. H. PETTIT & L. J. REED. 1969. Proc. Natl. Acad. Sci. USA **62:** 234–241.
15. LINN, T. C., F. H. PETTIT, F. HUCHO & L. J. REED. 1969. Proc. Natl. Acad. Sci. USA **64:** 227–234.
16. WIELAND, O. H. 1983. Rev. Physiol. Biochem. Pharmacol. **96:** 123–170.
17. RANDLE, P. J. 1986. Biochem. Soc. Trans. **14:**799–806.
18. KERBEY, A. L., P. M. RADCLIFFE & P. J. RANDLE. 1977. Biochem. J. **164:** 509–519.
19. HUTSON, N. J. & P. J. RANDLE. 1978. FEBS Lett. **92:** 73–76.
20. FULLER, S. J. & P. J. RANDLE. 1984. Biochem. J. **219:** 635–646.
21. CATERSON, I. D., S. J. FULLER & P. J. RANDLE. 1982. Biochem. J. **208:** 53–60.
22. HUE, L., L. MAISIN & M. H. RIDER. 1988. Biochem. J. **251:** 241–245.
23. FRENCH, T. J., A. W. GOODE, M. J. HOLNESS, P. A. MACLENNAN & M. C. SUGDEN. 1988. Biochem. J. **256:** 935–939.
24. ISSAD, T., L. PENICAUD, P. FERRE, J. KANDE, M. A. BAUDON & J. GIRARD. 1987. Biochem. J. **246:** 241–244.
25. BAXTER, M. A. & H. G. COORE. 1978. Biochem. J. **174:** 553–561.
26. KERBEY, A. L. & P. J. RANDLE. 1982. Biochem. J. **206:** 103–111.
27. KERBEY, A. L., L. J. RICHARDSON & P. J. RANDLE. 1984. FEBS Lett. **176:** 115–119.
28. DENYER, G. S., A. L. KERBEY & P. J. RANDLE. 1986. Biochem. J. **239:** 347–354.
29. FATANIA, H. R., T. C. VARY & P. J. RANDLE. 1986. Biochem. J. **234:** 233–236.
30. MARSHALL, S. E., J. G. MCCORMACK & R. M. DENTON. 1984. Biochem. J. **218:** 249–260.
31. THOMAS, A. P. & R. M. DENTON. 1986. Biochem. J. **238:** 93–101.
32. HOLNESS, M. J. & M. C. SUGDEN. 1987. Biochem. J. **241:** 421–425.
33. FERRE, P., A. LETURQUE, A. F. BURNOL, L. PENICAUD & J. GIRARD. 1985. Biochem. J. **228:** 103–110.
34. BERGMEYER, H. U. 1974. Methods of Enzymatic Analysis, 2nd ed. Academic Press, New York.
35. BLACKSHEAR, P. J., P. A. HOLLOWAY & K. G. M. M. ALBERTI. 1975. Biochem. J. **148:** 353–362.
36. GOODMAN, M. W. 1975. Biochem. J. **150:** 137–139.
37. SUGDEN, M. C., D. I. WATTS, T. N. PALMER & D. D. MYLES. 1983. Biochem. Int. **7:** 329–337.
38. CORI, C. F. 1931. Physiol. Rev. **11:** 143–275.
39. WHITEHOUSE, S., R. H. COOPER & P. J. RANDLE. 1974. Biochem. J. **141:** 761–774.
40. HOLNESS, M. J., T. J. FRENCH & M. C. SUGDEN. 1986. Biochem. J. **235:** 441–445.
41. NEWGARD, C. B., L. J. HIRSCH, D. W. FOSTER & J. D. MCGARRY. 1983. J. Biol. Chem. **258:** 8046–8052.
42. NIEWOEHNER, C. B., D. P. GILBOE & F. Q. NUTTALL. 1984. Am. J. Physiol. **246:** E89–E94.
43. KUWAJIMA M., C. B. NEWGARD, D. W. FOSTER & J. D. MCGARRY. 1984. J. Clin. Invest. **74:** 1108–1111.
44. LANDAU, B. R. & J. WAHREN. 1988. FASEB J. **2:** 2368–2375.
45. HEMS, D. A., P. D. WHITTON & E. A. TAYLOR. 1972. Biochem. J. **129:** 529–538.
46. KATZ, J., S. GOLDEN & P. A. WALS. 1976. Proc. Natl. Acad. Sci. USA **73:** 3433–3437.
47. KATZ, J., S. GOLDEN & P. A. WALS. 1979. Biochem. J. **180:** 389–402.
48. NEWGARD, C. B., S. V. MOORE, D. W. FOSTER & J. D. MCGARRY. 1984. J. Biol. Chem. **259:** 6958–6963.

49. CLAUS, T. H., F. NYFELER, H. A. MUENKEL, M. G. BURNS, T. PATEL & S. J. PILKIS. 1984. Biochem. Biophys. Res. Commun. **125:** 655–661.
50. CHEN, K. S. & J. KATZ. 1988. Biochem. J. **255:** 99–104.
51. WINDMUELLER, H. G. & A. E. SPAETH. 1978. J. Biol. Chem. **253:** 69–76.
52. SHAPIRO, A. & B. SHAPIRO. 1979. Biochim. Biophys. Acta **586:** 123–187.
53. NICHOLLS, T. T., H. J. LEESE & J. R. BRONK. 1983. Biochem. J. **212:** 183–187.
54. MERCER, S. W. & D. H. WILLIAMSON. 1987. Biochem. J. **242:** 235–243.
55. COX, D. J. & T. N. PALMER. 1987. Biochem. J. **245:** 903–905.
56. HOLNESS, M. J., M. J. L. SHUSTER-BRUCE & M. C. SUGDEN. 1988. Biochem. J. **254:** 855–859.
57. SPITZER, J. J. 1974. Am. J. Physiol. **226:** 213–217.
58. SUGDEN, M. C., D. I. WATTS, C. E. MARSHALL & J. G. MCCORMACK. 1982. Biosci. Rep. **2:** 289–297.
59. STANSBIE, D., R. W. BROWNSEY, M. CRETTAZ & R. M. DENTON. 1976. Biochem. J. **160:** 413–416.
60. BRUNENGRABER, H., M. BOUTRY & J. M. LOWENSTEIN. 1978. Eur. J. Biochem. **82:** 373–384.
61. SALMON, D. M. W., N. L. BOWEN & D. A. HEMS. 1974. Biochem. J. **142:** 611–618.
62. BOYD, M. E., E. A. ALBRIGHT, D. W. FOSTER & J. D. MCGARRY. 1981. J. Clin. Invest. **68:** 142–152.
63. AGIUS, L. & D. H. WILLIAMSON. 1981. Biochim. Biophys. Acta **666:** 127–132.
64. SUGDEN, M. C., D. I. WATTS & C. E. MARSHALL. 1981. Biosci. Rep. **1:** 469–476.
65. HOLNESS, M. J., I. N. PALMER, E. B. WORRALL & M. C. SUGDEN. 1987. Biochem. J. **248:** 969–972.
66. LAVIONNE, A., A. BAQUET & L. HUE. 1987. Biochem. J. **248:** 429–437.
67. GOODMAN, M. N. & M. GOMEZ. 1987. Am. J. Physiol. **253:** E52–E58.
68. FREMINET, A., C. POYANT, L. LECLERC & M. GENTIL. 1976. FEBS Lett. **61:** 294–297.
69. HOLNESS, M. J. & M. C. SUGDEN. 1988. Biochem. Soc. Trans. **16:** 554.
70. MINDEROP, R. H., W. HOEPPNER & J. H. SIETZ. 1987. Eur. J. Biochem. **164:** 181–187.
71. SPENCE, J. T. & A. P. KOUDELKA. 1986. J. Biol. Chem. **260:** 1521–1526.
72. HUE, L. & M. H. RIDER. 1987. Biochem. J. **245:** 313–324.
73. HUE, L., F. SOBRINO & L. BOSCA. 1984. Biochem. J. **224:** 779–786.
74. HOLNESS, M. J., E. B. COOK & M. C. SUGDEN. 1988. Biochem. J. **252:** 357–362.
75. TRISCARI, J. & A. C. SULLIVAN. 1977. Lipids **12:** 357–363.
76. HOLNESS, M. J., T. J. FRENCH, P. S. SCHOFIELD & M. C. SUGDEN. 1987. Biochem. J. **247:** 621–626.
77. NISHIKORI, K., N. IRITANI & S. NUMA. 1973. FEBS Lett. **32:** 19–21.
78. MARCHINGTON, D. R., A. L. KERBEY, A. E. JONES & P. J. RANDLE. 1987. Biochem. J. **246:** 233–236.
79. MACAULAY, S. L. & L. JARETT. 1985. Arch. Biochem. Biophys. **237:** 142–150.
80. PARKER, J. C. & L. JARETT. 1985. Diabetes **34:** 92–97.
81. WIELAND, O. H., C. PATZELT & G. LOFFLER. 1972. Eur. J. Biochem. **26:** 426–433.
82. MCGARRY, J. D., J. M. MEIER & D. W. FOSTER. 1973. J. Biol. Chem. **248:** 270–278.
83. SUGDEN, P. H., N. J. HUTSON, A. L. KERBEY & P. J. RANDLE. 1978. Biochem. J. **169:** 433–435.
84. SALE, G. J. & P. J. RANDLE. 1982. Biochem. J. **206:** 221–229.
85. GRANTHAM, B. D. & V. A. ZAMMIT. 1986. Biochem. J. **239:** 485–488.
86. FRENCH, T. J., M. J. HOLNESS, P. A. MACLENNAN & M. C. SUGDEN. 1988. Biochem. J. **250:** 773–779.
87. SMADJA, C., J. MORIN, P. FERRE, & J. GIRARD. 1988. Am. J. Physiol. **254:** E407–E413.

Isolated and Combined Deficiencies of the
α-Keto Acid Dehydrogenase Complexes[a]

BRIAN H. ROBINSON, KATHY CHUN,
NEVENA MACKAY, GAIL OTULAKOWSKI,
ROUMYANA PETROVA-BENEDICT,
AND HUNT WILLARD

Departments of Genetics and Biochemistry
University of Toronto and
The Research Institute
Hospital for Sick Children
Toronto, Canada
M5G 1X8

Interest in the inborn errors of pyruvate metabolism increased substantially with the demonstration by Blass *et al.*[1] that defects in the pyruvate dehydrogenase complex could be demonstrated in cultured skin fibroblasts. Improved assay systems, documentation of the clinical picture, development of specific antibodies, and, eventually, the isolation of cDNA and genomic clones have recently given us a much clearer view of the spectrum of defects that occur in this complex. We have covered the earlier literature extensively in recent reviews,[2,3] and much of it can be interpreted in a new light in view of the findings presented here. Most of this contribution will deal with the spectrum of patients we have diagnosed in our "Lactic Acidemia" program, since we are able to correlate biochemical, clinical and molecular data on all of them.

The two major sources of inspiration for us in working with the α-keto acid dehydrogenase complexes were the fundamental protein and enzymological work done by Lester Reed and his group[4] and the parallel studies by Phillip Randle and colleagues,[5] which concentrated more on the metabolic control functions of these complexes.

PYRUVATE DEHYDROGENASE COMPLEX DEFICIENCY: 51 CASES

The most common form of pyruvate dehydrogenase (PDH) complex deficiency seems to be that located in the E_1 component. We identified 46 cases in which the first component of the complex was deficient. They can be divided up roughly into three major groups, according to the clinical course of the disease (FIG. 1). The first group suffer from severe bouts of lactic acidosis, i.e., the lacticacidemia resulting from the PDH defect is extensive enough to cause a significant and often life-threatening acid-base disturbance. The members of this group expire in the neonatal period or, if aggressive supportive therapy is given, they can be kept alive until a few months of age. The second group, although they have lactic acidemia, do not have a major acid-base disturbance. However, as the members of this group develop, it becomes apparent that

[a]This work was supported by the Medical Research Council of Canada, the National Foundation, the March of Dimes, and the Beta Sigma Phi Sorority.

337

they are developmentally delayed from both a motor and a psychological point of view. This psychomotor retardation progresses in many cases to a neurodegenerative course, and death ensues, often due to an apneic episode. In other cases, spasticity and cortical blindness accompany the descent into a totally or partially vegetative state. There are structural changes to the brain that are present at birth in some individuals with neonatal lacticacidosis, these being manifest as either cystic lesions in the cerebral hemispheres or as cerebral atrophy (TABLE 1). In the group with psychomotor retardation, 5 out of the 7 that died before three years of age were found to have the cystic lesions present in the basal ganglia and brain stem, typical of Leigh's disease; the

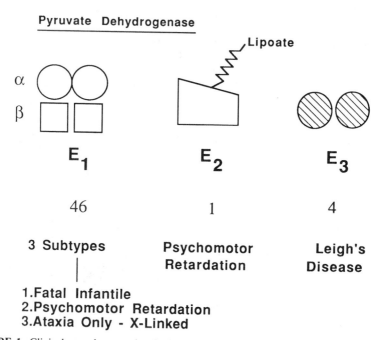

FIGURE 1. Clinical sequelae associated with defects in the pyruvate dehydrogenase (PDH) complex. Depicted are the subcomponent parts of the PDH complex: E_1, the decarboxylase; E_2, the dihydrolipoyl transacetylase; and E_3, the dihydrolipoyl dehydrogenase. We have skin fibroblast cultures from 46 patients with E_1 deficiency which can be divided into three groups; fatal infantile, psychomotor retarded, and ataxic. E_2 deficiency has been documented once. E_3 deficiency results in a clinical course identical with Leigh's disease.

other two had cystic lesions but in the cerebral hemispheres. In the remaining 21 cases of psychomotor retardation, 16 were found to have cerebral atrophy and ventricular enlargement, while 4 of these 16 also had basal ganglia hypodensities on CT scanning. One patient in this group of survivors had basal ganglia hypodensities alone. The third group of patients are not seriously neurologically compromised and suffer only from bouts of ataxia, often in association with ingestion of carbohydrates. The members of this group are all boys, and, unlike the previous groups, they do not develop the lesions in the central nervous system.

As might be expected, the residual activity of the PDH complex showed some

TABLE 1. Clinical Presentation of Children with Pyruvate Dehydrogenase-E_1 Deficiency

	Neonatal and Infant Deaths	Psychomotor Retardation		Ataxic Episodes Only
		With Death (age 10 mo–3 yr)	Still Living	
n	11 cases	7 cases	21 cases	7 cases
Residual activity of PDH complex (nmol/min/mg; ave ± SEM)	14.6 ± 4.8	21.9 ± 5.1	27.9 ± 3.9	29.8 ± 8.1
Agenesis corpus callosum (n)	4	1	1	0
Ratio, male:female	5:6	3:4	7:14	7:0
Neuropathology	Cystic lesions in cerebral hemispheres or cerebral atrophy (7); Cystic lesions in basal ganglia (2)	Autopsy-proven Leigh's disease (5); Cerebral atrophy and cerebral cysts (2)	Cortical atrophy and ventricular enlargement (16); Hypodensities in basal ganglia by CT (5)	No neuropathology evident
Lacticacidemia	Severe	Moderate	Mild	Mild, carbohydrate sensitive

gradation with severity of disease, activity was lowest in the group with neonatal deaths and highest in the group with ataxic episodes only. In 1984,[6] we pointed out that a significant number of children with PDH-E_1 deficiency had mildly dysmorphic features, a finding that has recently been confirmed by others.[7] The characteristic features are a wide nasal bridge, slightly bossed forehead, anteverted nares, and a long filtrum. It has been suggested that part of this dysmorphic appearance may be due to lack of brain growth, leading to distortion of the facial features and microcephaly.[7] An alternative hypothesis we have proposed is based on the similarity of the dysmorphism seen in PDH complex deficiency to that seen in the fetal alcohol syndrome. We proposed that low PDH activity in the fetus, due to the presence of the potent inhibitor acetaldehyde or due to a genetic defect, causes abnormal growth associated with dysmorphic facial development.[3] Fourteen of our patients had facial dysmorphism, most of them from birth, 4 of them later developing microcephaly. Eleven out of these 14 patients were girls. Six patients were found to have either partial or total agenesis of the corpus callosum, 5 of them girls. Of the eleven patients who developed seizures, nine were girls.

We have shown one patient to have deficient activity of transacetylase activity while possessing normal activity of E_1 and E_3. This patient, who is psychomotor retarded, appears by evidence from Western blotting to have an abnormal protein X rather than an abnormal E_2 protein. We have encountered four patients with a defect in PDH-E_3 (lipoamide dehydrogenase). Two had severe defects, the others partial. All cases exhibited combined deficiency in the activities of the PDH, α-ketoglutarate dehydrogenase (αKGDH), and branched-chain keto acid dehydrogenase (BCKADH) complexes. This is consistent with the observation that elevations of pyruvate, lactate, α-ketoglutarate, and the branched-chain amino acids are observed in most of these patients.[8-11] The branched-chain amino acids are not elevated to the extent seen in classical maple syrup urine disease. Urine organic acids show significant quantities of lactate, pyruvate, α-hydroxybutyrate, α-hydroxyisovalerate, and α-ketoglutarate.[9,12,13] In one case, α-ketoisocaproate was detected in the urine.[14] Postmortem examination of the brain in three cases showed myelin loss and cavitation in discrete areas of the basal ganglia, thalamus and brain stem, giving a picture typical of Leigh's disease.[8,9,15]

In four cases that have been reported, the combined defect in the α-keto acid dehydrogenase complexes is definitely the result of low activity of the lipoamide dehydrogenase component,[8,9,12,14] which was between 0 and 20% of controls. In other cases we have examined, the activity of lipoamide dehydrogenase was about 60% of normal, despite the fact that all three keto acid dehydrogenase complexes were deficient and present at only 25% of normal.[10,13] This paradox can be explained if it is postulated that the abnormal E_3 protein can carry out the lipoamide dehydrogenase reaction reasonably well, but that its ability to interact with the E_2 transacetylases is compromised by the mutation.

PROTEIN COMPOSITION OF THE PDH COMPLEX IN CULTURES OF PDH COMPLEX–DEFICIENT SKIN FIBROBLASTS

Western blotting of cultured skin fibroblast extracts has been used to visualize the protein components of the PDH complex by a number of investigators. Two patients have been reported with missing E_1 subunits: one of them, a male patient who died of neonatal acidosis, had a missing α subunit,[16] the other, a patient with central hypoventilation syndrome who had lesions typical of Leigh's disease,[17] appeared to have neither α nor β subunits. Anomalies in the electrophoretic behavior of the α subunit of E_1 have been reported in a total of four female patients.[16,18] This anomolous behavior almost certainly relates to alterations in charge because of the phosphorylation state of the α subunit.

FIGURE 2 shows the results obtained on Western blotting of skin fibroblast extracts from a group of patients diagnosed with PDH (E_1) complex deficiency. On this one blot can be seen the variety of patterns that can be obtained. The antibody used is one we raised to purified porcine heart PDH complex, which cross-reacts well with the

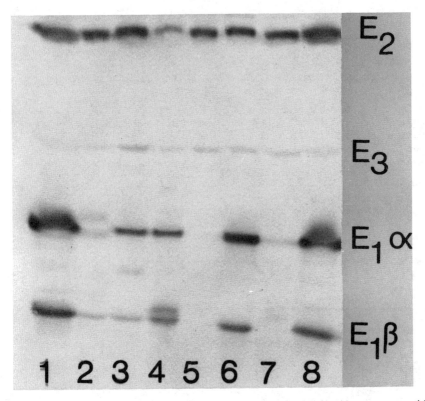

FIGURE 2. Western blotting of PDH-E_1-deficient cultured skin fibroblast extracts with anti–PDH complex antibody. Each cell line was subjected to digitonin and Triton X-100 extraction, and the Triton extracts were resolved on a 10% polyacrylamide gel. This gel was electroblotted onto Hybond support matrix and stained with anti–PDH complex antibody. Immunoreactive proteins were visualized by goat anti-rabbit IgG and horseradish peroxidase staining. (**Lanes 1–7**) PDH deficient cell lines 2638, 2653, 2654, 2645, 2641, 2595, and 2583, respectively; (**lane 8**) control cell line 2491.

human PDH complex subunits $E_1\alpha$, $E_1\beta$, and E_2 but rather weakly with E_3.[18] The most common observation is that all protein components are present in adequate amounts (lanes 1, 6, and 8). Sometimes a double band of protein is seen for either the $E_1\alpha$ (lane 2) or $E_1\beta$ (lane 4) subunits. Two cell lines on this blot have both $E_1\alpha$ and $E_1\beta$ subunits missing (lanes 5 and 7). Reduced amounts of $E_1\beta$ may be present in lanes 2 and 3. Visualization of lipoamide dehydrogenase either by Western blotting or by immunoprecipitation of proteins from ^{35}S-methionine labeled cells[19] revealed no major abnormalities in the amount or the mobility of this protein.

Examination of mRNA levels for $E_1\alpha$ and $E_1\beta$ subunits on Northern blotting with cDNA probes revealed normal message levels for the β subunit in all deficient cell lines (FIG 3). One cell line, that of a boy with ataxia, consistently displayed low or absent levels of the mRNA for the α subunit. One girl with severe deficiency also displayed an anomalous intermediate size species of mRNA (FIG. 3, lane 2) not seen in any other cell line. This phenomenon was also seen, in Northern blots with E_3 cDNA, in one cell line with partial lipoamide dehydrogenase deficiency and defective activity of all three α-keto acid dehydrogenase complexes (FIG. 4, lane 3). Other lipoamide dehydrogenase–deficient cell lines appeared to have normal mRNA levels.[20]

CHROMOSOMAL LOCATION OF PDH COMPLEX GENES

Using man/mouse hybrid panels, we have mapped the chromosomal location of the genes for the $E_1\alpha$, $E_1\beta$ and E_3 components of the PDH complex. cDNA clones have now been isolated for the $E_1\alpha$ component,[21–23] the $E_1\beta$ component,[23–25] the E_2 component,[26] and the E_3 component.[27,28] Using the clones we have isolated, we located $E_1\alpha$ to the X chromosome,[29] $E_1\beta$ to chromosome 3,[29] and E_3 to chromosome 7.[30]

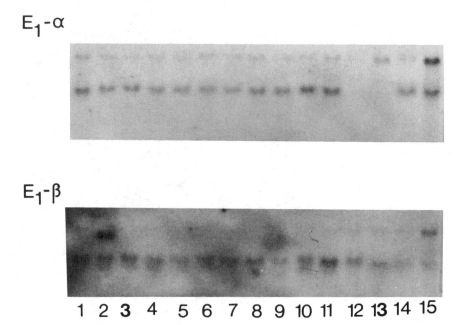

FIGURE 3. Northern blotting of total RNA from cultured skin fibroblast cell lines of patients with PDH complex deficiency. Total RNA (20 μg per cell line) were electrophoresed on a 2.2 M formaldehyde/1% agarose gel and transferred to Hybond support membrane. This blot was then probed with ^{32}P-labeled cDNA probes for $E_1\alpha$ and $E_1\beta$ in separate experiments. (Lanes 1–3) PDH-deficient cell lines 2641, 2645, and 2554, respectively. (Lanes 5 and 6) control cell lines 1206 and 1286. (Lanes 7–15) PDH-deficient cell lines 825, 1558, 1588, 1956, 2451, 2278, 1861(a), 1861(b), 1863(a), and 1863(b), respectively.

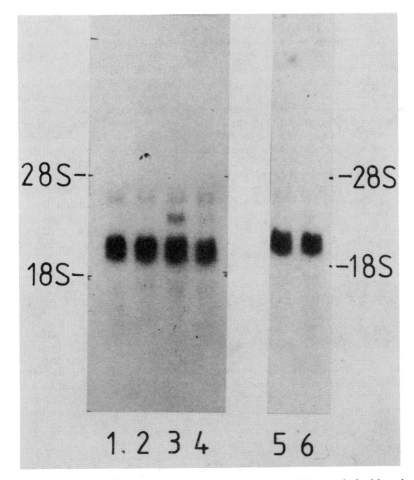

FIGURE 4. Northern blots of total RNA from human skin fibroblasts probed with a cloned cDNA probe for E_3 (lipoamide dehydrogenase). Blots of 20 μg of total RNA were prepared as described for FIGURE 3 and blotted with ^{32}P-labeled lipoamide dehydrogenase cDNA. (**Lane 1**) control cell line 1685; (**lanes 2–5**) E_3-deficient cell lines 584, 1111, 1376, and 1532, respectively. (**Lane 6**) cell line 1069, from the mother of patient 1111, an obligate heterozygote.

How do these chromosomal assignments influence our thinking about the groups of patients we have described with different clinical presentation? First of all, we have a discrete group of patients whose pattern would fit with an X-linked syndrome, that is, the group of boys with ataxia. In addition to the six patients we have described, there are another four described in the literature with this presentation of PDH deficiency, all of them boys.[31-33] This group also tend to be very carbohydrate-sensitive compared to the other patients with PDH complex deficiency. One of the members of this group is the only patient to show an abnormality in mRNA levels for the $E_1\alpha$ subunit. Thus, the evidence is very much in favor of an association of the PDH deficiency in this group with defects in the α subunit. There may be another group of male patients that are affected more severely who also have defects in the α subunit. This is suggested by the occurrence in one family of two half-brothers, both with severe deficiency causing infant death. Their mother is mentally retarded, with an IQ of 70 and mild lacticacidemia, suggesting that she, as a carrier of the X-linked α defect, exhibits abnormal pyruvate metabolism in some cells at least, due to Lyonization. There are several female patients in our cohort that have a severity of CNS disease out of keeping with mildness of their PDH complex defect. These patients, we suspect, may also have defects in the α subunit, which have severe metabolic effects in some tissues due to Lyonization. Some male patients with ataxia due to an α-defect may also be mosaic, although there is no evidence for this at this time. Severely affected female patients are almost certain to have a defect in the β subunit. Though there should be equal numbers of girls and boys with this severe form of the defect, there seems to be an excess of girls (24:15) and a predominance of girls in the groups with agenesis of the corpus callosum, in the group that develop seizure activity, and in the group with dysmorphic facial features. The explanation for this female predominance is not forthcoming at this point. Finally, the picture that has emerged is consistent with the results of the Western blotting experiments, where abnormal α-subunit patterns were seen in boys, abnormal β-subunit patterns were seen in girls, and totally missing α and β subunits were also seen in girls (with very low PDH complex activity).

TYPES OF MUTATIONS PRESENT IN PDH COMPLEX DEFICIENCY

Because mRNAs for both $E_1\alpha$ and $E_1\beta$ subunits are present in all our cases but one, it seems likely that most of the proper size mutations in this deficiency are single-base-change point mutations. The one exception to this, the cell line with a very low titre of $E_1\alpha$ mRNA, almost certainly has a splicing mutation, because we see a small amount of α protein on Western blotting. With the great variety of presentation within the different groups with PDH deficiency, the presence of multiple distinct alleles within each group is a certainty. Analysis of mutation at the molecular level will shed some light on this problem.

REFERENCES

1. BLASS, J. P., R. A. P. KARK, & W. K. ENGEL. 1971. Clinical studies of a patient with pyruvate decarboxylase deficiency. Arch. Neurol. 25: 449–460.
2. ROBINSON, B. H. 1985. The lacticacidemias. In Genetic and Metabolic Disease in Pediatrics. J. K. Loyd & C. R. Scriver, Eds.: 111–139. Butterworth & Co., London.
3. ROBINSON, B. H. 1989. The lacticacidemias. In The Metabolic Basis of Inherited Disease, 6th ed. C. R. Scriver, A. L. Beaudet, W. S. Sly & D. Valle, Eds.: 869–888. McGraw Hill. New York.
4. REED, L. J. 1981. Regulation of mammalian pyruvate dehydrogenase complex by a phosphorylation-dephosphorylation cycle. Curr. Top. Cell. Regul. 18: 95–106.
5. RANDLE, P. J. 1983. Mitochondrial 2-oxoacid dehydrogenase complexes of animal tissues. Philos. Trans. R. Soc. Lond. 302: 47–57.
6. ROBINSON, B. H. & W. G. SHERWOOD. 1984. Lactic acidemia, the prevalence of pyruvate decarboxylase deficiency. J. Inherited Metab. Dis. 7(Suppl 1): 69–73.
7. BROWN, G. K., E. A. HAAN, D. M. KIRBY, R. D. SCHOLEM, J. E. WRAITH, J. G. ROGERS & D. M. DANKS. 1988. "Cerebral" lactic acidosis: Defects in pyruvate metabolism with profound brain damage and minimal systemic acidosis. Eur. J. Pediatr. 147: 10–14.
8. ROBINSON, B. H., J. TAYLOR & W. G. SHERWOOD. 1978. Deficiency of dihydrolipoyl dehydrogenase. A cause of congenital lactic acidosis in infancy. Pediatr. Res. 11: 1198–1202.

9. ROBINSON, B. H., J. TAYLOR, S. G. KAHLER & H. N. KIRKMAN. 1981. Lacticacidemia, neurologic deterioration and carbohydrate dependence in a girl with dihydrolipoyl dehydrogenase deficiency. Eur. J. Pediatr. **136:** 35–39.

10. MUNNICH, A., J. M. SAUDUBRAY, J. TAYLOR, C. CHARPENTIER, C. MARSAC, F. ROCCI-CHIOLI, O. AMEDEE-MENESME, J. FREZAL & B. H. ROBINSON. 1982. Congenital lactic acidosis, α-ketoglutaric aciduria and variant form of maple syrup urine disease due to a single enzyme defect. Dihydrolipoyl dehydrogenase deficiency. Acta Paediatr. Scand. **71:** 167–171.

11. MATUDA, S., A. KITANO, Y. SAKAGUCHI, M. YOSHINO & T. SAHEKI. 1984. Pyruvate dehydrogenase subcomplex with lipoamide dehydrogenase deficiency in a patient with lactic acidosis and branched chain ketoaciduria. Clin. Chim. Acta **140:** 59–64.

12. MATALON, R., D. A. STUMPF, K. MICHALS, R. D. HART, J. K. PARKS & S. I. GOODMAN. 1983. Lipoamide dehydrogenase deficiency with primary lactic acidosis: Favourable response to treatment with oral lipoic acid. J. Pediatr. **104:** 65–69.

13. YOSHIDA, I., L. SWEETMAN, W. L. NYHAN & B. H. ROBINSON. Effects of lipoic acid in a patient with defective activity of pyruvate dehydrogenase, 2-ketoglutarate dehydrogenase and branched chain keto dehydrogenase. Pediatr. Res. In press.

14. KUHARA, T., T. SHINKA, Y. INOUE, M. MATSUMOTO, M. YOSHINO, Y. SAKAGUCHI & I. MATSUMOTO. 1983. Studies of urinary organic acid profiles of a patient with dihydroli-poyl dehydrogenase deficiency. Clin. Chim. Acta **133:** 133–140.

15. TAYLOR, J., B. H. ROBINSON & W. G. SHERWOOD. 1978. A defect in branched-chain amino acid metabolism in a patient with congenital lacticacidosis due to dihydrolipoyl dehydro-genase deficiency. Pediatr. Res. **12:** 60–62.

16. WICKING, C. A., R. D. SCHOLEM, S. M. HUNT & G. K. BROWN. 1986. Immunochemical analysis of normal and mutant forms of human pyruvate dehydrogenase. Biochem. J. **239:** 89–96.

17. HO, L., C. W. C. HU, S. PACKMAN & M. S. PATEL. 1986. Deficiency of the pyruvate dehydrogenase component in pyruvate dehydrogenase complex deficient human fibro-blasts—immunological identification. J. Clin. Invest. **78:** 844–847.

18. ROBINSON, B. H., H. MACMILLAN, R. PETROVA-BENEDICT & W. G. SHERWOOD. 1987. Variable clinical presentation in patients with deficiency of the pyruvate dehydrogenase complex. A review of 30 cases with a defect in the E_1 component of the complex. J. Pediatr. **111:** 525–533.

19. OTULAKOWSKI, G., W. NYHAN, L. SWEETMAN & B. H. ROBINSON. 1985. Immunoextrac-tion of lipoamide dehydrogenase from cultured skin fibroblasts in patients with combined α-ketoacid dehydrogenase. Clin. Chim. Acta **152:** 27–36.

20. OTULAKOWSKI, G. & B. H. ROBINSON. 1988. Human lipoamide dehydrogenase: Northern and Southern analysis of RNA and DNA from normal and combined α-keto acid dehydrogenase deficient cultured skin fibroblasts. Am. J. Hum. Genet. Manuscript submitted.

21. DAHL, H., S. M. HUNT, W. M. HUTCHISON & G. K. BROWN. 1987. The human pyruvate dehydrogenase complex: Isolation of cDNA clones for the E_1-α subunit, sequence analysis and characterization of the mRNA. J. Biol. Chem. **262:** 7398–7405.

22. DE MEIRLEIR, L., N. MACKAY, A. M. LAM HON WAH & B. H. ROBINSON. 1988. Isolation of a full-length complementary DNA coding for human E_1 α-subunit of the pyruvate dehydrogenase complex. J. Biol. Chem. **263:** 1991–1995.

23. KOIKE, K., S. OHTA, Y. URATA, Y. KAGAWA & M. KOIKE. Cloning and sequencing of cDNAs encoding α and β subunits of human pyruvate dehydrogenase. Proc. Natl. Acad. Sci. USA **85:** 41–45.

24. HO, L., A. A. JAVED, R. A. PEPIN, T. J. THEKKUMKARA, C. RAEFSKY, J. E. MOLE, A. M. CALIENDO, M. S. KWON, D. S. KERR & M. S. PATEL. 1988. Identification of a cDNA clone for the β-subunit of the pyruvate dehydrogenase component of human pyruvate dehydrogenase complex. Biochem. Biophys. Res. Commun. **150:** 904–908,

25. MACKAY, N. & B. H. ROBINSON. 1988. Isolation and sequence of a full-length cDNA for the E_1β-subunit of the human pyruvate dehydrogenase complex. In press.

26. THEKKUMKARA, T. J., B. W. JESSE, L. HO, C. RAEFSKY, R. A. PEPIN, A. A. JAVED, G. PONS & M. S. PATEL. 1987. Isolation of a cDNA clone for the dihydrolipoamide acetyltransferase component of the human liver pyruvate dehydrogenase complex. Biochem. Biophys. Res. Commun. **145:** 903–907.

27. OTULAKOWSKI, G. & B. H. ROBINSON. 1987. Isolation and sequence determination of cDNA clones for porcine and human lipoamide dehydrogenase: Homology to other disulphide oxidoreductases. J. Biol. Chem. **262:** 17313–17318.
28. PONS, G., C. RAEFSKY-ESTRIN, D. J. CAROTHERS, R. A. PEPIN, A. A. JAVED, B. W. JESSE, M. K. GANAPATHI, D. SAMOLS & M. S. PATEL. 1988. Cloning and cDNA sequence of the dihydrolipoamide dehydrogenase complexes. Proc. Natl. Acad. Sci. USA **85:** 1422–1426.
29. ROBINSON, B. H., K. CHUN, N. MACKAY & F. H. WILLARD. 1988. Pyruvate dehydrogenase complex-E$_1$ deficiency. α and β subunits, coded on the X chromosome and chromosome 3, respectively, lead to distinguishable entities. Am. J. Hum. Genet. Manuscript submitted.
30. OTULAKOWSKI, G., B. H. ROBINSON & H. F. WILLARD. 1988. Gene for lipoamide dehydrogenase maps to human chromosome 7. Somatic Cell Mol. Genet. **14:** 411–414.
31. FALK, R. E., S. D. CEDERBAUM, J. P. BLASS, G. E. GIBSON, R. A. P. KARK & R. E. CARREL. 1976. Ketogenic diet in the management of pyruvate dehydrogenase deficiency. Pediatrics **58:** 713–721.
32. KODAMA, S., R. YAS, M. NINOMIYA, K. GOJI, T. TAKAHASHI, Y. MONSHITA & T. MATSUO. 1983. The effect of high fat diet on pyruvate decarboxylase deficiency without involvement of the central nervous system. Brain Dev. **5:** 381–389.
33. MIYABAYASHI, S., T. ITO, K. NARISAWA, K. IINUMA & K. TADA. 1985. Biochemical study in 28 children with lactic acidosis, in relation to Leigh's encephalomyelopathy. Eur. J. Pediatr. **143:** 278–283.

Genetic Defects in Human Pyruvate Dehydrogenase[a]

LAP HO,[b] ISAIAH D. WEXLER,[c] DOUGLAS S. KERR,[c]
AND MULCHAND S. PATEL[b,d]

Departments of [b]Biochemistry and [c]Pediatrics
Case Western Reserve University School of Medicine
Cleveland, Ohio 44106

INTRODUCTION

Human pyruvate dehydrogenase complex (PDC) deficiency is a potentially severe inborn error of oxidative metabolism. There have been more than 100 reported cases of human PDC deficiency identified by measurements of PDC activity.[1-4] The clinical presentation of these subjects varied greatly but had in common lactic acidosis and neurological disabilities ranging from lethal brain stem dysfunction to moderate ataxia with otherwise normal mental development.[1-5]

Due to the multisubunit structure of PDC, a variety of genetic defects are possible. Most PDC defects appear to involve the pyruvate dehydrogenase (E_1) component.[2,4-6] Defects involving the dihydrolipoamide acetyltransferase (E_2)[7] and dihydrolipoamide dehydrogenase (E_3)[8-10] catalytic components, as well as the phospho-E_1 phosphatase,[11,12] have also been reported.

Presently, no treatment for PDC deficiency has been proven to have long-term benefit, although various dietary and pharmacological approaches have been used.[1,7,13-15] The choice of a specific clinical intervention and assessment of its benefits may require early and exact localization of the genetic defect. Diagnosis of specific PDC component deficiencies is laborious, and the techniques required are available only at a limited number of facilities. Assays for detection of heterozygous states and for prenatal diagnosis of defects of PDC are still under development. Further advances in diagnosis, intervention, and genetic counseling for this disorder will depend on exact localization of various defects and better understanding of the basic mechanisms responsible for these defects. The prospect of relating specific mutations which alter enzyme activity and regulation to changes in protein subunits, gene structure, and gene expression offers an opportunity to increase basic understanding of this mitochondrial multienzyme complex.

HUMAN PDC DEFICIENCY

Human Subjects and the Prevalence of PDC Deficiency

The diagnosis of PDC deficiency is based on assays of the catalytic activity of "total" PDC in cultured skin fibroblasts, lymphocytes, and/or tissue specimens

[a]The work performed in this laboratory and reported in this review was supported by Public Health Service Grant AM 20478 and Metabolism Training Grant AM 07319 (to L. H. and I. D. W.).

[d]Address correspondence to Mulchand S. Patel, Ph.D., Department of Biochemistry, Case Western Reserve University School of Medicine, 2119 Abington Road, Cleveland, OH 44106.

347

obtained from biopsy or autopsy.[15,16] "Total" PDC activity (hereafter referred to as PDC activity) in cells or isolated mitochondria is determined by measuring decarboxylation of [1-^{14}C]pyruvate after PDC is activated by preincubation in the presence of dichloroacetate (DCA). For extracts of frozen tissues, assays are done either after activation by preincubation with purified phospho-E_1 phosphatase (provided by Dr. T. Roche, Kansas State University, Manhattan, KS) or without preincubation. We have determined the normal ranges of PDC activity on the basis of activity measurements performed on large numbers of fibroblasts, lymphocytes and other tissues from controls (TABLE 1). The diagnosis of PDC deficiency is based on finding in subjects' cultured fibroblasts, fresh lymphocytes and/or tissue specimens PDC activity below the normal range in the presence of normal activities of citrate synthase, pyruvate carboxylase, and phosphoenolpyruvate carboxykinase. During the past 5 years, samples from 200 subjects with unexplained lactic acidosis have been tested for PDC deficiency and other disorders of energy metabolism. Twenty-one (approximately 10%) of these subjects with lactic acidosis have been identified to be PDC deficient (TABLE 1). With the exception of three cases (RC, CHa, and JHa), deficiency of PDC had been evident in subjects' cultured fibroblasts, lymphocytes, and all other tissues tested (TABLE 1). In contrast, PDC deficiency in these three cases is manifested in a tissue-specific manner. This observation will be discussed in more detail below.

Clinical Features of PDC Defects

At the time of evaluation, the ages of the 21 PDC-deficient subjects ranged from 2 days to 24 years. All of the subjects had elevated blood lactate and all had a varying degree of central nervous system dysfunction (TABLE 1). Six subjects had died by or before 1 year of age; 3 succumbed at older ages. Respiratory failure, indicative of brain stem dysfunction, was present in 9 subjects. Signs of central nervous system dysfunction including seizures, hypotonia, ataxia and congenital malformations of the brain occurred in 20 subjects (TABLE 1). Developmental delay was evident in 15 subjects (TABLE 1). In two of the subjects, neuropathological findings consistent with Leigh's necrotizing encephalomyelopathy were evident at autopsy.[13,17] The predominance of central nervous system pathology among PDC-deficient patients has been noted by others.[2-4] There was no correlation between the clinical severity of a subject's condition and the level of PDC activity measured in fibroblasts, lymphocytes, liver, or muscle (TABLE 1). The lack of correlation between residual levels of PDC activity in fibroblasts and clinical severity has been observed by others.[3,4]

Localization of Defects to Specific PDC Catalytic Components

The enzymatic activity of the components E_1, E_2, and E_3 was assessed using partial reactions.[17,18] The E_1 component of PDC was assayed after preincubation with DCA by thiamin pyrophosphate–dependent decarboxylation of [1-^{14}C]pyruvate in the absence of coenzyme A and NAD^+. E_2 was assayed by acetylation of reduced lipoamide with [1-^{14}C]acetyl-coenzyme A. E_3 was assayed by the reduction of NAD^+ in the presence of reduced lipoamide. All three assays are dependent on non-physiological reactions that result in the formation or use of non–enzyme-bound intermediates. The E_1 assay is of questionable significance, as the measured rate is less than 5% of the overall PDC reaction (TABLE 2). Measurement of these PDC catalytic components in cultured fibroblasts showed that 14 of the PDC-deficient patients had low E_1 activity in the presence of normal activity of E_2 and E_3 (TABLE 2). However, finding low levels of E_1

TABLE 1. Activity of Total PDC in Cells and Tissues from PDC-Deficient Patients

Source	Sex	Age[a]	Clinical Status[b]	Total PDC Activity (nmol/min/mg protein)[c]			
				Fibroblasts	Lymphocytes	Liver	Muscle
Controls							
Mean ± SD				2.46 ± 0.89	1.87 ± 0.68	2.23 ± 0.78	2.54 ± 1.26
Range				1.1–6.7	0.9–3.8	1.0–3.7	1.0–5.5
n				74	93	11	8
Patients							
LA	F	9 m[†]	C, D, R, U	0.53	0.37		
AB	F	2 d[†]	C, R	0.37	—	0.57	
JB	M	24 y	D, S	0.17	0.05		0.06
BC	M	4 m	C, D, H, R, S	0.33	0.36		
CC	F	12 y	D, S	0.23	0.33		0.70
RC	M	13 y	D, H, R	1.86	0.37		
TF	M	11 m	D, H, R	0.02	0.14		0.26
BF	M	1 d[†]	R	0.00	—		
MG	M	1 m	D, H, S	0.41	0.05		
CHa[d]	M	3 y[†]	D, S	2.01	0.14	0.11	0.01
JHa[d]	M	4 y	D, S	4.39	0.08		
PH	M	14 y[†]	H, S	0.75	—		0.13
JH	M	8 y	H	0.58	0.30		
BK	M	4 m[†]	C, R, S, U	0.09	0.13	0.09	0.14
CP	F	4 y	D, S	0.05	0.90		
KPi[d]	F	17 y	D, S	0.14	0.49		
RPi[d]	M	20 y	D, S		0.34		
DR	M	1 y	D, H	0.30	0.20		
JS	M	8 y[†]	H, D, L, S	0.46	—		
EU	M	1 y[†]	D, L, R, S	0.71	0.16	0.20	
BW	M	2 d[†]	C, R	0.39	—		

[a] d, day; m, month; y, year; [†], age at which patient expired.
[b] C, congenital malformation of brain; D, developmental delay; H, hypotonia/ataxia; L, Leigh's disease (autopsy proven); R, respiratory failure (central); S, seizure disorder; U, sudden unexpected death.
[c] PDC activity in samples activated with dichloroacetate (cells) or PDH phosphatase (tissues). Dash, no activity detected.
[d] CHa and JHa, and KPi and RPi, are siblings.

TABLE 2. PDC Component Activity, Immunoreactivity, and mRNA in Cells and Tissues from PDC-Deficient Patients

| | Fibroblasts | | | | | | | Tissues | | | | | | | | |
| | Activity (nmol/min/mg protein) | | | Immunoreactivity[a] | | | | Immunoreactivity[a] | | | | | mRNA[c] | | | |
Source	E_1	E_2	E_3	$E_1\alpha$	$E_1\beta$	E_2	E_3	Tissues Tested[b]	$E_1\alpha$	$E_1\beta$	E_2	E_3	Tissues Tested[b]	$E_1\alpha$	$E_1\beta$	E_3
Controls																
Mean ± SD	0.08 ± 0.02	3.0 ± 1.0	38 ± 16	+	+	+	+	L, M, H, K, B	+	+	+	+	F, L, H, M	+	+	+
Range	0.06–11	1.3–5.3	19–67													
n	*16*	*19*	*15*													
Patients																
LA	0.04	1.7	27	+	+	+	+									
GB	0.01	2.5	28	+	+	+	+									
JB		2.6	26					L	+	+	+	+				
BC	0.01	1.5	24	+	+	+	+									
CC	0.03	5.7	65	+	+	+	+						M	+	+	
TF		0.3	26		+	+	+									
BF	0.02	2.2	22													
CHa	0.08	4.4	34	+	+	+	+	L, M, H	–	–	+	+	F, L, M	+	+	+
JHa		2.6	84										F	+	+	+
PH	0.04	1.7	24	–	–	+	+	M	–	–	+	+	F, M	+	+	+
JH	0.03	3.5	28	–	–	+	+						F	–	+	+
BK	0.01	1.6	91	+	+	+	+						F		+	+
CP	0.03	5.6	36	+	+	+	+						F	+	+	+
KPi	0.02	2.6	19	+	+	+	+									
DR	0.03	2.2	2													
JS	0.01	4.6	19	–	–	+	+									
EU	0.04	2.9	61	–	–	+	+	L, H, K, B	–	–	+	+	F	–	+	+
BW	0.01	2.8	40	+	+	+	+						F, L	+	+	+

[a] Western blot.
[b] F, fibroblasts; L, liver; M, muscle; H, heart; K, kidney; B, brain.
[c] Northern blot.

activity does not localize the defect to E_1. Mutations of the phospho-E_1 phosphatase may also result in decreased E_1 activity. Phospho-E_1 phosphatase mutations can be demonstrated by the restoration of E_1 activity *in vitro* after the addition of phospho-E_1 phosphatase or non-specific phosphatase.[12,16,19] In 8 of the subjects (AB, JB, RC, BF, CHa, PH, BK and EU), preincubation of tissue extracts with purified phospho-E_1 phosphatase did not restore PDC activity (data not shown). In some of these cases, the specificity of the E_1 defect was independently corroborated by immunological and RNA blot analyses (TABLE 2). The predominance of defects involving the E_1 component among cases of PDC deficiency has been reported by others,[3,20] although the possibility of phospho-E_1 phosphatase defects was not eliminated in most of these cases. Naito *et al.*[12] reported that PDC activity was restored in fibroblasts from three out of four PDC-deficient patients by pretreatment with a non-specific phosphatase, but not by DCA. In contrast, we have not yet detected any case of phospho-E_1 phosphatase deficiency in our series of patients.

We found one case with low activity of the E_3 component (DR; TABLE 2); E_2 activity was normal but apparent E_1 activity was also below the normal range. Urinary metabolite analysis showed elevated levels of α-ketoglutarate and metabolites of branched-chain α-keto acids (data not shown), which is consistent with an E_3 deficiency. In another subject (TF, TABLE 2), E_2 activity was well below the normal range; E_3 activity was normal. The nature of genetic defects in these subjects is under investigation.

Immunological Assessment of PDC Deficiency

Immunological assessment of PDC deficiency by Western blot analysis offers a complementary approach in characterizing genetic defects of PDC. This approach discriminates between a change in enzyme content and a change affecting only the catalytic efficiency of the enzyme. In addition, mutations resulting in significant changes in the size of the defective protein could be identified. We generated specific rabbit antisera against the individual components E_1, E_2, and E_3, using highly purified bovine kidney E_1 and bovine heart E_2 (both enzymes were generously provided by Dr. L. Reed) and a commercially available porcine heart E_3.[21] All antisera are highly cross-reactive with their respective human antigens.[21]

Cultured fibroblasts from 12 patients with low E_1 catalytic activity were further characterized by Western blot analysis using the specific antisera or affinity-selected antibodies.[5,17,21] In four cases (PH, JH, JS and EU), E_1 deficiency was associated with dramatically reduced immunoreactivity corresponding to the E_1 component, reflecting the presence of abnormally low levels of $E_1\alpha$ and $E_1\beta$ proteins in these fibroblasts (TABLE 2). Both the $E_1\alpha$ and the $E_1\beta$ peptides were simultaneously affected (FIG. 1 shows as an example the immunoblot analysis of subjects PH and JH). These observations indicated that genetic mutations in these four CRM⁻ (cross-reactive materials negative) subjects specifically affected the expression of the E_1 peptides. Simultaneous reduction of both $E_1\alpha$ and $E_1\beta$ peptides in another PDC-deficient patient has been reported recently.[6] Observation of this phenomenon indicates that expression of the two E_1 peptides is in some way coordinated. Possible sites for the coordination of these two mature mitochondrial peptides could exist at the transcriptional, post-transcriptional, translational, or post-translational levels (FIG. 2). The two E_1 proteins are normally assembled into an $\alpha_2\beta_2$ tetramer in the mitochondria.[22,23] We believe that the most likely explanation for the simultaneous reduction of both E_1 peptides is that in the absence of one peptide, the other peptide is not able to assemble into the stable

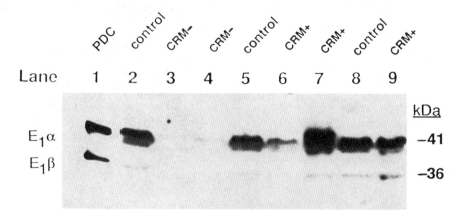

FIGURE 1. Immunoblot analysis of E_1 from cultured fibroblast extracts using affinity-purified anti-E_1 antibodies followed by ^{125}I-labeled protein A. (**Lane 1**) 0.4 μg purified bovine PDC. (**Lanes 2–9**) 500 μg total protein per lane from three different controls (**lanes 2, 5,** and **8**) and five E_1-deficient subjects (**lanes 3, 4, 6, 7,** and **9**). CRM$^+$ (cross-reactive material–positive) subjects are GB (**lane 6**), BK (**lane 7**), and LA (**lane 9**). CRM$^-$ subjects are JH (**lane 3**) and PH (**lane 4**).

tetrameric conformation and is rapidly degraded. A similar phenomenon has been observed for cyclic AMP–protein kinase.[24]

In one case (BK), Western analysis of PDC in fibroblasts revealed the presence of an additional approximately 43-kDa E_1 peptide (FIG. 1). The approximately 43-kDa peptide could represent a large $E_1\alpha$ peptide produced by mutation which results in the expression of either a larger mature mitochondrial $E_1\alpha$ or a defective precursor $E_1\alpha$ peptide that is not properly processed by the mitochondria. This finding localizes the genetic defect specifically to the $E_1\alpha$ peptide. In contrast, 3 cases of E_1 deficiency were previously identified which have a smaller $E_1\alpha$ protein.[25] These cases indicate that genetic mutations specific to the $E_1\alpha$ peptide may exhibit polymorphism at the protein level.

Western blot analysis of cultured fibroblasts from the remaining seven E_1-deficient patients showed that the molecular sizes as well as the levels of the $E_1\alpha$ and $E_1\beta$ peptides appeared to be normal (TABLE 2). Further resolution by 2-dimensional gel electrophoresis may show additional variation among the CRM$^+$ subjects. In one reported case, Western blot analysis combined with 2-dimensional gel electrophoresis and use of phospho-E_1 phosphatase showed that the E_1 component was resistant to dephosphorylation.[19]

RNA-Blot Analysis of E_1-Deficient Subjects

To characterize PDC mutations at the mRNA level, individual human cDNA clones for $E_1\alpha$, $E_1\beta$, E_2, and E_3 were isolated using specific antisera and a human liver λgt11 cDNA library (provided by Drs. T. Chandra and S. L. C. Woo, Baylor College of Medicine, Houston, TX). The isolation, identification, and analysis of these cDNA clones have been previously described.[5,26–30] Three different cDNA sequences for human $E_1\alpha$ have been published recently.[31–33] Two of these sequences were generated from human liver cDNAs,[31,32] and the third one was from a human foreskin fibroblast cDNA.[33] These two human liver $E_1\alpha$ cDNA sequences and our $E_1\alpha$ cDNA sequence are essentially identical. The minor differences noted are most likely due to cloning or sequencing artifacts. In contrast, 93 consecutive deoxynucleotides that were present in the coding region of all three human liver $E_1\alpha$ cDNAs were not present in the foreskin fibroblast $E_1\alpha$ cDNA.[33] Although no explanation was provided for this difference, it may reflect a tissue-specific expression of $E_1\alpha$ mRNA or an artifact of cloning.

In RNA-blot analysis of normal cultured skin fibroblasts (FIG. 3), the $E_1\alpha$ cDNA hybridized intensely with an approximately 1.6-kb species and less intensely with an approximately 3.3-kb species. Dahl *et al.* have demonstrated that these two mRNA species contain the same coding and 5' untranslated region but differ in the length of the 3' untranslated region.[31] The $E_1\beta$ cDNA also hybridized to two species of RNAs from human heart, a major and a minor hybridizable species of approximately 1.6 and

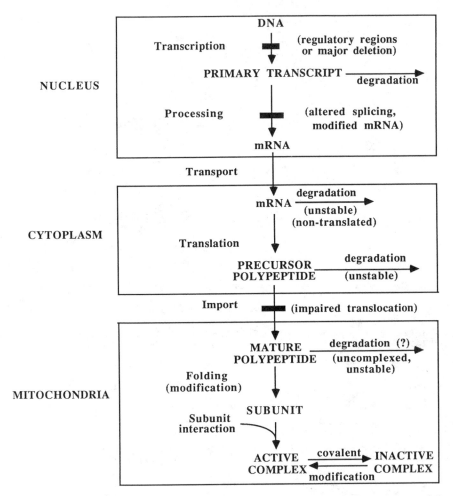

FIGURE 2. An outline of the multiple processes involved in the expression of a nuclear-encoded mitochondrial enzyme. Various points where mutations may affect the availability of specific mRNAs and/or the mature mitochondrial proteins are noted.

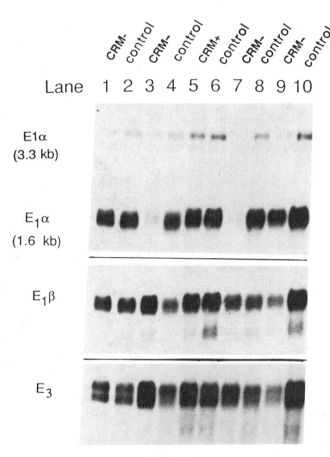

FIGURE 3. RNA-blot analysis of total RNA from fibroblasts of E_1-deficient subjects. Total RNA (15 μg) was loaded onto each lane. The membrane was hybridized with radiolabeled deoxyoligonucleotide probes generated using cDNAs for $E_1\alpha$ (*upper panel*), $E_1\beta$ (*middle panel*) and E_3 (*lower panel*). (**Lanes 2, 4, 6, 8** and **10**) total RNA from five different human control fibroblast cell lines. (**Lanes 1, 3, 5, 7** and **9**) total RNA from E_1-deficient subjects. Subject BK is CRM⁺. The CRM⁻ subjects are EU (**lane 1**), JS (**lane 3**), JH (**lane 7**), and PH (**lane 9**). CRM, cross-reactive material.

5.2 kb, respectively.[29] In RNA-blot analysis of normal cultured skin fibroblasts, the 5.2-kb $E_1\beta$ RNA species is often visible only upon prolonged exposures (data not shown). The physiological significance of multiple $E_1\alpha$ and $E_1\beta$ mRNA species is not known.

Fibroblast RNA from all four CRM⁻ subjects had apparently normal amounts and sizes of specific $E_1\beta$ mRNAs (FIG. 3). This finding rules out the possibility that absence of the two E_1 peptides is due to a defect in coordinately regulated transcription. However, two different patterns of specific $E_1\alpha$ mRNA expression were identified among the four CRM⁻ subjects (FIG. 3). The levels of both specific $E_1\alpha$ mRNAs were decreased in two CRM⁻ cases (JH and JS). This observation indicates that genetic defects in these two cases specifically affect the expression of $E_1\alpha$. The cause(s) for decreased levels of $E_1\alpha$ mRNAs has not yet been determined. Genetic mutations in these subjects could adversely affect transcription of the $E_1\alpha$ gene, post-transcriptional processing, or stability of the gene product (FIG. 2).

Specific $E_1\alpha$ mRNAs were present at normal levels in cultured fibroblasts from the other two CRM⁻ subjects (PH and EU) (FIG. 3), and the electrophoretic mobility of these mRNAs was indistinguishable from normal (FIG. 3). The nature of the genetic defects in these two cases is not known. It is possible that mutations could impair effective translation of one of the E_1 peptides, preventing the other E_1 peptide from complexing into a stable tetramer.

As expected, the CRM⁺ patients tested also expressed normal levels of $E_1\alpha$ and $E_1\beta$ mRNAs (TABLE 2), and the apparent molecular sizes of their E_1 mRNAs were indistinguishable from normal. Further analysis of E_1 mRNAs in these cases would be expected to provide information regarding the nature of their genetic defects.

Variable Expression of E_1 Deficiency

The first case of severe systemic deficiency we reported was subject EU (TABLES 1 and 2; FIG. 4). PDC and component E_1 activity was below normal ranges in this subject's cultured fibroblasts, lymphocytes, liver, muscle, kidney, heart, and brain (FIG. 4). This is associated with reduced amounts of both immunoreactive $E_1\alpha$ and $E_1\beta$ peptides (TABLE 2). Component E_2 and E_3 activities, as well as the amount of immunoreactive E_2 and E_3 peptides, were normal. In most other cases, PDC deficiency was also expressed in cultured fibroblasts, lymphocytes, and other tissues tested (TABLES 1 and 2). In contrast, three cases (CHa, JHa and RC; CHa and JHa are

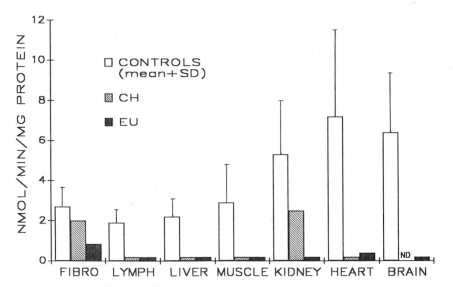

FIGURE 4. Total PDC activity in cells and tissues of two PDC-deficient subjects. Control values represent averages ± S.D. from normal subjects.[5,15,17] Subject EU had low PDC activity in all cells and tissues tested. In subject CHa (CH), PDC deficiency was manifested in lymphocytes (LYMPH), liver, muscle, heart, and brain but was normal in fibroblasts (FIBRO). Kidney PDC activity was approximately 50% of the average control value. ND, not determined.

brothers) have been identified in which E_1 deficiency is expressed in a tissue-specific manner. In all three cases, PDC activity measured in freshly prepared lymphocytes was abnormally low, whereas PDC activity in cultured fibroblasts was normal (TABLE 1).

In the case of CHa, several tissues were obtained at autopsy. PDC activity in heart, liver, and muscle was severely reduced (FIG. 4). Catalytic activities of individual components were measured in cultured fibroblasts and isolated liver mitochondria. Individual component activities for E_1, E_2, and E_3 in this subject's cultured fibroblasts were normal (TABLE 2), but E_1 was specifically low in liver mitochondria.[15] E_1 deficiency in patient CHa was confirmed by Western blot analysis, which showed the simultaneous absence of both $E_1\alpha$ and $E_1\beta$ peptides in liver, heart, and muscle specimens (TABLE 2). However, a kidney specimen from the patient showed approximately 50% of average control PDC activity (FIG. 4). This result was corroborated by Western blot analysis, which showed the presence of significant levels of $E_1\alpha$ and $E_1\beta$ proteins in the kidney.[15] The mother also had reduced PDC activity (approximately 50% of controls) in her lymphocytes but no reduction in the activity in her fibroblasts.[15] Therefore, variable expression of E_1 deficiency in this family was not the result of an artifact or compound series of experimental errors.

Current knowledge of regulation of PDC and E_1 expression in differentiated cells is insufficient to provide an explanation for these observations of variable E_1 deficiency. One possible explanation could be tissue-specific expression of E_1 isozymes. Previous studies of the kinetic properties of purified PDC or peptide fragments of purified E_1 have indicated that the E_1 components from bovine kidney, brain, and heart are very similar to each other.[23,34,35] However, the possibility of tissue-specific E_1 isozymes has not been excluded. An alternative explanation for variable expression of E_1 deficiency could be the existence of multiple gene copies for specific E_1 subunits which are differentially expressed in various tissues and are separately affected by mutations.

Previous reports of PDC deficiency have been based predominantly on enzymatic activity measurements in cultured fibroblasts. Our findings demonstrate that dependence on fibroblasts alone for the diagnosis of PDC deficiency could be misleading. In three cases among our series of subjects, severe systemic E_1 deficiency would have escaped detection if biochemical analyses had been restricted to cultured fibroblasts. Diagnostic assessments should be performed in more than one cell or tissue type whenever possible. Even in the case of EU, with severe systemic deficiency of PDC, the defect was not accurately reflected by his cultured fibroblasts; residual PDC activity was approximately 30% of the average control (TABLE 1, FIG. 4). Differential expression of PDC in various tissues or cell types could play a role in the variable severity of clinical presentations observed among subjects.

Multiple Patterns of Inheritance of E_1 Deficiency

Immunological analysis of our series of E_1-deficient subjects showed two overall patterns: (i) the presence of normal levels of cross-immunoreactive $E_1\alpha$ and $E_1\beta$ (CRM$^+$) and (ii) dramatically reduced non-detectable levels of cross-immunoreactive $E_1\alpha$ and $E_1\beta$ (CRM$^-$). We identified five CRM$^-$ subjects (CHa, PH, JH, JS, and EU) and noted that they all are males. In contrast, five of the seven CRM$^+$ subjects are female. Based on these findings, we have considered the possibility that some genetic defects of E_1 may be X-linked.[15]

An opportunity was presented for analysis of PDC activity in relatives of CRM$^-$ subjects, CHa and his brother JHa, in whom PDC activity was normal in fibroblasts but low in lymphocytes.[15] Their sister had normal PDC activity in her lymphocytes.

Their father had normal PDC activities in both fibroblasts and lymphocytes. In contrast, their mother's lymphocytes showed half the normal levels of PDC activity, indicative of a heterozygous state. However, lymphocytes from both the maternal grandmother and great-grandmother were found to have normal PDC activity. These results are consistent with X-linked inheritance due to a mutation in the germ cell line from which the mother was derived. Alternatively, the maternal ancestors could be heterozygous for the defect but do not express reduced activity due to skewed lyonization of their X-chromosomes.

Heterogeneity of the inheritance pattern for E_1 deficiency may be due, in part, to the fact that the two subunits are encoded by different genes. Other yet unidentified regulatory factor(s) could also be involved in the expression of $E_1\alpha$ and $E_1\beta$. Presently, there is no established example of a specific $E_1\beta$ defect. In our series of patients and in previously reported cases are six examples of E_1 deficiency which specifically involve $E_1\alpha$.[25] In two of these cases (PH and JS, two males from our series), specific reduction of the level of $E_1\alpha$ mRNAs localized these defects to $E_1\alpha$. However, the possibility of mutation of a yet unidentified regulator of $E_1\alpha$ expression cannot be ruled out. A female subject has been reported by Brown *et al.*, in whom there was simultaneous absence of both $E_1\alpha$ and $E_1\beta$ peptides and no detectable $E_1\alpha$ mRNAs; the presence of $E_1\beta$ mRNAs was not assessed.[6] In the remaining four cases, genetic mutations appeared to be located within the structural $E_1\alpha$ gene, as mobility of the $E_1\alpha$ protein

TABLE 3. Summary of the Types of Heterogeneous Expression of E_1 Proteins and mRNAs among E_1-Deficient Subjects

			Protein		mRNA	
Type	Cases (n)	E_1 Activity	α	β	α	β
I	7	−	+	+	+	+
II	3	−	−	−	+	+
III	2	−	−	−	−	+

was altered (BK from our series and three others from McKay *et al.*[25]). A recent preliminary report identified the gene for human $E_1\alpha$ on the X chromosome, between regions Xq24 to Xp22.[36] The finding of structural defects of $E_1\alpha$ in females is not necessarily inconsistent with the location of this gene on the X chromosome, since the unaffected X chromosome could be predominantly inactivated. Alternatively, the genetic defect might impair a yet unidentified autosomal factor affecting expression of the $E_1\alpha$ gene.

SUMMARY AND CONCLUSIONS

The nature of PDC deficiency has been characterized at the levels of total and component catalytic activities as well as at the levels of component proteins and specific mRNAs. Defects in 14 cases were shown to involve the E_1 component, and there was one case each of an apparent E_2 and E_3 deficiency.

Defects involving the E_1 component exhibit heterogeneous expression of E_1 proteins and mRNAs (TABLE 3), indicating that different types of mutations cause E_1 deficiency. E_1 deficiencies can occur either in the presence or absence of E_1 proteins, representing catalytic mutations or mutations affecting the expression of E_1 proteins, respectively. In every case where the content of E_1 proteins is reduced, both the $E_1\alpha$ and the $E_1\beta$ peptides are simultaneously affected. This is likely to be due to rapid degradation of any E_1 peptide that is not complexed into the $\alpha_2\beta_2$ conformation. Among subjects with reduced levels of both E_1 peptides, some had normal amounts of specific $E_1\alpha$ and $E_1\beta$ mRNAs. In these subjects, the primary mutations affect either translational or post-translational processes leading to the formation of mature E_1 proteins in the mitochondria. In contrast, two cases of simultaneous reduction of both $E_1\alpha$ and $E_1\beta$ proteins had decreases in the amounts of $E_1\alpha$ mRNA only. Mutations in these cases may impair the transcription, nuclear processing, or stability of $E_1\alpha$ mRNA.

E_1 deficiency may manifest in a variable manner. Further characterization of this phenomenon might provide insight into the discrepancy between the clinical severity of the defect and the residual level of PDC catalytic activity. Available information indicates that the $E_1\alpha$ gene is located on the X chromosome, but sex distribution of $E_1\alpha$ defects suggests that the mode of inheritance may not follow a simple X-linked pattern. The availability of specific PDC antibodies and cDNA clones, as well as the application of molecular biological techniques, should facilitate the characterization of the molecular basis of various PDC deficiencies. This information should provide better understanding of the function of PDC, pathophysiology of PDC deficiency, and mechanisms of inheritance and expression of these genes.

ACKNOWLEDGMENTS

We are grateful to M. Lusk for technical assistance. We appreciate the cooperation of Drs. M. Lipson (Kaiser Permanente, Sacramento, CA) K. Johnston (Stanford University, Palo Alto, CA), M. Bofinger (University of Cincinnati, Cincinnati, OH), P. Lubens (Memorial Medical Center, Long Beach, CA), W. Grover (Temple University, Philadelphia, PA), K. McCormick (University of Rochester, Rochester, NY), R. Wappner (Indiana University, Indianapolis, IN), S. Cederbaum (University of California, Los Angeles, CA), N. Buist (University of Oregon Health Science Center, Portland, OR), C. Berlin (Pennsylvania State University, Hershey, PA), and S. Packman (University of California, San Francisco) in sending us skin fibroblasts from PDHC-deficient subjects.

REFERENCES

1. BLASS, J. P. 1983. *In* The Metabolic Basis of Inherited Disease, 5th ed. J. B. Stanbury, D. S. Wyngaarden, D. S. Fredrickson, J. L. Goldstein & M. S. Brown, Eds.: 193–203. McGraw-Hill Company. New York.
2. BUTTERWORTH, R. F. 1985. *In* Cerebral Energy Metabolism and Metabolic Encephalopathy. D. M. McCandless, Ed.: 121–141. Plenum Company. New York.
3. STANSBIE, D., S. J. WALLACE & C. MARSAC. 1986. J. Inherited Metab. Dis. **9:** 105–119.
4. ROBINSON, B. H., H. MACMILLAN, R. PETROVA-BENEDICT & W. G. SHERWOOD. 1987. J. Pediatr. **111:** 525–533.
5. WEXLER, I. D., D. S. KERR, L. HO, M. M. LUSK, R. A. PEPIN, A. A. JAVID, J. E. MOLE, B. W. JESSE, T. J. THEKKUMKARA, G. PONS & M. S. PATEL. 1988. Proc. Natl. Acad. Sci. USA **88:** 7336–7340.
6. BROWN, G. K., R. D. SCHOLEM, S. M. HUNT, J. R. HARRISON & A. C. POLLARD. 1987. J. Inherited Metab. Dis. **10:** 359–366.
7. CEDERBAUM, S. D., J. P. BLASS, N. MINKOFF, W. J. BROWN, M. E. COTTON & S. H. HARRIS. 1976. Pediatr Res. **10:** 713–720.
8. HAWORTH, J. C., Y. L. PERRY, J. P. BLASS, S. HANSEN & N. URQUHART. 1976. Pediatrics **58:** 564–572.

9. KURODA, Y., J. J. KLINE, L. SWEETMAN, W. NYHAN & T. D. GROSHONG. 1979. Pediatr. Res. **13:** 928–931.
10. MATUDA, S., A. KITANO, Y. SAKAGUCHI, M. YOSHINA & T. SAHEKI. 1984. Clin. Chim. Acta. **140:** 59–64.
11. ROBINSON, B. H. & W. G. SHERWOOD. 1975. Pediatr. Res. **9:** 935–939.
12. NAITO, E., Y. KURODA, E. TAKEDA, J. YOKOTA, H. KOBASHI & M. MIYAO. 1988. Pediatr. Res. **23:** 561–564.
13. JOHNSTON, K., C. J. L. NEWTH, K-F. R. SHEU, M. S. PATEL, G. P. HELDT, K. A. SCHMIDT & S. PACKMAN. 1984. Pediatrics **74:** 1034–1040.
14. MATALON, R., D. A. STUMPH, K. MICHAELS, R. D. HART, J. K. PARKS & S. I. GOODMAN. 1984. J. Pediatr. **104:** 59–64.
15. KERR, D. S., S. A. BERRY, M. M. LUSK, L. HO & M. S. PATEL. 1988. Pediatr. Res. **24:** 95–100.
16. SHEU, K-F. R., C-W. C. HU & M. F. UTTER. 1981. J. Clin. Invest. **67:** 1463–1471.
17. KERR, D. S., L. HO, C. M. BERLIN, K. F. LANOUE, J. TOWFIGHI, C. L. HOPPEL, M. M. LUSK, C. M. GONDEK & M. S. PATEL. 1987. Pediatr. Res. **22:** 312–318.
18. CHUANG, D. T., C-W. C. HU & M. S. PATEL. 1983. Biochem. J. **214:** 177–181.
19. WICKING, C. A., R. D. SCHOLEM, S. M. HUNT & G. K. BROWN. 1986. Biochem. J. **239:** 89–96.
20. ROBINSON, B. H., J. TAYLOR & J. G. SHERWOOD. 1980. Pediatr. Res **14:** 956–962.
21. HO, L., C-W. C. HU, S. PACKMAN & M. S. PATEL. 1986. J. Clin. Invest. **78:** 844–847.
22. REED, L. J. 1973. Acc. Chem. Res. **7:** 40–46.
23. BARRERA, C. R., G. NAMIHARA, L. HAMILTON, P. MUNK, M. H. ELEY, T. C. LINN & L. J. REED. 1972. Arch. Biochem. Biophys. **148:** 343–358.
24. UHLER, M. D. & G. S. MCKNIGHT. 1987. J. Biol. Chem. **262:** 15202–15207.
25. MCKAY, N., R. PETROVA-BENEDICT, J. THOENE, B. BERGEN, W. WILSON & B. ROBINSON. 1986. Eur. J. Pediatr. **144:** 445–450.
26. PONS, G., C. RAEFSKY-ESTRIN, D. CAROTHERS, R. A. PEPIN, A. A. JAVED, B. W. JESSE, M. K. GANAPATHI, D. SAMOLS & M. S. PATEL. 1988. Proc. Natl. Acad. Sci. USA **85:** 1422–1426.
27. THEKKUMKARA, T. J., B. W. JESSE, L. HO, C. RAEFSKY, R. A. PEPIN, A. A. JAVED, G. PONS & M. S. PATEL. 1987. Biochem. Biophys. Res. Commun. **145:** 903–907.
28. HO, L., D. S. KERR, I. D. WEXLER & M. S. PATEL. 1988. FASEB J. **2:** A1550 (Abstr.).
29. HO, L., A. A. JAVED, R. A. PEPIN, T. K. THEKKUMKARA, C. RAEFSKY, J. E. MOLE, A. M. CALIENDO, M. S. KWON, D. S. KERR & M. S. PATEL. 1988. Biochem. Biophys. Res. Commun. **150:** 904–908.
30. THEKKUMKARA, T. J., L. HO, I. D. WEXLER, T-C. LIU & M. S. PATEL. 1988. FEBS Lett. **240:** 45–48.
31. DAHL, H-H. M., S. M. HUNT, W. M. HUTCHISON & G. K. BROWN. 1987. J. Biol. Chem. **262:** 7398–7403.
32. DEMEIRLEIR, L., N. MACKAY, H. W. A. M. LAM & B. H. ROBINSON. 1988. J. Biol. Chem. **263:** 1991–1995.
33. KOIKE, K., S. S. OHTA, Y. URATA, Y. KAGAWA & M. KOIKE. 1988. Proc. Natl. Acad. Sci. USA **85:** 41–45.
34. HALDANE, G. C. & B. FIELD. 1974. Biochem. J. **142:** 87–95.
35. SHEU, K-F. R. & Y. T. KIM. 1984. J. Neurochem. **43:** 1352–1358.
36. SHEU, K-F. R., P. SZABO, R. ROBINSON, M. E. WEKSLER & J. P. BLASS. 1988. Trans. Am. Soc. Neurochem. **19:** 232 (Abstr.).

The Clinical and Biochemical Spectrum of Human Pyruvate Dehydrogenase Complex Deficiency

G. K. BROWN,[a,b] R. M. BROWN,[c] R. D. SCHOLEM,[c]
D. M. KIRBY[c] AND H-H. M. DAHL[c]

[c]Murdoch Institute for Research into Birth Defects
Royal Children's Hospital
Melbourne, Australia
and
[a]Department of Paediatrics
University of Melbourne
Melbourne, Australia

Pyruvate dehydrogenase complex (PDC) deficiency is a major cause of primary lactic acidosis in infants and young children.[1] In almost all cases, the basic defect appears to be in the E1 component of PDC and, in particular, in the E1α subunit.[2-4] In spite of numerous reports of PDC deficiency in humans, there is still significant controversy concerning the incidence and the clinical and biochemical spectrum of this condition.[5]

Some of the confusion regarding PDC deficiency in humans has arisen because of difficulties in establishing the diagnosis by assay of the enzyme complex in readily available samples from patients. However, the development of more reliable assays,[6] the availability of immunochemical methods for analysis of structural changes in specific components of the complex,[3,4,7] and the isolation of recombinant DNA probes for studies of the underlying genetic defects[8-10] have greatly improved the accuracy of diagnosis. The heterogeneity of PDC deficiency can be assessed from recently reported cases with confidence that the patients described do indeed have a primary genetic defect in the PDC.

The following discussion will be limited to patients with defects in the E1α component of PDC. From our own experience and from recently reported cases, it is apparent that this form of PDC deficiency in humans is an extremely heterogeneous condition. The characteristic features of the disorder are metabolic acidosis and neurological dysfunction. In contrast with many other inborn errors of metabolism which affect cerebral function, PDC deficiency is distinguished by the presence of significant structural abnormalities in the central nervous system (CNS). Within this general clinical presentation, however, there is a wide range in the severity of symptoms and the clinical course of the condition.

In the most severe form of PDC deficiency, lactic acidosis develops within hours of birth and the blood lactate concentration rapidly attains levels as high as 10–20 mM.[4] The lactic acidosis is almost always refractory to all attempts at specific therapy, and most of these patients die in the newborn period. Patients with less severe forms of PDC deficiency generally present later, and their clinical course is characterized by episodes of severe lactic acidosis, often precipitated by intercurrent illness.[11] Blood pyruvate and

[b]Address correspondence to Dr. G. K. Brown, Murdoch Institute, Royal Children's Hospital, Parkville, Vic., 3052, Australia.

lactate concentrations often remain slightly above the normal range in the periods between acute episodes of acidosis.

At the other extreme, some patients with PDC deficiency never develop significant systemic metabolic acidosis, and the blood lactate concentration is normal or only slightly raised throughout their course.[12] In these patients, neurological symptoms predominate, and impairment of pyruvate metabolism in the CNS is reflected in concentrations of pyruvate and lactate in the cerebrospinal fluid (CSF) which are disproportionately elevated compared with those in the blood.

The neurological symptoms of PDC deficiency also vary considerably between patients, in both their nature and severity. In patients with profound lactic acidosis in the newborn period, there is usually generalized CNS depression with altered conscious state and seizures. There are more specific patterns of neurologic dysfunction in patients with persistent or episodic lactic acidosis. Some have recurrent episodes of cerebellar ataxia at times when their blood pyruvate and lactate concentrations are raised, while others have a chronic neurodegenerative disorder with neurological regression, muscular hypotonia, and focal brain stem signs which fall within the clinical spectrum of Leigh's syndrome.[13,14]

Patients with the "cerebral" form of PDC deficiency have a prolonged clinical course, with gross cerebral pathology.[12] Neurological symptoms, including feeding difficulties, seizures, and abnormalities of motor function, develop soon after birth and progress to profound mental retardation, microcephaly, spastic tetraparesis, and blindness. Several patients with this form of PDC deficiency have survived to adolescence.[12]

Structural defects in the CNS are a major feature of PDC deficiency and, again, there is considerable variation. Patients who die in the newborn period often have generalized cerebral pathology with edema or multiple hemorrhages. However, in all other forms of PDC deficiency, more localized structural abnormalities are commonly found. Two different pathological processes appear to be involved: degeneration of apparently normally formed cerebral tissue and abnormal development of particular regions of the brain.

In some patients, there are cystic lesions with areas of spongiform change and reduced myelination. These may be localized to the brain stem in the typical pattern of Leigh's syndrome[13] or may be found in the basal ganglia or cerebral cortex.[11] Neurodegeneration in other patients manifests as cerebral atrophy and dilated ventricles.[12] Maldevelopment of specific regions of the brain most commonly involves the corpus callosum, medullary pyramids, and inferior olives.[11,15]

Biochemical studies of PDC deficiency have not resolved any of the problems of heterogeneity in this condition. Variability of assay results in cultured fibroblasts and tissues has made it difficult to establish a diagnosis of PDC deficiency with any degree of certainty in many patients with lactic acidosis. Even with reliable assay methods, there is an extremely poor correlation between the amount of residual enzyme activity and the clinical severity of the condition (FIG. 1), and between the activity in different tissues from the same patient.[16] In the most extreme examples of heterogeneity, assay results have even suggested the existence of tissue-specific forms of PDC deficiency.[17]

Numerous studies of patients with PDC deficiency and of their families failed to reveal the mode of inheritance of the condition. In a large published series of cases,[11] and in our own experience, the numbers of affected males and females are approximately equal. There are relatively few cases of multiple sibs affected in one family,[16] and it has been extremely difficult to establish that the parents of affected individuals have intermediate levels of activity.[11] In spite of these results, it has been widely assumed that PDC deficiency is inherited as an autosomal recessive.

Family studies of patients with Leigh's syndrome should also be taken into account

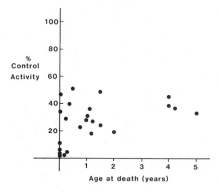

FIGURE 1. PDC activity and clinical severity of the PDC-deficient condition. The clinical severity in patients with PDC E1 deficiency, as reflected in the age at death, is plotted as a function of PDC activity in their cultured fibroblasts. Enzyme activity is presented as a percentage of normal controls, to allow for differences in assay methods. The results are derived from our own unpublished data and information contained in Refs. 11 and 14.

when considering the genetics of PDC deficiency, as there is now good evidence that a proportion of these patients have a primary defect in PDC. These studies indicate that, in a subset of Leigh's syndrome patients, the mode of inheritance is X-linked.[18] However, even in these families, the pattern is unusual. In most cases, the disorder is restricted to one generation, and there are very few male patients with affected uncles.

After isolating cDNA probes for the E1α subunit of PDC,[8] we have been able to map the gene for this subunit using both *in situ* hybridization to human metaphase chromosomes (FIG. 2) and Southern blot analysis of human-mouse somatic cell hybrids with varying human chromosome constitutions.[19] The results indicate that a DNA sequence corresponding to the E1α subunit is located on the human X chromosome at position Xp22.13–22.2. In addition, a weaker signal has been detected on the long arm of chromosome 4. It was confirmed that the locus on the X chromosome contains the functional PDC E1α gene by demonstrating that females who are heterozygous for

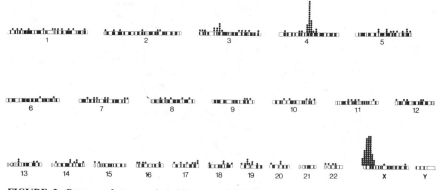

FIGURE 2. Pattern of *in situ* hybridization of PDC E1α cDNA to human chromosomes. Distribution of grains over normal human male metaphase chromosomes following *in situ* hybridization of the PDC E1α cDNA probe and washing at a stringency of 0.5 × SSC. In this analysis, a total of 90 metaphases were scored and 19% of the grains fell on the X chromsome in the region Xp22.13–22.2. A secondary peak of grains was detected on the long arm of chromosome 4.

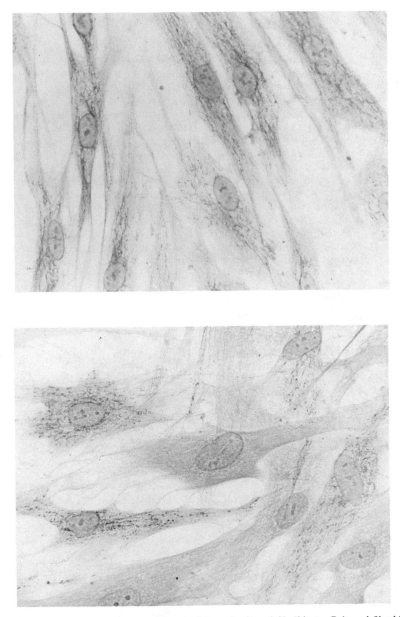

FIGURE 3. PDC E1α immunoperoxidase staining of cultured fibroblasts. Cultured fibroblasts from a normal female (**upper panel**) and a female patient with PDC E1α deficiency and reduced E1α immunoreactive protein (**lower panel**) were incubated with an affinity-purified anti-E1α antibody, and the reaction product was localized with peroxidase–anti-peroxidase complex. In the normal control, reaction product in the mitochondria appears as discrete granules. Two distinct populations of cells are seen in the patient, one with the normal level of PDC E1α immunoreactive protein, the other completely deficient.

PDC E1α deficiency are mosaics with two populations of cells, one normal, the other expressing the defect (FIG. 3).

The X-chromosome location of the PDC E1α gene necessitates a complete review of the clinical, biochemical, and genetic features of PDC deficiency. At the same time, it also provides possible explanations for many of the variations in the clinical and biochemical presentations of the disorder. In males with PDC E1α deficiency, all cells of the body will be affected and, as a result, early onset of severe systemic disease should be the most likely presentation. Female patients, as manifesting heterozygotes, will have two populations of cells, one normal, the other deficient. The proportion of these will differ in different tissues, depending on patterns of X-inactivation. In general, this should lead to less severe disease, with later onset, less systemic acidosis, and more localized pathology.

When the various clinical features of PDC E1α deficiency are reconsidered, a number of differences between male and female patients are indeed observed. In general, males with PDC deficiency do have more severe systemic disease and die at a younger age than do females (FIG. 4). Although some females present with the acute neonatal form of PDC deficiency, the majority have episodic acidosis or the chronic neurodegenerative form of the condition which is compatible with prolonged survival.

In comparison with the clincal presentation, it may appear paradoxical that females often have more extensive structural abnormalities in the CNS. In our experience, gross degrees of cerebral atrophy and ventricular dilatation are rare in male patients, as are developmental defects such as absence of the corpus callosum and medullary pyramids. Most males with the severe neonatal form of PDC deficiency have comparatively little localized cerebral pathology. By contrast, all six of our patients with "cerebral" lactic acidosis[12] were female.

As PDC is a major enzyme of aerobic energy metabolism, a significant impairment of function would be expected in cells which are deficient in PDC activity. The defect in energy metabolism should be greatest in the brain because of its obligatory requirement for aerobic glucose oxidation, and this would account for the frequency of predominantly "cerebral" forms of PDC deficiency. As peripheral tissues have alternative energy sources, the threshold for clinically significant involvement may be much higher but could become important when the activity of the complex is grossly reduced. Overall, the clinical and biochemical abnormalities will be determined by the degree of enzyme deficiency, the extent to which different tissues depend on aerobic oxidation of glucose for their energy requirements, and, in females, the pattern of X-inactivation in different tissues.

When considering the expression of deleterious mutations on the X chromosome in heterozygous females, non-random inactivation of X chromosomes or selective death of cells expressing the mutant X chromosome are often proposed to explain unexpected behavior. In the case of isolated PDC E1α deficiency, we have found no evidence of non-random X-inactivation, either *in vivo* or *in vitro*.

Cultured fibroblasts from females who are heterozygous for PDC E1α mutations which lead to reduced levels of immunoreactive protein can be separated into two populations, one normal, the other deficient (FIG. 3). The proportion of cells of each type remains constant in culture over many cell divisions, indicating that the mutant cells do not have any selective disadvantage. However, since cells in culture grow under relatively anaerobic conditions, these results may not reflect the situation *in vivo*, where aerobic pathways are of greater importance.

With respect to the clinical presentations of PDC E1α deficiency in females, it is therefore more important to determine the fate of cells expressing the mutant gene *in vivo*. Again, there is no evidence of non-random X-inactivation in the patients. Instead, there is a wide variation in the residual activity, the amount of immunoreactive protein, and the proportion of cells expressing the mutant X chromosome in different tissues.

However, in any one tissue, there is a good correlation between all of these parameters of PDC E1α gene expression.

Even in cells of the early embryo which are destined to form the central nervous system, isolated PDC E1α deficiency is apparently compatible with random X-inactivation, as both PDC-positive and PDC-negative cells can be demonstrated in the brain of heterozygous females (FIG 5). However, it is not possible to determine whether the structural defects which are so prominent in these females arise only from

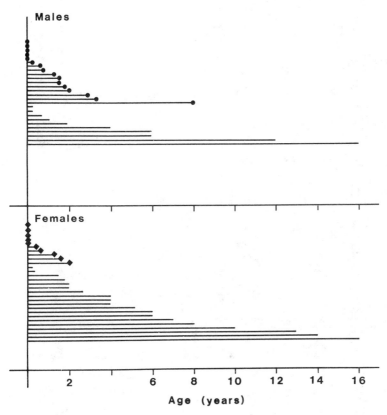

FIGURE 4. Course and outcome in PDC E1 deficiency. A comparison of the course and outcome of PDC E1 deficiency in males and females. The age at death (●, ♦) or the age at which the patient was last known to be alive is shown. The data were generated from our own cases and patients described in Refs. 11 and 14.

cells which are PDC deficient. Cells which degenerate and contribute to cerebral atrophy or which fail to develop normally are not available for analysis, nor is it possible to determine the potential fate of PDC-deficient cells at the time of death of the patient.

Affected males, including those with the more severe forms of the disease and significant systemic lactic acidosis, may only represent a small proportion of those who inherit a mutant PDC E1α gene. Mutations which completely prevent the synthesis of PDC E1α protein may be incompatible with normal fetal development in the male. In

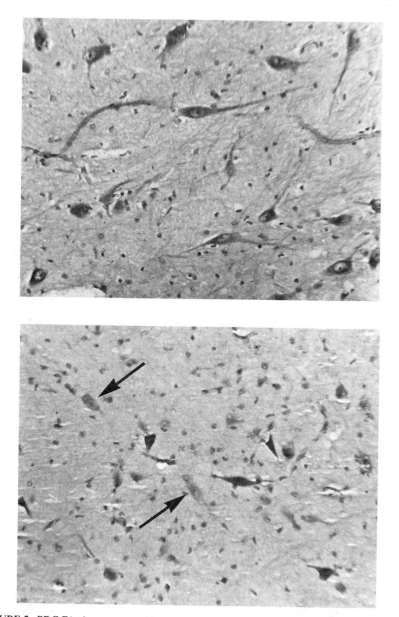

FIGURE 5. PDC E1α immunoperoxidase reaction in brain. Sections of brain stem were reacted with affinity-purified anti-E1α antibody, and the product was localized with peroxidase–anti-peroxidase complex. Part of a section from a normal control (**upper panel**) and a comparable region from a female patient with PDC E1α deficiency (**lower panel**) are shown. This patient had approximately 25% of the normal level of PDC activity in brain, and a corresponding reduction in PDC E1α immunoreactive protein. Brain cells in the patient can be divided into two populations, one with the normal amount of PDC E1α immunoreactive protein, the other (examples indicated by *arrows*) with no detectable cross-reacting material.

our experience, even males who die in the newborn period with profound lactic acidosis, and who have no detectable PDC E1α protein in cultured fibroblasts, have some residual PDC activity in metabolically active tissues such as the heart. Females heterozygous for mutations which completely abolish PDC E1α synthesis could survive fetal life if they have sufficient cells expressing the normal X chromosome to support the energy requirements of development.

The pattern of cerebral pathology should also be different in males compared to females with PDC E1α deficiency. Generalized reactions to impaired energy metabolism, such as cerebral edema, should be more common, and localized structural defects might be more uniform, reflecting vulnerability of particular areas of the brain to the metabolic stress imposed by PDC deficiency.

Diagnosis of PDC E1α deficiency by assay of activity and by analysis of immunoreactive protein is also affected by the X-chromosome location of the gene for this subunit. In females, the pattern of X-inactivation which determines tissue differences in the severity of the defect also presents a sampling problem for diagnosis. The skin biopsy from which fibroblasts are cultured or the tissue biopsy sample may not reflect the pattern of X-inactivation in other parts of the body, particularly the brain. In the most extreme examples of sampling problems, normal results in available tissues may hide the true diagnosis completely. The poor correlation observed between PDC activity and clinical severity may be due in large part to this problem of obtaining representative samples for diagnostic testing.

In the male, diagnosis of PDC E1α deficiency should be more reliable because of the uniform nature of the defect. In these cases, it is much more important to try to establish whether the mother is an asymptomatic carrier of PDC E1α deficiency for counseling and future antenatal diagnosis. So far, we have not detected any obligate female carriers of this condition and have not found any heterozygotes among the mothers of our patients. These studies have included mothers of all our patients, both male and female, who have a clear reduction in PDC E1α–immunoreactive protein. In these cases, the genetic status of the mother can be assessed by immunoperoxidase analysis of cultured fibroblasts with an anti-E1α antibody. These results suggest that most females who are heterozygous for PDC E1α deficiency manifest the condition. However, the possibility of asymptomatic female carriers cannot be excluded without more extensive family surveys.

As long as antenatal diagnosis of PDC E1α deficiency is based on enzyme assay and immunochemical analysis, there will be a significant risk of misdiagnosis of female fetuses. The sampling problems described above could lead to normal results in an affected fetus, and this will be the case with either amniotic cells or chorionic villi. In the latter case, the complex patterns of X-inactivation in human extra-embryonic tissues[20] could further complicate interpretation of the results. Confident antenatal diagnosis will be restricted for the present to male fetuses and those female fetuses who have clearly abnormal results.

PDC E1α deficiency is a complex and heterogeneous disorder. The localization of the E1α gene to the human X chromosome provides a genetic basis for much of this complexity and clearly suggests lines of future investigation which should lead to a better understanding of this important inborn error of metabolism in humans.

ACKNOWLEDGMENTS

We wish to thank Rosa De Fazio of the Murdoch Institute and Elizabeth McKinnon and Tracey Tucker of the Department of Pathology, Royal Children's Hospital, for preparing the cultured fibroblasts and tissue sections for immunoperoxidase studies.

REFERENCES

1. ROBINSON, B. H., J. TAYLOR & W. G. SHERWOOD. 1980. The genetic heterogeneity of lactic acidosis: Occurrence of recognizable inborn errors of metabolism in a pediatric population with lactic acidosis. Pediatr. Res. **14:** 956–962.
2. ROBINSON, B. H. & W. G. SHERWOOD. 1984. Lactic acidaemia. J. Inherited Metab. Dis. 7(Suppl. 1): 69–73.
3. MCKAY, N., R. PETROVA-BENEDICT, J. THOENE, B. BERGEN, W. WILSON & B. ROBINSON. 1986. Lacticacidaemia due to pyruvate dehydrogenase deficiency, with evidence of protein polymorphism in the α-subunit of the enzyme. Eur. J. Pediatr. **144:** 445–450.
4. WICKING, C. A., R. D. SCHOLEM, S. M. HUNT & G. K. BROWN. 1986. Immunochemical analysis of normal and mutant forms of human pyruvate dehydrogenase. Biochem. J. **239:** 89–96.
5. STANSBIE, D., S. J. WALLACE & C. MARSAC. 1986. Disorders of the pyruvate dehydrogenase complex. J. Inherited Metab. Dis. **9:** 105–119.
6. SHEU, K-F. R., C-W. C. HU & M. F. UTTER. 1981. Pyruvate dehydrogenase complex activity in normal and deficient fibroblasts. J. Clin. Invest. **67:** 1463–1471.
7. HO L., C-W. C. HU, S. PACKMAN & M. S. PATEL. 1986. Deficiency of the pyruvate dehydrogenase component in pyruvate dehydrogenase complex-deficient human fibroblasts. J. Clin. Invest. **78:** 844–847.
8. DAHL, H-H. M., S. M. HUNT, W. M. HUTCHISON & G. K. BROWN. 1987. The human pyruvate dehydrogenase complex. Isolation of cDNA clones for the $E1\alpha$ subunit, sequence analysis, and characteriztion of the mRNA. J. Biol. Chem. **262:** 7398–7403.
9. DE MEIRLEIR, L., N. MACKAY, A. M. LAM HON WAH & B. H. ROBINSON. 1988. Isolation of a full-length complementary DNA coding for human $E1\alpha$ subunit of the pyruvate dehydrogenase complex. J. Biol. Chem. **263:** 1991–1995.
10. KOIKE, K., S. OHTA, Y. URATA, Y. KAGAWA & M. KOIKE. 1988. Cloning and sequencing of cDNAs encoding α and β subunits of human pyruvate dehydrogenase. Proc. Natl. Acad. Sci. USA **85:** 41–45.
11. ROBINSON, B. H., H. MACMILLAN, R. PETROVA-BENEDICT & W. G. SHERWOOD. 1987. Variable clinical presentation in patients with defective E1 component of pyruvate dehydrogenase complex. J. Pediatr. **111:** 525–533.
12. BROWN, G. K., E. A. HAAN, D. M. KIRBY, R. D. SCHOLEM, J. E. WRAITH, J. G. ROGERS & D. M. DANKS. 1988. "Cerebral" lactic acidosis: Defects in pyruvate metabolism with profound brain damage and minimal systemic acidosis. Eur. J. Pediatr. **147:** 10–14.
13. KRETZSCHMAR, H. A., S. J. DEARMOND, T. K. KOCH, M. S. PATEL, C. J. L. NEWTH, K. A. SCHMIDT & S. PACKMAN. 1987. Pyruvate dehydrogenase complex deficiency as a cause of subacute necrotizing encephalopathy (Leigh disease). Pediatrics **79:** 370–373.
14. MIYABAYASHI, S., T. ITO, K NARISAWA, K. IINUMA & K. TADA. 1985. Biochemical study in 28 children with lactic acidosis, in relation to Leigh's encephalomyelopathy. Eur. J. Pediatr. **143:** 278–283.
15. CHOW, C. W., R. MCD. ANDERSON & G. C. T. KENNY. 1987. Neuropathology in cerebral lactic acidosis. Acta Neuropathol. **74:** 393–396.
16. KERR, D. S., S. A. BERRY, M. M. LUSK, L. HO & M. S. PATEL. 1988. A deficiency of both subunits of pyruvate dehydrogenase which is not expressed in fibroblasts. Pediatr. Res. **24:** 95–100.
17. PRICK, M., F. GABREELS, W. RENIER, F. TRIJBELS, H. JASPER, K. LAMERS & J. KOK. 1981. Pyruvate dehydrogenase deficiency restricted to brain. Neurology (NY) **31:** 398–404.
18. BENKE, P. J., J. C. PARKER, M-L. LUBS, J. BENKENDORF & A. E. FEUER. 1982. X-linked Leigh's syndrome. Hum. Genet. **62:** 53–59.
19. BROWN, R. M., H-H. M. DAHL & G. K. BROWN. 1989. X chromosome localisation of the functional gene for the $E1\alpha$ subunit of the human pyruvate dehydrogenase complex. Genomics **4:** 174–181.
20. MIGEON, B. R., S. F. WOLF, J. AXELMAN, D. C. KASLOW & M. SCHMIDT. 1985. Incomplete X chromosome dosage compensation in chorionic villi of human placenta. Proc. Natl. Acad. Sci. USA **82:** 3390–3394.

Molecular Genetic Basis for Inherited Human Disorders of Branched-Chain α-Keto Acid Dehydrogenase Complex[a]

DEAN J. DANNER, STUART LITWER,
W. JOSEPH HERRING,[b] AND LOUIS J. ELSAS

Division of Medical Genetics
Department of Pediatrics
Emory University School of Medicine
Atlanta, Georgia 30322

INTRODUCTION

Branched-chain α-keto acid dehydrogenase complex (BCKDC) exists as a multienzyme complex in the mitochondria of all human cells.[1] Inherited disorders in humans which affect the function of BCKDC were first described over 30 years ago, yet the specific genetic variations resulting in the disorder known as maple syrup urine disease (MSUD) remain to be defined. Clinically, MSUD patients show a widely varied picture of expression, ranging from the "classic" cases presenting in the neonate with physical and mental impairment and early death to the cases of a late-onset, milder form with better prognosis. Early detection of MSUD through newborn screening programs and strict dietary management of these individuals after diagnosis has lead to an excellent prognosis for most MSUD patients.[1] The identification of a thiamin-responsive subgroup within the population of those expressing MSUD has provided an alternative course of management for this group.[2,3] With supplementation of the protein-restricted diet by pharmacologic doses of thiamin, fewer clinical complications occur in the thiamin-responsive group than in the thiamin–nonresponsive patients. Still, the specific mutation for any form of MSUD has not been described.

Explanations for the widely varied clinical picture became evident with the purification of BCKDC and the characterization of the protein components. To date BCKDC has been purified from several tissues and species, including humans.[4–9] The complex is highly conserved in the size of the proteins and their amino acid composition. Three proteins are unique to BCKDC, the branched-chain acyltransferase (E2b) core protein of 52 kilodaltons (kDa) and the two subunits of the decarboxylase component, E1bα, of 46 kDa, and E1bβ, of 36 kDa. Two other proteins specifically interact with the E1bα subunit: a kinase[5,7] which adds phosphate and thus inactivates the complex and a phosphatase[10,11] which removes the phosphate, reactivating the complex. It is the phosphorylation state of BCKDC which accounts for the varied activity in different tissues.[12–14]

One can therefore envision an inherited change in any one of the three main subunits as a probable cause of MSUD. Defects in the kinase or phosphatase proteins also could result in varied expression of BCKDC activity and present as a mild form of

[a]This research was supported by NIH Grant DK 38320.
[b]Recipient of Predoctoral Graduate Training Fellowship 18-88-20 from the March of Dimes.

MSUD. Inheritance patterns in families show autosomal recessive transmission for the disorder. This pattern does not vary with the clinical phenotype, suggesting that all components of BCKDC are nuclear encoded. Since BCKDC resides on the matrix side of the mitochondrial inner membrane, another mechanism for MSUD could be a defect in the mitochondrial import mechanisms. Presumably this would involve a gene or genes other than those encoding the proteins for BCKDC. An antigenic absence of a protein in the complex remains the only defined mechanism for MSUD but does not describe the specific molecular genetic defect.

RESULTS AND DISCUSSION

Over the years different approaches have been used in attempts to understand the molecular genetic basis for MSUD. Newborn screening methods are still used to identify individuals at risk for MSUD. Newborn blood samples are tested for elevated leucine concentration by growth of *Bacillus subtilis* in medium containing the leucine analog, β-2-thienyl DL-alanine. If the blood contains >2 mg leucine/dl, the bacteria will grow. Confirmation of the diagnosis for MSUD is done by quantifying BCKDC activity in isolated peripheral white blood cells from the individual. Neither test addresses the molecular basis for the disorder.

A recent advancement in diagnosis has been the Western blot analysis using antibodies which specifically recognize E2b, E1bα, and E1bβ. This technique has demonstrated the antigenic absence of either E2b, E1bα, or E1bβ in cells from different families expressing MSUD.[15,16] However, the bulk of the MSUD patients show Western blots with protein patterns indistinguishable from that in wild type cells. No antigenic proteins with abnormal migration have been detected by this procedure. However, density gradient gels can distinguish the phosphorylated E1bα from the dephosphorylated protein and may be useful in screening individuals suspected to have kinase or phosphatase defects. Japanese investigators have attempted to use this distinctive E1bα mobility diagnostically to differentiate MSUD families.[15,17]

Other investigators have attempted to assay individual components of BCKDC for enzyme activity.[18] These assays in skin fibroblasts are difficult and lead to questionable results. A cell line, GM612, from a patient with "classic MSUD" was reported to have E2b activity indistinguishable from that in wild-type cells. Later it was shown that this same cell line antigenically lacked E2b.[16] These examples are used, not to discredit any previous work, but only to point out the difficulty with this type of analysis. Better methods for describing the specific defects in MSUD are necessary.

The recent molecular cloning of cDNAs which encode human pre-E2b[19,20] and E1bα[21] has made possible the investigation of specific genetic mutations in humans which result in MSUD. We used antibodies against BCKDC proteins to select cDNA clones for E2b from human expression libraries.[19,20,22] Similar methods were used to isolate cDNAs for E2b from bovine tissue[23,24] and cDNA clones for E1bα from human and rat.[21,25] Our studies described here focus on the human mutations affecting the E2b gene.

Initially, several cDNAs for E2b were selected which made antigenically recognized fusion proteins in λgt11. From two independently isolated cDNAs we engineered a single cDNA (pSL5) which encodes the entire pre-E2b protein[19,20] (FIG. 1). Transcripts from the SP6 promoter were translated *in vitro* with a rabbit reticulocyte lysate system to produce an immunoprecipable protein which migrated with an apparent molecular mass of 57 kDa in SDS–polyacrylamide gel electrophoresis (PAGE). This protein was imported by mitochondria and processed to an immunoprecipable protein of 52 kDa indistinguishable from authentic E2b (FIG. 2). Only the

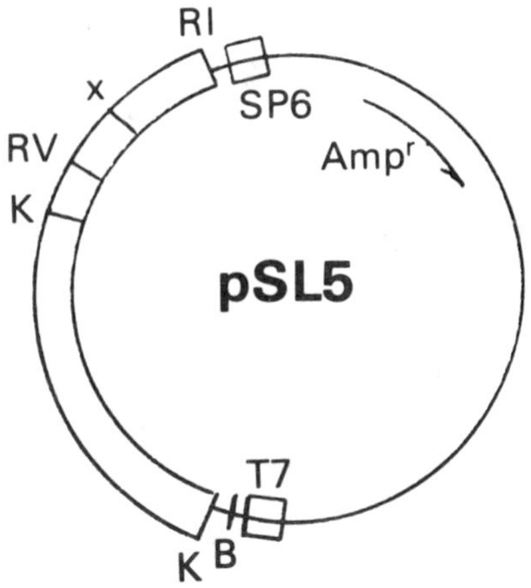

FIGURE 1. pSL5. An 1882-bp cDNA containing the entire open reading frame for the human pre-E2b, branched-chain acyltransferase, in pGEM 4 vector. RI, *Eco*R I; X, *Xba* I; RV, *Eco*R V; K, *Kpn* I; B, *Bam*H I.

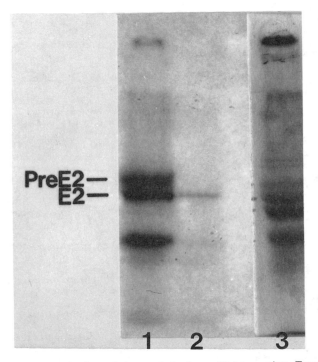

FIGURE 2. Autoradiograph of translation products from pSL5 transcripts. Transcripts from pSL5 were translated with a rabbit reticulocyte lysate using [^{35}S]methionine as the radiolabel. (**Lane 1**) Mouse liver mitochondria were incubated with *in vitro* translation products for 40 min at 30°C. After lysis of the mitochondria, proteins were immunoprecipitated with antibodies to E2b. Precipitates were resolved by SDS-PAGE, and an autoradiograph was made from the dried gel. (**Lane 2**) Samples were prepared as for lane 1, but after incubation of mitochondria and translation products, the mitochondria were treated for 10 min with 1.25 mg trypsin/ml, followed by the addition of 2.5 mg soybean tryspin inhibitor/ml. (**Lane 3**) Coomassie blue–stained gel pattern of bovine liver BCKDC.[20]

```
1                    30                        60                        90
ATGCTGAGAACCTGGAGCAGGAATGCGGGGAAGCTGATTTGTGTTCGCTATTTTCAAACATGTGGTAATGTTCATGTTTTGAAGCCAAAT
M  L  R  T  W  S  R  N  A  G  K  L  I  C  V  R  Y  F  Q  T  C  G  N  V  H  V  L  K  P  N
                     120                      150                      180       LEADER
TATGTGTGTTTCTTTGGTTATCCTTCATTCAAGTATAGTCATCCACATCACTTCCTGAAAACAACTGCTGCTCTCCGTGGACAGGTTGTT
Y  V  C  F  F  G  Y  P  S  F  K  Y  S  H  P  H  H  F  L  K  T  T  A  A  L  R  G  Q  V  V
                     210                      240                      270
CAGTTCAAGCTCTCAGACATTGGAGAAGGGATTAGAGAAGTAACTGTTAAAGAATGGTATGTAAAAGAAGGAGATACAGTGTCTCAGTTT
Q  F  K  L  S  D  I  G  E  G  I  R  E  V  T  V  K  E  W  Y  V  K  E  G  D  T  V  S  Q  F
                     300                      330                      360
GATAGCATCTGTGAAGTTCAAAGTGATAAAGCTTCTGTTACCATCACTAGTCGTTATGATGGAGTCATTAAAAAACTCTATTATAATCTA
D  S  I  C  E  V  Q  S  D  K  A  S  V  T  I  T  S  R  Y  D  G  V  I  K  K  L  Y  Y  N  L    LIPOATE
                     390                      420                      450
GACGATATTGCCTATGTGGGGAAGCCATTAGTAGACATAGAAACGGAAGCTTTAAAAGATTCAGAAGAAGATGTTGTTGAAACTCCTGCA
D  D  I  A  Y  V  G  K  P  L  V  D  I  E  T  E  A  L  K  D  S  E  E  D  V  V  E  T  P  A
                     480                      510                      540
GTGTCTCATGATGAACATACACACCAAGAGATAAAGGGCCGAAAAACACTGGCAACTCCTGCAGTTCGCCGTCTGGCAATGGAAAACAAT
V  S  H  D  E  H  T  H  Q  E  I  K  G  R  K  T  L  A  T  P  A  V  R  R  L  A  M  E  N  N
                     570                      600                      630       E3
ATTAAGCTGAGTGAAGTTGTTGGCTCAGGAAAAGATGGCAGAATACTTAAAGAAGATATCCTCAACTATTTGGAAAAGCAGACAGGAGCT
I  K  L  S  E  V  V  G  S  G  K  D  G  R  I  L  K  E  D  I  L  N  Y  L  E  K  Q  T  G  A
                     660                      690                      720
ATATTGCCTCCTTCACCCAAAGTTGAAATTATGCCACCTCCACCAAAGCCAAAAGACATGACTGTTCCTATACTAGTATCAAAACCTCCG
I  L  P  P  S  P  K  V  E  I  M  P  P  P  P  K  P  K  D  M  T  V  P  I  L  V  S  K  P  P
                     750                      780                      810
GTATTCACAGGCAAAGACAAAACAGAACCCATAAAAGGCTTTCAAAAAGCAATGGTCAAGACTATGTCTGCAGCCCTGAAGATACCTCAT
V  F  T  G  K  D  K  T  E  P  I  K  G  F  Q  K  A  M  V  K  T  M  S  A  A  L  K  I  P  H
                     840                      870                      900
TTTGGTTATTGTGATGAGATTGACCTTACTGAACTGGTTAAGCTCCGAGAAGAATTAAAAACCCATTGCATTTGCTCGTGGAATTAAACTC
F  G  Y  C  D  E  I  D  L  T  E  L  V  K  L  R  E  E  L  K  P  I  A  F  A  R  G  I  K  L
                     930                      960                      990
TCCTTTATGCCTTTCTTCTTCTTAAAGGCTGCTTCCTTGGGATTACTACAGTTTCCTATCCTTAACGCTTCTGTGGATGAAAACTGCCAGAAT
S  F  M  P  F  F  L  K  A  A  S  L  G  L  L  Q  F  P  I  L  N  A  S  V  D  E  N  C  Q  N
                     1020                     1050                     1080
ATAACATATAAGGCTTCTCATAACATTGGGATAGCAATGGATACTGAGCAGGGTTTGATTGTCCCTAATGTGAAAAATGTTCAGATCTGC
I  T  Y  K  A  S  H  N  I  G  I  A  M  D  T  E  Q  G  L  I  V  P  N  V  K  N  V  Q  I  C
                     1110                     1140                     1170
TCTATATTTGACATCGCCACTGAACTGAACCGCCTCCAGAAATTGGGCTCTGTGGGTCAGCTCAGCACCACTGATCTTACAGGAGGAACA
S  I  F  D  I  A  T  E  L  N  R  L  Q  K  L  G  S  V  G  Q  L  S  T  T  D  L  T  G  G  T
                     1200                     1230                     1260
TTTACTCTTTCCAACATTGGATCAATTGGTGGTACCTTTGCCAAACCAGTGATAATGCCACCTGAAGTAGCCATTGGGGCCCTTGGATCA
F  T  L  S  N  I  G  S  I  G  G  T  F  A  K  P  V  I  M  P  P  E  V  A  I  G  A  L  G  S
                     1290                     1320                     1350
ATTAAGGCCATTCCCCGATTTAACCAGAAAGGAGAAGTATATAAGGCACAGATAATGAATGTGAGCTGGTCAGCTGATCACAGAGTTATT
I  K  A  I  P  R  F  N  Q  K  G  E  V  Y  K  A  Q  I  M  N  V  S  W  S  A  D  H  R  V  I    CoA
                     1380                     1410                     1440
GATGGTGCTACAATGTCACGCTTCTCCAATTTGTGGAAATCCTATTTAGAAAACCCAGCTTTTATGCTACTAGATCTGAAATGAAGACTG
D  G  A  T  M  S  R  F  S  N  L  W  K  S  Y  L  E  N  P  A  F  M  L  L  D  L  K  *
                     1470                     1500                     1530
ATAAGACATTCTTGAACTTTTTGAGCTTCCAAAGAGTATGTAAACCCTAGCTGTGCCAGCACATGTTCATCTTTACAATTTATATTGTAA
                     1560                     1590                     1620
ACGATTTGTATCGTATGATTAAGGATCTAAGGCACAATATTTGTCACTGTTCTATTAGACTTTTTACTGAAAATGAATAATGGTGTAATG
                     1650                     1680                     1710
GTTCTCCTGGGGCTGTCACATTTTATAGGTCAGAGTGTGACTTCTTAATATGGTGCTGATGTTTTTGTGTCAATGGCTTGAAACTGGCAA
                     1740                     1770                     1800
GATTAACAAAATTAGGCCGGGCATGGTGGCTCACGCCTGTAATCCAGCACTTTGGGAGGCCCAGGTGGGGCGATCACCTGAGGTTAGAAG
                     1830                     1860                     1882
TTTGAGACCAGCCTGGCCAACATGGTGAAACCTGGCCTCTACCTAAAAAATACAAAATTGACCGGGTGTGGTGGTGGGTACC
```

FIGURE 3. Nucleotide sequence of the cDNA in pSL5, with the deduced amino acid sequence for the open reading frame. Amino acids in the leader sequence are **underlined,** the lipoate-binding region is **boxed,** the E3-binding region is enclosed in an **open box,** and the CoA-binding region is **double underlined.**

52-kDa protein was protected from mild trypsin digestion of the mitochondria, confirming that the 52-kDa protein was inside the inner mitochondrial membrane. The nucleotide sequence of the entire cDNA construct was determined and the amino acid sequence deduced[20] (FIG. 3). The leader sequence contains 56 amino acids, with the remaining 421 amino acids defining the mature E2b protein. When this protein was compared to other acyltransferase proteins, the general similarity in architecture of the various proteins was evident (FIG. 4). All the proteins were aligned for comparison. In order, from the amino-terminal end, they contain a lipoate-binding region, an E3-binding region, a catalytic domain, and the CoA-binding region.[20] The two mammalian proteins compared here, human E2b and human E2p, have an amino-terminal extension (leader) which directs these proteins to the mitochondria. No amino acid sequence similarity exists between these two leaders. Despite the similarity among these proteins, antibodies against the individual proteins show absolute specificity.

We are now producing monoclonal antibodies for use in comparing the structure of

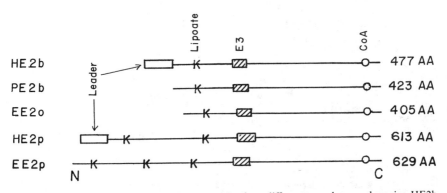

FIGURE 4. Comparison of acyltransferase proteins from different complexes and species. HE2b, human pre–branched-chain acyltransferase; PE2b, *Pseudomonas putida* branched-chain acyltransferase; EE2o, *Escherichia coli* succinyltransferase; HE2p, human pre-acetyltransferase; EE2p, *Escherichia coli* acetyltransferase. The **open box** represents the leader sequence for targeting these proteins to mitochondria. **K** represents the lysine residue which binds lipoate. The **hatched box** represents the E3-binding region, and the **circle** represents the CoA-binding region. At the end of each line is listed the number of amino acids (AA) present in each protein.

mutant E2b proteins with that of the wild-type protein. Recently it was shown that E2b is antigenically recognized by sera from humans with primary biliary cirrhosis or with some forms of dilated cardiomyopathy.[26] We do not know why these proteins are specifically recognized in these autoimmune disorders, but the mechanisms and specific epitopes for recognition of E2b are being investigated. It is anticipated that antibodies from these patients will be useful in this approach to studying the mutant E2b proteins in MSUD patients.

In other studies we are using our cloned cDNA for pre-E2b to explore the E2b⁻ phenotype in MSUD families. Cultured skin fibroblasts and lymphoblasts are available from three independent families with this phenotype. Initially, three hypotheses were proposed for the molecular genetic basis of this phenotype: (1) a gene deletion may exist in these families; (2) the gene could be present but not transcribed; (3) the gene could be transcribed, but the transcripts produce no protein or a protein which is unstable or can't enter the mitochondria.

To begin our investigations we first constructed a 608-bp fragment (pJH1) from the 5′ end of the cDNA in pSL5 to use as a probe (FIG. 5). This nucleotide sequence encodes the leader, lipoate- and E3-binding domains (see FIG. 3). The 608-bp DNA fragment was radiolabeled and used to probe genomic DNA from the three E2b⁻ mutants and wild-type cells by Southern blotting. Autoradiographs revealed identical banding patterns for all the different DNA digests. This suggests that gene deletion was not responsible for the E2b⁻ phenotype in these families.

To test the second hypothesis, we asked whether poly(A)⁺ RNA for pre-E2b was being produced by the mutant cells. Antisense RNA transcripts from the T7 promoter in pJH1 were prepared with radiolabeled [α-³²P]UTP. Poly(A)⁺ RNA was prepared from the three E2b⁻ mutant cell lines and control cells by standard methods and used in Northern blot analysis. As seen in FIGURE 6, autoradiographs showed that wild-type cells produce a 3.4- and a 2.5-kb hybridizing species. Currently we do not know if both transcripts produce protein. Probes which include the 3′ untranslated portion of the pre-E2b cDNA were uninformative in hybridization studies of this type, since this region contains an *Alu* repeat sequence. Inspection of the lanes containing poly(A)⁺ RNA from the E2b⁻ cells showed that one family had no detectable poly(A)⁺ RNA, while cells from another family gave the same pattern as the wild-type cells. From these data it was evident that more than one mutation could result in MSUD with the E2b⁻ phenotype. A mutation affecting transcription would account for those families without detectable mRNA by Northern blot analysis. A second group of mutations must exist for families with mRNA for E2b but no E2b protein. Several mechanisms could explain the latter situation. The protein could be unstable, a termination codon could have been created early in the coding sequence, or the leader sequence could be abortive and not direct the protein to the mitochondria. Alternatively, a mutation could have occurred in the gene encoding the receptor protein for translocation of pre-E2b across the mitochondrial membrane, thus specifically preventing import of pre-E2b.

To compare the nucleotide sequences of mutant transcripts with that of wild-type transcripts, we prepared cDNA from RNA isolated from these cells and amplified the DNA by the polymerase chain reaction (PCR). This procedure was also done with RNA from the cell line which did not have detectable mRNA for E2b by Northern blot analysis. Interestingly, from the latter cell line, DNA of the correct size was produced which hybridized to probes for pre-E2b. These data imply that transcripts are produced in low copy number in this mutant. The results also suggest that the mutation in this cell line may involve the promoter or regulatory region of the gene. To explore

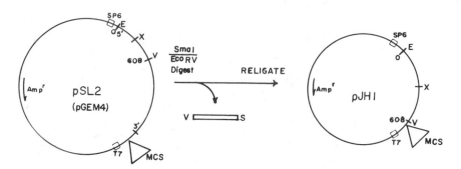

FIGURE 5. Construction of pJH1 from pSL2. pJH1 is used to produce cDNA and antisense probes for analysis of the E2b gene and its transcripts. E, *EcoR* I; X, *Xba* I; V, *EcoR* V; S, *Sma* I; MCS, multiple cloning site.

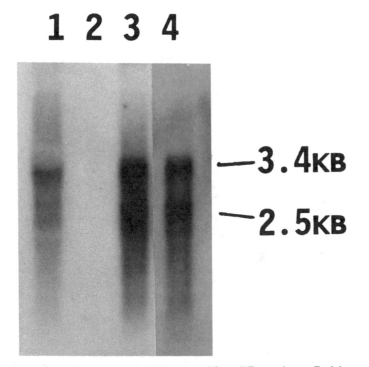

FIGURE 6. Northern blot of poly(A)$^+$ RNA prepared from different tissues. Each lane contains 10–20 μg of poly(A)$^+$ RNA which was resolved in a formaldehyde denaturing agarose gel. The RNA was transferred to a Zeta-Probe membrane and hybridized to antisense RNA from pJH1 labeled with [α^{32}P]UTP. (**Lane 1**) RNA from the E2b$^-$ fibroblast line 328, (**lane 2**) RNA from E2$^-$ lymphoblast line GM1366, (**lane 3**) RNA from a wild-type lymphoblast line, (**lane 4**) RNA from human liver.

this possibility, we are comparing the nucleotide sequence upstream from the transcriptional start site in the mutant and wild-type genes; the results are still pending.

Nucleotide sequences from all the E2b$^-$ mutants are being compared by direct analysis of PCR-amplified cDNA. DNA has been amplified using primers within the reading frame sequence. Thus far we have found no base-pair changes in the nucleotide sequence from bp-608 to bp-810 (see FIG. 3 for reference). We might anticipate a base change in the leader sequence which directs these proteins to the mitochondria or a change which creates a stop codon early in the coding sequence. This analysis is continuing.

To explore the possibility that a defect was present in the mitochondrial receptor specific for the import of pre-E2b, we isolated mitochondria from the different mutant cells and used them to test for import. Transcripts from pSL5 were translated as described in FIGURE 2. No cell line has been found to have a mitochondrial defect for import of wild-type pre-E2b.

In summary, we have demonstrated that gene deletion is not a basis for any of the E2b$^-$ MSUD phenotypes studied by us thus far. Our data indicated that at least two different mutations can result in the E2b$^-$ phenotype. One mutation affects the promoter or regulatory region of the E2b gene, since cells from one family with the E2b⁻ phenotype express low amounts of these transcripts. One or more mutations must be responsible for the phenotype in which normal amounts of the RNA transcripts are present but the translation products are not. The different possibilities for this latter situation are being tested. The mutations appear to affect the pre-E2b gene, and not the import mechanism, since we can demonstrate mitochondrial uptake and processing of wild-type pre-E2b using mitochondria prepared from tissue with this E2b⁻ phenotype.

ACKNOWLEDGMENT

Special thanks are given to Dr. A. A. Ansari for his help with the studies on patients with autoantibodies against the proteins of BCKDC.

REFERENCES

1. DANNER, D. J. & L. J. ELSAS. 1989. Disorders of branched chain amino acid and keto acid metabolism. *In* The Metabolic Basis of Inherited Disease. C. R. Scriver, A. L. Beaudet, W. S. Sly & D. Valle, Eds.: Chap. 22. McGraw-Hill Book Company. New York.
2. ELSAS, L. J. & D. J. DANNER. 1982. The role of thiamin in maple syrup urine disease. Ann. NY Acad. Sci. **378:** 404.
3. FERNHOFF, P. M., D. LUBITZ, D. J. DANNER, P. P. DEMBURE, H. P. SCHWARZ, R. HILLMAN, D. M. BIER & L. J. ELSAS. 1985. Thiamine responsive maple syrup urine disease. Pediat. Res. **19:** 1011–1016.
4. SHIMOMURA, Y., R. PAXTON, T. OZAWA & R. A. HARRIS. 1987. Purification of branched chain α-ketoacid dehydrogenase complex from rat liver. Anal. Biochem. **163:** 74–78.
5. LAWSON, R., K. G. COOK & S. J. YEAMAN. 1983. Rapid purification of bovine kidney branched-chain 2-oxoacid dehydrogenase complex containing endogenous kinase activity. FEBS Lett. **157:** 54–58.
6. PETTIT, F. H., S. J. YEAMAN & L. J. REED. 1978. Purification and characterization of branched chain α-ketoacid dehydrogenase complex of bovine kidney. Proc. Natl. Acad. Sci. USA **75:** 4881–4886.
7. PAXTON, R. & R. A. HARRIS. 1982. Isolation of rabbit liver branched chain α-ketoacid dehydrogenase and regulation by phosphorylation. J. Biol. Chem. **257:** 14433–14439.
8. ONO, K., M. HAKOZAKI, H. NISHIMAKI & H. KOCHI. 1987. Purification and characterization of human liver branched-chain α-ketoacid dehydrogenase complex. Biochem. Med. Metab. Biol. **37:** 133–141.
9. HEFFELFINGER, S. C., E. T. SEWELL & D. J. DANNER. 1983. Identification of specific subunits of highly purified bovine liver branched-chain ketoacid dehydrogenase. Biochemistry **22:** 5519–5522.
10. DAMUNI, Z. & L. J. REED. 1987. Purification and properties of the catalytic subunit of the branched-chain α-ketoacid dehydrogenase phosphatase from bovine kidney mitochondria. J. Biol. Chem. **262:** 5129–5132.
11. DAMUNI, Z., M. L. MERRYFIELD, J. S. HUMPHREYS & L. J. REED. 1984. Purification and properties of branched-chain α-ketoacid dehydrogenase phosphatase from bovine kidney. Proc. Natl. Acad. Sci. USA **81:** 4335–4338.
12. WAGENMAKERS, A. J. M., J. T. G. SCHEPENS, J. A. M. VELDHUIZEN & J. H. VEERKAMP. 1984. The activity state of the branched-chain 2-oxoacid dehydrogenase complex in rat tissues. Biochem. J. **220:** 273–281.
13. PAXTON, R., M. KUNTZ & R. A. HARRIS. 1986. Phosphorylation sites and inactivation of branched-chain α-ketoacid dehydrogenase isolated from rat heart, bovine kidney, and rabbit liver, kidney, heart, brain, and skeletal muscle. Arch. Biochem. Biophys. **244:** 187–201.

14. HARRIS, R. A., R. PAXTON, S. M. POWELL, G. W. GOODWIN, M. J. KUNTZ & A. C. HAN. 1986. Regulation of branched-chain α-ketoacid dehydrogenase complex by covalent modification. *In* Advances in Enzyme Regulation. 219–237. Academic Press. New York.

15. INDO, Y., A. KITANO, F. ENDO, I. AKABOSHI & I. MATSUDA. 1987. Altered kinetic properties of the branched-chain α-keto acid dehydrogenase complex due to mutation of the α-subunit of the branched-chain α-keto acid decarboxylase (E_1) component in lymphoblastoid cells derived from patients with maple syrup urine disease. J. Clin. Invest. **80:** 63–70.

16. DANNER, D. J., N. ARMSTRONG, S. C. HEFFELFINGER, E. T. SEWELL, J. H. PRIEST & L. J. ELSAS. 1985. Absence of branched chain acyl-transferase as a cause of maple syrup urine disease. J. Clin. Invest. **75:** 858–860.

17. INDO, Y., I. AKABOSHI, Y. NOBUKUNI, F. ENDO & I. MATSUDA. 1988. Maple syrup urine disease: A possible biochemical basis for the clinical heterogeneity. Hum. Genet. **80:** 6–10.

18. CHUANG, D. T., W-L. NIU & R. P. COX. 1981. Activities of branched-chain 2-oxo acid dehydrogenase and its components in skin fibroblasts from normal and classical-maple-syrup-urine-disease subjects. Biochem. J. **200:** 59–67.

19. HUMMEL, K. B., S. LITWER, A. P. BRADFORD, A. AITKEN, D. J. DANNER & S. J. YEAMAN. 1988. Nucleotide sequence of a cDNA for branched chain acyltransferase with analysis of the deduced protein structure. J. Biol. Chem. **263:** 6165–6168.

20. DANNER, D. J., S. LITWER, W. J. HERRING & J. PRUCKLER. 1988. Construction and nucleotide sequence of a cDNA encoding the full-length preprotein for human branched chain acyltransferase. J. Biol. Chem. **264:** 7742–7745.

21. ZHANG, B., D. W. CRABB & R. A. HARRIS. 1988. Nucleotide and deduced amino acid sequence of the $E1\alpha$ subunit of human liver branched-chain α-ketoacid dehydrogenase. Gene **69:** 159–164.

22. LITWER, S. & D. J. DANNER. 1985. Identification of a cDNA clone in λgt11 for the transacylase component of branched chain ketoacid dehydrogenase. Biochem. Biophys. Res. Commun. **131:** 961–967.

23. LAU, K. S., T. A. GRIFFIN, C-W. C. HU & D. T. CHUANG. 1988. Conservation of primary structure in the lipoyl-bearing and dihydrolipoyl dehydrogenase binding domains of mammalian branched-chain α-keto acid dehydrogenase complex: Molecular cloning of human and bovine transacylase (E2) cDNAs. Biochemistry **27:** 1972–1981.

24. GRIFFIN, T. A., K. S. LAU & D. T. CHUANG. 1988. Characterization and conservation of the inner E2 core domain structure of branched chain α-keto acid dehydrogenase complex from bovine liver. Construction of a cDNA encoding the entire transacylase (E2b) precursor. J. Biol. Chem. **263:** 14008–14014.

25. ZHANG, B., M. J. KUNTZ, G. W. GOODWIN, R. A. HARRIS & D. W. CRABB. 1987. Molecular cloning of a cDNA for the $E1\alpha$ subunit of rat liver branched chain α-ketoacid dehydrogenase. J. Biol. Chem. **262:** 15220–15224.

26. SURH, C. D., D. J. DANNER, A. AHMED, R. L. COPPEL, I. R. MACKAY, R. DICKSON & M. E. GERSHWIN. 1988. Reactivity of PBC sera with a human fetal liver cDNA clone of branched chain α-ketoacid dehydrogenase (BCKD) dihydrolipoamide acyltransferase, the 52 kD mitochondrial autoantigen. Hepatology **9:** 63–68.

Abnormalities of Pyruvate Dehydrogenase Complex in Brain Disease[a]

KWAN-FU REX SHEU,[b] PAUL SZABO,[c] LI-WEN KO,[b]
AND LOIS M. HINMAN[b]

[b]Cornell University Medical College
Burke Rehabilitation Center
White Plains, New York 10605
and
[c]Department of Medicine
Cornell University Medical College
New York, New York 10021

INTRODUCTION

Abnormalities of pyruvate dehydrogenase complex (PDHC) have been found in a number of diseases affecting brain. Congenital pyruvic and lactic acidemia and Leigh's subacute necrotizing encephalomyelopathy (Leigh's disease) in newborns and young children may be caused by a structural aberration of a component of PDHC, suggesting that the corresponding gene may be abnormal.[1,2] Deficits of PDHC have also been found in subgroup(s) of young adults with hereditary ataxia,[3–5] which includes a clinically and biochemically heterogeneous spectrum of degenerative disorders. There is evidence that PDHC is structurally abnormal in at least some patients with intermittent ataxia.[6] As for the more common hereditary ataxic syndromes, including Friedreich's disease, whether PDHC plays a causal role has been controversial.[7,8] A marginal deficit of PDHC is found in some of the ataxic patients,[4,5] as are deficits of other mitochondrial constituents.[4,5,9,10] Furthermore, PDHC appears to be immunochemically normal in some ataxic patients with reduced PDHC activity.[5] Thus, the deficit of PDHC may well reflect a general abnormality of mitochondria. Finally, a deficit of PDHC activity was demonstrated in brains obtained at autopsy from patients who had died of Alzheimer's disease,[11,12] a degenerative disorder of aging. Since the level of PDHC in the peripheral tissues, such as blood platelets, from Alzheimer patients appears to be normal,[13] the deficit of brain PDHC may reflect a selective cell death in Alzheimer brain. This notion is supported by the immunocytochemical data showing a selective enrichment of PDHC in cholinergic and other neurons.[14] In the first portion of this paper, we present results of enzymatic and immunochemical characterization of the abnormality of PDHC in fibroblasts from patients with abnormal pyruvate metabolism.

Identification of PDHC deficiency has been based mostly on enzyme activity and immunochemical assays. Recent advances in elucidating the structure of cDNAs for PDHC components[15–18] further point to the potential for the analysis of PDHC mutation at the genomic level. To obtain information for genetic analysis of the inheritance of PDHC mutation, we have mapped the gene of the E1α component to the X chromosome. This somewhat surprising result is also presented below.

[a]Supported in part by grants from the National Institutes of Health (AG03853 and NS22952) and the March of Dimes Birth Defect Foundation (6-406).

TABLE 1. Effect of Basic Compounds (Polyamines, Monoamines, and Amino Acids) on Pyruvate Dehydrogenase Complex Activity

Compound[a]	Concentration (mM)	Effect[b]	
		Difference from Control (%)	p
Procaine	0.1	10 ± 3	< 0.005
	0.01	10 ± 2	< 0.01
Lidocaine	0.1	0	NSD
3-(β-morpholinopropionyl)benzo[b]thiophene (**VII**)	0.1	10 ± 2	< 0.0005
	0.01	29 ± 10	< 0.05
3-(β-piperidinopropionyl)benzo[b]thiophene (**VI**)	0.1	−10 ± 3	< 0.005
3-(β-morpholinopropionyl)naphthaline	0.1	0	NSD
Spermine	0.1	10 ± 3	< 0.005
Spermidine	0.1	10 ± 2	< 0.0005
Putrescine	0.1	10 ± 3	< 0.01
Lysine	0.1	20 ± 4	< 0.01
Tryptophan	0.1	10 ± 4	< 0.02
	0.01	10 ± 2	< 0.005
Arginine	0.1	0	NSD
Poly-L-lysine			
M_r 4,000	0.1	−32 ± 3	< 0.002
M_r 14,000	0.1	−53 ± 4	< 0.002

[a]Mitochondria (60 μg/ml) were preincubated with 25 μl of the basic compound prepared in 50 mM potassium phosphate buffer, pH 7.4, or with the buffer alone (basal activity = 0.9 ± 0.03 nmol/mg/min for all compounds, except poly-L-lysine = 1.3 ± 0.02 nmol/mg/min). The concentration of Ca^{2+} and of Mg^{2+} was 0.05 mM.

[b]The results are from two experiments, each performed in triplicate. NSD (no statistical significance) indicates that $p > 0.05$ as determined by the unpaired Student's t test.

TABLE 2. Effect of Varying the Mg^{2+} Concentration on Stimulation of Pyruvate Dehydrogenase Complex Activity by Basic Compounds

Mg^{2+} (mM)	% Difference from Control[a]			
	Spermine (0.5 mM)	Lysine (0.5 mM)	Procaine (0.01 mM)	VII (0.01 mM)
0.05	16 ± 3[c]	8 ± 2[b]	9 ± 1[b]	18 ± 2[c]
0.3	32 ± 2[d]	3 ± 1	0	11 ± 2[b]
0.75	36 ± 1[d]	0	0	−18 ± 3[b]
1.0	27 ± 1[d]	−11 ± 2[b]	0	−6 ± 2
4.5	22 ± 1[d]	−9 ± 2[b]	−9 ± 3	−3 ± 2

[a]Mitochondria (30 μg/ml) were preincubated in 0.05 mM Ca^{2+} and the indicated Mg^{2+} concentration and cationic compound prepared in 50 mM potassium phosphate buffer, pH 7.4, or in buffer alone (basal activity). Basal activity increased from 2.0 ± 0.05 nmol/mg/min at 0.05 mM Mg^{2+} to 7.0 ± 0.05 nmol/mg/min at 4.5 mM Mg^{2+}. The results are from a representative experiment.

[b]$p < 0.05$.

[c]$p < 0.01$.

[d]$p < 0.005$.

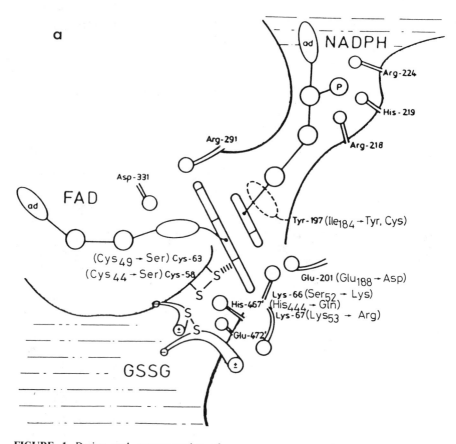

a

NADPH

Arg-224

His-219

Arg-291   Arg-218

Asp-331

FAD

Tyr-197 (Ile$_{184}$ → Tyr, Cys)

(Cys$_{49}$ → Ser) Cys-63
(Cys$_{44}$ → Ser) Cys-58

Glu-201 (Glu$_{188}$ → Asp)
Lys-66 (Ser$_{52}$ → Lys)
His-467' (His$_{444}$ → Gln)
Lys-67 (Lys$_{53}$ → Arg)

His-467'

Glu-472'

GSSG

FIGURE 1. Design and overexpression of lipoamide dehydrogenase mutants. **(a)** Schematic diagram of the human glutathione reductase catalytic center[6] showing important residues in GR and, in parentheses, the substitutions made at equivalent sites in *E. coli* LPDH. In LPDH, Lys-53–Glu-188 forms the salt bridge equivalent to Lys-66–Glu-201 in GR.[10] **(b)** Coomassie blue–stained gel showing the overexpression of altered LPDH enzymes from the plasmids listed in TABLE 1. Transformants of an *aceEF-lpd* deletion strain (JRG1342) were harvested after 3.5-hr induction at 42°C and disrupted by sonication; supernatant samples containing 25 µg protein were analyzed by SDS–polyacrylamide gel electrophoresis. The gel shows that LPDH is expressed to approximately the same extent from the mutant and wild-type (pGS239) genes.

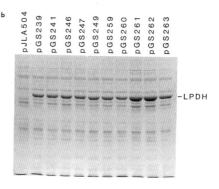

b

pJLA504 pGS239 pGS241 pGS246 pGS247 pGS249 pGS259 pGS260 pGS261 pGS262 pGS263

–LPDH

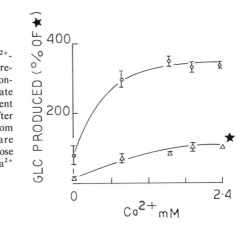

FIGURE 2. Effect of phorbol ester on Ca^{2+}-sensitivity of gluconeogenesis. Cells were pretreated for 5 min in Ca^{2+}-free medium containing EGTA and 45 μM phorbol dibutyrate (O). Controls (△) received similar treatment except for the omission of phorbol ester. After washing, glucose (GLC) production from pyruvate was monitored. The data are expressed as a percentage of the rate of glucose production by the controls at 2.4 mM Ca^{2+} (shown at ★).

the bathing medium. The use of ATP^{4-} permeabilization[6] to raise the cytosolic Ca^{2+} concentration to 1.8 μM enabled maximal stimulation of GNG at 2.5 mM Ca^{2+} in the bathing medium (FIG. 1). Phorbol ester greatly increased the sensitivity to Ca^{2+} (FIG. 2).

Cytosolic P_i seems to be carefully buffered.[2] It is probable that an efflux of P_i from mitochondria plays a part in stabilizing the cytosolic concentration under conditions of P_i depletion. The consequent fall in intramitochondrial P_i may affect the activity of pyruvate carboxylase and/or pyruvate dehydrogenase and thereby influence the conversion of pyruvate to glucose, and/or influence the flux of important intermediates of GNG between the cytosol and mitochondrial matrix.

PTH stimulates diacylglycerol formation in proximal tubules.[7] Assuming that phorbol mimics diacylglycerol action, it seems likely that PTH regulation of GNG involves stimulation of protein kinase C.

REFERENCES

1. GMAJ, P. & H. MURER. 1986. Physiol. Rev. **66:** 36–70.
2. BUTTERWORTH, P. J. 1987. Mol. Aspects Med. **9:** 289–386.
3. NAGATA, N. & H. RASMUSSEN. 1970. Proc. Natl. Acad. Sci. USA **65:** 368–374.
4. ROOBOL, A. & G. A. D. ALLEYNE. 1973. Biochem. J. **134:** 157–165.
5. JAHAN, M. &. P. J. BUTTERWORTH. 1988. Biochem. J. **252:** 105–109.
6. GOMPERTS, B. D. 1983. Nature **306:** 64–66.
7. HRUSKA, K. A., M. GOLIGORSKY, J. SCOBLE, M. TSUTSUMI, S. WESTBROOK & D. MOSKOWITZ. 1986. Am. J. Physiol. **251:** F188–F198.

Rapid Postnatal Induction of the Pyruvate Dehydrogenase Complex in Rat Liver Mitochondria[a]

ELENA SERRANO,[b] ANA MARÍA LUIS,[b]
PILAR ENCABO,[b] AGUSTÍN ALCONADA,[b] LAP HO,[c]
MULCHAND S. PATEL,[c] AND JOSÉ M. CUEZVA[b,d]

[b]Departamento de Biología Molecular
Centro de Biología Molecular
U.A.M.-C.S.I.C.
Universidad Autónoma de Madrid
28049-Madrid, Spain
and
[c]Department of Biochemistry
Case Western Reserve University School of Medicine
Cleveland, Ohio 44106

Postnatal structural, enzymatic, and bioenergetic development of mitochondria in the tissues of the newborn mammal is a key metabolic process necessary for adaptation to extra-uterine life. We have recently shown that postnatal mitochondrial differentiation in rat liver[1] and brown adipose tissue[2] is a rapid process that takes place during the first postnatal hour and depends on the increase in rates of synthesis for inner mitochondrial membrane proteins involved in respiration and oxidative phosphorylation. After birth until effective suckling begins, pyruvate is the main energy substrate oxidized by the tissues of the newborn rat.[3] Irreversible oxidation of pyruvate to acetyl-CoA is catalyzed by mitochondrial matrix–located pyruvate dehydrogenase complex (PDC) which contains multiple copies of three catalytic and two regulatory components and a protein X.[4] Pyruvate oxidation depends on the activity of "active" PDC. "Active" PDC in newborn rat liver increases transiently during the first postnatal hour,[5] whereas "total" PDC activity increases gradually over the entire neonatal period.[6] Because of the physiological importance of the PDC in metabolic adaptation after birth and because mitochondrial differentiation has not been defined at the level of matrix-located enzymes, the aim of the present investigation was to study the mechanism(s) responsible for the rapid postnatal increase of PDC activity in the newborn rat liver during the first postnatal hour.

PDC activity was measured as previously described[5] in freeze-clamped liver samples of newborn rats during the first 6 hr following birth. "Total" PDC activity was assayed after maximum dephosphorylation of the complex with an exogenously added partially purified phosphatase from pigeon acetone powder.[7] FIGURE 1 shows that maximum activation of PDC activity was achieved by 20 min preincubation with this

[a]This work was supported by Grant PB85-0199 from the Comisión Asesora de Investigación Científica y Técnica; by an institutional grant to the Centro de Biología Molecular from the Fundación R. Areces, Spain; and by U.S. Public Health Service Grant DK 20478.
[d]Address correspondence to Dr. J. M. Cuezva, Dep. Biología Molecular, Centro de Biología Molecular, Universidad Autónoma de Madrid, 28049-Madrid, Spain.

phosphatase preparation. Quantitation of the amount of PDC $E1\alpha$ subunit protein was carried out by Western blot analysis[8] of isolated rat liver mitochondrial proteins[1] during the first 2 postnatal hours. FIGURE 2A shows the linear correlation (slope = 0.048; Y intercept = 1.364; r = 0.988; $p < 0.01$) between the amount of fractionated mitochondrial protein transferred to the membrane and the densitometric area of the resulting 41-kDa immunoreactive band visualized by stain deposition from the oxidation of 4-chloro-1-naphthol by a rabbit anti-goat IgG conjugate with horseradish peroxidase used to detect the goat antisera against bovine PDC.

The results obtained with newborn rat liver extract showed a 5-fold increase in the "active" PDC activity during the first postnatal hour (0.069 ± 0.007 and 0.332 ± 0.020 mU/mg protein at 0 and 1 postnatal hour, respectively). Furthermore, a 2-fold

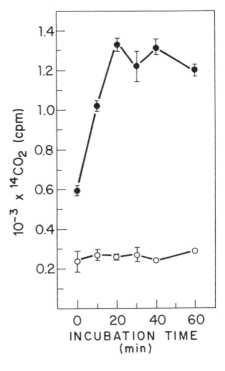

FIGURE 1. Time-course of the activation of PDC by a partially purified phosphatase from pigeon liver. The activity of PDC was assayed by measuring the formation of $^{14}CO_2$ from [1-^{14}C]pyruvate.[5] PDC activation was achieved by preincubating 400 μl of newborn rat liver extract with 100 μl of the 40–60% $(NH_4)_2SO_4$ fraction of the partially purified phosphatase.[7] The $^{14}CO_2$ radioactivity released during a 4-min incubation of stoppered vials containing newborn rat liver extracts (●) or the corresponding blanks (○), assayed in triplicate, is indicated.

increase in "total" PDC activity was observed during the same time period (0.680 ± 0.055 and 1.253 ± 0.120 mU/mg protein at 0 and 1 postnatal hour, respectively). The rapid postnatal increase in "total" PDC activity at 1 hr was paralleled by a similar degree of increase in the amount of PDC $E1\alpha$ protein (226 ± 30% over the 0-hr value). A representative example is shown in FIGURE 2B. No further significant changes were detected either in the "total" PDC activity up to 6 postnatal hours or in the immunologically detectable $E1\alpha$ protein. This finding is consistent with our previous observation showing that in the newborn rat the liver is one of the tissues involved in the rapid oxidation of lactate during the first two postnatal hours.[9] Further, postnatal mitochondrial differentiation also involves matrix-located proteins, as was previously

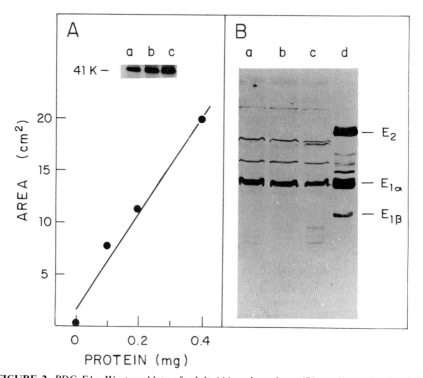

FIGURE 2. PDC E1α Western blots of adult (A) and newborn (B) rat liver mitochondrial extracts. (A) Standard curve for adult rat liver mitochondrial extracts fractionated on a 9% SDS–polyacrylamide gel and transferred to PVDF membranes (Millipore, USA). The amount of PDC E1α protein was detected as described in the text (**a:** 100, **b:** 200, and **c:** 400 μg of mitochondrial protein). (B) Immunoblot of PDC components in isolated newborn rat liver mitochondrial extract. 800 μg of isolated mitochondrial proteins was fractionated and quantitated as described above. Samples in **lanes a, b,** and **c** correspond to liver mitochondria from neonates 2 hr, 1 hr, and 0 hr old, respectively. Sample in **lane d** corresponds to 20 μg of purified bovine heart pyruvate dehydrogenase complex (Sigma, USA).

shown for membrane function–related proteins,[1,2] most likely by an increase in their rates of synthesis.

REFERENCES

1. VALCARCE, C., R. M. NAVARRETE, P. ENCABO, E. LOECHES, J. SATRÚSTEGUI & J. M. CUEZVA. 1988. Postnatal development of rat liver mitochondrial functions. The role of protein synthesis and of adenine nucleotides. J. Biol. Chem. **263:** 7767–7775.
2. LUIS, A. M. & J. M. CUEZVA. 1989. Rapid postnatal changes in F₁-ATPase proteins and in the uncoupling protein in brown adipose tissue mitochondria of the newborn rat. Biochem. Biophys. Res. Commun. **159:** 216–222.
3. CUEZVA, J. M., C. VALCARCE & J. M. MEDINA. 1985. Substrates availability for maintenance of energy homeostasis in the immediate postnatal period of the fasted newborn rat. *In* The Physiological Development of the Fetus and Newborn. C. T. Jones & P. W. Nathanielsz, Eds.: 63–69. Academic Press. New York.

4. REED, L. J. 1974. Multienzyme complexes. Acc. Chem. Res. **7:** 40–46.
5. CHITRA, C. I., J. M. CUEZVA & M. S. PATEL. 1985. Changes in the "active" pyruvate dehydrogenase complex in the newborn of normal and diabetic rats. Diabetologia **28:** 148–152.
6. KNOWLES, S. E. & F. J. BALLARD. 1974. Pyruvate dehydrogenase activity in rat liver during development. Biol. Neonate **24:** 41–48.
7. KSIEZAK-REDING, H., J. P. BLASS & G. E. GIBSON. 1982. Studies on the pyruvate dehydrogenase complex in brain with the arylamine acetyltransferase-coupled assay. J. Neurochem. **38:** 1627–1636.
8. HO, L., C-W. C. HU, S. PACKMAN & M. S. PATEL. 1986. Deficiency of the pyruvate dehydrogenase component in pyruvate dehydrogenase complex-deficient human fibroblasts: Immunological identification. J. Clin. Invest. **78:** 844–847.
9. MEDINA, J. M., J. M. CUEZVA & F. MAYOR. 1980. Non-gluconeogenic fate of lactate during the early neonatal period in the rat. FEBS Lett. **114:** 132–134.

Developmental Regulation of the Pyruvate Dehydrogenase Complex in the Rat Brain

G. D. A. MALLOCH, I. R. PHILLIPS, AND J. B. CLARK

Biochemistry Department
Medical College of St. Bartholomew's Hospital
University of London
Charterhouse Square
London EC1M 6BQ
United Kingdom

Studies concerning the development of the pyruvate dehydrogenase complex (PDHC) in the rat brain have established that increases in the enzyme activity of this complex are due partly to an increase in enzyme protein per mitochondrion and partly to an increase in mitochondrial numbers. There is no evidence for a change in the active proportion of the enzyme or for a qualitative alteration of the subunit composition.[1]

Comparison of the development of PDHC and citrate synthase in isolated mitochondria shows that most of the detectable increase in citrate synthase (56%) occurs between birth and 10 days postpartum. However, for PDHC about 60% of the increase in PDHC activity and immunochemically reactive protein occurs between 10 and 15 days postpartum.[1] This latter period is a particularly significant period of rat brain development, during which there is markedly increased oxygen consumption by the brain and pronounced advances in neuromuscular coordination. Our earlier studies suggest that the development of enzyme activities associated with the full aerobic oxidation of glucose correlates with this onset of neurological competence.[2] In addition, all our previous studies demonstrate to some extent that the development of PDHC lags behind that of numerous glycolytic and tricarboxylic acid cycle enzymes.[1-4] This implicates PDHC development as an important influence in brain maturation, particularly as the complex connects the flux of glycolytic products to the tricarboxylic acid cycle, which becomes the predominant pathway for energy metabolism in the brain during development. The relatively earlier development of citrate synthase is consistent with the need for tricarboxylic acid cycle flux during the early postnatal period of ketone-body utilization. The later development of PDHC protein levels and their associated enzyme activities suggests that the transcriptional regulation of PDHC is a crucial factor in the development of fully active aerobic glycolysis and acquired neurological competence.

cDNA clones that code for components of PDHC are currently being characterized and will be used to investigate the developmental regulation of PDHC in the rat brain.

REFERENCES

1. MALLOCH, G. D. A., L. A. MUNDAY, M. S. OLSON & J. B. CLARK. 1986. Biochem. J. **238:** 729–736.
2. BOOTH, R. F. G., T. B. PATEL & J. B. CLARK. 1980. J. Neurochem. **34:** 17–25.
3. LAND, J. M., R. F. G. BOOTH, R. BERGER & J. B. CLARK. 1977. Biochem. J. **164:** 539–544.
4. LEONG, S. F. & J. B. CLARK. 1984. Biochem. J. **218:** 139–145.

Polyamines, Monoamines, and Amino Acids Alter Pyruvate Dehydrogenase Complex Activity in Mitochondria from Rat Adipocytes[a]

FREDERICK L. KIECHLE,[b] JANET B. McGILL,
DIANE M. DANDURAND, AND HALINA MALINSKI

Department of Clinical Pathology
William Beaumont Hospital
Royal Oak, Michigan 48072

Damuni *et al.*[1] demonstrated that polyamines activate purified pyruvate dehydrogenase (PDH) phosphatase from bovine kidney and heart, using ^{32}P-labeled pyruvate dehydrogenase complex (PDC) as substrate. Spermine[1] and insulin[2] decrease the K_m of PDH phosphatase for Mg^{2+}, and polyamine concentrations are rapidly altered following insulin treatment.[3] Therefore, cationic compounds, like spermine, may represent intracellular mediators of insulin action.[1,3] An increase in PDC activity (assayed with [^{14}C]pyruvate as substrate, plus 0.05 mM Ca^{2+} and 0.05 mM Mg^{2+}) has been used to detect the presence of insulin mediator. However, some of these mediator preparations may have been contaminated with polyamines.[3] Therefore, the effect of a variety of basic compounds on PDC activity was investigated.

Mitochondria were prepared from rat epididymal adipocytes obtained from 100–120-g male Sprague-Dawley rats. PDC activity in mitochondria was assayed as the release of $^{14}CO_2$ from [1-^{14}C]pyruvic acid[4] in the presence of 0.05 mM Ca^{2+} and 0.05 mM Mg^{2+}, unless otherwise indicated. Basal activity varied between 0.6 and 2.0 nmol/mg/min. Non-enzymatic decarboxylation of [1-^{14}C]pyruvic acid was measured by quantitating the amount of $^{14}CO_2$ released in 50 mM potassium phosphate buffer, pH 7.4, in the presence or absence of various basic compounds (TABLE 1).

Nine of the 12 basic compounds tested caused a significant increase (procaine, VII, spermine, spermidine, putrescine, lysine, tryptophan) or decrease (VI, poly-L-lysine) in PDC activity (TABLE 1). None of the 12 compounds non-enzymatically decarboxylated [1-^{14}C]pyruvate to release $^{14}CO_2$, ruling out the involvement of induction of spontaneous decarboxylation by these basic compounds. Log-dose response experiments (0.001–10 mM) performed with the seven PDC-activating compounds demonstrated that three exhibited maximal stimulation either at 0.01 mM (VII) or at both 0.01 and 0.1 mM (tryptophan, procaine) (TABLE 1). The stimulatory effects of 0.1 mM procaine, tryptophan, and VII, as well as those of 10 mM spermine and spermidine were completely suppressed by 100 mM NaF. Since NaF is an inhibitor of PDH phosphatase, these five compounds appear to stimulate PDC activity through activation of the PDH phosphatase. Varying the Mg^{2+} concentration from 0.05 to 4.5 mM in

[a]Supported by a grant from the William Beaumont Research Institute.
[b]Address correspondence to Frederick L. Kiechle, M.D., Ph.D., Department of Clinical Pathology, William Beaumont Hospital, 3601 West 13 Mile Road, Royal Oak, Michigan 48072.

TABLE 1. Effect of Basic Compounds (Polyamines, Monoamines, and Amino Acids) on Pyruvate Dehydrogenase Complex Activity

Compound[a]	Concentration (mM)	Effect[b] Difference from Control (%)	p
Procaine	0.1	10 ± 3	< 0.005
	0.01	10 ± 2	< 0.01
Lidocaine	0.1	0	NSD
3-(β-morpholinopropionyl)benzo[b]thiophene (**VII**)	0.1	10 ± 2	< 0.0005
	0.01	29 ± 10	< 0.05
3-(β-piperidinopropionyl)benzo[b]thiophene (**VI**)	0.1	-10 ± 3	< 0.005
3-(β-morpholinopropionyl)naphthaline	0.1	0	NSD
Spermine	0.1	10 ± 3	< 0.005
Spermidine	0.1	10 ± 2	< 0.0005
Putrescine	0.1	10 ± 3	< 0.01
Lysine	0.1	20 ± 4	< 0.01
Tryptophan	0.1	10 ± 4	< 0.02
	0.01	10 ± 2	< 0.005
Arginine	0.1	0	NSD
Poly-L-lysine			
M_r 4,000	0.1	-32 ± 3	< 0.002
M_r 14,000	0.1	-53 ± 4	< 0.002

[a]Mitochondria (60 μg/ml) were preincubated with 25 μl of the basic compound prepared in 50 mM potassium phosphate buffer, pH 7.4, or with the buffer alone (basal activity = 0.9 ± 0.03 nmol/mg/min for all compounds, except poly-L-lysine = 1.3 ± 0.02 nmol/mg/min). The concentration of Ca^{2+} and of Mg^{2+} was 0.05 mM.

[b]The results are from two experiments, each performed in triplicate. NSD (no statistical significance) indicates that $p > 0.05$ as determined by the unpaired Student's t test.

TABLE 2. Effect of Varying the Mg^{2+} Concentration on Stimulation of Pyruvate Dehydrogenase Complex Activity by Basic Compounds

Mg^{2+} (mM)	% Difference from Control[a] Spermine (0.5 mM)	Lysine (0.5 mM)	Procaine (0.01 mM)	VII (0.01 mM)
0.05	16 ± 3^c	8 ± 2^b	9 ± 1^b	18 ± 2^c
0.3	32 ± 2^d	3 ± 1	0	11 ± 2^b
0.75	36 ± 1^d	0	0	-18 ± 3^b
1.0	27 ± 1^d	-11 ± 2^b	0	-6 ± 2
4.5	22 ± 1^d	-9 ± 2^b	-9 ± 3	-3 ± 2

[a]Mitochondria (30 μg/ml) were preincubated in 0.05 mM Ca^{2+} and the indicated Mg^{2+} concentration and cationic compound prepared in 50 mM potassium phosphate buffer, pH 7.4, or in buffer alone (basal activity). Basal activity increased from 2.0 ± 0.05 nmol/mg/min at 0.05 mM Mg^{2+} to 7.0 ± 0.05 nmol/mg/min at 4.5 mM Mg^{2+}. The results are from a representative experiment.

[b]$p < 0.05$.
[c]$p < 0.01$.
[d]$p < 0.005$.

the presence of 0.05 mM Ca^{2+} resulted in increased stimulation (spermine), loss of effect (procaine), or inhibition (lysine, VII) of PDC activity (TABLE 2).

In conclusion, the data demonstrate that a variety of cationic compounds may alter PDC activity when assayed in the presence of 0.05 mM Ca^{2+} and 0.5 mM Mg^{2+}. Magnesium enhanced the stimulatory effect of only one of the four compounds tested, spermine, consistent with the hypothesis that spermine lowers the K_m of PDH phosphatase for Mg^{2+}.[1] However, the results of the experiments with NaF imply that spermine, as well as spermidine, procaine, tryptophan and VII, activate PDH phosphatase. Therefore, a mechanism different from lowering the K_m for Mg^{2+} may mediate the effect of some basic compounds on PDH phosphatase activity. Monobasic and/or polybasic compounds may play a physiologic role in the regulation of PDC activity by insulin and other hormones.

REFERENCES

1. DAMUNI, Z., J. S. HUMPHREYS & L. J. REED. 1984. Stimulation of pyruvate dehydrogenase phosphatase activity by polyamines. Biochem. Biophys. Res. Commun. **124(1):** 95–99.
2. THOMAS, A. P. & R. M. DENTON. 1986. Use of toluene-permeabilized mitochondria to study the regulation of adipose tissue pyruvate dehydrogenase *in situ*. Biochem. J. **238:** 93–101.
3. GOLDSTONE, A. D., H. KOENIG, C. Y. LU & W. KABAT. 1987. Insulin stimulation of pyruvate dehydrogenase & mitochondrial function is mediated by polyamines. Fed. Proc. **46:** 645.
4. SYKES, E., S. GHAG & F. L. KIECHLE. 1987. Effect of S-adenosylhomocysteine on insulin-dependent release of pyruvate dehydrogenase activator from rat adipocyte plasma membranes. Biochem. Biophys. Res. Commun. **143:** 832–836.

Differential Inhibition of Mitochondrial Dehydrogenases by Fatty Acyl-CoAs[a]

JAMES C. K. LAI, KARIN RIMPEL-LAMHAOUAR, AND
ARTHUR J. L. COOPER

Departments of Biochemistry and Neurology
Cornell University Medical College
New York, New York 10021

In organic acidemias, Reye's syndrome, and several other metabolic encephalopathies, tissue accumulation of fatty acids leads to the formation of their CoA derivatives.[1] Fatty acids and their CoA derivatives are known toxins.[1,2] However, the biochemical mechanisms underlying their toxic effects have not been fully elucidated. To investigate the possibility that fatty acyl-CoAs selectively inhibit mitochondrial rate-limiting and/or tightly regulated dehydrogenases, we have studied the effects of butyryl-, octanoyl-, and palmitoyl-CoA on the brain mitochondrial α-ketoglutarate dehydrogenase complex (KGDHC), NAD^+- and $NADP^+$-isocitrate dehydrogenases (NAD-ICDH and NADP-ICDH), and NAD^+-malate dehydrogenase (MDH). We have also investigated the effects of the three fatty acyl-CoAs on purified bovine heart KGDHC and pyruvate dehydrogenase complex (PDHC).

TABLE 1. Effects of Fatty Acyl-CoAs on Activities of Brain Mitochondrial Dehydrogenases

Fatty Acyl-CoA (μM)	Enzymatic Activity (% of control)[a]			
	KGDHC	NAD-ICDH	NADP-ICDH	MDH
Butyryl				
250	21	ND	73	ND
1000	5	80	61	92[+]
Octanoyl				
250	1	93[+]	100[+]	ND
1000	6	54	69	74
Palmitoyl				
63	38	ND	ND	ND
250	9	96[+]	79	ND
1000	9	53	31	83

[a]Values are the means of 3 or more experiments. All, except those values marked with $+$, are significantly different [$p < 0.05$ by analysis of variance (ANOVA)] from corresponding control (100%) values. The control values are α-ketoglutarate dehydrogenase complex (KGDHC), 50 mU/mg protein; NAD^+-isocitrate dehydrogenase (NAD-ICDH), 120 mU/mg protein; $NADP^+$-isocitrate dehydrogenase (NADP-ICDH), 23 mU/mg protein; NAD^+-malate dehydrogenase (MDH), 8 U/mg protein. ND, not determined. Variations of data are $\leq 10\%$ of the means.

[a]This study was supported by NIH grants NS 24592 and AM 16739.

TABLE 2. Inhibition of Purified Bovine Heart KGDHC and PDHC by Fatty-Acyl CoAs

Fatty acyl-CoA	Enzymatic Activity (% of control)[a]	
(μM)	KGDHC	PDHC
Butyryl		
250	85	57
1000	44	28
Octanoyl		
12	70	102+
100	73	56
250	0	18
Palmitoyl		
25	40	ND
50	ND	4
63	25	ND

[a] Values are the means of 4 determinations and are, except for value marked with +, significantly ($p < 0.05$ by ANOVA) different from corresponding control (100%) values. Variations of data are $\leq 10\%$ of the means.

The isolation of rat forebrain non-synaptic mitochondria was carried out by the procedure of Lai and Clark.[3,4] The assays of the activities of NAD-ICDH, NADP-ICDH, MDH, KGDHC, and PDHC were as described previously.[3-7]

All these acyl-CoAs inhibit the brain mitochondrial dehydrogenases to differing degrees (TABLE 1). The susceptibility of the enzymes to inhibition by the fatty acyl-CoAs is in the order: KGDHC $\gg$ NADP-ICDH > NAD-ICDH $\gg$ MDH (TABLE 1). For the fatty acyl-CoAs studied, the inhibitory potency apparently increases with increasing chain length (TABLE 1). The inhibitor concentration that gives rise to 50% inhibition (i.e., the IC$_{50}$) for butyryl- and octanoyl-CoA inhibition of brain mitochondrial KGDHC is < 250 μM, whereas that for palmitoyl CoA is $\leq 60 \mu M$ (TABLE 1).

The fatty acyl-CoAs also inhibit the purified bovine heart PDHC and KGDHC, PDHC being more sensitive to inhibition than KGDHC (TABLE 2). The IC$_{50}$ values for the butyryl-, octanoyl- and palmitoyl-CoA inhibition of PDHC are, respectively, ≤ 250 μM, ca. 100 μM, and $\leq 25 \mu M$ (TABLE 2). The corresponding IC$_{50}$ values for the fatty acyl-CoA inhibition of KGDHC are, respectively, $\leq 1000 \mu M$, < 250 μM, and ≤ 25 μM (TABLE 2). Of the fatty acyl-CoAs studied, the inhibitor potency of the CoAs apparently increases with increasing chain length (TABLE 2).

In summary, our results are consistent with the notion that fatty acyl-CoAs selectively inhibit rate-limiting and/or highly regulated mitochondrial dehydrogenases. Since the reaction mediated by KGDHC is thought to be the slowest step of the tricarboxylic acid cycle, the sensitivity of KGDHC to inhibition by fatty acyl-CoAs may have pathophysiological importance in Reye's disease, organic acidemias, and several other metabolic encephalopathies.

REFERENCES

1. STUMPF, D. A., W. D. PARKER, JR., & C. ANGELINI. 1985. Neurology 35: 1041–1045.
2. ZIEVE, L. 1985. *In* Cerebral Energy Metabolism and Metabolic Encephalopathy. D. W. McCandless, Ed.: 163–177. Plenum Press. New York-London.

3. LAI, J. C. K., J. M. WALSH, S. C. DENNIS & J. B. CLARK. 1977. J. Neurochem. **28:** 625–631.
4. LAI, J. C. K. & J. B. CLARK. 1979. Methods Enzymol. **55(F):** 51–60.
5. LAI, J. C. K. & J. B. CLARK. 1976. Biochem. J. **154:** 423–432.
6. LAI, J. C. K. & K.-F. R. SHEU. 1985. J. Neurochem. **45:** 1861–1868.
7. LAI, J. C. K. & A. J. L. COOPER. 1986. J. Neurochem. **47:** 1376–1386.

Calcium Loading of Brain Mitochondria Alters Pyruvate Dehydrogenase Complex Activity and Flux[a]

JAMES C. K. LAI AND K-F. REX SHEU

Departments of Biochemistry and Neurology
Cornell University Medical College
New York, New York 10021
and
Burke Rehabilitation Center
White Plains, New York 10605

Calcium plays critical role(s) in cell injury and death.[1] Impairment of mitochondrial function as a consequence of Ca^{2+} loading may be one of the important mechanisms that leads to neuronal death after an ischemic insult.[1,2] To assess the metabolic effects of excess Ca^{2+}, pyruvate dehydrogenase complex (PDHC) activity and flux ([1-^{14}C]pyruvate decarboxylation) were studied in brain mitochondria upon loading with Ca^{2+} *in vitro*.

TABLE 1. Accumulation of $^{45}Ca^{2+}$ by Brain Mitochondria

	$^{45}Ca^{2+}$ Accumulation[a] (nmol/mg protein/2 min)		
$^{45}CaCl_2$ (μM)	Pyruvate	Pyruvate + ADP	Pyruvate + ATP
2.5	0.7 ± 0.1	1.1 ± 0.2	1.6 ± 0.1
125	3.1 ± 0.6	12.4 ± 1.0	23.3 ± 6.1

[a]Values are the means ± SD of 3 experiments. Mitochondria were incubated for 2 min with the indicated concentrations of $^{45}CaCl_2$ (specific activity, 25,500 dpm/nmol) in the presence of 5 mM pyruvate plus 1 mM malate and with or without adenine nucleotides (1 mM), as indicated. At the end of the incubation, the mitochondrial suspension was chilled on ice and mixed with an equal volume of 0.32 M sucrose and 10 mM MOPS (K) buffer, pH 7.4 (isolation medium). The chilled suspension was centrifuged at 9,000 × g for 1 min at 4°C. The pellet was resuspended in 1 ml of isolation medium and recentrifuged at 9,000 × g for 1 min. The radioactivity of the pellet was determined by liquid scintillation counting.

Brain mitochondria of nonsynaptic origin were isolated from adult male Wistar rat cerebrocortices.[3-5] [1-^{14}C]Pyruvate decarboxylation and PDHC activation state were determined as detailed by Lai and Sheu.[4,5] PDHC was isolated from bovine kidney and purified to near homogeneity.[6,7]

Brain mitochondria accumulated $^{45}Ca^{2+}$ in a concentration-dependent manner in the presence of pyruvate (i.e., in state 4; TABLE 1). This $^{45}Ca^{2+}$ accumulation was

[a]This study was supported, in part, by NIH grants AG03853 and NS22952 and by grants from the Will Roger Institute and Winifred Masterson Burke Relief Foundation.

accelerated in the presence of added ADP (i.e., in state 3) and was further enhanced when ATP was added instead of ADP (TABLE 1).

In state 3, 10 μM Ca^{2+} inhibited brain mitochondrial $[1\text{-}^{14}C]$pyruvate decarboxylation by greater than 85%: this Ca^{2+} inhibition was even more pronounced at 100 μM (data not shown). However, the inhibition was less in state 4 than in state 3, being 39% and 54%, respectively, at 10 and 100 μM Ca^{2+} (data not shown).

In state 4, the Ca^{2+} inhibition of flux through PDHC (i.e., $[1\text{-}^{14}C]$pyruvate decarboxylation) closely paralleled the Ca^{2+}-induced reduction of the PDHC activation state (TABLE 2), implicating a Ca^{2+}-mediated change in the PDHC phosphorylation. Consistent with this notion is our finding that the concentration-related, Ca^{2+}-induced depression of the PDHC activation state (at a Ca^{2+} level of 100 μM or higher) was greater in the presence of ATP than in state 3 (TABLE 2). On the other hand, in state 3, the Ca^{2+} inhibition of PDHC flux was more than the corresponding depression of the PDHC activation state, suggesting that mechanism(s) other than the phosphorylation of PDHC may also contribute to the Ca^{2+} inhibition of pyruvate oxidation by brain mitochondria.

An additional mechanism underlying the Ca^{2+}-induced decreases in the PDHC flux could be a direct inhibition of the enzymatic activity without involving effects on

TABLE 2. Effect of Calcium on the Activation State of Pyruvate Dehydrogenase Complex (PDHC) in Brain Mitochondria

	Activation State of PDHC (%)[a]		
CaCl$_2$ added (μM)	Pyruvate	Pyruvate + ADP	Pyruvate + ATP
0	83 ± 9	59 ± 10	60 ± 7
10	66 ± 6*	57 ± 9	53 ± 9
100	61 ± 9*	55 ± 13	46 ± 6*
500	51 ± 5*	46 ± 4*	36 ± 16*

[a]Values are the means ± SD of 6–8 experiments. *, $p < 0.005$ vs. incubations without added Ca^{2+}. In the mitochondrial incubations, the substrates were 5 mM pyruvate plus 1 mM malate, in the presence or absence of 1 mM ADP or ATP, as indicated. Other procedures were as described previously.[4,5]

phosphorylation, possibly in a manner similar to that of the inhibition of α-ketoglutarate dehydrogenase complex by pathological levels of Ca^{2+}.[8] Indeed, at levels higher than 1 mM, Ca^{2+} inhibited purified bovine kidney PDHC, with an IC$_{50}$ of 8 mM (data not shown).

In conclusion, our results indicate that, in state 4, Ca^{2+}, at pathophysiological levels, inhibits pyruvate metabolism by brain mitochondria primarily through a Ca^{2+}-mediated increase in the PDHC phosphorylation state. However, in state 3, the Ca^{2+} inhibition of pyruvate metabolism is likely to be mediated by more than one mechanism: in addition to Ca^{2+}-induced phosphorylation, one possible mechanism is the direct Ca^{2+} inhibition of the catalytic activity of the complex. Our data suggest that disruption of pyruvate metabolism may assume pathophysiological importance in Ca^{2+}-induced cell injury and in neuronal death in ischemia.

REFERENCES

1. SIESJÖ, B. K. 1981. J. Cereb. Blood Flow Metab. **1:** 155–185.
2. DESHPANDE, J. K., B. K. SIESJÖ & T. WIELOCK. 1987. J. Cereb. Blood Flow Metab. **7:** 89–95.

3. LAI, J. C. K. & J. B. CLARK. 1979. Methods Enzymol. **55(F):** 51–60.
4. LAI, J. C. K. & K.-F. R. SHEU. 1985. J. Neurochem. **45:** 1861–1868.
5. LAI, J. C. K. & K.-F. R. SHEU. 1987. Neurochem. Res. **12:** 715–722.
6. SHEU, K.-F. R. & Y. T. KIM. 1984. J. Neurochem. **43:** 1352–1358.
7. SHEU, K.-F. R., J. C. K. LAI, Y. T. KIM, J. BAGG & G. DORANTE. 1985. J. Neurochem. **44:** 593–599.
8. LAI, J. C. K. & A. J. L. COOPER. 1986. J. Neurochem. **47:** 1376–1386.

Organization of the Operon Encoding Components of the Branched-Chain Keto Acid Dehydrogenase Multienzyme Complex of *Pseudomonas putida*

JOHN. R. SOKATCH, GAYLE BURNS,
AND KENNETH HATTER

Department of Biochemistry and Molecular Biology
The University of Oklahoma Health Sciences Center
Oklahoma City, Oklahoma 73190

The branched-chain keto acid dehydrogenase multienzyme complex of *Pseudomonas putida* consists of four proteins: the E1 component, composed of α and β subunits; E2, and E3. The E3 component, LPD-val, is unique because it is specific for this

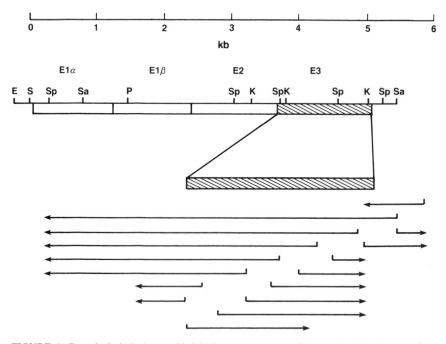

FIGURE 1. Branched-chain keto acid dehydrogenase operon of *P. putida*. Numbering of the nucleotides begins with the *Sst* I site immediately preceding the start of the gene encoding E1α. The structural gene for LPD-val (E3) is enlarged twofold to show the clones which were used for sequencing. *Arrows* represent the length of the clones and the direction of reading of the nucleotide sequence. Restriction sites shown are E, *Eco*R I; K, *Kpn* I; P, *Pst* I; S, *Sst* I; Sa, *Sal* I; Sp, *Sph* I.

P. putida bckad E1α   GPHSTSDDPSKYRPADDWSHF

                             :.::::::.: :: ...:. ..

Rat liver bckad E1α   GHHSTSDDSSAYRSVDEVNYW

                             ::.:: . .::. .:..

Human pdh E1α   HGHSMSDPGVSYRTREEIQEV

FIGURE 2. Comparison of primary sequences of the 21 amino acid region subject to phosphory-lation in E1α subunits of branched-chain keto acid dehydrogenase (bckad) from *P. putida*[2] and rat liver and of E1α from human pyruvate dehydrogenase (pdh). Identities are indicated by a *colon* and conservative amino acid changes are indicated by a *dot*. The phosphorylated serines of the rat liver enzyme are *underlined*.

multienzyme complex. The *bkd* operon has been cloned into pKT230 and expressed in *P. putida;* it has also been cloned into pUC, and the individual genes isolated and expressed in *Escherichia coli*. The gene order and direction of transcription are E1, E2, and LPD-val (FIG. 1). When the nucleotide sequence of the operon was determined, four open reading frames were found, *bkdA1*, *bkdA2*, *bkdB*, and *lpdV*, which encoded E1α, E1β, E2, and LPD-val, respectively. The complete coding region consists of 4947 bases and is transcribed from a single message of 6.2 kb.[1] Determination of the amino-terminal amino acid sequence of the encoded proteins revealed that E1α, E1β, and E2 all lack amino-terminal methionine, while LPD-val retains this amino acid. *bkdA1* consists of 1233 bp encoding a protein with a molecular weight of 45,158.[2] There was considerable primary sequence similarity of the E1α from *P. putida* to the E1α of rat liver branched-chain keto acid dehydrogenase, including at the region of the latter which is phosphorylated (FIG. 2). There was also distinct similarity to the phosphorylated region of E1α from human pyruvate dehydrogenase; however, the two branched-chain keto acid dehydrogenase subunits were much more closely related. There are 40 bases between *bkdA1* and the start of *bkdA2*. The translated sequence of *bkdA2* encoded a protein with an M_r of 37,007, which was identified as E1β from its amino-terminal sequence. The amino acid sequence of E1β has considerable similarity to that of the E1β subunit of human pyruvate dehydrogenase. The *bkdB* gene encoded a protein with an M_r of 45,134,[3] which was identified as the E2 component by its similarity to the sequences of the E2 components of the pyruvate and 2-ketoglutarate dehydrogenases of *E. coli*. The E2 component had a single lipoyl domain, in contrast to the E2 component of the pyruvate dehydrogenase of *E. coli*. the *lpdV* gene encoded a protein with an M_r of 48,164 (48,949, including FAD), which was identified from its amino-terminal sequence.[1] There was a typical rho-independent terminator down-stream from *lpdV*, which agrees with the evidence from Northern blots that the operon is transcribed from a single message. LPD-val contains the same domain structure found in other lipoamide dehydrogenases and in glutathione reductase. There was no feature of the amino acid sequence which would account for the specificity of LPD-val for the branched-chain keto acid dehydrogenase of *P. putida*.

REFERENCES

1. BURNS, G., T. BROWN, K. HATTER & J. R. SOKATCH. 1988. Sequence analysis of the lpdV gene for lipoamide dehydrogenase of branched chain oxoacid dehydrogenase of *Pseudomonas pituda*. Eur. J. Biochem. **179:** 61–69.
2. BURNS, G., T. BROWN, K. HATTER, J. M. IDRISS & J. R. SOKATCH. 1988. Similarity of the E1 subunits of branched-chain-oxoacid dehydrogenase from *Pseudomonas putida* to the

corresponding subunits of mammalian branched-chain-oxoacid and pyruvate dehyroge-
nases. Eur. J. Biochem. **176:** 311–317.

3.   BURNS, G., T. BROWN, K. HATTER & J. R. SOKATCH. 1988. Comparison of the amino acid
sequences of the transacylase components of branched chain oxoacid dehydrogenase of
Pseudomonas putida, and the pyruvate and 2-oxoglutarate dehydrogenases of *Escherichia
coli.* Eur. J. Biochem. **176:** 165–169.

Oligonucleotide-Directed Mutagenesis of the *lpd* Gene of *Escherichia coli*

G. C. RUSSELL, N. J. ALLISON, C. H. WILLIAMS, JR.,
AND J. R. GUEST

Department of Microbiology
University of Sheffield
Western Bank
Sheffield S10 2TN
United Kingdom

Lipoamide dehydrogenase (LPDH) is the flavoprotein (E3) component of the pyruvate (PDHC), 2-oxoglutarate, and branched-chain 2-oxo acid dehydrogenase multienzyme complexes. It reoxidizes the lipoamide cofactors bound to the acyltransferase (E2) components, with the reduction of NAD^+.[1,2] LPDH belongs to a family of enzymes possessing a disulphide bridge which is reversibly oxidized in the catalytic cycle.[1]

In *Escherichia coli*, LPDH is the product of the distal gene of the *aceEF-lpd* operon, which encodes all three components of the PDHC. The *lpd* gene has been cloned and sequenced.[3,4] Extensive sequence homology between *E. coli* LPDH and human glutathione reductase (GR),[5] another disulphide oxido-reductase, together with extensive mechanistic studies on these enzymes, has allowed the design of mutations to examine the roles of specific residues in the structure and catalysis of LPDH. The corresponding amino acid substitutions are superimposed on a schematic of the GR active site in FIGURE 1a.

The strategy for oligonucleotide-directed mutagenesis and overexpression of the *lpd* gene from λ promoters in derivatives of pJLA504[7] has been published.[8] Nine *lpd* mutants have so far been constructed, and a preliminary characterization of their LPDH activities has been made using crude extracts in which the enzymes have been amplified to 20% of total protein (FIG. 1b). The properties of the mutant enzymes are summarized in TABLE 1.

Changing each of the active site cysteine residues to serine (pGS261 and pGS262) abolished LPDH activity, confirming the critical role of the redox-active disulphide in catalysis (TABLE 1).

His-444 is thought to act as a member of a charge-relay system important for catalysis.[6] Substituting glutamine for His-444 in pGS246 reduced the LPDH activity some 27-fold with NAD as the cofactor (TABLE 1). However, the presence of some residual activity suggests that Gln-444 can function to a limited extent in charge transfer.

The postulated Lys-53–Glu-188 salt bridge[5,6] was converted to an Arg-53–Asp-188 salt bridge (pGS263) by combining the Glu-188→Asp (pGS241) and the Lys-53→Arg (pGS260) mutations. This should maintain the total length of the salt bridge but move the charged groups relative to the flavin ring. The activity of the mutant enzymes expressed by pGS241, pGS260, and pGS263 may indicate that this salt bridge is important in the reduction of the pyridine nucleotide cofactor. This suggestion is further supported by the reduced activity of the Ser-52→Lys mutant (pGS247) with NAD (TABLE 1).

The side chain of Tyr-197 in GR is believed to protect the face of the flavin ring of FAD after its reduction by NADPH.[6] The direction of the reaction catalyzed by

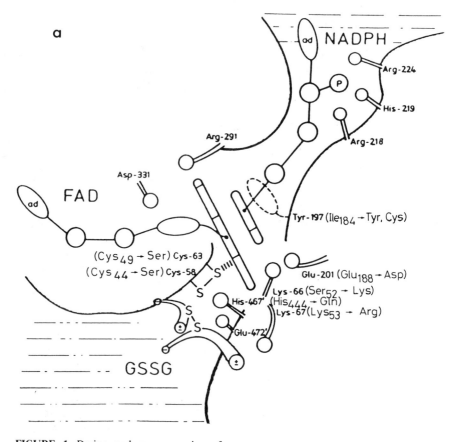

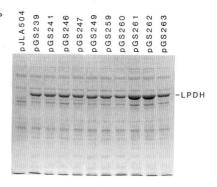

FIGURE 1. Design and overexpression of lipoamide dehydrogenase mutants. (a) Schematic diagram of the human glutathione reductase catalytic center[6] showing important residues in GR and, in parentheses, the substitutions made at equivalent sites in *E. coli* LPDH. In LPDH, Lys-53–Glu-188 forms the salt bridge equivalent to Lys-66–Glu-201 in GR.[10] (b) Coomassie blue–stained gel showing the overexpression of altered LPDH enzymes from the plasmids listed in TABLE 1. Transformants of an *aceEF-lpd* deletion strain (JRG1342) were harvested after 3.5-hr induction at 42°C and disrupted by sonication; supernatant samples containing 25 μg protein were analyzed by SDS–polyacrylamide gel electrophoresis. The gel shows that LPDH is expressed to approximately the same extent from the mutant and wild-type (pGS239) genes.

TABLE 1. Plasmids Expressing Wild-Type and Mutant *lpd* Genes
from Thermoinducible λ Promoters and the LPDH Activities
of the Corresponding Extracts

Plasmid	Mutation	*Lpd* Phenotype Conferred[a]	Specific Activity[b] (NAD:APAD)
pGS239	wild-type	+	70:8.9
pGS241	Glu-188→Asp	±[c]	13:97
pGS246	His-444→Gln	±	2.6:1.4
pGS247	Ser-52→Lys	+	35:4.6
pGS249	Ile-184→Cys	+	70:5.6
pGS259	Ile-184→Tyr	+	84:4.6
pGS260	Lys-53→Arg	+	55:8.7
pGS261	Cys-44→Ser	−	nd[d]:0
pGS262	Cys-49→Ser	−	nd[d]:0
pGS263	Glu-188→Asp	±	14:28
	Lys-53→Arg		

[a]The Lpd phenotype conferred by each plasmid was determined in the *aceEF-lpd* deletion strain JRG1342, using the ability to grow on glucose minimal medium supplemented with acetate as an indicator of *in vivo* LPDH activity.

[b]Specific activity of crude extracts is expressed as μmol/hr/mg protein, assayed at 30°C with dihydrolipoamide as substrate and the indicated cofactor.

[c]Poor growth (±) correlates with low *in vitro* LPDH activity with NAD as cofactor.

[d]nd, not determined.

LPDH (oxidation) is the reverse of that catalysed by GR, so the auto-oxidation of FAD is less important, and Tyr-197 is replaced in LPDH by Ile-184, which may not perform an FAD-protective role. In order to investigate catalysis of the reverse reaction by LPDH, Ile-184 was replaced by Tyr (pGS259). This substitution has no significant effect on the forward reaction with either cofactor (TABLE 1).

Further studies with the mutant proteins are being done in the laboratory of Dr. C. H. Williams, Jr., and preliminary results of this work are presented elsewhere in this volume.[9]

REFERENCES

1. WILLIAMS, C. H., JR. 1976. *In* The Enzymes. P. D. Boyer, Ed. Vol. **13**: 89–173. Academic Press. New York.
2. MASSEY, V. & C. VEEGER. 1961. Biochim. Biophys. Acta. **48**: 33–47.
3. GUEST, J. R. & P. E. STEPHENS. 1980. J. Gen. Microbiol. **121**: 277–292.
4. STEPHENS, P. E., H. M. LEWIS, M. G. DARLISON & J. R. GUEST. 1983. Eur. J. Biochem. **135**: 519–527.
5. RICE, D. W., G. E. SCHULZ & J. R. GUEST. 1984. J. Mol. Biol. **174**: 483–496.
6. PAI, E. F. & G. E. SCHULZ. 1983. J. Biol. Chem. **258**: 1752–1757.
7. SCHAUDER, B., H. BLOCKER, R. FRANK & J. E. G. McCARTHY. 1987. Gene **52**: 279–283.
8. ALLISON, N., C. H. WILLIAMS, JR., & J. R. GUEST. 1988. Biochem. J. **256**: 741–749.
9. WILLIAMS, C. H., JR., N. ALLISON, G. C. RUSSELL, A. J. PRONGAY, L. D. ARSCOTT, S. DATTA, L. SAHLMAN & J. R. GUEST. 1989. Ann. N.Y. Acad. Sci. This volume.
10. SCHIERBEEK, A. J. 1988. Ph.D. Thesis. University of Groningen. The Netherlands.

Characterization and Conservation of the Inner E2 Core Domain Structure of the Bovine Branched-Chain α-Keto Acid Dehydrogenase Complex[a]

THOMAS A. GRIFFIN,[b] KIM S. LAU,
AND DAVID T. CHUANG[c]

Departments of Medicine and Biochemistry
Case Western Reserve University
Cleveland, Ohio 44106

A cDNA clone encoding the entire transacylase (E2b) precursor of the bovine branched-chain α-keto acid dehydrogenase complex has been constructed from two shorter, overlapping cDNA clones.[1] This clone is 2701 bp in length and has an open

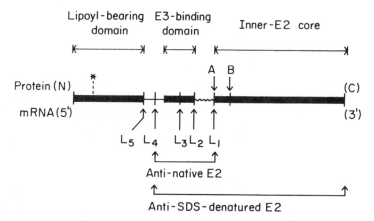

FIGURE 1. A linear model for the domain structure of bovine E2b. *Solid boxes* represent the three folded domains of the mature E2b polypeptide. The *wavy* and *solid lines* represent the first and second hinge regions of the E2b polypeptide, respectively. A, B, L1, L2, L3, L4, and L5 represent sites of tryptic cleavage of native E2b under conditions of limited proteolysis. The A and L1 sites are identical. The *asterisk* indicates the position of the lipoyllysine residue. The regions of E2b recognized by antibodies made against either SDS-denatured E2b or native E2b are indicated.

[a]This work was supported by Grants DK 37373 and DK 26758 from the National Institutes of Health, by Grant 1-796 from the March of Dimes Birth Defects Foundation, and by the Veterans Administration.

[b]Medical Scientist Trainee supported by Grant 07250 from the National Institutes of Health.

[c]To whom correspondence should be addressed at the Department of Biochemistry, The University of Texas Southwestern Medical Center, 5323 Harry Hines Blvd., Dallas, Texas 75235.

A ♦   B ♦

Bovine E2b   T I P I P I S K P P V F I G K D R T E P V K G F H K A M V K T M S A A L
Rat E2p   F I D I P I S - - - - - - - - - - - - - - N I R R V I A Q R L M Q S K Q
E. coli E2p   K V D F S K F G E I E E V E L G R I Q K I S G A N L S R N W V M I P H -
E. coli E2k   E K R V P M T - - - - - - - - - R L R K R V A E R L L E A K N S T A M -

Bovine E2b   K I P H F G Y C D E V D L T E L V K L R E E L K P I A F A R G I K L S F
Rat E2p   T I P H Y Y L S V D V N M G E V L L V R K E L N K M L E - G K G K I S V
E. coli E2p   - V T H F D K T D I T E L E A F R K Q Q N E E A A K R K - L D V K I T P
E. coli E2k   - L T T F N E V N M K P I M D L R K Q Y G E A F E K R - - H G I R L G F

Bovine E2b   M P F F L K A A S L G L L Q F P I L N A S V D E N C Q N I T Y K A S H N
Rat E2p   N D F I I K A S A L A C L K V P E A N S S W M - D - T V I R Q N H V V D
E. coli E2p   V V F I M K A V A A A L E Q M P R F N S S L S E D G Q R L T L K K Y I N
E. coli E2k   M S F Y V K A V V E A L K R Y P E V N A S I D - - G D D V V Y H N Y F D

Bovine E2b   I G I A M D T E Q G L I V P N V K N V Q I R S I F E I A T E L N R L Q K
Rat E2p   V S V A V S T P A G L I T P I V F N A H I K G L E T I A S D V V S L A S
E. coli E2p   I G V A V D T P N G L V V P V F K D V N K K G I I E L S R E L M T I S K
E. coli E2k   V S M A V S T P R G L V T P V L R D V D T L G M A D I E K K I K E L A V

Bovine E2b   L G S A G Q L S T N D L I G G T F T L S N I G S I G G T Y A K P V I L P
Rat E2p   K A R E G K L Q P H E F Q G G T F T I S N L G M F G I K N F S A I I N P
E. coli E2p   K A R D G K L T A G E M Q G G C F T I S S I G G L G T T H F A P I V N A
E. coli E2k   K G R D G K L T V E D L T G G N F T I T N G G V F G S L M S T P I I N P

Bovine E2b   P E - - - V A I G A L G T I K A L P - R F N E K G E V C K A Q I M N V S
Rat E2p   P Q A C I L A I G A - S E D K L I P - A D N E K G F D V A S - V M S V T
E. coli E2p   P E - - - V A I L G V S K S A M E P - V W N G K E F V P R L - M L P I S
E. coli E2k   P Q - - - S A I L G M H A I K D R P M A V N G Q V E I L P - - M M Y L A

Bovine E2b   W S A D H R I I D G A T V S R F S N L W K S Y L E N P A F M L L D L K ·
Rat E2p   L S C D H R V V D G A V G A Q W L A ...
E. coli E2p   L S F D H R V I D G A D G A R F I T I I N N T L S D I R R L V M ·
E. coli E2k   L S Y D H R L I D G R E S V G F L V T I K E L L E D P T R L L L D V ·

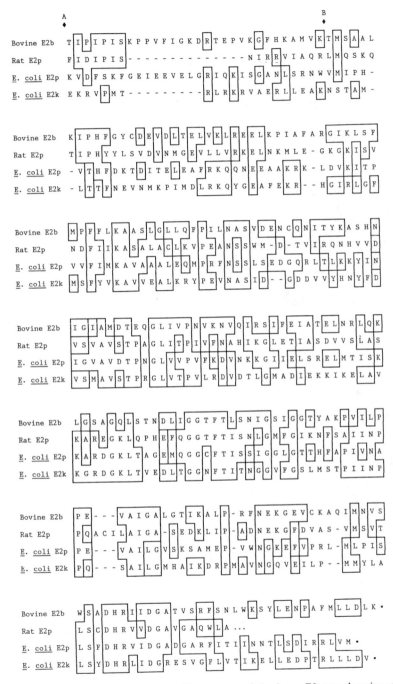

FIGURE 2. Comparison of the amino acid sequences of the inner E2 core domains of four different E2 proteins. The deduced primary structures of the inner E2 core domains of bovine E2b, rat E2p,[4] E. coli E2p,[5] and E. coli E2k[6] are aligned for maximal identity. The *boxed residues* are those which are identical between any two of the domains. The trypsin-sensitive sites A and B of bovine E2b are indicated at the *top* of the figure.

reading frame of 1446 bp, which codes for the 482 amino acid residue long bovine pre-E2b. The mature E2b polypeptide consists of 421 amino acid residues with a calculated molecular mass of 46,518 daltons. The first 61 amino acids of bovine pre-E2b represent a cleavable mitochondrial targeting presequence, as the amino-terminal glycine of mature E2b is the 62nd residue of pre-E2b.[2]

The molecular mass of native bovine E2b as determined by sedimentation equilibrium is 1,100,000 daltons. This supports the proposal of a 24-subunit model for the quaternary structure of bovine E2b, for which the deduced molecular mass of a 24-mer is 1,116,432 daltons.[3] The model in FIGURE 1 indicates the three folded domains of bovine E2b, which are connected by two hinge regions. The trypsin-sensitive sites A and B were located by amino-terminal sequencing of fragments A and B. Fragment A comprises the inner E2 core domain, encompassing residues 175 to 421 of mature E2b; it has transacylase activity and retains the 24-mer quaternary structure. Fragment B comprises residues 205 to 421; it retains the 24-mer quaternary structure but does not possess any transacylase activity.[3] The 30 residues at the amino terminus of fragment A appear to be critical for transacylase activity.

The deduced primary structure of the inner E2 core domain of bovine E2b is compared in FIGURE 2 with the primary structures of the inner E2 core domains of rat E2p,[4] *Escherichia coli* E2p,[5] and *E. coli* E2k.[6] There are 31 residues which are conserved among all four domains. This high degree of similarity suggests that these domains are structurally and evolutionarily related.

REFERENCES

1. GRIFFIN, T. A., K. S. LAU & D. T. CHUANG. 1988. J. Biol. Chem. 263: 14008–14014.
2. LAU, K. S., T. A. GRIFFIN, C.-W. C. HU & D. T. CHUANG. 1988. Biochemistry 27: 1972–1981.
3. CHUANG, D. T., C.-W. C. HU, L. S. KU, P. J. MARKOVITZ & R. P. COX. 1985. J. Biol. Chem. 260: 13779–13786.
4. FUSSEY, S. P. M., J. R. GUEST, O. F. W. JAMES M. F. BASSENDINE & S. J. YEAMAN. 1988. Proc. Natl. Acad. Sci. USA. 85: 8654–8658.
5. STEPHENS, P. E., M. G. DARLISON, H. M. LEWIS & J. R. GUEST. 1983. Eur. J. Biochem. 133: 481–489.
6. SPENCER, M. E., M. G. DARLISON, P. E. STEPHENS, I. K. DUCKENFIELD & J. R. GUEST. 1984. Eur. J. Biochem. 141: 361–374.

Expression and Assembly of Active Bovine Dihydrolipoyl Transacylase (E2b) Precursor in *Escherichia coli*[a]

THOMAS A. GRIFFIN[b] AND DAVID T. CHUANG[c]

Departments of Medicine and Biochemistry
Case Western Reserve University
Cleveland, Ohio 44106

A cDNA clone encoding the entire transacylase (E2b) precursor of bovine branched-chain α-keto acid dehydrogenase complex was cloned into the prokaryotic expression vector pKK233-2 (Pharmacia). The details of the construction of this vector, pKKbE2-11, are presented in FIGURE 1. Recombinant pre-E2b was expressed in *Escherichia coli* JM105 cells transformed with pKKbE2-11. Recombinant pre-E2b has a molecular mass of 50 kDa on SDS–polyacrylamide gel electrophoresis, which is less than that of natural mature E2b (52 kDa). This anomaly could be explained by possible amino-terminal processing of the recombinant pre-E2b polypeptide and/or the lack of attached lipoic acid on the recombinant molecule. The lack of lipoic acid attachment was demonstrated by the absence of ^{3}H incorporation into the recombinant pre-E2b when it was expressed in the presence of [^{3}H]lipoic acid.

The recombinant pre-E2b possesses transacylase activity and appears to be assembled with a 24 subunit quaternary structure. Both of these properties are functions of the inner E2 core domain. These data suggest that this domain has folded correctly in *E. coli*.

The pKKbE2-11 vector was deleted between various *Pst* I sites to produce three deleted vectors. Linear models of the three deleted polypeptides are shown in FIGURE 2. These recombinant proteins were expressed in *E. coli* JM105 and assayed for transacylase activity and reactivity with antibody to E2b. These data, summarized in FIGURE 2, suggest that specific amino acid sequences in the span of residues 115 to 207

[a]This work was supported by Grants DK 37373 and DK 26758 from the National Institutes of Health, by Grant 1-796 from the March of Dimes Birth Defects Foundation, and by the Veterans Administration.

[b]Medical Scientist Trainee supported by Grant 07250 from the National Institutes of Health.

[c]To whom correspondence should be addressed at the Department of Biochemistry, The University of Texas Southwestern Medical Center, 5323 Harry Hines Blvd., Dallas, Texas 75235.

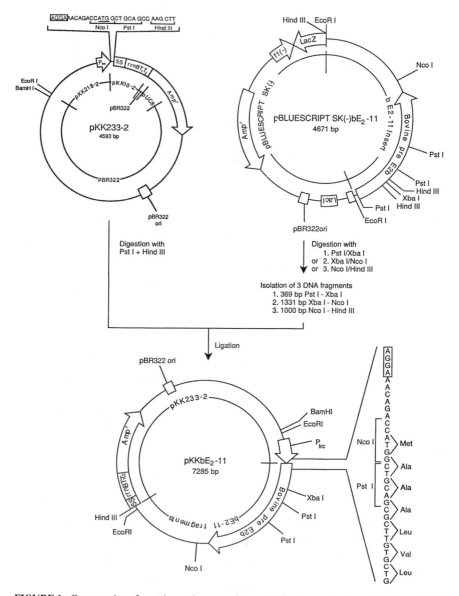

FIGURE 1. Construction of a prokaryotic expression vector for the production of bovine pre-E2b in *E. coli*. The diagram details the construction of the vector pKKbE2-11, which is used to express recombinant pre-E2b in *E. coli*. Three fragments of the vector pBLUESCRIPT SK(−)bE2-11, which includes the cDNA insert that codes for the entire bovine pre-E2b, were directionally cloned into the prokaryotic expression vector pKK233-2 (Pharmacia). This construction utilized a convenient *Pst* I site to produce an open reading frame in the expression vector that did not alter the region coding for the amino terminus of bovine pre-E2b.

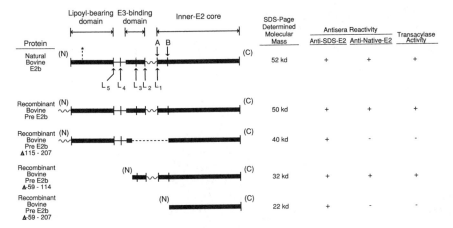

FIGURE 2. Linear models for natural bovine E2b, recombinant bovine pre-E2b, and three deleted recombinant bovine pre-E2b polypeptides. The diagram presents linear models of the domain structure of nature E2b and four recombinant molecules. The three deleted recombinant pre-E2b polypeptides were expressed using pKKbE2-11 vectors which had deletions between various *Pst* I sites. The molecular mass determined by SDS-PAGE, the reactivity with antibodies to E2, and the presence of transacylase activity for each polypeptide are indicated.

are required for transacylase activity and are the epitopes for antibodies made against native bovine E2b.

Calculated on the basis of specific activities, yields of up to 10% of total *E. coli* protein have been obtained for recombinant pre-E2b. The large amounts of recombinant protein produced by this expression system will be used to investigate lipoic acid attachment, structure-function relationships, and subunit and complex assembly.

Gene Structure of the Promoter Region for the Human Pyruvate Dehydrogenase $E_1\alpha$ Subunit and Regulation of Its Gene Expression

SHIGEO OHTA,[a] HITOSHI ENDO,
KAKUKO MATSUDA, AND YASUO KAGAWA

Department of Biochemistry
Jichi Medical School
Minamikawachi-machi
Tochigi-ken, 329-045, Japan

Mitochondria vary in number and morphology, depending on the developmental stage and the internal or external conditions. Therefore, expression of the nuclear genes encoding mitochondrial proteins should be coordinate. For investigating the coordinating mechanism, it is essential to analyze the promoter regions of the genes. We have cloned several cDNAs for nuclear-coded mitochondrial proteins, including the human pyruvate dehydrogenase (PDH) E_1 α and β subunits.[1-4] Here, we show the O_2-dependent expression of the PDH genes and the nucleotide sequence of the 5' upstream region of the genomic gene for the human PDH α subunit. The nucleotide sequence determination revealed the presence of a consensus sequence to the sequences of the nuclear genes for some other mitochondrial proteins.

For investigating the regulatory system for expression of a gene, it is necessary to find an artificial treatment by which expression of the gene can be changed in cultured cells. A Northern blot experiment was performed with HeLa cells cultured under a low pressure of oxygen (2%) by using the cloned cDNAs as hybridization probes. As shown in FIGURE 1, the amounts of mRNAs for the ATP synthase β subunit and the PDH α subunit were reduced by exposing the cells to the low oxygen pressure for 1.5 days (lane b), restored after 5 days (lane c), and then markedly increased by treatment with 20% oxygen for 1 day (lane d). The level of β-actin mRNA, used as a control, was not changed throughout these treatments. Coordinate expression was also found in the cytochrome c_1 gene. Therefore, expression of the PDH gene was coordinated with that of the other genes for mitochondrial proteins.

The genomic gene for the human PDH α subunit was cloned and sequenced; the sequence for its 5' upstream region is shown in FIGURE 2. An *in vitro* run-off transcription assay confirmed this 5' upstream region had promoter activity. In addition, this region contained a consensus sequence to some of the other nuclear genes of mitochondrial proteins, such as the ATP synthase β subunit[5] and cytochrome c_1[6] (FIG. 2, lower panel). Detailed analysis of this region of the ATP synthase gene revealed that the consensus sequence works as an enhancer for transcription (Tomura *et al.*, manuscript in preparation). Therefore, some nuclear genes encoding mitochondrial proteins may be regulated by this enhancer in coordinate fashion.

---

[a]Address correspondence to Dr. S. Ohta, Department of Biochemistry, Jichi Medical School, Minamikawachi-machi, Tochigi-ken, 329-04, Japan.

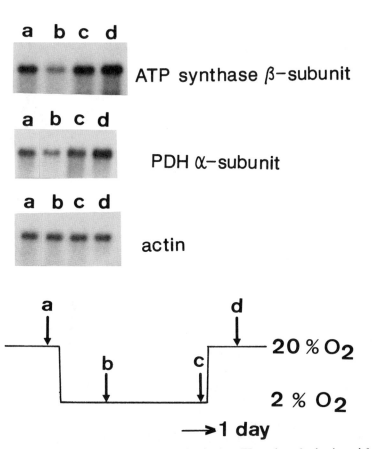

FIGURE 1. Northern blotting for the PDH α subunit, the ATP synthase β subunit, and β-actin. HeLa cells were cultured under 2% O_2 and 5% CO_2 for 1.5 days (**lane b**) or for 5 days (**lane c**), or they were cultured under the low O_2 pressure for 5 days and then under 20% O_2 and 5% CO_2 for 1 day (**lane d**). **Lane a** shows the untreated cells. Poly(A^+) RNA was isolated from the indicated cells and 3 μg of the poly(A^+) was applied to gels for electrophoresis for Northern blotting.

```
AAGCTTTGAGAGCCGGTTTAAATGATCCCTTTTCTCTTCATCCATGAGACAAGCTAAGTTCCAGAGAGAGGGTGCCACGCTGTGAGGGACCTGTGTTACG  -961

AGTACGATGGCTCGCGTCACTTCAAATTCTTGAAATCACTGAAATTTGGAGGTCAGTTGTTACATCATAACCCAGCCAATTCTAGTTAGCCTGTTTTCTT  -861

CCTAACTTCTTTAATCGTTCTTCATAAGTCACAATCGCAGCCCCTCACCGTTCTGACCACTGTCCCCTGGATTCCACTCAGTTTACTCATTATCCCCCTT  -761

AAAATGTGGAGCCCAAATCTGAACCCGGAACCCCAGGTGCAATCCCACTAGGACACAACACAATGGGTTCCTGAGCCCTTTGATCCTCTGAATAGAGCCC  -661

CTTGTTGCTT TGGTG TT TTGTCTCT GTGTGTGCTTTTATCATCGGCTGAGCCACGCTGTTAACTCGCAGTGAGCCTGTGAACCAATAACTAGAGAAAAAA  -561
           CONSENSUS SEQ.  Z-DNA
GATTTTTCCCATTGTCCTCTCGACATATATTGGGAAACAAATTTTTTGATCCGCGTTCAAGTAGACAGGGCAGAACTGTCCAACTGCTACGTGATCTTTT  -461

AAAGACAAAGTTAGTGGCAGACCATTTACAGAAACCAGATGTTCTGTCTTTTGGCTCTGAGCATGCTGCTAATCTTCATCATCTAGTGTACTGAACGAGA  -361

TGTACTGAACGAGGGCTGCAGAGCTGCAGCACCGGCAGGAGTAGGCGCTCGGTAGGACGGGGCCTGCACAACCTCCCCGGTAGTCAGCAGAGCGGAATCC  -261

AGGAAGGCTCCTTTCCCGCGGCGCCCTGGAGGCGGGGGCCCCACCTTCCCACGCAGGCGCTATCAAGCCCCGCCTCCTCAC CCGCCG GCGGCGTGGCGTC  -161
                                                                                 GC-BOX
GGAAAGAGCCCTCAGCCCCTTCCCTCTCTGGCGCTGATACCCAATGGGCAGCCTCAGGCCTTTAGCGG GGGCGG GGCACCCCCTGGACGCCGTTCTGGTT  -61
                                                                 *+1   GC-BOX
GGCCCGCGGCCCGGCGCAGCGCATGACGTTATTACGACTCTGTCACGCCGCGGTGCGACTGAGGCGTGGCGTCTGCTGGGGCACCTGAAGGAGACTTGGG   40

GGCACCCGTCTGTGCCTCCTGGGTTGTGAGGAGTCGCCCGTGCCGCCACTGCCTGTGCTTC ATGAGGAAGATGCTCGCCGCCGTCTCCCGCGTGCTGTCT  140
                                                              *INITIATION SITE FOR TRANSCRIPTION
                                                             MetArgLysMetLeuAlaAlaValSerArgValLeuSer
GGCGCTTCTCAGAAGCCG GTGAGACCTCCCGGGCCGGGCCGGGCCATGGGGCGCGAGTGGGGCTGAGGCGGGGCCGGAGGGCA GGGCGG GCCAGGCCGGG  240
GlyAlaSerGlnLysPro  INTRON                                                           GC-BOX
CCACCCAGAGCGGGGTGGAAGGCGCCAGGGGAGCCGGGGAGCCTTTACTTCGCCTCCGCGCCCTGCATTCCGTTCCTGGCCTCGGGAGAAGCGGCACGGA  340

CCGGGATCACGCCAAGGTCCGTGTGAACTTCCCCCTTCTCGACACCCACCTC CCGCCG CCGGGCCCAGCTGTGCGCCAGGCGAAGTCGGTGTGCTCAAGA  440
                                                     GC-BOX
GGTGCCTGTTGGGTTACAGGACACGGAAAGGGTGGCCTCGGCCTCCTTCGAGTCTCCAATTGACCCCACTCATTTCGGATCTTCTAACTTAATTTCTCTT  540

GACCGAGAGGCTTTGTAATAGCGTAGAATCTGGAGACAGGGTGGCTTCGTTCAAACAGCACCCTCACCATTGACTAGCCCTGTGACCTTGAGCAAGTTTT  640
```

A consensus sequence
_____

```
TGGTGAAACCTTGTCTCT    (ATP synthase beta-subunit)   inverted

TGGTGAAACCTTGTCTCT    (cytochrome c₁)        inverted

TGGTG T T TTGTCTCT    (pyruvate dehydrogenase alpha-subunit)
```

FIGURE 2. (Upper panel) Nucleotide sequence for the 5' upstream region of the human PDH $E_1\alpha$ subunit gene. The *numbers* start from the initiation site for transcription, which was determined by a primer extension method. **(Lower panel)** Consensus sequence found in the nuclear genes for some mitochondrial proteins.

REFERENCES

1. OHTA, S. & Y. KAGAWA. 1986. J. Biochem. (Tokyo) **93:** 135–141.
2. KOIKE, K., S. OHTA, Y. URATA, Y. KAGAWA & M. KOIKE. 1988. Proc. Natl. Acad. Sci. USA **85:** 41–45.
3. OHTA, S., K. GOTO, H. ARAI & Y. KAGAWA. 1987. FEBS Lett. **226:** 171–175.
4. NISHIKIMI, M., S. OHTA, H. SUZUKI, T. TANAKA, F. KIKKAWA, M. TANAKA, Y. KAGAWA & T. OZAWA. 1988. Nucleic Acids Res. **16:** 3577.
5. OHTA, S., H. TOMURA, K. MATSUDA & Y. KAGAWA. 1988. J. Biol. Chem. **263:** 11257–11262.
6. SUZUKI, H., Y. HOSOKAWA, M. NISHIKIMI & T. OZAWA. 1989. J. Biol. Chem. **264:** 1368–1374.

Identification of the Acyltransferase (E2) Components of Branched-Chain α-Keto Acid Dehydrogenase and Pyruvate Dehydrogenase Complexes as Autoantigens in Primary Biliary Cirrhosis

P. A. DAVIS,[a] D. R. FREGEAU,[a] J. VAN DE WATER,[a]
C. SURH,[a] A. ANSARI,[b] R. COPPEL,[c] D. DANNER,[d]
AND M. E. GERSHWIN[a]

[a]Division of Rheumatology-Clinical Immunology
TB192
University of California, Davis
Davis, California 95616

Departments of [b]Pathology and [d]Pediatrics
Emory University
Atlanta, Georgia 30322

[c]Walter and Eliza Hall Institute for Medical Research
Victoria, 3050 Australia

Primary biliary cirrhosis (PBC) represents an enigmatic human disease with a diverse set of clinical findings in addition to a puzzling incidence and disease course. It is thought to be an autoimmune disease, particularly given that the population affected by PBC is predominantly female and that signs of immune dysfunction are evident.[1] The disease is characterized by an inflammation of the intrahepatic bile ducts with the destruction, in some but not all patients, of these ducts, leading to cholestasis and liver cirrhosis. One of the hallmarks of this disease is the presence in patients' sera of antibodies directed against self antigens. Specifically, these sera contain high-titer anti-mitochondrial antibodies (AMA), which appear to be pathomnemonic for primary biliary cirrhosis, although their role in the disease process remains unknown.

Using a variety of biochemical and molecular biological approaches, we have sought to identify and characterize the target antigens for PBC-associated AMA in order to better understand the roles, if any, of these antibodies in the disease process. The antigens recognized by over 90% of PBC sera are found at molecular masses of 74 and 52 kDa, using for assay beef heart mitochondria resolved by SDS–polyacrylamide gel electrophoresis (SDS-PAGE) followed by immunoblotting.[2] The 74- and 52-kDa antigens are approximately the size of the E2 subunits of pyruvate dehydrogenase complex (PDC) and branched-chain α-keto acid dehydrogenase complex (BCKDC), respectively, from bovine heart mitochondria. This similarity, along with a sequence analysis of a 74-kDa antigen clone which revealed areas of homology with *Escherichia coli* PDC E2[3] led us to test mammalian PDC E2 as a candidate AMA target antigen. Several different approaches were used to prove that the bands recognized were the E2 subunits. PBC sera were tested by SDS-PAGE/immunoblotting before and after being absorbed with PDC or BCKDC E2 (either as the purified proteins or as recombinant fusion proteins). The 74-kDa and 52-kDa bands seen in the immunoblot analysis of

TABLE 1. PBC Sera Reactivity to PDC and Inhibition of PDC Enzyme Activity

PBC Serum No.	Reactivity[a] (ELISA: OD)	PDC Enzyme Activity (% control)	
		Unabsorbed Serum	Absorbed Serum[b]
3	0.769	5	80
6	0.666	38	97
7	0.747	7	71
24	0.590	61	88
71	0.806	0	76
78	0.490	46	95
88	0.715	10	100
90	0.823	22	95
91	0.686	52	86
96	0.705	45	88

[a]Antibody reaction tested in an ELISA using a recombinant protein containing rat PDC E2.
[b]Sera absorbed with recombinant PDC E2.

PBC sera dissappeared or were markedly diminished in assays with absorbed PBC sera.[4,5] PBC sera displayed high amounts of antibody when assayed using either recombinant PDC E2 or BCKDC E2 as the target antigen in an ELISA (TABLES 1 and 2). Further, PBC sera inhibited the activity of PDC and BCKDC upon addition to the enzyme assay mixtures (TABLES 1 and 2), and the degree of enzyme inhibition correlated with the OD values in the ELISA ($r = 0.719$, $p < 0.02$, and $r = 0.87$, $p < 0.05$, for PDC and BCKDC, respectively). Absorption of PBC sera with recombinant PDC E2 resulted in a decrease in the inhibition of PDC (TABLE 1) and BCKDC (not shown) enzyme activity. Absorption of PBC sera with purified BCKDC E2 and testing by ELISA using recombinant BCKDC E2 as the target antigen demonstrated a decline in reactivity as assessed by ELISA (TABLE 2), although reactivity towards PDC did not decline (TABLE 2). In addition to the nature of the antigen, the epitope recognized by these AMA is of interest. Two differing approaches were employed to generate peptides which contained candidate epitopes; peptides were generated either synthetically or after fragmenting the clone of the 74-kDa antigen using restriction

TABLE 2. PBC Sera Reactivity to BCKDC, Inhibition of BCKDC Enzyme Activity, and Reactivity to Both PDC and BCKDC after Absorption of PBC Sera with BCKDC

PBC Serum No.	Reactivity[a] (ELISA: OD)	BCKDC Enzyme Activity (% control)	Reactivity after Absorption[b] (ELISA: % initial OD)	
			Anti-BCKDC	Anti-PDC
11	1.027	41	60	101
36	1.449	10	49	100
41	0.996	35	18	106
54	1.135	32	37	105
106	1.141	23	52	93
128	0.948	70	56	89

[a]Antibody reaction tested in an ELISA using a recombinant protein containing human BCKDC E2.
[b]Sera absorbed with purified BCKDC E2 and then tested in an ELISA with recombinant human BCKDC E2 (anti-BCKDC) or with recombinant human PDC E2 (anti-PDC).

enzymes and then expressing those fragments. Using these peptides to absorb PBC sera and testing the sera by both immunoblotting and ELISA, we found that the site of antibody attachment to PDC E2 appears to be at or near the lipoic acid attachment region of the enzyme.[6] The findings that antibodies are present in PBC sera that recognize both PDC and BCKDC and inhibit enzyme activity suggest, given that enzyme-bound lipoic acid plays a crucial role in the reactions catalyzed by these transacylases, that the BCKDC E2 epitope also is a lipoic acid attachment site.[5] Further strengthening the identification of the lipoic acid attachment site as the epitope are data[2] demonstrating that protein X, a component of PDC which contains a lipoic acid attachment site similar to that of PDC E2, shares a common AMA epitope with PDC E2. In summary, the internally self-consistent nature of the data with regard to the identity of the antigens recognized and the epitope targeted, along with the data on the ability of the antibodies to inhibit enzyme activity, provides strong evidence for the identification of the PDC E2 and BCKDC E2 components as target antigens in patients with PBC.

The characterization of these high-titer, highly specific antibodies not only provides us with approaches to investigate the pathology of PBC, but also provides us with additional tools with which to examine the basic biochemistry and biophysics of these enzymes fundamental to cellular energy metabolism.

REFERENCES

1. GERSHWIN, M. E., R. L. COPPEL & I. R. MACKAY. 1988. Hepatology **8:** 147–151.
2. SURH, C. D., T. R. ROCHE, D. J. DANNER, A. ANSARI, R. L. COPPEL, T. PRINDIVILLE, E. R. DICKSON & M. E. GERSHWIN. 1989. Hepatology **10:** 127–133.
3. GERSHWIN, M. E., I. R. MACKAY, A. STURGESS & R. L. COPPEL. 1987. J. Immunol. **138:** 3525–3537.
4. VAN DE WATER, J., D. FREGEAU, P. DAVIS, A. ANSARI, D. J. DANNER, P. LEUNG, R. L. COPPEL & M. E. GERSHWIN. 1988. J. Immunol. **141:** 2321.
5. FREGEAU, D. R., P. A. DAVIS, D. J. DANNER, A. ANSARI, R. L. COPPEL, E. R. DICKSON & M. E. GERSHWIN. 1989. J. Immunol. **142:** 3815–3820.
6. VAN DE WATER, J., M. E. GERSHWIN, P. LEUNG, A. ANSARI & R. L. COPPEL. 1988. J. Exp. Med. **167:** 1791–1799.

The Lipoate-Containing Domain of PDC E2 Contains the Main Immunogenic Region of the 70-kDa M2 Autoantigen in Primary Biliary Cirrhosis

SHELLEY P. M. FUSSEY,[a,b] MARGARET F. BASSENDINE,[c]
OLIVER F. W. JAMES,[c] AND STEPHEN J. YEAMAN[a]

[a]Department of Biochemistry and Genetics
and [c]Department of Medicine
University of Newcastle upon Tyne
Newcastle upon Tyne NE2 4HH
United Kingdom

Primary biliary cirrhosis (PBC) is a chronic, progressive, and often fatal cholestatic liver disease, characterized by inflammatory obliteration of the intrahepatic bile ducts.[1] The diagnostic marker for the disease is the presence of anti-mitochondrial antibodies in the sera. The targets of these autoantibodies are trypsin-sensitive antigens of the inner mitochondrial membrane (M2), but until recently their precise identity remained unknown. By Western immunoblotting we have demonstrated that four of the autoantigens in this disease are the E2 components of the pyruvate dehydrogenase (PDC), branched-chain 2-oxo acid dehydrogenase, and 2-oxoglutarate dehydrogenase complexes, respectively, and protein X of PDC.[2]

These proteins contain an essential cofactor, lipoic acid, which is covalently bound to the polypeptide via a lysine sidechain. All the E2 components have a highly segmented structure, with the catalytic and subunit binding domains forming a central symmetrical core, from which protrude one or more flexible, lipoyl-containing domains.

The aim of this study was to identify the immunogenic domain within PDC E2, as this is the major M2 autoantigen in PBC.

PDC E2 was acetylated using [2-^{14}C]pyruvate in the presence of N-ethylmaleimide and limiting amounts of PDC E1, and the labeled protein was subsequently subjected to limited proteolysis by trypsin. Two major fragments were produced, the structural inner core domain and the lipoyl-containing domain, the production of which was monitored by SDS–polyacrylamide gel electrophoresis (SDS-PAGE) followed by autoradiography (FIG. 1).

Immunoblotting of PBC patients' sera against the products of the tryptic digest revealed that the lipoyl-containing domain is exclusively recognized in 119/119 cases and therefore contains the immunodominant region (FIG. 2). Free lipoic acid and lipoamide do not absorb out the reactivity of the sera, and lipoate-containing H-protein from the glycine cleavage system[3] is not recognized by PBC sera, indicating that a

---

[b]Address for correspondence: Department of Biochemistry and Genetics, The Medical School, Framlington Place, Newcastle upon Tyne University, Newcastle upon Tyne, NE2 4HH, United Kingdom.

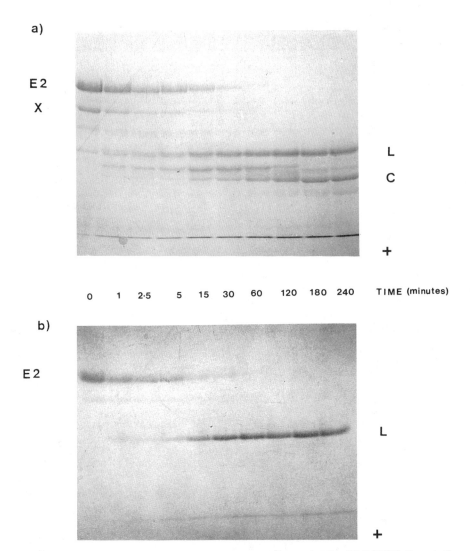

FIGURE 1. Time-course of limited tryptic digestion of ^{14}C-labeled E2. PDC E2(X) (2 mg/ml) was incubated at 25°C in 50 mM potassium phosphate; 1 mM EDTA, pH 6.5; with 0.2 mg/ml PDC E1; 0.4 mM thiamin pyrophosphate; 2 mM MgCl$_2$; 0.5 mM N-ethylmaleimide; and 0.2 mM [2-^{14}C]pyruvate (30,000 cpm/nmol). After incubation for 30 min, dithiothreitol was added to a final concentration of 1.5 mM. [^{14}C]E2 (2 mg/ml) was incubated with trypsin (1%, w/w) in an ice bath and 13-μl aliquots were taken at the times indicated and added to 0.14 μg of soybean trypsin inhibitor and 20 μl of Laemmli sample buffer. Samples of digested protein were subjected to polyacrylamide gel electrophoresis in the presence of sodium dodecyl sulphate (SDS-PAGE) on 10% gels and subsequently autoradiographed. (**a**) The resultant gel stained with Coomassie brilliant blue R, (**b**) the corresponding autoradiograph. E2 and X are intact component enzymes; L, the lipoyl-containing domain of E2; and C, the E2 structural core domain.

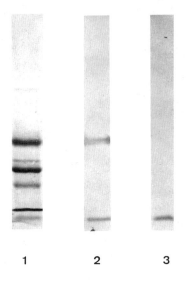

L

FIGURE 2. Reactivity of PBC sera with the domains of PDC E2 produced by tryptic digestion. [^{14}C]E2 was subjected to proteolysis by trypsin for 4 hr (as in FIG. 1); the digested protein was resolved by SDS-PAGE and electrophoretically transferred to nitrocellulose. (**Lane 1**) 10 μg of protein stained with Amido black. (**Lanes 2 and 3**) 1 μg of protein incubated with (**2**) PBC sera at a dilution of 1:1000, or (**3**) control sera at a dilution of 1:100. Detection of human IgG antibodies was by means of secondary goat anti-human IgG (γ-chain–specific) peroxidase-conjugated antibodies, with 4-chloro-1-naphthol as substrate. L, lipoyl-containing domain.

1   2   3

feature unique to the lipoyl-containing domain of the E2 polypeptide is a target in this autoimmune disease.

Further analysis of the precise nature of the antigenic element(s) may have important implications as to our understanding of not only the immunopathogenesis of PBC but also the molecular processes underlying the perturbation of self-tolerance mechanisms in all autoimmune disorders.

REFERENCES

1. KAPLAN, M. M. 1987. N. Engl. J. Med. **316:** 521–528.
2. FUSSEY, S. P. M., J. R. GUEST, O. F. W. JAMES, M. F. BASSENDINE & S. J. YEAMAN. 1988. Proc. Natl. Acad. Sci. USA **85:** 8654–8658.
3. FUJIWARA, K., K. OKAMURA & Y. MOTOKAWA. 1979. Arch. Biochem. Biophys. **197:** 454–462.

Cellular and Subcellular Branched-Chain Keto Acid Decarboxylase in Rat Brain and Its Response to Hyperammonemia

J. JESSY AND CH. R. K. MURTHY

School of Life Sciences
University of Hyderabad
Hyderabad 500 134
A.P. India

Hyperammonemia is a pathological condition associated with cerebral dysfunction. The exact biochemical mechanisms involved in ammonia toxicity in the central nervous system (CNS) remain elusive. Ammonia is mainly detoxified in brain by way of glutamine formation in astrocytes.[1] It has been previously suggested that the branched-chain amino acids (BCAA; leucine, isoleucine, and valine) may serve as precursors for the glutamate necessary for glutamine biosynthesis.[2] Reports have appeared on the efficacy of BCAA for ameliorating the clinical symptoms in hyperammonemia. Mans *et al.*[3] observed an enhanced transport of BCAA across the blood-brain barrier of portacaval-shunted rats. Earlier studies from this laboratory have shown enhanced BCAA-transaminase activity in hyperammonemia.[4] In the present study, the activity of branched-chain keto acid decarboxylase (BCKA-DC),

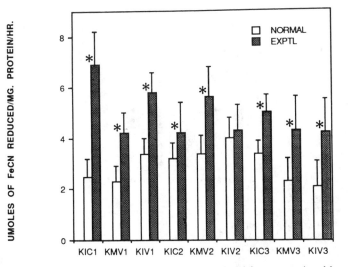

FIGURE 1. BCKA-DC activity in subcellular fractions isolated from normal and hyperammonemic rats. Values shown are mean ± SD of 5–7 experiments for subcellular fractions from control (NORMAL) or ammonia acetate–treated (EXPTL) rats. Fractions: (**1**) mitochondria, (**2**) cytosol, (**3**) synaptosomes. BCKA used: (**KIC**) ketoisocaproic acid, (**KMV**) ketomethylvaleric acid, (**KIV**) ketoisovaleric acid. *, significant difference from control.

the enzyme for the rate-limiting step of BCAA metabolism in the CNS, was determined in cellular and subcellular fractions.

Subcellular fractions, ie., synaptosomes, mitochondria, and cytosol, were prepared from rat brain cerebral cortex by the method of Cotman.[5] BCKA-DC activity was assayed by the procedure of Gubler.[6] The activity levels of BCKA-DC with the three

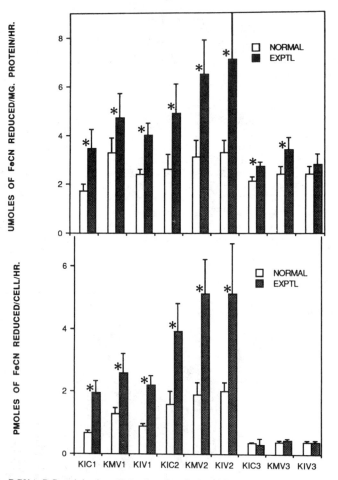

FIGURE 2. BCKA-DC activity in cellular fractions isolated from normal and hyperammonemic rats. Values shown are mean ± SD of 5 experiments for cellular fractions of (**1**) neurons, (**2**) astrocytes, and (**3**) oligodendrocytes from control (NORMAL) or ammonia acetate–treated (EXPTL) rats. BCKA used: (**KIC**) ketoisocaproic acid, (**KMV**) ketomethylvaleric acid, (**KIV**) ketoisovaleric acid. *, significant difference from control.

branched-chain keto acids (BCKA) as substrates were found to be similar in these fractions (FIG. 1). Neurons and astrocytes were isolated by the method of Farooq and Norton[7] and oligodendrocytes by that of Snyder *et al.*[8] The specific activity of BCKA-DC in the three cell types was similar. When expressed on a per-cell basis, the distribution profile of activity was astrocytes > neurons > oligodendrocytes (FIG. 2).

Upon acute administration of ammonium acetate, BCKA-DC activity was enhanced in all fractions except oligodendrocytes, where the activity remained unaltered when expressed per cell (FIGS. 1 and 2). These results are in accordance with the observation of Shiota[9] on enhanced decarboxylation of [1-^{14}C]leucine in brain homogenates of animals treated with CCl_4. Brain has a substantial potential for reamination of essential keto acids.[10] Enhanced BCKA-DC activity would prevent the reamination of BCKA, the glutamate produced by BCAA transamination being channeled towards glutamine biosynthesis. Moreover, elevated BCKA-DC activity would lead to production of more acetyl-CoA and succinyl-CoA, thus providing additional ATP and glutamate for glutamine synthesis, resulting in more efficient detoxification of ammonia.

REFERENCES

1. BENJAMIN, A. M. 1982. *In* Handbook of Neurochemistry, 2nd ed. A. Lajtha, Ed. Vol. 1: 117–137. Plenum Press. New York.
2. COOPER, A. J. L., J. M. McDONALD, A. S. GELBARD & R. F. GLEDHILL. 1979. J. Biol. Chem. **254:** 4982–4992.
3. MANS, A., J. F. BIEBUYCK & R. A. HAWKINS. 1983. Am. J. Physiol. **245:** C74–C77.
4. JESSY, J., & CH. R. K. MURTHY. 1985. Neurochem. Int. **7**(6): 1027–1031.
5. COTMAN, C. W. 1974. Methods Enzymol. **31:** 445–452.
6. GUBLER, C. J. 1961. J. Biol. Chem. **236:** 3112–3120.
7. FAROOQ, M. & W. T. NORTON. 1978. J. Neurochem. **31:** 887–894.
8. SNYDER, D. S., C. S. RAINE, M. FAROOQ & W. T. NORTON. 1980. J. Neurochem. **34:** 1614–1621.
9. SHIOTA, T. 1984. Acta Med. Okayama **38:** 219–226.
10. BRAND, K. 1981. Biochim. Biophys. Acta **677:** 126–132.

Chronic Acidemia Due to a Pyruvate Dehydrogenase Deficiency in the Pyruvate Dehydrogenase Complex, with Evidence of Abnormalities of the α and β Subunits of the Enzyme[a]

KICHIKO KOIKE AND YOSHISHIGE URATA

Department of Pathological Biochemistry
Atomic Disease Institute
Nagasaki University School of Medicine
Nagasaki, 852, Japan

It has been reported that a genetic pyruvate dehydrogenase (PDH) deficiency in infants results in progressive neurological disease with persistent lactic and pyruvic acidemia and growth retardation. In Japan, among more than 400 patients with increased blood levels of pyruvate and lactate, we have diagnosed over the past ten years eight patients in whom there is substantial biochemical evidence for abnormalities of the PDH component of the PDH multienzyme complex. This work was based on our development of highly sensitive enzyme assay procedures closely dependent on pyruvate metabolism and by analytical procedures for α-keto acids in blood and urine.[1] These studies were aimed at providing information concerning the nature of genetic mutants leading to molecular diseases (PDH deficiency) and at aiding in carrier detection, prenatal diagnosis, and treatment.

The eight cases of PDH deficiency were further characterized by immunoblotting of the two subunit proteins (PDHα and PDHβ) with specific antisera directed to the two porcine heart subunits. As shown in FIGURE 1, anti-porcine PDHα serum highly cross-reacted not only with porcine PDHα (A, lanes 6 and 7), but also with human liver PDHα (A, lane 1); and, similarly, anti-porcine PDHβ serum cross-reacted with both porcine PDHβ (B, lanes 6 and 7) and human PDHβ (B, lane 1). In the immunoblots of the liver extract from patient M, the PDHα and PDHβ bands were absent, in contrast to the other two components of PDH complex, and new, larger bands appeared. In liver extract from patient S, no bands were detected; however, in extracts from patients H and T, two normal size bands were detected. These results strongly suggested that impairments in the PDH complex of patients M and S are due to absence or abnormalities of the PDH component and that further studies of PDH on the gene level are indispensable.

Recently we have succeeded in the cloning and sequencing of human PDHα and PDHβ cDNAs.[2] Preliminary studies of the genomic structure of PDHα and PDHβ by Southern blot analysis using the two nick-translated radiolabeled cDNAs as probes have revealed simple digested fragment patterns with restriction enzymes, as shown in

[a]This work was supported in part by Grants-in-Aid for Scientific Research on Priority Areas of "Bioenergetics," Grants-in-Aid for Scientific Research from the Ministry of Education, Science and Culture, and grants from the Vitamin B Research Committee.

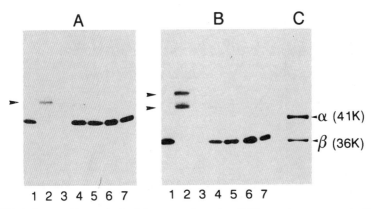

FIGURE 1. Immunoblot analysis of human and porcine PDH complex components. Samples extracted from normal human liver (**lane 1**); liver from patient M (**lane 2**), S (**lane 3**), H (**lane 4**), and T (**lane 5**); purified porcine PDHα (**lane 6**); or PDH complex (**lane 7**) are analyzed. (**A**) Anti-PDHα immunoblot, (**B**) anti-PDHβ immunoblot, (**C**) size markers PDHα and PDHβ stained with Coomassie Brilliant Blue R-250. Positions of new, larger bands in samples from patient M (**lane 2**) are indicated by *arrowheads*.

FIGURE 2. Restriction fragment length polymorphisms for PDHα and PDHβ genes were observed as the presence or absence of specific bands in patterns from *Xba* I, *Bgl* II, and *Msp* I digests for the PDHα gene (FIG. 2A) and from *Eco*R I, *Pvu* II, *Xba* I, and *Msp* I digests for the PDHβ gene (FIG. 2B). However, we have not succeeded in demonstrating a specific pattern of fragments from the genomes of patients with PDH deficiency. Further studies are in progress.

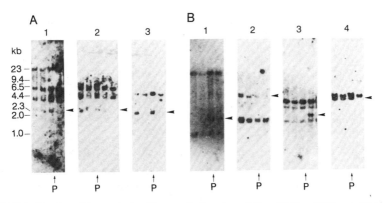

FIGURE 2. Southern blot analysis of human leukocyte and liver DNAs. DNA extracted from normal human leukocytes and from liver from patient M (P) were digested with a number of different restriction enzymes and probed with PDHα cDNA (**panel A**) and PDHβ cDNA (**panel B**). *Arrowheads* indicate positions of the specific bands involved in the polymorphism. **Panel A**: (**1**) *Xba* I, (**2**) *Bgl* II, (**3**) *Msp* I. **Panel B**: (**1**) *Eco*R I, (**2**) *Pvu* II, (**3**) *Xba* I, (**4**) *Msp* I. Positions indicated for size markers are based on an analysis of a *Hind* III digest of λDNA.

REFERENCES

1. KOIKE, K. 1988. Enzymatic studies of the genetic defect of pyruvate dehydrogenase in chronic pyruvic and lactic acidemia. *In* Thiamin Pyrophosphate Biochemistry. A. Schellenberger & R. L. Schowen, Eds. Vol. 2: 105–113. CRC Press. Boca Raton, Fla.
2. KOIKE, K., S. OHTA, Y. URATA, Y. KAGAWA & M. KOIKE. 1988. Cloning and sequencing of cDNAs encoding α and β subunits of human pyruvate dehydrogenase. Proc. Natl. Acad. Sci. USA **85:** 41–45.

Molecular Phenotypes in Cultured Maple Syrup Urine Disease Cells

CHARLES W. FISHER, JACINTA L. CHUANG,
THOMAS A. GRIFFIN, KIM S. LAU, RODY P. COX,
AND DAVID T. CHUANG

Department of Biochemistry
The University of Texas Southwestern
Medical Center at Dallas
Dallas, Texas 75235

The activity of the branched-chain α-keto acid dehydrogenase complex (BCKADC) is deficient in patients with inherited maple syrup urine disease (MSUD). MSUD is heterogeneous, as the BCKADC is encoded by at least six structural genes. A mutation at any one of these genetic loci could result in an MSUD phenotype. We[1-5] and others[6] have shown that the E1 activity of the BCKADC is deficient in several classical MSUD patients who were studied. The E2 polypeptide has been shown to be absent in cultured cells derived from other classical MSUD patients.[6,7]

To further identify the molecular basis of this metabolic disorder, we have isolated three overlapping cDNA clones for the E1α subunit of the human enzyme complex (FIG. 1). The clone for human E1α (hE1α-1) and the previously isolated E2 cDNA[8] were used as probes in Northern blot analysis with cultured fibroblasts or lymphoblasts

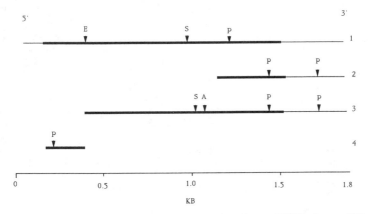

FIGURE 1. Alignment of the restriction maps of the three human cDNA clones of E1α (**2–4**) with the bovine cDNA clone (**1**) previously isolated. The longer hE1α-2 clone (**3**) is 1550 bp in length with an open reading frame encoding 378 amino acids. An alignment with the bovine E1α cDNA (**1**) indicates that this cDNA begins at Ile-23 and continues through the carboxyl terminus of the coding region. A 198-bp clone, hE1α-4, (**4**) was similarly aligned and found to encode the amino-terminal sequence (residues −44–22). Thus, a composite human E1α cDNA consists of 1,748 bp encoding the entire mature E1α peptide, with calculated M_r of 45,552. (**2**) hE1α-1 clone. *Thin lines,* non-coding sequence; *heavy lines,* coding sequence. A, *Acc* I; E, *Eco* R I; P, *Pst* I; S, *Sma* I.

TABLE 1. Molecular Phenotypes in Cultured Cells from MSUD Patients

Cell Line	MSUD Phenotype	Molecular Phenotype	E1α mRNA[a]	E1α Subunit[a]	E1β Subunit[a]	E2 mRNA[a]	E2 Subunit[a]
F.J.	Classical	I	+	+	+	+	+
P.K.	Classical	II	+	−	−	+	+
Lo	Classical	III	−	−	−	+	+
GM-1366	Classical	IV	+	+	N.D.	−	−
Ech	Classical	V	+	+	+	+	−
A.L.	Classical	V	+	+	+	+	−
WG-34[b]	Thiamin-responsive	V	+	+	+	+	−

[a]+, present in normal size and abundance; −, absent or much reduced in abundance; N.D., not determined.
[b]The original thiamin-responsive MSUD patient described by C. Scriver.

from seven MSUD patients. Polyclonal antibodies were used as probes to measure subunit contents of the enzyme complex in Western blots of cultured fibroblasts or lymphoblasts. This approach has allowed us to detect distinct molecular phenotypes for MSUD at mRNA and protein levels. The results (summarized in TABLE I) have identified the affected gene in these MSUD patients. Five distinct molecular phenotypes were defined on the basis of mRNA and protein subunit contents: Type I, where the levels of E1α mRNA and E1α and E1β subunits are normal in cells but E1 activity is deficient; Type II, where the E1α mRNA is present in normal quantity, but the contents of E1α and E1β subunits are reduced; Type III, where the level of E1α mRNA is markedly reduced with a concomitant loss of E1α and E1β subunits; Type IV, where the contents of both E2 mRNA and E2 subunits are markedly reduced; and Type V, where the E2 mRNA is normally expressed, but the E2 subunit is completely absent in cells. This latter type comprises classical and thiamin-responsive (WG-34) MSUD cells. The existence of different molecular phenotypes supports the proposal of genetic heterogeneity in MSUD, as demonstrated previously by complementation studies.[9,10] Thus, there appears to be no correlation between clinical[11] and molecular phenotypes, since multiple molecular phenotypes are observed within classical MSUD.

REFERENCES

1. CHUANG, D. T., et al. 1981. Biochem. J. **200:** 59–67.
2. CHUANG, D. T., et al. 1982. Am. J. Hum. Genet. **34:** 416–424.
3. CHUANG, D. T., et al. 1982. Proc. Natl. Acad. Sci. USA **79:** 3300–3304.
4. GONZALES-RIOS, M. C., et al. 1985. Clin. Genet. **27:** 153–159.
5. HU, C.-W. C., et al. 1988. J. Biol. Chem. **263:** 9007–9014.
6. RÜDIGER, H. W., et al. 1972. Humangenetik **14:** 257–263.
7. INDO, Y., et al. 1987. J. Clin. Invest. **80:** 63–70.
8. LAU, K. S., et al. 1988. Biochemistry **27:** 1972–1981.
9. LYON, L. B., et al. 1973. Nature **243:** 533–535.
10. SINGH, S., et al. 1977. Clin. Genet. **11:** 277.
11. TANAKA, K. & L. E. ROSENBERG. 1983. In The Metabolic Basis of Inherited Disease. pp. 440–473. McGraw-Hill Inc. New York.

Cloning and Characterization of Human Pyruvate Dehydrogenase Genes

B. J. SONG, Y. T. CHI, T. L. HUH, J. P. CASAZZA,
B. SUMEGI, P. A. SRERE, AND R. L. VEECH

Laboratory of Metabolism and Molecular Biology
National Institute of Alcohol Abuse and Alcoholism
12501 Washington Avenue
Rockville, Maryland 20852
and
Basic Biochemistry Division
Veterans Administration Medical Center
Dallas, Texas 75216

Certain alcoholics have elevated serum levels of 2,3-butanediol with or without the presence of ethanol.[1,2] Butanediol may be produced in animals by the reduction of acetoin formed by pyruvate dehydrogenase (PDH) in brain and testis.[3] In a program aimed at studying the genetics of human alcoholism, probes for the subunits of PDH were made and the genes cloned.

Oligodeoxynucleotide probes for PDH E1α and E1β were synthesized and used for screening λgt11 cDNA libraries of human brain and liver using published methods.[4] The cDNAs for the entire protein coding region of PDH E1α were cloned from human brain and liver libraries, and the nucleotide sequences compared to the three previous clones from human fetal liver,[5] human foreskin,[6] and human hepatoma[7] (FIG. 1). Our clones for E1α from adult human liver and brain are highly homologous and hybridized with brain mRNA, in contrast to a previous report.[5] Partial nucleotide sequencing of our clones verified that they were 99% homologous with the clones from fetal liver[5] and hepatoma.[7] However, our clones differed from the clone of human fetal liver,[5] which

FIGURE 1. Comparison of cDNA clones for PDH E1α isolated from various tissue libraries. The restriction endonuclease maps of full-length cDNA clones for PDH E1α from human brain (pHBPAF) and liver (pHLPAF) are compared to other full-length cDNA clones reported from fetal liver,[5] foreskin,[6] and hepatoma.[7] The *closed bars* indicate the E1α protein–coding region including the leader sequences, while 5' and 3' untranslated regions are shown in *open bars*. The *hatched areas* and *gray area* represent the locations of frame-shift mutations and the 94-base deletion, respectively, compared to the largest clone of fetal liver, PDHE.[5] Restriction endonuclease cleavage sites are marked and designated as follows: H, *Hind* III; P, *Pst* I.

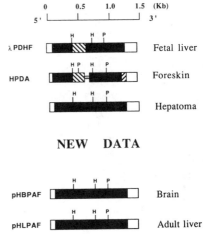

455

had a partial frame-shift mutation. Our clones also differed from the human foreskin clone,[6] which had two partial frame-shift mutations and a 94-base deletion mutation within the protein-coding region. Genomic Southern blots showed simple patterns of DNA fragments identical for liver and brain DNAs. This suggests that PDH E1α in liver and brain are derived from very similar genes.

At least three full-length cDNA clones for PDH E1β, ranging from 1.1 to 4.0 kb, were isolated from a human liver library (FIG. 2). Two have identical coding regions but different sizes for the 3'untranslated region, and the third has a 142-base insertion within the coding region, which yielded a mutant RNA transcript. The coding regions of our three clones are highly homologous, with the exception noted above, but differ from the clone isolated from foreskin,[6] which appeared to have three small frame-shift mutations. Genomic Southern blots yielded a simple pattern of hybridization, suggesting that PDH E1β is not the product of a multiple-gene family.

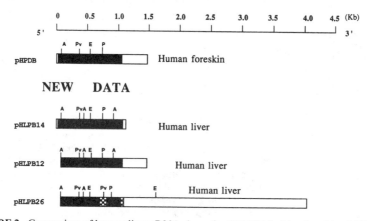

FIGURE 2. Comparison of human liver cDNA clones for PDH E1β with a foreskin cDNA clone. The restriction endonuclease maps of three different human liver cDNA clones for PDH E1β are compared to a full-length cDNA clone from human foreskin.[6] The *closed* and *open* bars indicate the E1β protein coding and untranslated regions, respectively, as in FIGURE 1. The *checkered areas* in clone pHLPB26 indicate locations of inserted nucleotides, compared to other cDNA clones. Various restriction endonuclease cleavage sites are marked and designated as follows: A, *Ava* II; E, *EcoR* I; P, *Pst* I; Pv, *Pvu* II.

The present study shows that we have confirmed the sequences of normal PDH E1α and E1β. On the basis of the similar nucleotide sequences and genomic DNA Southern blot data, we propose that brain and liver enzymes do not represent separate isozymes as suggested in earlier data.[5,8]

REFERENCES

1. FELVER, M. E., M. R. LAKSHMANAN, S. WOLF & R. L. VEECH. 1980. *In* Alcohol and Aldehyde Metabolizing Systems IV. R.G. Thurman, Ed.: 229. Plenum Press. New York.
2. CASAZZA, J. P., J. FRIETAS, D. STAMBUK, M. Y. MORGAN & R. L. VEECH. 1987. Alcohol. **Suppl. 1:** 607.
3. VEECH, R. L., M. E. FELVER, M. R. LAKSHMANAN, M. T. HUANG & S. WOLF. 1981. Curr. Top. Cell. Regul. **18:** 151. Academic Press. New York.

4. SONG, B. J., H. V. GELBOIN, S. S. PARK, C. S. YANG & F. J. GONZALEZ. 1986. J. Biol. Chem. **261:** 16689.
5. DAHL, H. H. M., S. M. HUNT, W. M. HUTCHINSON & G. K. BROWN. 1987. J. Biol. Chem. **262:** 7398.
6. KOIKE, K., S. OHTA, Y. URATA, Y. KAGAWA & M. KOIKE. 1988. Proc. Natl. Acad. Sci. **85:** 41.
7. DEMEIRLEIR, L., N. MACKAY, A. M. L. H. WAH & B. H. ROBINSON. 1988. J. Biol. Chem. **263:** 1991.
8. PRICK, M., F. GABREELS, W. RENIER, F. TRIJBELS, H. JASPAR. K. LAMERS & J. KOK. 1981. Neurology **31:** 398.

Identification of a Gene for the Pyruvate Dehydrogenase $E_1\alpha$ Subunit with a Deletion of Four Nucleotides from a Patient with Pyruvate Dehydrogenase Complex Deficiency

HITOSHI ENDO,[a] KIYOSHI HASEGAWA,[b]
KUNIAKI NARISAWA,[c] KEIYA TADA,[b]
YASUO KAGAWA,[a] AND SHIGEO OHTA[a,d]

[a]Department of Biochemistry
Jichi Medical School
Minamikawachi-machi
Tochigi-ken 329-04, Japan
and
[b]Department of Pediatrics and
[c]Department of Biochemical Genetics
Tohoku University School of Medicine
Seiryo-machi
Sendai 980, Japan

A considerable number of patients with pyruvate dehydrogenase complex (PDHC) deficiency have been reported.[1,2] Recently, the cDNAs encoding the α subunit and the β subunit of the PDHC E_1 enzyme have been cloned in several laboratories, including ours.[3-5] Here we report on the structure of the cDNA encoding the α subunit of PDHC from a PDHC-deficient patient.

This patient fatigued easily on exercise from the age of 3 years and had a slight lactic acidosis. His fibroblasts showed 24.6% of the normal amount of E_1 activity.[6]

Poly(A^+) RNAs were obtained from the patient's lymphocytes transformed by Epstein-Barr virus. The cDNA encoding the $E_1\alpha$ subunit was cloned and sequenced. FIGURE 1 (panel A) shows that the sequence lacked 4 base-pairs at the second codon upstream from the termination codon. The deletion should lead to a reading-frame shift in the protein and make a new termination codon at the 33rd codon downstream from the "normal" termination codon. The deduced sequence suggests that the polypeptide from the patient is larger than the normal one. The presence of this deletion in his mRNA was confirmed by an S1-nuclease protection experiment.

To determine whether the 4-nucleotide deletion is present in an exon or is caused by an abnormal splicing at the intron/exon junction, genomic DNA fragments from the patient's and his parent's blood cells were amplified around the region containing the deletion in the patient's cDNA by the polymerase chain reaction method. In FIGURE 1 (panel B), the size of the amplified DNA from the patient was shorter than that from the control, and it was the same as that of the cloned cDNA from the patient. This

[d]Address correspondence to Dr. S. Ohta, Department of Biochemistry, Jichi Medical School, Minamikawachi-machi, Tochigi-ken 329-04, Japan

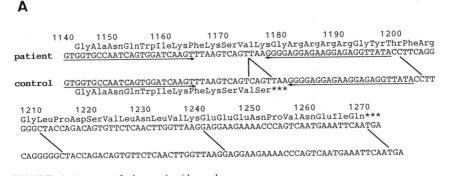

A

```
      1140      1150      1160      1170      1180      1190      1200
            GlyAlaAsnGlnTrpIleLysPheLysSerValLysGlyArgArgArgArgGlyTyrThrPheArg
patient  GTGGTGCCAATCAGTGGATCAAGTTTAAGTCAGTTAAGGGGAGGAGAAGGAGAGGTTATACCTTCAGG


control  GTGGTGCCAATCAGTGGATCAAGTTTAAGTCAGTCAGTTAAGGGGAGGAGAAGGAGAGGTTATACCTT
            GlyAlaAsnGlnTrpIleLysPheLysSerValSer***

  1210      1220      1230      1240      1250      1260      1270
GlyLeuProAspSerValLeuAsnLeuValLysGluGluGluAsnProValAsnGluIleGln***
GGGCTACCAGACAGTGTTCTCAACTTGGTTAAGGAGGAAGAAAACCCAGTCAATGAAATTCAATGA


CAGGGGGCTACCAGACAGTGTTCTCAACTTGGTTAAGGAGGAAGAAAACCCAGTCAATGAAATTCAATGA
```

FIGURE 1. A part of the nucleotide and deduced amino acid sequences of the cDNA encoding the PDHC-deficient patient's E₁α subunit and analysis by the polymerase chain reaction. (**Panel A**) Nucleotide and deduced amino acid sequences are copaired with those of the control. The patient's cDNA lacks 4 nucleotides at the second codon upstream from the "normal" termination codon. Oligonucleotide sequences used for the polymerase chain reaction are underlined by *solid lines with arrows*. (**Panel B**) Polymerase chain reaction in the region containing the 4-nucleotide deletion for genomic DNAs and cDNAs from the control, the patient, and his parents. The genomic DNAs were obtained from peripheral blood cells. The DNA fragments were amplified by the use of synthetic oligonucleotides, as indicated in **panel A**.

B

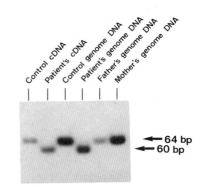

←64 bp
←60 bp

result indicates that the deletion takes place in an exon and that the gene is homozygous for this deletion. Furthermore, his parents both looked normal. These findings suggest that this deletion was sporadic and that the E₁α gene is located on the X-chromosome.

The next question is why the extra peptide caused by the frame shift affects

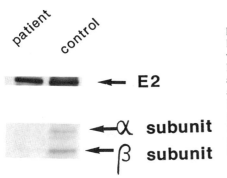

← E2

←α **subunit**
←β **subunit**

FIGURE 2. Immunoprecipitation with anti-E₂ antibody. The transformed lymphocytes were pulse-labeled with [³⁵S]methionine for 2 hr. The mitochondrial fraction was isolated and dissolved, then incubated with anti-E₂ antibody. Immunoprecipitates were pelleted by the addition of Protein A. The resulting pellets were taken up into a 2% SDS solution for electrophoresis on a 10% polyacrylamide gel. ³⁵S-labeled protein bands were visualized by autoradiography.

enzymatic activity. For the purpose of addressing this question, we examined complex formation by an immunoprecipitation method with anti-E_2 antibody. FIGURE 2 shows that α and β subunits were coprecipitated with E_2 in the normal cells, while they were not in the patient's. This result suggests that the abnormal additional peptide disturbed the normal assembly of this complex.

In conclusion, this is the first report on cloning and sequencing a defective gene of the PDHC. The four-nucleotide deletion should lead to a reading-frame shift and make an abnormal, large polypeptide form of the $E_1\alpha$ subunit. A polymerase chain reaction experiment showed that this deletion site was located in an exon and that this deletion was not inherited but sporadic.

REFERENCES

1. MCKAY, N., R. PETROVA-BENEDICT, J. THOENE, B. BERGEN, W. WILSON & B. ROBINSON. 1986. Eur. J. Pediatr. **144:** 445–450.
2. HO, L., C.-W. C. HU, S. PACKMAN & M. S. PATEL. 1986. J. Clin. Invest. **78:** 844–847.
3. DAHL, H.-H. M., S. M. HUNT, W. M. HUTCHINSON & G. BROWN. 1987. J. Biol. Chem. **262:** 7398–7403.
4. KOIKE, K., S. OHTA, Y. URATA, Y. KAGAWA & M. KOIKE. 1988. Proc. Natl. Acad. Sci. USA. **85:** 41–45.
5. MEIRLEIR, L. D., N. MACKAY, A. M. L. H. WAH & B. H. ROBINSON. 1988. J. Biol. Chem. **263:** 1991–1995.
6. MIYABAYASHI, S., T. ITO, K. NARISAWA, K. IINUMA & K. TADA. 1985. Eur. J. Pediatr. **143:** 278–283.

Biochemical Basis of Pyruvate Dehydrogenase Complex Deficiency: Polypeptide Heterogeneity of E1α Subunit

A. KITANO, F. ENDO, AND I. MATSUDA

Department of Pediatrics
Kumamoto University Medical School
Kumamoto 860, Japan

Pyruvate dehydrogenase (PDH) complex deficiency is a disease of autosomal recessive inheritance, representing a severe lactic acidemia. Most of the deficiency was attributed to a lack of the E1 component of the PDH complex. However, there are difficulties in the measurement of the E1 component by use of ferricyahide as electron acceptor in crude tissue or extracts of cultured cells. An immunochemical method has been developed and applied to analysis of PDH complex abnormalities. We report here the immunochemical analysis of the PDH complex in skin fibroblasts or Epstein-Barr–transformed lymphoid cells derived from four patients with the deficiency.

Characteristics of the patients are given in TABLE 1. Activated PDH complex activity was measured as described by Sheu et al.[1] Western and Northern blot analyses of the PDH complex were performed as described by Towbin et al.[2] and by Dahl et al.[3]

TABLE 1. Clinical Features of 4 Patients with PDH Complex Deficiency

Patient	Sex	Onset Age	Consanguinity	Mental State	Acidosis	Brain Atrophy
Case 1	F	1 Day	−	Severe retardation	+	+ +
Case 2	F	1 Month	−	Severe retardation	+	+
Case 3	M	9 Years	−	Almost normal	−	−
Case 4	M	4 Months	−	Mild retardation	+	+

TABLE 2 shows the results of measurement of PDH complex activity in the four patients. The PDH complex activities measured for case 1 and case 2 were profoundly decreased and the reductions of activity for case 3 and case 4 were moderate. In Western blot analysis using antibody against the bovine heart PDH complex, the band corresponding to the E1α component was not detectable in samples from cases 1 and 2. In case 3, the E1α band was also missing, and an additional band was detected below protein X. The intensity of both the E1α and E1β bands in the sample from patient 4 were reduced as compared with the control. In Northern blot analysis using PDH E1α cDNA, it was shown that the mRNA for the E1α protein (in cases 1, 2 and 3) had a level and pattern similar to that of the control.

A loss of cross-reacting protein corresponding to the E1α component in case 1 and case 2 indicates the primary involvement of the enzyme was attributable to a defect of the E1α protein of the PDH complex. On the other hand, case 3 and case 4 had, respectively, a mutation which changed the mobility of the E1α component, and a reduction of the E1α and E1β components. The kinetics of the PDH complex in cell

461

TABLE 2. Dichloroacetate-Activated PDHC Activities in Fibroblasts and Lymphoid Cells from Patients with PDHC Deficiency

	PDHC Activity[a]	
Patient	Fibroblasts	Lymphoid Cells
Case 1	0.19	
Case 2	0.41	
Case 3		1.43
Case 4	1.42	
Controls	3.35 ± 0.60^{b}	3.79 ± 0.82^{b}
n	4	3

[a]Activities are expressed as nmol/min/mg protein.
[b]Mean ± SD.

lines from these two patients didn't differ from that of the control. This finding suggests that the conformation of the active site in the PDH complex in these patients is similar to that of the control.

In Northern blot analysis, the pattern and molecular size of the E1α mRNA of cell lines from cases 1, 2, and 3 were similar to that of the control. These findings indicate that a defective synthesis or rapid degradation of the E1α component may explain the disease in cases 1 and 2, whereas normal (or near normal) synthesis with a relatively increased degradation rate can explain the results of the analysis of case 3.

ACKNOWLEDGMENT

We wish to thank Dr. H-H.M. Dahl for the supply of PDH E1α cDNA.

REFERENCES

1. SHUE, K.-F. R., C.-W. C. HU & M. F. UTTER. 1981. Pyruvate dehydrogenase complex activity in normal and deficient fibroblasts. J. Clin. Invest. **67:** 1463–1471.
2. TOWBIN, H., T. STAEHELIN & J. GORDON. 1979. Electrophoretic transfer of proteins from polyacrylamide gels to nitrocellulose sheets: Procedure and some applications. Proc. Natl. Acad. Sci. USA **76:** 4350–4354.
3. DAHL, H-H. M., S. M. HUNT, W. M. HUTCHISON & G. K. BROWN. 1987. The human pyruvate dehydrogenase complex: Isolation of cDNA clones for the E1α subunit, sequence analysis, and characterization of the mRNA. J. Biol. Chem. **262:** 7398–7403.

Subject Index

Index of Contributors